THE NATIONAL INVESTIGATIONS COMMITTEE ON AERIAL PHENOMENA (NICAP)

THE UFO EVIDENCE

EDITED BY RICHARD M. HALL

BARNES
&NOBLE
BOOKS
NEW YORK

1997 Barnes & Noble Books

ISBN 0-7607-0627-1

Printed and bound in the United States of America

97 98 99 00 01 M 9 8 7 6 5 4 3 2 1

RRDC

CONTENTS

CONTENTS (Con't)

ABSTRACT

A synthesis is presented of data concerning Unidentified Flying Objects (UFOs) reported during the past 20 years through governmental, press and private channels. The serious evidence is clarified and analyzed. The data are reported by categories of specially trained observers and studied by patterns of appearance, performance and periodic recurrence.

During the process of selecting the most reliable and significant reports, emphasis was placed on the qualifications of the observer and on cases involving two or more observers. This resulted in 746 reports being selected, after consideration of over 5000 signed reports and many hundreds of reports from newspapers and other publications.

An overall look is taken at the UFO problem: The historical development of the mystery, Congressional attitudes and activity, consideration of the problems and dangers involved, and discussion of what is needed in the way of organized scientific research.

Evidence is presented in support of the hypothesis that UFOs are under intelligent control, making plausible the notion that some of them might be of extraterrestrial origin.

Foreword

Over thirty years ago I compiled this documentary report for the leading UFO investigation group, the National Investigations Committee on Aerial Phenomena (NICAP) in Washington, D.C. Few people at that time were aware of the scope and consistency of UFO reports by credible witnesses such as scientists, professional pilots, police officers, and even U.S. Air Force personnel. The Air Force was officially charged with conducting a UFO investigation, but maintained that nothing of any importance was being observed.

When *The UFO Evidence* was released in July 1964, coinciding with a new wave of sightings after a lull of several years, it received national and international news coverage as well as serious attention in the U.S. Congress. Less than two years later, as the sightings increased, the Air Force UFO project came under heavy fire and the House Armed Services Committee held hearings.

Late in 1966, with prodding from Congress, an investigation of the Air Force Project Blue Book was undertaken through a contract with the University of Colorado. When Dr. E. U. Condon, the scientific director, repeatedly made public statements ridiculing the UFO subject before the investigation was completed, the Colorado Project became equally controversial.

In short, nobody could agree on the evidence or how to go about studying it. Proponents like NICAP insisted that the focus should be on the apparent "signal" (credible reports from qualified witnesses showing strong patterns), while detractors tended to see only "noise" (many witnesses were fooled by common phenomena such as aircraft strobe lights and bright meteors). Despite obvious patterns and consistencies among the data after weak reports were screened out, scientists and public officials failed to recognize them or shied away from the subject because it was too controversial.

In one sense, little has changed since 1964. Skeptics have hardened their attitudes, science and government seem unable to deal with the issue, and many people continue to make poor and unconvincing UFO reports. However, significant reports by highly credible witnesses have multiplied. All of the patterns set forth in *The UFO Evidence* (1964) have been strongly confirmed by repeated observations, and several new patterns have emerged as well.

This report comprises a cross section of the UFO mystery as it appeared then. Sightings are presented by witness category and special types of evidence. *The UFO Evidence* remains a valuable resource and reference work, cited in nearly every major book on the subject published in the past thirty years.

A new volume that will cover the years since 1964 is now in preparation and will be a companion volume to the original report, bringing the subject up to date. New tables and case summaries will demonstrate that expert witnesses have continued to report exactly the same kind of objects: geometric shapes (typically disks, ellipses, or cigars) that perform in typical ways and leave typical physical traces or other evidence.

The new volume will also report the history of the Air Force Project Blue Book after 1964, the University of Colorado Project study, and other new developments in the history of UFOs. It will also address the so-called UFO abduction phenomenon, reported interactions of human beings with apparent alien beings. Abductions first began coming into public awareness late in the 1960s and 1970s, and have dominated the UFO subject in recent years.

This reprint of *The UFO Evidence* (1964) affords recent generations an opportunity to read and study a report that has been widely hailed as a classic of the UFO literature. Copies of the original report have become quite scarce, and those few that can be found sell at a premium on the UFO "black market." The content was eye-opening at the time, and remains even now an important summary of the case for real UFOs. Over thirty years of data since then have totally replicated its findings.

—Richard Hall
Brentwood, Maryland

SECTION I.

A Cross-section of significant cases and guide to additional examples in other sections.

Most people are unaware that UFO sightings, many by exceptionally good witnesses, have been reported regularly in recent years. Contrary to popular belief, the reports have continued into the 1960's. The last fully publicized series of sightings was in November 1957 [Section XII; November 1957 Chronology]. At that time the cases involving electromagnetic effects on automobile motors and lights made headlines all over the country for two weeks.

Before that, UFO sightings were reported and discussed widely through 1952; in that year, the Air Force (officially charged with investigation of UFO reports) investigated a record number of cases—1,501. UFOs violated the restricted air spaces over Washington, D.C., on two consecutive weekends in July, were tracked on radar, and pursued by jet interceptors [Section XII; July 1952 Chronology].

Since 1957, the newswire services and national radio and television have rarely mentioned UFO sightings. As a result, few people outside the immediate area of occurrence ever learn about a report. Local newspapers and stations continue to report UFO activity, but it has been considered "local" rather than "national" news, in general.

The misconception that UFOs are no longer being sighted, and other erroneous beliefs, are challenged in this Section. Sample reports are given, representing a cross-section of the entire report, and providing a digest of the type of evidence which constitutes the UFO problem. The cases also were chosen to furnish examples of features of UFO sightings, such as maneuver patterns [Section XII] and UFOs tracked by instruments [Section VIII].

ARE UFOs STILL BEING SEEN?

This is probably the most common question asked by casually interested persons. The answer is "yes." But the sighting reports do not receive the publicity they once did. [See Section XI for chronology of recent sightings].

A grayish disc-shaped object which hovered, wobbling on its axis, then evaded pursuit, was sighted October 2, 1961 at Salt Lake City, Utah, airport. Private pilot Waldo J. Harris, a real estate broker, investigated the object in his light aircraft as 8-10 ground personnel at the airport watched. Mr. Harris signed a NICAP report form on October 10, and later answered additional questions by a NICAP Subcommittee member. His report: "I was preparing to take off in a Mooney Mark 20A from the North-South runway at Utah Central Airport when I noticed a bright spot in the sky over the southern end of the Salt Lake Valley. I began my take-off run without paying much attention to the bright spot as I assumed that it was some aircraft reflecting the sun as it turned. After I was airbourne and trimmed for my climb-out, I noticed that the bright spot was still about in the same position as before. I still thought it must be the sun reflecting from an airplane, so I made my turn onto my cross-wind leg of the traffic pattern, and was about to turn downwind when I noticed that the spot was in the same spot still.

"I turned out of the pattern and proceeded toward the spot to get a better look. As I drew nearer I could see that the object had no wings nor tail nor any other exterior control surfaces protruding from what appeared to be the fuselage. It seemed to be hovering with a little rocking motion. As it rocked up away from me, I could see that it was a disc shaped object. I would guess the diameter at about 50 to 55 feet, the thickness in the middle at about 8 to 10 feet. It had the appearance of sand-blasted aluminum. I could see no windows or doors or any other openings, nor could I see any landing gear doors, etc., protruding, nor showing.

"I believe at the closest point I was about 2 miles from the object, at the same altitude or a little above the object. It rose abruptly about 1000 feet above me as I closed in, giving me an excellent view of the underneath side, which was exactly like the upper side as far as I could tell. Then it went off on a course of about 170 degrees for about 10 miles where it again hovered with that little rocking motion.

"I again approached the object, but not so closely this time, when it departed on a course of about 245 degrees climbing at about 18 to 20 degrees above the horizon. It went completely out of sight in 2 or 3 seconds. As you know I can keep our fastest jets in sight for several minutes, so you can see that this object was moving rather rapidly."

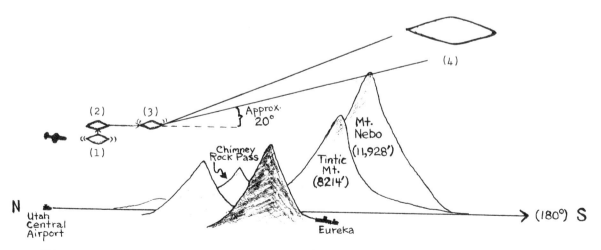

(1) UFO hovered with rocking motion at about 6000 ft. south of the airport.
(2) UFO rose abruptly estimated 1000 ft. as Harris closed in.
(3) UFO quickly moved away an estimated 10 miles, stopped and hovered, rocking motion.(SSE).
(4) As Harris closed in second time, UFO took off at high speed on 245° course (WSW) climbing at an angle of about 20°, completely out of sight in 2-3 seconds.(Copy of observer's sketch).

"All the time I was observing the object, after getting visual confirmation from the ground, I was describing what I saw on radio unicom frequency. I was answering questions from the ground both from Utah Central, and Provo. The voice at Provo said that they could not see the object, but at least 8 or 10 people did see it from the ground at Utah Central Airport.

"As to seeing it again, I was returning to the field after it had departed when I was asked over radio if I still could see the object, and I reported that I could not. They said they had it in sight again. I turned back and saw it at much greater distance only for about a second or two when it completely vanished. The guys on the ground said it went straight up as it finally left, but I didn't see that departure."

On the NICAP report form, Mr. Harris pointed out that the UFO at one time "passed below the horizon in front of mountains to the south." This fact rules out any astronomical explanation.

Later that month, an engineer in Pennsylvania saw a formation of four disc-shaped objects, with apparent lights or ports on the rims.

HAVE SCIENTISTS REPORTED UFOs?

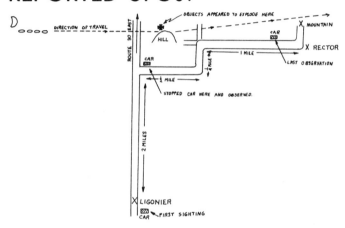

NATIONAL INVESTIGATIONS COMMITTEE ON AERIAL PHENOMENA
1536 Connecticut Avenue N. W.
NOrth 7-9434   Washington 6, D. C.

REPORT ON UNIDENTIFIED FLYING OBJECT(S)

This form includes questions asked by the United States Air Force and by other Armed Forces' investigating agencies, and additional questions to which answers are needed for full evaluation by NICAP.
After all the information has been fully studied, the conclusion of our Evaluation Panel will be published by NICAP in its regularly issued magazine or in another publication. Please try to answer as many questions as possible. Should you need additional room, please use another sheet of paper. Please print or typewrite. Your assistance is of great value and is genuinely appreciated. Thank you.

1. Name   Carl H. Geary, Jr.   Place of Employment Elliott Co., Jeannette, Pa.
   Address 228 Ridge Ave., Derry, Pa.   Occupation Engineer (Div. of Carrier Corp.)
                                                 Education Pennsylvania State University
                                                 Special Training
   Telephone OXbow 4-2678   Military Service U. S. Army, C.I.C.

2. Date of Observation October 30, 1961   Time 12:20 AM   XXXX   Time Zone Eastern

3. Locality of Observation Ligonier, Pa.

4. How long did you see the object?   0   Hours 45 Minutes   Seconds

5. Please describe weather conditions and the type of sky; i.e., bright daylight, nighttime, dusk, etc.
   Nighttime - sporadic cloud cover - moon approximately 1/2 full.

6. Position of the Sun or Moon in relation to the object and to you.
   Moon E-N-E position about 30° above horizon - objects passed just below moon - they

7. If seen at night, twilight, or dawn, were the stars or moon visible? were below cloud cover mentioned
   Moon   above.

8. Were there more than one object? 4   If so, please tell how many, and draw a sketch of what you saw, indicating direction of movement, if any.

9. Please describe the object(s) in detail. For instance, did it (they) appear solid, or only as a source of light; was it revolving, etc? Please use additional sheets of paper, if necessary.   See attached sheet.

10. Was the object(s) brighter than the background of the sky? Yes.

11. If so, compare the brightness with the Sun, Moon, headlights, etc.   See attached sheet.

12. Did the object(s) —   (Please elaborate, if you can give details.)
    a.   Appear to stand still at any time? No.
    b.   Suddenly speed up and rush away at any time? No.
    c.   Break up into parts or explode? Seemed to explode, but obviously did not.
    d.   Give off smoke? No.
    e.   Leave any visible trail? No.
    f.   Drop anything? No.
    g.   Change brightness? Yes.
    h.   Change shape? No.
    i.   Change color? No change in color, only in intensity of color.

13. Did the object(s) at any time pass in front of, or behind of, anything? If so, please elaborate giving distance, size, etc, if possible.
    See attached sheet.

14. Was there any wind? Yes.   If so, please give direction and speed. Approx. 15 mph from West to East.

15. Did you observe the object(s) through an optical instrument or other aid, windshield, windowpane, storm window, screening, etc? What? Observed objects through car windshield - open window - and out in the open.

16. Did the object(s) have any sound? No.   What kind?   How loud?

17. Please tell if the object was (were) —
    X.   Fuzzy or blurred.
    X.   Like a bright star.
    c.   Sharply outlined.

18. Was the object —
    a.   Self-luminous?   self-luminous
    b.   Dull finish?
    c.   Reflecting?
    d.   Transparent?

19. Did the object(s) rise or fall while in motion? They oscillated in a seemingly sideward motion from direction of travel.

20. Tell the apparent size of the object(s) when compared with the following held at arm's length:
    a.   Pinhead   d.   Nickel   g.   Orange
    b.   Pea   *a.   Half dollar   h.   Grapefruit
    c.   Dime   f.   Silver dollar   i.   Larger

    Or, if easier, give apparent size in inches on a ruler held at arm's length.

21. How did you happen to notice the object(s)? Am interested in astronomy. Noticed the 4 objects in a straight line across sky, at same magnitude & altitude - very seldom see celestial
22. Where were you and what were you doing at the time of sighting?   configurations like this.
    Driving car at first sighting.
23. How did the object(s) disappear from view? Objects seemed to float over mountain top.

24. Compare the speed of the object(s) with a piston or jet aircraft at the same apparent altitude. Compares more with speed of a piper cub. I paced them in car, nearly parallel at about 20 mph.
25. Were there any conventional aircraft in the location at the time or immediately afterwards? If so, please elaborate. No.

26. Please estimate the distance of the object(s). 1/2 to 3/4 mile

27. What was the elevation of the object(s) in the sky? Please mark on this hemisphere sketch:

28. Names and addresses of other witnesses, if any. None. Tried to get Wm. Huskey of Rector, Pa. out it
    time to see them, but they had disappeared over mountain by then.
29. Please draw a map of the locality of the observation showing North; your position; the direction from which the object(s) appeared and disappeared from view; the direction of its course over the area; roads, towns, villages, railroads, and other landmarks within a mile.

30. Is there an airport, military, governmental, or research installation in the area? Nearest civilian airport about 10 miles from area.
31. Have you seen other objects of an unidentified nature? If so, please describe these observations, using a separate sheet of paper.
    Yes - see attached sheet.
32. Please enclose photographs, motion pictures, news clippings, notes of radio or television programs (include time, station and date, if possible) regarding this or similar observations, or any other background material. We will return the material to you.
    None.
33. Were you interrogated by Air Force investigators? By any other federal, state, county, or local officials? If so, please state the name and rank or title of the agent, his office, and details as to where and when the questioning took place. Did not report to Air Force. Have read Maj. Keyhoe's books & disagree with A.F. handling of situa-
    Were you asked or told not to reveal or discuss the incident? If so, were any reasons or official orders mentioned? Please   tion.
    elaborate carefully.

34. We should like permission to quote your name in connection with this report. This action will encourage other responsible citizens to report similar observations to NICAP. However, if you prefer, we will keep your name confidential. Please note your choice by checking the proper statement below. In any case, please fill in all parts of the form, for our own confidential files. Thank you for your cooperation.

    You may use my name. (X)   Please keep my name confidential. ( )

35. Date of filling out this report: Signature: Carl H Geary Jr
    November 16, 1961

Skeptics have often claimed in public forums that "no astronomer has ever seen a UFO," sometimes implying that this proved UFOs do not exist. Astronomers, other scientists, and experienced observers of many types have often made reports [Section V, VI].

One detailed report by trained observers, describing a maneuvering elliptical UFO, has been reported briefly in the literature. The full, copyrighted story is here reproduced, with permission of the publisher.

[J. Gordon Vaeth, "200 Miles Up — The Conquest of the Upper Air," Second Edition, Revised Printing. Copyright (c) 1956, The Ronald Press Company, N. Y., ppg. 113-116.]

The General Mills, Inc., balloon personnel, who launched and tracked most of the large plastic research balloons during the 1940's and 1950's took little stock in UFO reports until April 24, 1949.

"On that date, a balloon crew was at the White Sands Proving Ground in New Mexico, together with personnel from the U.S. Navy Special Devices Center for a special Skyhook flight to be undertaken for that Office of Naval Research activity. The author was present as Navy representative in charge of the ground handling and balloon phases of the operation.

"As part of this particular project, a balloon launching site had been established three miles north of Arrey, New Mexico. Charles B. Moore, Jr., an aerologist, graduate engineer and balloonist, and four enlisted personnel from the Navy Unit, White Sands Proving Ground, had set up facilities there to observe and record local weather data preparatory to the Special Devices Center Skyhook operation. Instrumentation on hand consisted of a stop watch and a ML-47 (David White) theodolite, a tracking instrument consisting of a 25-power telescope so mounted as to provide readings of vertical (elevation) and horizontal (azimuth) bearings.

"At 10:20 A.M. on April 24th, this group of five released a small 350-gram weather balloon for observation of upper wind velocities and directions. The balloon was followed by Moore with the theodolite until immediately after the 10:30 reading, when he relinquished the tracking instrument to look up to find the balloon with the naked eye.

"Searching the sky for the balloon, he thought he had found it when he saw a whitish spherical object right along the direction the theodolite was pointed (45 degrees elevation and 210 degrees azimuth). The object was moving east at a rate of 5 degrees of azimuth change per second.

"When the difference in angle between the theodolite and the supposed balloon became apparent, Moore took over the theodolite and found the true balloon still there, whereupon he immediately abandoned it and picked up the unidentified object as it came out of the sun. At the time, the sun was at a computed bearing of 60 degrees elevation and 127 degrees azimuth. The object was moving too fast to be kept in the scope through cranking the theodolite around; one of the men, therefore, had to point the theodolite while Moore observed the object through the telescope.

"The object was an ellipsoid about 2-1/2 times as long as it was wide. It had a length of about .02 degrees subtended angle and was gleaming white in color. It did not have metallic or reflected shine. Toward the underside near the tail, the gleaming white became a light yellow.

"The object, readily visible to the naked eye and seen by all the members of the group, filled the field of the theodolite's 25-power scope. Its rapid movement, unfortunately, prevented Moore from obtaining a hard or clear focus, and no good detail was observable.

"The azimuth angle decreased as the object continued on a north heading (it originally came out of the southwest). Becoming smaller in size it moved to an azimuth reading of 20 degrees to 25 degrees, at which point the azimuth held constant. Coincidentally with this constant azimuth, the elevation angle suddenly increased from 25 degrees minimum to 29 degrees, at which point the object was lost to sight. It disappeared in a sharp climb after having been visible to Moore and his group for about 60 seconds.

"Fifteen minutes after the object had disappeared, Moore sent up another pibal weather balloon to check wind values. This balloon burst after an 88-minute flight to 93,000 feet and traveled only 13 miles in a southerly direction during that time. This was positive proof that the object could not have been a balloon moving at such angular speed below 90,000 feet.

"The object was seen under conditions of a cloudless sky and no haze. It left no vapor trail or exhaust. It was observed from an isolated mud flat in the New Mexico desert where there was extreme quiet; no noise of any kind was heard in connection with the sighting, and there were no cars, airplanes, or other noises nearby which might have blotted out sound coming from the object.

"As the day progressed and airplanes flew over and near the balloon launching site, Moore's group was able to identify them by appearance and engine noise. They saw nothing again that day which bore any resemblance to the white elliptical, unidentified object.

"Moore's sighting was an extremely fortunate one in that tracking instrumentation was set up and a weather balloon airbourne at the time. It represents one of the best substantiated and authentic unidentified object sightings on record.

"The foregoing discussion of 'flying saucers' does not represent any desire by the author to become involved in this controversial subject. The saucers have been mentioned because there has been in a number of cases a close relationship between reported sightings and the flight trajectories of Skyhook balloons. The description of Moore's instrumented sighting of an unidentified object has been included because it is authentic, details have not been previously published, and it occurred during a Skyhook operation.

"The author, and indeed Moore himself, make no claim that the unidentified object was a 'flying saucer.' The details have been set forth. Let the reader take the sighting for what it is worth and evaluate it for himself!" [1.]

Dr. Seymour L. Hess, who sighted a UFO in 1950, is a meteorologist and astronomer. He is currently head of the Department of Meteorology, Florida State University, and is considered an expert on planetary atmospheres. [2.] See letter next col.

Another sighting by General Mills, Inc., personnel in the vicinity of White Sands, New Mexico, was reported by Capt. Edward J. Ruppelt, former Chief of the Air Force Project Blue Book UFO investigation. [3.] Two General Mills employees and four others at Artesia, New Mexico, were watching a Skyhook balloon, January 16, 1951. Suddenly they noticed two tiny specks on the horizon moving rapidly toward them. The objects shot

I saw the object between 12:15 and 12:20 P.M. May 20, 1950 from the grounds of the Lowell Observatory. It was moving from the South-east to the Northwest. It was extremely prominent and showed some size to the naked eye, that is, it was not merely a pinpoint. During the last half of its visibility I observed it with 4-power binoculars. At first it looked like a parachute tipped at an angle to the vertical, but this same effect could have been produced by a sphere partly illuminated by the sun and partly shadowed, or by a disc-shaped object as well. Probably there are still other configurations which would give the same impression under proper inclination and illumination. I could see it well enough to be sure it was not an airplane (no propeller or wings were apparent) nor a bird. I saw no evidence of exhaust gases nor any markings on the object.

Most fortunately the object passed between me and a small bright cumulus cloud in the Northwest. Thus it must have been at or below the cloud level. A few seconds later it disappeared, apparently into the cloud.

Against the sky it was very bright but against the cloud it was dark. This could be produced by a grey body which would be bright against the relatively dark sky, but dark against the bright cloud. Alternatively, if the object were half in sunlight and half shadowed the sunlit part might have had no detectable contrast with the cloud while the shadowed part appeared dark.

I immediately telephoned the U.S. Weather Bureau (2-3 miles S.W. of the Observatory). They were estimating the cloud to be 6000 feet above the ground. Now estimates of cloud heights are rather risky, but I obtained their observations of temperature and dew point, and from the known lapse rates of these quantities in a convective atmosphere, calculated the cloud base to be at 12,000 ft. I believe this latter figure to be the more accurate one because later in the afternoon the cumulus clouds thickened but at all times remained well above the tops of our nearby mountains. These are about 6000 feet above us.

Thus, having some idea of the object's elevation and its angular diameter through the binoculars (about equivalent to a dime seen at 50 ft. with the naked eye), I calculated its size to be 3 to 5 ft. for a height of 6-12 thousand feet, and a zenith angle of about 45°. This size estimate could easily be in error by a factor or two, but I am sure it was a small object.

The clouds were drifting from the SW to the NE at right angles to the motion of the object. Therefore it must have been powered in some way. I did not time it but for that elevation I would estimate its speed to be about 100 miles per hour, perhaps as high as 200 m.p.h. This too means a powered craft. However, I could hear no engine noise.

Seymour L. Hess
Seymour L. Hess

This is a copy of the account which I set down within an hour of the sighting.

straight toward the balloon, tipped on edge revealing their disc shape, circled the balloon once and flew off over the horizon. In comparison with the known size of the balloon, the discs were estimated to be 60 feet in diameter.

A particularly detailed account of a lens-shaped disc was obtained from an experienced engineer by the NICAP Assistant Director in personal correspondence during 1955. [4.]

Date: October 1954, about mid-month
Location: Cherry Valley, New York
Time: About 4:00 p.m.
Witness: Major A. B. Cox, graduate of Yale University, member of the American Society of Mechanical Engineers, and Society of American Engineers.

Excerpts from letter dated December 28, 1955 from Major A. B. Cox to Richard Hall:

"The sky was more or less covered with streaks or layers of clouds, with blue sky between, so that the rays of the sun came through almost horizontally, the time being not far from sunset in the Valley. I was walking in a NE direction, having been an airplane spotter for a long time, I have formed the habit of looking at the sky, quite naturally.

"I happened to be looking at the West in the direction of my farm buildings, perhaps a half mile distant, and saw something which at first glance was about over my farm buildings. It was quite low, and did not seem to be more than a few hundred feet above the earth. I thought at first it was a large airplane not moving very swiftly. . . . It was moving horizontally in a direction parallel to my own direction. Then I noticed that it seemed to make no noise, and then I could not see any wings or tail or fuselage generally.

"It seemed to be a large disc or lens-shaped object, and in comparison with the objects below I estimated it to be perhaps 30 or 35 feet in diameter. . . . It was moving like a wheel sliding sidewise and not rotating, and in perspective presented an elliptical appearance such as any circular object would when viewed from an angle; the degree of ellipticity varying as it came up and then passed me. I must have seen it for 20 seconds or a little more. Then it got ahead of me and it presented the appearance of a circular disc, perhaps five or six feet thick. The color was grey, and I think perhaps a little darker on the rim or edge; not much but enough to make the edge sharply defined.

"Suddenly it stopped and seemed to be going in a direction more or less at right angles to its first motion, but still in an upright direction. . . This sudden stop interested me as an engineer, because any sudden retardation or acceleration requires in so large an object the application of a very considerable force, and seemed a much shorter turn and a more rapid turn than any airplane I had ever seen could be capable of.

"It then began to ascend in a direction of perhaps at right angles to its first direction and at an upward angle of perhaps 30 or 35 degrees from the horizontal. . . . There were some fleecy clouds above it, and it entered them and was lost to sight for perhaps a second or so, to emerge into vision again above this first layer of clouds. Its direction had not changed, and shortly after it entered some more layers of cloud, which were thicker, and was lost to view.''

ARE UFOs INTELLIGENTLY CONTROLLED?

The definitive answer to this question must await a full-fledged investigation by scientists using appropriate instrumentation, as NICAP advocates [Section XIV]. However, the accumulation of reports by good observers and some of the special evidence such as radar trackings [Section VIII] strongly suggest this hypothesis. How else can one explain the maneuvers of the disc which pilot Waldo Harris attempted to investigate? The "curiosity" evidenced by the two discs which circled the Skyhook balloon? The powered flight indicated by the reports of Dr. Hess, Engineer Cox, and others? Section II discusses this question in detail.

How else can one explain reports such as the following of objects approaching at meteorlike speed, then hovering or maneuvering? When these reports come from pilots, scientists, engineers, and police officers they deserve far more serious, scientific attention than they have yet received.

> Date: May 13, 1952
> Location: National City, California
> Time: Approximately 8:55 p.m. PDT
> Witnesses: Donald R. Carr, aeronautical engineer, and at least six others in separate locations, including a teacher who is a former Navy pilot.
> Excerpts from Mr. Carr's report. [5.]

"I saw what I thought was the trail of a large meteor appear, approximately 5 degrees of arc East of a line between the two pointers and almost exactly in the center of the bowl of the Big Dipper. [See diagram.] The trail was of a red color and appeared to be coming down at about an angle of 20 degrees to my line of sight and in a southwesterly direction. Only the red trail was visible for about two seconds and then a small white dot became visible, from which the trail was emanating. The speed appeared to be meteoric and so I still thought the object was what is commonly called a 'shooting star.' [After 2 or 3 seconds] the white object had an apparent diameter of 1/64 to 1/32 inch. The trail faded and the object still continued coming down. The speed appeared to be decreasing and I noted a certain erratic quality to the flight of the object, which now appeared to have a self-luminous or fluorescent quality. . . [for about 10 more seconds] the object was following a gradual curved path in process of levelling off. . . [then] the object was flying level on a course almost due West. . . . I estimated the altitude of the object at this point of its trajectory to be from 10,000 to 15,000 feet. Its speed at this time appeared to be within the range of known aircraft speeds. To the naked eye the object appeared as a sphere of about 1/16 inch diameter. . . . Through the [6 power] telescope the object presented a larger disc but the brightness did not appreciably increase. . . . In level flight the object seemed to dart from side to side in an oscillating motion without diminishing of forward speed. . . . After travelling a course almost due West for approximately one mile, the object turned toward the Northwest and appeared to circle over San Diego Bay and Point Loma and disappeared travelling North at a constant altitude and speed. During the entire time the object was visible there was absolutely no apparent sound created by it. Despite its terrific speed in its dive there was no shock wave or noise from its power source.''

About 9:25 p.m., Mr. Carr observed what appeared to be the same object returning from the North, and circling West. It passed over downtown San Diego, where bright ground lights seemed to reflect off a metal hull.

"It is my conviction," Mr. Carr stated, "that since this object followed an apparently controlled course it was not moving under the influence of gravity, and must have been guided by an intelligence unknown to us. Its dive from an extreme altitude at possibly meteoric speed, its deceleration, levelling off, and circle of the city twice indicate that it arrived from interplanetary space and was under intelligent control.''

The former Navy Pilot, Harold Strawn, with a group of students in La Mesa also witnessed the meteoric appearance, the levelling off and circling.

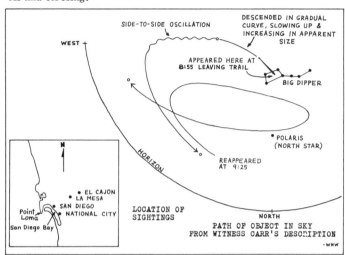

A multiple visual and multiple radar sighting, similarly suggesting controlled flight, occurred August 12, 1953; near Rapid City, South Dakota. The UFO was first spotted hovering in the eastern sky by the Ground Observer Corps. It moved in over the city, then back to its original position. Then ground radar began tracking the UFO, and an F-84 was scrambled and vectored in on the object, chasing it for 120 miles. Both the UFO and the jet showed plainly on the GCI radar screen. Each time the jet began to close in, the UFO would move ahead with a burst of speed. When the pilot gave up and turned back to base, the UFO turned and followed.

A second F-84 scrambled and chased the UFO 160 miles, obtaining a radar lock-on. The UFO again stayed just out of reach. When the pilot switched on his radar-ranging gunsight, and the red light blinked on showing something real and solid was ahead of him, the pilot was scared. ("When I talked to him, he readily admitted that he'd been scared. . .he asked the controller if he could break off the intercept." [6., p. 305].) This time the UFO continued on course to the north. The Ground Observer Corps on the path ahead was notified, and reported seeing a light speeding north.

At the climax of the sighting, when the pilot became frightened, ground radar showed the jet and the UFO; the pilot's gunsight radar showed the UFO, and the pilot could see with his own eyes a speeding unidentified light in front of him.

A NICAP member later queried the Air Force about the case, and received a written reply on September 17, 1958 stating: "Photos of the radar scope and gun camera photos were made but were not sufficiently clear for evaluation. The Ellsworth Air Force Base case is still listed as unknown or unsolved." [7.]

NICAP Note: The fact that the gun camera photos showed an image at all is further proof that something real and solid was outspeeding jet interceptors. In conjunction with the multiple radar and multiple visual observations, an image on the film is close to complete proof of the reality of UFOs.

Capt. W. J. Hull, veteran Capital Airlines pilot, was a UFO skeptic. He had written an article entitled "The Obituary of the Flying Saucers" for The Airline Pilot magazine. At 10:10 p.m., November 14, 1956, Captain Hull was a pilot of Capital Flight No. 77, approaching Mobile, Alabama, enroute from New York City [8.] Suddenly, he and his co-pilot, Peter MacIntosh, noticed a bright light through the upper part of the windshield. The plane was on a southwesterly course, and the object, looking like a meteor, was falling across their path from left to right. But instead of burning out, the "meteor" halted abruptly directly in front of the plane.

"What the hell is it, a jet?" MacIntosh shouted.

As the UFO remained a constant distance in front of the plane, Captain Hull grabbed his microphone and called Mobile Tower:

"Bates Tower, this is Capital 77. Look out toward the north and east and see if you can see a strange white light hovering in the sky."

Mobile quickly answered that a thick cloud layer was obscuring vision, and asked Captain Hull if he thought the object was in the vicinity of Mobile.

"Affirmative," Hull replied. "It is directly ahead of us and at about our altitude or slightly higher. We are right over Jackson and have descended to 10,000 feet. . ."

Immediately after the radio exchange, the UFO began to move. It darted back and forth, rising and falling, making extremely sharp turns, sometimes changing course 90 degrees in an instant. The color and size remained constant.

"MacIntosh and I sat there completely flabbergasted at this unnerving exhibition," Captain Hull reported. After 30 seconds or more, the UFO ceased its violent maneuvers and again appeared to hover ahead of the plane. About this time Mobile Tower called back:

"Capital 77, we are trying to raise the Brookley AFB Tower."

At this moment, the UFO began another series of "crazy gyrations, lazy 8's, square chandelles. . ." and then shot out over the Gulf of Mexico rising at a steep angle. It diminished rapidly to a pinpoint and disappeared in the night. (Elapsed time: At least two minutes.)

"The one thing which I can't get over," Captain Hull stated, "is the fact that when it came, it came steeply downward; when it departed after its amazing show, it went steeply upward!"

December 19/20 of 1958 was a cloudless night in Dunellen, New Jersey. At 12:55 a.m., Patrolmen LeRoy A. Arboreen and B. Talada were on night patrol, cruising west on Center Street. From an area elevated about 15 to 20 feet they had an unobstructed view to north, south, and west.

In a signed report to NICAP, [9] Patrolman Arboreen (ex-Navy man and graduate of the New Jersey State Police Academy) described the experience:

"This object came at us from the west. At first it looked like a red hot piece of coal about the size of a quarter held at arm's length. In a matter of seconds it was as large as a ruler held at arm's length. That is when it came to a complete stop. . .

"The shape of the object was distinct. (See illustration.) The body of the object was solid bright red and it gave off a pulsating red glow completely around the object. The object hovered a few seconds, then made a left turn and again hovered for a few seconds, then went straight up like a shot. We watched it until it completely faded beyond the stars."

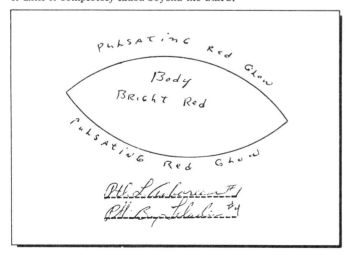

In this matter-of-fact manner, the two officers described an occurrence which is totally inexplicable. Meteors do not hover or shoot upward. No known aircraft is elliptical, and glows bright red in flight, not to mention the observed performance.

Nor does any known phenomenon descend through the atmosphere like a meteor, then circle around, as Engineer Carr observed. Nor does the gyrating light observed by Captain Hull, descending, pacing the airliner, then ascending, have any natural explanation.

HAVE UFOs BEEN SEEN IN OTHER COUNTRIES?

This surprising misconception, that UFOs are exclusively a native phenomenon of the United States, is completely refuted in the Foreign Reports Section [X]. Part of the reason for this erroneous belief is the lack of information on foreign sightings reported by newswire representatives abroad. In 1962, for instance, a major concentration of sightings occurred in Argentina [Section XII, Argentine Chronology], beginning in May and lasting almost all year. A few of the May sightings were reported briefly in the New York Times (June 3, 1962) from a Reuters dispatch, but in a manner implying that the sightings lasted only one day. In general, U.S. news coverage of these sightings was practically nonexistent. Reuters apparently was the only news agency to report them at all outside of Argentina.

Most major countries of the world for years have had either official or unofficial investigations of UFO sightings [Section X]. American servicemen overseas have contributed many reports.

At 11:20 a.m. March 29, 1952, an Air Force pilot was flying a T-6 north of Misawa, Japan. It was a bright cloudless day. Lt. D. C. Brigham was in the T-6 target plane in a practice intercept mission, with a flight of two F-84's pursuing him.

As the first F-84 overtook him at 6000 feet, Brigham noticed a flash of sunlight behind it and saw a small shiny disc-shaped object gaining on the interceptor. The UFO curved toward the F-84, decelerating rapidly to the Thunderjet's air speed (150 to 160 mph) and flipping up on edge in a 90 degree bank. Then it fluttered along close to the interceptor's fuselage (between the two aircraft) for 2 to 3 seconds, and pulled away around the starboard wing, flipping once, apparently as it hit the slipstream. Finally, the object passed the F-84, crossed in front, pulled up abruptly, accelerated, and shot out of sight in a near vertical climb.

Lieutenant Brigham estimated that the UFO at its closest point was 30 to 50 feet away from his plane. It was round, shiny as polished chromium, and seemed to be about 8 inches in diameter. Throughout the observation, the disc rocked back and forth in 40 degree banks at about one-second intervals. [See Section XII, Flight Characteristics.] Lieutenant Brigham saw no exhaust or protrusions, but reported a ripple in the apparently metal skin around the edge of the disc. [10]

Foreign pilots, scientists, and engineers also have observed UFOs many times. Around sunset June 30, 1954, south of Goose Bay, Labrador, a British Overseas Airways (BOAC) airliner was paced by a large "parent" object and about six satellite objects [See Section X, Foreign Reports]. Later that night (about 2:15 p.m. local time near Oslo, Norway), two UFOs operating in tandem were observed and filmed under especially favorable conditions. [11.] A solar eclipse was in progress, and three planes carrying scientists and technicians on a scientific expedition were flying through the moon's shadow. About 50 people in the three aircraft saw two "enormous" silvery discs swoop down from some clouds 15 to 20 miles away (estimate based on fact UFOs were in sunlight).

The objects sped along the horizon keeping an exact distance from each other, one slightly behind and above the other, both with forward edge tilted down. The observers detected apparent rotation, as the UFOs levelled off and disappeared into the distance after about 30 seconds. The chief cameraman of the expedition, John Bjornulf, managed to expose about 10 seconds of movie film which showed the UFOs. The films, released by Gaumont, a British firm, were shown on American television September 26, 1954. Still photographs of the UFOs have also been printed. Ernest Graham, one of the witnesses, stated that 50 persons afterwards wrote reports on what they had seen. [12]

Another unexplainable disc was observed, tracked on radar, and chased by two U. S. Air Force jet pilots somewhere in the Far East. [13.]

"On____ December 1956 two USAF jet pilots were practicing ground radar positioned intercepts on each other in the vicinity of_____.

During one run, the report states, the intercepting pilot picked up a large unexplained radar blip; he estimated the UFO to be as large as a B-29 bomber. Radar showed it to be 20 miles away and 30 degrees to the left.

"Pilot called the GCI [Ground Control Intercept] site to ask if they had a target which would correspond to the unidentified blip. After receiving an answer in the negative, he asked for and received permission to determine the nature of the source of the radar return."

The pilot closed in at over 700 mph; at 8 miles range a round object became visible exactly where the radar showed it. The apparent size was very large. The pilot described it as "the size of a lead pencil eraser if placed against the windscreen." [Using figures supplied by North American Aviation, the diameter of the UFO was computed to be about 350 feet.] [14.]

The pilot got a radar "lock-on" (automatically guiding his plane toward the UFO). As he continued to close in, his radar was suddenly jammed by a strong interference. Using antijam procedure, the pilot switched frequency. For 10 seconds, this eliminated the mysterious interference pulses, then they began again. But the pulsations were not strong enough to break the radar lock-on, and the jet held its course.

"The jet closed to within 5 nautical miles of the object and could not close further. When the pilot was closest to the unidentified object, it appeared to make a shallow left turn. It had the appearance of being circular on the bottom."

The color of the UFO was described as a golden tan, with no reflection from the sun. After the UFO began turning, the pilot's radar indicated that the object was "moving up and away at from 1,500 to 1,800 knots [1,700 to over 2,000 mph]."

The Air Force report states that this is an estimate, since the UFOs' rate of departure was faster than the jet's radar could track. The blip "disappeared by moving rapidly off the top of the scope."

The Intelligence Report shows that the jet and all of its equipment was immediately checked, and all systems were satisfactory. Under "Comments of the interrogation officers," the Report states:

"The observing pilot, Lt._____, had many flying hours as of the time of the incident. Over half had been logged in this type of jet. He appeared to be conscientious and reported the incident in a straightforward, slightly embarrassed manner, saying that he would doubt the possibility of such an occurrence if it hadn't actually happened to him.

"The fact that no unidentified tracks were observed by ground radar should not be given much weight in evaluating this report. Both the jet aircraft involved required IFF in order that the controlling GCI site could plot them." ["IFF" is an identification code transmitter system developed in World War II called "Identification, Friend or Foe." The fact that IFF signals were required for ground radar to plot the jets indicates that the Air Force planes otherwise would not have shown up on the ground radar.]

The above sample cases contain examples of most of the recurring features of reported UFOs:

√ Reports from competent observers such as scientists and pilots.

√ Flight characteristics such as a disc wobbling on its axis.

√ Maneuver patterns such as hovering and terrific acceleration.

√ Physical evidence such as radar trackings and electromagnetic effects.

Typically, the majority of reports describe disc-shaped or elliptical objects. [See Section XII, Patterns, for additional details.]

COULDN'T THEY BE U.S. OR SOVIET SECRET DEVICES?

When a person who has been a skeptic first becomes convinced that UFOs are, or might be, real, his usual first reaction is that they must be secret devices. While space activity in the past six years undoubtedly has caused some false UFO reports,

the activity of secret test devices on the other hand would necessarily be confined to restricted test areas. The arguments against the secret device theory, then, are:

a. Test devices of one nation would not be observed worldwide [see Section X, Worldwide UFO Reports].

b. If secret devices were operational in the scope necessary to account for UFO reports, the technology implied would cause all current jets and rockets to be completely outmoded. Yet, the direction of our research and experimentation does not reflect such a breakthrough.

c. Perhaps most damaging to the secret device theory is the fact that UFOs apparently have been observed for a very long time [see Section XI, Chronology]. Soviet aerial technology through and after World War II was not impressive. German technology at the end of World War II was impressive, and this has caused advocates of this theory to attribute UFOs to captured German scientists and engineers working secretly for the U.S. or Russia. American technology was making rapid strides at the close of the war, but our hottest operational aerial devices were propeller-driven aircraft, and our few guided missiles were hardly out of the laboratory.

However, NICAP examined this possibility thoroughly, consulting scientists and engineers (including Prof. Dr. Hermann Oberth, famous German rocket expert) and found not the slightest evidence to confirm the rumors of secret devices developed by former Nazi scientists.

The antiquity of UFO sightings, especially, rules out the possibility of any sort of test devices, secret or otherwise, accounting for more than a handful of UFO reports.

Explorer Nicholas Roerich, on an expedition in the Himalayan Mountains, August 5, 1926, and others in his caravan, saw a shiny oval-shaped object [15.] While watching a soaring eagle, they noticed the object far above moving south at high speed and observed it through binoculars. The UFO then made a turn to the southwest and moved out of sight in the distance.

An early postwar observation by an unusually well-trained observer was reported to NICAP Board Member, the Rev. Albert Baller: [See photostat].

ANDREW A. TITCOMB, ARCHITECT
"HILLWINDS"
PERKINSVILLE, VERMONT
TELEPHONE: 2300
MEMBER
AMERICAN INSTITUTE OF ARCHITECTS

April 4, 1955

Rev. Albert Baller
Munson Street
Greenfield, Mass.

Dear Mr. Baller: Re: "Flying Saucer"sighting.

The circumstances of the sighting of an unknown flying object by me were as follows:-

It was in May 1946, at my wife's family home, at La Grange, 4 miles north of Titusville, Florida, where I was spending my terminal leave as Lieutenant j.g. U.S.N.R., having just returned from the Pacific and Far East.

I had spent over a year aboard a destroyer escort as senior watch officer, gunnery officer and radar officer, and was very familiar, both in training and practice to ship and aircraft recognition, night and day under combat circumstances.

I was picking oranges in the forenoon about 100 feet from the house, when a distinct wavering whistling noise of a fast moving body through air made me look up.
Directly overhead I saw a dark "Flying football" shaped thus:-

flying from west to east at about 1000 feet elevation, possibly less, at the speed of a light plane - say 125 m.p.h. It appeared dark against the bright cloud layer which had a ceiling of perhaps 1500 feet - there was no blue sky showing. The sight astonished me, as the only sound was its passage through the air. There was no sound of any engine, it had no wings or other appendages, no props, and no trail of smoke in back. It appeared about 15 or 20 feet long, perhaps less, and as I watched it curved smoothly in an arc to the southeast and vanished forever in a lower cloud bank.

My wife and the rest of the family heard this queer noise and all rushed out to see what it was, and my wife glimpsed it as it vanished in the clouds, confirming my story.

I had never heard of flying saucers and had no idea what we had seen, but assumed that it was some secret device of the Air Force, and so never reported it.

It was not a MAD (magnetic airborn detector) used for anti-submarine work, as it was attached to no cable to a plane above, and there was the noise of no other plane or blimp at the time that could have been hidden, say, in the clouds above.

So that is the story of my "Flying Football", still as much a mystery today as it was to me 9 years ago.

Sincerely yours,   Andrew A. Titcomb

NOTES:

1. For other examples of UFO sightings by General Mills balloon personnel, see J. J. Kaliszewski reports, Section VI.
2. Sample contributions to astronomy literature:
   Hess, Dr. Seymour L., "A Meteorological approach to the question of water vapor on Mars and the mass of the Martian atmosphere," Publications of the Astronomical Society of the Pacific, 60, 289, (1948).
   _____, "Some Aspects of the Meteorology of Mars," Journal of Meteorology, 7, 1, (1950).
   _____, "Blue Haze and the Vertical Structure of the Martian Atmosphere," The Astrophysical Journal, 127, 743, (1958).
3. Ruppelt, Edward J., The Report on Unidentified Flying Objects, (Doubleday, 1956), p. 161.
4. Letter on file at NICAP.
5. Report on file at NICAP.
6. Ruppelt, Edward J., op. cit., p. 303; True, May 1954.
7. Air Force letter on file at NICAP.
8. Quotes taken from Capt. Hull's report to John DuBarry, former associate editor of True magazine, published in CSI Newsletter by a New York UFO group of which DuBarry is president.
9. Report on file at NICAP.
10. From U.S. Air Force Intelligence Report.
11. Chapman, Robert, London Evening News, December 21, 1955; Frame from movie film reproduced in RAF Flying Review, London, July 1957.
12. It is not known whether any of these reports have been published.
13. All quotes taken from unclassified U.S. Air Force Intelligence Report. Exact date, names, and location were deleted in accordance with Air Force policy.
14. The average distance from the pilot's face to the windscreen was determined to be 2.27 feet for the F-86-D Sabrejet, and about 2.50 feet maximum for most jets in operation at the time. The average pencil eraser is one-fourth of an inch in diameter. If the pilot's face was 2.50 feet from the windscreen, the diameter of the UFO was about 352 feet. Even allowing for appreciable error in the pilot's estimation of size, the true size of the UFO would be well over 100 feet diameter.
15. Roerich, Nicholas, Altai-Himalaya, (Fred Stokes, N.Y., 1929), Part II, ppg. 361-362.

SECTION II

INTELLIGENT CONTROL

What is "intelligence"? In reference to human behavior, we usually use the word to mean the application of logic and reason to understand nature or solve human problems. However, we observe "intelligence" by observing the behavior of people as they go about their affairs. We infer that they are intelligent or unintelligent by noticing their apparent awareness of their environment, and how they cope with problems in their environment. We note their behavior as individuals, and in groups. The ability of people to act in concert to accomplish mutual goals generally is considered to be intelligent activity.

In regard to the question of whether aerial devices are intelligently controlled, how is intelligence indicated by the performance of aircraft? If we did not know that the airliners and military jets we see coursing through the sky were guided by pilots, how would their actions lead us to suspect this? First, we might observe some jets rendezvousing, joining formation, then proceeding to act in concert. Then we might see a jet depart from its course and circle a balloon, apparently curious about it, before continuing on its way. Finally, we might notice indications (smoke trails, mechanical parts, high performance, etc.) which suggest to us that these are powered mechanical objects. This would imply intelligent construction and guidance.

UFOs have shown all of these features:
  √ Inquisitiveness, and reaction to environment.
  √ Powered flight.
  √ Formations in coordinated flight.

Reasoning by analogy to human devices and intelligence, the hypothesis that UFOs are intelligently operated is explored below. Caution is required in using this method of reasoning, because it is conceivable that actions which we normally associate with intelligence may not seem so to alien beings, and vice versa. However, there is a good chance that there would be an overlap of "intelligent behavior" between human and alien beings. In particular, we should expect any intelligent beings to be fundamentally curious about things in their environment. Curiosity underlies the acquisition of useful knowledge, which is necessary to intelligence.

In addition to the evidence advanced in this section, other sections contain data showing (a) that UFOs show repeating patterns suggesting a unique and unexplained phenomenon [Section XII], (b) that the observed objects and patterns have no counterparts among atmospheric phenomena which could account for them in terms of known events [Section XII: Maneuvers and Flight Characteristics], and (c) that the hypothesis of intelligently operated devices is reasonable, and adequate to explain the data.

Inquisitiveness

and Reaction to Environment

In case after case, UFOs singly or in formation have paced or followed automobiles, trains, airplanes, and rockets. Often the UFOs have circled the device and taken "evasive action" when pursued.

A Monon Railroad freight train was proceeding through Clinton County, Central Indiana, October 3, 1958. About 3:10 a.m. a formation of four odd white lights crossed ahead of the train. The UFOs turned and traversed the full length of the train, front to back (about a half mile) observed by the entire crew.

After passing the rear of the train, the objects swung east, turned back and followed the train. The bright glow concealed the exact shape of the UFOs, but they appeared flattened and sometimes flew on edge. Operating part of the time in-line abreast with coordinated motions, the objects followed the train until

the conductor shone a bright light on them. Immediately, the UFOs sped away, but returned quickly and continued to pace the train. Total time of observation: about 1 hour 10 minutes.

Finally the UFOs moved away to the northeast and disappeared.

The coordinated maneuvers in formation, reaction to a bright beam of light, and pacing of the train, all suggest some form of intelligence. [1]

Similar cases of vehicles being paced by UFOs also have been reported by experienced observers such as pilots and missile trackers. At White Sands, New Mexico, June 10, 1949, a missile had just been launched when two circular UFOs appeared. As the missile accelerated to about 1,430 mph, the UFOs climbed after it, passed through its exhaust, passed the missile and climbed out of sight. Five separate observation and tracking posts, scattered around the nearby mountains and not in communication with one another, reported observing this performance. One of the posts tracked a similar UFO several minutes later, as it sped west against the wind. [2]

Inquisitiveness and Reaction

Fifty sample cases in which UFOs displayed apparent awareness of their environment, charted here, are divided into two basic types: (a) UFOs which paced vehicles or otherwise appeared to be inquisitive about human devices; (b) UFOs which evaded or otherwise reacted to human devices. (All reports on file at NICAP.)

FEB. 28, 1904 U.S.S. SUPPLY

INQUISITIVENESS AND REACTION CASES

Date & Location	Reported Shape or Appearance	Witnesses	Action
(b) 7-23-48 near Montgomery, Ala.	Cigar	Pilots	Came head-on toward airliner, veered to side, shot straight up into clouds. [Section V]
(a) 10-1-48 Fargo, N.D.	Disc	Pilot, control tower operators	"Dogfight" with National Guard plane, intricate maneuvers, head-on passes, finally shot up out of sight. [Section V]
(b) 11-18-48 near Washington, D. C.	Oval	Pilot, ground crew	Led USAF pilot through "astounding maneuvers." When pilot flashed landing lights on UFO, it streaked away. [Section III]
(b) 3-26-50 near Washington, D. C.	Disc	Private pilot	Pilot spotted UFO below him, dove toward it, object shot up into overcast. [Section V]
(a) & (b) 4-27-50 Goshen, Ind.	Red disc	Pilot, passengers	Overtook airliner, paced it alongside, fled when plane turned toward it. [Section V]
(a) 5-29-50 near Washington, D. C.	Ellipse, bright body light	Pilots	Approached airliner head-on, circled it completely stopping once on each side, suddenly sped away. [Section V]
(a) 1-16-51 Artesia, N.M.	2 discs	Balloon tracking crew	Two discs approached rapidly from horizon, tipped on edge and circled balloon, then sped away. [Section I]
(a) 1-20-51 Sioux City, Iowa	Cigar with body lights	Pilots, passengers	Circled, came head-on toward airliner which was investigating, abruptly reversed direction and paced plane for few seconds, finally shot straight up. [Section V]
(b) 9-11-51 near Sandy Hook, N.J.	Disc	Pilots	First seen descending by USAF pilots in T-33; when pursued levelled off, accelerated, outsped jet and curved away. [Section III]
(b) 10-9-51 near Paris, Ill.	Oblate spheroid	Pilot	Pilot saw UFO hovering motionless, turned directly toward it, object shot away. [Section V]
(a) 1-29-52 Wonsan, Korea	Disc	Bomber crew	Paralleled USAF bomber for 5 minutes, pulled ahead, shot away at angle. [Section III]
(a) 3-29-52 near Misawa, Japan	Disc	T-6 Pilot	Made pass at USAF F-84, slowed and paced it, passed in front, climbed away vertically. [Section I]
(a) 6-18-52 California	Not specified	Bomber crew	Paced USAF B-25 for 30 minutes [Officially reported to AF UFO Project; see Section III]
(a) & (b) 7-13-52 Nr. Washington, D.C.	Ball of light	Pilot	Approached airliner and hovered. When pilot switched on all lights, UFO "took off, going up and away." [Section XII; July 1952 Chronology]
(b) 8-1-52 Dayton, Ohio	Round	Pilots	Jets climbed up to investigate hovering UFO, it streaked away at high speed. [Section III]
(a) 8-28-52 LeRoy, N.Y.	Disc	Family	Observed from ground making tight vertical circles around airliner. [3]
(a) 9-19-52 Topcliffe, England	Disc	Airbase ground observers	Followed meteor jet to base, descended, hovered rotating, suddenly sped away. [Section X]

Date & Location	Reported Shape or Appearance	Witnesses	Action
(b) 10-11-52 Newport News, Va.	Disc	Woman	Hovered in one spot 20 minutes. As jet interceptors neared, UFO tilted up and shot away.
(a) & (b) 12-29-52 Northern Japan	Circular	Pilots	Paralleled USAF F-84; when jet tried to close in, UFO sped away disappearing in seconds [Section III]
(a) 1953 Anaco, Venezuela	Round gray	Pilot	Approached airliner, paced it for 40 minutes, ascended out of sight. [Section X]
(b) 1-28-53 near Albany, Georgia	Circular	Pilot	USAF F-86 pursued UFO; it sped up (confirmed by radar) and disappeared. [Section III]
(a) & (b) 2-16-53 near Anchorage, Alaska	Bright red light source	Transport crew	Approached USAF C-47, stopped and hovered 5 minutes; when plane gave chase, UFO accelerated and quickly vanished. [Officially reported to AF UFO Project; see Section III]
(b) 2-17-53 Elmendorf AFB, Alaska	Red light source	Air Base ground observers	Observed near end of runway climbing; jet gave chase; UFO accelerated "noticeably" and climbed vertically away. [Officially reported to AF UFO Project; see Section III]
(a) & (b) 8-12-53 Rapid City, S.D.	Light source	Pilots, GOC	USAF F-84 chased UFO, turned back and UFO followed. Second jet gave chase, turned back, UFO continued on course seen by Ground Observer Corps post. [Section I]
(b) 3-24-54 Florida Missile range	Round	Pilot	Descended and hovered at 3,000 feet. Marine Corps jet banked toward UFO, it accelerated and sped away. [Section IV]
(a) & (b) 6-23-54 Ohio	Round white light	Pilot	Followed Air National Guard F-51 from Columbus to Vandalia; "took off" when pilot gave chase. [Section V]
(a) & (b) 6-30-54 near Goose Bay, Labrador	Large dark object with smaller satellites	Airliner crew	Paralleled BOAC airliner for 80 miles; disappeared when F-86 interceptor neared to investigate [Section X]
(b) 9-7-54 Origny, France	Luminous disc	Motorists	Disc maneuvered up and down, hovering; as it hovered, motorists turned headlights on it. UFO took off at high speed and dwindled into distant speck.
(a) 10-3-54 near Waben, France	Light source	Motorists, others	UFO followed car at estimated distance of 100 yards, slowed when car did; finally accelerated and sped away, observed by independent witnesses.
(b) 11-26-54 Millville, N.J.	Disc, with 4 body lights forming rectangle	Several	Circled town; when search-light hit it, UFO sped away (large V-formation of round UFOs sighted 70 miles to NE same night).
(a) & (b) 2-2-55 near Merida, Venezuela	Round, "ports" above & below central ring	Pilots	Approached airliner; when plane turned toward it, UFO dove, leveled off, sped away. Radio transmitter failed as pilot tried to report sighting. [Section X]
(a) 5-25-55 London, England	Round, luminous	Man	Sped toward B-47 from SW, hovered above it about 5 seconds; glided away to SE, reversed direction and hovered 8 seconds, suddenly shot away to SW.
(a) & (b) 11-14-55 San Bernardino, Calif.	Globe of white light	Pilot	Approached small plane; pilot blinked landing lights, UFO blinked twice in seeming response. UFO came closer, pilot blinked lights three times; UFO blinked three times, "suddenly backed up in mid-air." [Section V]

11

Date & Location	Reported Shape or Appearance	Witnesses	Action
(b) 12-56 Far East	Circular	Pilot	USAF F-86 investigated unidentified radar blip. Experienced radar interference as he saw and tried to close on circular UFO. When pursued, object shot up and away [Section I]
(a) 3-8-57 Beaumont-Houston, Texas	Large object with 3 brilliant white body lights	Pilots	Approached and passed plane S to N, hovered; moved away when plane neared. Swooped up and down at high speed. [Section V]
(b) 11-5-57 Transvaal, Africa	Cylinder	Many	Hovered, tracked by South African Air Force searchlights; witnesses said UFO "withdrew" behind clouds when light hit it. [Section X]
(a) & (b) 5-5-58 San Carlos, Uruguay	Top-like	Pilot	Approached plane, hovered (pilot felt heat); when plane attempted to close in, UFO darted away and disappeared. [Section X]
(b) 5-17-58 Ft. Lauderdale, Fla.	Orange light	Man and son	Approached from N at low altitude; high-powered spotlight turned on it, UFO flared brilliantly, shot out of sight.
(a) & (b) 10-3-58 near Rossville, Ind.	4 objects, elongated	Train crew	Approached ahead of train, traversed full length, swung around and followed for over an hour. Once darted away when conductor shone spotlight at them. [Section II].
(a) 1-13-59 Pymatuning Lake, Pa.	Blindingly brilliant light	Truck driver	Approached truck, hovered above it (truck electrical system failed); after 3 to 4 minutes, UFO shot away. [Section VIII]
(a) & (b) 7-14-59 Minas Gerais State Brazil	Luminous object	Pilot, airport observers	Followed Brazilian Air Force B-26, frightening pilot; hovered near airport after plane landed. When airport personnel fired flares in direction of UFO, it changed color then shot up and disappeared. [Section X]
(a) 7-2-60 near Maiquetia, Venezuela	Bright light source	Pilots	Followed airliner on parallel course angling toward plane; suddenly shot away at terrific speed. [Section X]
(a) 5-61 near Rio de Janeiro, Brazil	Luminous disc	Airline pilot	Observed circling at sea level; UFO ascended "with incredible speed" to level of plane, circled plane, followed it for over an hour. [Section X]
(b) 10-2-61 Salt Lake City, Utah	Disc	Private pilot, airport observers	Hovered near airport; private pilot approached to investigate, UFO moved up like an elevator and away to S, hovered again; finally rose and shot away to West. [Section I]
(a) 10-21-61 near Datil, N.M.	Four light sources	Man and wife	One UFO flashed ahead of car on Highway 60; as car entered dark canyon, UFO was there; object split into four parts which paced car. As car neared service area, objects flashed up into sky and disappeared.
(b) 9-20-62 Hawthorne, N.J.	Object with two body lights	Night watchman	Hovered over quarry; watchman approached in jeep to investigate, UFO maneuvered out of headlight beams.
(b) 9-24-62 Hawthorne, N.J.	Bright light source	Police, others	Hovered, moved away when police shone spotlight on it.

Powered, Controlled Flight

Many observations by competent observers (including engineers and aeronautical experts) suggest that the UFOs they saw were powered objects. The observations sometimes have included visual signs of mechanical-functional construction, in addition to other indicators of the UFOs' being, literally, machines.

Most of the cases cited previously in this section contain descriptions of observed "maneuvers." However, the following group of reports by unusually well-qualified observers is worth special mention.

UFO Formation Tracked Above Security Area at over 4,500 mph.

During the Fall of 1949 at a key atomic post, five apparently metallic objects in formation were tracked by radar. The UFOs crossed the 200-mile scope in less than 4 minutes. The officer in charge, who held a top military post, reported to Intelligence that this was a legitimate radar contact with unidentified objects. [4] (Official secrecy conceals other details of this case, in particular information on tracking and other detection of the UFOs by separate military posts. Nevertheless, it tends to substantiate the many other reports by reputable people of UFOs, and UFO formations, moving at spectacular speeds).

Technicians at Secret Test Base Observe Mechanical UFO

At Muroc AFB (now Edwards AFB) and adjacent Rogers Dry Lake, scientists and engineers test and develop the latest aircraft, including secret projects. Although thoroughly familiar with anything that flies, the base technical personnel had no explanation for the UFOs which maneuvered over the area July 8, 1947. Twice that morning, disc-shaped objects were observed cavorting overhead. Then about 11:50 a.m., a crew of technicians at Rogers saw a round white, apparently metallic object descending, moving west northwest against the wind. They observed thick projections on top which crossed each other at intervals, suggesting either rotation or slow oscillation. In their official report they stated: "It was man-made, as evidenced by the outline and functional appearance." [5] (Next day, near Boise, Idaho, a disc-shaped object maneuvering in front of a cloud bank was observed from a plane by Dave Johnson, aviation editor of the Idaho Statesman. See Section VII.)

Top Astronomer Reports "Novel Airborne Device"

On July 10, 1947, one of the country's top astronomers reported an elliptical UFO. At 4:47 p.m. in southern New Mexico, the astronomer observed a smooth ellipse with firm regular outline, motionless near some clouds, but wobbling. [See Section XII; Flight Characteristics.] The UFO then moved into the clouds, reappeared and rose quickly at an estimated speed of 600 to 900 mph. In his report to the Air Force, the astronomer stated: "The remarkably sudden ascent convinced me it was an absolutely novel airborne device." [4]

Scientist Observes Powered UFO

A very similar observation was made nearly three years later by an eminent meteorologist and astronomer. On the grounds of Lowell Observatory, Arizona, May 20, 1950, Dr. Seymour L. Hess, now head of the Department of Meteorology, Florida State University, noticed a disc (or partly illuminated sphere) moving across the front of some cumulus clouds at about 12:15 p.m. Studying the UFO with four-power binoculars, Doctor Hess could see no evidence of exhaust or markings on the object. "The clouds were drifting from the southwest to the northeast at right angles to the motion of the object. Therefore it must have been powered in some way. . . I would estimate its speed at 100 mph., perhaps as high as 200 mph. This too means a powered craft. However, I could hear no engine noise." [Full statement, Section I.]

High-Speed Disc Arcs Above Airliner

Airline pilots, although not necessarily technically trained in the sense of being scientists or engineers, are experienced observers of the sky, familiar with most atmospheric and astronomical displays. At 9:29 p.m., March 31, 1950, a Chicago & Southern Airlines plane was flying at 2,000 feet on a southwesterly course near Little Rock, Arkansas. Captain Jack Adams and Co-pilot G. W. Anderson, Jr., suddenly noticed a distinct circular object, apparently disc-shaped approaching from the left. The UFO passed in an arc above their plane, proceeding north at an estimated 700 to 1,000 mph. Eight to 10 lighted windows or ports were visible on the underside, and "the strongest blue-white light we've ever seen" flashed intermittently from the top. The pilots told official investigators they believed they had witnessed some secret experimental craft. To this date, the sighting remains unexplained. [6]

Aeronautical Engineer Amazed by UFO Performance

Another particularly well-qualified observer was "amazed" by a UFO performance he witnessed on the night of July 16, 1952. Paul R. Hill, an aeronautical research engineer of Hampton, Virginia, at 9:00 p.m. saw two amber-colored lights speed in from the south over the Hampton Roads channel. The UFOs slowed and circled rapidly around each other. Two similar objects then approached and joined the first two, one from the south and one from the north, and the formation moved off toward the south. "Their ability to make tight circling turns was amazing," Mr. Hill said. [Full report in Section VI.]

Formations and Coordinated Flight

A prime indicator of intelligence behind the maneuvers of UFOs is the observation that they often fly in formation, which requires coordination and mechanical control. (Aircraft and birds also fly in formations, but these can often be ruled out as cause of the sightings.) In UFO reports, the formations are of three general types: (a) Geometrical (V's, lines, etc.); (b) clusters, and (c) object with smaller objects maneuvering around it.

(a) Geometrical

1904: Circular UFOs Maneuvered Near Ship

One of the earliest formation cases was reported February 28, 1904, by a ship in the North Pacific off San Francisco. Three members of the crew of the USS Supply, at 6:10 a.m. local time, sighted an echelon formation of three "remarkable meteors" which appeared near the horizon below clouds, moving directly toward the ship. As they approached, the UFOs began soaring, rose above the cloud layer, and were observed climbing into space, still in echelon. The lead object was egg-shaped and about the size of six suns (about 3 degrees of arc). The other two were smaller and appeared to be perfectly round. They remained visible for over two minutes. [7] (Meteors, of course, do not travel in echelon formation, change course and climb, nor remain visible for two minutes).

Precise Formation, Sharp Turn Near Airliner

Perhaps the most detailed and instructive formation case on record is the sighting by Capt. William B. Nash, Pan American Airways pilot, and his co-pilot, William Fortenberry, July 14, 1952, near Newport News, Virginia. [See Section V.] In addition to being an example of precise formation flight, the report contains several other elements suggesting intelligent control. When an in-line formation of discs made an abrupt stop, two of the rear objects overrode the front one. This could be interpreted as a sign of pilot error or lag in reaction time. After the six discs flipped over and reversed course, two more sped up and joined the formation.

GEOMETRICAL FORMATION CASES

(All reports on file at NICAP)

Date	Location	Witnesses	Number	Type	Other Features
2-28-04	North Pacific	Crew, U.S.S. Supply	3	In-line, echelon	Changed course, climbed
6-23-47	Cedar Rapids, Iowa	Railroad engineer	10	In-line	Fluttered
6-24-47	Mt. Ranier, Wash.	Pilot	9	In-line	Zig-zag, skipping flight
7-4-47	Portland, Ore.	Police,	2	Unspecified	Oscillating motion
		Pilot	3	Unspecified	Oscillating motion
Summer 1948	Easton, Pa.	Scientist	3	In-line	Last zig-zagging [Section VI]
3-30-50	Selma, Ala.	Radio engineer & others	3	In-line	Middle disc pulled ahead, shot up out of sight
11-27-50	Evansville, Wis.	Pilot	6	Echelon	
8-11-51	Portland, Ore.	Pilot	3	V	Flew north in perfect formation
2-20-52	Greenfield, Mass.	Minister	3	V	[Section VII].
3-10-52	Oakland, Calif.	Inspecting engineer	2	Side-by-side	One on steady course, one swaying back and forth. [Section VI]
5-13-52	Greenville, S.C.	Amateur astronomers	"several"	Diamond	Wobbled in flight
7-14-52	Newport News, Va.	Airline pilots	6 + 2	In-line	Flip over, 120 degrees turn. [Section V]
7-16-52	Hampton, Va.	Aeronautical engineer	4	Varied; in-line	2 made tight circling turns [Section VI]
7-17-52	Staten Island, N.Y.	Citizens	5	V	
7-24-52	Near Carson Sink, Nev.	2 USAF colonels	3	V	UFOs were delta shaped [Section III]
8-1-52	Albuquerque, N.M.	Scripps-Howard staff writer	About 10	Cluster, V, 2 rows in-line	Shifted formation with precision. [Section VII]
8-5-52	Baltimore, Md.	Amateur Astronomer	2 + 2	Paired	[Section VI]
10-12-52	Palo Alto, Calif.	A/C maintenance man	6	V	Edges of discs glowing. [Section VI]
11-22-52	Bocaranga, Africa	Missionary	4	Rectangle	Sometimes moved singly, returned to formation
2-22-54	York, Pa.	GOC	14	Unspecified	
3-10-54	San Francisco, Calif.	Pilot, executive	12	V	
3-24-54	Baltimore, Md.	Civil Defense official	14	V; in-line	Changed to in-line as airliner passed, moved toward it. [Section VII]
5-5-54	Minneapolis, Minn.	Astronomy students	Unspecified	V	
5-6-54	Heppner, Ore.	Several	Unspecified	V	Oscillating motion
5-15-54	Southampton, England	Amateur astronomer	18	V	"Windows" visible in some through telescope
6-30-54	Near Oslo, Norway	Scientists	2	Echelon	First in tilted position, then levelled off. [Section I]
8-28-54	Oklahoma City, Okla.	Hundreds	15	Triangle, semi-circle	Changed to semicircular and sped up when pursued. [Section III]
9-6-54	Baltimore, Md.	Amateur Astronomer	4	In-line, echelon	One left, 3 changed formation
11-26-54	Manasquan, N.J.	Professor	15-20	V	[Section VII]
4-10-55	Baltimore, Md.	Several	Unspecified	(1) V (2) T	Two separate sightings
8-25-55	Birmingham, England	Ex-Navy officer	15	In-line	Groups of 3 in-line
11-9-55	Philadelphia, Pa.	Newspaperman, many others	12	V, A	Changed to A in flight [Section VII]
8-56	Boulder City, Nev.	Research technician	5	Staggered V	Spaced one diameter apart. [Section VI]
9-12-56	New Orleans, La.	Watchman	4	Y	Hovered, formed vertically, scattered
11-19-56	Frankfurt, Germany	Engineering student	7	V	[Section X]

Date	Location	Witnesses	Number	Type	Other Features
1-24-57	Indianapolis, Ind.	Airline pilot	4	In-line	Last larger, egg-shaped [Section V]
5-7-57	Sioux City, Iowa	Several	7-11	V	
6-18-57	North Pacific	Ship's captain and crew	3	V	Paced freighter [Section X].
7-17-57	Cuyahoga Falls, Ohio	Two	5	V	
8-57	Brooklyn, N.Y.	Singer	7	V	
10-22-57	Pittsburgh, Pa.	Family	3 + 3	In-line, Vertical V	Second group 2 hovering, third made V, moved away
11-11-57	San Fernando, Calif.	Engineers	3	V	Accelerated, ascended. [Section VI]
11-20-57	Murphysboro, Ill.	Housewife	3	V	
1-5-58	Beechwood, Ohio	Housewife	3	V	Elliptical rotation around vertices of triangle, departed in different directions
1-9-58	Marion, Ill.	Construction workers	7	In-line	Slow, some pulsated
4-9-58	Cleveland, Ohio	Family	9	V	Split to 2 groups, 5 & 4
4-9-58	Tucson, Ariz.	Bus driver	4-6	V	
8-7-58	Near Fairlington, Va.	Translator	4	In-line	Pulsated rapidly
8-28-58	Darlington, Ind.	Two persons	3	V	Changed course, SW to NW
10-3-58	Central Indiana	Train crew	4	In-line abreast	Paced train, reacted to light. [Section II]
10-6-58	Near Mt. Vernon, Ohio	Family	6	In-line	Jets passed above UFOs, which then took off.
6-11-59	Henderson, Nev.	Security guards	4	Square, in-line	Changed to in-line [Section VII]
7-8-59	Columbus, Ind.	Family	3	V	Pulsating, maneuvered
2-3-60	Intervale, N.H.	Former PT Boat Cmdr.	3 + 2	In-line	2 joined formation [Section VII]
3-4-60	Dubuque, Iowa	Flying Instructor	3	In-line	[Section V]
5-24-60	Ocumare..., Venezuela	Doctors, police	3	In-line	Last UFO largest, ovoid
9-5-60	Sonoma County, Calif.	Sheriffs	6	V	Bouncing motion. [Section VII]
8-17-61	Stillwater, Minn.	Five persons	Unspecified	V	Vertical orientation
10-30-61	Derry, Pa.	Engineer	4	In-line	Band of lights or "ports" [Section I]

(b) Clusters

In some cases clusters, or groups, of UFOs not in any clear geometrical pattern have acted in concert.

Discs Filmed by Navy Officer

The best known case of this type was documented on film by Navy Warrant Officer Delbert C. Newhouse, July 2, 1952. [See Section VIII, Photographs.] About 10 or 12 disc-shaped objects milling around in a group were observed by Newhouse and his wife near Tremonton, Utah. The 16 mm. color film shows bright round lights, occasionally tilting and appearing elliptical in outline. From film analysis report: The UFOs "often seem clustered in constellations, or formations which are recognizable for as long as 17 seconds. . .[they] seem to cluster in groups of two's and three's. . . the edges of the images are sharp and clear on many of the properly exposed frames. . . their pattern of motion is essentially a curvilinear milling about. . . sometimes the objects appear to circle about each other." [8]

Airliner Crew Watches Flight of Discs

An early cluster case, also from responsible witnesses, took place July 4, 1947. At about 9:12 p.m. Capt. E. J. Smith and the crew of a United Airlines plane were enroute to Portland, Oregon

(where earlier that day formations of disc-shaped UFOs had been reported; see chart). Five disc-shaped objects in a loose group or formation were seen silhouetted against the western sky for several minutes, opening and closing formation. Then a second group of objects appeared, three discs together and one off by itself. [9]

Other examples of cluster or group formation cases appear in the UFO Chronology in Section XI.

(c) Satellite Objects

Some of the most startling formation cases on record are those in which a large central object is observed in the process of launching or taking on board smaller objects, very much like an aircraft carrier or "mother ship." An example of this was observed by Maj. Paul A. Duich, Air Force Master Navigator, and other officers, September 8, 1958 at Offutt AFB, Omaha, Nebraska. [See Section III.] An elongated object tilted at an angle was seen in the western sky. Then small dark objects were seen maneuvering around the large object. Finally, the formation moved away to the west, the parent object still tilted at an angle.

In at least one instance, this phenomenon apparently was recorded on radar. December 6, 1952, over the Gulf of Mexico, the crew of a B-29 on a training mission repeatedly tracked UFOs moving at high speed past the plane, and crew members reported brief visual sightings of fast-moving lights. Finally the UFOs were seen on the radarscope to merge with a gigantic blip (radar target) which shot off the scope at about 9,000 mph. [Section VIII, Radar].

There is only one aerial phenomenon which remotely resembles the description and performance of the UFOs in these cases: aerial refueling operations by jets and tanker aircraft. In the cases cited, no such operations were reported in progress in the area of the sightings.

SATELLITE OBJECT CASES

(All reports on file at NICAP)

Date	Location	Witnesses	Description
Summer 1944	Grenada, Miss.	Artist	Parent Object (oval) emitted 3 smaller discs from underside, which hovered, moved away in different directions
Fall 1951	Birmingham to Chattanooga	Pilot	Parent Object (5 smaller flew out of it) paralleled plane, but when pilot pressed radio button to report sightings UFOs disappeared quickly
Early Oct. 1951	Anderson, Ind.	Family	Parent Object (Wing-shaped UFO) trailed by circular formation of over 30 evenly spaced dark objects which tilted back and forth in unison (app. discs).
1952	San Mateo, Calif.	Engineers	Parent Object (flat oval) emitted 5 smaller objects from one end
April 29, 1952	Singapore	Hundreds	Parent Object (silver cigar) leaving fiery exhaust, emitted bright lights after slowing; lights formed in clusters, sped away in various directions
July 23, 1952	Culver City, Calif.	Aircraft Plant employees	Parent Object (silvery elliptical) moved NW over city, stopped launched 2 small discs which circled area, went back on board, climbed straight up at high speed
Aug. 28, 1952	Denham, Bucks, England	3 residents	Parent Object (unspec.) ejected small object, minutes later 2 more small, 3 flew off in different directions
Oct. 17, 1952	Oloron College France	School Supt. & others	Parent Object (narrow cylinder inclined 45°) plus 30 Saturn-like discs, small, moved in pairs, zig-zagged, angel's hair fell
Oct. 27, 1952	Gaillac, France	Hundreds	Parent Object (cigar-inclined 45°) plus 16 discs with "domes", small, flew in pairs, zig-zagged, angel's hair fell
June 30, 1954	nr Labrador	Crew of BOAC airliner	Parent Object (variously described) plus about 6 small shiny objects sometimes appearing to enter and leave object
July 8, 1954	Abbey Lakes, Lanc. Eng.	Astronomer	Parent Object (apparently cylindrical) accompanied by 15-20 smaller lights moving around independently
Aug. 23, 1954	Vernon, France	Businessman, police, engineer	Parent Object (vertical cigar) emitted 5 discs from lower end which moved away horizontally.
Sept. 14, 1954	Vendee, France	Farmer, others	Parent Object (cigar) appeared out of clouds horizontally, tilted vertically, emitted shiny disc which spiralled around cigar, darted away; finally returned, re-entered cigar, which returned to horizontal, flew away into clouds.
Sept. 22, 1954	Fontainbleu, France	Woman	Parent Object (luminous ball) emitted several smaller ball-like objects from underside, which flew away in all directions. As plane approached, large object rose into clouds at high speed.
Sept. 27, 1954	Rixheim, France	Three; two independent sightings	Parent Object (cigar) with 10 or more small luminous objects navigating in all directions
Oct. 3, 1954	Lievin & Ablain-St. Nazaire, France	Many; two independent sightings	Parent Object (elongated luminous) hovered, something detached from bottom, descended to ground, rose and rejoined hovering object
Oct. 10/11 1954	Riom, France	Night watchman	Parent Object (cigar) moving S to N; three glowing objects detached, sped away
Feb. 16, 1955	nr Pinchincha volcano, Peru	Pilot, Air Force officer, others	Parent Object (hemispherical, domed) hovered, descended, emitted small lighted object just before speeding away.
Oct. 6, 1957	Tucson, Arizona	Engineer	Parent Object (oval-shaped) 5 smaller objects emerged, flew away
Dec. 15, 1957	Alminde, Jutland, Denmark	three youths	Parent Object (oval-shaped) 2 smaller emitted, parent object flew up out of sight leaving exhaust trail.

Date	Location	Witnesses	Description
Jan. 11, 1958	Vista, Calif.	Student	Parent Object (spindle-shaped) 8-10 smaller dropped from it, hovered, all disappeared upward.
March 3, 1958	nr Marshall, Texas	Family	Two Parent Objects (bright lights) 6-7 smaller lights clustered and moved around stationary large ones.
Sept. 10, 1960	N. Scituate, Mass.	Store Proprietors	Parent Object (dark cigar) with two large discs apparently resting on top; 3 in cluster flying nearby.
Oct. 4, 1960	Cressy, Launce-ton, Australia	Minister & wife	Parent Object (cigar with vertical bands) 5-6 smaller discs. Parent object descended from clouds, followed in about 2 minutes by discs, which stopped around cigar; finally rose rapidly in clouds.
May 3, 1961	Toonpang, N.S.W., Australia	5 men	Parent Object (round, domed) 4 small silvery v-shaped objects left and returned to parent object after maneuvering around at high speed.
June 4, 1961	Blue Ridge Summit, Pa.	Librarian	Parent Object (cigar or long ellipse) and cluster of smaller hovering objects; small objects streaked toward parent object, and all moved out of sight behind trees.

NOTES

1. Witnesses interviewed by NICAP Board Member Frank Edwards: Cecil Bridge, fireman; Harry Eckman, engineer; Morris Ott, head brakeman; Paul Soshey, flagman; and Ed Robinson, conductor.
2. True Magazine, March 1950. (Case confirmed by Capt. (then Cdr.) Robert B. McLaughlin, USN, head of Navy missile tracking crew.)
3. Interview report by Walter N. Webb, NICAP Adviser, on file at NICAP.
4. Life Magazine, April 17, 1952, from Air Force Intelligence Report.
5. Ruppelt, Edward J., Report on Unidentified Flying Objects, Doubleday, 1956, p. 38.
6. Flying, July 1950 (including pilot's sketch). See also Memphis Commercial Appeal, March 22, 1950.
7. Monthly Weather Review, March 1904.
8. Baker, Robert M. L., Jr., "Analyses of Photographic Material; Photogrammetric Analysis of the Utah Film Tracking UFOs," p. 2. (Copy on file at NICAP.)
9. Flying, July 1950; Life Magazine, July 21, 1947.

SECTION III

Air Force Observations

Before the issuance of Air Force Regulation 200-2 in 1953 (see extracts), a large number of significant UFO sightings by active Air Force personnel were made public. During the early 1950's, dozens of Intelligence Reports describing amazing UFO performances were released to the present NICAP Director. [1.] An article in LIFE, April 7, 1952, suggesting UFOs were interplanetary, represented the opinion of "several very high-ranking officers in the Pentagon," according to the former Air Force UFO project chief. [2.] After an early phase of official confusion and secrecy following the first publicized U.S. sightings in 1947, the Air Force was openly treating UFOs as a serious and important problem.

As indicated in the following chart, UFOs have been sighted regularly at dozens of Air Force bases in the United States and in foreign locations. Since 1953, however, Air Force UFO reports have steadily diminished. The effect of AFR 200-2 (and other Air Force policies; see Section IX) has been to dry up this source of current information about UFOs. With Air Force fliers active all over the globe, it is easy to imagine the amount of information which has been lost to the public.

In spite of the repressive effects of AFR 200-2 in recent years, a considerable number of good UFO sightings by Air Force witnesses has accumulated. These reports are a matter of public record. Others from unofficial and private sources have been obtained by NICAP.

Within the Air Force there is a strong difference of opinion about the official policies toward UFOs. Many officers and airmen do not agree with them, and favor more public disclosure of UFO information. A number have supplied NICAP with information when this could be done without violating security.

After NICAP was formed in 1956, Air Force officers (active and retired) began to visit the office. Some had personal ex-

---

9. Exceptions. In response to local inquiries resulting from any UFO reported in the vicinity of an Air Force base, information regarding a sighting may be released to the press or the general public by the commander of the Air Force base concerned only if it has been *positively identified as a familiar or known object.*

11. Contacts. Private individuals or organizations requesting Air Force interviews, briefings, lectures, or private discussions on UFO's will be referred to the Office of Information Services, Office of the Secretary of the Air Force. Air Force personnel, other than those of the Office of Information Services, will not contact private individuals on UFO cases nor will they discuss their operations and functions with unauthorized persons unless so directed, and then only on a "need-to-know" basis.

Air Force Regulation 200-2
Intelligence. Unidentified Flying Objects Reporting

DEPARTMENT OF THE AIR FORCE
WASHINGTON, 26 AUGUST 1953

---

periences to relate, others had general information about the UFO project. The visitors have included several former Project Blue Book (the UFO project) personnel and intelligence officers; a Master Navigator who had sighted several UFOs while on active duty; and a fighter pilot still on active duty. All expressed general agreement with NICAP's goals, and offered encouragement and support.

The reports from Air Force sources, many taken directly from Intelligence Reports, constitute good evidence that unexplained aerial objects are seen with regularity by observers who spend more time than the average person scanning the sky. (This is also true of airline crews; see Section V).

AIR FORCE UFO SIGHTINGS

UFO Sightings by U. S. Air Force Personnel
(All Reports on File at NICAP. Cases shaded in gray are detailed following chart).

Date & Location	Witnesses	Description
8-29-42 Columbus, Miss.	Michael Solomon, Control tower operator	Two round reddish objects descended near Army (Air Corps) Flying School, hovered, accelerated and sped away
3-44 Carlsbad, N.M.	B-17 pilot (conf. report certified by Bluegrass NICAP Affiliate)	High-speed glowing green object lit cockpit, moved out of sight over horizon.
8-10 Sumatra	Capt. Alvah Reida, B-29 pilot	Pulsating spherical object paced bomber, maneuvered.
11-44 France	Lt. Ed Schlueter, pilot, 415th Night Fighter Squadron	Eight to ten orange ball-like objects in-line formation, sometimes moving at high speed. [3.]
12-44 Austria	Maj. William D. Leet, B-17 pilot	Bomber paced by amber-colored disc.
1-45 Germany	415th Night Fighter Squadron pilot	Plane followed by three red and white lighted objects; UFOs followed plane's evasive maneuvers. [4.]
Abt. 1-2-45 France	Lt. Donald Meiers, pilot	Two UFO sightings reported; one object paced plane at 360 mph., "then zoomed up into the sky." [5.]
8-1-46 Florida	Capt. Jack Puckett, pilot	Cigar-shaped UFO maneuvered near AF transport plane

Date & Location	Witnesses	Description
6-28-47 Maxwell AFB, Alabama	Two pilots, two intelligence officers	Bright light source zig-zagged with bursts of speed, made 90 degree turn [6.]
6-28-47 near Lake Meade, Nevada	F-51 pilot	5-6 circular UFOs in formation off right wing. [6.]
7-6-47 ------	B-25 crew	Disc-shaped UFO below plane. [8.]
7-6-47 Fairfield-Suisun AFB, Calif.	Pilot	UFO "oscillating on its lateral axis" shot across sky in few seconds. [9.]
7-8-47 Muroc AFB, Calif.	Four separate sightings by at least four officers, and a crew of technicians	Circular or disc-shaped UFOs sighted at 9:30 a.m., 11:50 a.m., 12:00 noon, 3:50 p.m. [See Chronology, Sect. XI].
8-47 Media, Penna.	Single engine pilot	Hovering disc.
5-28-48 ------	C-47 crew	Three UFOs dove at transport. [10.]
Summer 1948 Labrador	Major Edwin Jerome, Command Pilot	Reports tracking of UFO at about 9000 mph., by U.S. and Canadian radar [See Section VIII, Radar].
10-15-48 Japan	F-61 crew, radar	Elongated UFO which alternately moved slowly, accelerated to about 1200 mph. [See Section VIII, Radar].
11-18-48 Washington, D. C.	Lt. Henry G. Combs, Lt. Kenwood W. Jackson, pilots	"Dogfight" with glowing oval UFO which put on bursts of speed up to est. 600 mph. [11.]
11-23-48 Fursten-Feldbruck, Germany	Two F-80 pilots	Bright red light source, tracked on radar at 900 mph. [See Section VIII, Radar].
12-3-48 Fairfield-Suisun AFB, Calif.	Pilot	Ball of light flashed into view, ascended rapidly out of sight. [12.]
11-3-49 Baja, Mexico	Capt. William H. Donnelly, pilot	Four discs in "cavorting" flight
Fall 1949 Atomic Base	Radar officer	Five apparently metallic UFOs tracked at approx. 4500 mph. [Section II]
2-2-50 Davis-Monthan AFB, Arizona	Lt. Roy L. Jones B-29 pilot	Chased unidentified object which was leaving smoke trail. [13.]
3-8-50 Dayton, Ohio	Two F-51 pilots, several airline pilots	Round UFO observed from ground, tracked on radar, climbed away from interceptors through clouds. [See Section VIII, Radar].
6-21-50 Hamilton AFB, Calif.	S/Sgt. Ellis Lorimer (control tower operator), Cpl. Garland Pryor (cto), and S/Sgt. Virgil Cappuro	Fiery object made several passes at the control tower. [14.]
12-50 near Cheyenne, Wyoming	Capt. J. E. Broyles	Aluminum-like oval with conical tail streaming behind, moving slowly.
2-14-51 Alamagordo, N.M.	Capt. J. E. Cocker, Capt. E. W. Spradley, pilots	Flashing white disc observed while tracking a balloon. [15.]
6-1-51 Dayton, Ohio	Unit Chief, Wright-Patterson AFB	Disc observed making rightangle turn. [Confidential report to NICAP, certified by NICAP Director and Ass't. Director].
Summer 1951 Augusta, Ga.	Lt. George Kinman, F-51 pilot	Large disc about twice the size of F-51 made repeated passes at plane.
9-10-51 Sandy Hook, N.J.	Capt. Edward Ballard, Lt. Wilbert S. Rogers, flying T-33	Chased silvery disc which evaded them at speeds est. over 900 mph. [16.]
9-23-51 March AFB, California	F-86 pilots	Attempted to intercept UFO in apparent orbit at 50,000 feet. [17.]
1-20-52 Fairchild AFB, Wash.	Two M/Sgt's, intelligence specialists	Blue-white spherical object sped below overcast; speed computed at 1400 mph. [18.]
1-29-52 Wonsan, Korea	B-29 crew	Disc paced bomber for 5 minutes, shot away at angle. [19.]
3-29-52 near Misawa, Japan	Lt. D. C. Brigham, T-6 pilot	Watched small disc maneuver around an F-84. [See Section I].
4-17-52 Nellis AFB, Nevada	T/Sgt. Orville Lawson, other airmen	18 circular UFOs in group, one zig-zagging. [20.]
6-18-52 Calif.	B-25 crew	UFO paced bomber for 30 minutes. Official "unknown" [21.]
7-12-52 Chicago, Ill.	Captain, weather officer	Reddish object with small white body lights, made 180 degree turn, disappeared over horizon. [22.]

Date & Location	Witnesses	Description
7-20-52 Andrews AFB, Md.	Betty Ann Behl, WAF, Weather observer	High-speed UFOs tracked on radar during Washington, D.C., sightings. [See Section VIII, Radar; Section XII, 1952 Chronology].
7-22-52 Uvalde, Texas	- - - - - - - - - - - - - - - - - -	Round silvery UFO spinning on vertical axis sped across 100 degrees of sky in 48 seconds, passing between two banks of cumulus clouds. [24.]

Note: Assuming various altitudes, it is possible to compute the speed of the UFO for those altitudes: 2 miles = about 250 mph.
         5 miles = about 635 mph.
         10 miles = about 1270 mph.

Date & Location	Witnesses	Description
7-23-52 South Bend, Indiana	Capt. Harold W. Kloth, Jr. (over 2000 hours flying time)	Two blue-white objects, changed course. [25.]
7-23-52 Braintree, Mass.	F-94 pilot, others	Pilot vectored in on UFO by radar, saw blue-green light, got radar lock-on, UFO sped away. [26.]
7-24-52 near Carson Sink, Nevada	Two Pentagon Colonels in B-25	Three silvery triangular UFOs sped past bomber at est. speed over 1000 mph. Official "unknown." [27.]
7-26-52 Washington, D. C.	Lt. William L. Patterson F-94 pilot	Chasing UFOs detected by CAA radar saw glowing objects all around his plane. [28.]
7-26-52	F-94 pilot	Chased UFO detected by radar, saw large yellow-orange light, got radar lock-on. UFO repeatedly pulled away at high speed, slowed again until jet caught up. Official "unknown." [29.]
7-28-52 near St. Paul, Minn.	Pilot, others	Several UFOs tracked on radar, pilot saw fast-moving lights, which accelerated, sped away. [30.]
7-29-52 Albuquerque & Los Alamos, N.M.	Jet pilots, reserve Colonel	Jets chased two UFOs, which maneuvered around behind planes; Colonel saw elliptical UFO. [31.]
Summer 1952 MacDill AFB, Florida	Colonel, pilot; co-pilot & scanner	Investigated radar target, saw maneuverable egg-shaped object.
8-1-52 Dayton, Ohio	Major, 1st Lt., pilots	Chased UFO detected by radar, saw and photographed circular object. [See Section VIII, Radar].
8-1-52 near Yaak, Montana	radar crew	Saw dark cigar-shaped object right where radar indicated a UFO. [See Section VIII, Radar].
8-3-52 Hamilton AFB, California	Lt. Duane Swimley, jet pilot; others	Two discs "dogfighting," joined by six others; took diamond formation and moved away. Also tracked on radar [See Section VIII, Radar].
8-5-52 Oneida AFB, Japan	Control tower operators	Dark circular UFO with brilliant white body light hovered, maneuvered over base, tracked on radar. [See Section VIII, Radar].
8-13-52 Tucson, Ariz.	Capt. Stanley W. Thompson, USAFR	Three V's of large bright UFOs in "perfect formation." [32.]
8-24-52 near Hermanas, N.M.	Colonel, F-84 pilot	Two high-speed maneuvering discs. [33.]
10-13-52 Oshima, Japan	Maj. William D. Leet, on C-54 mission	Disc hovered in clouds 7 minutes, sped away disappearing in seconds.
10-29-52 Hempstead, L. I.	F-94 pilots	High-speed maneuvering, "controlled" UFO evaded interceptors. [34.]
12-4-52 Laredo, Texas	F-51 pilot	Glowing object made several passes at plane, maneuvered in tight turns, climbed steeply at high speed. [35.]
12-6-52 Gulf of Mexico	B-29 crew	Radar-visual sighting; UFOs tracked at 9000 mph. [See Section VIII, Radar].
12-29-52 No. Japan	Col. Donald J. Blakeslee, Command pilot	UFO with rotating red, green and white lights, 3 fixed beams of white light, outsped F-94. [36.]
1-9-53 Santa Ana, Calif.	B-29 pilots	V-formation of blue-white lights approached plane, banked, climbed away. [37.]
1-26-53 New Mexico	Radar crew	Brilliant reddish-white light tracked on radar moving slowly (12-15 knots) into wind. [See Section VIII, Radar].
1-28-53 near Albany, Ga.	F-86 pilot	Circular UFO accelerated away from jet, observed on ground radar. [See Section VIII, Radar].
1-29-53 Presque Isle, Maine	F-94 and other pilots	Gray oval UFO. [38.]
2-1-53 Terre Haute, Indiana	T-33 pilot	Visual UFO sighting. [39.]
2-6-53 Rosalia, Wash.	B-36 crew	Circling UFO with flashing lights. [40.]
2-7-53 Korea	F-94 pilot	Radar-visual sighting of bright orange light which changed altitude pulled away from jet at high speed. [See Section VIII, Radar].

Date & Location	Witnesses	Description
2-11-53 Tunis-Tripoli	C-119 crew	UFO approached plane, fell back, paced plane for long period. [41.]
2-13-53 Ft. Worth, Texas	B-36 crew	Radar-visual UFO sightings. [42.]
2-16-53 near Anchorage, Alaska	C-47 pilots	Bright red light approached plane, hovered, sped away when pursued. [43.]
2-17-53 Elmendorf AFB, Alaska	Five Air Police	Red light near end of runway, climbed away rapidly when jet scrambled. [44.]
3-7-53 Yuma, Arizona	Over 20 officers	About a dozen disc-shaped UFOs dove, hovered over base, during gunnery meet. [45.]
Spring 1953 Laredo, Texas	1st Lt. Edward B. Wilford III (jet pilot instructor) in T-33	Dark cigar-shaped UFO leaving contrail; speed estimated at Mach 2.
8-9-53 Moscow, Idaho	F-86 pilots	Large glowing disc spotted by Ground Observer Corps, sped away from jets. [46.]
8-12-53 Ellsworth AFB, So. Dak.	F-84 pilots	Radar-visual "cat and mouse" pursuit. UFO fled jet, turned and followed it back to base. [Section I].

August 26, 1953 - Air Force Regulation 200-2 issued by Secretary of Air Force: "Intelligence. Unidentified Flying Objects Reporting." Paragraph 9 forbids public release of unexplained sightings. Paragraph 8 requires classification of radar-scope photographs of UFOs. Air Force personnel instructed to discuss sightings only with "authorized personnel."
(Note rapid drop-off of officially reported sightings after this date.)

Date & Location	Witnesses	Description
11-23-53 Kinross AFB, Michigan	F-89 crew	F-89 chasing UFO; blips of plane and UFO merged on radar screen, plane never found. [See Section IX].
1954 Dayton, Ohio	Lt. Col. USAFR, Senior Pilot	Two UFOs which hovered, took evasive action
5-24-54 near Dayton, Ohio	RB-29 crew	Brilliant circular UFO sped below plane at est. 600 mph., photographed by crew. Photograph never made public. [47.]
6-30-54 Brookley AFB, Alabama	Control tower operators	Radar-visual sighting of silvery UFO; streaked in from Gulf, circled, moved away northeast. [48.]
7-3-54 Albuquerque, New Mexico	Radar crew	Nine greenish spherical UFOs, hovered, sped away, tracked at about 2600 mph. [See Section VIII; Radar].
7-11-54 Hunterdon, Pa.	Jet bomber crews	Disc paced four bombers. [49.]
7-23-54 Franklin, Indiana	Two jet interceptor pilots, 97th Interceptor Squadron	Four large glowing UFOs seen by GOC; jets closed in on one, then veered away and left scene. Incident officially denied. [50.]
8-28-54 Tinker AFB, Oklahoma	Jet interceptor pilots	Radar-visual, 15 UFOs in precise triangular formation, changing to semi-circular formation. [See Section VIII, Radar].
6-16-55 Eastern United States	Dozens of interceptor pilots	UFOs reported seen over wide area of Eastern U. S., jets scrambled from many points. [51.]
8-23-55 Cincinnati, Ohio	Jet pilots	Three round and disc-shaped UFOs, evasive maneuvers as jets tried to catch them; first detected by radar [See Section VIII; Radar].
11-24/25-56 Rapid City, So. Dak.	Jet pilots	Maneuverable UFOs seen widely. Unofficial reports of sightings by 54th Fighter-Interceptor Sqdn., radar trackings. [52.]
12-56 Far East	Jet pilot	Pilot got radar lock-on, chased circular UFO which climbed away at over 1800 mph. [See Section VIII; Radar].
2-27-57 Houston, Texas	Lt. J. R. Poole	At radar site, UFO trailing fiery exhaust observed making several sweeps across sky at est. 2000 mph. [53.]
11-5-57 Keesler AFB, Miss.	A/1C William J. Mey	Elliptical UFO which accelerated and entered clouds. Report coincided with Coast Guard Cutter Sebago sighting. [See Section VIII; Radar].
11-5-57 Long Beach, California	Maj. Louis F. Baker, others	Six shiny circular UFOs maneuvering "like planes in a dogfight." [54.]
4-14-58 Albuquerque, New Mexico	S/Sgt. Oliver Dean	About 12-18 golden orange lights, V-formation with smaller irregular formation on each side in steady flight. CAA reported no aircraft flights in area.
7-17-58 Hokkaido, Japan	Control tower operator, others	Reddish star-like UFO circled over base, tracked on radar. Sighting officially denied. [55.]
9-8-58 Offutt AFB, Nebraska	Maj. Paul A. Duich, Master Navigator, others	Elongated object tilted at angle, small satellite objects.
5-20-61 Tyndall AFB, Florida	Air Police, others	Radar-visual report, UFO maneuvered over base, dove and climbed. Reported by NICAP in summer 1961. Later analysis by Adviser Webb determined radar reports did not coincide with visual. Reports still unexplained. [Confidential report to NICAP. Certified by NICAP Director, Ass't Director, and Adviser Walter N. Webb].

Bomber Paced by UFO

(Capt. Alvah M. Reida, during his military flying career, was an Airplane Commander on B-26's, B-24's and B-29's. At the time of the sighting, he was based at Kharagapur, India, in the 468th Bomb Group, 792nd Squadron, XX Bomber Command, All quotes from his report, on file at NICAP).

"I was on a mission from Ceylon, bombing Palembang, Sumatra. The date was August 10, 1944, time shortly after midnight. There were 50 planes on the strike going in on the target at about 2 or 3 minute intervals. My plane was the last one in on the target and the assignment was for us to bomb, then drop photoflash bombs, attached to parachutes, make a few runs over the target area, photographing damage from the preceding planes. The weather was broken clouds, with an overcast above us. Our altitude was 14,000 feet, indicated air speed about 210 mph.

"While in the general target area we were exposed to sporadic flak fire, but immidiately after leaving this area it ceased. At about 20 or 30 minutes later the right gunner and my co-pilot reported a strange object pacing us about 500 yards off the starboard wing. At that distance it appeared as a spherical object, probably 5 or 6 feet in diameter, of a very bright and intense red or orange in color. It seemed to have a halo effect. Something like this:

> At that distance it appeared as a spherical object, probably 5 or 6 feet in diameter, of a very bright and intense red or orange in color. It seemed to have a halo effect. Something like this My gunner reported it coming in from about the five o'clock position at our level. It seemed to throb or vibrate constantly. Assuming

"My gunner reported it coming in from about five o'clock position at our level. It seemed to throb or vibrate constantly. Assuming it was some kind of radio controlled object sent to pace us, I went into evasive action, changing direction constantly as much as 90 degrees and altitude about 2000 feet. It followed our every maneuver for about 8 minutes, always holding a position of about 500 yards out and about 2 o'clock in relation to the plane. When it left, it made an abrupt 90 degree turn, up and accelerating rapidly; it disappeared in the overcast."

Capt. Reida added: "During the strike evaluation and interrogation following this mission, I made a detailed report to Intelligence, thinking it was some new type of radio controlled missile or weapon."

Cigar-Shaped UFO Near AF Transport

(Capt. Jack Puckett, at the time of his UFO sighting, was Flying Safety Officer, Hdq., Tactical Air Command, 300th Base Unit, Langley Field, Va. His duties included supervision of flying operations and training, investigation of all aircraft accidents in his command. He has served as an instructor pilot, four engine aircraft, and flew a tour of combat in the European Theater, World War II).

"I was making a scheduled flight from Langley Field, Virginia [August 1, 1946] to MacDill Field, Tampa, Florida. At approximately 6 p.m. while flying a C-47 at 4000 feet northeast of Tampa

I observed what I thought to be a shooting star to the southeast over the Atlantic Ocean. My copilot, Lt. Henry F. Glass and my engineer both observed this object at the same time.

"This object continued toward us on a collision course at our exact altitude. At about 1000 yards it veered to cross our path. We observed it to be a long, cylindrical shape approximately twice the size of a B-29, with luminous portholes."

The UFO seemed to be rocket propelled, Capt. Puckett stated. The object trailed a stream of "fire" about one-half its own length, and remained in sight 2 1/2 to 3 minutes.

Pilot Has "Dogfight" With Oval Object

About 9:45 p.m., November 18, 1948 Lt. Henry G. Combs was approaching Andrews AFB, Maryland, near the Nation's Capital, in a T-6. Suddenly he noticed an odd light over the base, so he closed in to check on it. Abruptly, the light "began to take violent evasive action." Repeatedly, Combs tried to close in on the maneuvering object. But each time it would turn so sharply that he couldn't turn with it.

In his official report on the incident, Lt. Combs stated: "I chased the light up and down and around for about 10 minutes, then as a last resort I made a pass and turned on my landing lights. Just before the object made a final tight turn and headed for the coast I saw that it was a dark gray oval-shaped object, smaller than my T-6."

The UFO moved at variable speeds, vertically and horizontally. Lt. Combs estimated it traveled as fast as 600 mph.

TECHNICAL INTELLIGENCE CENTER OFFICIAL OBSERVES DISC, SHARP TURN

On June 1, 1951, about 10:00 p.m., an official at Wright-Patterson AFB, Ohio, sighted an apparently disc-shaped UFO. Because of his sensitive position, he has requested that his name be kept confidential. The report is certified by the NICAP Director and Assistant Director. (Note: All confidential reports in this document, certified by NICAP officials, will be made available to any authorized Congressional investigators.)

"While driving West near Dayton, Ohio, I suddenly became aware of a large blue-white light moving parallel to me. It was parallel and to the left at 30 to 45 degrees elevation. I can best describe it as being similar to the flame trail from a rocket power plant. It was a clearly defined outline similar to a stubby cigar. It was much brighter at the leading end, and gradually dimmer toward the trailing end. After 10 to 15 seconds it made approximately a right angle turn, became circular and even-colored, and rapidly disappeared. I detected no trace of yellow, orange, red or purple in the color. The speed was faster than an airplane, slower than a meteor."

Disc Buzzes Fighter Plane

The following case was reported by Cleveland Press Aviation Editor Charles Tracy, a former wing operations officer in the Air Force. (Originally reported in Cleveland Press, picked up by United Press International, July 30, 1952).

During the Summer of 1951, Lt. George Kinman was flying over Augusta, Georgia, on a clear, sunny day. At the time, he was a seven year flying veteran, since a jet pilot at overseas bases.

"I was cruising at about 250 mph.," Lt. Kinman told Tracy. "All of a sudden I noticed something ahead, closing in on me, head on. Before I could take evasive action - before I even thought of it, in fact - this thing dipped abruptly and passed underneath just missing my propeller. The thing was definitely of disc shape. . . white. . . pretty thick. . . it looked like an oval. . . it was about twice as big as my plane. It had no visible protrusions like motors, guns, windows, smoke or fire."

Lt. Kinman swung his F-51 around, but the disc was out of sight. Within about 15 seconds, he said, the disc came at him again, dipping at the last minute. This performance was repeated several times for a period of 5 to 10 minutes. Finally, on its last pass, the UFO zoomed upward instead of down, just missing his canopy.

MAJOR WILLIAM D. LEET
UNITED STATES AIR FORCE
Reserve
Rt. 1, Lexington, Ky.

11 March 1958

Major Donald E. Keyhoe, Director
National Investigating Committee
on Aerial Phenomena
Washington, D. C.

Dear Major Keyhoe:

Long before your book, "Flying Saucers Are Real",
was published, my B-17 and my crew and I were kept company
by a "Foo Fighter", a small amber disc, all the way from
Klagenfurt, Austria to the Adriatic Sea. This occurred on
a "lone wolf" mission at night, as I recall, in December,
1944 in the 15th Air Force, 5th Wing, 2nd Bomb Group. The
intelligence officer who debriefed us stated that it was a
new German fighter but could not explain why it did not fire
at us or, if it was reporting our heading, altitude and air-
speed, why we did not receive anti-aircraft fire.

On about 13 October 1952, while I was copilot on a
C-54 Troop Carrier mission out of Tachikawa and heading
South toward Oshima at dusk, I noticed in the strato-cumu-
lus formation Westward what appeared to be a perfectly
round cloud. After watching it for about a minute, and
deciding it wasn't a cloud, I called it to the attention
of the pilot and engineer. The pilot was intent upon his
flight plan but the engineer got several good glimpses of
the object. Seven minutes after I first saw it, it took
an elliptical shape and sped off to the West, disappearing
within a few seconds, toward Mount Fuji.

While stationed at McClellan AFB near Sacramento,
California from July, 1955 to December, 1957, I noticed a
tremendous number of luminous blue-green objects trans-
cending the sky from horizon to horizon in an instant. On
an AOC mission one night off the California Coast I had
the radio operator report such an observation. He, and
a day or two later one of our intelligence officers, told
me that the same object was reported by an airline pilot.

As a crusader for truth I believe that I understand
the difficulties under which you and your associates labor,
and I would like to offer my services. I am coming to Washington soon for an appointment with Senator Cooper and if it
is not inconvenient would like an appointment with you. I
am enclosing a copy of Form 57 for your information.

Sincerely,

William D. Leet

24

Radar, Pilot, Spot Elliptical UFO

One of the former Project Blue Book personnel who have visited NICAP is Don Widener. During 1952, he was a Staff Sergeant, senior information specialist in the Strategic Air Command, stationed with the 809th Air Base Group, MacDill AFB, Florida. Mr. Widener was assisting a Captain who was doing investigative work. When the Captain was called off base, Widener kept track of all sightings in the area for Project Blue Book.

Extracts from a letter to NICAP signed by Mr. Widener: "One of the key sightings which I was involved in was a radar sighting in the summer of 1952. Captain_____was off base and the operations officer notified me of the UFO, which radar had picked up at 40,000 feet proceeding at a speed of 400 knots. A check showed only two aircraft in the area; one a commercial airliner 300 miles out and the other a B-29 on the downwind leg to land.

The B-29 was piloted by a Colonel who reported he had five hours fuel and would investigate. The craft searched until midnight and finally reported a visual sighting at 20,000 feet. The object was at 40,000 feet flying at about 220 knots. The sighting was witnessed by the co-pilot and scanner. The Colonel and other witnesses described the object as a glowing white light shaped like a football. The B-29 turned to give chase, but the object reversed its field and disappeared at high speed. . . The weather that night was excellent. Bright moonlight, no inversion. Perfect for flying."

Jet Instructor Observes Circling UFO

A former Air Force jet pilot instructor, in a signed report to NICAP, detailed a sighting of a cigar-shaped UFO which left a contrail of constant length. 1st Lt. Edward B. Wilford III, a West Point graduate, was on a maintenance test flight in a T-33 from Laredo AFB, Texas, in about April 1953.

"While flying, I noticed a contrail at least 100 miles southeast coming in my direction. I had previously seen B-36's in our area, but within 5 minutes the contrail approached so rapidly that I thought it must be a B-47." He had just passed through 20,000 feet in a climbing spiral over the field.

Lt. Wilford gave the following log of the sighting:

T.   First sighting, 100+ miles ESE of Laredo. [Approached from over Gulf in direction of Corpus Christi].

T+5. Passed north of air base (my altitude, approx. 25,000 ft.)

T+10. Almost out of sight WNW of Laredo (my altitude 30,000 ft.), appeared to make 90 degree left turn.

T+17. Passed south of Laredo. I passed object through sun, but could not see any wing or tail structures. (My altitude, approx. 35,000 ft.)

T+20. Passed north of Laredo. I saw waves in contrail for first time. (My altitude, 37,000 ft.+)

T+25. Contrail disappeared to NW 100 miles away. (My altitude 41,000 ft.+).

Part of the time the UFO was sharply outlined, appearing as a "solid brown cigar-shaped object with contrail beginning one ship length behind," Lt. Wilford stated. "The contrail was a constant 2-1/2 or 3 ship lengths, disappearing as rapidly as it was forming, thus keeping constant length."

Based on the fact that the visibility at altitude exceeded 100 miles, Lt. Wilford estimated the UFO's speed at 1200 m.p.h. After circling the base, it took the UFO 5 minutes to speed out of sight to the NW. The object was as much as 45-50 degrees above his plane, and when he reached 40,000 feet it still seemed to be at least 20,000 feet above him.

Pilot Reports Two "Intelligently Controlled" Objects

In a letter to NICAP, Lt. Col. Richard T. Headrick, USAFR, Senior Pilot, described briefly a sighting of two UFOs in Dayton, Ohio, during 1954. A full report was made at the time to Project Blue Book. Col. Headrick outlined his views in this manner:

1. "Saucers exist. (I saw two).

2. They were intelligently controlled or operated. (Evasive tactics, formation flight, hovering flight.)

3. They are not propelled on any thermodynamic principle. (No contrails while jet intercept aircraft left heavy ones).

4. They are mechanisms rather than hallucinations, optical illusions, natural phenomena.

Col. Headrick added his evaluation of UFOs in general:

5. They are not U.S. secret weapons, for if they were, many contracts I am now working on would be dropped. [56.] Also they would not fly outside military test reservations.

6. They are not Russian for similar reasons. Russians have complained about their flying over their borders. They would not risk malfunction over our territory.

7. I presume they are extraterrestrial.

8. Provided they are, interstellar navigation would likely present little more complication than navigation within our solar system. Therefore, discussion on whether or not planets in the solar system are capable of supporting life are not material.

9. Judging from all evidence I have read, personal contact has not yet been established either on the ground or by radio transmission."

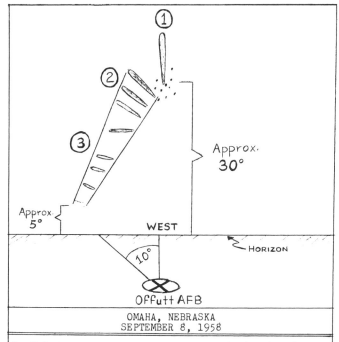

OMAHA, NEBRASKA
SEPTEMBER 8, 1958

1. UFO first appeared as vapor streak, bright flare of light. Then turned red-orange, solid shape became distinct. Black specks appeared, cavorted, near lower end.

2. Specks disappeared, object tilted to 45 degrees from horizontal, began moving slowly WSW.

3. Object tipped to horizontal, then as it moved into distance tilted upwards again.

SAC Officers Watch UFO With Satellite Objects

At SAC headquarters in 1958, a group of officers, airmen, and missile engineers observed an elongated UFO with satellite objects for about 20 minutes. The case was reported to NICAP by Major Paul A. Duich, USAF (Ret.), one of the witnesses, who was then on active duty. Until recently, Major Duich was an Air Force Master Navigator, accumulating 4000 flying hours and 300 combat hours. During World War II he was one of those who saw "foo-fighters," while crew member of a B-29 making bomb runs on Japan.

The time was approximately 1840. The date: 8 September 1958. I had just ordered dinner at the Officers Club, Strategic Air Command Headquarters, Offutt Air Force Base, Omaha,

WAYNE THOMAS, JR.
P. O. BOX 831
PLANT CITY, FLORIDA

October 3, 1963

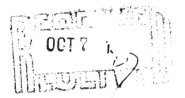

Mr. Richard Hall
NICAP
1536 Connecticut Avenue N. W.
Washington 6, D. C.

Dear Mr. Hall:

Pardon my delay in answering your letter of August 27 reqesting information on UFOs seen by B-29 crews during World War II.

I was a group intelligence officer stationed on Tinian, and the cases
I recall were all night-time sightings.

These lights, ranging from green to orange and yellow, would approach
and move along with the bombers for several minutes at a time before
breaking off. The crews were sure they were not reflections on plexi-
glass, or stars, or the moon.

I recall of no case where an aircraft or form was distinguished as
such, just the lights.

These "Foo-fighters" were so common, that they were discussed in the
various unit publications around the island.

I also remember no discussions about the possibility of space-craft;
just strange unidentified lights.

It is hoped that this small bit of fragmentary information may be of
help.

Very truly yours,

Wayne Thomas, Jr.

WTJr:v

Nebraska. I excused myself from my friend and co-worker, Major_____, and went out the side door to cross the open space between the club and the Visiting Officers Quarters next door. I wanted to buy a newspaper in the lobby of the VOQ to read after dinner.

As I crossed the open area, something caught my eye. Glancing up and to the west, I noticed what appeared to be a short vapor trail in an otherwise clear, blue sky. There were no clouds. The sun had just set. I continued walking but somehow that vapor trail didn't register properly. I have seen thousands of vapor trails but this one was peculiar. I did a double take at that point for suddenly the short 'vapor trail' became a brilliant source of light, much the same as a magnesium flare. I stopped dead in my tracks and watched.

The light was intense, but the "vapor trail" hung motionless. Even a short trail shows generation and dissipation as the aircraft moves across the sky. I watched for several minutes-- maybe 2 or 3--before I called to another officer: "Hey, what do you make of that?", pointing to the spot in the sky. He replied, "Looks like a short vapor trail." I pointed out that it wasn't moving or growing or diminishing in size. He stopped to gape and several others joined us.

By then, I decided this called for a better look. What we all agreed, rather quickly, was that the vapor was reflecting sunlight, the effect being similar to a sun-dog, even though the sun had already slipped below the horizon.

As the small crowd gathered, I hurried into the VOQ office and called the Offutt tower. I asked the tower operator to look west, about 30 degrees from the horizontal and tell me what he saw.

"Looks like a short vapor trail. Very odd."

"Vapor trail my foot! Look at it now."

I could see it through the window as I talked to the tower operator. The glow was now diminishing and changing to a dull red-orange and at the same time the fuzzy appearance gradually took on a solid look, in the distinct shape of a pencil or slender cigar. The upper end was blunter than the lower end.

By then all those in the office were curious and we all stepped outside to join the 10 or 20 others who had gathered to gape at the thing. All of a sudden we all started checking each others faces for some silly reason--for assurance of reality, perhaps, for as we watched there appeared at the lower end of the object a swarm of black specks cavorting every which way, much like a swarm of gnats. This procedure continued for a minute or so before they (the black specks) disappeared.

Then the object, which had hung motionless on the same spot, slowly changed attitude from an upright position to a 45 degree angle with the horizontal and started moving slowly toward the west. At the same time there was no drastic change in the coloring, but a perceptible color change did take place. It remained a dull orange-red color and continued its westerly movement.

We watched in awe for several minutes--perhaps 5--and then the object changed attitude, again very gradually, until its longitudinal axis appeared parallel to the horizon. The westward movement continued, slightly to the southwest. The apparent size of the object diminished gradually and the color faded. About 5 minutes before we lost it completely (as it faded into the haze just above the horizon) the object changed attitude again, back toward the 45 degree position, but not quite.

As it continued on its westerly path, it maintained this last attitude until completely swallowed up by the haze. It never did drop below the horizon--just faded away. The fading, of course, was due to the many miles of hazy atmosphere between us and the object. The sky was cloudless, but the western horizon did have a slight haze, readily apparent against the bright background.

About 10 minutes after I sighted the object, a full colonel set up a tripod and 35 mm camera with color film and took several photographs of the object. He later denied getting any successful exposures after I asked him on several occasions.

Immediately after the object faded away, we asked one another what it was we saw. The popular answer was, "I don't know, but I saw something."

The crowd was composed of airmen, officers and civilians (at least 25 officers and airmen were present). Several of the officers (and possibly a few civilians) were from the Air Force

Ballistic Missile Division in Los Angeles. Several more, like myself, were Operations personnel engaged in a SAC planning session at the time. All except a few of the airmen were seasoned, veteran flyers or highly trained missile engineers. We concluded that what was seen by all was no conventional vehicle, nor was it an atmospheric phenomenon.

I collected a few names of individuals present, as I intended to report the UFO to the proper authorities. I called the filter center and reported the facts over the telephone in the presence of a fellow officer and co-worker. I was told that I would be contacted within 48 hours by ATIC [Air Technical Intelligence Center] representatives. I am still waiting--5-1/2 years later.

NOTES

1. Keyhoe, Donald E., Flying Saucers From Outer Space, (Henry Holt, 1953).
2. Ruppelt, Edward J., Report on Unidentified Flying Objects, (Doubleday, 1956), ppg. 177-178.
3. American Legion Magazine; December 1945.
4. Ibid.
5. New York Times; January 2, 1945.
6. Ruppelt, Edward J., op. cit., p. 36.
7. Ibid., p. 35.
8. Ibid., p. 37.
9. Ibid., p. 37.
10. Ibid., p. 61.
11. Ibid., p. 96. (See also Saturday Evening Post, May 7, 1949.)
12. Keyhoe, Donald E., Flying Saucers Are Real, (Gold Medal Books, 1950), ppg. 79, 158.
13. Los Angeles Daily Mirror; February 2, 1950.
14. Associated Press; June 21, 1950.
15. New Yorker; September 6, 1952.
16. International News Service; September 12, 1951. (See also Ruppelt, Edward J., op. cit., p. 127).
17. From USAF Intelligence Report. (See also Ruppelt, Edward J., op. cit., p. 131).
18. Ruppelt, Edward J., op. cit., p. 26.
19. Newsweek; March 3, 1952. LIFE; April 7, 1952.
20. Report on file at NICAP. (See also International News Service; April 18, 1952.)
21. Ruppelt, Edward J., op. cit., p. 195.
22. Ibid., p. 204.
23. Ibid., p. 205.
24. From USAF Intelligence Report.
25. United Press; August 1, 1952.
26. From USAF Intelligence Report. (See also Ruppelt, Edward J., op. cit., p. 217).
27. Ruppelt, Edward J., op. cit., p. 24.
28. Tape recorded statement by Al Chop, former Air Force press official. (See also LIFE; August 4, 1952).
29. Ruppelt, Edward J., op. cit., p. 222.
30. From USAF Intelligence Report.
31. From USAF Intelligence Report. (See also Ruppelt, Edward J., op. cit., p. 217).
32. Associated Press; August 14, 1952.
33.-42. From USAF Intelligence Reports
43. True; May 1954.
44. Ibid.
45. Associated Press; March 9, 1953.
46. Keyhoe, Donald E., Flying Saucer Conspiracy, (Henry Holt, 1955), p. 30.
47. Ruppelt, Edward J., op. cit., p. 312.
48. United Press; June 30, 1954 (from Major James Zicherelli, public information officer).
49. Keyhoe, Donald E., Flying Saucer Conspiracy, op. cit., p. 190.
50. Ibid., p. 191.
51. Ibid., p. 270.
52. Associated Press; November 26, 1956.
53. Associated Press; February 28, 1957.
54. Los Angeles Times; November 6, 1957.
55. Japan Times; July 20, 1958.
56. Col. Headrick is Field Engineer and West Coast Military Coordinator for Bowser Inc., Engineers & Manufacturers.

SECTION IV
Army, Navy & Marine Corps

The other armed services, required by law to channel UFO reports to the Air Force, have also contributed some important cases to the public record. It is impossible to determine how many additional military reports have <u>not</u> been made public. Several of the cases in this section, however, strongly suggest that the on-the-record reports are only a small sample.

Several Navy cases can be detailed here primarily because of the background and personal connections of the NICAP Director. As a graduate of the U. S. Naval Academy (class of 1920) and former Marine Corps aircraft and balloon pilot, Major Keyhoe knows many active and retired officers, including Admirals who have held important positions. Some have taken an active part, supporting NICAP's investigations.

Rear Admiral Delmer S. Fahrney, USN (Ret.) - still a NICAP member - served for a time as Chairman of the Board of Gov-

ernors. Adm. Fahrney, credited with important aeronautical and guided missile development work, has obtained several highly significant UFO reports from his associates in aerospace activities.

Vice Admiral R. H. Hillenkoetter, USN (Ret.), a long-time acquaintance of Major Keyhoe, also served on the NICAP Board of Governors for five years. His service as a former Director of the Central Intelligence Agency (CIA), coupled with a distinguished Naval record in war and peace, cause his statements about UFOs to be of unusual interest. In 1960, Adm. Hillenkoetter said the UFOs appeared to be intelligently controlled. "They wouldn't be maneuvering accidentally. I think they are under intelligent guidance from all things seen." In 1961, Adm. Hillenkoetter joined with a majority of the NICAP Board in urging a Congressional investigation of the UFO problem.

RECEIVED
SEP 20 1957

Hq Sq Sec, First Air Force
Mitchel Air Force Base, NY
20 September 1957

Mr. Donald E. Keyhoe
Director NICAP
1536 Connecticut Ave, N. W.
Washington 6, D. C.

Dear Sir:

The following is a quote:

"Sighting of unconventional objects was made at Ft. Devens, Mass. between 2015 and 2055 hours, 17 Sep 57. Sky conditions varied from clear to partly scattered clouds. During the period a total of 8 objects, round in shape, were sighted from the ground. One went from East to West and then South. Two went from West to Northeast. Two went from East to West. One from West to East.

'' Exact time for each of the foregoing sightings was not reported, but they are listed in the order which sighted. Sometime after the sightings were made two conventional aircraft were sighted in the area and identified as such.

'' The color of the unidentified objects was orange, speed unknown, but reportedly faster than conventional aircraft and approximately of jet aircraft.

'' Altitude of objects varied with the lowest altitued estimated 5,000 feet. Just one object was sighted at this altitude, the remaining 7 appeared to be considerably higher. The objects made no sound and left no vapor trail. Bedford Air Force Base reported that they had only one jet aircraft up during the period. The Fort Devens Airport Duty Officer reported sighting a jet aircraft which was further to the north than the unidentified objects. These objects which changed direction did so in a gradual swing. All objects except the first one sighted appeared in steady flight. The first object appeared to be oscillating up and down. Lights utilized by conventional aircraft were not sighted on the objects. The objects appeared to be very small in size. The G-2 at Fort Devens reported that the objects were sighted by several people in one area and two people from a different location. "

UNCLASSIFIED

HEADQUARTERS
KAGNEW STATION
APO 843, New York, New York

KS2.001   11 February 1957

SUBJECT: Unidentified Objects

TO: Chief, US Army Security Agency
          Arlington Hall Station
          Arlington 12, Virginia
          ATTN: GAS22

1. The following, a summary of statements given by several members of this organization pertaining to unusual objects in the sky, is submitted for your information and any action deemed necessary.

2. At approximately 1045 hours, 21 January 1957, M/ Sgt Billy J. Woodruff, Sgt Frank Haverly, SP2 Robert O. Clewell, SP2 George R. Dean and SP3 Gerald L. Fennell, while returning to the 4th USASA Operations Area, noticed an unusual object in the sky. M/Sgt Woodruff was the first to see it, and brought it to the attention of the others. They all stated that at first they thought it was an airplane flying either directly toward or directly away from them, at an altitude of about 2000 feet. However, upon further observation they saw that it was not a plane, but rather an object with the appearance of a large shiny metal ball. The object was not moving, and even after they had changed their position on ground several times, the object still appeared to be motionless and to have the same shape. Suddenly the object disappeared. A few minutes later they saw what they believed to be the same or a similar object. This time the object acted in the same manner as stated above; it remained motionless for a few minutes and then suddenly disappeared. Later in the day M/Sgt Woodruff and Capt Jesse M. Strong observed two brownish objects maneuvering in close formation at high altitude. They first thought the objects to be birds; then one of the objects broke formation and took off at a right angle from the other object, in level flight, at a very high rate of speed. M/Sgt Woodruff stated that he knew that it was not a bird because it was disk shaped.

3. Several other persons have reported unusual objects in the sky, both prior to and after this incident, but their statements have been hazy and of little value, because the objects were always seen during the hours of darkness, and no clear discription could be given.

FOR THE COMMANDER:

/s/James A. Muncie
/t/JAMES A. MUNCIE
Capt, MI(Arty)
Intelligence Officer

U.S. ARMY INTELLIGENCE REPORTS ON UNIDENTIFIED FLYING OBJECTS

Rear Admiral Herbert B. Knowles, USN (Ret.), currently is a NICAP Board Member. Adm. Knowles held important submarine commands in World War II. He has also been active in encouraging witnesses to report sightings to NICAP.

Major Keyhoe also has obtained information on UFO sightings and official attitudes from top-level Naval officers on active duty in the Pentagon. Other Navy and Marine Corps officers on active duty contact him from time to time, and report personal sightings or related information.

NICAP has fewer connections with Army personnel, but some Army cases are on record. Of particular interest are two unclassified Army Intelligence Reports describing UFO activity. These were submitted to NICAP by members in the armed services.

OTHER MILITARY SIGHTINGS

ARMY

Date & Location	Witness	Description
Summer 1944 Normandy, France	George Todt, now Los Angeles columnist, other officers	Pulsating red object approached front lines, hovered, moved away.
October 1944 Holland	Capt. J. B. Douglas, Jr., 489th Field Artillery.	Brilliant light source observed moving across sky for 45 minutes.
3-13-50 Clarksburg, Calif.	Maj. Herbert W. Taylor, USAR (Signal Corps)	Droning sound heard; saucer-shaped object descended, hovered, swayed back and forth; later sped away. [1]
3-17-50 Farmington, N.M.	Capt. Clayton J. Boddy, USA (Ret.), Army Engineers; dozens of others	Shiny "saucer-like discs" cavorted around sky, hovered, moved with sudden bursts of speed. [2]
1-21-57 Army Base, A.P.O., N.Y.	M/Sgt. Billy J. Woodruff, others.	Two separate sightings; one of a disc which accelerated rapidly. (See above)
5-12-57 Nr. La Sal, Utah	Lt. Col. Samuel E. Craig, USAR	Round blue-green UFO viewed below observers' altitude moving at high speed. [3]
9-17-57 Ft. Devens, Mass.	First Army Intelligence Report	Eight round "unconventional objects" observed, one UFO oscillating up and down. (See above)
11-3-57 White Sands, N.M.	Army Jeep Patrol 3:00 a.m.	Egg-shaped UFO descended slowly, brightened and appeared to land. [Section XII; Nov. 1957 Chronology]
11-3-57 White Sands, N.M.	Separate Army jeep patrol, 8:00 p.m.	Hovering UFO took off at 45 degree angle, pulsating. [Section XII; Nov. 1957 Chronology]

NAVY & MARINE CORPS

Date & Location	Witness	Description
March 1945	U.S.A.T. Delarof (attack transport)	Dark sphere observed rising out of ocean, circled, flew away.
May 1946 LaGrange, Florida	Lt. (j.g.) Andrew A. Titcomb, gunnery and radar officer	Elliptical UFO banked overhead. [Section I.]
6-29-47 White Sands, N.M.	C. J. Zohn, Naval rocket expert	Silvery disc observed moving northward at estimated 10,000 feet. [4]
Summer 1947 Pittsburgh, Kansas	Cmdr. L. H. Witherspoon	Disc-like UFO flashed over airport. [5]
7-3-49 Longview, Wash.	Cmdr. M. B. Taylor, pilot	Disc maneuvered over air show
2-22-50 Key West, Fla.	Pilots, ground observers, radar at Naval Air Station	Two glowing objects streaked over field at height too great for pursuit. (From USAF Intelligence Report). [6]
3-16-50 Dallas, Texas	C.P.O. Charley Lewis	Oblong disc approached B-36, followed under it briefly, sped away at 45 degree angle. [7]
6-24-50 Nr. Daggett, Calif.	Navy transport pilot and crew	Cigar-shaped object maneuvered above desert, also seen by airline pilots.
7-11-50 Nr. Osceola, Ark.	Lt. (j.g.) J. W. Martin, pilot; enlisted pilot R. E. Moore	Domed disc crossed path of Navy planes, confirmed by radar
Fall 1951 Korea	Fleet radar sighting	UFO circled fleet, paced aircraft, departed at over 1000 mph. [Section VIII; Radar]
1-21-52 Mitchel AFB, N.Y.	Navy TBM pilot	Chased dome-shaped UFO which turned, accelerated, pulled away. [8]
6-52 Tombstone, Ariz.	Lt. Cmdr. John D. Williams, pilot	Domed disc, made sharp turns, "unbelievable" speeds
7-2-52 Nr. Tremonton, Utah	C.P.O. Delbert C. Newhouse, aviation photographer	Group of 12-14 maneuvering discs; 16 mm. color movies obtained. [Section VIII; photographs]
1953	Squadron of carrier-based attack planes	Rocket-shaped UFO swooped down, hovered over flight; sped away when pursued

Date/Location	Observer	Description
2-9-53 Virginia-No. Car. border	Lt. Ed Balocco, USMC; pilot	Rocket-like object chased in jet for 3-4 minutes; white with red glow at rear
9-7-53 Vandalia, Ohio	Lt. (j.g.); FG-1D pilot	UFO sped under plane, pulled up, climbed out of sight. (cf., Section V; July 4-5, 1961)
1-4-54 Quantico, Va.	Marine details	Story broke this date that red-lighted UFOs had hovered, maneuvered over base for past six nights. [9]
3-24-54 Florida	Capt. Don Holland, USMC, pilot	Round UFO descended, hovered at about 3000 feet; pilot banked to attempt gun camera photos, UFO sped away. (Report verified by Gen. William G. Manly, USMC).
5-14-54 Nr. Dallas, Texas	Maj. Charles Scarborough, USMC	Sixteen UFOs in groups, evaded pursuit by jets
Winter 1954 Pohang, Korea	John A. Potter, Marine Corps weather observer	Formation of about seven discs, moved with side-to-side oscillation. [Section XII]
1955 Virginia, Near Washington, D. C.	Cmdr.; pilot, missile expert	Disc with illuminated dome on top paced aircraft
12-11-55 Nr. Jacksonville, Fla.	Navy jet pilots, others	Dogfight with round, orange-red UFO; confirmed on radar
1956 North Atlantic	Cmdr., Senior pilot; other flight crews as passengers	Large disc climbed up to R7V-2, paced it, pulled away
8-15-57 Woodland Hills, Calif.	Eugene S. Allison, Chief Aviation Pilot (ret)	Disc-shaped UFO hovered, rocked back and forth, ascended rapidly
7-12-59 Nr. Ridgecrest, Calif.	Albert Guerrero, electronics mechanic, U.S. Naval Ordnance Test Station, China Lake	Three round lights, apparently oscillating discs, maneuvered SW of Test Station. [10]
10-20-59 Key West Florida	Two enlisted men (names on file)	Star-like UFO slowed, joined by second at high speed; two objects sped away. [11]
7-10-62 New Iberia, La.	Confidential Report (certified by NICAP Director & Ass't Director)	Disc buzzed Naval Air Station

UFOs Observed by Navy & Marine Corps Pilots

July 3, 1949. Longview, Wash.; Cmdr. M. B. Taylor, USN (former Officer-In-Charge of guided missile work under R. Adm. D. S. Fahrney) was giving the commentary at the beginning of an air show at Longview Fairgrounds, when he and others spotted an object above a sky-writing biplane. The UFO moved against the wind with an undulating motion, made right-angle turns and appeared like a discus of bright metal when viewed through field glasses. Cmdr. Taylor estimated its size as equal to a 50-foot object at an altitude of 20,000 feet. Among those who watched it and confirmed his description were many qualified airmen. While they saw but one object, others in the surrounding area reported seeing up to a dozen UFOs at the same time. Cmdr. Taylor concluded, "The sighting was definitely of some flying object unlike anything then or even presently [1957] known."

June 24, 1950. The crews of two commercial airliners and a Navy transport sighted a cigar-shaped object about 100 miles northeast of Los Angeles, Calif. The pilot of the Navy plane (name confidential) spent 22 years in Naval aviation and now is a project administrator with a West Coast electronics firm. He was alerted by a United Airlines pilot who had seen the object and they both discussed the matter with CAA (now FAA) ground stations at Daggett and Silver Lake, Calif. The co-pilot of the Navy plane was the first to see it, and pointed it out to the pilot and navigator.

The pilot described the object as cigar-shaped, dark gray or gunmetal in color and giving off a faint shimmering heat radiation appearance at the tail end. He judged its apparent size as about 1/8th that of the full moon. Estimated altitude 50,000-100,000 feet, speed 1000-1500 mph. for the three minutes it was in view. At first it was traveling north, but then turned west presenting a tail end view as it sped out of sight.

Signed report on file at NICAP, (Case certified by Paul Cerny, Chairman, Bay Area NICAP Subcommittee).

July 11, 1950. Near Osceola, Arkansas, the crews of two Navy planes saw a disc-shaped UFO whose presence was confirmed by airborne radar. Lt. (j.g.) J. W. Martin, enlisted pilot R. E. Moore, and electronics technician G. D. Wehner said the object first appeared as a round ball, ahead and to the left of their planes. As it crossed their flight path, disappearing in the distance to the right, the UFO resembled "a World War I helmet seen from the side, or a shiny, shallow bowl turned upside down." Wehner said he "caught it on the radar scope;" at the closest point, it was estimated to be about a mile away. [12]

June, 1952. Tombstone, Ariz. Lt. Cmdr. John C. Williams, USN (Ret.), his wife, Josephine, and a guest were watching the sunset when they saw "a huge circular object flying toward us from the direction of Tucson. . . Suddenly it stopped in midflight, seemed to hover, then reversed its direction and retraced its course. In a matter of seconds, however, it returned, stopped again, appeared to oscillate and tilt from one side to another. Again it reversed itself and apparently returned in the same straight line. It reappeared and acted in exactly the same manner two or three times." Cmdr. Williams graduated from the Naval Academy in 1919, completed flight training at Pensacola in 1922 and spent 10 years flying with the Navy. In a 1956 letter to the NICAP Director, he stated, "We had a perfectly clear view of the object which looked something like a cup and saucer, or a derby hat. Its speed was unbelievable. . . it diminished to a tiny speck [the last time it flew away] and then out of sight in the space of about four seconds."

1953. During off-shore combat maneuvers, a squadron of carrier based Navy AD-3 attack planes was approached by a rocket-shaped UFO which swooped down on the flight from above. The object levelled off about 1000 feet overhead, slowed and paced the aircraft. When the Squadron Commander led his flight in pursuit of the UFO, it turned sharply so that its tail was pointed away, and shot upwards out of sight in seconds. (Confidential report acquired by Adm. Fahrney, Adviser Lou Corbin).

Feb. 3, 1953. A Marine Corps fighter pilot, alerted by a Navy signal tower at Norfolk, Va., chased a silver object which had been sighted from the ground over an area near the Virginia-North Carolina border. After cruising in his F9F Panther for half an hour without seeing anything unusual, 1st Lt. Ed Balocco was returning to his base. "Over Washington, North Carolina," he said, "I saw what looked like an airplane with red lights which

31

appeared below me. I was cruising at about 20,000 feet. What caused me to look back at the object was the fact that it moved from below me 10,000 feet vertically in a matter of seconds.''

He turned and chased the object at better than 500 mph., but was unable to gain on it. Balocco estimated the UFO was about 10 miles from him during the 3-4 minute chase. At that distance, he said, it appeared about 1/4'' wide and about 3'' long. ''The object was the color of white heat and it threw out a red glow behind it. It had two red lights on the left hand side, bounding and flashing off the end, encircling an arc.'' The Marine officer said he seemed to gain on the object for a time, but it then dropped from his altitude and disappeared toward the coast.

Another pilot involved in the search, Capt. Thomas W. Riggs, reported he sighted an object flying low near the Carolina coast, but couldn't identify it. [13]

September 7, 1953. Near Vandalia, Ohio, U.S. Navy Reserve Lt. ''S.D.S.'' was flying to Indianapolis from Columbus with his wingman, both in FG-1D Corsairs. Shortly after 8 p.m., he ''noticed a brilliant white flashing light pass directly below us from south to north, traveling extremely fast at about 2000 feet.'' He was at 4000 feet. ''I called my wingman, but he did not see it. After passing beneath us, it pulled up and climbed rapidly out of sight to the north. The light was much like burning magnesium.

''Returning from Indianapolis (about 9 p.m.) I was leading the flight. I noticed the same brilliant white light at 12 o'clock high and called my wingman again. This time he saw it. It stayed motionless relative to the airplane's movement for about two minutes, then disappeared. It reappeared again quickly at 9 o'clock level. It again remained motionless for about two minutes and then dove and pulled up ahead of us and climbed out of sight. At no time were we close enough to see any concrete object or shape. Both of us were at a loss to explain this phenomenon.''

(Case reported by L. H. Stringfield, Ground Observer Corps official; see Section VII)

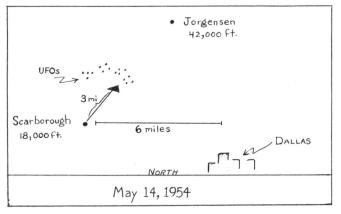

May 14, 1954

May 14, 1954. Near Dallas, Texas, a flight of Marine Corps jets led by Maj. Charles Scarborough, was headed north in mid-afternoon. At a point 6 miles west of the city, Major Scarborough sighted 16 unidentified objects in groups of four, dead ahead but at higher altitude, 15 degrees above. He radioed Capt. Roy Jorgensen, whose jet he had in sight by its contrail. Captain Jorgensen, at higher altitude, saw the UFOs below his left wing. Just as the two pilots tried to box in the UFOs, Major Scarborough saw them fade from glowing white to orange and disappear, apparently speeding away due north. (See sketch) Based on Captain Jorgensen's position the UFOs were 3 miles ahead of Major Scarborough's plane, and 15 degrees above him. Triangulation shows that the UFOs were at about 32,000 feet.

1955. A Navy Commander stationed at Anacostia Naval Air Station, was flying over Virginia, when he looked back over his shoulder and saw a huge disc flying formation on him, about 75 feet away. The Commander, also a Navy missile expert, described it as ''two saucers, face to face,'' apparently metallic about 100 feet in diameter, thick at the center with a domed top through which shone an amber light. When he tried to ease his plane in for a closer look, the disc tilted upward and accelerated away, leaving the clouds swirling behind it. (Report acquired by Rear Adm. Delmer S. Fahrney, USN, Ret.)

Dec. 11, 1955. At about 9 p.m., along the Atlantic Coast near Jacksonville, Florida, a fast-maneuvering, round, orange-red ob-

ject was reported by the crews of two airliners and by persons on the ground. Two Navy jets, on a night practice mission, were directed to the area by the Jacksonville Naval Air Station control tower. The jets located the object, but when they attempted to close in, it shot up to 30,000 feet and then dived back, circling and buzzing the jets, while Naval Air Station officers and tower controlers watched via radar. (Reported by Capt. Joe Hull, Capital Airlines pilot).

1956. A Navy R7V-2 Super Constellation, approaching Gander, Newfoundland, on its way from the other side of the Atlantic, carried its regular crew, the relief crew and two other crews being returned home from foreign duty -- almost 30 airmen in all. The senior pilot, a Commander, spotted a cluster of lights below and an estimated 25 miles ahead; this was confirmed by the co-pilot, navigator, radioman, and several others called to the cockpit for the purpose. As the pilot banked to give them a better look, the lights dimmed and several colored rings appeared and began to spread out. At this point, the Commander realized the lights were not on the ocean surface, but climbing toward him. He levelled out and began a full-power climb, in an effort to avoid what by this time looked like a giant disc. Just before the impact was due, the disc tilted, slowed and went by the transport's wing. As the Navy pilot began a bank, he saw the disc was flying alongside, about 100 yards away. He estimated its diameter as 3-4 times his plane's wingspan (370-500 feet) and thickness as at least 30 feet at the center. It looked like one dish atop another. Gradually the object pulled away then tilted upward, accelerated and was lost to sight among the stars. After it left, the pilot contacted Gander by radio and was informed they had watched both his aircraft and the other object on radar, but were unable to get a radio reply from the other ''aircraft.''

(Report acquired by Rear Adm. Delmer S. Fahrney USN, Ret.)

August 15, 1957. In Woodland Hills, Calif., Eugene E. Allison, Chief Aviation Pilot (ret.), his wife, son and a relative were around the family swimming pool, late in the afternoon, when they saw what appeared to be a solid white disc-shaped object hovering between two drifting cirro-stratus clouds. After about six minutes, ''the object appeared to rock from side to side, rising straight up out of sight in approximately three seconds'' according to the 10-year Navy veteran and Pensacola graduate. [14]

July 10, 1962. On the U. S. Naval Auxiliary Air Station, New Iberia, La., a Navy man (name confidential) was watching a group of S-2 Trackers in the landing pattern. ''Suddenly, a discus shaped object came in very fast and low about 1500 feet, slowed over the area of the runway and hangar, and then went out of sight while climbing at a 20 degree to 30 degree angle. It passed across the station heading northeast, and as it came directly ahead, I stopped the car to try to time it. It was accelerating rapidly at this time, however. The only unusual feature of the object, aside from the fact that it was no conventional aircraft, was a rotating dome on top that appeared to be equally divided into two sections, one half light gray in color, the other half black. The estimated speed of rotation was about 90 rpm.'' [15]

NOTES

1. True; March 1950
2. San Diego Journal, March 16, 1950; newswire reports; etc.
3. Report on file at NICAP
4. Keyhoe, Donald E., Flying Saucers Are Real. (Gold Medal Books, 1950), p. 27
5. Report on file at NICAP
6. True; December 1952
7. Ruppelt, Edward J., Report on Unidentified Flying Objects. (Doubleday, 1956), p. 106
8. Ibid., ppg. 162-165
9. United Press; January 4, 1954
10. Report on file at NICAP
11. Report on file at NICAP
12. New York Post, New York Journal-American, July 12, 1950
13. Associated Press; February 12, 1953
14. Report on file at NICAP
15. Report on file at NICAP

SECTION V

PILOTS & AVIATION EXPERTS

If UFOs had not been reported by pilots of scheduled airliners, and military pilots in operation all over the globe, there might be some justification in writing off reports of ground observers as mistaken observations. For, if unknown objects are maneuvering in our skies, pilots would be among the most likely to see them. (Others whose professions cause them to spend many hours watching the skies, such as General Mills Corporation balloon trackers, also have reported numerous UFOs. [1])

Airline and military pilots are among the most experienced observers of the sky. Their profession requires them to spend hundreds of hours per year in the air. Few, if any, occupations require more practical knowledge of weather, other aircraft, and unusual activity such as missile tests. Undoubtedly, few groups of observers have seen more meteors or watched planets under a wider variety of sky conditions. In addition, professional pilots normally are trained in rapid identification of anything which may endanger a flight. Therefore, it is significant that airline and military pilots have reported a large number of totally unexplained UFO sightings.

Recognizing that airline pilots have special training and are in a unique position for observation, the Defense Department includes them in the military system of reporting vital intelligence sightings (CIRVIS), as detailed in the Joint Chiefs regulation JANAP-146(D). [See Section IX.] In 1954, the groundwork for CIRVIS reports was laid by meetings between representatives of the airlines and Military Air Transport Service (MATS) intelligence branch. The reason? "The nation's 8,500 commercial airline pilots have been seeing a lot of unusual objects while flying at night, here and overseas," Scripps-Howard reported. "But," the report continued, "there hasn't been much of an or-ganized system of reporting to military authorities. . . [the airlines and MATS] agreed to organize a speedy reporting system so that a commercial pilot spotting strange objects could send the word to the Air Force in a hurry. The Air Force could then send jet fighters to investigate." [2]

With a few exceptions, most UFO reports on record from military pilots have come from the World War II and Korean War eras, or from recently retired officers. Military pilots, naturally, are restricted from discussing the sightings freely while they are on active duty. But airline pilots (although in recent years sometimes under pressure from their companies not to discuss sightings) have contributed some of the best reports on record.

There had been scattered reports by airline pilots previously but "In the Spring of 1950," the former Chief of the Air Force UFO project reported, "the airline pilots began to make more and more reports -- good reports. . . In April, May, and June of 1950 there were over thirty-five good reports from airline crews." [3] That June, Capt. Eddie Rickenbacker said in an interview: "Flying saucers are real. Too many good men have seen them, that don't have hallucinations." Flying magazine, July 1950, published a roundup report on pilot sightings, giving them very serious treatment (as did other aviation journals in later years; for example, see RAF Flying Review, July 1957).

When NICAP was formed in 1956, four airline pilots (two of whom had personally sighted UFOs) joined the NICAP Panel of Special Advisers. Federal Aviation Agency personnel, aviation industry engineers, and other aviation experts also related their sightings and offered their services. Why are UFOs taken so seriously by professional pilots and aviation experts?

WHAT THE PILOTS HAVE SEEN

This chart lists over 100 UFO sightings by pilots (AL=Airline pilot; M=Military; P=Private), the majority of whom reported typical geometrical objects such as discs and ellipses. The resulting patterns of the observations, and their strong similarity to reports by other reliable witnesses, are readily apparent.

Code	Date	Location	Witness	Description
M	8-10-44	Sumatra	Capt. A.M. Reida, USAF bomber pilot	Spherical object with halo paced B-29 during mission; maneuvered sharply, climbed away vertically. [Section III]
M	12-44	Austria	Maj. W.D. Leet, USAF bomber pilot	Amber disc followed B-17 across Austria. [Section III]
M	8-1-46	nr Tampa, Fla.	Capt. Jack Puckett, USAF 4-engine pilot	Cigar with "portholes" approached C-47 head-on, veered across path. [Section III]
P	6-24-47	Mt. Ranier, Wash.	Kenneth Arnold, businessman, pilot	Nine flat shiny objects in line, zig-zagged. [4]
AL	7-4-47	nr Portland, Oregon	Capt. E.J. Smith, United Airlines; Ralph Stevens, Co-pilot	Two groups of discs.
M	7-6-47	Fairfield-Suisan AFB, Calif.	Pilot (name deleted by Air Force)	UFO sped across sky "oscillating on lateral axis." [5]
M	7-8-47	nr Los Angeles, Calif.	F-51 pilot (name deleted by Air Force)	Flat, light-reflecting UFO passed above fighter. [6]
P	7-9-47	nr Boise, Idaho	Dave Johnson, pilot & aviation editor; others on ground	Large disc, maneuvered erratically. (Section VII)
M	8-47	Media, Pa.	W. Boyce, USAF fighter pilot	Hovering disc. [7]

Code	Date	Location	Witness	Description
M	1-7-48	Ft. Knox, Ky.	Capt. Thomas Mantell, Air National Guard (A.N.G.); many on ground	Pilot killed in crash of F-51 while chasing "huge . . . metallic" circular object. [8]
P	7-48	Pasco, Wash.	Don Newman, 6-year USAF veteran of WW II and Korean War	Disc diving and climbing.
AL	7-23-48	nr Montgomery, Ala.	Capt. C.S. Chiles, F/O J.B. Whitted, Eastern Airlines	Cigar with lights like portholes approached head-on, accelerated, climbed away.
M	10-1-48	Fargo, N.D.	Lt. George F. Gorman, A.N.G.; 3 others	"Dogfight" with disc; UFO outsped F-51. [9]
P	1-1-49	Jackson, Miss.	Tom Rush	Cigar crossed path of plane, accelerated rapidly.
M	7-3-49	Longview, Wash.	Cmdr. M.B. Taylor, USN; many others at air show	Round UFO wobbling on axis, sharp maneuvers. [Section IV]
M	11-3-49	nr Baja, Calif.	Capt. William H. Donnelly, USAFR	Four discs which cavorted in an "astounding manner. [Section III]
AL	3-8-50	Dayton, Ohio	TWA Captains W.H. Kerr, D.W. Miller, M.H. Rabeneck; plus USAF pilots	Round UFO tracked on radar, observed from ground and air, climbed away through clouds. [Section VIII, Radar]
P	3-18-50	nr Bradford, Ill.	Robert Fisher and family	Oval UFO, self-illuminated, sped past plane at estimated 600 to 1,000 mph.
AL	3-20-50	nr Little Rock, Ark.	Capt. Jack Adams, F/O G.W. Anderson, Jr.	Disc with apparent "portholes" flew above airliner in arc. [Section II]
P	3-26-50	nr Washington, D.C.	B.A. Totten, former USAF aircraft inspector	Disc flew below plane; when pilot dove at it, UFO "zoomed up into overcast." [10]
AL	4-27-50	nr Goshen, Ind.	Capt. Robert Adickes, Capt. Robert F. Manning, TWA; passengers	Disc paced plane, sped away when pursued.
AL	5-29-50	nr Washington D.C.	Capt. Willis T. Sperry, F/O Bill Gates, American Airlines	Elliptical object circled plane, raced away.
AL	6-24-50	California desert	F/O David Stewart, United Airlines	Cigar-shaped object paced plane for 20 miles. [11]
M	6-24-50	nr Daggett, Calif.	Navy transport pilot	Cigar-shaped object above desert [Section IV]
M	7-11-50	nr Osceola, Ark.	Lt(jg) J.W. Martin; Enlisted Pilot R.E. Moore, USN	Domed circular UFO passed in front of two Navy planes [confirmed by radar]. [Section IV]
AL	10-5-50	nr San Fernando, Calif.	Capt. Cecil Hardin, F/O Jack Conroy, California Central Airlines	UFO with body lights came head-on at plane, dipped down and passed below; "It appeared to be a wing," Captain Hardin said. "It had no fuselage." Bands of blue light were visible across its width. [12]
P	11-27-50	Evansville, Wisc.	Bill Blair, commercial pilot & flight instructor	Six elliptical objects in loose echelon formation, made sound similar to helicopters. Appeared to be at about 10,000 feet, travelling about 500 mph. [13]
AL	12-27-50	nr Bradford, Ill.	Capt. Art Shutts, TWA	Light source, making erratic and violent maneuvers.
AL	1-20-51	Sioux City, Iowa	Capt. Lawrence Vinther, F/O James F. Bachmeier, Mid-Continent Airlines; plus control tower operators.	Cigar with bright body light approached, reversed direction, climbed away.
AL	2-19-51	Mt. Kilimanjaro, Africa	Capt. Jack Bicknell, Radio Officer D.W. Merrifield, East African Airways; plus 9 passengers	Cigar-shaped object with vertical bands hovered for long period, ascended vertically at high speed. [Section X]
AL	5-22-51	nr Dodge City, Kans.	Capt. W.R. Hunt, American Airlines	Blue-white star-like object gyrated around airliner, "moved backward and forward, then up and down" and finally dove below plane and sped away. [14]
P	8-11-51	Portland, Ore.	R.O. Dodge, former USAF P-47 pilot	Three disc-like UFOs in formation. [15]

Code	Date	Location	Witness	Description
M	1-21-52	Mitchel AFB, N.Y.	Navy TBM pilot	Chased dome-shaped UFO [Section IV]
M	3-29-52	Misawa, Japan	Lt. D.C. Brigham, USAF	Small disc observed maneuvering around F-84. [Section I]
M	6-52	Tombstone, Ariz.	Lt. Cmdr. John C. Williams, USN (Ret.); others	Disc hovered in plain sight, sped away. [Section IV]
AL	7-5-52	Richlands, Wash.	Capts. John Baldwin, George Robertson, plus two co-pilots, Conner Airlines	"perfectly round disc" observed hovering above Hanford atomic plant
AL	7-13-52	nr Washington, D.C.	Capt. W. Bruen, National Airlines	Light source approached plane, hovered, fled when pilot turned on lights. [Section XII, July 1952 Chronology]
AL	7-14-52	Newport News, Va.	Capt. William B. Nash F/O William Fortenberry, PAA	Six discs flew below airliner, executed sharp turn in formation, sped away joined by two more discs.
AL	7-18-52	Denver, Colo.	Capt. Paul Carpenter, American Airlines	Three observations of speeding lights in period of 2 minutes, maximum of 3 UFOs seen at one time; objects appeared to reverse direction [16]
AL	7-20-52	Washington, D.C.	Capt. Casey Pierman, F/O Charles Wheaton	Lights moving rapidly, up, down, and horizontally, also hovered; coincided with radar targets. [Section XII, July 1952 Chronology]
M	7-23-52	South Bend, Ind.	Capt. Harold W. Kloth, USAF	From ground saw two blue-white light sources; one veered sharply. [Section III]
M	7-26-52	Washington, D.C.	Lt. William Patterson, USAF	Glowing objects surrounded his interceptor, confirmed on radar. [Section III; Section XII, July 1952 Chronology]
M	8-1-52	Dayton, Ohio	Maj. James B. Smith, Lt. Don Hemer, USAF F-86 pilots	Saw and photographed round hovering object, tracked on radar; UFO sped away. [Section III]
M	8-13-52	Tucson, Ariz.	Capt. Stanley W. Thompson, USAFR	Nine UFOs in three V's. [Section III]
AL	8-13-52	Dallas, Texas	Capt. Max M. Jacoby, Chief Pilot; Capt. J.W. McNaulty, Pioneer Airlines.	Chased unidentified light, which turned and dove.
M	Summer 52	MacDill AFB, Fla.	USAF Colonel, B-29 pilot	Investigated radar target, saw elliptical UFO. [Section III]
AL	10-29-52	nr Richmond, Va.	Capt. Francisco Rivas, Venezuelan	Bright, luminous object with apparent exhaust, travelled from 45° above plane, over horizon in 8 minutes [17]
M	10-29-52	Hempstead, L.I., N.Y.	Two USAF F-94 pilots	Chased object which maneuvered at high speed. [Section III]
AL	Fall, 1952	New York to Puerto Rico	Capts. Charles Zammett, Robert Harris, William Hutchins PAA	Large green sphere which hovered, then sped away.
M	12-8-52	Chicago, Ill.	Ernie Thorpe, Co-pilot H.S. Plowe	String of lights, 5 or 6 white, one rapidly blinking red, flew alongside plane [18]
P	1-27-53	nr Livermore, Calif.	J.B. Bean	Shiny circular object, climbed steeply at "terrific rate."
M	2-9-53	nr Washington, D.C.	Lt. Ed Balocco, USMC	Alerted by ground sightings, searched, saw luminous UFO with red glow, climbing rapidly. [Section IV]
M	4-53	Laredo, Texas	Lt. E. Wilford, USAF jet instructor	Cigar-shaped UFO leaving contrail of constant length, made right angle turn. [Section III]
P	5-21-53	Prescott, Ariz.	Bill Beers; two others	Eight disc-like objects maneuvered overhead for about an hour. Beers, a veteran pilot, said the UFOs "swooped around in formation, peeled-off, and shot directly up and down in a manner that could not be duplicated by a plane." [19]
M	8-12-53	Rapid City, S.D.	Two USAF jet pilots; ground observers	Multiple radar and visual sighting. [Section I]
M	9-7-53	Vandalia, Ohio	Navy fighter pilots	Brilliant light maneuvered around plane. [Section IV]
AL	10-18-53	English Channel	Capt. Peter Fletcher; F/O R.L. Lemon	UFO "like two shallow saucers with their rims together."

Code	Date	Location	Witness	Description
AL	12-17-53	Sweden	Capt. Ulf Christiernsson	"Unorthodox, metallic...circular" UFO. [Section X]
AL	1-1-54	Victoria, Australia	Capt. D. Barker	Large "metallic" elliptical UFO, speed estimated over 700 m.p.h.
M	1954	Dayton, Ohio	Lt. Col. Richard Headrick, USAFR, Senior Pilot	Two UFOs which hovered, flew in formation, evaded pursuing jets. [Section III]
M	3-24-54	Florida	Capt. Don Holland, USMC	Chased round UFO, which sped away. [Section IV]
M	5-14-54	nr Dallas, Texas	Maj. Charles Scarborough, USMC	Sixteen UFOs, in groups, evaded pursuit by Marine jets. [Section IV]
AL	6-1-54	nr Boston, Mass.	Capt. Charles Kratovil, TWA	White disc paced airliner.
M	6-23-54	Ohio	Lt. Harry L. Roe, Jr.	F-51 paced by unidentified light.
AL	6-30-54	nr Goose Bay, Labrador	Capt. James Howard; crew, British Overseas Airways Corporation	Large dark UFO with several satellite objects, paced airliner; disappeared as jet interceptor neared to check. [Section X]
M	10-4-54	Essex, England	Flt. Lt. J.R. Salandin Royal Air Force	Disc (Saturn-shaped) approached head-on veered to one side. [Section X]
M	10-24-54	Porto Alegre, Brazil	Brazilian Air Force pilots	Formation of silvery circular UFOs over base. [Section X]
AL	11-21-54	nr Rio de Janeiro Brazil	Captain; crew; passengers	About 19 discs rushed by close to airliner, causing panic among passengers. [Section X]
M	12-54	Nowra Air Base, Australia	Royal Australian Navy Pilot	Aircraft paced by two UFOs, ground radar confirmed sighting. [Section X]
M	1955	Virginia, nr. Washington, D.C.	Cmdr., Navy pilot	Disc with dome on top paced aircraft. [Section IV]
AL	1-2-55	nr Punta San Juan, Venezuela	Captain & crew, National Airlines	Orange light source approached plane, beam of light shone in cockpit. [Section X]
AL	2-2-55	nr Merida Venezuela	Capt. Dario Celis, Aeropost Airlines	Top-like UFO with central ring and "portholes" paced airliner. [Section X]
AL	2-11-55	Miami to New York City	Capt. J. King, PAA	Two reddish-green UFOs shot by close to airliner. (20)
AL	10-31-55	nr Auckland, New Zealand	Capt. W.T. Rainbow, Co-pilot S.G. Trounce, National Airways	Brilliant pulsating light overtook and passed airliner. [Section X]
P	11-14-55	San Bernardino Mts., Calif.	Gene Miller	Globe of light, blinked in apparent pattern.
AL & M	12-11-55	nr Jacksonville, Fla.	Navy jet pilots, airline pilots, others	Jets in dogfight with round, reddish UFO, confirmed on radar. [Section IV]
M	1956	North Atlantic	Cmdr. Senior Pilot, other flight crews as passengers	Large disc climbed up to R7V-2, paced it, moved away. [Section IV]
AL	2-17-56	Paris, France	Air France pilot	Investigated radar target, saw odd maneuvering light. [Section VIII, Radar]
AL	4-8-56	Schenectady, N.Y.	Capt. Raymond Ryan, F/O William Neff, American Airlines	Bright light source hovered, sped through 90° arc.
AL	9-6-56	Pasadena, Calif.	Western Airlines pilot	Reported UFO to Air Defense Command; erratically moving white light source confirmed visually from ground by 1st Lt. Mark Matlock, USAF. [21]
AL	11-14-56	nr Mobile, Ala.	Capt. W.J. Hull, F/O Peter MacIntosh, Capital Airlines	Bright light source descended, gyrated near airliner, climbed away. [Section I]
M	12-56	Far East	USAF jet pilot	Radar-visual sighting of disc, radar jammed by interference. [Section I]
AL	1-24-57	Indiana	Commercial pilot; others on ground	Four UFOs, in-line formation, last one larger and egg-shaped. [22]
P	3-8-57	nr Houston, Texas	Victor Hancock and Guy Miller	UFO with three brilliant white lights sped past DC-3, kept just ahead of plane, speeding up each time plane closed in. [23]
AL	3-9-57	nr San Juan Puerto Rico	Capt. Matthew Van Winkle, F/O D.W. Taylor, PAA; other airliners in area	Round greenish-white object came toward airliner; outer ring appeared to reflect light from center; pilot took violent evasive action. [24]

Code	Date	Location	Witness	Description
AL	3-29-57	Off East Coast of Florida	Capt. Kenneth G. Brosdal, F/O George Jacobson, PAA	Observed brilliant pulsating light, confirmed by radar. Visual sighting lasted 4 to 5 minutes.
AL	6-30-57	Belo Horizonte, Brazil	Capt. Saul Martins; passengers	Disc-like object paced airliner, maneuvered around it. [Section X]
AL	7-4-57	nr Campos, Brazil	Cdr. Delgado, REAL Airlines	Disc with dome and "portholes" paced airliner, shot away. [Section X]
AL	8-14-57	nr Joinville, Brazil	Cdr. Jorge Campos Araujo, Varig Airlines	Disc with dome, alternately hovered and moved at high speed; aircraft engines affected. [Section X]
P	8-15-57	Woodland Hills, Calif.	Eugene Allison, Chief Aviation Pilot, USN (Ret.)	Disc hovered, rocked back and forth, shot straight up out of sight. [Section IV]
AL	10-8-57	nr Boston, Mass.	Capt. Joseph L. Flynn, PAA	Brilliant planet-like object (in daylight) moving at high speed on steady course.
AL	11-4-57	Ararangua, Brazil	Capt. Jean Vincent de Beyssac, Varig Airlines	Red light source approached below plane, made erratic jump; electrical equipment on aircraft burnt out. [Section X]
AL	11-6-57	Nebraska	Capt. Irving Kravitz, TWA	Bright light source in high speed flight. [25]
AL	11-9-57	Lafayette, La.	Capt. Truman Gile, Eastern Airlines	Flaring bright light source, visible several minutes. [26]
AL	12-12-57	Chatham-Windsor area, Canada	Capt. J.A. Miller, Trans-Canada Airlines; police officers, others, on ground	Oval disc, changed course. [Section X]
P	5-5-58	San Carlos, Uruguay	Carlos Alejo Rodriguez	Brilliant UFO approached plane, hovered (pilot felt intense heat); when pilot tried to pursue object, it sped away. [Section X]
AL	5-27-58	Bahia State coast, Brazil	Cdr. Bittar, Varig Airlines	Luminous circular object maneuvered, hovered, below airliner. [Section X]
AL	2-4-59	Off New Orleans, La.	Capt. H. Dunker, PAA	Reddish light source sped back and forth across path of DC-6B, shot straight up.
AL	2-24-59	Pennsylvania	Capt. Peter Killan F/O John Dee American Airlines; other airliners; ground observers	Three glowing UFOs paced airliner.
AL	7-11-59	Pacific Ocean	Capt. George Wilson, PAA; several other aircraft	Formation of bright lights sped toward plane, veered away. [Section X]
M	7-14-59	Pampulha, Minas Gerais, Brazil	Brazilian Air Force pilot	Luminous object paced B-26, hovered near airport, reacted to flares. [Section X]
M	10-7-59	nr Forrest City, Ark.	Lt. E.L. Barksdale, Kentucky Air National Guard	Glowing UFO passed plane, pilot turned to chase it, object sped away. [27]
M	1960	Cincinnati, Ohio	Kentucky Air National Guard pilot	Pilot pursued UFO which pulled away each time plane closed to within about 10 miles. (Confidential report, certified by Bluegrass NICAP Affiliate, William D. Leet, President.)
P	3-4-60	Dubuque, Iowa	Charles Morris, flight instructor	Three elliptical UFOs, in-line formation.
AL	7-2-60	nr Maiquetia, Venezuela	Captain & crew Venezuelan Airlines	Bright light source, paralleled plane for 20 minutes, shot away. [Section X]
P	8-16-60	Oak Forest, Ill.	Harry J. Deerwester, former USAF pilot	Disc-like UFO hovered, bobbed around in various directions. [28]
P	1-10-61	Benjamin, Texas	W. K. Rutledge, Passenger George Thomas	Glowing red UFO changed course, descended, appeared to land.
P	7-4/5-61	Akron, Ohio	Ernest Stadvec, owner of flying service, former USAF bomber pilot; others	Light source dove toward plane, climbed away; similar experience next night, confirmed by radar.
AL	7-24-61	Ilha Grande, Brazil	Cdr Jose G. Saez and crew, VASP Airlines	Light source approached plane, bobbed around making angular turns. [Section X]
AL	9-21-61	Pacific Ocean nr Wake Island	Capt. R. F. Griffin, BOAC; also PAA crew; ship at sea	Ring-like UFO, passed above plane and over horizon at high speed. [Section X]

Code	Date	Location	Witness	Description
P	10-2-61	Salt Lake City, Utah	Waldo J. Harris, several others	Disc hovered, wobbled, moved away when pursued. [Section I]
M	1-29-62	Eastern Holland	Royal Dutch Air Force pilot in F-86	UFO sighted, confirmed by radar, fled when pursued. [Section X]
AL	5-21-62	England	Capt. Gordon Pendleton, Irish International Airlines	Globular UFO with antenna-like projections, streaked below his Viscount. [Section X]
M	5-22-62	Argentina	Several Navy pilots	Series of sightings by flight of aircraft. [Section XII, Argentine chronology]
AL	8-2-62	Liberal, Kans.	Capt. Jack Metzker, Central Airlines; airport observers	Brilliant light source, hovered, streaked west; airport alerted, also saw UFOs. [29]
AL	12-22-62	Buenos Aires, Argentina	Pilots of Panagra and Aerolineas Argentina airlines; control tower operators	Bright circular UFO observed near end of Ezeiza Airport runway, took off rapidly. [Section X]
P	2-5-63	nr Washington, D.C.	Carl Chambers, passenger	Pulsating yellow-white light source, maneuvered around plane.
M	3-11-63	Hawaii	Air National Guard jet pilots	Rocket-like UFO sped over high above jets, which were at 40,000 feet. [30]

THE PATTERNS

What professional and private pilots have seen is readily classifiable into three general types of UFO phenomena (corresponding very well with the Air Force Project Grudge Report; see Section XII):

* Geometrical objects, generally circular (disc, oval, ellipse)
* Maneuvering or gyrating lights
* Cigar-shaped or rocket-like objects

(Since military pilot sightings are covered in previous sections, they will not be detailed here. In general, they correspond to non-military reports, so the latter are discussed in this section as typical pilot sightings.)

Geometrical Objects

The earliest recorded UFO sighting by an airline pilot, during the initial flurry of sightings in the United States, was the report by Capt. E. J. Smith, United Airlines, July 4, 1947. Flying a DC-3 from Boise, Idaho, to Portland, Oregon, Captain Smith and his crew observed two separate groups of flat round objects ahead, silhouetted against the sunset. The UFOs were visible for about 10 minutes over a distance of about 45 miles, opening and closing formation. In the second group of UFOs, three operated close together, and a fourth was off to one side by itself. [31]

Since that date, dozens of pilots on all the major airlines have reported UFOs.

Private pilots, also, have witnessed typical geometrical UFOs. During July 1948, in Pasco, Washington, Don Newman (former Air Force pilot) watched a disc-shaped UFO with a dome on top maneuvering over the city at 1:00 p.m. "The exterior finish appeared to be spun or brushed aluminum," Newman said in his report to NICAP. The UFO alternately slowed and accelerated rapidly, diving, and climbing over the area. [32]

On March 18, 1950, Robert Fisher was flying his family from Chicago to Keokuk, Iowa. Near Bradford, Illinois, at 8:40 a.m., he spotted an oval, metallic-appearing disc ahead and slightly to the left of his Bonanza NC 505B. The UFO was moving on a course of about 120 degrees true. (Fisher was flying a southwesterly course, approximately 225 degrees.) The UFO shone in the sunlight, but when it flew below an overcast continued to glow, indicating that it was self-illuminated. It quickly moved off into the distance, at a speed estimated to be 600 to 1,000 mph. [33]

Near Goshen, Indiana, April 27, 1950, a bright orange-red disc paced a Trans World Airways DC-3, which was piloted by Capts. Robert Adickes and Robert F. Manning. As the crew and many passengers watched, the UFO pulled alongside the plane. It looked "like a big red wheel rolling along." Each time the pilot moved toward the object, it moved away as if controlled by repulse radar. When the pilot turned, the disc dove (presenting an edge-on view) and sped off to the north toward South Bend. [34]

A month later (May 29), an American Airlines plane departed Washington, D. C., enroute south over Virginia. About 9:30 p.m., First Officer Bill Gates noticed a light approaching the airliner head-on and notified Capt. Willis T. Sperry. Flight Engineer Robert Arnholt also witnessed what followed. An unidentified object with a brilliant bluish light on the leading edge neared, and seemed to stop. Suddenly it darted to the left of the plane, stopped for a few seconds, then circled around to the right. There it was silhouetted against the moon, revealing a torpedo-shaped or narrow elliptical body. Finally the UFO sped away to the east. Captain Sperry called the speed "fantastic," and said it was "without a doubt beyond the limits of any known aircraft speeds." [35]

A "perfectly round disc" hovering above the Hanford atomic plant, Richland, Washington, was observed by four veteran pilots July 5, 1952. The four Conner Airlines pilots were interviewed by United Press when they landed in Denver, Colorado, and their story was put on the newswires that day.

Capt. John Baldwin (former Air Force pilot, with 7000 hours airline pilot experience at the time) said he was flying near the Hanford atomic plant at about 9000 feet. The UFO was noticed above the plane about 6:00 a.m. It was "just below a deck of wispy clouds about 10,000 to 15,000 feet directly above us," Baldwin said. He described it as "a perfectly round disc, white in color and almost transparent with small vapor trails off it like the tentacles of an octopus." [cf., September 24, 1959 FAA case below]

Capt. George Robertson, D. Shenkel (both former Air Force pilots) and Steven Summers confirmed Baldwin's report. "All of us have been flying a number of years," Baldwin said, "and we've seen all kinds of clouds and formations, but none of us had ever seen anything like this before."

At first, the UFO was hovering. Then it "seemed to back away" and tilt edge-on. "It became flat, gained speed and then disappeared quickly," Baldwin reported.

DISC FORMATION

On the evening of July 14, 1952, a Pan American Airways DC-4 airliner, flying at 8,000 feet, was approaching the Norfolk, Virginia, area enroute to Miami. The senior Captain was back in the cabin and Capt. William B. Nash, temporarily acting as First Officer, was at the controls. In the righthand cockpit seat was Second Officer William Fortenberry. The night was clear and visibility unlimited. Norfolk lay about 20 miles ahead, on the plane's course of 200 degrees magnetic. Off to the right were the lights of Newport News.

About 8:10 p.m. EST, both men noticed a red brilliance in the sky, apparently beyond and to the east of Newport News. The light quickly resolved itself into six bright objects streaking toward the plane, at lower altitude. The UFOs were fiery red. "Their shape was clearly outlined and evidently circular," Captain Nash stated. "The edges were well-defined, not phosphorescent or fuzzy in the least." The upper surfaces were glowing red-orange.

Within seconds, "we could observe that they were holding a narrow echelon formation--a stepped-up line tilted slightly to our right, with the leader at the lowest point and each following craft slightly higher," Captain Nash said.

Abruptly, the leader seemed to slow. The second and third objects wavered slightly and almost overran the leader. The pilots estimated that the UFOs were a little more than a mile below them, at about 2,000 feet, and about 100 feet in diameter.

When the line of discs was almost directly underneath the plane and slightly to the right front, the UFOs abruptly flipped up on edge in unison and reversed direction. (See diagram.) Captain Nash described the maneuver: " . . . they flipped on edge, the sides to the left of us going up and the glowing surfaces facing right. Though the bottom surfaces did not become clearly visible, we had the impression that they were unlighted. The exposed edges, also unlighted, appeared to be about 15 feet thick, and the top surface, at least seemed flat. In shape and proportion, they were much like coins.

"While all were in the edgewise position, the last five slid over and past the leader so that the echelon was now tail foremost, so to speak, the top or last craft now being nearest to our position. Then, without any arc or swerve at all, they all flipped back together to the flat attitude and darted off in a direction that formed a sharp angle with their first course, holding their new formation. . .

"Immediately after these six lined away, two more objects just like them darted out from behind and under our airplane at the same altitude as the others."

As the two additional discs joined the formation, the lights of all eight blinked out, then came back on again. Still in line, the eight discs sped westward north of Newport News, climbed in a graceful arc above the altitude of the airliner. Then the lights blinked out one by one, though not in sequence.

Captain Nash also noted that the original six discs had dimmed slightly before their angular turn, and brightened considerably after making the turn. The two discs speeding to join the formation were brightest of all. Captain Nash and Third Officer Fortenberry radioed a report of the sighting to be forwarded to the Air Force.

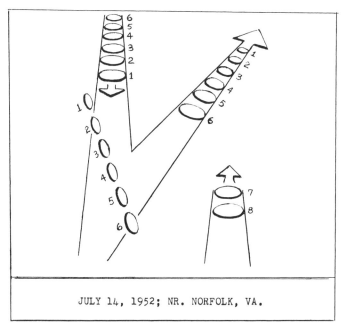

JULY 14, 1952; NR. NORFOLK, VA.

"At 7:00 a.m. the morning after the sighting," Captain Nash reported, "we were telephoned by the Air Force. . . to come for questioning. There were five men, one in uniform; the others showed us I.D. cards and badges of Special Investigators, USAF. In separate rooms, we were questioned for one hour and 45 minutes--then about a half hour together. We made sketches and drew the track of the objects on charts. . . the tracks matched. . . the accounts matched. . . all conversation [was] recorded on a stenotype machine.

"They had a complete weather report. . . it coincided with our visual observations. . . our flight plan. The investigators also advised us that they already had seven other reports. One was from a Lieutenant Commander and his wife. . . They described a formation of red discs travelling at high speed and making immediate direction changes without turn radius. . .

"Regarding speed: We tried again to be very conservative in our computations. The objects first appeared about 10 miles beyond Newport News. . . They travelled to within about a half mile of our craft. . . changed direction, then crossed the western suburban edge of the town areas. . . out over a dark area at least 10 miles beyond the lights, then angled up at about 45 degrees. . .

"We drew a line through the lighted area, measured the distance from our aircraft (and we knew our exact position both visually and by VAR navigation using an ILS needle) to the line through the lighted area. The distance was 25 miles. We had seen them cross this line twice, so we knew they had travelled at least 50 miles. . . . To get a time, we, seven times, separately, using our own panel stopwatch clocks, pushed the button, mentally went through the time, even to saying to ourselves again, 'What the hell's that!' Each time we came up amazingly close to 12 seconds. To be conservative, we increased it to 15 seconds. . . 50 miles in 15 seconds equals 12,000 miles per hour." [36]

Hovering Green Sphere

During the Fall of 1952, three airliners 15 minutes apart sighted a UFO simultaneously. Pan American Airways Captains Charles Zammett, Robert Harris, and William Hutchins were flying DC-4 aircraft about 600 miles south of New York, enroute from New York City to San Juan, Puerto Rico. Suddenly they all saw ahead of them a huge green ball, extremely brilliant and much larger than a full moon in apparent size. The object seemed to be absolutely stationary.

The sighting was not reported to anyone until several years later when one of the pilots happened to fly with Capt. William B. Nash, PAA pilot and NICAP Adviser. Captain Nash describes what happened next:

One ship called to one of the others: "Do you see that?"

"I'll say I see it! What the devil is it?"

Then the third crew broke in: "We see it too. Who could miss it!"

The three pilots continued to watch the amazing sight for about 45 seconds, as the UFO stood perfectly still. Then one pilot started to ask: "Do you think we'll pass it-----wow! Look at it go!"

Just then the bright green orb suddenly sped off to the west at fantastic speed. They watched it move straight away from them on a horizontal path gradually diminishing in size, seemingly due to perspective diminishment.

DISC SIGHTINGS

John B. Bean, a flyer with 17 years experience, made the following report in a letter dated February 7, 1953. [37]

"On the afternoon of January 27, 1953, after stopping at the Purchasing Office of the Atomic Energy Commission Research Facilities near Livermore, California, I was driving north on the road which runs parallel to the eastern fence bounding the Commission properties. Immediately opposite the northeast corner of the fence, I pulled over to the side of the road in order to stop and check some papers which I had in my briefcase behind the front seat of my car. In order to do this, I opened the door and stepped out of the car, thus facing southward. Having finished removing the papers from the briefcase, I was about to climb into the car again when I heard the sound of airplane engines overhead coming in from an easterly direction. . . . It was a DC-6 letting down in the direction of Oakland Municipal Airport, which is to the west of Livermore. Estimated altitude of this aircraft was 2,500 to 3,000 feet.

"As the DC-6 proceeded westward, I was about to take my hand down from my eyes when I noticed a small, whitish object proceeding southward on a course which had just brought it across the Commission property. My initial reaction was that it was some sort of plant fiber floating in the air. Since this was the first clear, sunny day in several weeks and the atmosphere was very springlike, it was a perfectly natural reaction.

"It suddenly occurred to me that we are still in the middle of winter and, insofar as I knew, there were no plants which were giving off any white fibrous substance into the air at this time. As this realization came to me, I also noticed that this object was moving directly away from me at a very rapid rate of departure.

"It began a shallow left turn and at that point I could see that it was perfectly round and had a metallic sheen somewhat similar to that of aluminum with a satin finish. I believe another term for this type of finish on aluminum is known as brushed aluminum. It did not have a sharp glint which one often sees when light is reflected from a conventional aluminum aircraft. The light was more diffused and whitish in color. . . . Having gathered my wits about me to this extent, I followed its course and suddenly it began to alter direction, at first seemingly heading due south again, and then suddenly making a steep righthand turn. It also began to climb at the most terrific rate of ascent that I have ever witnessed. I should like to say parenthetically at this point that only the week previously I had watched two swept-wing F-86's chasing tails near Hamilton Field late one evening. The two F-86's had remained relatively stationary over one spot and I had an excellent opportunity to watch them in several merry-go-rounds. A number of times they each climbed almost vertically, but their speed was insignificant compared to the speed at which this object was able to climb and execute a sharp right turn.

"The moment the object began its climb, I started a count of 1,000-2,000-3,000. By the time the count of 3,000 had been reached the object disappeared from sight.

"At this moment, coming in from the East on a due westerly heading, at an altitude somewhat lower than that at which I had sighted the disc, was a jet. It was leaving a very definite contrail all the way across the sky and was on a collison course with that of the disc prior to its rapid ascent. When I say collison course, I mean that directionally the two objects were on a collision course but that actually they were separated by several thousand feet of altitude. However, it occurred to me that the disc might have taken evasive action in order to avoid the jet.

"The jet proceeded on its course due west and to the south of the Atomic Energy Commission grounds and at a point approximately over Hayward or Castro Valley turned and headed due north.

"The interesting facts about this sighting were that I had three distinct types of aircraft within my sight range simultaneously so that it was possible to evaluate their relative speeds. Thus there was no question that the disc-like object had far more power and far more rapid maneuverability than the other two. An additional interesting factor to be kept in mind is that, whereas the jet was leaving a distinct contrail at the higher altitude, the white disc left no contrail whatsoever. Neither of the two higher aircraft made any sound. However, both of them were well to the south of my position and the wind was blowing from me toward them at about 15 to 20 knots. Actually I imagine the correct direction of the wind was approximately north-northwest.

"As soon as the sighting was over, I glanced at my watch and noticed the time to be 1343. The date again was the afternoon of January 27, 1953 and the atmospheric conditions were CAVU . . . . In closing, there is one other factor which may be of interest. The whole elapsed time from the original sighting to the disappearance of the disc was approximately nine seconds in my estimation. It may have been slightly longer, but certainly no shorter. Three of those seconds were counted time, three or four of them were observed time when I had my wits about me, and the other two to four were initial-reaction time."

A disc-shaped UFO paced a Trans-World Airways plane June 1, 1954. United Press reported the incident (newswire copy on file at NICAP):

FLYING SAUCER OR A WEATHER BALLOON...THAT SEEMS TO BE THE ISSUE BETWEEN AN AIRLINES PILOT AND THE AIR FORCE.

TRANS-WORLD AIRWAYS PILOT CHARLES KRATOVIL OF PORT WASHINGTON, NEW YORK, SAYS HE SAW AN UNIDENTIFIED OBJECT . . . LARGE, WHITE-COLORED, AND DISC-SHAPED.

HE SAYS HE AND HIS TWO CREW MATES SPOTTED THE OBJECT 10 MILES NORTH OF BOSTON THIS MORNING . . . THAT IT WAS PURSUING THE SAME COURSE AS HIS PLANE BUT THAT IT WAS OBSCURED BY HIGH CLOUDS.

KRATOVIL SAYS HE RECEIVED A MESSAGE FROM THE AIRLINES BOSTON OFFICE QUOTING THE AIR FORCE AS SAYING THE OBJECT PROBABLY WAS A WEATHER BALLOON.

HOWEVER, THE PILOTS PUT IT THIS WAY:

"IF THIS IS A WEATHER BALOON . . . IT'S THE FIRST TIME I EVER SAW ONE TRAVELING AGAINST THE WIND."

Elliptical Objects

Charles R. Morris of Dubuque, Iowa, attempted (unsuccessfully) to film three elliptical objects observed by him and his wife on March 4, 1960. The 8 mm kodachrome film, which he exposed in late afternoon, failed to show the UFOs. At 5:57 p.m. while watching one of his flying students perform aerobatics, Morris first noticed the three UFOs in the southeast sky. They moved in line, glowing a neon-like blue-white and arced from about 25 degrees elevation in the southeast toward the northeast. In about 4 minutes, the objects covered an arc of about 135 degrees. During that time, Morris ran into the house for his camera while his wife continued to watch the UFOs. As the objects disappeared in the distance to the northeast, they appeared to be climbing slightly. [38]

NICAP Member Lex Mebane telephoned Morris and interviewed him at length a few days after the sighting, obtaining some additional information. At their largest, the UFOs appeared to be about one-eighth the apparent size of the moon. They made no sound and left no trails. The third UFO lagged behind occasionally. [cf., February 24, 1959, American Airlines case, following.]

Morris was interrogated by the Air Force, who told him there were no aircraft scheduled in the vicinity. He had checked independently with Cedar Rapids Air Traffic Control and determined the same.

Maneuvering or Gyrating Lights

The typical disc-shaped or elliptical UFOs seem to fly a recognizable course, though they do hover, alter direction abruptly and accelerate rapidly. The second main category of sightings, however, displays a characteristically different pattern of flight in a number of cases. This pattern has been compared to the gyrations of a hummingbird--alternately hovering and flitting here and there, horizontally and vertically. Whether some of the erratically maneuvering lights seen at night are in fact different from the geometrical UFOs observed in daylight is an open question. In some cases the lights have proved to be body lights on discs or ellipses; in others no definite silhouette could be seen.

TWA Pilot Reports Gyrating Light

December 27, 1950: A TWA flight was enroute from Chicago to Kansas City. Shortly after sunset Capt. Art Shutts, at the controls, noticed a bright white light ahead of the plane, also flashing to green and red occasionally. The aircraft was on a heading of approximately 200 degrees. At first Captain Shutts thought it was a star, until it began to "wobble and swerve unsteadily." Then the UFO began to streak back and forth in a north-south line, through an arc of 10 degrees to 30 degrees, changing direction abruptly. The UFO would move at terrific speed, hover oscillating slightly, then speed up. Captain Shutts noticed that the visible horizon near the UFO appeared to vibrate as if light were being distorted, especially after the object put on a burst of speed.

Finally the light dimmed to a pinpoint and began to move slowly south in a straight line. Suddenly it "lurched," accelerated rapidly and zoomed upward at a 45 degree angle, made a nearly square turn, plunged downward and disappeared below the horizon on a north heading. It had been visible for 25 minutes. [39]

Chief Pilot Chases Unidentified Light

The following is an exact copy of a 1952 United Press newswire report:

DALLAS, TEX., AUG. 15--(UP)--A VETERAN AIRLINES PILOT TOLD TODAY HOW HE CHASED A MYSTERIOUS ORANGE LIGHT THROUGH THE SKY NEAR DALLAS IN AN ATTEMPT TO LEARN WHAT IT WAS HE HAD SIGHTED SKIMMING THROUGH THE AIR.

THE PILOT, CAPT. MAX M. JACOBY, MERELY CALLED THE OBJECT A "LIGHT." HE SAID HE WAS AFRAID HE WOULD BE LAUGHED AT.

JACOBY, CHIEF PILOT FOR PIONEER AIRLINES, SAID HE SAW THE LIGHT WHILE ON A ROUTINE TEST FLIGHT WEDNESDAY NIGHT. HE SAID HE DELAYED TELLING OF THE INCIDENT BECAUSE HE FEARED HE WOULD BE RIDICULED.

JACOBY SAID HE MADE AN EFFORT TO INTERCEPT THE LIGHT BUT IT ELUDED HIM AND FINALLY DISAPPEARED.

HE SAID HE FIRST SPOTTED IT 15 TO 25 MILES FROM LOVE AIR FIELD AT AN ALTITUDE OF ABOUT 3,000 FEET.

THE PILOT SAID THE OBJECT TURNED AND DIVED BUT THE APPEARANCE OF ITS BODY "DID NOT CHANGE WHEN IT TURNED . . . I COULDN'T TELL WHETHER IT WAS JUST A LIGHT OR A LIGHT COMING FROM SOME OBJECT."

HE SAID HE WAS ACCOMPANIED ON THE FLIGHT BY CAPT. J.W. MCNAULTY, ALSO A PILOT.

June 23, 1954: An Air National Guard pilot, flying an F-51 Mustang fighter, was trailed by a UFO over Ohio. The incident was reported to Leonard H. Stringfield, then director of an Ohio-based UFO investigation organization. [See Section VII; Ground Observer Corps]. Lt. Harry L. Roe, Jr., first noticed the object about 8:00 p.m. near Columbus, and kept it in sight for 45 minutes all the way to Vandalia. Lt. Roe repeatedly tried to maneuver so that he could see a silhouette behind the "round white light," but "it kept maneuvering around so it was against the darkened part of the sky." When Roe swung the F-51 around to give chase, the UFO "took off" and sped away.

November 14, 1955: Another UFO which gave the appearance of intelligence behind its actions was observed at night above the San Bernardino Mountains of California. Gene Miller, a former Air Force instructor, was enroute from Phoenix, Arizona, to Banning, California. His passenger, Dr. Leslie Ward (Redlands physician) also witnessed the UFO.

A "globe of white light" appeared ahead of Miller's plane, moving very slowly. Assuming it was an airliner, he blinked his landing lights twice. The "white globe" went out twice, in apparent acknowledgment. As the light grew larger, closing on his plane, Miller flashed his landing lights three times. The UFO, he said, blinked three times, then "suddenly backed up in mid-air."

The sighting by Miller, who later became a NICAP member, was reported in the Los Angeles Times, November 26, 1955.

Commercial Plane Follows UFO

April 8, 1956: A very brilliant light was followed across New York State by an American Airlines plane. The pilots were Capt. Raymond Ryan and First Officer William Neff. The chase was described by radio to Air Force and civilian control tower operators. The following account of the sighting is taken from a tape-recorded interview program, "Meet the Millers," on WBEN-TV, Buffalo, New York, April 16, 1956 (tape on file at NICAP). Mr. and Mrs. Miller are the interviewers (Int.); Captain Ryan, F/O Neff, and Bruce Foster (a Bell Aircraft Company engineer) are the guests:

Int: Was that a regular flight of American Airlines?
Ryan: Yes, it was.
Int: From Buffalo to New York?
Ryan: This flight comes out of New York and lands at Albany, Syracuse, Rochester, and terminates in Buffalo.
Int: What was your first idea that anything was happening-- that you were seeing something?
Neff: This very brilliant white light, like an approaching aircraft with its landing lights on. Naturally we moved away from it thinking that's what it was. Then we noticed it was standing still at the time and we got sort of curious.
Int: Just about what location was this?
Ryan: This was just about over Schenectady. We were coming out of Albany. We took off north and we made a left turn and we noticed this light over Schenectady. It seemed to be standing still.
Int: A light? Now, when you say a light do you mean a light like a light bulb--about that color?
Ryan: Oh yes, very fluorescent--a very bright light. . .
Int: A big what?
Ryan: A large light. It looked more like a light coming into Albany airport.
Int: And both of you saw it? At the same time?
Int: How close were you to it, do you think?
Ryan: We turned a little bit to pass to the south of it, and we were probably 2 or 3 miles from it.

Int: And the thing was just standing there?
Ryan: Just about standing; it was off our wingtip.
Int: Was there anyone else on the flight with you?
Ryan: Oh, we had Miss Reynolds, our stewardess was with us.
Int: Did she happen to notice it too?
Ryan: She came up. We called her and she came up and looked at it later on after this had taken off at this terrific speed from where we first noticed it. . .
Int: How long was it stationary there?
Neff: We couldn't say that it was actually stationary. . .
  Several talking at once

Ryan: . . . from the time we were off the ground at Albany, until we--it's about 15 miles by air to Schenectady and it was off our wingtip, and we watched it go through a ninety degree arc, go right straight to the west, and it was-- how many seconds does it take to go through a ninety degree arc?
Int: Bruce?
Foster: How fast would you say it appeared to be going? Did it change speed very radically during the time that you saw it?
Ryan: The initial speed I would say probably was 800 to 1000 miles an hour. How fast can it--it's hard to say, just to compute that speed.
Neff: Certainly much faster than another airplane would.
Ryan: Oh much faster, much faster than a jet.
Int: Faster than a jet?
Ryan: Yes ma'am.
Neff: Couldn't be a jet, not at that altitude because their fuel is so critical.

. . . . . .

Foster: Did it appear to change color at all?
Ryan: Yes it did. It changed color after it got to the west of us, probably 8 to 10 miles. It appeared--the light went out, that's what had Bill and I concerned. It went out momentarily, and we knew there was something up there, and now here we were with a load of passengers with something on our course up ahead, and what are we going to do, so we watched this where the light went out and this orange object came on--this orange light.

. . . . . .

Ryan: We looked at one another a little bit amazed, so we decided we'd call Griffiss Air Force Base, and I thought they had the radar on. . . And they didn't have it on-- It would take them 30 minutes to energize the set.

. . . . . .

Neff: They asked us to keep it sighted and we did, and we kept calling out our location and as we told them where we were we turned all our lights on. They asked us to turn them off and they could see us, and they asked if this object you see is orange in color. We said it was--
Int: This is after it turned on I understand
Ryan: Yes. They said "we have a definite silhouette in sight south of the field." Now those fellas are observers who are in the tower. They said that they could see a silhouette.

. . . . . .

Neff: Watertown could see it and they're quite a ways north of Griffiss, and Albany saw it--two men in the tower at Albany--one an Air Force man and one a CAA man. And they saw it after we first called them, and noticed--and they looked over to the west and saw it right away.
Int: And when they saw it was it moving?
Neff: Well, we didn't get to talk with them--
Int: But to you it was moving?
Neff: Oh yes.
Int: Real fast?
Ryan: It stayed just that far ahead of us, and they asked us what our point of next intended landing was, and I told them Syracuse, and they wanted to be identified--our aircraft, number and serial number, and they said "well abandon that next landing temporarily and maintain the course and your altitude," so we did. They were calling scramble.

. . . . . .

Int: When you said ****(garbled), was it low, or was it low for a jet?

Neff: Well, it was low and it was also low for a jet. There happened to be an overcast that evening which eliminated the possibility of a star right off the bat, and ****(garbled) the way I understand it a jet burns up three or four times the amount of fuel at low altitude than it does at high altitude. I don't think a jet could stay down that long without using up a considerable amount of gas.

. . . . . .

Int: How fast were you going?

Ryan: About 250 miles per hour.

Int: ****(garbled) then did they slow down or why didn't**** (garbled)

Ryan: They must have slowed down. "They" or "it" must have slowed down.

. . . . . .

Neff: We trailed out as far as Oswego which is right on the south shore of Lake Ontario and we passed up our point of landing at Syracuse and we weren't sure we should hold the passengers up any longer, and of course we didn't advise them.

. . . . . .

Ryan: We called them (Griffiss AFB) and they said they were "about off," and that was about 8 minutes and we couldn't work them any longer, and we turned over with Syracuse tower, and they were giving--relaying the messages back and forth, and it was then about 10 to 12 minutes and they're still not off yet. And we can't--I don't know, we'd probably still be flying. I just don't know where the jets were. Why didn't they get the jets up?

Int: Well what happened to the object?

Ryan: It went off, it just went to the northwest and it went out of sight.

Foster: Was it more rapid? All of a sudden did it accelerate its speed?

Ryan: It did appear to--after it got over the water it appeared really get out of sight very fast.

Neff: It did, in the direction of Toronto--in that direction.

. . . . . .

Int: Was this object saucer-shaped or not?

Ryan: Oh I don't know; I couldn't say.

Neff: There was no definite shape to it, it was just a brilliant light.

. . . . . .

Radar-Visual Sighting by PAA Flight

March 29, 1957: About 7:30 p.m. local time, Pan American flight 206A was northbound off the east coast of Florida, at 30 degrees N. Latitude. The plane was enroute to New York from Nassau at 16,000 feet, moving through the tops of cumulus clouds, on a heading of 25 degrees magnetic. At the controls was Capt. Kenneth G. Brosdal. The engineer, John Wilbur, was in the co-pilot's seat. The co-pilot, George Jacobson, was navigating.

"About 50 miles east of Papa-3, a checkpoint between Nassau and Tuna," Capt. Brosdal stated, "we (the co-pilot, engineer and myself) saw this very bright white light. It seemed to grow in intensity to the point where it would be about 3 or 4 strengths of a rising Venus, then would subside. This happened about 3 or 4 times, during which I came to enough to check on the radar screen. Sure enough, a target showed up at 3 o'clock between 45-50 miles away.

"Using the curser on the face of the radar, I checked the angle of sighting and it checked with the visual angle. This light appeared to be stationary, or moving in a N.E. direction (same as us). I observed this on the scope long after the light went out. I checked with Miami ATC [Air Traffic Control] but no other traffic or firing was in the area, to their knowledge." [40]

The radar set, tuned to the 50 mile range, tracked the unidentified target for 20 minutes. The visual observation lasted 4-5 minutes. The blip on the scope, Capt. Brosdal added, indicated an apparent size in excess of the size of normal aircraft. The altitude of the light, on the basis of angle of sight and radar ranging, was estimated to be 20,000 to 25,000 feet.

Capt. Brosdal indicated that he was most impressed by the exceptional intensity of the light during the bright phase of pulsation.

Pilot Reports High-Speed Light

October 8, 1957: Another Pan American pilot sighted an unidentified light. Capt. Joseph L. Flynn, bringing a DC-7C flight into New York from Paris, noticed the UFO at 7:05 a.m. about 25 miles southwest of Boston. The object, "like a star travelling very fast," showed up to the right of the plane. "The sun was directly behind the plane and the object glowed a very bright silver," Captain Flynn said. "It was much brighter than the morning star." The pilot turned the plane and, for five minutes, tried to follow the UFO. But it sped out of sight.

At first Captain Flynn assumed the object was the Russian satellite, Sputnik I. But a check with the Smithsonian Institution's astrophysical observatory revealed that the satellite had passed over the New York area at 8:03 a.m., nearly an hour after the UFO sighting. [41] Nor would a satellite be so readily visible or appear to travel at high speed as described.

Gyrating Light Ascends After Crossing Path of Plane

February 4, 1959: Over the Western Caribbean, 3:00 a.m., Capt. H. Dunker, Pan American Airways, was piloting a DC-6-B from New Orleans to Panama. He and the crew saw a reddish light speed across their course from right to left (west to east). About 45 degrees to their left the light stopped suddenly, fading in luminosity. Seconds later it sped back across and stopped about 10 degrees to the right. Then the UFO moved again to the left. After remaining visible about 45 seconds, the object went straight up out of sight at tremendous speed. [42]

Airliners Paced by Three UFOs

The sighting of three glowing objects by several airline crews February 24, 1959 is one of the most thoroughly investigated (and, ironically, one of the most controversial) on record. The key witness, Capt. Peter W. Killian, was interviewed by NICAP personnel. A detailed investigation report, including weather data, air navigation maps, etc., was submitted to NICAP by the New York City Affiliate. The Akron UFO Research Committee cooperated in the investigation, adding valuable details. Other published references are listed in the Section Notes [43].

The Air Force later attributed the sighting to a refueling mission involving a tanker aircraft and jet bombers flashing brilliant lights. Discrepancies in this explanation are discussed in Section IX.

February 24, 1959: Captain Killian and First Officer James Dee, American Airlines, were flying a DC-6B nonstop from Newark to Detroit. It was a clear night, with stars brightly visible and no moon. At 8:20 p.m. EST the plane was approximately 13 miles west of Williamsport, Pennsylvania, flying on a heading of 295 degrees at 8,500 feet. Off the left wingtip, Captain Killian noticed three bright lights, which he first thought were the three stars making up the belt of the constellation Orion. But then he realized that Orion was also visible, higher overhead. The UFOs were about 15 degrees above the plane.

As he and F/O Dee continued to watch, the objects pulled ahead of the wingtip. At this point, in the vicinity of Erie, Pennsylvania, Captain Killian contacted two other American Airlines planes in the area. One at the Dolphin checkpoint (over the northern shore of Lake Erie) saw the objects directly to the south over Cleveland. The other aircraft, near Sandusky, Ohio, and headed toward Pittsburgh, spotted the objects a little to the left of their heading, to the southeast. [See map in Section IX]

As the DC-6B continued west, the UFOs occasionally pulled ahead and dropped back until they were in their original position with respect to the left wingtip. Then Captain Killian began letting down for landing in Detroit, and the crew no longer had time to watch the objects.

During the 45 minute observation, the UFOs continuously changed brightness, flashing brightly "brighter than any star," and fading completely. This did not occur in any apparent pattern. The color fluctuated from yellow-orange to a brilliant blue-white at their brightest. The last object in line moved back and forth at times, independently of the generally western motion of the formation.

Visibility was unlimited. The pilots agreed, "It could not be any clearer than it was that night above 5,000 feet."

When the plane began letting down for landing, about 9:15 p.m., Captain Killian and F/O Dee lost sight of the objects. At 9:30 p.m. in Akron, Ohio, George Popowitch of the UFO Research Committee received a phone call from a contact at the Akron airport. A United Airlines plane (Flight 937) had just landed for a 15-minute stop, and reported sighting three UFOs which had followed their plane for 30 minutes. Popowitch had already received 9 reports from local citizens between 9:15 and 9:20 of three UFOs seen in the area, so he arranged to interview the crew of the airliner.

Capt. A. D. Yates and Eng. L. E. Baney said they had tracked the objects from the vicinity of Lockhaven, Pennsylvania, to Youngstown, Ohio, between 8:40 and 9:10 p.m. United Airlines flight 321, also, had discussed the objects by radio. Captain Yates had seen the UFOs pacing his plane to the south. But in the vicinity of Warren, Ohio the objects passed the aircraft, veered to the right, and finally disappeared to the northwest.

UFO Landing Reported

Early in 1961, a private pilot in Texas witnessed an apparent landing of a UFO. NICAP Member Jack Varnell, Knox City, Texas, conducted an extensive investigation into the sighting and the resulting USAF interest. [44] An employee of the Agricultural Stabilization and Conservation office, he joined the search for the landed object shortly after noon of the day following the sighting, and observed proceedings firsthand from then on.

January 10, 1961: Pilot W. K. Rutledge and passenger George Thomas, both of Abilene, Texas, were enroute to Abilene from Tulsa, Oklahoma. At 6,500 feet over Wichita Falls, Texas, about 9:00 p.m. they spotted a red object about 1,500 feet above the plane, glowing brilliantly in the night sky. Rutledge changed course to follow it at about 180 mph, establishing radio contact with the control tower at Shepard AFB, Wichita Falls, during the chase. He followed it WSW to Munday, then north to Vera (where several persons on the ground saw it). Then the object moved WSW again, toward Benjamin, finally turning SW. When beyond Benjamin, the object began to reduce its speed and altitude, going into a glide and apparently landing 4 to 5 miles SW of the town in a heavily wooded area.

The pilot circled in his single-engine Beech "Debonair" while law officers, alerted by radio, sped to the scene. Included were Knox County Sheriff Homer T. Melton (now a Texas Ranger), one of his deputies, and the police chiefs of Knox City and Munday. Rutledge radioed his position to the Shepard AFB control tower when he began to circle, and the word was relayed to the converging patrol cars.

Poor communication between air and ground hampered Rutledge in his efforts to direct the search cars. At one point, a cruiser ·driven by Deputy Stone came within 100 yards of the landing spot, but the pilot was unable to direct him closer. During this period the glow from the UFO, which had been visible to Rutledge on the ground, was diminishing to a dull red. About the time Stone approached it (unknowingly) and blinked his lights, the glow from the UFO vanished completely.

After about 90 minutes of chasing and circling, Rutledge noticed he was running low on fuel and decided to go on to Abilene.

AIR FORCE INVESTIGATION

Next morning the search was resumed by police, about 20 high school boys, and several other citizens of the area. Despite a cold drizzle, they hunted until 3:00 p.m., when Rutledge and Thomas flew back from Abilene. Since there was no convenient airport, Rutledge landed on a highway near Benjamin. When they got into town they were immediately met by USAF Lieutenant McClure and a Sergeant; the four retired to a restaurant nearby for the questioning. NICAP Member Jack Varnell listened from the next table.

The Air Force officer's opening implications that the object might have been a balloon or meteorite were quickly shortcut by Rutledge's firm statement: "What I saw last night was certainly not a meteorite or a weather balloon." He then made it clear that the object "came down slowly," and did not "fall." The lieutenant changed his tone at this point, Varnell reported, and became much more serious and interested.

As the interview progressed, the cafe began to fill, since the

sighting was by this time the chief topic of conversation in the small Texas town. Questions were posed and answers noted for more than a half hour, but the muffled voices were hard to hear in the crowded room.

The USAF men expressed an interest in locating the site of the landing, so the group returned to Rutledge's parked airplane. While Jack Varnell and the sheriff stopped traffic, Rutledge, Thomas, and Lieutenant McClure took off from the highway. The sergeant and the enlisted driver of the USAF car drove off.

The small plane made three or four passes over the 1,000 acre tract of mesquite where the object had reportedly landed, and then flew off. Contrary to expectations, the other USAF men did not join the ground search party, which broke up about the time the plane departed.

Shortly after 5:00 p.m., the three airmen, the pilot and his companion were seen at a drive-in restaurant near Knox City. Rutledge was observed by Jack Varnell to be filling out what appeared to be the standard USAF Technical Information Sheet with Lieutenant McClure.

July 4-5, 1961: On two consecutive nights while flying in the Cleveland-Akron area, Ernest Stadvec encountered strangely maneuvering lights which he could not identify. A World War II bomber pilot, he now owns a flying service in Akron, Ohio.

"I have been flying since 1942 both day and night," he stated, "and currently own a flying business that requires us to fly day or night in all types of weather. Over the years I have seen many falling stars and other phenomena associated with atmospheric conditions as well. What we saw was not an astronomical or meteorological phenomenon."

On the first night, over northwest Akron, Stadvec and two passengers spotted a brilliant green and white light apparently suspended to the right of the plane, about 10:15 p.m.

"The object we saw dived at us on a collison course to the extent that I actually called out to my passengers that the object was going to ram us," Stadvec said. "After the object came at us it reversed course and climbed rapidly into a clear night sky."

And he continued: "This happened again the next night [about the same time] when the object flashed up from in front of us and again climbed into a clear sky. In both instances, the object climbed at tremendous speeds, levelled off and disappeared to the northwest."

On the second night about the time of the sighting, radar at Cleveland Hopkins airport detected a meteor-like object, which flared up on the screen and faded out within a few minutes. [46]

A similar experience was reported more recently by a private pilot from Williamsport, Penna., and his passenger, John P. Campbell, reporter for the Williamsburg Sun-Gazette.

February 7, 1963: Returning to Pennsylvania from Danville, Virginia at 11:45 p.m. (near Charlottesville, Virginia, about 95 miles SW of Washington, D.C.) Carl Chambers noticed a starlike light, and soon realized it was moving toward his plane. "After noting that its altitude and position changed rapidly, I radioed the Washington FAA and reported the incident," Chambers said in a signed report to NICAP.

"For nearly an hour after, we stayed in contact with Washington. During that time, the object hovered off the right wing [easterly] and moved toward, under, and above the aircraft. Then it dropped off and a few minutes later appeared about 35 miles south of Washington, where it seemingly hovered over a missile defense base. From that position and less than a half-minute later it reappeared some 10 or 15 miles north of the capital."

FAA tower personnel confirmed to Chambers that they had received a similar report from another pilot in the area at the same time. The object had an intermittent yellow-white glow, and at its closest point appeared to be about three feet in diameter.

Cigar-Shaped or Rocket-Like UFOs

The third general category of UFO types which pilots and others have reported is the rocket or cigar shape, sometimes leaving a flame-like exhaust. Reports of this type are comparatively rare, but they have been seen by enough competent witnesses to establish them as a distinct type. (Some objects reported as "cigar-shaped" have, on closer investigation, turned out to be elliptical in shape, i.e., tapered to a point--or nearly so--on the ends. The term "cigar-shaped" is used here to apply to spindle or cylindrical shaped objects with somewhat blunted ends).

The "classic" case of this type is the sighting by Eastern Airlines pilots C. S. Chiles and J. B. Whitted, July 23, 1948. At 2:45 a.m. in the vicinity of Montgomery, Alabama, Captain Chiles and his co-pilot noticed a brilliant light loom up in front of the DC-3, hurtling head-on toward them. The UFO swooped down, veered to the right of the airliner, emitted a long red exhaust blast and shot straight up into clouds. Captain Chiles later described the UFO as torpedo-shaped, about 100 feet long, with two rows of brightly-lit apparent windows along the side.

The USAF currently contests the fact that the airliner was rocked when the UFO climbed away, but the statement that it was appears in the Air Force Project "Saucer" Report from the witnesses' original descriptions. [47] At Robbins AFB, Georgia on the same night, about 2:00 a.m., a "long, dark wingless tube" was seen rushing overhead spurting flame from the stern.

Similar maneuvering rocket-shaped objects have been reported by military pilots [see August 1, 1946 case, Capt. Jack Puckett, Section III] and private pilots.

January 1, 1949: Tom Rush of Jackson, Mississippi, saw a cigar-shaped object while approaching to land at Dixie Airport. The UFO crossed in front of his plane, accelerated and flew out of sight. [48]

January 20, 1951: A bright light, source unknown, was observed from the control tower at Sioux City, Iowa, airport about 8:30 p.m. Chief Controller John Williams cautioned a Mid-Continent Airlines DC-3, which was about to take off; thinking it was another aircraft approaching the field.

Shortly after take-off, Capt. Lawrence W. Vinther and Co-pilot James F. Bachmeier, in the DC-3, were startled to see the bright light closing on them very rapidly. Before they could take any action, the light flashed past the airliner and the pilots saw a clear silhouette of a cigar-shaped object behind the light.

The Co-pilot turned quickly, and there was the UFO pacing the airliner. The object had apparently reversed direction in an instant. Bachmeier called out to Captain Vinther, and he turned and looked. Then the UFO shot straight up and disappeared. [49]

One of the passengers who also witnessed the UFO was a full colonel of Air Force Intelligence, who filed a report along with the pilots. He was reportedly greatly impressed by what he had seen. [50]

AVIATION PERSONNEL OTHER THAN PILOTS

Aviation personnel other than pilots--Federal Aviation Agency (FAA) [51] control tower operators and flight controllers, flight crew members, ground crews, airport supervisors, etc.--have made regular reports of UFOs. The FAA often has cooperated with NICAP, in some cases furnishing logs, teletype reports, and other documentary material. Some of the information has come from NICAP members employed by the FAA, other from public servants (not NICAP members) who apparently have no prejudices about UFOs and merely believe that the subject should be treated frankly and openly.

September 24, 1959: Redmond Airport, Oregon, is situated southeast of the city. (see sketch map). Just before dawn, policeman Robert Dickerson was cruising the city streets when he noticed a bright falling object like a meteor. Instead of "burning out," the object took on a larger, ball-like appearance, stopped abruptly, and hovered about 200 feet above the ground. Its glow lit up juniper trees below it.

The patrolman watched the UFO for several minutes, then drove toward it on Prineville Highway, turning in at the airport. The UFO, meanwhile changed color from bright white to a duller reddish-orange color, and moved rapidly to a new position NE of the airport.

At the FAA office, Flight Service Specialist Laverne Wertz had just completed making weather observations minutes before, and had seen nothing unusual. Now Patrolman Dickerson, Wertz, and others studied the hovering object through binoculars. The UFO was round and flat, with tongues of "flame" periodically extending from the rim.

At 1310Z (5:10 a.m. PST), official logs show, the UFO was reported to Seattle Air Route Control Center. Logs of the Seattle center show that the report was relayed to Hamilton AFB. The Seattle log continues: "UFO also seen on the radar at Klamath

Falls GCI [Ground Control Intercept] site. F-102's scrambled from Portland."

As the Redmond observers studied the UFO, they noticed a highspeed aircraft approaching from the southeast. The log continues: "As aircraft approached, UFO took shape of mushroom, observed long yellow and red flame from lower side as UFO rose rapidly and disappeared above clouds."

The UFO was seen again briefly, hovering about 25 miles south of the airport. Radar continued to show the UFO south of Redmond for about two hours. [See FAA log, Section IX.]

October 9, 1951: An earlier UFO, rated an "unknown" by the Air Force after investigation of similar evidence (apparently without radar confirmation) was reported at Municipal Airport, Terre Haute, Indiana. About 1:43 p.m., CAA Airways Operations Specialist R. L. Messmore noticed an unusual object approaching from the SE, and quickly called another witness. C. W. Sonner, Chief of Interstate Airways Communication Station, ran outside to watch. "I have been working at airports for 16 years." Sonner said, "and never before have I seen an aircraft like it." The flattened round object sped overhead, disappearing to the NW after 15 seconds. Using the angle of sighting, Messmore and Sonner calculated that the UFO was travelling at 2,880 mph, assuming it was at treetop level; 18,000 mph if at 3,000 feet; etc.

Because of the experience of the observers, this would have been a good sighting as it stood. But two minutes later, near Paris, Illinois (19 miles to the NW), a private pilot encountered a hovering UFO shaped like a flattened sphere. (See diagram.) When the pilot turned directly toward the UFO, it accelerated and shot away to the NE. [53]

In the next two days, General Mills, Inc., balloon personnel spotted UFOs over Wisconsin and Minnesota. [Section VI]

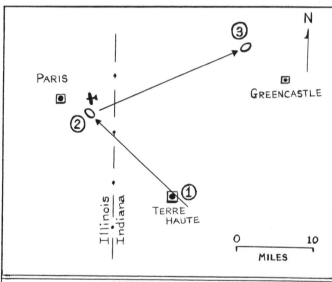

OCTOBER 9, 1951

1. Time: 1:43 p.m. UFO sped over airport, visible 15 seconds.

2. Time: 1:45 p.m. Private pilot enroute from Greencastle to Paris encountered hovering UFO.

3. When pilot turned toward it, object accelerated and shot away northeast.

OTHER SAMPLE CASES

March 13, 1950; Mexico City, Mexico. Santiago Smith, chief weather observer for the Mexican Aviation Company, J. de la Vega of the airport commander's office, and others saw a total of four UFOs passing over the airport during the day. Smith caught one in a theodolite telescope, and described it as resembling the "shape of a half-moon." [54]

March 26, 1950; Reno, Nevada. Mrs. Marie H. Matthews, CAA Tower Operator (over four years experience in aircraft observation with Navy and as a civilian), others in the tower, and United Airlines employees Robert Higbee and Fred Hinkle at about 8:50 p.m. saw a brilliant light NE of Hubbard Field which was "so bright it was impossible to determine shape." Visible on each side of it was a green light. The UFO appeared to hang motionless for 5 or 6 minutes; then it began moving slowly across the sky, and suddenly shot upward into a cloud bank. [55]

March 29, 1950; Ironwood, Michigan. Tom Christensen, airlines representative for Wisconsin Central Airlines, and six other persons at the airport (all pilots or with flying experience) viewed a round UFO through binoculars at 2:55 p.m. It was moving directly into a north wind at "pretty good" speed. As it travelled, the UFO made a "slipping and sliding sideways" motion. [56]

July 1950; Cincinnati, Ohio. At 1:45 p.m., a C.A.A. flight engineer with 11 years of aeronautical experience observed a "wingless, fuselage-shaped" object which maneuvered in a sunny sky. The UFO climbed at a steep angle, hesitated, dove and sped away to the west. Estimated speed: 5,000 m.p.h. The object made no sound and left no trail. (Confidential report obtained by NICAP Adviser L. H. Stringfield, Cincinnati, Ohio).

November 27, 1950; Huron, South Dakota. In the early morning, Gene Fowler of the Weather Bureau, Winfield Henry of CAA, and two Western Airlines ground crew members watched a UFO which alternately hovered and darted around the sky. The UFO changed color, red to white to green. At Aberdeen, 75 miles north, William B. Hiller, CAA Aircraft Communicator, also, saw a lighted UFO that changed colors. [57]

July 8, 1952; near Wilkes-Barre, Pennsylvania. Joseph J. Greiner, CAA equipment provider (experienced as radio operator weather observer, and traffic controller) at 10:00 p.m. saw a domed UFO speed overhead below a high overcast. The object was visible about 10 seconds, travelling at an estimated 1,000 mph. The main body was green, with a reddish domed portion on top. [58]

Early 1952; Cleveland, Ohio. Clark Croft, chief of the CAA Tower staff, stated to the Associated Press July 22 that "several months ago" a member of his staff had sighted a red light hovering in the sky in the direction of nearby Berea. He asked a pilot taking off for Akron to watch for it. The pilot saw it first below and ahead of him. "Suddenly it took off at a very rapid rate," Croft said. "He tried to catch it, but couldn't. It was faster than any jet aircraft we know about."

Washington, D.C., Sightings

On two consecutive weekends in July 1952, UFOs swarmed over Washington, D.C. Maneuverable, erratically performing objects were seen visually by pilots where radar showed them to be. Among the aviation personnel who either tracked the UFOs on radar or sighted them visually were the following:

July 19, 11:40 p.m. CAA radar operators at National Airport control center and in tower; 8 unidentified targets moving 100 to 130 mph.

July 20, midnight to 5:40 a.m. Harry G. Barnes (senior air route traffic controller), Ed Nugent, Jim Copeland, and Jim Ritchey (radar controllers); up to 10 unidentified targets at one time on radar; motions coincided with visual sightings by Capt. Casey Pierman, Capitol Airlines pilot, who about 1:00 a.m. saw a total of 7 UFOs which maneuvered in all directions, sometimes hovering.

July 20, early a.m. Howard Cocklin, CAA control tower operator, saw yellow-orange light gyrating low in NW sky where control center radar indicated it was.

July 20, 3:00 a.m. Capt. Dermott, Capitol Airlines pilot, watched unidentified light follow his plane to within 4 miles of National Airport; radar also showed object.

July 26, 9:08 p.m. Jim Ritchey and other radar personnel saw 12 unidentified targets move onto scope from NW headed SE; helped vector in jet interceptors, which reported glimpses of high speed lights. Commercial pilot reported yellow light that turned to red, then back to yellow, pacing his plane about two miles away; "Radar confirmed that he was between two and three miles from the object," Ritchey stated.

[For additional details, see Section XII, July 1952 Chronology.]

October 12, 1952; Palo Alto, California. Harry C. Potter, aircraft maintenance man for United Airlines, was standing talking to friends at 1:00 a.m. Suddenly they noticed a V-formation of six apparent discs speeding overhead from N to S, travelling about 120 degrees in about 8 seconds. One separate UFO crossed at the same time from W to E. The UFOs appeared as rings of very bright blue-white light, apparently dark discs lighted only on the outer rim. [59]

1952; San Mateo, California. At 6:30 a.m., Leonard L. Musel, United Airlines mechanic, was one of five persons in a car pool who saw a large flat UFO take on board five smaller objects of similar shape. [See Section II, Satellite Object Cases.] All six UFOs were roughly diamond-shaped, the main object nearly elliptical as it hovered 50 to 75 feet above salt flats visible from Hillsdale Boulevard. When the smaller objects were on board, the parent object flipped over flat side down (presenting an elliptical outline) and took off eastward at fantastic speed, going out of sight in seconds. [60]

December 3, 1954; Wilmington, North Carolina. About 12:30 p.m. Luther H. O'Banian and J. B. Bradley, CAA traffic controllers, and others at the airport saw a round yellowish UFO which sped overhead on a southwesterly course. The two controllers studied the object through binoculars, but could not identify it. The UFO, visible about 45 seconds, seemed to be moving at a downward angle at an estimated speed of 500 mph or more. [61]

January 8, 1959; near Walworth, Wisconsin. Gordon Higgins, a draftsman who has had two years USAF experience as control tower operator and flight controller, watched a UFO descend and then speed away horizontally. (See self-explanatory diagram with number keys.)

September 29, 1960; Arlington, Texas. J. Rodriguez, Jr., flight radio officer for Pan American Airways, reported to NICAP: "At 6:23 p.m. CST while watching 8 or 9 kids (ages 10 to 16) play fast ball in front yard across street from my home, I looked up, east, elevation 50 degrees approximately, and I saw a bright pinpoint of orange-colored light travelling toward the south; its speed was faster than a high flying jet aircraft, but slower than a meteor. As it reached a point below the moon it slowed down very rapidly, at which time I turned and ran toward my house for my field glasses. [see sketch, position "A" to "B"].

"Upon returning with my field glasses (7 power) the kids had now taken up the watch. Mr. Louis Via, my neighbor across the street, was also out in his front yard where we all were. While the kids insisted that it was up there just below a bright star, Mr. Via and myself said 'no it's just another star.' [See sketch, position "C"]

"Soon we all realized that the stars were moving, as though around each other clockwise. I took up a position where I could use the house roof for reference to see if one was moving.

"Mr. Via and myself soon agreed that the bottom one was slowly moving upward and clockwise around the star, which I then realized was the planet Jupiter. The movement between positions 'B' and 'C' was seen by the 8 or 9 kids. While watching the movement between positions 'C' and 'D', Mrs. Via came outside and also saw the orange colored point of light moving. My field glasses did nothing for seeing what it was, still a bright point of light.

"At about 6:35 another neighbor came over from two houses down, Mr. and Mrs. Rowmach. Mrs. Rowmach said: 'Rod, I've been watching that very fast moving light since you ran toward your house a while ago.' We all stood there and watched it slowly moving up and getting smaller, but still bright. . . "

About 6:37 p.m. while trying to point out the UFO to another neighbor, Rodriguez saw it take off suddenly toward the west and vanish "as fast as a meteor."

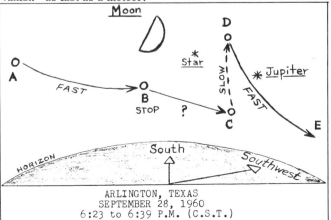

ARLINGTON, TEXAS
SEPTEMBER 28, 1960
6:23 to 6:39 P.M. (C.S.T.)

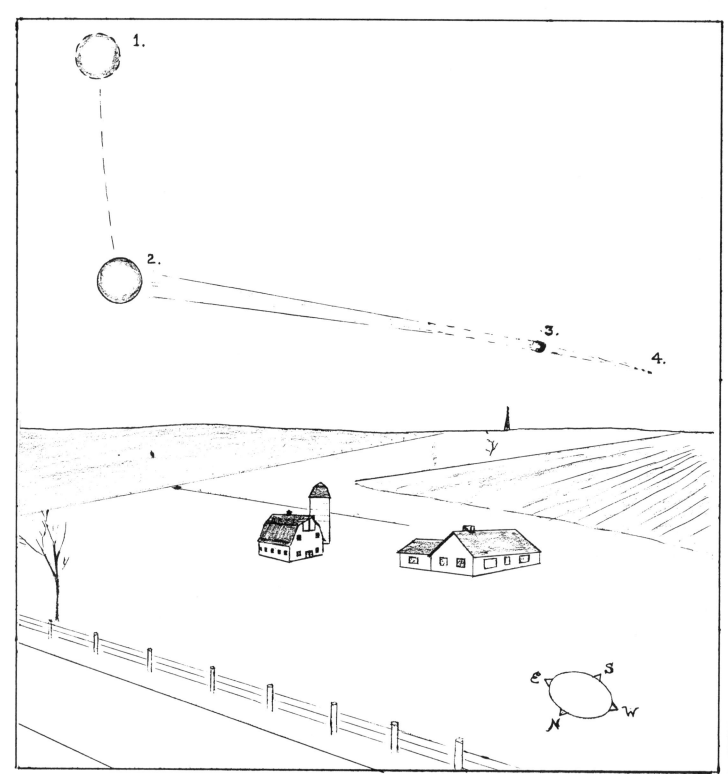

TIME OF SIGHTING: 5:15 P.M. THURSDAY JANUARY 8, 1959
POSITION: 1 MILE NORTH OF ILLINOIS-WISCONSIN STATE LINE
          ON U.S. 14
1. 40° FROM HORIZON   100° FROM NORTH
2. 20°   "   "   100°   "   "
3. 15°   "   "   130°   "   "
4. 10°   "   "   135°   "   "
     WHILE TRAVELING EAST AT 5:15 P.M. THE OBJECT WAS SIGHTED AT
POSITION №1. AS IT STARTED TO DESCEND SLOWLY THE AUTOMOBILE
WAS BROUGHT TO A STOP TO GET A BETTER VIEW. IT TOOK APPROXIMATELY
15 SECONDS FOR THE OBJECT TO REACH POSITION №2. IT STILL GLOWED A
BRIGHT WHITE AS IN POSITION №1. THEN IT SHOT OFF AT TREMENDOUS SPEED
LEAVING A TRAIL OF SPARKS CHANGING FROM THE ORIGINAL BRILLIANT
WHITE, TO ORANGE, AND SEEMED TO EITHER GO OUT OF SIGHT, DISAPPEAR, OR DISINTEGRATE.

NOTES

1. See Sections I, VI; Also Ruppelt, Edward J., Report on Un-identified Flying Objects, (Doubleday, 1956), p. 161.
2. Washington Daily News; February 23, 1954.
3. Ruppelt, Edward J., op. cit., p. 109.
4. Flying, July 1950. (For contemporary accounts, see Life, July 21, 1947; Time, July 14, 1947).
5. Ruppelt, Edward J., op. cit., p. 37.
6. Ibid., p. 38.
7. Report on file at NICAP.
8. Saturday Evening Post; April 30, 1949. New Yorker; September 6, 1952.
9. U.S. Air Force, Project "Saucer" Report, April 27, 1949. (Other sources: Saturday Evening Post, May 7, 1949; Reader's Digest, July 1952).
10. Washington Post; March 27, 1950.
11. Associated Press; June 27, 1950.
12. San Francisco Chronicle; October 7, 1950.
13. Report on file at NICAP.
14. United Press; May 23, 1951.
15. Report on file at NICAP.
16. United Press; July 18, 1952.
17. New York Journal-American; October 30, 1952.
18. Chicago Sun-Times; December 10, 1952.
19. Prescott Evening Courier; May 22, 1953.
20. Keyhoe, Donald E., Flying Saucer Conspiracy. (Henry Holt, 1955), p. 259.
21. C.R.I.F.O. Orbit, October 5, 1956; Case 210. (L.H. String-field, Ed., 4412 Grove Avenue, Cincinnati, Ohio).
22. Independent reports to NICAP Board Member Frank Edwards (WTTV, Indianapolis, Indiana).
23. United Press; March 10, 1957.
24. Tape recorded interview with pilot, on file at NICAP.
25. Chicago Daily News; November 6, 1957.
26. New Orleans Times-Picayune; November 10, 1957.
27. Memphis Press-Scimitar; October 8, 1959.
28. Report on file at NICAP.
29. Report on file at NICAP.
30. Honolulu Advertiser; March 12, 1963.
31. Flying, July 1950.
32. Report on file at NICAP.
33. Air Facts; May 1, 1950, ppg. 29-30.
34. Case personally investigated by NICAP Director. For detailed account, see Keyhoe, Donald E., Flying Saucers From Outer Space (Henry Holt, 1953), ppg. 145-148. See also Flying, July 1950.
35. Flying, September 1950 (includes pilot's sketch). See also Ruppelt, Edward J., op. cit., p. 120; Popular Science, August 1951.
36. Capt. Nash is a member of the NICAP Panel of Special Advisers; correspondence on file. (For detailed account of his sighting, see True, October 1952).
37. Report on file at NICAP.
38. Report on file at NICAP.
39. Air Facts; September 1, 1951, p. 37 ff.
40. Interviewed by CSI, N.Y. (67 Jane Street, New York 14).
41. New York World Telegram & Sun; October 8, 1957. New York Daily Mirror; October 9, 1957.
42. Reported to Capt. William B. Nash, Pan American Airways, NICAP Adviser.
43. Published accounts of the February 24, 1959 sighting by American and United Airlines crews:
    Flagship News, American Airlines, March 9, 1959, (Vol. 14, No. 4). Keyhoe, Donald E., Flying Saucers: Top Secret. (Putnam's, 1960), Chapter II, "The Killian Case."
    Akron UFO Research Committee, (Box 5242, Akron 13, Ohio) Report on Unidentified Flying Objects Observed February 24, 1959 by American/United Airline Pilots, (c. 1960).
    Detroit Times; February 25, 1959. Front page story: "Mystery Sky Objects Trail Detroit Airliner."
    Detroit Times; February 26, 1959. "Saucers Might Be Just That." (Follow-up story, quoting opinions of Lt. Col. Lee B. James, army ordnance, Huntsville, Alabama).
    Long Island Newsday; February 26, 1959. "Strange Lights In Sky Make Pilot, Crew Blink." (Interview with Capt. Killian).
    Long Island Daily Press; March 24, 1959. "Those Mystery Lights in the Sky Were NOT Jets, LI Pilot Insists." (Capt. Killian is quoted as being familiar with refueling operations, and rejecting this and other Air Force explanations of his sighting).
    New York Journal-American; March 25, 1959. "Airline Pilot Insists He Saw Saucers." (Essentially same as above).
44. Report on file at NICAP.
45. Statement on file at NICAP.
46. Statement to Cleveland Plain Dealer; July 8, 1961, by Airport Operations Supervisor John M. Gieb.
47. For additional details, see Flying, July 1950; Saturday Evening Post, May 7, 1949.
48. Menzel, Donald H., Flying Saucers. (Harvard, 1953), P. 15.
49. Flying, June 1951.
50. Ruppelt, Edward J., op. cit., p. 119.

Aviation Personnel

51. The FAA formerly was CAA (Civil Aeronautics Administration). This designation appears in some of the reports.
52. The FAA freely admitted observations of a glowing, high-speed UFO, and stated that Air Force radar had confirmed the sighting. The Air Force denied the radar tracking, and suggested the UFO was "probably a balloon."
53. Terre Haute Star; October 10, 1951. Ruppelt, Edward J., op. cit., ppg. 152-153.
54. United Press; March 14, 1950.
55. Reno Evening Gazette; March 27, 1950.
56. Ironwood Daily Globe; March 30, 1950.
57. New York Times; November 27, 1950.
58. Report on file at NICAP.
59. Report on file at NICAP.
60. Interviewed by Bay Area NICAP Subcommittee, report on file at NICAP.
61. Associated Press; December 3, 1954.

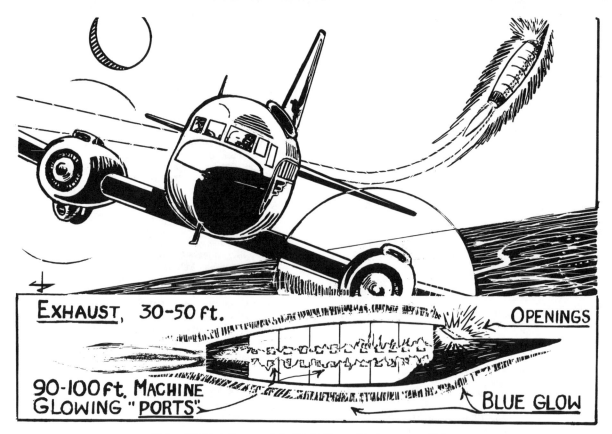

EXHAUST, 30-50 ft.

OPENINGS

90-100 ft. MACHINE GLOWING "PORTS"

BLUE GLOW

Chiles–Whitted Case — July 23, 1948; nr Montgomery, Alabama

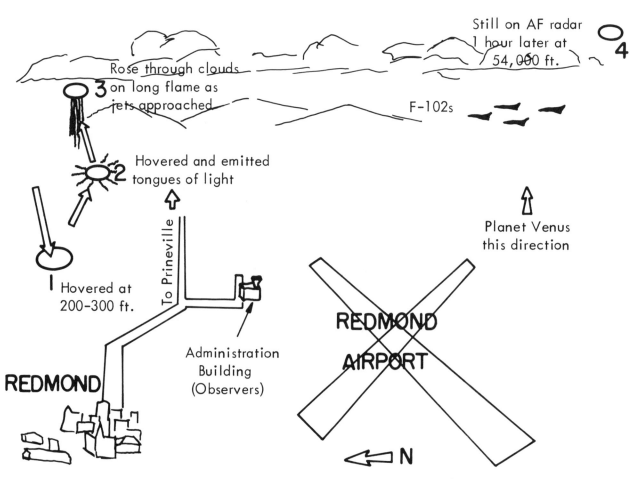

Still on AF radar 1 hour later at 54,000 ft.

Rose through clouds on long flame as jets approached

F-102s

Hovered and emitted tongues of light

Planet Venus this direction

To Prineville

Hovered at 200–300 ft.

Administration Building (Observers)

REDMOND

REDMOND AIRPORT

N

Federal Aviation Agency Case — September 24, 1959; Redmond, Oregon

SECTION VI
SCIENTISTS & ENGINEERS

One of the many current myths about UFOs is that no trained observers have reported them. Often this argument is used by skeptics to imply that UFO reports result only from careless observations. This attitude is reflected in a question often posed in newspaper articles: "If UFOs are real, why haven't astronomers seen them?" The answer is that they have, on many occasions.

The ridicule evoked by the reporting of a UFO sighting definitely has taken its toll among professional scientists and engineers who value their reputations. A significant number of scientists have told NICAP privately that it would be professional suicide for them to discuss the subject openly among their colleagues. Nevertheless, a number of good UFO reports by scientific observers are on record.

Another myth is that only amateurs and pseudo-scientists consider UFOs worth further investigation. One scientist who took early notice of UFO reports was Dr. Anthony O. Mirarchi, chemist employed by the Air Force in its geophysical laboratory. In 1951 Dr. Urner Liddel, a Navy scientist, insisted all UFOs were Skyhook balloons. Dr. Mirarchi challenged this conclusion and urged a full investigation of UFOs which, he said, could be foreign experiments of some kind. Dr. Mirarchi rejected the idea that UFOs were only misidentified conventional phenomena and said he had recommended a "considerable appropriation" to investigate them. After studying Air Force reports, he said UFOs appeared to have "maneuvered motion" and their vertical and horizontal motions could not be reconciled with natural phenomena. [1.]

A former German rocket scientist, Dr. Walther Riedel, headed the now defunct Civilian Saucer Investigation of Los Angeles, which attained national prominence in 1952 after being publicized in Life and Time. Dr. Riedel stated his opinion that UFOs were of extraterrestrial origin. [2.] (Some of the cases gathered by CSI are incorporated in this report).

Three world-famous scientists have expressed similar views:

Prof. Hermann Oberth, whose pioneering studies paved the way for space travel, has stated his complete conviction that UFOs are piloted by super-intelligent beings from another planet. [3.]

Admiral Delmer S. Fahrney, U.S.N. (Ret.), "father of guided missiles," and former NICAP Board Member, in a 1957 press conference stated that there was an urgent need to know the facts about the apparently controlled objects reported to be entering our atmosphere. His statement received wide coverage in the world press.

Dr. Carl Jung, famous Swiss psychologist, shortly before his death in 1961, sent a personal communication to the NICAP Director. In it he stated he had come to the opinion that UFOs did appear to be space ships. [4.] (Previously he had been embroiled in international publicity, accidentally misquoted as believing UFOs were real when he still considered this an open question).

UFO Sightings by Scientists

(All Reports on File at NICAP)

Date & Location	Name	Field	Description
7-10-47; S. New Mexico	"top astronomer"	Astronomy	Elliptical object which hovered, wobbled, ascended suddenly. [Section II.]
Summer 1948; Easton, Penna.	Carl A. Mitchell	Physics	Three luminescent greenish discs one second apart, passed across sky from N to S and over horizon.
8-49; Las Cruces, N.M.	Clyde W. Tombaugh	Astronomy	Circular pattern of rectangular lights, keeping fixed interval.
5-20-50; Flagstaff, Arizona	Seymour L. Hess	Meteorology, Astronomy	Disc or sphere in apparent "powered" flight. [Section I.]
6-12-50; California	John Zimmerman	Geology	Silvery discs looping around aircraft, disrupting its vapor trail.
10-3-50; Pomona, California	J. D. Laudermilk	Geochemistry	Disc moving with wobbling motion passed behind mountain peak; minimum speed computed to be 720 mph.
8-3-51; near Pinckney, Mich.	Walter N. Webb	Astronomy	Bright glowing light moving in undulating path.
1952; London, Ont., Canada	W. Gordon Graham	Astronomy	UFO "like a smoke ring, elliptical in shape, and having two bright pinpoints of light along its main axis;" sailed overhead from W to E. [5.]
7-27-52; Ann Arbor, Mich.	Dr. Charles H. Otis	Biology	Formation of rocket-like objects leaving constant length trails.
8-5-52; Baltimore, Md.	Dr. James C. Bartlett, Jr.	Astronomy*	During daylight observation of Venus, saw a flight of two discs diameter about 30 minutes of arc; passed overhead to S, turned E. Then two more discs with dome-like protrusions in center.
1-30-53; near Yuma, Arizona	Wells Alan Webb	Chemistry	Gyrating light which ascended steeply.
5-5-53; near Yuma, Arizona	Wells Alan Webb	Chemistry	Silvery disc, turned sharply; observed through Polaroid glasses, dark circular bands around object became visible.

*Technically an amateur astronomer; member Association of Lunar and Planetary Observers, frequent contributor to scientific journals.

Date/Location	Witness	Field	Description
6-11-54; near Atlanta, Georgia	H. Percy Wilkins	Astronomy	Two silvery objects "like polished metal plates" moving against wind; third grayish oval arced across sky.
11-25-54; Cordoba, Argentina	Dr. Marcos Guerci	Meteorology	Two luminous objects observed from airport; one apparently semi-circular, other circular. [Section X.]
12-7-54; Upington, Cape Province, So. Africa	R. H. Kleyweg	Meteorology	Hemispherical disc tracked through theodolite. [Section X.]
11-1-55; Mojave Desert, California	Frank Halstead	Astronomy	Cigar-shaped object followed by domed disc.
6-18-57; Jackson, Mississippi	Prof. Henry Carlock	Physics	Observing sky with telescope; twice glimpsed UFO with halo around it and "what appeared to be three portholes."
11-10-57; Toulouse, France	Jacques Chapuis	Astronomy	At Toulouse Observatory observed maneuvering yellow star-like object for 5 minutes. "It was something I had never seen before." UFO finally ascended straight up out of sight.
10-2-58; near Blairstown, N.J.	Ivan T. Sanderson	Zoology	Maneuvering, banking disc.
10-26-58; La Fayette, Indiana	T. C. Shafer	Chemistry	While observing moon with 4 inch reflector telescope, saw three bright unidentified objects pass from East to West.
5-22-60; Majorca	Observatory staff	Astronomy	Triangular UFO about 1/4 apparent size of moon sighted at 9:33 a.m., spinning on its axis while on steady course. Report cabled to NASA in Washington. [6.]
6-8-60; New York City	Lee Ball	Biochemistry	Flat ellipse traversed about 15 degrees of sky; appeared about 8 times apparent size of moon.
11-24-60; Ohio	Confidential report, certified by NICAP Board Member.	---------	Ellipse in smooth silent flight; 5 minute observation.
3-16-61; Antarctica	R. J. Villela	Meteorology	Fireball-like object in slow level flight.
11-22-61; near Grafton, N.D.	Melvin C. Vagle, Jr.,	Metallurgy	Cigar-shaped UFO with "portholes", hovering tilted at angle.
5-20-62; Defiance, Ohio	Prof. C. A. Maney six others	Physics	Maneuvering light, turned sharply, made sudden change in speed.

DISCS CIRCLE AIRCRAFT

Source: "Mars, The New Frontier" by Wells Alan Webb, (Fearon Publishers, Calif., 1956) p. 124.

Witnesses: John Zimmerman, Geologist; Charles Fisher, civil engineer.
Date: June 12, 1950.
Location: California.
Time: About 4:00 p.m.

Working outdoors at a quarry, they had noticed a high-flying swept-wing aircraft leaving a vapor trail, and paused to watch it.

"He [Zimmerman] was startled to notice a rift form in the vapor trail not far behind the airplane and a wisp of cloud suddenly streak upward as if an object had come from below and cut upward through the vapor trail, disturbing it. Looking quickly for the object, Zimmerman saw a silvery disc of diameter about one-third the apparent length of the airplane's fuselage, flying rapidly in a circle above the airplane, overtaking it. With an exclamation he called Fisher's attention to the phenomenon, and together they watched two additional discs pass from below, dart up through the vapor trail, overtake the airplane and then dive down in front of it, making vertical loops around the airplane. Each object made several such loops in succession, each time coming up behind the airplane and cutting the vapor trail, each cut displacing a filament of the trail in an upward direction."

Date: August 3, 1951. Witness: Walter N. Webb, Chief Lecturer on Astronomy, Charles Hayden Planetarium, Boston, Mass., (former member of the Smithsonian Institution Satellite Tracking Program): "That summer I was a nature counselor at Camp Big Silver, the Toledo (Ohio) Boy's Club camp on the shores of Silver Lake in southern Michigan, three miles south of Pinckney. It was a clear, moonless night. I had been showing two boys various celestial objects through my 3-1/2 inch reflecting telescope and pointing out constellations. The time was about 11 p.m. or midnight. Suddenly I noticed a glowing yellow, or yellowish-red light moving in an undulating path (but on a straight course) over the hills south of Silver Lake. As the object traveled slowly westward in this peculiar manner, the three of us watched in fascination. It was at such a low elevation that its regular wavelike course caused it to dip behind the hills a few times. At first I frankly didn't realize that I might be seeing anything unusual and thought the object was a plane light. But something was disturbing about that flight path and by the time it dawned on me that planes don't fly on wavy paths, the thing was about to vanish for good behind trees in the foreground. I swung the telescope toward the hills, but it was too late.

"I had seen something strange in the sky that I could not explain. No known object I could think of followed a path like that. The remote possibility that the UFO might have been the reflection of a moving ground light from a rippling inversion layer was quickly rejected. An inversion reflection would appear as a hazy spot of light in the sky much reduced in brightness when compared with its original light source. My UFO appeared to be a bright, glowing object moving in a regular wavy pattern. It is impossible for an inversion layer to produce a smooth rhythmic reflection. A turbulent rippling layer of air would be required, and such a condition would not be capable of producing any image at all."

Formation of Rocket-like Objects

The following report was submitted to NICAP by Dr. Charles H. Otis, professor emeritus of Biology, Bowling Green State University.

"Place of observation: 3724 Dexter Rd., R.D. No. 1, Ann Arbor, Washtenew County, Michigan; a small acreage at the top of Lyon Hill, called Sleepy Hollow, situated about four miles west from Main Street (or the County Court House). Altitude at the road, about 975 feet (the place is easily located on the

Ann Arbor quadrangle, topographical map, U.S. Geological Survey), at the place of observation, in the hollow, probably 950 feet, or a little more. Along the west property line is a small woods and two low buildings. To the east is a wide expanse of sky.

"Date of sighting: July 27, 1952. Time of observation, about 10:40 a.m. Conditions for observation, perfect; a beautiful day, not a cloud in the sky (see an observation later); the sun at this time of day high in the heavens; no observable haze. Photographically speaking, conditions were probably those of maximum light for the year and suitable for the fastest exposure (only, no camera—what a picture, I think, could have been made, with a ray filter over the lens, and with telephoto equipment, either snapshot or movie—explanation will appear in the story).

"The story: (apologies for the use of ''I'').

"I was working on a lawn setee, giving it a coat of white enamel, in the shade of a walnut tree. My wife was sitting nearby . . . . For some reason—perhaps my back was tired—I stood up, laid down my brush, stepped out into the sunshine and glanced up and to the east. I was startled by what I saw. There in a pattern, were a number of objects, seemingly floating along, making no sound. My first thought was that something had been released from a plane that I remembered had passed overhead not long before (I refer to a noisy 4-engined plane that makes its regular east to west trip at about this time of day, and to which we never pay any attention, although it usually passes over the house, both coming and going), and I called to my wife to come and then I realized that these objects were probably much higher than the plane was flying and that there was no connection with it (I mention these reactions because, so far as I am aware, the pilot of the plane did not report on these strange objects, and, they might not even have been there at the time of his passing). It was my impression that the objects were as high as the highest fleecy white clouds, but it may be only an impression (later checking of the sky revealed only two small white clouds lying low on the horizon at the north, and there was nothing at the time to use as a gauge). I assumed that they were traveling over the city of Ann Arbor, as if a reconnaissance were being made; the direction appeared to be due south. They were travelling so slowly (but, of course, they may have been much higher than I supposed) that I told my wife to keep looking, while I ran to the house and seized a bird glass (magnification near 5X). From then on, with the glass, I studied the objects until they disappeared at my horizon.

"When first counted, the objects number 15; and they were traveling in the form of an organized flotilla, the horizontal distribution being something on this order (but probably not an exact duplication):

```
        X           X
           X      X
  X
              X
        X      X   X
  X
              X
        X      X
  X
              X
```

For this reason, I will hereafter refer to the objects as ''ships.'' The ''ships'' traveled so slowly that it seemed to me that I was able to study them for minutes (that may have been one of those times, however, when a minute may seem an hour; but, of course they were going farther away all the time). Before they reached my horizon, one ''ship'' as if receiving a signal, left the flotilla and, describing what to me seemed to be a wide arc, disappeared with a burst of speed that seemed incredible. I had the glass on it, and then it was gone. . . The mathematics has not been worked, but just after the episode the approximate angle of sight when first seen was determined to be 34 degrees with the horizontal, using level and planimeter, and if we knew the height, it could be calculated.

Description of a ''ship'':

The 15 ''ships'' appeared to be identical in size, shape, and other discernible characteristics. In the way in which they seemingly floated, one got the impression that they were of very light weight (unless someone has discovered some way to eliminate the force of gravity). There was no sound (even from 15 of them in a body). They maintained position in the flotilla

perfectly. The body appeared to be elongated, but split at the rear; there were no wings. Nothing like a cabin could be discerned, nor windows, nor persons. The sketch shown here is a copy of one hastily made in my notebook immediately after the ''ships'' had passed out of sight.

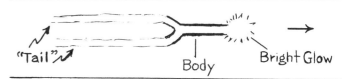

Two items stand out conspicuously. In the ''bow'' end of each ''ship'' was a relatively large and exceedingly bright glow (brighter than a star, even in the bright light of the day; - this might explain the reported ''lights over Washington'' episode, which occurred at night). Each ''ship'' also had, emanating from the ''stern'' portion, two ''tails'', seemingly streaming out horizontally, never changing in length, nor wavering. These ''tails'' had none of the aspects of vapor trails, and they cut off cleanly; i.e. they had definite ends. It was as if the ''ships'' laid down a caterpillar track, walked on it, but carried it along with them. They gave the appearance of the tail of a comet, like Halley's, which I once saw very beautifully one night (1910?), but in this instance, and strangely enough, in a bright sky. They gave somewhat the appearance of the Tyndall effect which the stereopticon beam gives in a darkened theater. But, if due to the Tyndall effect, why should the ''tails'' or ''beams'' have been visible in broad daylight? It is possible that the ''tails'' just described represent atomic or subatomic particles leaving the ''ship'' with terrific speed and with propulsive force, that they were luminous in themselves, and that they had a limited and short length of life (which could account for the definite length of the ''tail'' which has been mentioned previously). What other explanations are there which might account for the appearance and behavior of the ''ships'' upon which I am reporting?''

GYRATING LIGHT

Wells Alan Webb
B.S., M.S., Chemistry, University of California
Chemical Engineer & Research Chemist
Provided Univ. of Calif. with deuterium source for cyclotron research.

Source: ''Mars, The New Frontier'', by W. A. Webb (Fearon Publishers, 1956), page 125:

"On January 30, 1953, at approximately 7:25 p.m. the author was riding in the back seat of an automobile in which Felix Gelber and Grover Kihorny, both of Los Angeles, were passengers. The night sky appeared black except for stars. The desert air was clear and the stars and ground lights shone with brilliance. We were on Highway 80, traveling west toward Yuma, Arizona, 7 miles away at the approximate rate of 60 miles per hour. While looking through the windshield the writer noticed a half mile ahead among a group of steady bright ground lights there was one light which flickered and danced. At about 15 degrees above the horizon stood the evening star. All of these lights, the steady, the dancer and the star, had approximately equal brilliance in the field of vision at that moment. As we approached the ground lights, they resolved into floodlights on twenty foot poles illuminating the hangar area of Spain Flying Field. We saw through the side window a single engine Army trainer standing in this area with a man working over it. The dancing light, now apparently higher than at first, hovered directly over the airplane at about twice the height of the floodlights. Suddenly, looking out the side, then the rear window, we became aware of the dancing light's rising motion. It rose slowly at first, then gathering momentum it lifted rapidly. The author strained at the rear window and watched the light blink repeatedly, then vanish among the stars at an altitude of at least 60 degrees. This was not more than about ten seconds after we had passed the flying field, still traveling at 60 mph.

Gelber and Kihorney had also seen the light, their observation of the details had been the same as the author's, so the next morning the writer prevailed upon them to investigate the mysterious light. We returned to the place on the highway opposite the hangar. The airplane stood on the same spot as the night before. We paced off the perpendicular distance from the highway to the airplane. It was one hundred yards. Then we found a mechanic who said that he was the man who had been working on the airplane the evening before. He had not seen the dancing light; there had been no sound to attract his eyes overhead. Therefore the light had not been on a helicopter. He referred us to the U. S. Weather Station, one quarter of a mile eastward. There the weatherman said that he had released a lighted balloon at about the time we had seen our flickering light. He showed us one of the balloon lights, a very small flashlight blub without reflector. It did not flicker, it burned steadily the weatherman said, but its light could never appear to be of the same brightness as the glaring floodlights of the Spain Flying Field. Furthermore, the weather balloon had not hovered over the hangar of that flying field; at a uniform rate it had mounted steadily in the sky above the weather station. The weatherman proved this by showing us the chart he had plotted by taking telescope sightings of the altitude of the light at timed intervals.

When all of the facts about the light that Gelber, Kihorney and the writer had seen were laid before the weatherman, he said that ours must have been a UFO, that such things were a great mystery but had nevertheless been seen frequently in the neighborhood by the personnel of the Weather Station and also of the nearby Air Force Fighter Base."

Mr. Webb's second UFO sighting was on May 5, 1953. Time: 9:45 - 10:00 a.m.

"It was a clear sunny morning; the author was standing in a field near the Vacuum Cooling Company plant, not far from Spain Flying Field, and about a mile north of the Yuma Air Force Fighter Base. His attention was drawn by the buzzing of jet fighters taking off in quick succession, passing directly overhead traveling northward. As he scanned the northern sky, the author's attention became fixed upon what at first appeared to be a small white cloud, the only one in the sky at the time. The author was wearing Polaroid glasses having a greenish tint, and as was his custom when studying clouds he took the glasses off and put them on at intervals to compare the effect with and without Polaroid. The object was approximately oblong with the long axis in a horizontal plane. It floated at an elevation of about forty-five degrees. During the course of about five minutes the object traveled approximately 30 degrees toward the east. Then it appeared abruptly to turn and travel northward; at the same time its oblong shape changed to circular section. As a circular object it rapidly became smaller as if receding. While receding, the object did not noticeably lose any of its brightness. In about thirty seconds of this, its diameter became too small for the author to hold in his vision.

During the first period the writer had not noticed a change in the oblong nor in the field of view about it as a result of putting on and taking off his Polaroid glasses. But during the second period several uniformly spaced concentric circles appeared around the now circular object. The circles were distinct dark bands which enveloped the silvery disc. The largest of these circles was, perhaps, six times the diameter of the central disc. When the writer removed his polarizing glasses the silvery disc remained but the concentric rings vanished. When the glasses were put on again, the rings reappeared. The writer repeated this several times, each time with the same result. The rings with glasses on, faded to invisibility before the disc became too small to see."

ASTRONOMERS' REPORTS

The late Dr. H. Percy Wilkins, British lunar astronomer, relates several UFO reports including one of his own in his book "Mysteries of Space and Time", (F. Muller Ltd., London, 1955). Attributing most UFO reports to conventional objects, Dr. Wilkins states: ". . . a residuum remains which cannot be thus explained." [p. 4.]

Dr. Wilkins was flying from Charleston, W. Va. to Atlanta, Ga. on the morning of June 11, 1954. At 10:45 a.m. he noticed two brilliant oval-shaped objects apparently hovering above the tops of cumulus clouds an estimated two miles away. They were "sharp-edged objects," the color of polished brass or gold, and much brighter than the clouds. "They looked exactly like polished metal plates reflecting the sunlight," Dr. Wilkins reported, "and were in slow motion northwards, in contrast to the clouds which were drifting southwards." [p. 41]. Then he noticed a third object of the same description against the shadowed side of the cloudbank; it was grayish and not reflecting sunlight. The third UFO accelerated, and arced across the sky, disappearing behind another cloud mass.

The UFOs were about 15 minutes of arc in length [about 1/2 the apparent diameter of the moon], and the two bright ones maintained a separation of about five degrees. Based on his estimation of distance (2 miles) and apparent size (15 minutes of arc), Dr. Wilkins calculated the actual size of the UFOs to be nearly 50 feet in diameter.

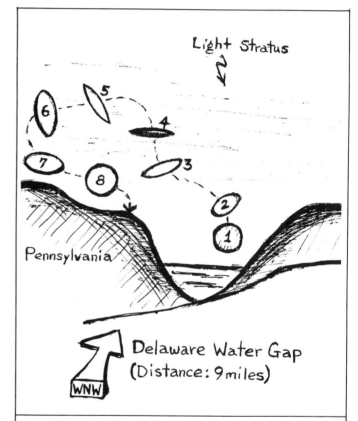

October 2, 1958; near Blairstown, New Jersey. Shortly after 5:00 p.m., noted Zoologist Ivan T. Sanderson observed a disc-shaped UFO maneuvering over the Delaware Water Gap. The flat disc looped back and forth, appearing sometimes edge-on (as a very thin line), sometimes oval to circular. It vanished once, but quickly reappeared, and continued its rapid gyrations, finally speeding away to the west.

Frank Halstead
Former Curator of Darling Observatory,
University of Minnesota

Mr. Halstead and his wife saw two UFOs while crossing the Mojave Desert on a Union Pacific train in 1955. He reported the experience to NICAP Board Member, Frank Edwards:

"It was the first day of November, 1955. We were on our way to California — about 100 miles west of Las Vegas when it happened. My wife Ann was sitting next to the window and she called my attention to an object which she saw — something moving just above the mountain range. Our train was running parallel to this range of mountains and this object was moving in the same direction as the train, just above the mountains. I first thought the thing was a blimp. . . But as I watched it I realized that it could not be a blimp — they are only about 200 feet long. And this thing was gigantic. It was about 800 feet long. I could estimate that because it was so close to the mountain ridge where trees and clumps of trees were visible for comparison.

While we were watching the cigar-shaped thing, for four or five minutes as it paced the train, we noticed that another object had joined it. This second object appeared very suddenly in back of the first one. It was a disc-shaped thing. Both of them were very shiny, we noticed. . . If my estimate of size on the cigar-shaped thing was correct then the disc-shaped object would have been about 100 feet in diameter, flat on the bottom with a shallow dome on top.

My wife and I watched them for another two or three minutes. They were moving at about the same speed as the train and they were very close to the top of the ridge, not more than 500 feet above it, I should say. Then they began to rise, slowly at first and then much faster. In a matter of seconds they had risen so high that we couldn't see them any more from the train window.

All over the world credible witnesses are reporting experiences similar to mine. Holding these people up to ridicule does not alter the existing facts. The time is long overdue for accepting the presence of these things, whatever they are and dealing with them and the public on a basis of realism.''

**NEW MEXICO COLLEGE
OF AGRICULTURE AND MECHANIC ARTS**

ADJACENT TO AND COOPERATING WITH
WHITE SANDS PROVING GROUND

10 September 1957

Mr. Richard Hall
SATELLITE
721 Burdette Street
New Orleans 18, La.

Dear Mr. Hall:

Regarding the solidity of the phenomenon I saw: My wife thought she saw a faint connecting glow across the structure. The illuminated rectangles I saw did maintain an exact fixed position with respect to each other, which would tend to support the impression of solidity. I doubt that the phenomenon was any terrestrial reflection, because some similarity to it should have appeared many times. I do a great deal of observing (both telescopic and unaided eye) in the backyard and nothing of the kind has ever appeared before or since.

As I have said before, I was so unprepared for such a strange sight that I was really petrified with astonishment. Consequently, some of the details I might have noted were missed.

Sincerely yours,

Clyde W. Tombaugh

CLYDE W. TOMBAUGH
Astronomer

CWT:ds

Antarctic Sighting

March 16, 1961; Antarctica. A Brazilian Meteorologist, recently employed at NASA Goddard Space Flight Center near Washington, D. C., observed a strange phenomenon while aboard an ice-breaker in Admiralty Bay, Antarctica on a scientific expedition. He noted the observation in his diary, and later filled out a NICAP report form. Though in some respects the phenomenon resembles a meteor, in other respects it does not. At any rate, it is worth recording as an unexplained aerial phenomenon, possibly related to UFO activity.

Rubens J. Villela, who also has experience as a glider pilot and Moonwatch observer, was on the deck of the U.S.S. Glacier about 6:15 p.m. The temperature was about 33 degrees, dew point 28, wind calm, sky overcast, visibility about 5 miles. Weak, yellowish sunset light was visible to the NW. About 50 degrees above the horizon he noticed a strange tear-shaped "luminous body" crossing the sky from NW to SE. It was "multi-colored, leaving long trail as tracer bullet; abruptly divided in two (in tandem) as if 'exploding', shone more brightly in bluish-white and red, and threw lateral rays radiating backwards at an angle. Appearance neither 'solid' nor purely 'light'; best described as 'corporified light', forms geometrical and not diffuse," The object was roughly tear-shaped before and after splitting.

The object travelled on a level course, completely disappearing "very suddenly" after about 10 seconds. It moved "rather slowly" leaving a long trail.

"I believe it was much too slow for a meteor," Mr. Villela stated, "also its appearance was 'out of this world.' I can think of nothing on earth which would reproduce the phenomenon."

Hovering Cigar-Shaped Object

A Minneapolis Honeywell metallurgist, Melvin C. Vagle, Jr., saw a cigar-shaped UFO on November 22, 1961. NICAP later learned of the sighting through the Honeywell newspaper [7.], and obtained a first-hand report from Mr. Vagle, as well as a detailed painting of the UFO done under his supervision. [See sketch.]

It was a clear starlit night about 7:00 p.m. (CST). Mr. and Mrs. Vagle were traveling north on U. S. Highway 81 approaching Grafton. A red light in the sky west of the highway up ahead attracted their attention, then other associated lights made them think it might be an aircraft. As they neared the site and pulled alongside they saw "a cigar-shaped object hovering at a sharp angle over a plowed field. . .At the lower end. . . there was a bright flashing white light and at the upper end there was a

steady red light. Along the length of the fuselage there was a row of square-appearing ports, illuminated with a white yellowish light."

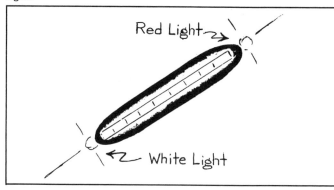

The UFO seemed to be motionless until, when the Vagle's son started crying, they drove on. Then the UFO appeared to drift westward across the highway. Earlier the same evening a farmer in the Grafton area had seen a reddish cigar-shaped UFO west of Grafton and reported it to an area newspaper. Accompanying Mr. Vagle's report to NICAP was a letter from the farmer confirming the basic points of his sighting, which occurred at sunset. The farmer could not see any "ports", only a dull reddish glow from the UFO. The object vanished behind a dark cloud after about 10 minutes.

THE DEFIANCE COLLEGE
DEFIANCE, OHIO

DEPARTMENT OF PHYSICS
CHARLES A. MANEY

I hereby certify that the following account of a UFO sighting, witnessed by a scientist known to me, on the faculty of a large university in the State of Ohio, a man of high standing, having grants for research, has been approved by him as an accurate statement. Charles A. Maney

"At about 10:00 A.M. on Thanksgiving Day. Thursday, November 24, 1960, I was driving my car south on a highway not far from the campus. A member of my family was a passenger. Low in the sky ahead of me appeared a black spot which I first assumed to be an approaching plane. But as the object got closer I could see that unlike a plane the object had no wings. My curiosity aroused I drove the car to the side of the road adjacent to a golf course, where I and my companion got out to get a better look at the approaching sky object. As it passed us at its closest point, the object was at a straight line distance of from 1200 to 1500 feet, at an altitude of approximately 70 degrees and clearly visible.

It was egg-shaped or elliptical, perfectly smooth, no protuberances or markings, clear curved edges, and a bright chalk-white on top with just a narrow band of shadow across the bottom.

The apparent diameter of the horizontal major axis of the ellipse shape viewed at arms length figured out to be approximately 100 feet.

The object moved at moderate speed like that of a conventional propeller-driven plane, but silently with no trace of noise whatever. The object traced a smooth arc of travel with no up or down motion. It was in sight some five minutes, moving toward the northwest until it disappeared from view."

NICAP Board Member, Prof. Charles A. Maney, was among seven witnesses to a UFO sighted in Defiance, Ohio, May 20, 1962. Prof. Maney is Head of the Defiance College Physics Department.

About 8:00 p.m., Don Reimund noticed a distinctly round unidentified object in the northwest sky, moving horizontally at an elevation of about 10 degrees. Knowing of Prof. Maney's interest in UFOs, Mr. Reimund telephoned him. Prof. and Mrs. Maney rushed to the Reimund residence, only to learn that the UFO had disappeared to the southwest minutes before.

As they discussed the sighting, the same or a similar object appeared in the southwest, moving north, at an elevation of about 20 degrees. Prof. Maney and the others present viewed the object through binoculars, and with the unaided eye. It appeared as a brilliant blue light, changing to brilliant yellow. Then the UFO stopped abruptly, hovered for 5-6 seconds, reversed course and headed south. Its motions continued to be erratic, sometimes moving rapidly, then apparently hovering. The UFO finally disappeared in the southwest about 9:00 p.m.

Prof. Maney later learned that near St. Johns, Ohio, 55 miles to the south, a UFO had been witnessed at about the same time. Mr. Quincy L. Dray, Jr., and a neighbor, had watched a similar performance between 8:10 and 8:30 p.m. "It moved erratically, seemed to dip or back up then start forward fast," Mr. Dray said. [8.]

UFO Sightings by Engineers

In addition to the detailed report by the crew of General Mills balloon technicians headed by aerologist Charles B. Moore on April 24, 1949 (Section I), dozens of professional engineers and technicians have reported UFOs. As indicated in these sample cases, their backgrounds include a cross-section of technological fields. Many are uniquely qualified to evaluate the appearance and performance of aerial phenomena in comparison to known devices or atmospheric effects. (All reports on file at NICAP).

Date & Location	Witnesses	Field	Description
7-6-47; S. Central Wyoming	David A. Kenney, two others	Instruments Engineer, Aviation Co.	Oval UFO in steady flight at high altitude.
7-8-47; Muroc, California	Several	Aircraft technicians	Oval object, apparently rotating [Section II].
Summer 1948; Erie, Penna.	Victor G. Didelot	Aircraft Instrumentation	Elliptical or oval UFO, sudden vertical ascent.
4-24-49; White Sands, N.M.	Charles B. Moore, Jr., Others	Aerology, balloon technicians	Elliptical UFO tracked with theodolite [Section I].
6-10-49; White Sands, N.M.	Guided missile unit	Missile tracking	Two white round UFOs paced missile [Section II].
1-16-51; Artesia, New Mexico	Six	Balloon technicians	Two discs, approached rapidly, circled balloon. [Section I].
8-51; Central New Mexico	Alford Roos	Mining engineer	Two discs descended, hovered, shot away.
10-10/11-51; near Minneapolis, Minn.	J. J. Kaliszewski, others	Aeronautical research	Maneuvering UFOs observed during balloon tracking flights.
3-10-52; Oakland, California	Clarence K. Greenwood	Inspector Engineering Metals	Two hemispherical discs, one in oscillatory flight.
4-8-52; near Big Pines, California	H. I. Smith	Staff Engineer television	Reddish disc-like UFO with raised portion like dome on top, observed through binoculars.
4-23-52; Lexington, Massachusetts	R. C. Munroe	Engineering Standards	UFO accelerated to meteor-like speed.
5-13-52; National City, California	Donald R. Carr, six others	Aeronautical engineer	Circular UFO descended at meteor-like speed, circled [Section I].
7-16-52; Hampton, Virginia	Paul R. Hill	Aeronautical research engineer	Four maneuvering lights rendezvoused, sped away.
7-27-52; Manhattan Beach, California	Former Navy Pilot, seven others	Aeronautical engineer	Large object separated like "stack of coins" into 7 round UFOs; three took V-formation, others followed in pairs flying abreast. [From USAF Intell. Report].
8-6/7-52; Kerkrade, Holland	Will Jansen	Marine engineer	Detailed observation of two domed discs. [Section X].
9-30-52; Edwards AFB, California	Dick Beemer, two others	Aviation photography	Two flattened spherical UFOs, hovering, turning sharply at variable speeds.
10-54; Cherry Valley, New York	Maj. A. B. Cox	Chemical & mechanical engineer	Disc, 90 degree turn, ascended at steep angle. [Section I].
8-56; Boulder City, Nevada	E. F. Carpenter	Aviation research technician	Six discs in V-formation.
11-11-57; San Fernando, California	Harold R. Lamb, 3 others	Rocketdyne engineers	Three oval UFOs ascending, est. speed: 5000 mph.
8-11-58; Chautauqua Lake, New York	Dr. Fred C. Fair, one other	Professor Emeritus of engineering, N. Y. University	Several observations; one apparent oval object.
9-4-60; Lexington, Kentucky	John R. Cooke	Electronics, former USAF radar technician	Glowing sphere, passed from horizon to horizon.
10-30-61; Ligonier, Pennsylvania	Carl H. Geary, Jr.	Engineer, Carrier Corp. division	Four discs with lights like portholes [Section I].

VERTICAL ASCENT, OTHER MANEUVERS

Summer 1958; Erie, Penna. Victor G. Didelot, B.S. Physics, research engineer in aircraft instrumentation and magnetics: "The object appeared to be elliptic or oval shaped, approximately twice as long about its longest axis as it was thick. The object maintained a course parallel to the ground for a visible arc of close to 120 degrees, and roughly parallel to the shore line of Lake Erie. The object moved at a very rapid pace from west to east. When it had reached what appeared to be a position directly over the city of Erie, it abruptly and at a speed at least three times its horizontal speed ascended vertically until it passed from my sight."

Mr. Didelot adds that the time was early afternoon, and the UFO was a silvery-white color. "I was also able to see that the object did wobble slightly, but when it changed course to the vertical, it seemed to lose this apparent instability. There was a complete absence of noise, and there was no discernible vapor trail."

Mid-August 1951; Central, N.M. At his ranch 10 miles east of Silver City, N.M., about 10:30 a.m., Alford Roos, mining engineer, heard a "swishing" noise, looked up and observed the performance of two lens-shaped UFOs in particularly interesting detail. Mr. Roos at the time had a Civil Service rating of senior mining engineer, was a project engineer for the U.S. Bureau of Mines and other government agencies, and a member of the American Institute of Mining & Metal Engineers. Extracts from his report:

"I saw an object swooping down at an angle of about 45 degrees, from southerly direction, travelling at immense speed, coming quite close to the earth over Ft. Bayard, 2 miles to the NW. Reaching the bottom of the swoop it hovered for moments, then darted up at an angle of about 70 degrees from vertical, in a northwesterly direction, directly over Ft. Bayard. . . . I neglected to state that there were two objects that [converged at the point of hovering] at which time they were in close proximity . . . . Over Ft. Bayard there was an isolated cloud island covering perhaps 3 degrees of arc and perhaps a mile across. The two objects shot up at this steep angle at incredible speed, both entering the cloud, and neither appeared beyond, and no trace after entering the cloud.

"Their track was as straight as a ruled line, no zig-zagging. The astonishing thing was that the cloud immediately split into 3 segments, ever widening, where the objects entered. . . Each object left a pencil-thin vapor trail."

At first, Mr. Roos continued, the UFOs appeared spherical, "but after the hovering and the turn up, they must have tipped, canted so I then saw the edge-on of the lens-like object. Going toward the cloud they were disc-shaped. There was no gathering of momentum from the low hover, to the lightning-like shoot. . . From almost stationary to instant about 500 mph., the shock of inertia would have made human (terrestrial) survival impossible.

"After the objects turned on their sides at the hover, there appeared to be a button, or some small protrusion on the upper side as viewed edge-on. . . the objects were quite close and we [Ed. Note: other witnesses named in report] could all detect some form of outer ornamentation or process or possibly orifices or port holes, on the lower side just below the rim of the lens, and these seemed to undergo change of iridescent color, almost like a blinking."

From: J. J. Kaliszewski

Subject: UNIDENTIFIED OBJECT OBSERVATION

Time: 1010, 10 October 1951
Place: 10 miles east of St. Croix Falls, Wisconsin
Observers: J. J. Kaliszewski and Jack Donaghue

We had just spotted our trajectory flight and were approaching from the north at an altitude of 4000 feet. We started a climb towards the balloon on a course of 230°. At 6,000 feet I noticed a strange object crossing the skies from East to West, a great deal higher and behind our balloon. I estimate that our balloon was at approximately 20,000 feet at the time.

Using our balloon for comparison, this object appeared to be about 1/4 the size of the balloon. We were climbing and about six miles northeast of the balloon. The object had a peculiar glow to it, crossing behind and above our balloon from East to West very rapidly, first coming in at a slight dive, leveling off for about a minute and slowing down, then into a sharp left turn and climb at an angle of 50° to 60° into the southeast with a terrific acceleration, and disappeared.

Jack Donaghue and I observed this object for approximately two minutes and it crossed through an arc of approximately 40°-50°. We saw no vapor trail and from past experience I know that this object was not a balloon, jet, conventional aircraft, or celestial star.

JJK:rj
cc: G. O. Haglund

/s/ J. J. Kaliszewski
[Supervisor of balloon manufacture
Aeronautical Research Laboratories
General Mills, Inc.]

From: J. J. Kaliszewski

Subject: SIGHTING OF UNIDENTIFIED OBJECTS

Time: 0630, 11 October 1951

Dick Reilly and I were flying at 10,000 feet observing the grab bag balloon when I saw a brightly glowing object to the southeast of the University of Minnesota airport. At that time we were a few miles north of Minneapolis and heading east. I pointed it out to Dick and we both made the following observation:

The object was moving from east to west at a high rate and very high. We tried keeping the ship on a constant course and using reinforcing member of the windshield as a point. The object moved past this member at about 5° per second.

This object was peculiar in that it had what can be described as a halo around it with a dark under surface. It crossed rapidly and then slowed down and started to climb in lazy circles slowly. The pattern it made was like a falling oak leaf inverted. It went through these gyrations for a couple minutes. I called our tracking station at the University of Minnesota airport and the observers there on the theodolite managed to get glimpses of a number of them, but couldn't keep the theodolite going fast enough to keep them in the field of their instruments. Both Doug Smith and Dick Dorion caught glimpses of these objects in the theodolite after I notified them of their presence by radio. This object, Dick and I watched for approximately five minutes.

I don't know how to describe its size, because at the time I didn't have the balloon in sight for a comparison.

Two hours later we saw another one, but this one didn't hang around. It approached from the west and disappeared to the east, neither one leaving any trace of vapor trail.

JJK:rj
cc: G. O. Haglund

/s/ J. J. Kaliszewski

Oscillatory Flight

March 10, 1952; Oakland, California. Two UFOs, one in oscillatory flight, were observed by Clarence K. Greenwood, an Inspector of Engineering Metals:

"About 6:45 a.m., as I waited for my bus to come along, I was examining the sky predicting the weather for the day, when two dark objects came into my line of vision apparently from my right rear. It was difficult to gauge their altitude. I estimated very roughly between five thousand and seventy-five hundred feet. The two dark objects flew — scooted would be a better description of their flight — diagonally away from me gradually picking up speed. One followed a direct or regular course while the other seemed to play at flight — a sort of pendulum motion. I could only estimate their size. I judged about forty-five feet. Their length about one-half the width. Below is a sketch of how they appeared to me."

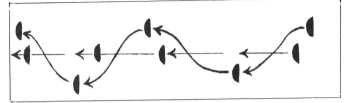

April 23, 1952; Lexington, Mass. Mr. R. C. Munroe (then Engineering Standards Section Head of Raytheon Manufacturing Company). While watching an AT-6 trainer aircraft about 9:30 a.m., noticed a second object nearby:

"Because of the speed at which this second aircraft was moving, I immediately concluded it was of the jet variety. I would estimate its altitude at approximately 40,000 feet. . . just below the cloud cover. My curiosity was aroused upon realizing that I could not distinguish a fuselage wing configuration. My curiosity was further aroused when this aircraft began to decelerate at an unbelievable rate. I observed the aircraft going into a flat turn, while continuing to decelerate and believe I saw the aircraft come to a stop. . .

"The observation that inspires writing this letter to you [i.e., to CSI of Los Angeles] was the speed of this aircraft, apparently accelerating from a stopped condition and flying in a northeast direction which would carry it over the north end of Boston. I would relate this speed to the apparent speed of a falling star. This speed was considerably in excess of that of any jet aircraft that I have observed.

"The altitude of this aircraft did not permit color identification. There was no apparent exhaust or vapor trail. It is inconceivable to me that any human being could have withstood the deceleration or acceleration displayed by this aircraft."

Aviation Expert

UFO RENDEZVOUS OBSERVED

July 16, 1952, Hampton, Virginia, 9:00 p.m. (EST). Mr. Paul R. Hill, an Aeronautical Research Engineer, holds a B.S. degree in mechanical and aeronautical engineering from the University of California. At the time of the report he had 13 years experience in aeronautical research.

Mr. Hill was aware of previous UFO sightings which had been headlined in July 1952, particularly the report by Capt. William B. Nash, Pan-American Airways pilot, who on the night of July 14 had sighted 8 circular UFOs while flying above Newport News, Va. [Section V]. Mr. Hill was situated on Chesapeake Avenue (near La Salle Avenue) on the north shore of Hampton Roads watching the sky. With him was his wife, Frances, who also witnessed what followed.

At 9:00 p.m., he noticed two amber-colored lights. He gave this description: "Two were seen first coming in over Hampton Roads at about 500 mph. from the south. These slowed down as they made a "U" turn at the southern edge of the Peninsula. They moved side by side until they revolved around each other at a high rate of speed in a tight circle 2 or 3 hundred feet in diameter. This appeared to be a rendezvous signal as a third UFO came racing up from the direction of Virginia Beach and "fell in" several hundred feet below the first two, forming a sort of "V" formation. A fourth UFO came in from up the James River and joined the group which headed on south at about 500 mph."

Mr. Hill added that the UFOs changed altitude "only when they revolved around each other, circling or spiraling rapidly (as fast as once per second).

"They moved jerkily when moving slowly. The speed varied from 50 to 500 mph. Their ability to make tight circling turns was amazing." [See diagram.]

At about 9:03 p.m., the four UFOs had moved into the distance out of sight to the south. The color and brightness of the objects, which did not change except apparently due to increase in distance, was compared to "an amber traffic light about 3 or 4 blocks away." The elevation angle of the UFOs covered a range of

about 50 degrees, from about 10 to 60 degrees, during the observation.

Mr. Hill was interrogated by an Air Force intelligence officer from Langley Air Force Base. [9.]

NICAP note: Four amber-colored UFOs were reported at Patrick Air Force Base, Florida later the same evening.

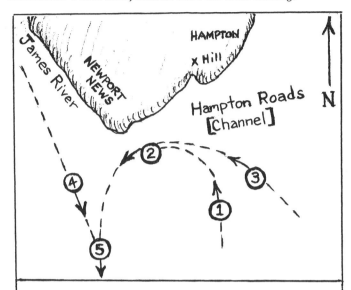

1. Two UFOs approached, slowed.

2. Point of fast circling.

3. Third UFO joined circling ones.

4. Fourth joined formation.

5. All four moved south in group.

Paul R. Hill - Hampton, Virginia
July 16, 1952

September 30, 1952; Edwards AFB, California. In a letter to the President of CSI of Los Angeles, Dick Beemer, aviation photographer for North American Aviation Company, described the following sighting. [Note that once again observation of a passing aircraft attracted the witnesses' attention to the sky. Otherwise they probably would not have noticed the UFOs]

"I went to Edwards Air Force Base [Muroc]. . . to direct the motion picture photography of a flight test. We had driven to the test site on the lake bed, and were standing outside. At 10:30 a.m., Carlos Garcia, one of our cameramen, looked up at a B-29 which was passing overhead. He said that he believed something had fallen from the plane. He then discovered that it was not from the plane, but seemed to be flying around. Then he noticed another. I thought he was joking and didn't pay much attention. Then Gene Pichler, the other cameraman looked up. He too observed them. By this time, I joined the watching party, and sure enough, there was really something there. We watched them for nearly ten minutes, and they appeared as follows:

"They were east of us at approximately a fifty degree angle from about the ground level, and just below the mid-morning sun. They were flying at a very high altitude, moved at an extremely high rate of speed (much faster than a jet plane), left no vapor trails, and made no sound. Each of us thought that there were at least three in flight, but we could see no more than two at one time. They moved in no definite direction. For a short time, fifteen seconds or more, one would hover while the other would zoom down past one side of it, make a sharp turn, and flash back above it on the opposite side.

"They seemed to be shaped more like flattened spheres, rather than thin saucers. In fact, they looked and behaved somewhat like yo-yo's. They moved about quickly, but seemed to have no particular destination.

"Although the sun was above them, the side away from the sun, that is, the side toward us, appeared as if it were reflecting the sunlight. They were somewhat metallic in appearance, but seemed whiter than modern aircraft.

"We had a color motion picture camera with us, but were waiting for them to fly away from the direct rays of the sun. Instead, they disappeared away from us, and we were left with nothing but memories."

Formation of Discs

Mid-August 1956; Boulder City, Nevada. A formation of five disc-shaped UFOs was seen about 10:15 p.m. (PDT) by Edison F. Carpenter, a research technician for a division of North American Aviation. At the time of the sighting, Mr. Carpenter was employed by the U.S. Bureau of Mines.

"My wife and I were sitting on the back step of our home. It was a clear night, not a cloud in sight and a slight breeze from the southwest. We were facing due south. . . Suddenly from directly overhead, they had come over the house from the north, we both became aware of a group of slightly glowing objects as they flew to the south. The group numbered five and was in roughly this formation:

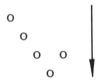

Their shape was perfectly round as viewed from below and they had a sort of phosphorescent glow (pinkish in color). The general shape must have been round and flat rather than round like a ball because as they drew away the shape was like this O rather than this O as a ball would appear from any angle.

"They held the formation illustrated while in view and maintained a spacing of approximately one diameter between ships. This diameter was about the diameter of a cigarette cross-section held at arm's length. They crossed approximately 60 degrees of sky, from the time they came into view over our roof until I lost sight of them, in about 6 seconds. I'm quite sure of the time element because pistol shooting is a hobby of mine and I've become accustomed to counting off 10 and 20 seconds for rapid and timed fire."

(In an accompanying letter to NICAP, Mr. Carpenter added an important point about the duration of some UFO sightings: "I am also aware that 10 seconds is a much longer interval than most people realize since it allows time for 5 aimed shots with a pistol." Some skeptics deny the validity of observations of several seconds duration, even when made by trained observers. Anyone in military service who has taken courses in aircraft and ship identification is also aware of how much detail can be observed in 2-3 seconds, and even in a fraction of a second with appropriate training).

Rocketdyne Engineers

During a large flurry of UFO sightings in November 1957, four engineers for Rocketdyne, near Canoga Park, California, observed three UFOs flying in formation in bright daylight. One of the engineers, Harold R. Lamb, Jr., filled out a NICAP report form. [10.]

November 11, 1957: at 4:20 p.m. the group was driving in a generally ESE direction from the Rocketdyne SanSu facility toward Canoga Park, with the late afternoon sun to their back. One of the men happened to look up and saw three shiny objects crossing their path, from NE to SW. He alerted the others, and they all clearly saw a large narrow oval object (almost cigar-shaped) accompanied by two smaller nearly circular objects (slightly oval, as if discs viewed at an angle). The large UFO was silvery on top, but bright orange underneath, possibly re-

flecting sunlight. The two smaller UFOs were solid silver colored. Keeping the same positions relative to each other, a V with one of the smaller objects slightly ahead and one slightly behind the large object, the three UFOs accelerated and climbed away into the distance.

The four men compared notes, and arrived at a consensus of opinion that the UFOs were first seen at about 10,000 feet altitude, climbing to 30,000 feet, at an estimated 5000 mph.

TELESCOPIC SIGHTINGS

August 11, 1958; Chautauqua Lake, N.Y.
Time: 9:15 to 10:30 p.m.
Observers: Fred C. Fair, Ph.D., and Gary Phillips.

Dr. Fair, a retired professor of Engineering, New York University, submitted the following log of observations of aerial phenomena. He and Gary Phillips were using a survey transit to observe the altitude and azimuth of certain stars.

"(1) A white light was observed moving across the sky to the right and away from the observers. When the transit telescope was sighted on the moving light, possibly a minute had elapsed since it was first observed. At first only one white light was seen, then a second was noted, then a third and finally a fourth light, all four being more or less in line, and each separated by an angular distance of about 2 degrees. It is the opinion of both observers that when the first of the four lights was seen, that there were no other moving lights in the vicinity. Which does not mean that the objects were not in the sky, but that they were not emitting visible light at that time.

Shortly after watching all four lights with the naked eye, the third light became about ten times as bright as the others, becoming brighter than Jupiter which was in the same sky area. The other three lights at this time were about as bright as a second magnitude star. A few seconds later this third light rather suddenly dimmed until it was the faintest of the four lights.

Due to the narrow field of view of a surveyor's transit telescope, it is rather difficult to locate and follow a rapidly moving object. By the time that Gary made his first observation through the telescope the moving lights had traveled from Northwest to Southwest, passing close to Jupiter. Gary made the statement that the objects were Flying Saucers, and that the telescope showed that what appeared to be a single light to the naked eye was several lights, and that there was a red light above the others. When Dr. Fair took his turn to observe the lights, three of the objects had already disappeared behind trees to the south. The very brief glance that Dr. Fair had showed several white lights, he thought there were five, and he observed a faint red light to the rear and above the white ones.

(2) Fifteen minutes later, while in a boat on Lake Chautauqua, while looking for meteors, a single white light was seen in the southeast sky traveling from south to north. The light slowly and continuously varied intensity, fluctuating from 5th to 3rd magnitude, but the time of the cycle was irregular, but of more than three-second duration per cycle. For several seconds the light appeared to be stationary and when it resumed its motion it was traveling in a direction opposite to when first observed. Total time of observation of this light was about five minutes. As it receded in the south it became too faint to be further seen.

At about this time a jet trail, making an arc of about 180 degrees was observed in a tighter radius than that described by the first four objects, but following essentially the same course. At the head of the jet trail Gary saw a red glow, possibly the exhaust from the jet.

(3) Still later a different type of lighting was seen close to the horizon in the western sky. We were still out on the lake at the time. A bright, rapidly blinking red and white light moved rapidly from right to left. Soon a similar blinking red and white light was seen to the right of this light, moving from right to left. It was fainter than the other which could have been due to being farther away. When the two lights passed each other they were separated by a vertical angle of about 2 or 3 degrees.

(4) After returning to the transit on shore, star observations were resumed but in a few minutes were interrupted to again observe a white light in the northwest traveling rapidly from west to north. The telescope showed this light to be similar to the first objects. Dr. Fair noted in particular that the five white lights were not arranged in a straight line, but appeared as though spaced on the circumference of an oval. [Emphasis added]. Again, a red light was noted above and slightly to the rear of the white lights. This was followed with the telescope until it disappeared behind some nearby trees. Gary who noticed this object first saw only two white lights. Probably fifteen seconds elapsed before Dr. Fair was sighted on the object and observed that there were five white lights.

No vapor trail was observed behind any of the sighted objects."

September 4, 1960; Lexington, Kentucky. John R. Cooke, currently owner of an automobile company, was a radar technician in the U. S. Air Force Strategic Air Command for four years, completing special electronics courses during Air Force service. His report was obtained by the Bluegrass NICAP Affiliate in Lexington, on a NICAP report form.

About 9:30 p.m., Mrs. Cooke noticed a bright light low on the horizon to the SW, and called it to the attention of her husband. As they watched, the UFO, appearing as a fiery-looking, glowing sphere, passed from horizon to horizon in about 2 minutes, fading from sight in the bright lights above the city. The UFO did not move particularly rapidly, but was unlike any conventional phenomenon, and flew parallel to the earth.

(Mr. Cooke also stated that in 1952, while a passenger in a B-25, he had listened on the radio to an F-86 jet pilot describing the maneuvers of a UFO).

NOTES

1. Associated Press; February 25, 1951
2. Time; March 3, 1952
3. American Weekly; October 24, 1954
4. Letter on file at NICAP
5. London, Ontario, Free Press; May 1, 1954
6. Copy of cable furnished to NICAP by member employed at Space Agency
7. The Honeywell World, Minneapolis; Vol. 2, No. 17 January 1, 1962
8. Defiance, Ohio, Crescent-News; June 2, 1962. See also May 21st edition.
9. See Ruppelt, Edward J., Report on Unidentified Flying Objects, (Doubleday, 1956), p. 210.
10. Names of other witnesses on file at NICAP

SECTION VII

Officials & Citizens

The reports of technically trained observers, military and civilian pilots, in themselves are sufficient to make a strong case for UFOs. However, when we also realize that a broad cross-section of reputable citizens has described identical phenomena, it seems incredible that UFOs are not an acknowledged fact. The disc-shaped, elliptical and other main types of UFOs observed by pilots and scientists have been reported with great frequency by such responsible persons as judges, civil defense officials, professors, lawyers and clergymen.

Some of these individual observer categories could fill another complete section of this report. From the hundreds of cases on file, the following have been selected to provide a survey of what has been seen by officials and private citizens of various backgrounds.

LAW ENFORCEMENT OFFICERS

Police switchboards normally and logically are the first to be swamped with calls during concentrations of sightings, since there is no established procedure for citizens to follow when they see a UFO. Examples abound of cases in which police responded to citizens' reports of UFOs, and saw the objects for themselves. Police Officers on patrol duty, too, have observed unexplainable objects maneuvering overhead.

During a six-day concentration of UFO sightings in northern California, August 13-18, 1960, at least 14 police officers were among the numerous witnesses. At 11:50 p.m. (PDT) August 13, State Policeman Charles A. Carson and Stanley Scott were patrolling near Red Bluff when they noticed an object low in the sky directly ahead of them. (Their report of the sighting was put on the police teletype, a copy of which was submitted to NICAP confidentially by a police source. Later, NICAP Adviser Walter N. Webb contacted Officer Carson and was sent another copy of the teletype report, a sketch of the UFO, and a letter giving additional information.)

Verbatim text of the police teletype report to the Area Commander:

"STATEMENT MADE BY OFFICER CHARLES A. CARSON CONCERNING OBJECT OBSERVED ON THE NIGHT OF AUGUST 13, 1960.

Officer Scott and I were E/B on Hoag Road, east of Corning, looking for a speeding motorcycle when we saw what at first appeared to be a huge airliner dropping from the sky. The object was very low and directly in front of us. We stopped and leaped from the patrol vehicle in order to get a position on what we were sure was going to be an airplane crash. From our position outside the car, the first thing we noticed was an absolute silence. Still assuming it to be an aircraft with power off, we continued to watch until the object was probably within 100 feet to 200 feet off the ground, when it suddenly reversed completely, at high speed, and gained approximately 500 feet altitude. There the object stopped. At this time it was clearly visible to both of us. It was surrounded by a glow making the round or oblong object visible. At each end, or each side of the object, there were definite red lights. At times about five white lights were visible between the red lights. As we watched the object moved again and performed aerial feats that were actually unbelievable.

At this time we radioed Tehama County Sheriff's Office requesting they contact local radar base. The radar base confirmed the UFO - completely unidentified.

Officer Scott and myself, after our verification, continued to watch the object. On two occasions the object came directly towards the patrol vehicle; each time it approached, the object turned, swept the area with a huge red light. Officer Scott turned the red light on the patrol vehicle towards the object, and it immediately went away from us. We observed the object use the red beam approximately 6 or 7 times, sweeping the sky and ground areas. The object began moving slowly in an easterly direction and we followed. We proceeded to the Vina Plains Fire Station where it was approached by a similar object from the south. It moved near the first object and both stopped, remaining in that position for some time, occasionally emitting the red beam. Finally, both objects disappeared below the eastern horizon. We returned to the Tehama County Sheriff's Office and met Deputy Fry and Deputy Montgomery, who had gone to Los Molinos after contacting the radar base. Both had seen the UFO clearly, and described to us what we saw. The night jailer also was able to see the object for a short time; each described the object and its maneuvers exactly as we saw them. We first saw the object at 2350 hours and observed it for approximately two hours and 15 minutes. Each time the object neared us we experienced radio interference.

We submit this report in confidence for your information. We were calm after our initial shock, and decided to observe and record all we could of the object.
Stanley Scott   1851
Charles A. Carson   2358."

Extracts from Officer Carson's letter of November 14, 1960, in answer to Adviser Webb's questions:

"We made several attempts to follow it, or I should say get closer to it, but the object seemed aware of us and we were more successful remaining motionless and allow it to approach us, which it did on several occasions.

"There were no clouds or aircraft visible. The object was shaped somewhat like a football, the edges (here I am confused as to what you mean by edges, referring to the outside visible edges of the object as opposed to a thin, sharp edge, no thin sharp edges were visible) or I should say outside of the object were clear to us . . . [the] glow was emitted by the object, was not a reflection of other lights. The object was solid, definitely not transparent. At no time did we hear any type of sound except radio interference.

"The object was capable of moving in any direction. Up and down, back and forth. At times the movement was very slow. At times it was completely motionless. It moved at high (extremely) speeds and several times we watched it change directions or reverse itself while moving at unbelievable speeds.

"When first observed the object was moving from north to south [patrol car moving almost due east]. Our pursuit led in an easterly direction and object disappeared on eastern horizon. It was approximately 500 feet above the horizon when first observed, seemingly falling at approximate 45 degree angle to the south . . .

"As to the official explanation [See Section IX.], I have been told we saw Northern lights, a weather balloon, and now refractions.

"I served 4 years with the Air Force, I believe I am familiar with the Northern lights, also weather balloons. Officer Scott served as a paratrooper during the Korean Conflict. Both of us are aware of the tricks light can play on the eyes during darkness. We were aware of this at the time. Our observations and estimations of speed, size, etc. came from aligning the object with fixed objects on the horizon. I agree we find it difficult to believe what we were watching, but no one will ever convince us that we were witnessing a refraction of light.

/s/ Charles A. Carson
Calif. Highway Patrol." [1]

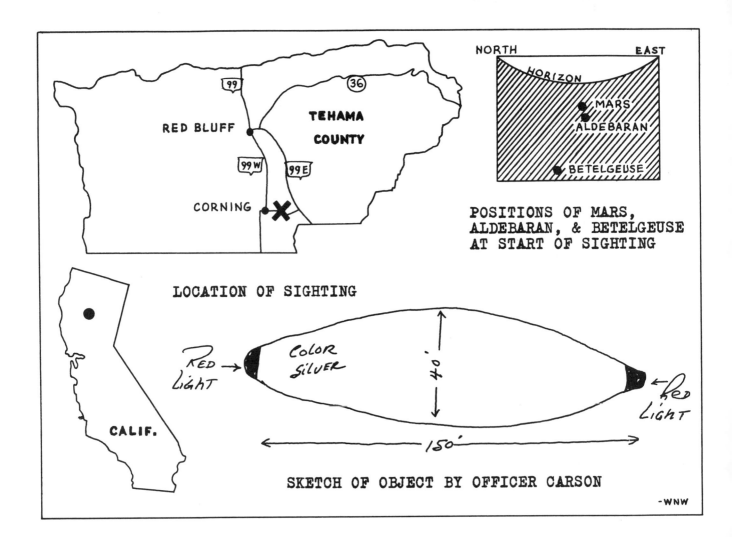

NORTH EAST

HORIZON

● MARS

ALDEBARAN

● BETELGEUSE

POSITIONS OF MARS,
ALDEBARAN, & BETELGEUSE
AT START OF SIGHTING

RED BLUFF

TEHAMA
COUNTY

99

36

99W 99E

CORNING

X

LOCATION OF SIGHTING

CALIF.

Red
Light →

Color
Silver

40'

150'

←Red
Light

SKETCH OF OBJECT BY OFFICER CARSON

-WNW

Police In Four Counties Sight UFOs

Six police officers in four adjoining counties of Northeast Ohio, in five separate locations, independently observed UFO activity within a 15 minute period September 18, 1962. The officers were: State Policemen Roger A. Stinard, and David McCurry; Mahoning County Deputy Sheriff Donald E. Corey, Carroll County Police Officers James Nelson and Delmus Earley; Ptn. Dave Richey of Canal Fulton. All reported a generally northeast or east direction, but in two of the observations the UFOs maneuvered across the sky. Comparison of the reports strongly suggests that associated phenomena were observed.

(1) State Policeman David McCurry, chasing a speeding car about 5:00 a.m. in the vicinity of Minerva, intermittently watched two white oval-shaped objects which he had noticed hovering in the sky just before the speeder came by. When he looked again he saw that one of the UFOs had descended and was glowing brilliantly. Suddenly the object took off at high speed to the NE. Later Officer McCurry checked with a patrol just across the County line in Carroll County, and learned they had seen essentially the same phenomenon.

(2) Ptn. James Nelson and Delmus Early, opposite Minerva across the County line in Carroll County, were cruising north on route 80 checking out various business establishments. Between 5:00 and 5:10 a.m., they noticed two UFOs, widely separated but apparently maneuvering in unison. The objects descended, seemed to stop momentarily, then accelerated and sped away NE. In a taped interview, the officers described the UFO closest to them as cone-shaped with a fiery exhaust, leaving a trail of smoke. The sighting lasted 4-5 minutes.

(3) Deputy Sheriff Donald E. Corey, Mahoning County, was cruising near Poland, about 35 miles north and east of Minerva at 5:00 a.m. He noticed a very bright light source hovering or floating slowly to the NE. The light disappeared in 30 seconds.

(4) Ptn. Dave Richey, Canal Fulton, about the same time sighted a stationary UFO, also in the NE sky. It was cone-shaped with a bright blue-white light on one end, visible about 45 seconds. After parking his car, Officer Richey looked again about a minute later and the object was gone.

(5) State Policeman Roger A. Stinard was cruising near Hudson, about 45 miles NNW of Minerva; it was cloudy and drizzling. He places the time at 5:15 a.m. A bright light in the sky attracted his attention, and he looked toward the E. Visible through the clouds was an "extreme white light, brighter than headlights." The light was completely stationary as long as he watched it, for 2-3 minutes. [2.]

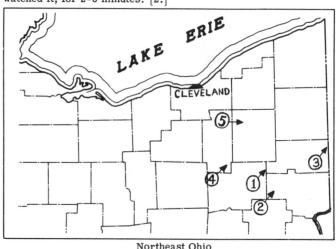

Northeast Ohio

September 18, 1962   5:00-5:15 a.m. EDT

1. Ptn. McCurry 2. Ptn. Nelson & Early 3. Dep'y Corey 4. Ptn. Richey 5. Ptn. Stinard.

Dispatcher, Officers, Watch Flashing Objects

Over the western slope of the Rocky Mountains, in an area about 60 miles in diameter, UFOs were seen on several occasions during the week of October 21-27, 1962. On the night of the 25th between 6:40 and 8:15 p.m., police officers in Delta and Cedaredge observed two bright objects "shaped like an inverted umbrella with a number of bright tail-like appendages." [cf., September 24, 1959, Redmond, Oregon; Section V.] Cedaredge Marshal Ed Marah and State Policeman Richard Kuta (who later declined to answer NICAP questions) watched the UFOs through binoculars, and said they changed color, at various times appearing blue, white and orange.

The sighting was confirmed to NICAP by another witness, Mrs. Helen G. Mitchell, Police Dispatcher at Delta County Court House. [3.] At 6:40 p.m., while on duty, she received a call from the Civil Defense Coordinator advising her to look out to see an object in the sky. Through the window of the Dispatcher's office she saw to the NE a bright white object, which changed color rapidly, "flashing or blinking."

"Since I was on duty in the Radio Room," Mrs. Mitchell told NICAP, "and under the rules of the F.C.C., I am unable to give any information which I received via short wave radio from Units reporting to me on these sightings."

The object she saw turned reddish, then to dark glowing red, and back to "dazzling white." It rose and lost altitude jerkily while moving slowly SW toward her position, then stopped and hovered for about 25 minutes. Finally it drifted out of her line of sight to the SE. She thought it might be some type of balloon "because of the jerky way in which it rose and lost altitude." However, weather balloons are only faintly visible, rise quickly and burst, and do not hover for 25 minutes. Larger high-altitude research balloons do remain in flight for days, but are not brilliantly lighted. Nor do they normally operate in pairs, as reported by Marshal Marah and Officer Kuta.

Disc On Edge Reported

During the early morning of September 26, 1963, a UFO was sighted by people in scattered locations around the San Francisco Bay area. Paul Cerny, Chairman of the Bay Area NICAP Subcommittee, conducted an investigation and located nine witnesses. (The sighting was reported September 26 in the San Jose Mercury News, Los Altos Times, and the San Francisco Chronicle.) A particularly detailed report was obtained from Officer Galen Anderson of the Sunnyvale Police Department, who observed the UFO for about 45 seconds.

About 4:20 a.m., Officer Anderson was patrolling the streets in a squad car. A radio call from other officers alerted him, and he stopped to watch the UFO. The object was traveling from east to west at an elevation angle of about 45 degrees, at about the speed of a propeller-driven aircraft. The leading edge was brightly illuminated, the main body grayish in color, with a small point of light visible on it. (See sketches and description prepared by Bay Area Subcommittee). The UFO then made a turn toward the northwest, was momentarily visible edge-on, then quickly disappeared from view.

In nearby Monta Vista about 4:15 a.m., George W. Scott was on the job as a supervisor at the Permanente Cement Company. One of the work crew called his attention to a strange object in the sky, and he watched its flight for about a minute. To him, it appeared that the UFO stopped briefly each time the small body light pulsed, then moved 3 to 4 degrees between pulses. The UFO continued on a westerly course, disappearing behind the coastal mountains.

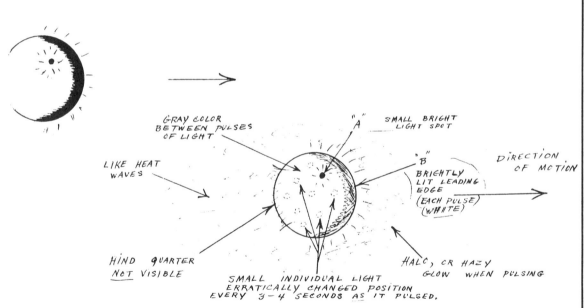

September 26, 1963; Sunnyvale, California

This object appeared larger than a full moon, according to Officer Anderson, about basketball size at about 8 feet away. It appeared as a disc on edge, with about 3/4 or more of its outline showing. The trailing 1/4 of the circle, if it were there, appeared more or less invisible. Police Officer Lt. Haag told Anderson that he saw what appeared as heat waves in this quarter area and further to the rear. The disc appeared grayish in color except when the small spot of light ("A") lighted up about every 3 to 4 seconds. The color then changed to yellowish - white, some trace of orange, but predominately along the front leading edge portion ("B"). This produced a pulsing effect every three or four seconds. This in turn gave an eerie lighted haze or mist illumination of the area just outside the disc circle itself as if it were glowing or surrounded by a gas, or thin cloud, halo, etc. At each 3-4 second pulse, the small inner bright light would move around erratically to various new positions within the disc area.

The object was visible about 45 seconds to Officer Anderson and traveled in a perfectly straight line over Sunnyvale toward Los Altos, then suddenly made a turn and was momentarily edgewise and vertical to Anderson's vision, then immediately disappeared from sight. Officer Anderson and Lt. Haag were only about a third of a mile apart at the time and Officer Girard was perhaps a mile to their northeast. Speed of the object was about that of a propeller driven military aircraft, elevation about 45° from Officer Anderson, estimated altitude 4000-6000 ft., visible about 45 seconds. Brighter than full moon.

(Names and addresses of other witnesses on file at NICAP.)

A somewhat similar case during the winter of 1943 or 1944 was reported by Harry G. Barnes, then a member of the Washington, D.C., Metropolitan Police Department stationed at No. 1 Precinct. About 3:00 p.m., Barnes saw three oval-shaped UFOs in V-formation speed eastward across the NE sky. The objects had pulsating greenish-red "exhausts", which occasionally flared and curled around them. [5.]

State Policeman Fred Porcello, Portville, N.Y., saw two UFOs of uncommon configuration July 24, 1960. He described the sighting to Olean, N.Y., newsman Bob Barry who relayed the report to NICAP.

While Officer Porcello was playing in the yard with his children between 8:30 and 9:00 p.m., his youngest son, Fred Jr. (age 7) pointed to the sky and said: "Look Daddy, two light bulbs in the sky." He looked and saw two glowing reddish objects which did resemble light bulbs, moving toward them in the southern sky.

As the UFOs changed angle relative to the sun, they appeared silvery and metallic (suggesting that the glow was reflected sunlight). They changed course to the NNW, then stopped and hovered for a short period of time. Then the objects made a fairly sharp right turn, heading east, swung back toward the south and moved out of sight in the distance. They had been visible 4-5 minutes. When not glowing, the UFOs appeared to be dumbbell-shaped, round on the ends with an oblong section between.

(On August 21, 1956, J. Gordon Campbell observed similar objects while flying between Sheridan, Wyoming, and Billings, Montana. Mr. Campbell is president of a Minneapolis machine tool and industrial supply company. Shortly after 8:00 p.m., a dark elongated object with knobs at each end rapidly approached his plane, hovered, then sped away. Seconds later, four similar objects maneuvered near his plane).

OTHER POLICE CASES

Date & Location		Names	Description	Notes
July 4, 1947	Portland, Ore.	Ptn. Kenneth A. McDowell	5 discs, up & down oscillation.	[7]
July 7, 1947	Tacoma, Wash.	Ptn. Evan Davis & Stan Johnson	3 spinning objects, sparks emitted, attracted back; hovered, changed direction.	[8]
Jan. 7, 1948	Kentucky	State Police	Huge round UFO reported to Godman AFB. Capt. Mantell case; [See Section V.]	
July 28, 1952	Shelby Co., Ind.	State Policemen Charles Longstreet & Norman Mellis	Star-like UFO "moved up and down, and back and forth, and at times it would hover."	[9]
Aug. 28, 1952	Atlanta, Ga.	Six officers including Ptn. M.J. Spears and A.L. Elsberry	UFO changing color, "every so often it would sprout a red flamed trail, then it would move up and down . . . it turned a flip a couple of times."	[10]
Sept. 22, 1952	Fairfax Co., Va.	Police Pvt's. Douglas Dunn, Julian Burke, Martin Eherill, and Sgt. Wall	1-4 glowing objects circled and maneuvered over area. Dunn saw 3-4 at one time: "Looked like a white ball of fire coming through the clouds . . . they would come and go . . . it was like tag." Burke: "One would pop out here, another there . . . Weird . . . weird indeed."	[11]
Sept. 11-13, 1953	Chiloquin, Ore.	Police Chief Lew Jones	Top-like UFOs, seen by many citizens over three nights, sighted once by Chief Jones. Watched through binoculars, appeared top-shaped with body lights.	[12]
Nov. 2, 1955	Williston, Fla.	Deputy Sheriff A.H. Perkins, Ptn. C.F. Bell	Perkins twice witnessed UFOs seen by over a dozen area residents. Bell saw 6 oval-shaped UFOs moving in spurts, felt stinging heat.	[13]
Nov. 24-25, 1956	So. Dakota	Sheriff Glen Best, State Policeman C.D. Erickson	Widespread sightings, rumors of radar contacts by Ellsworth AFB pilots; near Rapid City officers chased a UFO which had steady green light, flashing red light. UFO occasionally beamed a white light upwards.	[14]
Nov. 2, 1957	Levelland, Tex.	Sheriff Weir Clem, Deputy Pat McCullough	Bright red elliptical UFO, also seen by many others. [See Section XII; Nov. 1957 Chronology]	
Nov. 4, 1957	Elmwood Park, Ill.	Officers Joseph Lukasek, Clifford Schau, and Daniel DeGiovanni	Round, reddish object hovered over cemetery, moved away when pursued by police.	[15]
Nov. 6, 1957	nr. Danville, Ill.	State Policemen Calvin Showers, John Matulis	Brilliant white light, changing to amber and orange, viewed 20 minutes; cruiser radio failed.	[16]
Nov. 10, 1957	Hammond, Ind.	Capt. Dennis Becky, Officers Charles Moore, Charles Mauder, and Steve Betustak	Elongated object with one red, one white, body light; interference on police radio. Object eluded pursuing police.	[17]

(Many other police reports during November 1957)

Date & Location		Names	Description	Notes
April 9, 1958	Newport Beach, Calif.	Ptn. R. Gordon	Two flat objects with rows of six flashing lights on leading edge of each, low above ocean with light reflecting in water; maneuvered, made sharp turns.	[18]
Aug. 24, 1958	Westwood, N.J.	Ptn. Richard Schulz and Richard McCabe	Glowing orange circular UFO hovered, moved E rapidly disappearing in seconds.	[19]
Oct. 12, 1958	Aurora, Ill.	Ptn. William Hornyan and Jack Adams	Several yellow objects moving in all directions; many witnesses.	[20]
April 3, 1959	Ocoee, Fla.	John F. Wilmeth, retired U.S. Treasury enforcement officer, former Coast Guard Lieut.	Large greenish-yellow light ascending, reflecting on lake; faded, re-appeared descending, hovered . . . finally ascended out of sight.	[21]

CIVIL DEFENSE,
GROUND OBSERVER CORPS

The Ground Observer Corps was created in January 1950, and inactivated January 31, 1959. By that time the improvement of electronic detection equipment reduced the need for civilian volunteer observers to supplement the air detection network of the Air Defense Command. During the period of its operation, the GOC made a great contribution to the security of the United States. It also logged hundreds of sightings of unexplainable aerial phenomena.

NICAP Adviser Leonard H. Stringfield, during this period, was Director of an effective world-wide organization (C.R.I.F.O.) in Cincinnati, Ohio, which sifted and publicized reliable UFO information. In September 1955, the Air Defense Command Filter Center in Columbus designated Stringfield's home as an official "UFO reporting post." Thereafter, when UFOs were observed in the skies above Cincinnati, Stringfield would check out the reports. If the objects did not appear to be anything conventional, he would alert the Filter Center. On several occasions, Stringfield helped vector in jet interceptors to track down unidentified objects in the skies.

A similar incident occurred August 23, 1955. In a privately published book, [22.] Stringfield described what happened:

"About midnight, residents throughout the city were jarred by the roar of jets. From S.A.C., Lockburne AFB, south of Columbus, the Air National Guard jets were alerted, scrambled and were over Cincinnati in 12 minutes. The alert began when three UFOs were sighted and confirmed by radar somewhere between Columbus and Cincinnati.

"In the meantime, Walter Paner, Supt. of Hamilton County GOC, on duty at the Mt. Healthy Post, phoned the author of the existent alert and relayed the word that jet interceptors were due over the area. He said the UFOs had been active over Mt. Healthy and could be seen clearly by observers from the tower. In a short time, the jets, at approximately 20,000 feet, were over Cincinnati, but poor visibility prevented me and a visiting friend from Toronto, Canada, from seeing the UFOs which had deployed over a wide area. According to radar, the interlopers had extended 37 miles south, 24 miles north of the city, and as far as 10 miles east of Mt. Healthy.

"A later call from Paner disclosed that a UFO was seen hovering in pendulum-like motions directly over the tower. At about 12:10 a.m., the interceptors made contact, and swooping in, chased the UFO - which disappeared at incredible speed. In the meantime, the Forestville and Loveland GOC Post reported the erratic flights of UFOs to the Air Filter Center describing them as round brilliant white spheres and discs."

The Cincinnati-Columbus, Ohio, area has long been a scene of extensive UFO activity. During 1953 and 1954, another NICAP member, Don Berliner, logged UFO sightings at the Columbus Filter Center. A selection of the reports indicates the flavor and frequency of UFO observations:

July 9, 1953; Columbus, Ohio. "Circular, silver" object traveling at terrific rate of speed" at very high altitude seen by accountant at North American Aviation plant.

July 24, 1953; Mt. Vernon, Ohio. 0900 EST; "large silver object" circles over town and then leaves in SW direction at speed slightly faster than clouds. Altitude estimated at 30,000 ft.

July 31, 1953; Port Clinton, Ohio. White light; going east 45 degrees in 30-40 seconds; viewed through 7x field glasses; ceiling was 15-20,000 feet. 2050 EST.

August 1, 1953; Toledo, Ohio. 0030 EST; "amber to green or blue;" ... "flickers and jumps."

August 14, 1953; Columbus, Ohio. 2030 EST; lighted object came straight down out of the sky, stopped, then sped out of view; in sight 30 seconds; observed by two young boys. (From Ohio State Journal; 8-15-53).

August 15, 1953; Crestline, Ohio. 2030 EST; light: white, red, green; circling; clear and calm.

August 21, 1953; Maumee, Ohio. 2200-2300 EST; Black oval, beads of light with green and red around perimeter; going NW, 20 degrees above horizon.

August 23, 1953; Columbus, Ohio. 0415 EST; red and white, half dollar [apparent size], moving very slowly upward; observed 1-1/2 hours.

September 24, 1953; Columbus, Ohio. 1027 EST; round disk, silvery, few seconds, following plane.

October 30, 1953; Mt. Vernon, Ohio. 1725Z; round, silver, did not look like plane; héard motor sound; low altitude; circular motion; clear.

November 14, 1953; vicinity of Toledo, Ohio. 2330Z; orange, white, blue and red flashing; gaining altitude; very clear.

December 13, 1953; Central Ohio. 0030 EST; long with white lights at both ends. Altitude approx. 5000 feet. Clear.

December 16, 1953; Toledo, Ohio. 1920 EST. Small group of lights changing from red to white, each appearing to revolve; altitude very high. Disappeared to NW a few minutes prior to arrival of seven aircraft from east. Seven were in loose formation, 1 mile apart and at different altitudes. Four miles from point of observation, broke formation and flew off in different directions.

GOC, Radar,
Track UFO Across New York

From 1951 to 1955, NICAP Adviser James C. Beatty served as a civilian leader at the Air Force Filter Center in White Plains, N.Y. The Center covered parts of three states: A portion of southern New York, about one-half of Connecticut, and most of New Jersey. Approximately 15,000 Ground Observer Corps spotters reported to this Center. During this period, Beatty served as an instructor, a team supervisor, and also as alert crew supervisor. In the latter capacity, he would have been the civilian in charge at the Filter Center if New York had actually been attacked. In a tape recorded talk to the New York NICAP Affiliate, Beatty said that UFO sightings reported by GOC spotters were numerous; "It was a fairly frequent occurrence."

Beatty recalled in particular one sighting in which he helped track the UFO. It was late August or early September 1954, on the 8:00 p.m. to midnight shift. At first, all was quiet. Then about 9:30 p.m. a post about 20 miles southeast of Poughkeepsie, N.Y., reported that "a large round orange object" the apparent size of the moon had appeared suddenly in the sky. The moon was also visible in another sector of the sky, and was not full that night.

For 20-30 minutes, the ground observers watched the UFO. At first it appeared stationary, except for an oscillatory effect as if it were about to start moving. Then it began moving slowly in a southeasterly direction. As it moved the color changed slightly from orange to a more yellow-orange.

"During the next hour," Beatty reported, "our team at the Filter Center plotted the progress of this object across the board...This track as it began to evolve had a southeasterly direction. During this whole period of an hour it was under constant observation.

"While the object had been progressing across our board, I at that particular time was on the hot-line at the Filter Center... Two radar stations we were hooked into confirmed at that time that they had been holding an electronic fix on this same object... It coincided in position and movement with the object we had seen visually."

Over the hot-line, Beatty could hear the various ground bases talking to each other, and heard the "scramble" order go out from two different Air Force bases. Two jets were scrambled from Stewart AFB, Newburgh, N.Y., and two from the base at Newcastle, Delaware.

"At the time I was hearing the scrambles in the background, the plot was progressing more in a direction toward the state of Connecticut...then we began to pick up the jet patterns, coming in from the south in the case of the scramble from Delaware, and from the west in the case of the scramble from Stewart Field...We could track the jets as they closed in on this object.

"Shortly before the interception occurred, a strange thing happened to the orange object. This was reported both by the ground observer posts and by the pilots of the jets. It seemed to speed up in its motion - it had been oscillating or pulsating and moved rather slowly - and it changed to a rotational effect with also a change of lights. By this time the reports came in that it was a whirling combination of red, green and yellow lights... sort of a rainbow effect.

"Then at almost the same time we got reports from the posts which had been holding this object under ground observation, and jets themselves, that the object disappeared straight upward in a burst of speed...At that moment it also became apparent that not only the ground observers, but also the aircraft and airborne radar had lost visual and electronic contact with the object as it zoomed upward and vanished in the night sky."

Later the witnesses were requested by the Air Force to fill out standard UFO report forms. [23.]

Other GOC Reports

August 22, 1952; Chicago, Illinois. Associated Press reported (Chicago, August 23): "Two Air Force jet fighters, directed by ground observers, chased a yellowish light in the sky last night but reported that it blinked out when they started closing in on it. Air Force officers in the Chicago filter center said the blink-out of the light over nearby Elgin, Illinois, was reported simultaneously at 11:48 p.m., last night by the pilots and by D.C. Scott, Elgin, Supervisor of the Center's ground observers in the Elgin area...Ground observers said that when the planes gave up the chase the light reappeared and ascended rapidly in the night sky." A few minutes later, another GOC post about 20 miles to the NW reported a glowing object which hovered blinked twice, and ascended out of sight.

August 9, 1953; Moscow, Idaho. Mr. L.E. Towner, supervisor, and other GOC observers reported a large glowing disc. As three F-86's closed in to investigate, the UFO abruptly sped up and left the jets behind.

August 12, 1953; Rapid City, S.D. Two GOC posts observed a UFO which was chased twice by F-84 pilots, tracked by ground and airborne radar. [Section I.]

March 24, 1954; Baltimore, Md. A formation of UFOs was observed at night by a Civil Defense official. Adolph Wagner, Deputy Coordinator for the area, saw 13 sharply defined triangular objects in a V moving from west to east. They were glowing a fluorescent blue. From the north, a larger object approached and stationed itself in front of the V. At this point, Wagner noticed a commercial airliner approaching the airport. Suddenly the UFOs split formation. Six executed a sharp turn, their color turning to purplish, and headed toward the airliner in single file. The other 8 objects continued on to the east. [25.]

June 12 & 14, 1954; Nr Baltimore, Md. On two nights, Ground Observer Corps spotters and radar tracked a large glowing object hovering at over 75,000 feet. Jets circled below, unable to reach the object's altitude. Reports of the UFO came into the Baltimore Filter Center for about an hour the first night; two hours the second night. The object alternately moved in a square pattern at high speed, and hovered. [See Wilmington (Del.) Morning News; July 9, 1954].

July 29, 1955; Cincinnati, Ohio. A Ground Observer Corps post at Loveland, and many others in Cincinnati proper, saw a round UFO at 1:00 a.m. The bright ball-like object made a penetrating shrill sound, as it zig-zagged across the sky making sharp turns. (cf., July 26, 1958 case following) [26.]

November 23, 1955; Spirit Lake, Iowa. Earl Rose (a biologist) and Gay Orr (superintendent of schools) were on duty at the GOC post about 5:45 p.m. Attracted by a multi-motor sound on their amplifying pickup system, the two men scanned the sky with binoculars. A brilliant object at low altitude was visible maneuvering erratically to the southwest. As it moved, the UFO changed color from white to bluish-white to green and red. For about twenty minutes, Rose and Orr watched the gyrating object as it moved forward, up and down. At one point, the UFO hovered over Center Lake for about 10 minutes. Its maneuvers were totally unlike an aircraft, and it moved against the wind. [27.]

July 29, 1956; Pasadena, Calif. A brilliant white light moving at variable speeds was observed from Ground Observer Corps posts by Homer Clem, Ray La Roche and others at 8:43 p.m. The UFO appeared in the south sky, and moved northeast, alternately hovering and speeding up. According to a press report, "The Air Defense Filter Center at Pasadena reported that the mysterious object had been trailed with radar screens." [28.]

November 5, 1957; Haverhill, Mass. At 4:30 p.m., Kenneth Chadwick, Walter Downey and others at a GOC post saw a circular or spherical object hovering high in the sky. Lining the UFO with a chimney, they verified that it was vibrating up and down, and from side to side. This continued for 3 or 4 minutes. The object then disappeared, but reappeared quickly in a new position. The UFO was observed intermittently afterwards, at times resembling a cigar in shape. [29.]

November 22, 1957; Canutillo, Texas. The supervisor of the GOC post, Mrs. G.A. Baker, saw a UFO which appeared "metallic, like silver" about 4:00 p.m. When first noticed, the UFO was nearly stationary in the south sky. Then it "flew west rapidly," stopped, sped back toward the east, and finally zoomed upward out of sight after three minutes. [39.]

July 26, 1958; Durango, Colo. Another post supervisor, Mrs. Elton Highland, observed a spherical UFO about 9:45 a.m. The UFO, resembling a silver ball, was headed northwest "at a tremendous rate of speed" making a noise similar to a jet. It appeared to be at 35,000 to 40,000 feet. Within 45 seconds, the UFO had vanished in the distance. [31.]

PROFESSIONAL AND BUSINESS MEN

July 13, 1947; Gardner, Mass. A disc-shaped UFO which accelerated with a burst of speed was observed at 5:48 p.m. by Warren Baker Eames, A.I.D. Mr. Eames, president of an interior design company, is a magna cum laude graduate of Harvard University. While driving west on Route 2, Eames noticed a large bright object in the sky. The UFO seemed to be traveling in the same direction. It was "round, disc-shaped, exactly like a silver dollar in shape...silver, aluminum color."

After a few seconds, "the edge of the disc nearest me appeared to dip slightly down toward my direction, and then it sped off to the WNW with a huge burst of speed. When it dipped, I could see the edge very clearly," Eames said. [32.]

April 26, 1954; Newburyport, Mass. Russell M. Peirce, Architect, reported a circular object which made a right-angle turn.

"The time of day was between three and four o'clock in the afternoon, and the sky was clear overhead. I was standing at the rear of the local High School building talking with two friends... Suddenly we all heard a very loud deep roar as of many motors, which accelerated very rapidly and then faded out just as rapidly. The direction of the sound was from the sky and I instinctively turned my head and eyes upward. It just happened that the line of my vision was such that my eyes were almost instantly focused on the object, which was east, perhaps a little to the SE, from where I was standing. It was up high overhead, and from the angle at which I was looking up, about 60 degrees, with the earth, I would say that the object could have been out over the ocean as we are in about 4 miles from the coast...

"The object as I first saw it appeared as a flaming ring. The color was a little on the whitish tone but also had some suggestion of the orange-yellow of the common flame of burning wood, say. At the lower left quadrant of the ring there appeared a small, bright disc tangent with the ring, same color as the ring. The center of the remainder of the ring appeared dark. The object was headed earthward, not quite in a direct line toward me, but sort of downward and a little to the right. This direction was indicated by a short, grayish trail upward to the left. Then the object seemed to waver and 'skid around' for just a few seconds, apparently reversing its direction, because it next went upward and to the right, disappearing from sight very quickly.

"As it disappeared the appearance changed from that of a ring and internal concentric disc, to a solid silvery colored disc. . . The sound came and went synonymously with the object's appearance and disappearance. The size appeared slightly smaller than a full moon would appear high in the sky...The time of observation was short, say twenty seconds, but long enough to get a good clear view of what was visible...My daughter heard the roar from inside our home, and three other people called me, after seeing the newspaper article, to tell me they had heard the unusual sound from the sky at the same time I had heard it...

"It appeared as though the object were traveling earthward at a terrific speed, and then as though a tremendous force were applied to arrest the earthward direction and send the object back upward, and consequently it went rapidly out of sight and out of hearing distance...What the object was, where it came from, and where it went, are all a complete mystery to me but the sighting was as clear as a picture on a wall." [33]

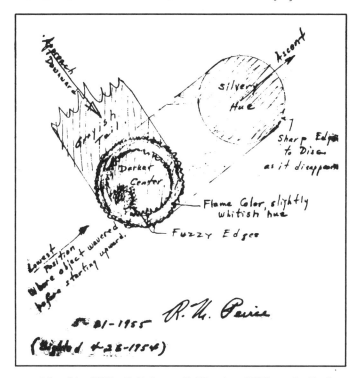

July 31, 1957; Calistoga, California. William J. Besler, president of Besler Corporation, Oakland, California, was relaxing in the natural hot springs mineral bath at Calistoga, about 9:30 a.m. "I happened to glance out the window," Besler said, "and was attracted by a very bright light behind a poplar tree on the top of a nearby knoll at an angle of about 20 degrees from the horizon. The light was climbing behind the branches and I thought it might be a brilliantly white bird, but discerned in a matter of seconds that it was ascending too slowly and deliberately for any bird. The bright light rose above the tree, and it was then apparent that there were two objects approximately a thumb-nail's height at arm's length above the tree and completely stationary. I wondered what kind of jet-jobs or objects could be reflecting the sun's light and remain so completely stationary but so brilliantly white and maintain such a fixed position relative to each other.

"The objects then started to rise higher above the tree and I began to wonder, so I got out of the tub and proceeded to the window for a better look, by which time the lights were no longer in their previous position relative to the tree. I looked around the horizon, left and right, and up; and there they were - now almost due north and at an angle of about 70 degrees from the horizontal, describing antics which no jet-jobs, guided missiles or airplanes could accomplish.

"I pushed the window open...and got a good look at the two bright lights which can be described as the size of the tip of a blue-head wood stick match at arm's length at a distance from each other equal to about 6 or 7 times their diameter. No better description can be given than that they were brilliantly white lights against an azure blue cloudless sky...

"To describe the antics they were going through is to first state that they made no pattern nor any sense. One could climb above the other, then the other would climb above the first, the lights sometimes blinking on and off at a surprising frequency of four blinks per second as they climbed. When the lights would blink out, there was absolutely nothing to see, indicating that they could hardly have been a somersaulting disc, black on one side and white on the other, as something would have shown up against the clear azure sky.

"The two lights then circled around each other twice and began moving in a more or less straight line due west and continued in this path at a speed I would estimate at 200 mph., for an arc of perhaps 15 degrees requiring some 8 seconds...as

I was watching them intently they mysteriously and instantaneously went out...I looked in all directions for the next 30 seconds but they didn't reappear..."

(Mr. Besler added a note about the natural tendency for a person to try to account for unusual observations in terms of familiar experiences. "I was aware from almost the first of the 18 seconds I had them in observation that these could well be UFOs. Nonetheless my mind was struggling at all times to identify them as planes, birds, pieces of tinfoil in the wind, or something familiar to this planet. Even after they disappeared my mind kept searching for an explanation other than the obvious that there had been a couple of brilliant flying unidentified objects (saucers?) under observation by the rare chance of a glance out of a window.") [34]

November 11, 1957; California Desert. During the surge of sightings in November 1957 [See Section XII; November 1957 Chronology], a silvery elliptical UFO was sighted flying below an airliner. Robert D. Hahn, a jewelry designer, was flying from Minneapolis to Los Angeles aboard Western Airlines flight #61.

"Flight #61 was over desert country approximately 30 to 45 minutes before landing at Los Angeles International Airport," Hahn reported. The sighting occurred approximately seven to ten minutes before we passed what appeared to be an Air Force base. My seat was just above the leading edge of the wing next to the window on the right side of the plane. We were at about 14,000 feet, or so it had been announced some time previously. I was observing several jets making vapor trails at high altitude, crossing and criss-crossing. The earth seemed rugged and deserted with no sign of roads or cultivation, with the exception of a meandering, apparently dirt, road approximately 10 to 12 miles to the right angling away from our line of flight.

"My first observation of the object struck me as a large, roughly elliptical, metallic building on the ground at the base of a hill that seemed to have dark patches, like brush or small trees. I wondered what such a structure was doing out there with no roads or sign of access appearing near it - it was, I should judge, eight to nine miles ahead and to the right of the plane. Suddenly, I observed it was moving

"Dark patches on the hill, probably scrub trees, were passing beneath it. It went up and over the hill angling toward the road. Its course was extremely erratic, seeming to zig-zag two or three hundred feet in an instant to the right or left while maintaining a general direction angle of about 45 degrees away from our course. Its overall speed seemed to me (pure 'guestimate') about one-third our own. It eventually disappeared from my view behind and under the wing, paralleling the road about a mile to the right...

"I would judge the size of the object to be approximately 200 to 250 feet in diameter - its height off the ground to be only a couple hundred feet as it went over the first hill and never over 1000 feet during my observation."

Mr. Hahn added that the UFO's surface resembled "sandblasted aluminum," and was not shiny. He saw no trail or exhaust from the object. [35.]

(That afternoon a group of Rocketdyne engineers sighted three elliptical UFOs over the San Fernando Valley; See Section VI).

September 7, 1958; Mission, Kansas. The publisher of The American Hereford Journal, Hayes Walker, Jr., and his wife saw a white disc speed across the sky about 5:30 p.m. The UFO, round and flat, passed nearly overhead traveling from southwest to northeast, disappearing over the horizon in 12-15 seconds. It was "more distinct than the daytime moon," Walker reported. [36]

Rendezvous of Two UFOs

February 16, 1960; Laguna Beach, Calif. Mr. Earl T. Ross, retired chemical manufacturing company executive (industrial chemist and engineer) reported the following case to NICAP.

"At 9:15 a.m., Tuesday, February 16, 1960, from my home... I saw, in a very clear and cloudless blue sky, an oval, light colored object move steadily toward the east from a point a little south of overhead. Then, perhaps two seconds later, I saw another similar object approach and overtake the first from a position lower in the southern sky; the second object wobbled or rather nodded, (on an axis through its center and at right angles to its course, the axis being parallel to the earth's surface), as it slowed down to join the first, and it altered its course and speed so as to take up a steady position that appeared to be behind and to the right of the first.

"The first object maintained its flight path steadily, without nodding, and after joining up the second object stopped its nodding; both objects then moved rapidly, that is, in a period of perhaps eight or ten seconds, to the local horizon which is a range of hills along the coast back of this town. I saw no vapor trails and heard no sound. There was no wind.

"The objects each appeared to be about a third of the apparent diameter of the full moon. They were sharply defined and had some sort of surface structure that made it appear to me as though they were flattened spheres having a thickness of about one-third their diameter. The objects were an off-white color, not silvery.

"During this sighting the sun was in the southeast, above the path of the objects, and as they moved along past the sun's apparent position, I observed a most peculiar darkening - to almost black - of the side of the objects that faced the sun, so that each object took on the appearance of a crescent. This dark crescent developed and moved around over the surface of the objects as they passed under the sun.

"The original light color of the objects then appeared to become transparent as the dark crescents developed. The appearance of the dark crescents on the sunny side of the objects of course seems to be at variance with our normal experience.

"The above account is from the detailed notes I made a few minutes after the sighting." [37.]

October 27, 1960; Lexington, Kentucky. B.L. Kissinger, Jr., Attorney, and his wife at 5:50 p.m. watched a circular object hovering in the sky to the southwest. After about ten minutes, the UFO took off toward the northwest (the shape changing to elliptical), at a speed "faster than a jet." The UFO departed on a rising course, leaving a visible trail. [38.]

February 7, 1961; Kennebunkport, Maine. During a flurry of sightings in northern New England, the president of an advertising agency was among the numerous witnesses. At 10:30 p.m., H. David Walley was returning home from a Chamber of Commerce meeting. As he rounded a curve in the road, he saw "what appeared to be the lower half of an orange-red ball in the sky. It was of such unusual brightness that I stopped and got out of my car to observe more closely," Walley said.

"My first impression was that this was a harvest moon because of its size and color. I observed this stationary object for at least two minutes and then saw it disappear at a tremendous speed, far in excess of the capabilities of any of our military aircraft.

"The object was at an angle of 20 to 30 degrees above the horizon and traveled in an easterly direction...As the UFO disappeared I could hear no sound or saw no contrails, or smoke of any kind." [39]

PUBLIC OFFICIALS

Carl J. Henry
Chairman, Industrial Commission of Missouri
Department of Labor and Industrial Relations

March 29, 1952 - 6:40 p.m.   Butler, Missouri (65 miles south of Kansas City
Mr. Henry, along with several others, saw a silver-colored cylinder-shaped object in the sky almost directly overhead. The object was moving slowly in a northwesterly direction leaving no trail or exhaust. It was definite and fixed in shape, and moved end-ways with a steady motion. The observers watched the object for approximately 2 minutes. Mr. Henry estimated its length at about 100 feet. The sky was clear and not yet dark at the time of the observation. No sound was heard. [40]

Marvin W. Skipworth
District Judge
District Court for Coos County, Oregon

1954 or 1955 - day Coos Bay, Oregon
"I was idly gazing at the blue sky and scattered clouds to the south, or maybe a little west of south. The sky was very blue and the air very clear, except for the scattered clouds, which were practically motionless. My attention was directed to two white irregular roundish clouds and the sky beyond.

"Suddenly, what appeared to be a huge aluminum discus appeared coming on a decline from above and beyond the cloud to my left and when it appeared to be about midway between and beyond the clouds and about even with the bottom of each cloud it suddenly turned a little to the left (my right) and soared upward and backward at a terrific speed...(cf., April 26, 1954 report above; Professional Men.)

"As it reversed and started up and back it flattened again so that it was traveling with its perimeter longitudinal to its diameter in my line of sight. The sun was to the right of the clouds and as I remember they may have been slightly pinkish on their western sides, but the object was remarkably clear and well defined - no fuzzy edges or vapor streaks, and it appeared to have ridged or terraced sides. An ordinary track and field discus describes it perfectly as to shape, as I saw it.

"I am not capable of judging how far away nor how high it was, but as I remember it appeared to be about two-thirds or three-fourths the area of the usual appearance of a full moon." [41]

Arnold W. Spencer
Former Town Selectman (12 years)

April 25, 1960 - 9:00 p.m.   Plymouth, N.H.
Mr. Spencer watched a bright hovering cigar-shaped object, "dark scarlet as the deepest red in a rainbow," with blunted ends. The UFO hung stationary low in the eastern sky, vertical bands of pulsating light visible along its length. (cf., Mt. Kilimanjaro sighting, 1951; Section X.) After about 25 seconds, the UFO suddenly moved off toward the south at high speed, illuminating the branches of trees as it passed. It left no trail and made no sound. [42]

Patrick McAley
Deputy Inspector, Weights & Measures
City of Chicago

October 3, 1962 - 9:25 p.m.   Chicago, Illinois
While watching for the Echo satellite, McAley and his son saw a domed disc cross the face of the moon traveling in a westerly direction. The object, tilted at an angle, "seemed to be floating." It appeared to be a small fraction of the apparent size of the moon and gave the impression of being far out in space. [43]

PROFESSORS AND TEACHERS

May 20, 1950; Flagstaff, Arizona. Dr. Seymour L. Hess, Head, Department of Meteorology, Florida State University. Observation of "powered" disc. [Section I]

July 27, 1952; Ann Arbor, Michigan. Dr. Charles H. Otis, professor emeritus of Biology, Bowling Green State University. Formation of elongated objects leaving constant length trails. [Section VI.]

November 26, 1954; Manasquan, N.J. Confidential report (certified by NICAP Director and Assistant Director); College professor with M.A. degree, from Columbia University. V-formation of 15-20 round luminous objects which moved overhead, north to south. (witness stated: "For professional reasons, I do not want my name used. I feel strongly that you are fighting something that should be fought, but at this time I cannot expose myself as a fellow combatant.") [44]

June 18, 1957; Jackson, Miss. Prof. Henry Carlock, Physics Department, Mississippi College. Reddish oval-shaped object with three "portholes" observed passing over city. [Section VI.]

August 26, 1960; Mesa, Arizona. Mr. Clete L. Miller, Science Department Head and Chemistry Teacher, Mesa High School. (Holds M.S. degree, served in Army Air Corps 1942-1946, single engine pilot.) At 8:00 p.m. Miller and his wife saw a hovering object in the southeast sky, emitting four beams of light; flashes of light, apparently from a beacon on top of the object also were visible. "Suddenly all four lights went out simultaneously,"

Miller said, "and reappeared in a like manner - standing still - much farther to the north." A rumbling noise appeared to be associated with the UFO.

When the local newspaper printed Miller's report next day, several other citizens called to confirm his sighting. Miller called nearby Williams Air Force Base, and determined that there were no unusual aircraft in the area at the time. [45]

CLERGYMEN

A formation of UFOs which paused, made a sharp turn, then sped away, was observed February 20, 1952 by Rev. Albert Baller, NICAP Board Member. Rev. Baller currently is pastor of the German Congregational Church, Clinton, Mass.

"[It] was an exceptionally beautiful day at Greenfield, Mass. There were no clouds and the sky was a 'cobalt blue.' Also, no wind. At three o'clock p.m., I boarded the New York train at the Greenfield station, took a seat away from the station and near a window opening onto a vast expanse of sky to the north and east. A minute or two afterward my attention was drawn to the sky by a sharp flash of light about 35 degrees or more above the horizon. Looking carefully toward this flash, I was quite astonished to see three, perfectly circular, silver objects approaching in V-formation...

[In an accompanying diagram, Rev. Baller added that the UFOs were "like highly polished silver; appeared approximately 2/3 size of a full moon."].

"They moved without vapor--or smoke--trail and at approximately the speed of a second hand on a watch. At this speed and in this formation they came to a point almost overhead but not quite, since I could still watch them from my window. There they stopped and hovered for perhaps ten seconds. Then I noted that the lead object was slowly reversing and appearing to pull into a line with the other two between them. After this brief shift, there was another quick motion by all three (I am not too sure just what) and they began to depart in a direction at right angles to their approach...

"My astonishment increased as I saw them leave, because they went with such speed that they dwindled to specks and were out of sight in not more than six seconds. I could not tell whether they made any noise, as there was such a racket about the station. However, I doubt that they did, since nobody standing on the station platform seemed to be aware of them...

"I first tried to fit it into the conventional--balloons, jets, etc. But it just would not fit. Obviously they were not planes, and on second thought, they were just as obviously not balloons..." [46]

Between 6:00 and 6:30 p.m., November 5, 1955, Rev. and Mrs. Kenneth R. Hoffman saw a large elliptical UFO, with light shining from square "ports" like windows. At the time, Rev. Hoffman was pastor of the Grace Lutheran Church, Cleveland, Ohio. Rev. and Mrs. Hoffman were interviewed by C. W. Fitch, NICAP member in Cleveland.

"We were driving south on Lee Road on our way to the Cleveland-Hopkins Airport just at dusk...Shortly after crossing Fairmount Boulevard our attention was attracted to a row of bright lights in the sky directly ahead over Lee Road...Mrs. Hoffman saw them approaching on an arc course and stop...

"We watched the lights as we drove, speculating the while on what they were and continued on across North Park and Shaker Boulevards. At a point on the south side of Shaker Blvd., we stopped the car in order to get a better look at them. We could then discern that the lights were coming from a huge oval-shaped object, similar in appearance to two saucers, the uppermost inverted and resting on the edges of the lower one. Around the portion of its perimeter visible to us were eight large windows from which shone an intense white light. It was the light shining from these windows that we had first seen.

"Viewed from this point the strange object appeared to be hovering almost directly over the Van Aken-Lee intersection at a height we estimated as not being over five hundred feet. From the fact that it filled the sky above the highway beyond the width of the street we felt it must have been close to one hundred feet in diameter.

"At this point, which was our closest approach to the craft, we were, in all probability, not more than half a mile away from it. The body appeared to be metallic and was of a light gray color,

similar in appearance to weathered aluminum. Mrs. Hoffman described it as being a pearly aluminum color.

"The windows were clearly defined as were the dark spaces between them. We estimated that each window must have been at least 8 feet by ten feet in size with a two foot space between them. An intensely white glow or beam of light shone steadily downward from each window at about a 45 degree angle. The light rays were so bright that we could see the air dust in them.

"We watched it for about ten minutes, then started the car and drove south on Lee Road hoping to get under it. When we were at Fernway Road, it began to slip westward over the tree-tops. It moved slowly and noiselessly and did not appear to rotate. It disappeared from view, the trees blocking our vision. When we reached the Van Aken intersection, which is an open area, within a matter of a minute or less, the object had completely disappeared."

(Rev. Hoffman then described their mental reactions to the experience: "We decided it would be best to keep the matter to ourselves since we felt it might have certain undesirable repercussions if it were made public, our principal concern being the possibility of ridicule and disparagement. As time passed and we heard and read of other persons having seen strange lights and objects in the skies, our feelings underwent a change. We hereby grant permission to publish or use this account, all or in part, as you may see fit to inform or enlighten others.") [47]

Rev. Jack L. Sanford, First Congregational Church, was among a group of people who witnessed an elliptical UFO October 9, 1960, in Longpoint, Illinois.

"When we turned west onto Longpoint Road [about 6:30 p.m.]," Rev. Sanford said, "It was very bright and clear and attracted our attention readily." There hovering in the sky in a tilted position was a football-shaped object. Its lower portion was distinct and golden-colored; the upper portion "hazy as when steam heat rises from a radiator." The bottom portion was tilted toward the observers.

Stopping the car, the group got out and watched the UFO for 8-10 minutes as it hung motionless. "Then when it pulled up horizontal," Rev. Sanford continued, "it began to become smaller. We knew it was moving, so we chased it in the car. It just pulled away rising slightly until it was too small to see anymore. We chased it 3-1/2 miles." [48]

NEWSMEN

After a three day aerial search during the first widespread UFO sightings in the United States, Dave Johnson, aviation editor of the Idaho Statesman, observed a maneuvering disc July 9, 1947. Ground observers at Gowan Field confirmed the sighting.

"For 45 seconds, I watched a circular object dart about in front of a cloud bank," Johnson reported. [49] The object was round...it appeared black, altogether, as it maneuvered in front of the clouds. I saw the sun flash from it once. "I was flying at 14,000 feet west of Boise, near the end of my third mission... Frankly, I had given up hope of ever seeing one of the objects. I turned the plane toward Boise, to begin a circular let-down over Gowan Field, and over the nose of the aircraft I saw the object... clearly and distinctly. I turned the plane broadside to it and pulled back the Plexiglas canopy so there would be no distortion. The object was still there.

"It was rising sharply and jerkily toward the top of the towering bank of alto-cumulus and alto-stratus clouds. At that moment it was so round I thought it was a balloon. The object was turning so that it presented its edge to me. It then appeared as a straight, black line. Then, with its edge still toward me, it shot straight up, rolled over at the top of the maneuver, and I lost sight of it.

"The object could have been ten miles away, or forty, I do not know. If it was a great distance from me, its speed was incredible...This circular thing was maneuvering very swiftly."

In a story dated line Albuquerque, N.M., August 2, 1952, Scripps-Howard Staff Writer Doyle Kline detailed a personal UFO sighting which "made a flying saucers believer out of me." [50]

At 9:50 p.m., August 1, Mr. Kline observed about 10 glowing objects which "resembled nothing I had seen before. Their flight was soundless and graceful." The UFOs shifted formation in a coordinated maneuver as they passed overhead, Kline reported. They appeared to be about 1/3 the size of the full moon.

At first the UFOs were clustered together, heading north. "Then they shifted to a perfect V. The shift was done with precision," Kline said. Within seconds, the objects took up a new formation: Two rows, with the UFOs in one row spaced evenly between those in the other row.

Assuming the UFOs were about 2500 feet above the city, Kline concluded their speed would be about that of an F-86 Sabrejet. But "their shifts in position were incredibly swift and fantastically violent--in terms of our experience." If the UFOs were higher than they appeared to be, Kline continued, "their performance takes on even more incredible aspects."

Mr. Kline reported his sighting to the 34th Air Defense Division, and was asked to describe the maneuvers to intelligence officers.

"I have witnessed both day and night rocket flights at White Sands...The saucers were something different altogether," he concluded.

A formation of 12 UFOs passing over Philadelphia was observed by photographers of the Inquirer and the Bulletin, and many others, November 9, 1955.

At 6:08 p.m., Charles W. James, of the Philadelphia <u>In</u>quirer, saw a V-formation of round, silvery-white objects pass overhead. During the observation, the objects shifted into an A-formation. The UFOs made no sound. The color did not change. (James was interviewed by a correspondent of C.R.I.F.O., headed by Leonard H. Stringfield, now a NICAP Adviser. See Ground Observer Corps, this section).

CROSS-SECTION

After the many sightings in 1952 [See Section XI, Chronology], UFO reports began to be publicized less and less. However, over the following years there was no lack of sightings. Of the many hundreds reported since 1952, the following selected cases comprise a cross-section of reports from observers of various backgrounds, from 1952 to 1962, inclusive.

<u>1953</u>: Cleveland, Ohio; Don P. Hollister, a technical writer for the Goodyear Aircraft Corporation, saw a UFO pass overhead about 6:30 p.m., September 7. While waxing his car in the back yard, Hollister happened to glance up and noticed a grayish-blue object directly overhead, headed north. The sky was completely overcast, and the UFO appeared to be at less than 3000 feet altitude. It was shaped roughly like an equilateral triangle, but rounded somewhat on the sides and angles, and was rotating around a central axis. The UFO continued on over the visible horizon at constant velocity, disappearing from view after about 5 seconds. [51]

<u>1954</u>: Grand Canyon, Arizona; Elbert Edwards (Superintendent of Schools in Boulder City, Nevada) and John Goddard (professional explorer) saw a cigar-shaped UFO April 16 about 10:20 p.m. While camped above Havasu canyon in the Grand Canyon, they noticed a very bright light approaching at high speed. For the next minute, Goddard studied the object through 8x binoculars. It was cigar-shaped and had a row of five bright lights along the side "like portholes." The brilliant light which they had first noticed was on the front of the object. The UFO travelled from north to south-southwest, in the direction of Mexico. [52]

<u>1955</u>: Ohio: UFO activity was observed over a wide area, October 2, by many witnesses in separate locations. So-called "angel's hair" fell the same day. (Walter N. Webb, NICAP Adviser, interviewed several of the witnesses and wrote the following report. Another Ohio report for the same day, discovered later, is appended.)

"A remarkable local [Alliance, Ohio] UFO sighting took place at sunset on Sunday, October 2, 1955. The sighting was confirmed by at least eight witnesses who saw the same object around the same time from three widely separated areas. Six of the eight observers were interviewed.

"I first received word of the UFO from a close friend of mine, James Ansley (Jr.) who called me right after he and his family had returned home from a drive in the country. Jim was an Alliance High School student and an amateur astronomer and photographer whom I consider to be an accurate observer. Two days after the sighting and Jim's report, Wilma Faye Barker, a chemistry major in her junior year at Mount Union College in Alliance, told me of the sighting she and her boy friend had made

that Sunday. Finally, in late November I was visiting another UFO investigator, Fred Kirsch of Cuyahoga Falls, and learned that an Akron couple, Donald J. Karaiskos and his wife, had also seen the same strange object at the same time, October 2. Mr. Karaiskos had phoned his uncle, Mr. George Popowitch, after his sighting, and several days later Mr. Popowitch in turn called Kirsch.

Ansley Report
"The Ansleys were driving west (more exactly, WSW) from Alliance on West Main Street when Jim noticed an orangish object hanging in the sky about 15 degrees above the west horizon. It was 6:10 p.m. (EST) just after sunset, and the sky was clear. At first Jim thought it might have been Mercury or Venus, but he soon realized that it could be no celestial object. The tiny round object was as bright as Venus. Everybody in the car saw it -- Mr. and Mrs. Ansley, Jim and his brother, Dave. After they turned north on the Sawburg Road, the UFO appeared to move south slightly but Jim couldn't be sure (probably an illusion of movement since the car itself was in motion and also had to make a turn).

When they pulled out on the Harrisburg Road, Route 173, the thing was hovering over the road straight ahead (far away) and soon began to change size and shape, becoming a darker orange, then lighter in color again. It changed from a small disc to an ellipse to a thin crescent and finally to a very thin, pointed cigar-like object perpendicular to the horizon. Jim estimated the cigar was 3/8" long, with dividers held at arm's length against the sky. This agrees with the Akron observer's estimate - 1/3 the length of a pin which is 3/8".

When the crescent stage was reached, the object began to straighten out to become the vertical cigar. To Jim, the whole change resembled the phases of the moon. It remained perpendicular for about 7 seconds (timed on Jim's navigators watch), then it started tilting downward, halting momentarily at an estimated inclination of 20 degrees. It then tipped to a level position, parallel to the horizon, and faded from view in this position -- like a plane vanishing behind a cloud, said Mrs. Ansley...Most of the phases were watched along Freshley Road, and the Ansleys saw it disappear from there.

The sighting lasted 10 minutes, from 6:10 to 6:20.

The observers said the cigar appeared solid and sharply defined.

Barker Report
Wilma Faye Barker and her boy friend, Rudolph Holloway, saw the same object. They were driving home from Guilford Lake, southeast of Alliance, around 6 p.m. and first noticed the thing at North Georgetown. She saw it as a very bright silver line or needle, solid and sharply outlined. She could not estimate its angular size or altitude except that it was big and low in the western sky, tilted slightly toward the north...and standing still all the time. They continued to watch it now and then as they drove along U.S. Route 62 into Alliance. Then they noticed that the thing had changed shape, to a flattened oval, roughly triangular, still hanging at a slant (Faye said they did not see the actual change in shape occur). The oval was not as sharply outlined as the needle and was duller in color. Driving north on Union Avenue (Route 80) she lost sight of it at intervals because of trees and finally discovered it was gone. She arrived home at 6:20. The object was probably observed during a 15 or 20-minute period.

Karaiskos Report
"In Akron a Kent State University student, Donald J. Karaiskos, 25, and his wife were driving west along Cole Avenue near Hammel Street at approximately 6 p.m. when they noticed a bright white sharply outlined cigar-shaped object (also described by him in his report as "rectangular, proportions of 1/3 the length of a pin") about 10 degrees above the horizon. It was tilted at a 45-degree angle and motionless. The sky was clear except for some clouds along the horizon below the object. The setting sun was partially obscured by the landscape and houses. Mr. Karaiskos drove about three blocks, then turned around and came back to the original spot to see if the object was still there. It was, so he parked the car, got out, and watched it for 5 minutes. They then went to his wife's sister's house in the nearby Cole Avenue housing project where he phoned the post supervisor of the Akron GOC, a Mrs. Sutter, and also called his uncle, Mr. George Popowitch (who later notified Fred Kirsch). Following the

two phone calls, Karaiskos and his brother-in-law went outside to see if the object was still there. It was dark. The UFO was gone. Karaiskos called Mrs. Sutter again, but she said no one at the GOC post had seen the object.

"The UFO was in view for approximately 10 minutes, according to the report, and was motionless the whole time.

"Mr. Karaiskos concludes: 'The object was definitely not a balloon nor a blimp. My first logical explanation was that it was a vapor trail. This theory was dispelled as it was too low in the sky to be a vapor trail, and it retained its shape for 10 minutes. A vapor trail would have scattered in a few minutes. It is the firm belief of myself and my wife that it was not any known object.'

"If the angular altitudes and azimuths given were absolutely dependable -- and they are not -- it might be possible to discover the object's actual size, distance, and height. It must have been huge -- several hundred feet in diameter -- to have been seen over such a wide area. Using the times and descriptions of all three groups of observers, it is possible to work out a continuous change-of-phase pattern for the UFO (see diagram). This apparent change in shape and size could have been due to a disc turning vertically in flight and presenting its edge to the observers. Or it may have been a real alteration...Whatever the explanation, it is evident that eight persons did see a UFO -- an extraordinary UFO -- from three different areas around the same time..."

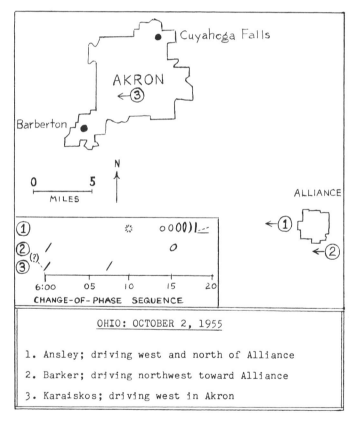

OHIO: OCTOBER 2, 1955

1. Ansley; driving west and north of Alliance

2. Barker; driving northwest toward Alliance

3. Karaiskos; driving west in Akron

Addenda

Later two additional reports for the same date were uncovered. Mrs. Albert Fanty, and her mother Mrs. Della Burroway of Uhrichsville (south of Akron and southwest of Alliance) reported two UFO sightings during the day.

In the morning, Mrs. Burroway saw seven disc-shaped objects bunched together at high altitude. About 1:00 p.m., Mrs. Fanty arrived for a visit. As her mother described the discs seen earlier, they searched the sky. Then they saw three or four silvery objects travelling at high speed in an irregular line. Shortly afterwards, the air was filled with 'fine silken-like silver cobwebs which floated everywhere,' Mrs. Fanty said. [53]

1956: Los Angeles, California; about 1:50 p.m., December 27, three silvery, spherical UFOs were observed by Jack

Telaneus, a Real Estate Investor. Chancing to look up, Telaneus noticed the objects at about 60 degrees moving westerly. The sides of the UFOs toward the sun were reflecting sunlight brightly; the other sides were shadowed. The objects moved on a slightly rising course. Two did not alter their velocity, but one reversed direction, seemed to speed up, and headed back toward the east. All three objects moved out of sight in the distance after about two minutes. [54]

1957: Toronto, Ontario, Canada; On the night of August 1, a hovering UFO was observed by many residents and a telescopic view of it broadcast on television. One of the witnesses was Eric Aldwinckle, a professional artist, who reported the sighting to NICAP. At 9:10 p.m., Aldwinckle saw the brilliant orange-yellow object, appearing as a sizeable light source, and studied it carefully for 20 minutes. In the center were two adjoining oblong orange lights, and these were surrounded by a paler yellow glow. The UFO then began moving toward the northwest, climbing "upward and outward" at "great speed" (estimated 2000 m.p.h.) [55]

1958: Nantucket Channel, Mass.; Joseph Gwooz, Master of the S.S. Nantucket, reported an October 7 sighting to NICAP (quoting from the ship's log): "Time 1455 (2:55 p.m. E.D.T.), entrance Nantucket Channel, while outbound from Nantucket for Martha's Vineyard, Woods Hole and New Bedford. Sighted unknown object hovering in the sky, estimated height 8,000 to 10,000 feet at an angle of about 160 degrees. Object remained stationary for a minute or more, then shot up and away to the N.E. and disappeared out of sight at a rapid rate of speed. Color of object grayish. Oval Shape." A sketch with the report shows an object approximately 2-1/2 times as long as its central width. [56]

1959: Henderson, Nevada; Ed D. Arnold and Berdell S. Haycock, security officers for a metal company, watched a formation flight of four elliptical UFOs about 7:45 p.m., June 11. While on duty at the plant, Arnold noticed the objects and pointed them out to Haycock, who confirmed the sighting. The objects were silvery-white and moving slowly from WSW to ENE, remaining visible about 5 minutes. Arnold, a former Navy air identification and anti-aircraft gunnery control officer, said the UFOs changed formation twice before disappearing. When first observed, the objects were in a circular pattern. "They changed from circular formation to in-line formation, held for two minutes, then back to a circular formation," Arnold stated. During the formation changes, two of the objects dipped slightly below the others. Arnold estimated that the UFOs were about 100 feet long and 25-30 feet in diameter, assuming they were within two miles distance. [57]

1960: Intervale, N.H.; At 8:53 p.m., February 3, William M. Kendrick (former PT Boat Commander) spotted three lighted objects travelling in an in-line formation. The first two were yellow-orange, the third brighter and pulsating from red to orange. As Kendrick continued to watch, the bright UFO appeared to launch a fourth object which joined the formation, which then moved quickly out of sight behind Mt. Washington and Mt. Adams. (Next night, three UFOs were seen near East Madison, N.H., travelling in-line, about 7:00 p.m. The third object pulsated from yellow to bright red.) [58]

1961: Blue Ridge Summit, Penna.; Mrs. James W. Annis, librarian, in the early afternoon of June 4 noticed a large, narrow elliptical object hovering low in the sky to the north. Farther to the east, a cluster of smaller objects hovered. The UFOs were just above treetops on the visible horizon. Mrs. Annis then saw the smaller objects "streak across the sky to the large one." All of the UFOs quickly moved out of sight behind trees to the NNW. Mrs. Annis said the UFOs "were extremely faster than any aircraft I have observed." The weather was clear, with bright sunlight shining on the objects from behind the observer. The large UFO "appeared like the flat end of a clam shell, seen in profile [i.e., elliptical]." [59]

1962: Pompano Beach, Fla.; Mrs. Elizabeth Scott, a housewife and college graduate, saw a hovering cigar-shaped object May 18. The UFO was first noticed about 7:00 p.m. in the northwest sky. The underside was brilliantly lighted, the top dark. For about 9 minutes, the object remained motionless." Then it moved very slowly south for 30 seconds, and then speeded up and disappeared into the southwest very rapidly," Mrs. Scott reported. As it sped away, the lighted underside dimmed suddenly. When it accelerated, it moved "like a flash of lightning," she said. [60]

NOTES

Law Enforcement Officers
1. Teletype report and letter on file at NICAP
2. Reports obtained by Cleveland and Akron UFO groups, on file at NICAP
3-6. Reports on file at NICAP
7. Saturday Evening Post; April 30, 1949. Popular Science; August 1951
8. Seattle Times; July 7, 1947
9. Associated Press; July 28, 1952
10. International News Service; August 28, 1952
11. Washington Times-Herald and Washington Daily News; September 22, 1952
12. Los Angeles Daily News; September 15, 1953
13. Associated Press; November 1, 1955
14. Associated Press; November 26, 1956
15. Chicago Sun Times; November 5, 1957
16. Chicago Sun Times; November 8, 1957
17. Hammond Times; November 11-13, 1957
18. Santa Ana Register; April 10, 1958
19. Bergen Evening Record; August 25, 1958
20. Chicago Daily News; October 13, 1958
21. Report on file at NICAP

Civil Defense, Ground Observer Corps.
22. Stringfield, Leonard H.; Inside Saucer Post...3-0 Blue. (Privately published, 1957; 4412 Grove Avenue, Cincinnati, Ohio), p. 26
23. Tape recorded report on file at NICAP
24. Keyhoe, Donald E., Flying Saucer Conspiracy. (Holt, 1955), p. 30

25. C.R.I.F.O. Newsletter, L.H. Stringfield, Ed.; July 2, 1954 (See address above)
26. Ibid., September 1955.
27. Des Moines Register; November 24, 1955
28. San Bernardino Telegram; July 30, 1956
29. Haverhill Gazette; November 6, 1957
30. El Paso Times; November 24, 1957
31. United Press International, July 26, 1958

Professional and Business Men
32-39. Reports on file at NICAP

Public Officials
40-43. Reports on file at NICAP

Professors and Teachers
44-45. Reports on file at NICAP

Clergymen
46-48. Reports on file at NICAP

Newsmen
49. Associated Press; July 10, 1947
50. Scripps-Howard newspapers; August 2, 1952

Cross-Section
51. Report on file at NICAP
52. Las Vegas Sun; April 22, 1954
53. Uhrichsville Evening Chronicle; October 6, 1955
54-60. Reports on file at NICAP

SECTION VIII

SPECIAL EVIDENCE

There are three basic types of UFO reports:

(1) UFOs detected by the unaided human senses.

(2) UFOs detected by instruments, but not by human senses.

(3) UFOs detected by the human senses, substantiated by instruments.

Of these, the cases of UFOs being detected by the senses and confirmed by instrument generally are considered the most significant. Examples would include UFOs observed visually, which apparently caused electro-magnetic interference at the same time; simultaneous radar-visual sightings; UFOs reliably observed and also photographed. The cases in this section generally involve detection of a UFO by more than one of the human senses, or by the human senses substantiated by some instrument.

The human organism itself is a rudimentary scientific instrument. When a person not only sees something, but also experiences physiological effects of it, an extra dimension is added to the observation. If the effects are objectively verifiable by other persons, so much the better. If a UFO is reliably observed, and also leaves physical markings or traces, this adds an objective factor to the report.

Another way of analyzing UFO sightings is to consider what they affect. A sighting may affect only the human senses; it may also affect machines or instruments (causing electro-magnetic interference in an automobile, leaving an image on film, or showing up on radar); or it may affect nature (leaving physical markings or substances on the ground). The strongest cases would be ones involving several of these aspects.

ELECTRO-MAGNETIC (E-M) EFFECTS

In June 1960 NICAP published a booklet listing and analyzing reported cases in which electrical circuits were disrupted in the presence of UFOs. [1.] This phenomenon was first widely reported during the widespread sightings of November 1957 [See Section XII], but subsequent research uncovered additional cases which occurred before and after the 1957 cases. The E-M report, concluding that the evidence was "sufficient to warrant a more thorough investigation of UFOs, and an attempt to learn more about the E-M phenomenon through deliberate instrumentation for that purpose," was circulated to several hundred interested parties, including scientists and members of Congress.

The E-M Report was a study of 81 main cases, plus 9 borderline cases which had some characteristics in common with the main cases. It was suggested that there were no doubt other similar experiences, either buried in the literature somewhere or unreported due to poor news coverage of UFO sightings at times. In the intervening 3-1/2 years, an additional 39 cases have been discovered. Thirty-two of these had occurred before the June 1960 publication date of the E-M Report; seven have occurred since. Where sufficient information was available to justify their inclusion, the newly discovered cases have been added to the original chronology. The combined listing of cases is reproduced below.

The recent discovery that electrical circuits were upset by upper atmosphere atomic tests during 1961-62 leads to interesting speculation, and makes a definite scientific experiment feasible, concerning the manner in which UFOs could affect electrical circuits. These points are discussed following the chronology of E-M cases.

Chronology of E-M Cases

The cases listed here represent reports in which a distinct UFO, either a plainly visible object or light source (not merely diffuse or intermittent flashes of light), was observed at the same time and place that a definite electro-magnetic effect (E-M) such as a car-stalling occurred. Cases added since publication of the June 1960 report are denoted by a plus sign (+). (Sources appear under Note 2 at the end of the section).

    1. August 28, 1945; near Iwo Jima, C-46 had engine trouble, lost altitude, as three UFOs were observed from plane. [2.]

    2. June 24, 1947; Cascade Mts., Oregon, compass needle waved wildly as UFO passed overhead.

    3. Fall 1949; New Mexico, music on car radio blanked out by static as UFO passed low over car.

(+)4. September 1950; Korea, Navy planes on mission approached by two large discs, radar jammed, radio transmitter blocked by buzzing noise each time new frequency tried.

(+)5. March 26, 1952; Long Beach, Calif. Two yellowish discs passed by slowly; "as they passed the radio was agitated twice."

    6. January 9, 1952; Kerrville, Texas. Odd "roaring" interference on radio as UFO circled town.

(+)7. September 29, 1953; Easton, Pa., Television picture "began going up and down real fast," as UFO emitting white vapor passed overhead.

    8. January 29, 1954; near Santa Ana, Calif., car radio quit and motor missed as UFO passed low over car.

    9. June 21, 1954; Ridgeway, Ontario, Canada, Car motor quit as UFO crossed highway ahead of car.

10. August 30, 1954; Porto Alegre, Brazil. House lights failed as UFO passed.

(+)11. September 16, 1954; Marion, Va. Radio station transmitter failed to operate properly as round shiny UFO passed tower.

12. September 18, 1954; New Mexico. Large green fireball observed; radio and television interference noted over wide area.

13. October 7, 1954; St.-Jean-d'Asse, France. Car motor and headlights failed; UFO over road.

14. October 9, 1954; Cuisy (Seine-Et-Marne), France. Car motor and headlights failed as cigar-shaped UFO passed above.

15. October 11, 1954; Fronfrede (Loire) France. Car motor and headlights failed as UFO crossed road ahead of car, below cloud cover.

16. October 11, 1954; Clamecy (Nievre), France. Car motor and headlights failed, passengers felt shock and numbness; round UFO took off from nearby field.

17. October 11, 1954; Chateauneuf-Sur-Charente, France. Car motor and headlights failed; two UFOs observed at low altitude ahead of car.

18. October 14, 1954; near Brosses-Thillot, Saone-Et-Loire, France. Motorcycle stalled, round lighted UFO observed about 50 yards ahead.

19. October 16, 1954; Baillolet, Seine-Inferieure, France. Four UFOs sighted at low altitude ahead of car. One descended toward road; driver felt shock and numbness, car motor and headlights failed.

20. October 18, 1954; Coheix, Puy-De-Dome, France. Driver of light truck felt half paralyzed, motor began missing; dark elongated object seen in nearby field. Police later searched field, found nothing.

21. October 20, 1954; Schirmeck, France. Motorist felt paralyzed, motor stalled, heat felt; UFO on road.

22. October 21, 1954; near La Rochelle, France. Motorist and child felt shock and heat, motor and headlights failed; then luminous UFO became visible ahead of car.

(+)23. October 23, 1954; Cincinnati, Ohio. Radio made harsh shrieking noise, volume increased; then reddish disc seen circling overhead.

24. October 27, 1954; near Linzeux, France. Headlights and motor failed, two passengers felt "electric shock"; UFO passed ahead of car.

25. November 14, 1954; Forli, Italy. Conventional and diesel tractors driving side by side, conventional stalled, diesel did not, as luminous UFO flew overhead.

26. December 5, 1954; North East, Pa. House radio "pulsated" as UFO observed hovering low over Lake Erie.

27. February 2, 1955; near Valera, Venezuela. Commercial airliner en route from Barquisimeto; radio went dead both at Valera and Barquismeto as pilot started to report a UFO sighting.

28. April 6, 1955; New Mexico. Three unusual green fireballs; heavy radio and TV disturbance.

29. June 26, 1955; Washington, D. C. National airport ceiling lights went out as round UFO approached. UFO caught in searchlight, searchlight went out.

30. August 25, 1955; Bedford, Indiana. House lights dimmed and brightened as hovering UFO pulsated.

(+)31. Sept. or Oct., 1955; Agrinion, Greece. Truck driver and hotel manager driving over mountain road saw luminous object fly overhead, truck engine stopped.

(+)32. May 1954; La Porte, Indiana. Car lights and radio went off, motorist saw three round or oval UFOs moving as unit, emitting beams of light toward ground.

33. May 1, 1954; Tokyo, Japan. TV pictures distorted as UFO passed over.

(+)34. July 28, 1954; Brentwood, Calif. "Sparkling green light" appeared to land in orchard, television reception interrupted.

35. October 1956; Oslo, Norway. Motorist felt "prickly sensation," wristwatch magnetized (according to jeweler) when UFO flew in front of car and hovered over road.

36. November 16, 1956; Lemmon, S.D. Railroad phones, automatic block system "mysteriously dead" as UFO passed over railroad yards.

37. December 1956; Far East. Visual and radar sighting of round UFO by Air Force jet pilot. Radar jammed by strong interference.

38. April 14, 1957; Vins-Sur-Caraney, France. Metal signs magnetized after being observed vibrating as UFO maneuvered nearby. Fifteen degree deviation of compass noted only in immediate area of sighting.

39. April 19, 1957; Maiquetia, Venezuela. Airliner en route to Maiquetia sighted UFO; strange radio signals received at Maiquetia airport at same time.

(+)40. April or May 1957; Moriah Center, N. Y. "Television started to have all sorts of trouble"; witness called outdoors in time to see red disc pass overhead.

41. May 31, 1957; Kent, England. Airliner suffered radio failure during UFO sighting. Normal functions returned when UFO left.

(+)42. June 25, 1957; Baltimore, Maryland. Car radio stopped playing and street lights went out as formation of seven white discs with red rims passed overhead.

43. August 14, 1957; near Joinville, Brazil. Airliner cabin lights dimmed and engine sputtered during UFO sighting.

44. October 15, 1957; Covington, Indiana. Combine engine failed as hovering UFO began to rise.

45. October 30, 1957; Casper, Wyoming. Car motor kept stalling as motorist tried to turn around to avoid UFO sitting on road.

46. October 31, 1957; Lumberton, N.C. Car motor failed as UFO observed.

47. November 2, 1957; near Seminole, Texas. Car motor and headlights failed, UFO seen on road.

48. November 2, 1957; Amarillo, Texas. Car motor failed, UFO seen on road.

49. November 2/3, 1957; Levelland, Texas. Many witnesses in series of sightings watched egg-shaped UFOs on or near ground, nine instances of car motors and lights failing.

50. November 3, 1957; near Calgary, Alta., Canada. Car motor missed, headlights flickered as UFO arced overhead.

51. November 3/4, 1957; Ararangua, Brazil. Airliner direction finder and transmitter-receiver burnt during UFO sighting.

52. November 3/4, 1957; Sao Vicente, Brazil. Itaipu Fort electrical system failed, sentries received burns as UFO approached and hovered.

53. November 4, 1957; Elmwood Park, Illinois. Squad car lights and spotlight dimmed as police pursued low-flying UFO.

54. November 4, 1957; Toronto, Ont., Canada. TV interference (audio); viewers called out by neighbors to see UFO.

55. November 4, 1957; Orogrande, N.M. Car motor stalled, radio failed, heat felt. (James Stokes, White Sands engineer).

56. November 4, 1957; Kodiak, Alaska. A "steady dit-dit-dit" interference on police radio during UFO sighting.

(+)57. November 5, 1957; Ft. Oglethorpe, Ga. Brilliant round orange object hovered, revolving; television blacked out.

(+)58. November 5, 1957; near San Antonio, Texas. Car radio quit, headlights dimmed, engine stopped; UFO seen hovering low over field.

59. November 5, 1957; Hedley, Texas. Farmer saw UFO; neighbor reported TV off at same time.

(+)60. November 5, 1957; Philadelphia, Penna. Apartment lights dead, electric clock stopped; bright light awakened couple. Milkman reported flaming disc.

61. November 5, 1957; Hobbs, N.M. Speeding car, motor failed, lights went out as UFO swooped over car.

62. November 5, 1957; Ringwood, Illinois. UFO followed car returning to town. TV sets in town dimmed, finally lost both picture and sound during same period of time.

63. November 5, 1957; S. Springfield, Ohio. Car and cab stalled as UFO observed.

64. November 6, 1957; Pell City, Alabama. Car motor stalled, as driver attempted to approach UFO hovering low over ground.

65. November 6, 1957; Houston, Texas. Car motor stalled, radio blanked with static, during UFO sighting.

66. November 6, 1957; Santa Fe, N.M. Car motor failed, car clock and wristwatch stopped as UFO passed low over car.

67. November 6, 1957; Danville, Illinois. Police chased UFO, unable to notify headquarters "because their radio went mysteriously dead."

68. November 6, 1957; Montville, Ohio. TV blurred, next day found automobile pockmarked. Night of Olden Moore's report of UFO on ground about one-half mile from viewer's house.

69. November 6, 1957; north of Ottawa, Canada. Battery radio and portable short wave radio failed, then single tone signal heard on one short wave frequency. UFO hovering below overcast. Radios worked normally after UFO departed.

70. November 7, 1957; Lake Charles, La. Car motor sputtered and failed as UFO hovered low overhead.

71. November 7, 1957; near Orogrande, N.M. Car traveling about 60 mph. Speedometer waved wildly between 60 and 110. UFO then sighted. (Car was 1954 Mercury with magnetic speedometer.)

72. November 9, 1957; Near White Oaks, N.M. Car lights failed as UFO observed.

73. November 10, 1957; Hammond, Indiana. Loud beeping caused radio interference as police chased UFO. TV blackout in city, motorist reported radio failure.

74. November 12, 1957; Rumney, N.H. Car motor and lights failed. Ground observer corps reported UFO at same time.

75. November 12 or 13, 1957; Hazelton, Penna. TV disrupted as UFO seen.

76. November 14, 1957; Tamaroa, Illinois. Power failed for 10 minutes in a four mile area, just after hovering UFO flashed.

77. November 15, 1957; Cachoeira, Brazil. Several car motors failed as drivers attempted to approach UFO hovering low above ground.

78. November 25, 1957; Mogi Mirim, Brazil. All city lights failed as three UFOs passed overhead.

79. December 3, 1957; Near Ellensburg, Washington. Truck motor "almost stopped," caught again, as UFO sighted. Sighting confirmed by police.

80. December 3, 1957; Cobalt, Ont., Canada. Radio static as several UFOs seen over area.

81. December 8, 1957; Near Coulee City, Washington. Automobiles stalled, headlights flickered and went out, as large fiery object passed overhead.

82. December 18, 1957; Sarasota, Florida. White light source glided overhead, TV interference noted.

83. January 13, 1958; Casino, N.S.W., Australia. Interference on car radio as UFO followed car.

84. January 30, 1958; near Lima, Peru. Truck, bus, and car passengers felt shock; motors of all three vehicles failed, as UFO descended and hovered.

(+)85. February 24, 1958; Near Santa Antonio de Jesus, Brazil. Car motor failed; passengers then noticed a Saturn-shaped disc hovering overhead.

(+)86. May 1958; Near Richmond, Va. Engine of car began running roughly, driver then noticed UFO following car.

87. August 3, 1958; Rome Italy. Luminous UFO observed passing overhead as city lights failed; one report of car radio failure.

88. August 31, 1958; La Verde, Argentina. Light aircraft (Piper) engine increased its revolutions abnormally during UFO sighting. Engine normal after UFO left.

(+)89. October 3, 1958; Fukushima-Ken, Japan. Portable radio emitted strange buzz as green fireball passed.

90. October 26, 1958; Baltimore, Maryland. UFO observed hovering over bridge ahead of car; motor and headlights failed, two passengers felt heat.

91. January 13, 1959; Pymatuning Lake, Penna. Truck motor, lights and radio failed as UFO hovered over truck.

92. January 13, 1959; Bygholm, Denmark. Car motor failed as UFO passed overhead; headlights and spotlight functioned normally.

93. February 25, 1959; Hobbs, N.M. Signals on car radio (steady succession of two dots and a dash) as UFO passed.

(+)94. March 19, 1959; Kyger, Ohio. Buzzing static-like sound on car radio. Lights dimmed; unidentified light source seen ahead of car.

95. June 22, 1959; Salta, Argentina. Luminous sphere observed passing in sky, city lights failed.

(+)96. July 14, 1959; Salisbury, N.C. Television sets blacked out, some lights reported off, as circular UFO observed; loud oscillating high frequency noise reported.

97. August 13, 1959; Freeport, Texas. UFO crossed road ahead of car at low altitude. Motor and headlights failed.

(+)98. August 17, 1959; Uberlandia, Minais Gerais, Brazil. Automatic keys at power station turned off as round UFO passed overhead following trunk line. After UFO left, keys turned back on automatically, normal functions resumed.

99. October 22, 1959; Cumberland, Maryland. Car motor, headlights, and radio failed as UFO hovered low over road ahead.

100. January 18, 1960; Near Lakota, No. Dak. Car lights dimmed as UFO descended toward field, apparently about a mile off highway.

(+)101. February 28, 1961; Lakeville, Mass. House lights dimmed three times, went out on two occasions as elongated UFO twice passed overhead.

(+)102. February 9, 1962; Ashton Clinton, Beds., England. Car motor lost power, headlights not affected, as UFO passed ahead of car.

(+)103. July 30, 1962; Near Pojucara, Belo Horizonte, Brazil. Car motor stopped, then oval UFO seen alongside road.

(+)104. September 20, 1963; Wonthaggi, Victoria, Australia. TV difficulty noted, viewer called outside to see UFO. Object hovered, darted around at high speed. TV interference noted over area of three towns.

(+)105. November 7, 1963; San Francisco, Calif. Fireball observed, shock wave felt, over Bay area. Unidentified signal picked up by local radio station.

(+)106. November 14, 1963; Carson City, Nevada. Disc with bluish-green glow hovered emitting beam of light which illuminated hilltop; house radio failed, came back on when UFO left.

E-M Cases (Continued)

Secondary Cases:
These borderline cases have some characteristics in common with those on the main chronology. In each case, a definite E-M effect was reported. However, either the associated aerial phenomenon was not distinct or it could not be determined that an E-M effect and a UFO sighted nearby coincided in time.

(a) July 6, 1947; Acampo, Calif. All lights in community went out, as citizens heard a roaring noise and saw a glow in the sky.

(b) July 20, 1952; Cumberland, Md. Engineer reported unusual type of TV interference. Occurred within a few hours of the famous Washington, D.C., UFO sightings all over D.C.-Virginia area.

(c) January 21, 1957; Bristol, England. TV pictures disrupted and noise heard on audio; same time as fiery light in sky with rays running through it. (Aurora?)

(d) January 27, 1957; Glendora, Calif. Unexplained power failure. Two UFOs reported same night in general area.

(e) May 7, 1957; New York, N.Y. TV disrupted, citizens complained about low-flying "aircraft". Commercial test plane blamed, but Air Force reported several unidentified blips on radar.

(f) September 1, 1957; LeMars, Iowa. Car motor and headlights failed, as flash of light seen in sky.

(g) November 2 or 3, 1957; Las Cruces, N.M. Car motor and headlights failed twice as witness, a UFO skeptic, saw flashes of light in the sky. Witness blamed it on "static atmosphere."

(h) November 28, 1957; Hakalau, Hawaii. Car motor failed, driver felt numb, as bright flash of light appeared in sky about 20 feet above highway ahead of car.

(i) December 1, 1957; Ann Arbor, Michigan. Telephone lines affected by odd noise in Detroit area, as numerous red lights observed in sky. (Aurora?)

(j) Approximately August 16, 1958; Olean, N.Y. and Eldred, Penna. Strange noise lasting one minute heard on short wave, 20 meter band, in Olean. UFO seen in nearby Eldred about same time.

(k) December 7, 1959; Bangor, Me. Airport runway lights went out, airliner circling over field reported unexplained blinding glow around plane.

During the summer of 1963 the story broke that Russian nuclear tests of 1961-1962 in the atmosphere had knocked out the electronic equipment on board a U.S. satellite in space. [3.] Publicity about this little-known side effect of high-yield nuclear explosions immediately led to speculation on the military applications of it. A prominent magazine on space activities later that year reported that the Soviet Union might be developing an anti-ballistic missile system based on the E-M effects of nuclear blasts. [4.]

The main significance of this discovery, in relation to UFOs, is that it provides a clue about how UFOs might affect the electrical systems of automobiles. American scientists have theorized that an "electromagnetic pulse" is emitted by large nuclear explosions at high altitude. John Crittenden, General Electric consultant on radiation, has stated: "The detonation of (nuclear) weapons produces radiation over the entire electromagnetic spectrum. The prompt gamma pulse will affect electronic devices sensitive to ionization, and the radio-frequency signal propagated carries enough energy to damage electronic circuits drastically. . ." Mr. Crittenden added that a one-megaton explosion in space could affect electronic systems over a radius of 110 miles or more.

In testimony before the House Committee on Science & Astronautics, major aerospace firms have strongly advocated the development of an atomic engine for use in the U.S. space program. [5.] Douglas Aircraft Corporation, for example, citing the inefficiency and great expense of normal rocket boosters, stated: "A gross reduction of these costs will come only with the development of a propulsion system with truly superior performance. Only then will extensive manned space travel on an interplanetary scale be practical. In our opinion, the greatest immediate hope for such an improvement may be found in nuclear propulsion systems. . ." [6.]

The energy locked up in matter, obviously, is universal. UFOs could plausibly have some nuclear propulsion component, perhaps controlled explosions which incidentally interfere with electrical circuits under certain conditions. (Another conceivable explanation for the E-M effects observed in the presence of UFOs is that some atomic device or weapon on board is used deliberately and selectively, as a test or for other purposes. However, this is purely speculative).

The fact remains that is is not necessary to postulate a "mysterious force" in some mystical sense to account for the observed effects. An atomic device capable of producing the observed effects is now technologically feasible. Even if this were not the case, it is false logic for a scientist to deny observations on the grounds that we cannot fully explain the mechanism involved in E-M effects. Taken in association with the other accumulated evidence about UFOs, the fact that we do have difficulty explaining the E-M effects could also mean that we are dealing with a superior technology about which we know very little.

RADAR UFO SIGHTINGS

Unidentified targets have been detected by radar on numerous occasions. Air Force radar-scope photographs of UFOs are classified (see box), but the facts of many radar observations have been published. The question is, what causes the unexplained "blips" on the scope? On the whole, theorists have tended to attribute all such reports to the vagaries of radar. This view is challenged here.

NICAP's position is that the radar-UFO reports, after all, were made largely by experienced radar operators who were convinced they had tracked something solid and unexplained. The conflict amounts to data versus theory, with most theorists all too prone to assume that radar operators are incompetent.

It is a well-known fact that false (or misleading) images can appear on radar scopes. However, if these could not be distinguished from the blips of solid targets, radar would be a useless instrument. Also, lights and objects have been observed visually in the positions where radar indicated the presence of unexplained objects. The theorists' ad hoc arguments to account for this aspect of the reports leave much to be desired.

What can radar detect? How do different phenomena appear on the scope? What are so-called radar "angels?" These questions are analyzed following the chart which includes the controversial cases under discussion.

Radar Cases

G = Ground Radar   V = Visual Sighting
A = Airborne Radar   P = Photograph

Code	Date & Location	Description	Speed	Altitude	Sources & References
G	Summer 1948 Goose Bay, Labrador	USAF and RCAF radar independently tracked unidentified target.	9000 mph.	60,000 ft.	[Details this Section]
A, V	October 15, 1948 Japan	Air Force F-61 night interceptor tracked and saw visually UFO shaped "like a rifle bullet." On one pass, F-61 got close enough to see silhouette 20-30 ft. long.	Abt. 200 mph. Accel. to est. 1200 mph.	5000 - 6000 ft.	[7]
G	November 1, 1948 Goose Bay, Labrador	UFO tracked	600 mph.		[8]
G	November 6, 1948 Japan	Air Force radar tracked two maneuvering UFOs for over an hour. On scope, looked like two planes dogfighting.			[9]
G, V	November 23, 1948 Fursten-Feldbruck, Germany	UFO tracked, reddish star-like object observed visually. Climbed 23,000 feet in few minutes.	900 mph.		[10]
G	Fall 1949 Key atomic base	Five UFOs in formation clocked covering 300 miles in less than 4 minutes	4500 mph. (average)		[11]
G, V	February 22, 1950 Key West, Fla.	Two glowing objects sped over Naval Air Station			[Section IV]
G, V	March 8, 1950 Dayton, Ohio	Two F-51 pilots saw "huge and metallic" UFO which ground radar detected. Object gave solid "blip", climbed vertically		15,000 ft.	[12]

76

Code	Date & Location	Description	Speed	Altitude	Sources & References
A, V	July 11, 1950 nr. Osceola , Arkansas	Disc-shaped UFO sighting visual-ly by Navy pilots, tracked by air-borne radar	200 mph.	Est. 8000 ft.	[Section IV]
G, V, P	July 14, 1951 White Sands, New Mexico	UFO sped near B-29, tracked on radar; 200 ft. of 35 mm film re-portedly shows bright round spot.			[13]
G, V	July 23, 1951 March Field, California	UFO tracked on radar, pilots saw silvery object circling above them		50,000 ft.	[14]
G	August 26, 1951 Washington State	Two radar sets tracked UFO headed northwest	900 mph.		[15]
G, A	Fall 1951 Korean area	Over 14 Navy radar sets tracked UFO circling above fleet. (signed report at NICAP)	Slow to over 1000 mph.	5000 ft.	[Details this Section]
G, A	January 22, 1952 Alaska	Three F-94s scrambled to inter-cept radar target; UFO maneu-vered, ground radar saw object streak away to west	1500 mph.	23,000 ft.	[16]
G	June 1, 1952 Los Angeles, Cal.	Hughes Aircraft radar tracked UFO which climbed at 35,000 ft. per min., levelled off, dove, pulled out, and headed southeast.	180-550 mph.	11,000 ft.	[17]
G, V	June 19, 1952 Goose Bay, Labrador	Red-lighted object approached base, radar blip enlarged as object seemed to wobble.			[18]
G, V	July 1, 1952 Ft. Monmouth, New Jersey	Two shiny objects tracked; moved slowly, hovered, burst of speed to southwest. Coincided with other visual observations.	Slow - "terrific burst of speed."	50,000 ft.	[19]
G, V	July 10, 1952 Near Korea	Canadian destroyer tracked two shiny discs; calculated altitude of 2 miles, 7 miles from ship.		2 miles	[20]
G, V	July 19/20, 1952 Washington, D. C.	UFO's tracked by CAA and Air Force radar; some visual sightings coinciding.	"On the order of 7500 mph." (Air Force "fact sheet")		[Section XII; July 1952 Chron-ology]
G	July 21, 1952 Dobbins AFB, Ga.	UFO tracked at 10:30 am.	1200 mph	Abt. 50,000 ft.	[21]
G, A, V	July 23, 1952 Braintree, Mass.	F-94 pilot obtained radar lock-on while chasing blue-green light which circled at high speed.			[22]
G, V	July 26/27, 1952 Washington, D. C.	Series of radar-visual sightings involving CAA airline and Air Force pilots.	Some "slow-moving," some "fast."		[Section XII; July 1952 Chron-ology]
G, A, V	July 26, 1952 California	F-94 interceptor obtained radar lock-on, UFO kept pulling away. Visually appeared as large yellow-orange light.	Slow to "terrific speed"		[23]
G, V	July 28, 1952 Wisconsin-- Minnesota	USAF jets chased UFO tracked by ground radar, UFO's sped up and evaded interceptors.	60 to over 600 mph		[24]
G	July 28/29, 1952 Washington, D. C.	Eight to twelve UFO's tracked at a time on CAA radar; airline pilot investigated, saw nothing but CAA said targets disappeared from screen when plane was in their area, then came in behind plane.			[Section XII; July 1952 Chron-ology]
G, A, V	July 29, 1952 Michigan	F-94's attempted to intercept radar traget, observed visually as flashing red and green light, then solid white. (From USAF Intelligence Report)	635 mph	20,000 ft.	[25]
G, V	Summer 1952 MacDill AFB,	UFO target tracked at base. Air Force bomber in area investigated saw maneuverable egg-shaped UFO.	400 knots (460 mph)	40,000 ft.	[Section III]
G, V, P	August 1, 1952 Wright-Patterson AFB, Ohio	UFO tracked, seen visually and photographed by F-86 pilot.	480 mph	Above 40,000 ft.	[26]

Code	Date & Location	Description	Speed	Altitude	Sources & References
G, V	August 3, 1952 Hamilton AFB, Calif.	Two silver discs "dogfighting" joined by six others, took diamond formation and sped away as jets scrambled.			[27]
G, A, V	August 5, 1952 Haneda AFB, Japan	Circular UFO tracked; ap- proached field and hovered visible from control tower. Sped away dividing into 3 parts.	300 knots		[28]
G	August 20, 1952 Congaree AFB, S.C.	Air Defense Command radar tracked UFO 60 miles from base	Over 4000 mph		[29]
G	During period of 9-51 to 11-52 Prominent east coast AF base.	Confidential report, certified by NICAP Board Member, Rev. Albert Baller. Moving object tracked about 15 miles from base. Stopped for long period of time, vanished as plane approached.			[Details this Section]
G	November 25/26, 1952 Panama Canal	two UFO's tracked by defense radar.			[30]
A, V	December 6, 1952 Gulf of Mexico	B-29 crew tracked several small, one large, object; saw speeding lights coinciding with radar tracks.	5240- 9000 mph.	18,000 ft.	[31]
A, V	December 10, 1952 Nr Hanford, Wash.	F-94 obtained radar lock-on, UFO seen as round, white, with "windows"			[32]
A, V	December 16, 1952 Goose Bay, Labrador	F-94 obtained radar lock-on; UFO observed visually as red light changing to white during maneuvers.			[33]
G, V	December 29, 1952 Japan	UFO spotted by B-29 crew, tracked on radar. Jet pilot investigated, saw rotating lights on UFO, and three fixed beams of light from it.		35,000 ft.	[34]
A, V	January 9, 1953 Japan	Second "rotating lights" case, similar to above.			[34]
G, V	January 26, 1953 New Mexico	Bright red-white UFO, official "unknown." Travelled steadily into the wind.	12-15 knots (abt. 17 mph)	10,000 - 15,000 ft.	[35]
G, V	January 28, 1953 Nr Albany, Ga.	Ground radar tracked UFO, inter- ceptor pilot saw circular object. UFO travelled slowly; radar indicated it sped up as interceptor neared.		Below 30,000 ft.	[36]
G, V	February 7, 1953 Korean area	F-94 scrambled after radar target, pilot saw UFO as bright orange light which changed altitude, sped away.			[37]
A, V	February 13, 1953 Fort Worth, Texas	Radar-visual sighting by B-36 crew			[38]
G	May 23, 1953 Cape, So. Africa	Air Force radar tracked UFO on six passes.	Over 1250 mph	5000 - 15,000 ft.	[39]
G, V	Summer 1953 Yaak, Montana	Six UFO's observed visually and tracked by USAF radar site; ob- jects changed formation repeated- ly.	1400 - 1600 mph		[Details this Section]
G, A, V, P	August 12, 1953 Rapid City, So. Dak.	Official "unknown". Cat-and-mouse jet chase. UFO fled, turned back and followed jet. Gun camera photo showed image.	Hover - over 500 mph	16,000 ft.	[40]
G, V	November 3, 1953 London, England	Circular, flattened white UFO tracked, seen by telescope, also by interceptor pilots.			[41]
G	November 23, 1953 Kinross AFB, Michigan	F-89 lost pursuing unidentified radar target, blip of aircraft seen to merge with UFO blip. No trace ever found.			[42]
G, V	May 13, 1954 Washington, D. C.	Several large glowing objects seen by National Airport police; tracked on airport radar.	Hover-abt. 200 mph.	Abt. 80,000 ft.	[43]
G, V	June 30, 1954 Brookley AFB, Alabama	Silvery UFO tracked, observed visually from base tower. Con- firmed by base PIO, Maj. James Zicherelli.			[44]

Code	Date & Location	Description	Speed	Altitude	Sources & References
G, V	July 3, 1954 Albuquerque, New Mexico	Nine green spheres hovered, sped away, tracked by radar.	About 2600 mph.	24,000 ft.	[45]
G, V	August 28, 1954 Tinker AFB, Oklahoma	Fifteen UFO's in triangle formation tracked on radar, chased by jets; changed to semi-circle formation and sped away.			[46]
G, A, V	August or September, 1954 White Plains, N.Y.	Circular UFO tracked across N. Y. by GOC, Air Force radar.		Above 45,000 ft.	[Section VII]
G, V	September 17, 1954 Rome, Italy	Italian Air Force radar tracked disc-like UFO sene by thousands.	About 150 mph; burst of speed upwards.	3600 ft.	[47]
G, V	November 12, 1954 Kentucky, (Indiana, Ohio)	Air Force interceptors chased spherical object seen over tri-state area; also followed by theodolite.			[48]
G, V	December 15, 1954 Nr Nowra, Australia	Royal Australian Navy pilot returning to base, joined by two "strange aircraft resembling flying saucers." Ground radar showed his Seafury, when pilot identified self by moving according to pattern, and also two other objects.			[49]
G, V	August 23, 1955 Cincinnati, Ohio	SAC radar detected UFO's Jets engaged in dogfight with three circular objects.			[Section VII]
G, V	December 11, 1955 Nr Jacksonville, Fla.	Navy Jets in dogfight with UFO, confirmed on radar.			[Section IV]
G, V	February 17, 1956 Paris, France	Orly Airport radar tracked UFO, larger than commercial airliner. Observed by Air France pilot as blinking red light. UFO maneuvered erratically, alternately hovering and moving with jet-like bursts of speed.			[50]
G, V	July 19, 1956 Hutchinson, Kansas	Naval Air Station tracked UFO, observed visually by State Police and pilots as erratically moving tear-drop shaped object.			[51]
G, V	July 29, 1956 Pasadena, California	GOC spotters sighted brilliant white UFO, tracked by Air Defense Command radar. GOC said UFO appeared to stop, then speed up again "faster than a conventional airplane."			[Section VII]
G	Aug.-Sept., 1956 Bornholm Island, Denmark	Report September 11 that NATO radar had been tracking UFO's for three weeks, curving over Baltic Sea.	2000-- 3500 mph.		[52]
G, V	September 4, 1956 Copenhagen, Denmark	Several "fireball"-like UFO's flew over, tracked by radar.	3000 km/h (abt. 1800 mph.)	5000 meters	[53]
G	November 8, 1956 Miami, Florida	Donald Freestone, Pan American master radar mechanic, tracked UFO maneuvering like "aerial tag" over tip of Florida. (Bendix RDR-1A weather radar.) "It had a definite shape and moved on a definite course so is not believed to have been a freak weather return." Object 4-5 times larger than any known aircraft.	Hover - 4000 mph.	7000 - 8000 ft.	[54]
G, A, V	November 25, 1956 Hot Springs, So. Dakota	Series of UFO sightings, one by state police of circular object swaying back and forth across road. Objects detected by radar, jets scrambled from Ellsworth AFB, S.D.			[55]
A, V	December 1956 Far East	USAF jet tracking UFO, radar jammed by interference; changed frequency and picked up UFO again, saw circular object climb away.	3600 mph.	Below 10,000 ft.	[Section I]

G, V	March 23, 1957 Long Beach, Calif.	Four UFOs tracked by CAA radar. (Confidential report certified by 6 NICAP Board Members) Coincided with visual reports by GOC, police and Oxnard AFB.			[Details this Section]
A, V	March 29, 1957	Pan American Airways flight #206A, saw pulsating UFO, radar target coincided.			[Section V]
G	April 4, 1957 Wigtownshire, Scotland	Three radar posts tracked UFO which dove and circled. Wing Cdr. W. P. Whitworth (at Scottish base): "Quite definitely this was no freak. It was an object of some substance and no mistake could have been made."		60,000 to 14,000 ft.	[56]
G, V	October 21 or 29, 1957 Nr London, England	UFO sighted visually by pilot near atomic base, tracked by ground radar; dimmed lights and sped away.			[57]
G, V	November 5, 1957 Gulf of Mexico	Coast Guard Cutter Sebago tracked UFO, brief visual sighting from deck.	1020 mph		[Details this Section]
G, V	December 12, 1957 Tokyo, Japan	GCI radar tracked UFO seen by ground observers as vari-colored object; jets scrambled.			[58]
G	March 8, 1958 Korea	USAF radar site tracked slowly de- scending UFO.		77,000 - 25,000 ft.	[59]
G, V	Summer 1958 Air Force Base, SW United States.	Two maneuverable UFOs tracked, evaded jet interceptors.			[60]
G	November, 1958 Dewline radar	UFO descended from maximum alt. range of radar, moved horizontally for 100 miles, ascended vertically.	500 knots (abt. 575 mph.)		[62]
G, V	January 23, 1959 Panama Canal	Bright silver object arced across sky, tracked by U.S. radar.			[63]
G, V	September 24, 1959 Redmond, Oregon	Air Force radar site reportedly tracked UFO, observed visually by FAA personnel at airport as disc- shaped object.			[Section V, IX]
G, V	August 13, 1960 Red Bluff, California	State Police observed egg-shaped UFO reported USAF radar site confirmed tracking it.			[Section VII, IX]
G	January 1961 Missile Base during missile test flight	UFO which alternately hovered and moved rapidly to new position, tracked.			[64]
G, V	June 19, 1961 Exeter, England; Edinburgh, Scotland	Large, bright shining UFO observed at Exeter airport, tracked on radar. Cigar-object and speeding light ob- served over Edinburgh twice during preceding night.	Hovered	50,000 ft.	[65]
G, V	July 5, 1961 Akron, Ohio	Former AF pilot saw maneuvering glowing UFO, also tracked by FAA radar at Cleveland airport.			[Section V]
G, A, V	January 29, 1962 Eastern Holland	Royal Dutch Air Force jet intercep- tor chased UFO detected by ground and airborne radar, and visually.			[Section X]

Official Speed Records: Aircraft

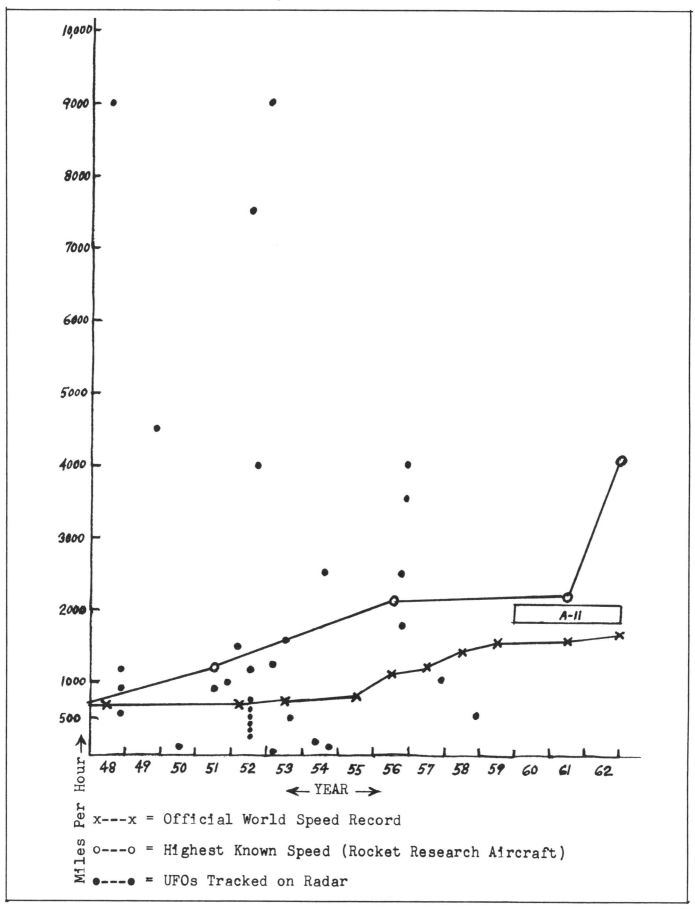

x---x = Official World Speed Record

o---o = Highest Known Speed (Rocket Research Aircraft)

●----● = UFOs Tracked on Radar

RADAR: THEORY & FACT

Except for cases of so-called "anomalous propagation"--false radar targets caused by bending or refraction of radar signals-- UFO targets on radar constitute objective confirmation of the reality of unexplained objects in the atmosphere. Some research reports have tended to explain-away radar UFO sightings as "false targets. . .[sometimes caused by] a low angle radar beam . . . reflected from one surface to another before retracing its path to the radar." [66] Unexplained radar targets have been observed since the early days of radar.

Some evaluations of this phenomenon appear to be more a rationalization of troublesome reports than objective studies of them. Facts of observation seemingly are ignored or glossed over in order to make a theory fit. A prime example of this procedure is the study by the Civil Aeronautics Administration (CAA) of the famous July 1952 radar sightings over Washington, D.C. [67] The CAA report concludes that the Washington sightings were "ground returns caused by reflection phenomena closely connected with the temperature inversions in the lower atmosphere."

Table 1 of the CAA report, "Tabulation of Unidentified Radar Targets and Visual Objects Reported to Washington ARTC Center," includes one case for May, twenty-two for July, and 11 for August. Yet the text goes into detail on, and bases its conclusions on, only reports for the nights of August 14/15 and August 15/16. Unlike the July cases, there were no visual sightings on these nights and the recorded speeds were extremely slow (about 24-70 m.p.h.) The characteristics of the phenomena on these nights, and the lack of visual sightings, do resemble so-called "angels" (which are themselves little understood non-visual phenomena). By contrast, many of the July cases involved objects tracked in high-speed flight and also observed visually by pilots exactly where radar showed the objects to be.

Evaluations of this kind, aside from their glaring omissions of data and questionable reasoning, fail to take into account two vitally important points: (1) Because of the long history of false radar targets, they and their characteristics are well-known to experienced radar operators. (2) The bending of radar beams and creation of false targets on the scope cannot explain sustained radar-visual sightings. If a pilot sees a light source or object which changes its angular position radically, and ground radar shows a target maneuvering as described right where the pilot is looking, this cannot be explained in terms of the erratics of radar.

Because it is known that false targets do occur on radar screens which can be misinterpreted by inexperienced operators, radar-visual sightings in general are more significant evidence than reports lacking visual confirmation. As in all other aspects of UFO investigation, it is necessary to weed out erroneous reports and to recognize that human error is possible. But the same logic often applied to UFOs in general seems to be used by skeptics on radar cases: Because error is possible, and because some people definitely have been mistaken, all the reports are false. This is known as throwing out the baby with the bath-water.

What Radar Shows

In general, a blip on radar always corresponds to a reflection off of some solid (or liquid) surface, though that surface may not be where the radar scope indicates it to be. The surface may be (a) a mass of raindrops in a cloud in the position where radar shows it to be; (b) a solid object in the air in the position where radar shows it to be; (c) something on the ground, reflecting back to the scope and only seeming to be an object in the air. The latter explanation commonly is invoked to account for all radar UFO reports.

This highlights the real problem of radar sightings: Interpretation of the scope by radar operators. The phenomenon most subject to misinterpretation is the "ducting" effect, where low-angle radar beams are bent around the earth's curvature. An object which would ordinarily be out of radar range might then be detected, and mistaken for something which seems to be closer and in a different position. A radar set can pick up echoes of its beam which have bounced around from more than one reflecting surface, and back to the antenna. In a case of this type, it would be severely strained coincidence for an unidentified object to be sighted visually in the same position as the false radar target.

Weather Targets on Radar

Weather targets on radar may be ruled out generally as a source of false UFO reports. Clouds and cold fronts are not detected by radar, except for rain-carrying clouds, in which case it is the moisture (precipitation) which is detected. An Air Force manual on the subject states " . . . in general, strong radar echoes will be returned only from air of high specific humidity in which intense convective activity releases water in large amounts." [68] The echoes received are "false" only in the sense of not representing solid airborne objects. They are real liquid objects collectively acting as reflectors of the radar beam.

Section II, Paragraph 15 of the Air Force manual discusses "Interpretation of Echoes." In general, weather targets show up as diffuse masses on the radar screen, and their origin is easily recognizable.

Dense nimbostratus from which rain is falling, the manual states, can be detected to short or moderate ranges. ". . . echoes from nimbostratus usually appear on the PPI [Plan Position Indicator] scope as a mass of brightness concentrated about the center of the scope and merging into the blackness of the outer rings. . . there are many breaks and irregularities in the pattern since rain does not fall uniformly over even a small area."

Radar Angels

A recent example of radar angels occurred at the NASA Wallops Island, Virginia, base during the Spring of 1962. The observations were analyzed by the Cornell University Center for Radiophysics and Space Research, for the Air Force Cambridge Research Laboratory. [69] The analysts theorized that "plate-like" objects could explain the observations, but commented: "It is difficult to conceive of foreign objects in the atmosphere having this plate-like shape. It is even more difficult to imagine that such objects would invariably maintain a consistent horizontal orientation while passing over the radar station. . ."

Although it is clear that radar angels have not been satisfactorily explained, the Center suggested that "most" of them were "caused either by very smooth layers of refractive index gradient or by a single intense [atmospheric] discontinuity. . ."

What are radar "angels?" Used in its broadest sense, the term applies to all unidentified targets on radar. But this terminology is misleading, since the targets have been of three basic and distinct types: (1) Diffuse and intermittent targets probably attributable to meteorological effects; (2) Sharp, "solid" targets which give a persistent blip exactly like that of a moving metallic aircraft (sometimes also observed visually); (3) groups of targets, usually in very slow-moving meandering swarms, for which there are no known visual observations. We prefer to adopt the terminology of CSI, a UFO investigation group in New York City, and call the third type "angels;" the second "UFOs."

The research section of CSI has published an excellent analysis of radar angels; pertinent extracts are quoted here.

"ANGELS" Explained by Two Experts
(Two Different Ways)

Typical "angels" are characterized by being gregarious, slow-traveling (30-60 mph.), and much more conspicuous to radar than to the eye - in fact, it may be that no one has ever seen them except on a radarscope. They have been observed ever since 1943, when microwave radar was first being developed, and they have never been acceptably explained.

The celebrated Washington radar sightings of July 1952 occurred during a period when typical angels were being seen there abundantly (for details, see C.A.A. Technical Report #180, Note 67). . .

The radar visibility of birds happens to be known; it is very much less than that of angels. Birds (and a fortiori, flocks of birds) can be detected on a powerful radar set - at distances up to a mile or two. Bonham and Blake, authors of an earlier claim that angels could be identified with birds (Scientific Monthly, April 1956), admitted that the visually-confirmed birds they were able to pick up on radar were at distances "considerably less than a mile." Yet all authors agree that angels are clearly visible at distances of 25 miles or even more. If the "bird" theory is correct, it must be possible to show that ordinary aircraft-control radar can "see" a bird 25 miles away. No evidence that this is true has ever been presented, and no practicing radar operator will take such a suggestion seriously for a moment. . .

Something that appears only sporadically, like angels, cannot - in the name of simple common sense - be identified with something that is around all the time, like birds. That the bird-theorists can ignore difficulties as fundamental as this one only shows us once again how irrational the human mind can be when confronted by facts that point to some conclusion it does not wish to accept. . .

The other leading "orthodox" idea about angels is that they are "refractive-index inhomogeneities of various types," in the words of a valuable though turgidly-written article by Vernon G. Plank of the Air Force's Cambridge Research Center (Bedford, Mass.) in Electronics of March 14, 1958. Plank, like Harper, nails his thesis to the mast in his title: "Atmospheric Angels Mimic Radar Echoes." As for birds, he informs us that they have "radar cross-sections as large as 20 sq. cm at S-Band. . . Radar cross-sections of the non-wind-carried sources range as large as 700 sq. cm at L-Band. . . birds cannot explain echoes with such large indicated radar cross-sections. There must be other sources." (In other words: the angels give a radar echo far stronger than that from a bird). This confirms what we have said above about the applicability of the bird theory.

But when Plank puts forward "convective bubbles, highly refractive portions of atmospheric layers and water-vapor or temperature anomaly regions" as his candidates, he is shutting his eyes to known impossibilities just as the bird-men have done. Not only are such atmospheric phenomena obviously incapable of flying counter to the wind, but they are known to be just as incapable as birds of producing the sharp, relatively intense "angel" echoes. To quote Herbert Goldstein in the authoritative Radiation Laboratory treatise Propagation of Short Radio Waves, ed. D. E. Kerr (McGraw-Hill, 1951): "In Section 7.4 it is shown that the refractive index gradients believed to exist in the atmosphere are much too low to account for the observed echoes." . . .

"Then there are radar flying saucers." Plank continues. Here he cites no detail, and has only two remarks to make. "The classic saucer incidents over Washington in July, 1952, for example, occurred when the atmosphere was exceedingly super-refractive and spotty anomalous propagation was definitely in order.". . . (In reality, there was only a moderate inversion on those nights, and "spotty anomalous propagation" is a purely imaginary phenomenon. It has never been known to occur, there is no theoretical basis for believing that it could occur, and it would have had no resemblance to the Washington sightings if it did occur.) Plank's other "saucer mechanism" (as he calls it) is the suggestion that real aircraft may generate ghost images by reflection to and back from some radar mirror on the ground, thus producing a phantom echo that might seem to accompany the plane. The accompanying diagram [in the original article] shows that Plank is unconscious of the optical grotesquerie of what he is proposing. Quite apart from that, he has not stopped to think that if this could happen at all, it would happen all the time, and would be a perfectly familiar nuisance to the radar men.

The idea that reflection from refractive index gradients could account for radar UFO reports is also challenged by Merrill J. Skolnik, a scientist associated with the Research Division of Electronic Communications, Inc. In a 1962 book on the subject of radar, Mr. Skolnik states: ". . . there must be a large change in the index of refraction over a very short distance [to account for the observed radar targets]. Unfortunately, the refractive-index gradients required by the theory are much greater than have been measured experimentally, and it has not been possible on this basis to account for the observed angel radar cross sections theoretically."

[70]

One of the persons consulted in preparing this report was a veteran Air Force radar operator, a Sgt. First Class, who has operated sets all over the world. He has also tracked unidentified targets, at White Sands, N.M.; in Detroit, Michigan; and during NATO maneuvers overseas. He stated that he had observed some "solid unidentified targets moving at variable speeds, up to 500 mph." He had observed targets which disappeared and reappeared on his scope. Sometimes the objects simply moved out of range.

Ionized air "islands," which are commonly invoked to explain radar-UFO reports, he said were easily recognizable. Their blips "pile up" and they tend to develop a comet-like tail on the screen. Birds, he said, cause no problem even to novice operators fresh out of radar school. The targets which caused problems were those which exactly resembled a solid object, when there was no known aerial device in the position indicated. Special records are kept of all such sightings. Usually, in a case of this type, jets are scrambled and other radar stations along the path of the UFO notified.

Another consultant, David L. Morgan, Jr. (physicist), Madison, Connecticut, submitted a paper to NICAP which he preferred to term "thoughts on the matter" rather than a detailed scientific study. In it, Mr. Morgan approached the question of radar-UFO targets theoretically, based on a general knowledge of physics. Citing hypothetical cases of different types of images which appear on radar screens, he analyzed each in terms of the probability that they could be explained by weather phenomena.

Mr. Morgan independently concluded that the cases of an unexplained radar target pacing an aircraft could not be explained by an echo from the aircraft to another surface, and back to the radar set. "If a large, stationary ground object did this," he states, "it would always do it and this would be familiar to the radar operator. If the [radar-detected] object were a meteorological condition such as an ionized layer of air, it is highly doubtful that the reflection would be regular enough to give a consistent appearance, and sharp enough to prevent the blip from spreading in a radial direction."

In summary, Mr. Morgan stated: "It may be said that highly specialized UFO patterns on radar scopes can be explained only by highly unlikely or even impossible meteorological conditions. In the case of inversions, it is further unlikely that a specialized condition would exist without the simultaneous presence of less specialized conditions that would immediately be recognized as coming from an inversion."

Having examined various known phenomena which produce blips on radar, and theoretical attempts to account for unknown targets, a closer look at some of the radar-UFO reports is in order.

Summer 1948; Goose Bay, Labrador

Major Edwin A. Jerome, USAF (Ret.) reported the following information to NICAP in 1961. Major Jerome was a Command Pilot, Air Provost Marshal for about 8 years, and also served as an Intelligence Officer and CID Investigator.

"My only real contact with the UFO problem was way back in the summer of 1948 while stationed at Goose Bay, Labrador. There an incident happened which is worthy of note. It seems that a high-ranking inspection team was visiting the radar facilities of this base whose mission at the time was to serve as a prime refueling and servicing air base for all military and civilian aircraft plying the north Atlantic air routes. GCA [Ground Control Approach radar] was a critical part of this picture, thus these high-ranking officers RCAF & USAF up to the rank of General as I recall.

"While inspecting the USAF radar shack, the operator noted a high-speed target on his scope going from NE to SW. Upon computation of the speed it was found to be about 9000 mph. This incident caused much consternation in the shack since obviously this was no time for levity or miscalculations in the presence of an inspecting party. The poor airman technician was brought to task for his apparent miscalculation. Again the target appeared and this time the inspectors actually shown the apparition on the radar screen. The only reaction to this was that obviously the American equipment was way off calibration.

"The party then proceeded to the Canadian side to inspect the RCAF GCA facility. Upon their arrival the OIC related

83

this most unbelievable target they had just seen. The inspecting officers were appalled that such a coincidence should happen. I was part of the meager intelligence reporting machinery at the base and I was called in to make an immediate urgent intelligence report on the incident. The prevailing theory at the time was that it was a meteor. I personally discounted this since upon interviewing the radar observers on both sides of the base they stated that it maintained an altitude of 60,000 feet and a speed of approximately 9000 mph.

"To make this story more incredible the very next day both radars again reported an object hovering over the base at about 10 mph, at 45,000 feet. The "official" story on this was that they were probably some type of "high-flying seagulls." You must remember all these incidents happened before the days of fast high flying jets and missiles and the now common altitude record-breaking helicopters."

(Maj. Jerome then added: "On my recent tour in Alaska [circa 1960], I became very familiar with the early warning and air defense systems on the DEW Line and Alaska Air Defense Sectors. Many times high speed unknown objects were discerned which could not be explained as normal air breathing vehicles penetrating our sectors. Many of the citizens of Alaska along the Bering Sea Coast have reported seeing missile-like aircraft flying at very low altitudes at very high speeds. The AF denied the presence of Russian aircraft vehemently. When it was suggested that they might be extra-terrestrial everyone clammed up.")

October 15, 1948; Japan

Capt. Edward J. Ruppelt reported the following case received by Project Sign (the original Air Force UFO investigation project) in October 1948.

An F-61 "Black Widow" night fighter on patrol over Japan, October 15, picked up an unidentified radar target. The UFO was traveling about 200 mph. between 5000 and 6000 feet. Each time the F-61 tried to close in, the object would accelerate to an estimated 1200 mph., outdistancing the interceptor before slowing down again. On one of six passes at the UFO, the crew of the F-61 got close enough to see its silhouette. The UFO appeared to be 20-30 feet long and shaped "like a rifle bullet."

November 23, 1948; Fursten-Feldbruck, Germany

An unidentified object resembling a reddish light was sighted east of the base at 2200 hours, local time. Capt._____[names deleted from Air Force reports] said the UFO was moving south across Munich, turned southwest, then southeast. Not knowing the height, the speed could not be estimated; but it appeared to be traveling between 200 and 600 mph.

Capt._____reported the sighting to base operations, and the radar station checked its scope. An unidentified target, traveling 900 mph., was detected at 27,000 feet about 30 miles south of Munich. Capt._____verified that the UFO was now visible in that area. Radar then reported that the target had climbed quickly to 50,000 feet and was circling 40 miles south of Munich.

March 8, 1950; Nr Dayton, Ohio

In mid-morning, the CAA received a report from Capt. W. H. Kerr, Trans-World Airways pilot, that he and two other TWA pilots had a UFO in sight. A gleaming object was visible, hovering at high altitude. CAA also had 20 or more reports on the UFO from the Vandalia area. Wright-Patterson AFB, near Dayton, was notified, and sent up four interceptors. The UFO was also visible to control tower operators and personnel of Air Technical Intelligence Center on the base. Radar had an unidentified target in the same position.

Two F-51 pilots reported that they could see the UFO, which presented a distinct round shape and seemed huge and metallic. But clouds moved in, and the pilots were forced to turn back. The Master Sergeant who tracked it on radar stated: "The target was a good solid return. . . caused by a good solid target." Witnesses reported that the UFO finally climbed vertically out of sight at high speed.

July 14, 1951; White Sands, N.M.

During the morning two radar operators at a missile tracking site caught a fast-moving object on their scope. At the same time a tracker watching a B-29 with binoculars saw a large UFO near the bomber. Another observer sighted the UFO and, with a 35 mm camera, shot 200 feet of film. The UFO showed on the film as a round, bright spot. (The film has never been released.)

Fall 1951; Korean Area

Following are extracts from a letter to NICAP dated May 16, 1957, signed by Lt. Cmdr. M. C. Davies, U.S.N., then stationed at the U. S. Naval Air Station, Jacksonville, Florida.

My background is a Naval Aviator with approximately 4000 hours. At the time of the incident I was deployed with an Anti-Submarine Squadron aboard a CVE class carrier. I was assigned Air Crew Training Officer and prior to deployment had attended CIC Air Controller School at Point Loma, also Airborne Air Controller School and Airborne Early Warning School both located at NAS, San Diego. . .

It was at night, I was riding with a radar operator which I often did to check on their proficiency. We were flying at 5000 feet, solid instruments, with our wingman flying a radar position about 3 miles astern and slightly to our right or left. The target, which was slightly larger than our wingman, I picked up on our scope, had been circling the fleet; it left the fleet and joined up on us a position behind our wingman, approximately the same position he held on us.

I reported the target to the ship and was informed that the target was also held on the ship's radars, 14 in number; and for us to get a visual sighting if possible. This was impossible because of the clouds. The target retained his relative position for approximately 5 minutes and then departed in excess of one thousand miles per hour. He departed on a straight course and was observed to the maximum distance of my radar which was two hundred miles.

Upon completion of my flight an unidentified flying object report was completed, at which time I was informed that the object was held on ship's radars for approximately seven hours.

July 1, 1952; Ft. Monmouth, N.J.

A radar tracking of two UFOs at Fort Monmouth, N. J. was one of a series of sightings which fit a definite pattern. It occurred at a time when the Air Force was swamped with UFO reports - good ones. [See Section XII, 1952 Chronology.] Also, it was the first of ten known incidents of UFOs tracked by radar during July 1952. (See chart).

The sequence of events, reported by the Air Force UFO project chief, was as follows.

7:30 a.m., Boston, Mass. A couple in nearby Lynn and an Air Force Captain in Bedford saw two F-94's which had been scrambled on an intercept mission. The Captain saw one and the couple saw two silvery cigar-shaped UFOs, which moved southwest across Boston, outspeeding the jets.

9:30 a.m., Ft. Monmouth, N. J. Radar tracked two UFO targets, also observed visually as two shiny objects. The UFOs approached slowly from the northeast, and hovered nearby at 50,000 feet for about 5 minutes.. Suddenly the blips on the scope accelerated and shot away to the southwest, confirmed by visual observation.

A few hours later, Washington, D. C. A physics professor at George Washington University, and dozens of others, saw a grayish UFO bobbing back and forth in the sky about 30-40 degrees above the north-northwest horizon.

None of the sightings could be explained.

August 5, 1952; Haneda AFB, Japan

Just before midnight, two Air Force control tower operators noticed a brilliant light in the sky, and joined others watching it through binoculars. The UFO approached the base slowly and hovered, plainly visible from the control tower. Behind the brilliant light, the observers could see a dark circular shape four times the light's diameter. A smaller body light was visible on the underside. The object was tracked by ground radar, and an F-94 interceptor obtained a radar lock-on while chasing it. At one point, the UFO suddenly raced away at a clocked speed of 300 knots (about 345 mph.), dividing into three separate radar targets at spaced intervals. Contact with the UFO either by radar or visually, was maintained for over 30 minutes. During this period, scattered witnesses saw the UFO exactly where radar showed it to be. Conclusion: Officially "unknown."

1951-1952 Period; East Coast Air Force Base

Period of September 1951 to November 1952; prominent east coast Air Force Base.

Confidential report, certified by Rev. Albert H. Baller, German Congregational Church, Clinton, Mass.

Extracts from letter by Air Force Control Tower Operator to Rev. Baller, dated March 10, 1954:

"About 3 a.m., on a clear moonlit night, a buddy of mine who was radar operator on the same night shift called me rather excitedly on the intercom, and asked me if I could see any object in the sky about 15 miles southwest of the base. Using a pair of powerful binoculars I carefully scanned the sky in that direction and assured him that I could see nothing. It was then that he told me why he was so concerned.

"For several minutes he had tracked an object on his radar scope, then all of a sudden it had stopped at a range of about 15 miles from the base and remained stationary. Being an experienced radar operator, he knew that whatever it was, it was of good size, at least as big as any of our larger transport planes. But what amazed him was the fact that it stopped and remained motionless on the scope. A full half hour passed and still this object remained in the same location on the radar screen. Remembering that I had an inbound C-124 Globemaster coming in from that direction, I thought that perhaps the pilot would see something out there that we couldn't. I gave the pilot a couple of calls and finally raised him just south of _____ on his way in. I told him what we had on radar and asked him if he would mind swinging off his course slightly so that he could take a look for us.

"I then turned him over to the radar operator who had picked up the inbound aircraft on radar and he guided the pilot to a new heading that would bring him directly into this blip that was still stationary on the screen. The pilot slowed his aircraft and he and his copilot and engineer started looking about them. I could hear the radar man giving the pilot directions on a monitoring speaker in the tower.

"The aircraft got onto a line on the radar screen that would intersect the blip that was unidentified; then as the minutes went by the aircraft slowly approached the object on the scope. Both blips were equally bright and distinct. Then when it seemed that the two would collide, at about a half mile separation on the scope, the stationary object simply disappeared, vanished seconds before the big Globemaster reached its location.

"None of the crew on the plane had seen anything at any time, although they were all observing closely at the time and were told how close they were getting all the way to the object.

"How anything could vanish so suddenly from a radar screen without even leaving a trace of what direction it went is really amazing. When you bear in mind that a radar scanner usually has a sweep of better than 50 miles, that would mean that whatever the object was it went from a dead standstill at 15 miles and disappeared from the scope covering over 35 miles in a split second. Remember also that this object was there for over a half hour and did not disappear until seconds before the aircraft reached its position: certainly this couldn't be any electrical disturbance or other phenomena. Why then would it disappear precisely when it did?"

Summer 1953; Yaak, Montana

Unidentified objects were tracked at an Air Force radar site several times. S/Sgt. William Kelly described the incidents in a taped interview with Olean, N. Y., newsman Bob Barry.

On one occasion Sgt. Kelly and other radarmen picked up six unidentified targets. In five sweeps of the antenna (about 1 minute), the UFOs changed direction 5 times, sometimes making 90 degree turns. When radar indicated the UFOs had approached within 10 miles of the station, the crew went outside to look for them. They saw six objects in trail formation, switching to in-line abreast, then stack formation. Other radar stations were notified and they also tracked the UFOs.

The radar crew calculated the objects' speed: 1400-1600 mph. (In 1953 the official world speed record for aircraft was 755.14 mph.; see table).

At other times, the station tracked UFOs making similar maneuvers. Sgt. Kelly had also tracked UFOs climbing vertically out of the radar beam, with height finder equipment confirming the rise, until the objects went off the scope.

July 3, 1954; Albuquerque, N.M.

Nine greenish spherical UFOs which invaded a restricted flying area were detected by Air Defense Command radar and sighted visually. The Albuquerque radar station's message on the sighting was accidentally intercepted at Chicago Midway Airport by an airline operations employee:

0105-C. . . NINE UNIDENTIFIED SPHERICAL OBJECTS GIVING OFF GREEN LIGHT REPORTED 20 MILES NORTH ABQ [Albuquerque] FIELD AT 24,000 FEET. OBJECTS HOVERED MOTIONLESS FOR 6 MINUTES THEN PROCEEDED 340 DEGREES AT APPROX 2600 MPH. ALTITUDE AND SPEED BY TRIANGULATION. . . ABQ ADIZ RADAR.

(NICAP Note: "ADIZ" means Air Defense Identification Zone; only aircraft which have filed a flight plan are allowed to fly through an ADIZ area.)

March 23, 1957; Los Angeles, Calif.

Confidential report obtained from CAA (now FAA) radar operator confirming visual sightings at Oxnard AFB and vicinity. Report certified by NICAP Board Members: Rev. Albert Baller; Dr. Earl Douglass; Mr. Frank Edwards; Col. Robert B. Emerson, USAR; Prof. Charles A. Maney; Rear Admiral H. B. Knowles, USN (Ret.).

At 9:55 p.m., Mr. K. E. Jefferson, Pasadena, saw a brilliant flashing object moving over Downey. Between that time and midnight, police switchboards throughout the Los Angeles area were flooded with hundreds of calls reporting a UFO. The reports poured into the Pasadena Filter Center.

According to Capt. Joseph Fry, commanding officer of the Center, the first official report came in at 11:10 p.m., at which time Capt. Fry notified Air Defense radar.

"Between 2310 (11:10 p.m.) and 2350," Capt. Fry said in a statement to newsman Russ Leadabrand, "we had many reports. We had reports that indicated the UFO was orange-red, flashing a bright white light. Some of the callers claimed they heard the 'sound of reports' when the light flashed from the object."

At the Filter Center itself, Air Force T/Sgt. Dewey Crow and newsman Les Wagner watched the UFO maneuver slowly around the area for over an hour. Just after midnight, Mrs. Robert Beaudoin, wife of an Oxnard AFB Captain, telephoned the base tower to report sighting the UFO. It was described as a large silent object, flashing a brilliant red light, and maneuvering above the Santa Rosa Valley.

An F-89 interceptor attempted to locate the object, but the Air Force denied it was able to make contact, although at the same time witnesses on the ground could see the UFO plainly near one of the Oxnard runways.

Reports continued into early morning hours, with witnesses in various locations describing objects which sometimes hovered, and sometimes moved swiftly.

The CAA radar report, obtained later, virtually proved that unexplained objects were operating over Los Angeles. The radar operator's report:

"At 2350 (11:50 p.m.) I was watching the radar scope, when I noticed a target about 15 miles northwest and moving northwest. At first I thought it was a jet, then I noticed it was moving much faster than anything I had ever seen on the scope. About 40 miles northwest it came to an abrupt stop and reversed course, all within a period of about three seconds. It then traveled back along its course for about 20 miles, reversed course again and disappeared off the scope at 50 miles (our radar reaches out only 50 miles).

"Approximately 5 minutes later 2 more targets appeared and disappeared off the scope in the same direction as the first; and these we had time to clock. They traveled 20 miles in 30 seconds which figures out to 3600 mph. A minute or so later a fourth target appeared in the same area as the other 3, 10 or 15 miles northwest, and went off the scope to the northwest at 3600 mph.

"Our radar does not give height of aircraft so I couldn't give you the height, however they had to be about 10,000 feet or lower because our radar's maximum height range is about 10,000 feet."

November 5, 1957; Gulf of Mexico

Just after 5:00 a.m. the U. S. Coast Guard Cutter Sebago was about 200 miles south of the Mississippi delta. At 5:10 the bridge radar suddenly showed an unidentified target at 246 degrees true, moving N to S, range 12,000 yards (almost 7 miles). On duty were Ensign Wayne Schotley, deck officer, Lt. (j.g.) Donald Schaefer, first class quartermaster Kenneth Smith, and radioman Thomas Kirk.

Interviewed in New Orleans, Ensign Schotley was asked how good the radar target was.

Schotley: "The ship's combat information center confirmed the sighting. At that point it was reported falling astern rapidly. It was a good pip [target]. It was a very strong contact, considered good."

Cmdr. James N. Schrader, spokesman in New Orleans, said that at one point "in two minutes it went 33 miles straight away from the ship." (About 1020 mph.)

At 5:14 contact was lost.

At 5:16 contact was regained, object about 22 miles north.

At 5:18 object faded off radar screen, range about 55 miles.

At 5:20 contact regained, object appeared stationary, seven miles due north.

About this time, A/1C William J. Mey, an Electronics technician at Keesler AFB, Mississippi (about 320 miles to the north on the Gulf Coast) spotted an elliptical UFO. In his signed report to NICAP, A/1C Mey gives the time as approximately 5:20 a.m. Looking south, he saw the UFO approach on a northerly course at about the speed of a propeller airliner, then accelerate rapidly and disappear into some clouds.

This suggests that more than one UFO may have been operating in the area, and that the Sebago's radar may have tracked more than one of them. A/1C Mey's report is fairly consistent with the 5:18 radar report of the UFO headed north at over 1000 mph. If Mey actually saw the UFO at 5:28, it would have averaged about 1590 mph., from the time it faded from the Sebago's radar screen. If he saw it precisely at 5:20 a.m., it would have had to accelerate to nearly 8000 mph. to cover the distance in that time).

At 5:21 the Sebago regained radar contact, and also saw the UFO visually for 3-5 seconds as a brilliant white object with no distinguishable shape. It was at a bearing of 270 degrees true (west), elevation about 31 degrees, moving horizontally from south to north. (A navigator obtained the elevation by noting a star at the same angle and taking a sextant reading of it). The UFO finally entered a cloudbank and disappeared.

At 5:37 the cutter reported its last radar contact with the object, about 175 miles to the north, traveling about 660 mph.

[See Section XII, November 1957 chronology, for other reports during the same period.]

January 1961; Missile Base

Confidential report certified by NICAP Director Donald E. Keyhoe and Assistant Director Richard Hall. During the test of a solid fuel missile, radar which was supposed to track the first stage instead tracked a UFO target. Test evaluation report in NICAP possession states "object unidentifiable." The UFO "appeared to be alternately hovering, then moving rapidly to a new location."

PHOTOGRAPHS

The photographic material listed below has been evaluated with this principle in mind: A still photograph purporting to show a UFO is, at most, approximately as reliable as the person who took it. If the witness is a reputable person and all pertinent data is provided, his photograph deserves careful analysis. Where character information about the witness is lacking, the photograph is of less value and it is necessary to suspend judgment about it. Still photographs can be faked very easily. In general, movie films are more valuable because they are more difficult to fake, and more subject to analysis independently of the character of the witness.

NICAP Adviser Ralph Rankow, a professional photographer in New York City, gave the following estimate of photographic evidence for UFOs:

"Everyone knows that photographs can be faked, but the real question is, to what extent can they be faked? We have seen Hollywood movies of realistic dinosaurs fighting one another. We have seen dams break and towns washed away by the flood waters. We have seen naval battles and ships blown up right before our eyes. In one movie I even saw Moses hold back the waters of the Red Sea. These were all very realistic scenes, and we had to keep reminding ourselves that what we were seeing was a Hollywood movie and not a real event.

If these complicated scenes can be photographed so realistically why can't a simple thing like a UFO be faked? The answer, of course, is that it can, and what's more it has--time and time again. A UFO can be any shape, not just saucer or cigar shaped. This makes it very easy to fake by anyone, and furthermore any unintentional mark on a film can be, and sometimes is claimed to be a UFO.

If model airplanes can be photographed to look real, then so can model UFO's. This does not mean that there are no airplanes, just because we are easily able to fake a picture to represent one. In the same way, the ability to fake a UFO photograph in no way implies that these things do not exist.

This is just to point up the extreme difficulty of determining whether or not a photograph is authentic on just the unsupported word of one or two witnesses who may or may not be reliable. In truth, no photograph, no matter how clear it may be, can be considered evidence of UFO reality without a reliable witness.

Now, this brings us to the question of what makes a reliable witness? One need not be a famous person whose name we all know, in order to be termed "reliable". A man's credentials give him reliability, not his vocation. Is he a mature individual or one given to playing tricks? What is the opinion of him held by those who know him best? Questions of this nature will help to determine how responsible and trustworthy an individual we are dealing with.

It is only when a photograph is vouched for by such a veracious individual that it becomes important as evidence."

In addition to the question of witness reliability, analysis of photographic evidence for UFOs is complicated by other factors. Many of the potentially most significant pictures were taken before NICAP was formed in 1956. Belated attempts to obtain all the necessary data for full analysis have proved extremely difficult. Since then, quite a few of the seemingly better movie films and photographs were submitted to the Air Force, rather than to NICAP, by citizens unaware of NICAP's existence. Secrecy and red tape thereupon obscured the facts. In some cases, because of the confusion surrounding the UFO subject and reports of tampering with or confiscation of films [Section IX], witnesses have refused to give up their films for analysis.

Because of these problems, we consider it appropriate merely to list photographic evidence known to exist. This will supply references to data which would need to be analyzed thoroughly in any complete scientific investigation of UFOs. We have also attempted to rate each case according to its probable significance as evidence. The codes below indicate rating, film data, and status of analysis by NICAP. Other description and comments follow with cases numbered to match the entries on next page.

(Inc)	1.	March 1946. Fred J. Stange, Bernardston, Mass.	bS/VN
(Inc)	2.	July 5, 1947. Frank Ryman, C. G., Seattle, Wash.	bS/VN
(Inc)	3.	February 23, 1949. Cmdr. A. V. Orrego, Chile.	M/NN
(*)	4.	October 23, 1949. Norwood, Ohio, searchlight case.	bM/NN
(Inc)	5.	April 24, 1950. Enrique Hausemann Muller, Balearic Islands.	S/VN
(#)	6.	April 27, 1950. White Sands theodolite photo.	M/NN
(*)	7.	May 11, 1950. Trent photographs, McMinnville, Ore.	S/VN
(#)	8.	May 29, 1950. White Sands theodolite photo.	M/NN
*	9.	August 15, 1950. Nick Mariana, Great Falls, Montana.	cM/VN
(*)	10.	July 14, 1951. Near White Sands, tracking camera film.	M/NN
(#)	11.	August 30, 1951. Carl Hart, Jr., Lubbock lights, Texas.	bS/VN
(Inc)	12.	May 7, 1952. Barra da Tijuca, Brazil. Ed Keffel.	bS/VN
*	13.	July 2, 1952. Warrant Officer Newhouse, Tremonton, Utah.	cM/VN
(#)	14.	July 16, 1952. Shell Alpert, Coast Guard, Salem, Mass.	bS/VN
(#)	15.	July 19, 1952. Peru.	bS/VN
(*)	16.	July 29, 1952. Ralph Mayher, Miami, Fla.	M/VN (few frames)
(#)	17.	August 1, 1952. Wright-Patterson AFB, Ohio. gun-camera	M/VN (few frames)
(*)	18.	September 19, 1952. Operation Mainbrace color photos.	cS/NN
(*)	19.	November 16, 1952. David S. Bunch near Landrum, S. C.	cM/NN
(X)	20.	December 13, 1952. Adamski "scout ship."	bS/VN
(#)	21.	August 12, 1953. Ellsworth AFB gun-camera, "best unknown" case.	M/NN
(#)	22.	August 31, 1953. Port Moresby, New Guinea, T. C. Drury	M/NN
(X)	23.	February 15, 1954. Stephen Darbishire, Coniston, England	bS/VN
(*)	24.	March 1954. Rouen, France. RAF Flying Review.	bS/VN
(*)	25.	May 24, 1954. USAF photo by RB-29 reconaissance plane	/NN
(*)	26.	June 30, 1954. Scandinavian eclipse photos.	cM/VN (few frames)
(*)	27.	September 9, 1954. K. M. Gibbons, New Zealand	bS/VN
(#)	28.	March 5, 1956. William L. Wannall, Hawaii (cS orig.)	bS/VN
(X)	29.	July 17, 1956. Elizabeth Klarer, S. Africa.	bS/VN
(X)	30.	July 19, 1956. Michael Savage, 15, San Bernardino, Calif.	bS/VN
(Inc)	31.	September 18, 1956. Ray Stanford, Calif.	cM/NN
(X)	32.	October 10, 1956. Joe Kerska, Twin Peaks, San Francisco, California	bS/VN
(#)	33.	August 20, 1957. Japan. S. Takeda	bS/VN
(Inc)	34.	November 6, 1957. Anaheim, California	bS/VN
(X)	35.	November 16, 1957. Near Holloman AFB, New Mexico	bS/VN
(#)	36.	December 1957. T. Fogl, radio officer, S.S. Ramsey	bS/VN
(#)	37.	December 1, 1957. Ralph Benn, Los Angeles, California	cM/NN
(*)	38.	January 3, 1958. Cliff DeLacey, Hawaii.	cM/NN
(*)	39.	January 16, 1958. Trindade Isle, Brazil, sequence.	bS/VN
(#)	40.	February 9, 1958. Troy, Michigan, airport	cS/VN
(Inc)	41.	June 23, 1958. Near England AFB, Louisana State police.	bS/NN
(X)	42.	July 28, 1959. Ray Stanford. Two movie films.	cM/AN
(Inc)	43.	October 16, 1958. Mike Schultz, Newark, Ohio.	bS/VN
(#)	44.	February 9, 1959. Purdon, Imperial Beach, California	cM/NN
(X)	45.	September 24, 1959. Redmond, Ore. FAA case.	bM/AN
(Inc)	46.	November 29, 1959. J. J. Rehill, USN, Miami, Florida	bS/VN
(X)	47.	February 13, 1960. Joe Perry, Grand Blanc, Michigan	cS/AN
(Inc)	48.	March 2, 1960. Schedelbauer, Vienna.	bS/VN
(X)	49.	April 11, 1960. Mary Jo Curwen, Hazel Green, Wisconsin	cM/AN
(Inc)	50.	August 3, 1960. Linz, Austria	bS/AN
(X)	51.	August 9, 1960. Jay Rees, San Francisco, California	cS/AN
(Inc)	52.	August 25, 1960. Grumman mystery satellite photo	bS/VN
(X)	53.	January 1, 1961. A/3c Bellett, Golden, Colorado	bS/AN
(*)	54.	January 22, 1961. Harry Caslar, Eglin AFB, Florida	M/NN
(X)	55.	May 27, 1961. Triangle, Nashville, Tenn.	bS/AN
(#)	56.	May 29, 1961. Craig Seese, Newark, Ohio.	cM/VN
(Inc)	57.	July 13, 1961. Bob Feldman, Akron, Ohio.	cS/VN
(Inc)	58.	September, 1961. Paccione moon photos	bS/AN
(Inc)	59.	September 29, 1961. Savage, Warrenton, Virginia	cM/VN
(X)	60.	March 9, 1962. Jeanne B. Johnson, Hawaii.	bS/AN
(Inc)	61.	May 25, 1962. F. DiMambro, Woburn, Mass.	bS/VN
(Inc)	62.	November 18, 1962. Bruce Fox, Bayonne, New Jersey	bS/VN
(X)	63.	December 15 & 16, 1962. Ronald Gounad, New Jersey	bS/VN
(*)	64.	December 21, 1962. Ali R. Diaz, Angel Falls, Venezuela.	cM/AN

PHOTOGRAPHIC CASES

1. Fred J. Stange, Bernardston, Mass. Photograph submitted in 1954 to Rev. Albert Baller (now NICAP Board member). Witness states he first saw three discs in a group, then two other single objects. Photograph shows all five, according to Leonard H. Stringfield (CRIFO Newsletter; Vol. II No. 3, June 3, 1955). Lead object of V-formation is largest image. Photo taken with box camera. Other camera data not available. The slide viewed by NICAP, a copy of the original, is of very poor quality.

Many splotches are apparent, but no easily discernible UFO images.

2. Frank Ryman, U.S. Coast Guard, Seattle, Wash. At 5:45 p.m. Mr. Ryman photographed a circular white object moving across the wind. (See Popular Science, August 1951; "Report on UFO", Ruppelt, p. 37). Photograph reproduced in "Coming of the Saucers", by Arnold & Palmer, shows small, white, elliptical image. Photo carries identification: "Acme Telephoto, SE 86-7/5 Seattle."

Photographic Cases (Continued)

3. <u>Cmdr. A. V. Orrego, Chilean Navy</u>. Reported sighting and photographing UFOs over an Antarctic base. Objects described as "one above the other, turning at tremendous speeds." Major Donald E. Keyhoe queried the Chilean Embassy and was told the films were classified. ("Flying Saucers From Outer Space," p. 44). Other sources indicate movie film was taken.

4. <u>Norwood, Ohio, searchlight case</u>. Rev. Gregory Miller, Norwood, Ohio, in the presence of other witnesses, with help of Norwood police officer, obtained 16 mm black and white movies of a large disc hovering in a searchlight beam. The disc emitted "two distinct groups of triangular-shaped objects." (<u>CRIFO Newsletter</u>, Vol. I No. 5, August 6, 1954). One of series of well-witnessed sightings logged by Army searchlight operator, Sgt. Donald R. Berger. Three 25 foot rolls of movie film were exposed, using a Hugo Meyer F-19-3 camera with telephoto lens; also several still photographs with a Speed-Graphic and 14 inch Wallensach telephoto lens, the best of which were submitted to <u>Time-Life</u> and reportedly never returned. One photograph reproduced in "Inside Saucer Post. . .3-0 Blue," by L. H. Stringfield, Cincinnati, 1957.

5. <u>Balearic Islands</u>. A United Press Newspictures photo reportedly taken by Enrique H. Muller is reproduced in "The Coming of the Saucers," by Arnold & Palmer, Amherst, Wisc., c. 1952. Shows large circular, fiery-looking UFO with rays of "flame" spinning off edge in pinwheel fashion. No reference points visible. No camera data available.

6. <u>White Sands, N.M. tracking station</u>, April 27, 1950, photographed UFO which had been observed visually. Reportedly shows smudgy dark object in motion. ("Report on UFOs," by Capt. E. J. Ruppelt, Doubleday, 1956, p. 123). Filmed by Askania Cine Theodolite.

7. <u>Paul Trent, McMinnville, Oregon</u>, obtained two of clearest UFO photographs on record. Both show disc with superstructure. Reproduced by <u>Life</u> magazine (June 26, 1950) with comment that Mr. Trent is "an honest individual" and "the negatives show no signs of having been tampered with." Images closely similar to UFO photographed over France in March 1954 (see below).

8. <u>White Sands, N.M.</u>, tracking station, May 29, 1950, photographed UFO which had been observed visually. Films by Askania Cine Theodolite cameras from two separate stations reportedly showed bright dots of light. ("Report on UFOs," Ruppelt, p. 124.)

9. <u>Nick Mariana, Great Falls, Montana</u>, obtained 16 mm color movies of two UFOs which appear as bright circular points of light. Footage of UFOs at closer range, confirming visual observation of discs with rotating rims, was reported missing from film when returned by Air Force. Remaining footage was contained in United Artists documentary movie "UFO" and compared to July 2, 1952, Trementon, Utah film showing similar images. Mr. Mariana used Daylight Kodachrome film in a Revere turret type camera and obtained 315 frames showing the UFOs. The film was examined by the Air Force and Navy, but no formal reports released. Report on Photogrammetric analysis by Dr. Robert M.L. Baker, Jr., Douglas Aircraft Corporation, on file at NICAP. Air Force explanation that UFOs were reflections off jet aircraft said to be "quite strained," and the analyst states no definite conclusion. However, UFOs could not be explained as any conventional objects.

10. <u>White Sands, N.M.</u>, tracking station, July 14, 1951. UFO tracked on radar, observed visually through binoculars, photographed on 200 feet of 35 mm movie film. Film reportedly shows round, bright spot. ("F.S. From Outer Space," p. 48).

11. <u>Lubbock (Texas) "Lights"</u> photographs by Carl Hart, Jr., show V-formation of large perfectly circular objects. (See "Report on UFOs", p. 144 et seq.). Capt. Ruppelt, head of Air Force Project Blue Book, reported that "In each photograph the individual lights in the formation shifted position according to a definite pattern." Main photograph reproduced in <u>True</u>, May 1954. Taken with Kodak 35 camera set at f/3.5, shutter at 1/10 of a second.

12. <u>Barra de Tijuca, Brazil</u>, photographs of disc, taken by magazine writers Ed Keffel and Joao Martins. NICAP has never obtained any negatives for analysis. Prints show disc from five different angles. Critics have pointed out that in main photograph shadows on object do not coincide with shadows on ground below.

Until this criticism is fully answered, photographs must be considered suspect.

13. <u>Utah Movie</u>. Warrant Officer D.C. Newhouse, USN, obtained 16 mm color movies of a group of UFOs which he and his wife observed visually near Tremonton, Utah. At relatively close range, UFOs appeared flat and circular "shaped like two saucers, one inverted on top of the other." Mr. Newhouse unpacked his Bell and Howell Automaster camera, with 3 inch telephoto lens, from the trunk of his car and obtained about 1200 frames of the UFOs on Daylight Kodachrome film. During the filming, Mr. Newhouse changed the iris stop of the camera from f/8 to f/16. The film was submitted to Navy authorities, who forwarded it to the Air Force at ATIC in Dayton, Ohio, where it was studied for several months. According to Mr. Newhouse, frames of the movie showing a single UFO moving away over the horizon (hence providing some ranging information) were missing when the film was returned. The hypothesis that the objects were out of focus sea gulls was considered by the Air Force, but could neither be confirmed nor denied. The report of Photogrammetric analysis by Dr. Robert M.L. Baker, Jr., Douglas Aircraft Corporation (which included a study of the 1950 Montana film--see above) also examined this possibility. He states: "The motion of the objects is not exactly what one would expect from a flock of soaring birds (not the slightest indication of a decrease in brightness due to periodic turning with the wind or flapping)." Dr. Baker reports that no definite conclusion could be reached, but "the evidence remains rather contradictory and no single hypothesis of a natural phenomenon yet suggested seems to completely account for the UFO involved." [See Section IX re: later Air Force statements on Utah film]

14. <u>Shell Alpert, U.S. Coast Guard, Salem, Mass.</u>, visually observed and photographed four UFOs in formation. Taken through window of laboratory, picture shows four roughly elliptical blobs of light. Photograph reproduced widely in newspapers and magazines. Date coincides with peak of Summer 1952 sighting "flap", in which four objects flying in formation were observed several times. Official Coast Guard letter, 8 August 1962 (copy in NICAP files): "...it never has been determined what caused the phenomenal lights shown [in the photograph]."

15. <u>Peru</u>. Round UFO observed by Sr. Pedro Bardi, agricultural engineer, and others on a farm about 4:30 p.m., in Madre de Dios, Peru, noticed when short wave radio went dead. Object also seen four minutes later near Porto Maldo where Sr. Domingo Troncosco, customs administrator, photographed it. Photo shows elongated object trailing smoke, passing over the top of a tree and in front of a cumulus cloud. Photograph submitted by James W. Moseley. (For story and picture, see UFO Investigator, Vol. I No. 2, August-September, 1957).

16. <u>Ralph Mayher, Miami, Fla.</u> Using 16 mm film exposed at 24 frames per second, Mr. Mayher obtained good footage of a high speed UFO. Calculations by a physicist at the University of Miami yielded the information that the object was about 27 feet in diameter and travelling about 7550 mph. Retaining a few frames for personal study, Mr. Mayher submitted the main portion of the film to the Air Force for analysis. The film was never returned and no analysis report was ever released. (For story and pictures, see PIC magazine, June 1954). Enlargements of a few frames show a fiery looking roughly circular object, symmetrical, with two small peaks or projection on opposite sides of the disc.

17. <u>Gun camera photos</u>. Nr. Wright-Patterson AFB, Ohio, August 1, 1952. Two jet interceptors chased a UFO which had been tracked on radar, and one obtained gun camera photographs of it before the object accelerated at high speed and disappeared. ("F.S. From Outer Space," p. 107-8; Hartford, Conn., Courant, August 2, 1952). Part of the 35 mm gun camera film is reproduced in <u>True</u>, December 1952, showing a faint, dark circular image. The Air Force says radar tracked a jet aircraft, while the pilots saw and chased a radiosonde balloon assuming it was the UFO which had shown on radar. The rapid acceleration of the object which the pilots observed (and filmed while stationary) would appear to rule out this interpretation.

18. <u>Operation Mainbrace</u>. During fleet maneuvers in the North Sea in September 1952, UFOs were sighted in the vicinity on several occasions. [See Section XII]. On September 19, American reporter Wallace Litwin, on board the aircraft carrier "Franklin Roosevelt", took three color photographs of a large silvery

Photographic Cases (Continued)

spherical object which reportedly moved rapidly across the sky above the fleet. The pictures showed a round object, according to press reports, but have not been released to our knowledge. ("The Truth About Flying Saucers", Michel, p. 130).

19. David S. Bunch film, Landrum, S.C. About 5:00 p.m. hundreds of people near Florence, S.C. had seen a large disc-shaped UFO. About six minutes later, a group of round glowing objects were sighted near Landrum. Among the witnesses were J.D. McLean and David S. Bunch. Mr. Bunch took 40 feet of color movie film, using an 8 mm camera with telephoto lens. The film was submitted to the Air Force, and viewed by Maj. Donald E. Keyhoe along with Air Force officers. It shows five glowing, oval-shaped objects.

20. Adamski "Scout Ship." Because of Mr. George Adamski's background as a self-styled "professor" of oriental mystical philosophy (later espoused by his "spacemen") and at least one claim of his which was conclusively proved false by NICAP investigators, his photographs are considered dubious. NICAP Board Member, Frank Edwards, (an experienced photographer) considers the Adamski pictures hoaxes. Mr. Adamski refuses to submit his negatives for analysis.

21. The Ellsworth AFB case, in which two jet interceptors chased a UFO which turned and followed the first jet back towards its base, was termed by Capt. E.J. Ruppelt "an unknown...the best." Later information obtained by a NICAP member indicates that the UFO was photographed by gun camera and that the film verified the presence of a UFO, making it an even stronger case. Maj. Lawrence J. Tacker, then Air Force Spokesman on UFOs, wrote to NICAP Member Alexander Overall: 17 September 1958, "Photos of the radar scope and gun camera photos were made but were not sufficiently clear for evaluation. The Ellsworth AFB case is still listed as unknown or unsolved." As in other gun camera and tracking camera cases, the film has not been released for outside scientific analysis.

22. New Guinea film. Mr. T.C. Drury, then Deputy Regional Director of the Civil Aviation Department at Port Moresby, obtained motion picture film of a UFO at high altitude leaving a clear vapor trail. (telephoto lens used). The UFO climbed steeply and disappeared. Reuters, on March 14, 1954, reported that the film had been sent to the United States for "special processing." (Other sources indicate it was sent to ATIC at Wright-Patterson AFB, Ohio.) On February 19, 1958, Mr. Drury, replying to a query by Max B. Miller, stated he had turned his film over to the Commonwealth Security Branch and had not seen it since.

23. The "Coniston Saucer" photograph was taken by Stephen Darbishire, 13, at Coniston, Lancs., England. His brother Adrian, 8, also reportedly witnessed the UFO. The boys' father is a doctor of good reputation. Using an inexpensive Kodak, extending bellows type, with only two lens settings ("bulb" and "infinity"), Stephen photographed a UFO rising low over a hillock.

The picture, although blurred and of poor quality, shows a bright object (lighter than the sky background) strongly resembling a side view of the Adamski "scout ship". (See No. 20 above.) An orthographic projection by Leonard G. Cramp confirmed that the Coniston and Adamski photographs were of identical proportions.

David Wightman, NICAP Adviser in England, has met the Darbishire family and now knows them very well. He found no reason to consider the incident a hoax. In spite of the above, we are inclined to be dubious of the photograph (a) because it is an exact copy of the Adamski-type "saucer", which is in itself dubious; (b) because it could easily be a cut-out or model of the Adamski "saucer", and in fact on the photograph a black marking extends from the object to the hilltop, which could be a support for a cut-out or model. Admittedly, no motive for a hoax is apparent, and the validity of the photograph is not disproved.

24. Rouen, France. In conjunction with an article "Something in the Sky," RAF Flying Review (July 1957) published a UFO photograph which was taken over Rouen, France. No camera or film data were given. The highly-respected aviation magazine termed it "one of the few [photographs] which seem authentic." The UFO resembles a disc viewed edge-on, and has a small projection on top. It closely resembles the May 11, 1950 Trent photographs. (No. 7).

25. RB-29 Photo. USAF photo taken as UFO was observed flying beneath an RB-29 near Dayton, Ohio. Picture reportedly showing unexplained circular light source, never made public. [See "Report on Unidentified Flying Objects," Ruppelt, pp. 310-312]

26. Scandinavian eclipse film. Three aircraft carrying scientists, newsmen and other observers were flying near Lifjell, Denmark, on an expedition to film and study a total eclipse of the sun. At 2:17 p.m. two shiny discs were noticed flying past the planes and witnessed by about 50 people on the three planes. John Bjornulf, chief cameraman of the expedition, managed to obtain about 10 seconds (of the approximately 30 second UFO flight) on 16 mm color film. The film was reportedly shown on American television December 26, 1954. [See Section I]

27. Gibbons film, N.Z. Three disc-like UFOs were observed simultaneously near Nelson, N.Z., at positions 5 miles apart by Mr. K.M. Gibbons and Mr. Alex Ingram. A third witness later saw 5 similar discs in the same general area. Mr. Gibbons took photographs (number unspecified) with a Cannon 35 mm miniature camera equipped with telephoto lens, as the UFOs hovered low over a mudflat, wobbling like tops and glowing blue-white. Two of the discs tilted on edge, streaked up vertically and disappeared. Then the third disc brightened, and also streaked away. (CRIFO Newsletter, L.H. Stringfield, November 5, 1954; CRIFO Case 29). One of the photographs, showing an apparent oblate spheroid with small dark projection on top, is reproduced in "Flying Saucers Uncensored", Wilkins, p. 96.

28. Wannall Photo, Hawaii. Mr. and Mrs. William L. Wannall, Honolulu, Hawaii were driving south on 10th Avenue at 8:45 p.m., when they noticed "three large lights flying in a wide formation over the Kaimuki area...sky was clear, and visibility unlimited, prevailing trade winds." (SAUCERS, Vol. IV No. 2). After watching the lights for about 1 minute, Mr. Wannall took a photograph of them with his Cannon 35 mm camera using Anscochrome color film (32 ASA), exposure 1/8, aperture f/1.8. NICAP has viewed only a black and white print, which shows three lights in a triangle pattern, two of which have sharply curving "trails". Off to one side is another, slightly larger, apparent light. There is a dark background with no visible landmarks. According to Max B. Miller, who examined a color print, the lights are bright yellow except for one of the "trails" which is bluish-green. The fourth "object" was not visible to the photographer. The light sources are surrounded by an "aureoletype effect."

29. Mrs. Elizabeth Klarer, Natal, South Africa, took three photographs showing a metallic-appearing disc against a cloud background. She used a Brownie box camera. (See Flying Saucer Review, November-December, 1956). Clearest photograph strongly resembles an automobile hubcap. Mrs. Klarer is also a "contactee" with claims of meeting spacemen, similar to George Adamski's story. Photographs considered dubious.

30. Savage Photo, California. Photograph taken by Michael Savage, 15, son of Dr. Phillip M. Savage, Jr., San Bernardino, California. Shows elliptical outline of apparent disc-like object, large apparent size, above trees and wires. Michael said the UFO appeared to be about 20 feet in diameter, with some "apparatus or portholes" visible near the trailing edge. He said it moved at high speed and climbed out of sight at about a 55 degree angle. The alleged UFO is barely in the frame of the picture, one end clipped off by the edge of the frame. Could be cardboard or other model held up in foreground and photographed. Dubious.

31. Ray Stanford, California. Using a Wollensak 8 mm camera with telephoto lens, Mr. Stanford shot about 6 feet of film of a "tiny, flickering object moving in and out of the field of view;" (as described by Max B. Miller). The sequence was accidentally considerably underexposed. He used Daylight Kodachrome. (Pictures and story, SAUCERS, Autumn 1958); originally described in "Look Up", privately published book by Ray Stanford).

32. Twin Peaks, California. Photograph showing dark disc-shaped object with lighter dome (about 1/5 diameter of the object) against light sky with city and mountains visible beneath. SAUCERS (Vol. V No. 1) reports the picture was taken by Joe Kerska, about 12:30 p.m., facing east on the south slope of Twin Peaks, San Francisco. No camera data or character information available. The alleged UFO strongly resembles a small model at relatively close range, thrown into the air and photographed. No meaningful analysis is possible because of lack of data, but the photograph is considered dubious.

Photographic Cases (Continued)

33. **Fujisawa City, Japan.** Taken by Shinichi Takeda near Enoshima Miami Beach at 11:28 a.m. Object reportedly also seen by his sister, who called his attention to it. UFO silvery in color, giving off brilliant glow at est. altitude of 3000-4000 feet, travelling N to S. When overhead, object made 90 degree left turn, sped up, and disappeared in clouds. A few minutes later 15 people on the beach reported a similar object which passed over at high speed. No camera data available. Picture shows capsule-shaped image near bank of cumulus clouds.

34. **Leadford Photo, Calif.** During the November 1957 "flap" [see Section XI; Chronology] Mr. Edwin G. Leadford, Anaheim, California, noticed an object giving off a reddish glow as he was driving home at about 12:10 a.m. Using his Graphic camera, at f/4.5 and 1/10, Mr. Leadford photographed the UFO. The picture was printed widely as a United Press telephoto, showing an irregular elongated mass with a round projection on the top near one end. The Garden Grove Daily News reported receiving about a dozen calls from people who had seen UFOs in the same area that night. Mr. Leadford reported on November 8 that he had turned the photograph over to the Air Force for analysis. (San Diego Union, November 9, 1957).

35. **Holloman AFB, N.M.,** photo taken by welfare nurse who filled out NICAP report form on sighting. (She requested anonymity, but her name has been published elsewhere). Photo shows white elongated object, huge in size, which did not move during the sighting. The color, size and lack of movement make it impossible to distinguish from a cloud, which it resembles. Conclusion: Probably a cloud.

36. **S. S. Ramsey Photo.** Mr. T. Fogl, while radio officer of the S.S. Ramsey, off the coast of California, about 2:30 p.m., was alerted by the Second Officer to come see a disc. According to the story, he grabbed his Yashica C reflex camera and ran to the bridge. A thick circular object with a flat dome and a pulsating red light on the bottom was visible in the distance. As it neared, Mr. Fogl managed a photograph before the UFO accelerated rapidly and disappeared toward the coast. (See "Flying Saucer Review", Jan.-Feb., 1959, for picture and story). NICAP's Adviser in England was unable to contact Mr. Fogl, and nothing is known of his character.

37. **Ralph Benn, Los Angeles, Calif.,** was alerted to some UFOs by his eight year old son at about 3:00 p.m. He ran outside, but the objects were gone. Judging by the reaction of the children, he figured they had seen something unusual, so he ran back to the house and got his 8 mm movie camera equipped with 3 power telephoto lens. Other people close by gathered to watch, as they scanned the sky. Suddenly Mr. Benn noticed six objects in formation, moving slowly west in the northern sky. They were oval in shape and dull white. He obtained about 6-1/2 feet of Kodachrome film, using a Keystone Capri camera. The telephoto lens was an Elgeet 1-1/2 inch f/3.5 fixed-focus. Four sizeable, but undefined, blobs of light show up on the film. Mr. Benn allowed the Air Force to develop his film, was promised and received a 16 mm enlargement copy. Later, the original film was returned and the UFOs were (according to the Air Force) identified as balloons. In his description of the case (SAUCERS, Spring 1958) Max B. Miller states: "We have carefully examined Ralph Benn's original film as returned by the Air Force. A pronounced number of very noticeable horizontal 'streaks' were prevalent on the UFO portion, and it was found that about three splices were made in the UFO sequence, unknown to Mr. Benn. Apparently no quantity of film is missing, and examination indicates that only two or three frames were taken out at the points of splice. . ." Other passes of the UFOs were witnessed by a number of people, in formations including a three-quarter circle, grouped pairs, and a straight line. In his account, Mr. Benn states: "Who ever heard of planets, meteors or balloons flying in formation and traversing the sky three times from horizon to horizon--and maintaining a different formation pattern with each pass?"

38. **Cliff DeLacey, Hawaii.** According to the Vallejo (Calif.) Times Herald of January 19, 1958, Mr. DeLacey obtained about 90 seconds of 8 mm color film showing some of nine UFOs which were sighted about 4:00 p.m. The maneuvers of the round UFOs, treetops and other reference points, reportedly were recorded. Mr. DeLacey did not answer queries from NICAP or

from Max B. Miller, former NICAP photographic adviser.

39. **Trindade Isle, Brazil.** NICAP has carefully studied prints (but not the negatives) of the four successful exposures of a Saturn-shaped UFO, the verbal accounts and relevant facts. The UFO was sighted about noon January 16, 1958, from the deck of the Brazilian IGY ship "Almirante Saldanha" by a retired Brazilian Air Force officer, Capt. Jose Teobaldo Viegas, and Amilar Vieira Filho, chief of a group of submarine explorers on board. They alerted Almiro Barauna, an expert submarine photographer, who managed to take four successful pictures. Many other officers and men, attracted by the commotion, soon witnessed the UFO, including Capt.-Lt. Homero Ribeiro, ship's dentist. Capt. Viegas later stated: "The First view was that of a disc shining with a phosphorescent glow, which--even in daylight--appeared to be brighter than the moon. The object was about the apparent size of the full moon. As it followed its path across the sky, changing to a tilted position, its real shape was clearly outlined against the sky: that of a flattened sphere encircled, at the equator, by a large ring or platform."

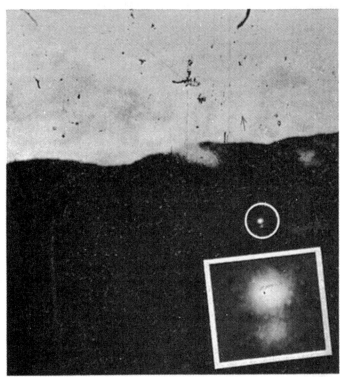

December 21, 1962; Venezuela (Case 64)

In his 1963 book ("The World of Flying Saucers"), Dr. Donald H. Menzel labels the Trindade photographs a hoax. His main reason appears to be that Mr. Barauna is a skilled photographer capable of faking a picture, and in fact, Dr. Menzel says, once did produce a fake "flying saucer" to illustrate an article. Further, Dr. Menzel notes, several of the witnesses, including Barauna were members of the same submarine explorers group on board ship (implying complicity in a hoax). However, other witnesses were not members of the explorer's group and there is no evidence of fakery in the case.

On February 25, 1958 (four days after the pictures were first publicized by the Brazilian press) United Press reported from Rio de Janeiro that the Brazilian Navy Ministry vouched for the Trindade photographs. The report went on: "Navy Minister Adm. Antonio Alves Camara said after meeting with President Juscelino Kubitschek in the summer Presidential Palace at Petropolis, that he also vouched personally for the authenticity of the pictures." This would be a curious statement to make to newsmen if the Navy had any suspicion of a hoax.

The pictures and negatives were analyzed by both the Navy Photo Reconnaissance Laboratory and the Cruzeiro do Sul Aerophotogrammetric Service, both agreeing the pictures were authentic. The latter's written conclusion stated: "It was established that no photographic tricks are involved. The negatives are normal."

Photographic Cases (Continued)

Correspondence between U.S. UFO groups and leading Brazilian investigators drew out many facts about the case, including background information about other similar sightings at Trindade Isle over a period of time, all of which tends to substantiate the January 16 sighting and photographs. No suspicion of hoax was uncovered by J. Escobar Faria, Sao Paulo attorney (NICAP Adviser), Dr. Olavo Fontes, M.D., in Rio de Janeiro (APRO Special Representative), or other Brazilian correspondents in a position to ascertain the facts. [See APRO Bulletins, January, March, and May 1960 for detailed series of articles about the Trindade photographs by Dr. Fontes].

Weighing all the facts, we conclude that the pictures appear to be authentic. They definitely are one of the potentially most significant series of UFO photographs on record, so that clarification of the incident and additional analysis is strongly desirable. In the interests of scientific investigation, we urge that secrecy about the case be lifted by the United States and Brazil and that a frank report of the facts be issued to the public. In particular, the full analysis reports by the Brazilian laboratories should be made available to scientists. Information currently withheld by the U.S. Air Force about its investigation of the case through the American Embassy in Rio de Janeiro also should be made available to the public.

Photographic data: Mr. Barauna used a Rolleiflex 2.8--Model E camera, speed 1/125, aperture f/8 (causing a slight overexposure).

40. Troy, Michigan airport. Photograph taken by H.M. Stump using an Argus C-3 camera, from a private plane landing at the airport. Picture shows yellow-white oval with slight trail. Verbal report states object hovered, then sped away to the west.

41. England AFB, La.--State Police case. Polaroid pictures taken by a state policeman at 12:20 p.m. were published by the Alexandria Daily Town Talk. The officer stated he saw "two glowing balls" in the sky and that it "scared hell out of me." He was not sure whether it was one double object, or two separate ones close together. The Air Force later stated the "UFO" was a reflection off the windshield of the patrol car. NICAP letters to the state police were not answered.

42. Ray Stanford Movies. NICAP first learned of the two color movies taken by Ray Stanford and a friend (one 8 mm, one 16 mm) in the Fall/Winter 1959-60 issue of SAUCERS (now defunct) by Max B. Miller. Mr. Miller, who later became a NICAP photographic adviser, examined the films and his evaluation is incorporated below. After preliminary correspondence with Mr. Stanford requesting the films for analysis, the films and a filled-out NICAP report form were received March 11, 1960. Additional report forms were sent to Mr. Stanford for some of the approximately 12 other witnesses to fill out, and he promised to try to obtain signed reports.

July 16, 1952; Massachusetts (Case 14)

Jack Brotzman, NICAP scientific adviser in the Washington area, projected the 8 mm film in the NICAP office and examined the 16 mm film frame by frame in the government laboratory where he is employed. Shortly thereafter, Max Miller became a NICAP photographic adviser, and since he had already examined the films he was consulted and asked for suggestions for further analysis. He gave NICAP some comments about the films, to the effect that they were not impressive in themselves, but together (because of some overlapping scenes) might have special significance. As he stated in SAUCERS, the overlap "makes simulation exceedingly improbable."

In June 1960, Mr. Stanford wrote inquiring about progress with the analysis. He also stated that, through an intermediary, the Air Force had requested copies of the films for analysis and permission for NICAP to forward the copies in its possession. Mr. Stanford granted permission. NICAP replied to Mr. Stanford, giving preliminary conclusions, and adding: "For a more thorough analysis, we would need the verbal reports you promised. . .to correlate the action described verbally with the action visible on the film. . .We also have [Max Miller's] analysis of your films to guide us. Our consensus so far is that the films appear to be authentic, and it now becomes a problem of interpretation. For this reason, I believe it would be best to forward the films to [the intermediary and the Air Force representative]. . ."

The films and Mr. Stanford's report form were forwarded, as generally agreed by all parties, to the intermediary in a city on the west coast. (Names and exact location are deleted here because the intermediary and Air Force representative both requested that their participation be kept confidential).

Over a year later, following an inquiry by Mr. Stanford, the films were returned to him by the Air Force representative with no comments about analysis results.

The Story:

The sighting and filming took place July 28, 1959, between 2:10 and 2:20 p.m. in Corpus Christi, Texas. There had been numerous UFO sightings in the area, and Ray Stanford and a friend had cameras ready. Mr. Stanford used a 16 mm Keystone K51 Executive camera on a tripod, with 75 mm Kern Yvar telephoto lens, and daylight Kodachrome film. The aperture setting was approximately f/10, and exposure was at 16 frames per second. The friend used an 8 mm Keystone K27 Capri camera with 25 mm lens, hand-held, and Type A Kodachrome film. The aperture setting was f/8, exposure 16 frames per second.

Mr. Stanford notified Max Miller by telephone, August 1, that he had the films, still unprocessed. Mr. Miller subsequently viewed the films, which were processed in Los Angeles, several days before they were forwarded to Mr. Stanford.

In his verbal report, Mr. Stanford states that three cigar-shaped UFOs were visible at one time, and a fourth appeared soon after. One of the objects reportedly "released" a small disc beneath it, and the disc sped upwards at about a 45 degree angle disappearing in the distance. Each of the objects was said to be sharply outlined, and blue-white in color. Only one object was photographed, appearing as a bright, slightly oblong light source. It does not maneuver.

Also visible on both films is the contrail of an airplane curving slightly around the UFO, after apparently moving in the direction of the UFO.

NICAP Comments: Examination of the films by NICAP showed no detail on the object, and no appreciable motion of the object. Venus, which was prominent at the time, was considered as an explanation, but ruled out because the image was enlarged considerably by the larger telephoto lens. The verbally described maneuvers, multiple objects, and launching of a disc were not confirmed by the films.

The many other reports from alleged additional witnesses were never received from Mr. Stanford. His background relative to the UFO subject was considered. (He and his brother co-authored a privately published book entitled "Look Up", in which alleged contacts with space ships, ESP, and a chapter on "how the craft are constructed, propelled and controlled" are included. One is an alleged personal close-up visual contact brought about by ESP experiments). Also, Mr. Stanford previously took an 8 mm color film, September 18, 1956, which purportedly shows two jet interceptors chasing a UFO.

Photographic Cases (Continued)

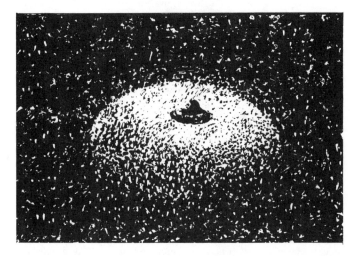

September 9, 1954; New Zealand (Case 27)
Drawing from photograph, by Eric Aldwinckle

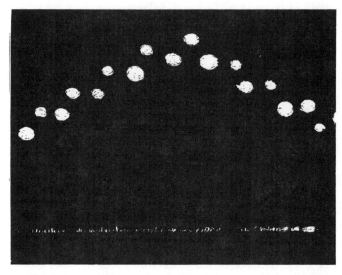

August 30, 1951; Lubbock, Texas (Case 11)
Drawing from photograph, by Eric Aldwinckle

With this background, there was some natural suspicion about the authenticity of the 1959 film. However, NICAP representatives who have talked to Mr. Stanford were impressed by his sincerity, and examination of the films by NICAP and Max B. Miller found no evidence of fakery or tampering with the films (which, as stated above, were processed in Los Angeles and examined by Max Miller before they were viewed by Mr. Stanford himself). We conclude that the films themselves are authentic records of some object in the sky, but that they do not substantiate the verbal report and do not constitute significant evidence of UFOs as the matter now stands.

Comments by Max Miller (quoted from SAUCERS, Vol. VII Nos. 3 & 4):

"The 8 mm footage lacks sufficient resolution. . .The 16 mm film is excellent, but the UFO sequence is extremely short, comprising not more than three or four feet. However, one or two scenes are identical in the 8 mm and 16 mm films, making simulation exceedingly improbable. . .

It is [my] not inexperienced opinion that the cameras did photograph a visible object, and that super-imposure or double-exposure could not account for the images produced. What the object was, of course, remains an enigma. The first possibility to cross our minds was a polyethelyne type balloon, but we have never heard of any of the shape recorded. . ."

43. Mike Schultz, Newark, Ohio. The Newark Advocate, Nov. 15, 1958 published three pictures and the story. Some excerpts from the article and a black and white print of the news-

paper photographs were forwarded to NICAP in January 1959 by a member. Using an inexpensive camera and telescope, Mr. Schultz photographed what looked like a bright star in the sky. Then the object moved and stopped, and he took the second picture. This was repeated once more. According to the member who submitted the photographs, each picture is a double-exposure of one object (the images are double in each case) because of unavoidable motion of the camera and telescope. The pictures in NICAP possession (poor copies with no negatives) strongly resemble internal reflections in the telescope as might be obtained by an inexperienced amateur astronomer using poor equipment. Without more complete data, no final judgment can be made.

44. James M. Purdon, Jr., Imperial Beach, Calif. Mr. Purdon, an engineer with a west coast aviation company, obtained several feet of color movie film of a bright object with a halo around it, observed by him and his family between 4:20 and 4:50 p.m. The equipment used was a Kodak camera with telephoto lens on a turret.

According to a report which Mr. Purdon submitted to NICAP, the UFO was first motionless for a long period of time. While he was phoning a newspaper, his wife saw the UFO disappear. Minutes later he obtained moving footage of a moving bright object (about 20 seconds of which, he states, "came out rather good").

According to his report, the UFO "hove into view from one direction, slowed up to almost a stop, then proceeded at a 90 degree angle toward the ocean. It accelerated quite rapidly at first. Then it oscillated up and down." A TV antenna in the foreground furnishes a reference point on the film, and the object moves behind a "Christmas tree" (presumably planted in his yard).

August 20, 1957; Japan (case 33)
Drawing from photograph, by Eric Aldwinckle

Photographic Cases (Continued)

March 1954; Rouen, France (case 24)
Drawing from photograph, by Eric Aldwinckle

May 11, 1950; Oregon (Case 7)
Drawing from photograph, by Eric Aldwinckle

January 16, 1958; Trindade Isle, Brazil
Drawing from photograph, by Eric Aldwinckle

Because the same film contained family scenes of great personal value to Mr. Purdon, he was not willing to risk loaning it for analysis. He did agree to show the film to any NICAP representative, but the nearest NICAP personnel were not able to make the trip for that purpose. To the best of our knowledge, the film has not been analyzed.

45. Redmond, Ore., FAA Case. After a great deal of difficulty and lengthy correspondence, a copy of motion picture film taken by an IGY "All-Sky" Camera site in Redmond, Oregon, was obtained from the Cornell University Aurora Archive, Ithaca,

N. Y. The camera had been in operation on the night of an important UFO sighting by Federal Aviation Agency personnel at Redmond airport [Section V], and it was felt that an unusual opportunity for objective confirmation of the sighting was available. However, the film was not received until August 1960 and the covering letter stated: "You have been a victim of the testing of the film copying process here at Ithaca, and we have just received the first copy. . .You should bear in mind that the camera gives a very small image of the sky, and it is seldom possible to see star sized objects unless they are very bright. . ."

Max B. Miller projected the film and viewed it frame by frame. In his report to NICAP, Mr. Miller stated the film was "in such deplorable condition as to be almost worthless. There are thousands of dust specks and processing specks. . .So unless the UFO were of spectacular brilliance or dimensions, or were recorded on at least three consecutive frames, you'd never find it. Moreover, internal lens reflections (also countless) create an additional problem." The attempt to find photographic confirmation was therefore totally inconclusive.

(For data about All-Sky cameras and their use, see IGY General Report Series, Numbers 5 & 6, September 1959, National Academy of Sciences, National Research Council, Washington 25, D. C. The instruments consist of a convex mirror and a 16 mm motion picture camera adjusted to time-lapse photography).

46. J. J. Rehill, Miami, Fla. According to a story in the Miami Herald, December 6, 1959, Seaman Rehill while on leave saw a flash of light in the sky while taking a picture in the city. He used an Argus C-3 camera and color film. When the picture was returned after processing, it showed five white spots, one disc-shaped followed by a white streak. The paper reports: "The transparency itself was undamaged. There was no evidence whatsoever of any monkey business with the original film."

Norbert Gariety, then editor of a UFO publication in Coral Gables, telephoned Rehill and interviewed him after the Herald story appeared. Mr. Rehill stated he had been interrogated by Air Force investigators, and they had examined his camera and the roll of pictures. NICAP wrote the public information officer at Mr. Rehill's base on January 4, 1960, but did not receive any reply.

47. Joe Perry, Grand Blanc, Michigan. The Detroit Times, March 9, reported the story of this photograph, stating that the FBI was investigating it. While pursuing his hobby of astronomical photography, Mr. Perry obtained a color photograph (slide) reportedly showing a UFO which was "disc-shaped with a dome and leaving a green trail." (The image on the print examined by NICAP is similar to a black disc viewed edge-on, but not perfectly symmetrical, and the "object" is surrounded by green coloration resembling a glow.)

The FBI turned Mr. Perry's slide over to the Air Force for analysis. Later the Air Force stated their opinion "that the blue spots [sic] on the slide are not images but result from damage to the emulsion during the developing process."

A color print of Mr. Perry's photograph was analyzed for NICAP by Max B. Miller, who reported September 18, 1960: The UFO "quite probably is a cinch mark. . . it could either be foreign matter which attached itself to the film during processing or undeveloped emulsion, and I'm inclined to say the latter. . . the

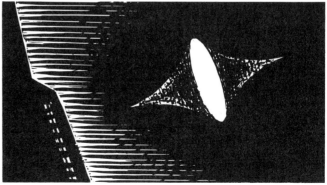

Appearance of typical lens flare sometimes mistaken for UFOs; caused by bright light source reflecting from camera lens.

(Drawing from photograph, by Eric Aldwinckle)

Photographic Cases (Continued)

greenish halation is sympathetic to the defect and is effected by one of the color developers overcompensating around the undeveloped emulsion (if a cinch mark) or foreign matter.''

48. Schedelbauer, Vienna. Edgar Schedlebauer, a reporter for the Vienna newspaper ''Wiener Montag'', photographed a round, glowing object which he said hovered low over the ground for ten seconds emitting heat. The newspaper, alleging that the photograph had been declared authentic by outside experts, printed the picture on the front page and labelled it ''the most sensational photograph of our century.'' The picture shows a bright white object something like a parachute canopy against a black background. There are no reference points.

NICAP wrote to Mr. Schedelbauer requesting the photograph and negative for analysis, but received no answer. Therefore the case must be considered incomplete. Since it is the type of photograph which could easily be faked, we are presently skeptical about it.

49. Mary Jo Curwen, Hazel Green, Wisconsin. A signed report form was received from Miss Curwen in July 1960, with a letter stating: ''When the Air Force returns our film [A copy of the original] we will be willing to lend it to you.'' After further correspondence, the film was finally submitted to the Minneapolis NICAP Subcommittee in April 1963. After analysis, it was then forwarded to NICAP Photographic Adviser Ralph Rankow in New York City, who also examined it. The film was returned to the Curwen family in June 1963.

The analyses established that the film was worthless as evidence of UFOs. The images were tiny, almost merging with the grain of the film, showed no appreciable motion other than typical movie film ''jump'' and were also visible in other scenes against the ground. The witnesses did not explain why a mundane farmyard scene appears between two scenes allegedly showing UFOs against the blue sky.

In the verbal report the witnesses stated they saw three saucer-shaped objects flying past in formation, oscillating up and down in flight, at 5:50 p.m. Miss Curwen attempted to film the UFOs with an 8 mm camera on a roll of color film which was being used primarily for family scenes.

It is possible that the attempt was unsuccessful, and that the family naturally misinterpreted routine film specks as being images of the UFOs they had seen. At any rate, the film does not verify the verbal report.

50. Linz, Austria. A photograph showing a globular UFO seemingly lighted more brightly on the underside, near what is apparently out-of-focus tree branches, was submitted to NICAP for analysis. Max B. Miller examined the picture, and stated: ''Knowing what camera and lens made the photo, we can determine that the object was approximately 6 degrees in diameter. . .it appears to be out of focus rather than blurred due to motion. . . having no further data additional evaluations cannot be made. My own opinion, however, is totally negative.''

51. Jay Rees, San Francisco. This is one of the few photographic cases involving ideal conditions for analysis: (1) An intelligent witness who saw and took good photographs of an unusual object in the sky; (2) Full cooperation between the witness and NICAP analysts uniquely fitted for the analysis work; (3) Thorough analysis and submission of detailed formal reports by NICAP analysts.

Mr. Rees first spotted the UFO at 1:45 p.m. (PDT), August 9, 1960, in the presence of other witnesses at the civic center plaza in San Francisco. The object moved slowly due west above a broken overcast which was being blown east by westerly winds of 10-20 mph (according to newspaper weather reports). The relatively rapid motion ruled out an astronomical explanation, and the wind direction seemed to rule out a balloon.

Mr. Rees watched the object for 30 minutes, wishing he had his camera to record it. By this time the UFO was about 70 degrees above the SE horizon. Finally he decided to get his camera in the hope the object would still be visible. He rushed home and picked up his Zeiss Tessar 2.8 35mm camera, with 45mm lens and Kodachrome color film, and found a location at which the overcast was broken. He then proceeded to take 12 photographs in succession, taking care to include known objects in the foreground of each picture for reference points.

In his initial report to NICAP, Mr. Rees stated: ''I changed exposure and f-stop every several frames--from 1/500 to 1/250 to 1/125 and from f/5.6 to f/14. By this time the UFO was still moving due west into a brisk wind and above the clouds in the direction of the sun's disc, about the zenith or 85 degrees from the southeast horizon. The slides were shot from 2:30 to 2:40. Thus in nearly an hour [from 1:45 to 2:40] of observation about 45 degrees of sky had been crossed.''

After using up his film, Mr. Rees began observing the UFO through 8 x 30 binoculars, but it was perfectly circular and had no distinguishable characteristics. It was extremely luminous and clearly visible through thin clouds (confirmed on one of the slides). To both the unaided eye and through binoculars, the object had a node of light brighter than the remainder of the object on the westward or leading edge. After 3:00 p.m. the UFO disappeared in the sun's rays and did not reappear.

In later correspondence with Max B. Miller, to whom the slides were sent for analysis, Mr. Rees cited six arguments against the balloon explanation:

(1) The extreme brightness for an opaque plastic balloon, suggesting emitted rather than reflected light.

(2) There was a brisk westerly wind from the ocean, strongly evidenced by movements of the low fog and broken overcast.

(3) The object suddenly vanished when near the sun's disc, not reappearing. There was no subsequent report of a balloon landing.

(4) Through binoculars there was no elongation of the object visible, and no instrument package, lines or other external apparatus.

(5) The UFO gave the impression of rotating around its vertical axis, though the position of the node did not change.

(6) The readily visible node and its constant orientation toward the west. (Node confirmed on photographic enlargements)

In addition to making a thorough analysis of the pictures themselves, and studying various enlargements, Max B. Miller (with assistance from Robert C. Beck, another NICAP Adviser) also checked weather records and balloon records. There were no Weather Bureau, Navy or Air Force balloons in the area at the time of the sighting. Winds aloft up to 50,000 feet were generally westerly and definitely inconsistent with the motion of the UFO. However, at 60,000 feet (the highest reading taken) winds were easterly at 9 knots.

Excerpts from Mr. Miller's detailed analysis report: ''The images of the object on the original slides varied between approximately .07mm and .09mm along their maximum axes. . . [Based on camera data] the object appears to have been between approximately 4.2 and 5.4 minutes of arc in angular diameter. [This variation in size could have been caused by additional grain structure in different exposures].''

Mr. Miller then considers and rules out Venus as the source of the light (too small and too close to the sun). ''An object 5 minutes in angular diamerter at 50,000 feet and 70 degrees above the horizon. . .would have been approximately 82 feet in diameter. . .''

''[My first] reaction was that Mr. Rees had photographed some type of aerial balloon.'' Mr. Miller then discusses the wind and balloon data, and cites a letter from the Weather Bureau giving fairly complete information. ''This statement did not, of course, rule out the possibility that a Skyhook or similar high altitude research balloon might have been photographed. . .'' Mr. Miller then cites Navy and Air Force letters stating none of their balloons were in the area.

Neither the Air Force nor local newspapers had any record of a UFO sighting in the area on that date, and no other witnesses turned up aside from the original group at the civic center.

''Mr. Rees'. . .objections [about the possibility the UFO was a balloon] seem to be well taken. . . . It seems logical to this writer that the usual appendage handing below these balloons would be relatively apparent, even under minimum magnification. However, I certainly do not feel qualified to adequately comment on this aspect, and therefore recommend that this phase of the evaluation be dispatched to someone experienced in balloon tracking.''

In conclusion, Mr. Miller stated he believed the following possibilities were eliminated: Aircraft, a bird, a cloud, foreign matter such as windblown newspaper, radiosonde or pilot weather balloons. ''Unfortunately, the possibility that Jay Rees may have

Photographic Cases (Continued)

photographed a high altitude research balloon has not been eliminated.''

The photographs subsequently were delivered to the Minneapolis NICAP Subcommittee since one of its members, Mr. Wallace Roepke, was formerly on the Skyhook balloon atmospheric research program and was still connected with General Mills. Also the Subcommittee has other scientists and a professional photographer. Mr. Roepke also filed a detailed report with NICAP on behalf of the Subcommittee.

In consultation with experienced balloon personnel Mr. Roepke and Mr. Hub T. Sherman (Chairman of the Subcommittee and an astronomer by training) obtained the following facts bearing on the case:

1. Although plenty of advanced warning is given to airports concerning balloon launchings, records of such are destroyed 72 hours after launching.

2. Release of payload usually causes a sudden rise of the balloon and a resulting explosion or fragmentation, but there are anomalous cases where the balloon survives for several days or even weeks.

3. The balloons become nearly spherical at their maximum altitudes where they are not normally seen by many people, are easily seen in more teardrop form at lower altitudes.

In view of the above, there was no way to check on the presence of a General Mills research balloon. One of the consultants believed the UFO definitely was a balloon at about 100,000 feet. It was observed that apparent direction of motion of the balloons can be misleading, due to cloud motion. ''The disappearance of the object can be explained in at least three ways: a. Proximity to the sun and its overpowering glare. b. Proximity to the sun causing most of the reflection to be at the back side of the object as seen from the position of the observer. c. The object could have exploded or fragmented.''

Mr. Roepke expressed his confidence that the analysts were skilled and impartial, and stated his conclusion as follows:

''In consideration of all the foregoing, it is concluded by one investigator that there is nothing of major significance in the Rees sighting to show that a balloon was not observed. One investigator considers that, in all probability, a balloon was sighted; while two investigators consider that the object was a balloon. Two other investigators were noncommital.''

Thus four out of six of the General Mills scientists and technicians consulted leaned heavily toward the balloon explanation. In view of this fact and the lack of any maneuvers which could not be attributed to a balloon, NICAP's conclusion is that the UFO probably was a large plastic research balloon at 60,000 feet or higher. If so, this would be one of the anomalous cases cited above when the balloon did not explode upon releasing its instrument package. It is conceivable that the ''node'' was a partial rupture--not quite sufficient to cause fragmentation--resulting from the sudden rise following release of the instruments.

52. August 25, 1960, ''mystery satellite'' photograph. Data received by NICAP from the Grumman Aircraft Corporation in Long Island were a contact print and enlargement showing the motion of the unknown object in relation to the star field. Grumman stated the object was moving at a speed comparable to previous satellites, but from east to west.

53. A/3C Bellett, Golden, Colorado. Photograph submitted in letter dated January 16, 1961. Negative requested and subsequently furnished. Both were forwarded to Max B. Miller for analysis. Mr. Miller stated: ''This is a very common negative defect. . .[which] occurs whenever a piece of foreign matter happens to collect on the negative at the moment of exposure.'' The picture shows a thin dark line (about the proportions of a thin cigar) against the sky high above a plateau. Nothing was observed visually.

54. Harry Caslar, Eglin AFB, Fla. At 4:45 p.m. while taking movies of his son on the beach at Eglin AFB reservation, Mr. Caslar noticed a UFO approaching from over the water. He managed to obtain footage of it with his 8mm camera. The film was viewed by the staff of a local newspaper. The film reportedly showed a cigar shaped or elliptical object making a U-turn and receding out over the Gulf. Both the Air Force and a NICAP member approached Mr. Caslar about borrowing the film

for analysis, but he refused to part with it. Based on the newspaper description, the film sounds like an important one. However, neither the film nor stills from it have been viewed by NICAP.

55. Nashville triangle. A shining object at very high altitude, appearing roughly triangular in shape, was viewed over a wide area near Nashville, Tenn., from about 5:00 p.m. to sunset. Data on the incident was gathered for NICAP by member Paul Norman, including photographs of the object. Navy jets tried to inspect the object, but couldn't reach its altitude, which appeared to be about 60,000 feet. Examination of the photographs and witness reports to NICAP led to the conclusion the object probably was a high altitude research balloon. Nothing contained in the photographs or reports strongly challenges this conclusion. Huge ''Moby Dick'' plastic balloons (named after Melville's legendary whale) used for high altitude research are pyramidal in form and can appear triangular in outline. Also, local authorities often know nothing about these balloons, which travel long distances glowing brightly in sunlight at times. When local airports are unaware of the nature of the objects, this sometimes adds to the mystery.

(The NICAP Assistant Director once experienced a sighting of a ''Moby Dick'' hovering and glowing brightly over New Orleans. No one could account for it, and the object still resembled a bright light source through 6 power binoculars. With the aid of an astronomical telescope, he was finally able to resolve it. The plastic material and instrument packages were clearly visible).

56. Craig Seese, Newark, Ohio. NICAP received a telegram in June 1961 notifying us about the existence of some color movies of a UFO taken by a 16 year old boy, Craig Seese. Our informant was Robert William Miller, a young man with serious interest in UFO investigation who had formed his own group for that purpose. Mr. Miller had been one of five witnesses to the UFO sighting and filming.

A meeting was arranged between the youths, and Mr. A. B. Ledwith, a NICAP member in the area with technical background (including photographic analysis work with Smithsonian Astrophysical Observatory). Mr. Ledwith was requested to advise NICAP whether he considered analysis of the film worthwhile. After talking to the youths and viewing the film, Mr. Ledwith recommended analysis of the film and advised Mr. Seese to have several copies made, storing the original in a cool safe place.

Mr. Miller was advised to forward one copy of the film to Max B. Miller in Los Angeles for analysis. (NICAP paid for the printing of one copy of the film for this purpose). The film was sent to Max Miller by registered mail August 7, 1961. About this time photographic analysis work began to pile up on Max Miller, and other committments began to make demands on his time. As a result several analyses in the past two years are either incomplete or still pending. Max Miller is no longer a NICAP Special Adviser, and other arrangements are being made to complete the analyses.

The color film was taken between 10:00 p.m. and midnight with a Brownie 8mm camera and telephoto lens (2.5 power), f/1.9. The UFO appeared to the unaided eye as a single white light, but the film indicates three objects, one slightly off-frame. Mr. Ledwith has tentatively ruled out reflections and film defects as the source of the images.

57. Bob Feldman, Akron, Ohio. Color photograph of alleged UFO taken by 12 year old boy forwarded to Max B. Miller for examination. No report received. Picture shows object resembling sky rocket, on Echtachrome film E-21.5 at 1/1250 seconds.

58. Paccione Moon Photos. A series of four photographs showing a dark spot moving across the face of the moon were submitted to NICAP by Ralph Rankow (now a NICAP photographic Adviser). A young employee, Michael Paccione, had taken them sometime around September 20, but could not recall the exact date. He used a Starmaster refractor telescope and 35mm single lens reflex camera, with Tri-X pan film exposures of 1, 2, & 3 seconds. The time was just after 8:30 p.m.

Mr. Rankow, a professional photographer, considers the negatives authentic. The photographs were then examined by Dr. James C. Bartlett, Jr., NICAP astronomy Adviser in Baltimore, and Mr. Sidney Parsons, professional astronomer and NICAP member. Dr. Bartlett determined that, based on the fraction of the moon's surface which was illuminated in the photographs, the

Photographic Cases (Continued)

data was consistent with conditions on September 17. Mr. Parsons made some rough computations of the size (diameter) and velocity of the object, assuming various distances from earth. The UFO travelled too slow for a conventional aircraft and was unlike a satellite. "The only conventional device which could comply with such an observation," Mr. Parsons concluded, "is a high-altitude balloon." Assuming the object was about 1/15th the angular diameter of the moon, and at an altitude of 10 miles (52,800 feet), its diameter would be 31 feet. If at 100 miles altitude, the diameter would be 306 feet, etc.

59. Savage, Warrenton, Va. While returning home from Washington, D.C. to Warrenton, Va. in a car pool, Mr. Harvey B. Savage, Jr., and his companions noticed an unusual object in the sky with an elongated pearshaped tail or trail. The object appeared to remain stationary until he reached home. When he started to photograph the UFO with his 16mm Bell & Howell camera using telephoto lens, the UFO changed position, then began moving rapidly. He managed to obtain several feet of film showing the object. (The above is a second-hand account from a close friend of Mr. Savage. The film was loaned to NICAP for analysis, a misunderstanding developed over the timing of the analysis, and Mr. Savage refused to fill out a NICAP form.)

The film was copied by NICAP, the original returned to Mr. Savage. As viewed at NICAP, the film showed what appeared to be a contrail. The film was nevertheless forwarded to Max Miller for closer examination, and is among the unprocessed material awaiting analysis.

60. Jeanne Booth Johnson, Hawaii. Following some UFO sightings in Hawaii during March 1963, the Honolulu Advertiser published Mrs. Johnson's UFO photograph taken about a year previously. NICAP contacted Mrs. Johnson about analyzing the picture and received full cooperation. She had taken five exposures of ships in Kahului harbor, and the final exposure, when developed showed a large, dark pear-shaped object with what appeared to be a vapor-like trail above it. (She had not seen anything visually, but was intent on photographing the harbor scene and had not looked closely at the sky).

The camera used was a Rolleicord, with 120 Tri-X (400) film. Camera settings f/5.6 and 1/250. All five prints and negatives were submitted to photographic Adviser Ralph Rankow. Enlargement of the UFO photograph revealed bubbles or spots caused by developmental defects elsewhere in the picture, making the authenticity of the UFO doubtful. Stating that it could have been coincidence, even though an unlikely one, that only this photograph of the series showed such defects, Mr. Rankow termed the case "undecided." However, the lack of visual sighting of such a large object (well within the frame of the picture) in addition to the detected defects on the negative cause us to conclude it is most likely not a real UFO, only a developmental defect.

61. F. DiMambro, Woburn, Mass. NICAP first learned of the existence of these four photographs in a news release form Mr. George Fawcett received in June 1962. The witnesses originally were anonymous, but Mr. Fawcett was contacted and obtained for NICAP the Polaroid prints and a signed report form in which Mr. DiMambro gave permission to use his name. This added considerable value to the case. The pictures were forwarded to Ralph Rankow who examined them, and made copies for NICAP.

The images are faint, due to overexposure, but readily visible. Mr. Fawcett's original report stated that the four pictures were taken in 30 seconds. Concerning this, Mr. Rankow said: "I sincerely question the ability of anyone to make 4 Polaroid photos on one camera in 30 seconds. It must have taken longer, or else they weren't developed for the full ten seconds. This is a possibility, since the streaks on the top and bottom of photos #2 and #3 would indicate improper developing. . ." (On the report form, Mr. DiMambro stated the UFO was observed for 40-50 seconds, but he gave no information about the actual filming).

Mr. Rankow also raised this question: "Why did he not adjust the lens setting differently after seeing how light the first one came out? It would have been better to get one good shot than 4 like this."

As NICAP stated to Mr. Fawcett, "If the witnesses are of sound character, I would say these are the most interesting pictures we've seen in a long time." Mr. DiMambro is a concrete and brick mason who was building a chimney on the rooftop of a new home when the sighting and filming took place. Reportedly, there were three other adult witnesses. Lacking information about the witnesses, we are forced to place the pictures in the incomplete category, pending additional data.

The first three photographs show no landmarks. The fourth shows the UFO close above a definite skyline including trees. The UFO, in one exposure, appears to be perfectly circular with a smaller circular marking in the center. However, the alleged UFO could also be one or more relatively small objects thrown in the air and photographed.

62. Bruce Fox, Bayonne, N.J. Mr. Fox submitted this photograph to NICAP in a letter dated November 19, stating he had seen a bright moving object in the sky about 8:15 p.m. and managed to take one successful photograph of it. The letter and photograph were forwarded to Ralph Rankow, NICAP Adviser, on November 20. Mr. Fox was asked to submit his negative, a signed report form, and to include camera data. All the requested information was provided, except the negative. The camera was a box type Spartus with fixed lens setting, using 620 black and white film. In a letter to Mr. Rankow, Mr. Fox stated that his original letter to NICAP had been in error, and that he had obtained two clear photographs. A second photograph was submitted directly to Mr. Rankow. No meaningful analysis of the photographs has been possible.

63. Ronald Gounad, Bayonne, N.J. Photographs showing groups of lights in the sky were submitted in January 1963. Lights resembling those on a Christmas tree were visible in the foreground. The UFOs reportedly were visible, and photographed two consecutive nights. The negatives were requested, and submitted in April. Meanwhile, Ralph Rankow examined the pictures and stated that nothing could be determined from them. It was deduced that the original light sources were three lights in a straight line one above the other. However, the camera was hand-held and the shutter snapped five times for each picture further confusing already nebulous photographs. Since the witness offered no comments or explanation about the needless multiple exposures, the photographs and negatives were returned to him with a rating of "dubious."

64. Angel Falls, Venezuela. Mr. Ali R. Diaz, Caracas, aboard a tourist plane on a vacation trip to the Angel Falls area of remote Venezuelan jungle, obtained color movies of a UFO rising from the base of a mountain into the sky. With the aid of Dr. Askold Ladonko, NICAP Adviser in Caracas, and other NICAP members in the area. Mr. Diaz was interviewed and still shots from the movie film were obtained.

Later a Spanish-speaking NICAP member, Mr. Jose' Cecin, was able to fly to Caracas from New York City, and persuaded Mr. Diaz to loan the film to NICAP for analysis. The U.S. Air Force attache' had already viewed the film, but had not been permitted to retain it.

As this Report is being written, the original film is in the possession of a professional scientist on the west coast who has previously analyzed UFO movies. An analysis report is expected sometime in 1964. Mr. Cecin has retained a protection copy, and plans are being made for independent analysis of it. A third protection copy is being stored for safe-keeping.

The movie, taken from the side window of a DC-3 as it passed Angel Falls, shows a yellowish tear-drop shaped object rising at a slight angle across the face of Auyantupuy Mountain. The object seems to oscillate from side to side, until it is lost in the sky, apparently moving into clouds. The falls and mountain provide landmarks throughout. The jungle area where the film was taken is so impenetrable that no one has ever been known to reach it on foot. While filming the falls, Mr. Diaz noticed a bright flash of light through his view finder, and the film appears to verify the presence of something unusual.

Physical & Physiological Effects

In addition to radar trackings, electro-magnetic effects, and photographs, there have been other indications of the physical reality of UFOs. These include markings or substances left on the ground, and physiological effects on the observers. (With a few exceptions, the physiological effects have been temporary and not severe.)

The following chart lists 35 sample cases; about half are taken from Aime Michel's account of the intensive concentration of UFO sightings in France during fall 1954, the remainder from other sources. The chart gives a cross-section of the types of physical and physiological effects which have been reported generally as resulting from UFOs.

In most cases, scientific investigation of these reports has been totally lacking. Therefore, it is not claimed that they prove anything. On the other hand, independent witnesses all over the world have reported very similar experiences. Their reports deserve far more attention than they have received to date. NICAP has tried to encourage more thorough investigation of them.

A comparison with the listing of electro-magnetic effects (this section) will show that there appears to be a relationship between E-M cases and physiological effects. *Hypothesis: That the presumed electro-magnetic radiation from UFOs which affects electrical circuits also affects the human body under certain conditions. If this hypothesis is correct, the importance of scientific investigation in this area is obvious.*

Date & Location		Physiological	Physical	Traces	Description	Notes
7-23-48	Montgomery, Ala.		X		Airliner rocked (Chiles-Whitted) as UFO passed	[Section V]
7-1-54	Walesville, N.Y.	X			Intense heat	[71]
9-10-54	Nr. Quarouble, France	X	X	X	Paralysis, markings, trees black	[72]
9-17-54	Vienne, France	X			Prickling sensation like "electric shock"	[73]
9-24-54	Correze, France		X		Tree branches dried and curled	[74]
9-26-54	Chabeuil, France		X		10. ft. circle; foliage crushed	[75]
9-27-54	Premanon, France		X		Holes in ground, grass flattened	[76]
9-28-54	Bouzais, France	X			Paralysis, lost consciousness	[77]
10-3-54	Nessier, France			X	Oily spots	[78]
10-3-54	Ronsenac, France		X		Grass flattened	[79]
10-4-54	St. Seine L'Abbaya, France		X		Crater over 4 feet long	[80]
10-7-54	Le Mans, France	X			Prickling, partial paralysis	[81]
10-7-54	Monteux, France	X			Paralysis	[82]
10-9-54	Briatexte, France			X	Brownish, sticky deposit	[83]
10-11-54	Clamecy, France	X			Electric shock, paralysis	[84]
10-14-54	Meral, France			X	Sticky deposit	[85]
10-15-54	Rovigo, Italy			X	20 ft. crater, trees "carbonized"	[86]
10-16-54	Nr. Baillolet, France	X			Electric shock	[87]
10-18-54	Auverne, France	X			Paralysis	[88]
7-22-55	Cincinnati, Ohio	X		X	Skin burned, tree petrified	[89]
8-6-55	Cincinnati, Ohio	X			Eyes badly irritated	[90]
8-25-55	Bedford, Indiana		X		Semicircular impressions in ground	[91]
11-2-55	Williston, Florida	X			Heat stung body	
7-31-57	Galt, Ontario, Canada		X		Burned patches, impressions in ground	[92]
11-3-57	Scotia, Nebraska	X			Paralysis, fumes left in air	[93]
11-4-57	Sao Vicente, Brazil	X			1st & 2nd degree burns, 10% of body	[94]
11-4-57	Alamagordo, New Mexico	X			Minor facial burns	[Section XII]
11-6-57	Nr. Merom, Indiana	X			Skin red, eyes swollen	[Section XII]
11-10-57	Madison, Ohio	X			Eye damage, shock, emotional upset	[Detailed in this Section]
2-20-58	Nr. Espanola, N.Mex.	X			Skin burns, reported radioactivity	[95]
5-5-58	Nr. San Carlos, Uruguay	X			Intense heat, E-M effect	[Section X]
9-7-59	Nr. Lexington, Kentucky			X	13 ft. stained ring	[96]
5-24-60	Ocumare del Tuy, Venezuela		X		Diamond-shaped scorched marks	[97]
5-12-62	Argentina	X			Intense glow injured eyes	[Section XII]
5-12-62	Nr. LaPampa, Argentina			X	Grayish stain on ground	[Section XII]
	TOTALS	20	10	8		

As in the fall 1954 French sightings, the November 1957 "flap" in the United States brought with it reports of physical and physiological effects from UFOs. On a farm in Scotia, Nebraska, November 3, Roger Groetzinger (10) was milking the cows when he noticed an oblong object circling low over the barn. He thought it was a plane about to land, and went outside to the pasture fence to watch. The object was at low altitude emitting a humming noise. Suddenly Roger found that he could not move. As the UFO gained altitude and started moving away, the paralysis left. When Roger's mother returned home, she found a thoroughly frightened son. Where the UFO was seen low above the ground, heavy fumes lingered in the air.

A week later, Mrs. Leita Kuhn in Madison, Ohio, observed a brilliant glowing object at close range. The physiological after-effects of her sighting were fairly serious. Between 1:00 and 2:00 a.m. on the morning of November 10, Mrs. Kuhn had been having difficulty with an overheating stove in her kennel. It was a dark night, snowing and windy, and she had to make several trips between her house and the kennel.

Finally, after she was sure all was well in the kennel, she shut the door and stepped outside. Suddenly she realized the sky was very bright. It had stopped snowing.

"I stepped away from the kennel," she told NICAP, "and there in back about 60 feet above ground was a huge glowing object. . . It was phosphorous in color. Base, forty feet wide and nine to ten feet thick, domelike top. Top seemed brighter than bottom. I looked the bottom over well. . ." Exhaust-like clouds were visible on the left side of the object.

"The top was brighter. I couldn't look at the top. My eyes burned so I closed them--orange sparks seemed to glow every-time I closed my eyes. . . The brilliance is beyond description."

Becoming frightened, Mrs. Kuhn fled to the house. She looked out the window and it was dark again. "I went back outside and it was gone. There was no noise, no odor. It was 1:55 a.m."

Mrs. Kuhn couldn't sleep, and wondered what to do about the sighting. UFOs were not supposed to exist; who could she report it to?

"I decided not to," she said. "A few days later I had to see a doctor. My eyes were troubling me, a rash was driving me insane and I hadn't slept since November 10. Upon hearing my story, he advised me to report it. Which I did--thank goodness. The publicity was tough but through it I met others who have seen these too."

UFO witnesses sometimes need psychological reinforcement. In the face of repeated official denials that UFOs exist, a person would begin to doubt his own sanity unless he knew that others had made similar reports. Mrs. Kuhn was shocked by her experience, and a little bitter toward those in authority.

"I surely wish they [the Air Force] would call on me. I've been wanting to tell them I'm mad--clear through. I feel duped and deceived."

Later NICAP contacted Mrs. Kuhn again to inquire about her health. In a detailed letter which she requested be treated as confidential, she described in detail what the physiological effects had been. Although ultra-violet radiation had been suggested as the cause at one point, the doctors she consulted treated her for a variety of ailments which had not been present prior to the UFO sighting. Some were painful and emotionally disturbing, and she began to fear for her life. In time, the symptoms began to clear up until, as of her January 1959 letter, her health was returning and she felt "rather well."

Aside from the physical effects, Mrs. Kuhn experienced several psychological problems. Local civil defense officials treated her report seriously, but why did the government deny the existence of UFOs? Some friends rebuffed her, curiosity seekers plagued her. Getting no satisfactory explanation from government or scientific authorities, she sought an answer among UFO believers. In the process, she encountered the inevitable crackpots who took every light in the sky to be a space ship bearing noble beings. She was repelled by their attitude toward UFOs, and felt they only obscured the truth.

Mrs. Kuhn seemed to be an intelligent and level-headed woman who was shocked and disturbed by an experience so immediate that it caused her to lose confidence in officialdom. She now feels it is urgent that the truth about UFOs be made public so that others may be prepared psychologically where she was not. At last report, she had given up her kennel to devote more time to establishing the truth about UFOs.

SOUND

The notion that UFOs are typically silent, unlike piston and jet aircraft, is true in general. In a surprising number of cases, however, UFOs have made noises of some kind. This aspect of the phenomena should be studied carefully in the future, since it could provide some important clues to the nature of UFOs. To date, the descriptions of the sounds have been sketchy. This line of questioning has not been pursued by investigators in as much detail as it might have been, probably because of the "silent UFO" stereotype.

Useful information for a study of UFO sounds would include careful estimations (or measurements when possible) of the distance of the object from the observer when the sound was heard; and ideally tape recordings of the actual sound, as well as information about the appearance of the UFO and what maneuvers it was making at the time. Sound detection and amplification equipment would be required for any complete scientific investigation.

The following chart is intended only to be descriptive, and to organize seeming patterns tentatively.

Date & Location	Type of UFO	Distance estimate	Sound & Maneuvers
8-1-52; Sharonville, Ohio	white disc	"low"	crackling, while ascending after level flight
9-17-54; Nr Rome, Italy	top-like	3600-6000 ft. (radar track)	series of staccato explosions [Section X.]
11-12-54; Oolitic, Ind.	white ball	--	hovered, exploded "like shotgun," took off at high speed
7-29-55; Cincinnati, Ohio	glowing ball	--	penetrating shrill noise while zig-zagging, making sharp turns [Section VII.]
1-27-57; Glendora, Calif.	2 amber discs	--	hovered, sped away making swishing noise
8-2-57; Sebago Lake, Maine	greenish glowing light	--	maneuvered, rapidly at times; hovered 30 minutes, making loud humming noise
11-2-57; Levelland, Texas	torpedo-shaped	first on ground, rose & sped low over truck	rush of wind, "noise like thunder"
11-5-57; Nr Ringwood, Ill.	luminous ball	2000 ft. altitude	noise "like swishing water"
11-6157; Dunn, N.C.	shaped like lamp-shade	--	sharp explosive sound attracted witness; saw UFO going straight up
11-6-57; Dugger, Ind.	est. 40 ft. diameter; no description	1000 ft. altitude	hovered, climbed straight up, moved away horizontally making "whirring" noise

Date & Location	Type of UFO	Distance estimate	Sound & Maneuvers
8-11-58; Acright, N. Y.	bright white light	--	moved with skipping motion, droning noise
9-21-58; Sheffield Lake, Ohio	glowing disc	6 ft. alt., 10 ft. distance	"whirring" or "whining" noise, constant
10-26-58; Baltimore, Maryland	glowing ellipse	320 ft. distance, hovering low over bridge	hovered, shot straight up making thunderous explosive noise
2-3-59; Oil City, Pa.	circular	below low cloud ceiling	high-speed pass, swishing noise
7-13-59; Blenheim, N.Z.	disc	below treetops	descended, hovered, low humming sound; rose vertically at high speed with "thin high-pitched whine" [Section XIV]
8-17-60; Folsom, Calif.	dark, body lights visible	--	whine "like spinning top"
8-18-60; Dunsmuir, Calif.	reddish oblong	--	sound "like rushing wind"
9-13-62; Nr Overfield, England	grayish disc	about height of telegraph poles	hovered, made "swishing" noise as it sped away

The eighteen cases above were selected from a larger sample (approximately 50) of readily available sound cases, in a manner designed to minimize the accidental inclusion of misidentified aircraft, etc., which may have been seen under unusual lighting conditions and reported as UFOs. This was done by taking cases in which the UFOs exhibited "typical" characteristics such as sharp turns, erratic maneuvers, and rapid acceleration. Cases involving simple straight line flight at moderate speeds, regardless of the physical appearance of the supposed UFO, were excluded. The result gives a wide distribution, both by date and geographical location, of fairly typical UFO sightings, with the added feature of sound from the objects.

These apparent patterns emerge:

✳ UFOs which make sharp explosive noise during rapid acceleration or high-speed flight.

✳ UFOs which emit a humming (whining or whirring) noise while hovering or moving relatively slowly.

✳ UFOs which make a whistling or "swishing" noise like rushing air.

Assuming that the sample of cases is representative, we next have to take into account variations in terminology used by different witnesses in describing what they have heard. We shall assume that "whirring," "whining," or "humming" constitute a single type of sound. This has sometimes been compared to the sound made by an electric motor or generator.

The French theorist, Lieutenant Plantier, has developed the concept of deriving propulsive force from primary cosmic rays by transforming the energy into "a local field of force that can be varied and directed at will." His theory has the merit of predicting some of the observed features of UFOs. However, it rules out sonic booms (postulating that an air cushion carried along with the UFO would buffer sound), when there is evidence that UFOs do make sonic booms.

Another similar approach, suggested by Prof. Dr. Hermann Oberth, is that whoever operates the UFOs has knowledge of the control of gravity. The UFOs' apparent circumvention of the laws of inertia, as we understand them, has been the single most difficult feature of UFO phenomena to account for. Could control of gravity explain how this is possible?

The above speculation may or may not be close to the truth. If we forget for the moment the problem of inertial effects and assume we are dealing with controlled devices which in some manner surmount that problem, we can hypothetically explain the UFO sounds as (a) actual sonic booms; (b) actual "engine" noises very similar to a "whirring" electric motor; and (c) whistling, rushing air effects of a solid body traveling through air.

There are indications that only the sonic booms are heard at any appreciable distance. At distances comparable to those attained by high-altitude aircraft, where we are able to hear jet or piston engines at least faintly, UFOs apparently are virtually silent. The July 13, 1959, New Zealand case (and similar data) suggests a direct relationship between the level of sound and acceleration, with increased intensity or shrillness when power is applied.

Angel's Hair

An interesting phenomenon which has been linked with UFOs is so-called "angel's hair." This gossamer-like substance has been observed falling from the sky, sometimes in great quantity. However, it (if indeed only one type of substance is involved) has only been observed in association with UFOs in about one-half of the cases. Also, it is obvious that in many cases the substance has been nothing but cobwebs spun by ballooning spiders. [Natural History, January 1951; "Those Things in the Sky."] On at least one occasion, small spiders have actually been found in the material leaving little doubt about the identification.

Although we do not presently consider angel's hair to be significant evidence of UFOs, (or for that matter to be clearly differentiated from spider webs in most cases) there are some surprising reports on record which cause us to suspend final judgment.

A typical angel's hair report (though not designated as such) is reported in the Humboldt (Calif.) Times, November 11 and 12, 1958. Residents of Trinidad, Rio Dell, and other northern California towns reported showers of cobweb-like material on November 9, some in strands 5 to 6 feet long. Two fishermen at sea, George Korkan and Jack Curry, said the substance settled on their boat in such quantity that it made the boat appear to be "a million years old."

A sample of the substance obtained at McKinleyville airport was examined by Dr. Erwin Bielfuss, assistant professor of biology at Humboldt State College. The newspaper quotes him as ruling out the possibility of it being a mold growth or animal product, and suggesting it is either plant life or a plastic material.

Although it was reported that strands up to 40 feet in length were draped over trees and wires, there were no reports of spiders being found.

A trained biologist witnessed a fall of angel's hair about 1957. He gave the following statement to NICAP:

"Several years ago, I would estimate close to the summer of 1957, two others and myself witnessed a phenomenon that could be best described as "a sky full of cobwebs" off the Florida coast a short distance south of Miami. At that time I held the position of curator of the Miami Seaquarium, and I was taking part in a specimen-collecting trip aboard the Seaquarium vessel Sea Horse, which was skippered by collections director Capt. W. B. Gray and his assistant, Emil Hanson.

"We were traveling northward after a successful day's collecting, somewhere between Soldiers Key and Key Biscayne and approximately three miles off the Florida mainland. The sky was clear on this particular day and little or no wind was blowing. For a period of two hours or more we observed occasional strands of what appeared to be very fine cobwebs up to two or more feet in length, drifting down from the sky and occasionally catching in the rigging of our craft. On being questioned by the others as to what might be the nature of these webs, I explained to the others that an oft-repeated statement in natural history books is that very young spiders on hatching will frequently pay out long strands of silk from their spinnerets until the wind catches them and they eventually become airborne, sometimes being transported many miles and even, as I seemed to recall, far out to sea on occasion.

"At the time I assumed that some phenomenon of temperature or timing had resulted in the mass hatching and exodus of a certain type of spider somewhere on the mainland, and that furthermore, these webs must be fragments of the original strands which in themselves may have been of considerable length. Spiders can and do at times produce vast lengths (in proportion to their size) of web material at little expense to their own metabolism, and I visualized the little spiderlets, wherever they might be, continuing to emit their silken trails during their airborne journey as the wind broke and blew the first ones away. Although we captured a number of these strands on our fingertips, no spiders were to be seen despite the likelihood that a certain percentage of them would still have spiders attached.

"With the intention of examining the strands under my laboratory microscope when we reached the Seaquarium, I carefully placed several of them inside a mason jar, allowing them to cling to the inside of the glass before I capped it. Under high power I had hoped to see the tiny adhesive droplets that adorn most but not all spider webs, and were these present, there would be little doubt of their true nature. However, when I uncapped the jar later in my office, no trace of the web material could be found.

"This phenomenon is to me still unexplained, and I have seen nothing comparable to it before or since. I will mention by way of information that I have always been interested in the biology of spiders and their webs, particularly the giant orb-weaver Nephilia, whose bright golden web is a fairly common sight through the Everglades. Strong enough to support small pebbles, this web has actually been woven into cloth by natives of the tropics.

"From the foregoing, I would say that it is possible that the strands we saw were something other than spider web, and I have no explanation for the apparent disappearance of the collected material in the mason jar."

/s/ Craig Phillips
U.S. Fish & Wildlife Service,
Department of the Interior; 11-5-63

The reported dissipation of the angel's hair in this case is commonly reported. Some analysts who do not think all angel's hair is cobwebs use this feature to differentiate "true" angel's hair from spider webs. If this assumption is correct, angel's hair unfortunately becomes a will-of-the-wisp which disappears before it can be analyzed properly, and therefore it does not constitute good physical evidence.

Biologists who have examined angel's hair which has subsequently dissipated have been unable to account for it in terms of spiders. The substances which have not dissipated so far show no particular pattern, and may be attributed to many different phenomena. The following chart includes all reported cases of falls of gossamer-like material which have been compiled by NICAP for specific dates.

ANGEL's HAIR AND/OR GOSSAMER FALLS

Date & Location	U.F.O. reported	Dissipation	Spiders	Remarks & Notes
9-21-1741; Bradly, England				Strands 5-6 inches long "fell with some velocity" for hours in great quantity. [From Charles Fort]
9-20-1892; Gainesville, Florida				Vast quantity "like great white sheets," some "50 yards or more in length." [Proceedings, Entomological Society of Washington, D.C., Vol. II (1892) ppg. 385-388.]
11-21-1898; Montgomery, Alabama				Strands several inches long fell in batches; reportedly phosphorescent. [From Charles Fort]
11-10-49; Depues Ferry, Pennsylvania	X			["Inside Saucer Post ... 3-0 Blue, " Stringfield, p. 49]
10-11-50; Butte County, California	X			Sample analyzed by Dr. Willis J. Gertsch, Museum of Natural History; identified as gossamer. [Natural History, January 1951]
10-11-50; Paradise, California	X	X		Partial dissipation reported, leaving "tough white threads--resembling a spiderweb, but of much tougher consistency." [Chico Enterprise-Record, October 12, 1950]
10-17-1952; Oloron, France	X	X		Fibres burned like cellophane when ignited. ["The Truth about flying Saucers," Michel, ppg. 146-7]
10-27-52; Gaillac, France	X	X		[Ibid., p. 148]
4-15-53; Auckland, N.Z.		X		["Challenge of UFOs," Maney & Hall, p, 59]
5-30-53; Christchurch, N.Z.	X			[Ibid., p. 59]
10-9-53; Melbourne, Australia		X		[Ibid., p. 59]
10-13-53; Pleasant Hill, California	X			[Ibid., p. 59]
11-16-53; San Fernando Valley, California	X	X		[Pageant, November 1954]
10-19-54; Fort Wayne, Indiana				[Stringfield, op. cit., p. 49]
10-22-54; Marysville, Ohio	X	X		[Maney & Hall, op. cit., ppg. 40-42]
10-28-54; Rome, Italy	X			[Ibid., p. 59]
11-4-54; Nelson, N.Z.	X			[Stringfield, op. cit., p. 49]
11-8-54; Florence, Italy	X			[Ibid., p. 59]
12-12-54; Christchurch, N.Z.	X			[Ibid., p. 49]
2-21-55; Horseheads, N.Y.				"White, fibrous and heavily impregnated with soot and dirt" No odor, did not burn rapidly. [AP, 2-22-55]

Date & Location	U.F.O. reported	Dissipation	Spiders	Remarks & Notes
7-29-55; Sacramento, California				[Stringfield, op. cit., p. 49]
9-1-55; Edmore, Mich.	X			Fell slowly in clumps, "some as large as big platters." [Edmore Times, 9-9-55]
10-2-55; Uhrichsville, Ohio	X			[Section VII]
10-10-55; Cincinnati, Ohio	X			[Stringfield, op. cit., p. 49]
10-27-55; Whitsett, N.C.	X			Analysts disagreed whether substance was of animal or synthetic origin. [Greensboro Daily News, Oct. 28, 1955]
7-10-56; Melbourne, Australia		X		"Millions of white web-like threads." [Bournemouth Echo; 7-10-56]
8-19-56; St. Louis, Mo.				[Stringfield, op. cit., p. 49]
9-25-56; Cincinnati, Ohio				Analyzed by AF, identified as rayon fibres. [CRIFO Orbit; Nov. 2, 1956 & Dec. 7, 1956]
9-30-56; Cherry Valley, Illinois	X			[CRIFO Orbit; Dec. 7, 1956]
10-15-56; Indianapolis, Indiana	X			[Stringfield, op. cit., p. 50]
10-16-56; Fond de Lac, Wisconsin				[Ibid., p. 50]
4-28-57; Christchurch, N.Z.				[Ibid., p. 50]
10-4-57; Ichinoseki City, Japan				[Flying Saucer Review (London), Jan.-Feb.. 1958]
10-17-57; Nr. Fatima, Portugal		X		[Irish News, from Lisbon, 10-23-57]
10-23/24-57; Portales, N.M.				Strands up to 50 feet long, enormous quantities. [Associated Press, Oct. 24-25, 1957]
10-9-58; Portales, N.M.				[Associated Press, Oct. 10, 1958]
11-9-58; Humboldt County, California				Strands of 5-6 feet, one report of 40 foot strand by airport dispatcher.
10-26/27-59; Savannah, Georgia				[Savannah Morning News; 11-4-59]
11-3-59; Centerville, Georgia			X	[Atlanta Journal; 11-5-59]
8-5-61; Mt. Hale, Australia	X	X		Visible objects traveled in pairs, as in Gaillac and Oloron cases cited above. Substance described as "a snowy white, fine mesh....." [Perth, Western Australia newspaper, 8-6-61]
10-14-61; Sunset, Utah	X			[Report from member]
11-11-62; Lakeland, Florida	X			"Loops and whorls" of "gossamer filaments" observed in sky (No reports of striking ground). [Lakeland Ledger; 11-12-62]
TOTALS: Number of cases 43	23	12	1	

Of the 43 cases of angel's hair, visible unidentified objects were reported in just over half (23). The most common descriptions of the UFOs have been "cigar-shaped" or like "silvery balls". Sudden accelerations and high speeds have been reported, but a person seeing something at relatively close range and thinking it is a larger object farther away could easily overestimate the speed. Nevertheless, the cases of cigar-shaped UFOs (sometimes accompanied by other round objects) observed in association with angel hair falls, are the most difficult to explain.

Rapid dissipation of the substance was reported in 12 of 43 cases. In seven of these 12 cases, there were also visual sightings of UFOs.

NOTES

Electro-Magnetic Effects.

1. "Electro-Magnetic Effects Associated With Unidentified Flying Objects (UFOs)," by Washington, D. C., Subcommittee of the National Investigations Committee on Aerial Phenomena. June 1960.
2. E-M Cases, by Case Numbers:
   E-1.   Stringfield, Leonard H.; Inside Saucer Post. . .3-0 Blue. (4412 Grove Avenue, Cincinnati, Ohio).
   E-2.   Time; May 9, 1949.

E-3.   Tulsa, Okla., Tribune; 12-1-57
E-4.   Lorenzen, Coral; The Great Flying Saucer Hoax. (William-Frederick Press, N.Y. 1962), ppg. 19-22.
E-5.   Report to NICAP
E-6.   Miller, Max B. (1420 So. Ridgley Drive, Los Angeles, Calif.).
E-7.   Report to NICAP
E-8.   Aerial Phenomena Research Organization (4145 East Desert Place, Tucson, Arizona).
E-9.   Report to NICAP

E-10. Faria, J. Escobar (Rua General Mena Barreto, 527, Sao Paulo, Brazil).

E-11. Lancaster, Pa., Intelligencer-Journal; 9-17-54.

E-12. New Orleans Item; 9-21-54.

E-13. Michel, Aime, Flying Saucers and the Straight Line Mystery. (Criterion, 1958), p. 143.

E-14. Ibid., p. 150.

E-15. Ibid., p. 157.

E-16. Ibid., p. 158.

E-17. Ibid., p. 160.

E-18. Ibid., p. 175.

E-19. Ibid., p. 185.

E-20. Ibid., p. 198.

E-21. Ibid., p. 203.

E-22. Ibid., p. 204.

E-23. CRIFO Newsletter; December 3, 1954 (Stringfield, Leonard H. See address above).

E-24. Michel, Aime; op. cit., p. 204.

E-25. Ibid., p. 211.

E-26. North East Breeze (weekly); week of December 5, 1954.

E-27. Keyhoe, Donald E.; Flying Saucer Conspiracy. (Holt, 1955), p. 249.

E-28. Ibid., p. 265.

E-29. CSI (67 Jane Street, New York, N.Y.); Michel, Aime; op. cit., p. 236.

E-30. Indianapolis Star; 8-27-55.

E-31. Flying Saucer Review; Sept.-Oct., 1955 (1 Doughty Street, W.C. 1, London, England).

E-32. Report to NICAP

E-33. Fulton, H. H., New Zealand NICAP Adviser (from Japan News).

E-34. CRIFO Orbit (formerly "Newsletter"); Sept. 7, 1956.

E-35. Trench, Brinsley le Poer; Ed.; World UFO Roundup. (Citadel, 1958), ppg. 96-97.

E-36. Mobridge, S.D., Tribune, 11-22-56; Bowman, N.D., Pioneer, 11-22-56.

E-37. Report to NICAP (from Air Force Intelligence Report).

E-38. Thirouin, Marc; Ouranos. (27 Rue Etienne-Dolet, Bondy, Seine, France).

E-39. Aerial Phenomena Research Organization (APRO).

E-40. Report to NICAP.

E-41. Trench, Brinsley le Poer; op. cit., ppg 162-163.

E-42. Report to NICAP.

E-43. APRO Bulletin; September 1959.

E-44. Associated Press; 11-4-57.

E-45. Casper, Wyo., Tribune-Herald; 11-5-57. Also Report to NICAP.

E-46. Charlotte, N.C., Observer; 11-4-57.

E-47. Hobbs, N.M., News-Sun; 11-5-57.

E-48. Amarillo Daily News; 11-4-57.

E-49. Associated Press; 11-3-57, etc.

E-50. Winnipeg Tribune; 11-7-57.

E-51. Faria, J. Escobar, Brazilian NICAP Adviser.

E-52. APRO Bulletin; September 1959.

E-53. Chicago Tribune; 11-5-57.

E-54. Toronto Daily Star; 11-5-57.

E-55. Clark, Terry; "The Day All Roads Led to Alamogordo," Writer's Digest, December 1957. Associated Press; 11-4-57, etc.

E-56. Anchorage, Alaska, Daily News; 11-4-57.

E-57. Report to NICAP

E-58. San Antonio Light; 11-6-57.

E-59. Amarillo News; 11-7-57.

E-60. Report to NICAP.

E-61. El Paso, Texas, Times; 11-7-57.

E-62. Aurora, Ill., Beacon-News; 11-7-57.

E-63. Marietta, Ohio, Times; 11-6-57.

E-64. Associated Press; 11-6-57.

E-65. Houston Chronicle; 11-6-57.

E-66. Santa Fe New Mexican; 11-6-57.

E-67. Hammond, Ind., Times; 11-7-57.

E-68. Report to NICAP.

E-69. CSI Newsletter #10 (see address above).

E-70. Michel, Aime; op. cit., p. 263.

E-71. APRO Bulletin; November 1957.

E-72. Ibid.

E-73. Hammond, Ind., Times; 11-13-57.

E-74. Plymouth, N.H., Record; 11-14-57.

E-75. Hazelton, Pa., Plain Speaker; 11-13-57.

E-76. Chicago American, 11-15-57; St. Louis Post Dispatch, 11-15-57; etc.

E-77. Faria, J. Escobar (Sao Paulo, Brazil).

E-78. Ibid.

E-79. Ellensburg, Wash., Daily Record; 12-4-57.

E-80. Ontario Daily Nugget; 12-4-57.

E-81. Grant County, Wash., Journal; 12-10-57.

E-82. Report to NICAP.

E-83. UFO Bulletin, March 1958. (Box 1120, G.P.O., Sydney, N.S.W., Australia).

E-84. La Prensa, 2-1-58; United Press.

E-85. Lorenzen, Coral; op. cit., ppg. 143-144.

E-86. Report to NICAP.

E-87. Faria, J. Escobar (from Italian newspapers).

E-88. Faria, J. Escobar.

E-89. Takanashi, June'Ichi; Modern Space Flight Association (8-9-2, Sakurazuka Higashi, Toyonaka-City, Osaka, Japan).

E-90. Report to NICAP. Also Baltimore newspapers, 10-27-58.

E-91. Greenville, Pa., Record-Argus; 1-31-59.

E-92. Flying Saucer Review; Sept.-Oct., 1959.

E-93. Associated Press; 2-26-59.

E-94. Gallipolis, Ohio, Daily Tribune; 3-20-59.

E-95. APRO Bulletin, November 1959.

E-96. Report to NICAP.

E-97. APRO Bulletin; September 1959.

E-98. Lorenzen, Coral; op. cit., ppg. 175-176.

E-99. Bolton, Whitney; Newark Evening News, 11-5-59.

E-100. Grand Forks, N.D., Herald; 1-21-60.

E-101. Report to NICAP.

E-102. Flying Saucer Review; March-April, 1962.

E-103. Ibid., Nov.-Dec., 1962.

E-104. Report to NICAP.

E-105. San Francisco Examiner; 11-8-63.

E-106. Carson City Nevada Appeal; 11-14-63.

(a) Portland Oregonian; 7-7-47.

(b) Associated Press; 7-23-52.

(c) Trench, Brinsley le Poer; op. cit., ppg. 115-116.

(d) Glendora, Calif., Press; 1-31-57.

(e) Washington Star; 5-8-57, 5-9-57.

(f) Miller, Max B. Saucers, Winter 1957/58 (see address above).

(g) Houston Chronicle; 11-7-57.

(h) Honolulu Star-Bulletin; 11-29-57.

(i) Ann Arbor, Mich., News; 12-2-57.

(j) Buffalo, N.Y., Courier Express; 8-16-58.

(k) Portland, Me., Press-Herald; 12-8-59.

3. St. Louis Globe-Democrat; July 30, 1963

4. Missiles & Rockets; September 16, 1963

5. Space Propulsion Technology, Hearings before the Committee on Science & Astronautics, U.S. House of Representatives, 87th Congress, 1st Session; No. 4, Committee Print, 1961

6. Ibid., p. 216.

Radar

7. Ruppelt, Edward J., Report on Unidentified Flying Objects. (Doubleday, 1956), p. 68.

8. Keyhoe, Donald E., Flying Saucers From Outer Space. (Henry Holt, 1953), p. 33. (From USAF Intelligence Report).

9. Ibid., p. 34. (From USAF Intelligence Report).

10. Ruppelt, op. cit., p. 68

11. Life, April 7, 1952. (From USAF Intelligence Report).

12. Ruppelt, op. cit., p. 103. True, August 1950.

13. Keyhoe, op. cit., p. 48. (From USAF Intelligence Report).

14. Ibid., p. 48. (From USAF Intelligence Report).

15. Ruppelt, op. cit., p. 135.

16. Ibid., p. 167.

17. Ibid., p. 190.

18. Keyhoe, op. cit., p. 52. (From USAF Intelligence Report).

19. Ruppelt, op. cit., p. 201.

20. Time, August 11, 1952.

21. International News Service, Atlanta; July 24, 1952.
22. Keyhoe, op. cit., p. 97 (From USAF Intelligence Report).
23. Ruppelt, op. cit., p. 222.
24. Keyhoe, op. cit., p. 98. (From USAF Intelligence Report).
25. Ibid., ppg. 105-106. (From USAF Intelligence Report).
26. Ibid., p. 107. (From USAF Intelligence Report).
27. Ibid., p. 120. (From USAF Intelligence Report).
28. Ibid., p. 95; Ruppelt, op. cit., p. 247.
29. Ibid., p. 96. (From USAF Intelligence Report).
30. Ibid., p. 258. (From USAF Intelligence Report).
31. Ibid., p. 161. (From USAF Intelligence Report).
32. Ruppelt, op. cit., p. 65.
33. Keyhoe, op. cit., p. 149. (From USAF Intelligence Report).
34. Ibid., p. 189-191. (From USAF Intelligence Report).
35. True; May 1954.
36. Ruppelt, op. cit., p. 295.
37. Keyhoe, op. cit., p. 257. (From USAF Intelligence Report).
38. Ibid., p. 257. (From USAF Intelligence Report).
39. Michel, Aime, The Truth About Flying Saucers. (Criterion, 1956), p. 123
40. Ruppelt, op. cit., p. 303. (Other data on file at NICAP).
41. Keyhoe, Donald E., Flying Saucer Conspiracy. (Henry Holt, 1955), p. 79.
42. Ibid., p. 13.
43. Ibid., p. 144.
44. United Press; June 30, 1954.
45. Report obtained by Leonard H. Stringfield, Cincinnati, Ohio (See Section VII).
46. Keyhoe, op. cit., p. 25.
47. Associated Press; September 18, 1954.
48. Louisville Courier-Journal; November 13, 1954
49. Auckland Star; December 16, 1954.
50. Associated Press, Paris; February 19, 1956.
51. United Press; July 19, 1956.
52. Altus (Okla.) Times-Democrat; September 11, 1956.
53. APRO Bulletin; November 1956.
54. CRIFO Orbit; January 4, 1957. The Clipper, Pan American Airways; January 1957. Miami Daily News; November 8, 1956.
55. CRIFO Orbit; January 4, 1957. Pierre Daily Capitol Journal, November 26, 1956.
56. Associated Press, United Press, London; April 6, 1957.
57. Unresolved discrepancy in dates. Flying Saucer Review (London), Jan.-Feb., 1958 gives October 21. APRO Bulletin, November 1957, gives October 29.
58. APRO Bulletin, January 1958.
59. Signed report on file at NICAP.
60. Signed report on file at NICAP. Visual sighting inferred from report.
61. Japan Times; July 28, 1958.
62. Confidential report obtained and certified by Calgary, Alberta, NICAP Subcommittee.

63. New York Times; January 25, 1959.
64. Confidential report certified by NICAP Director and Assistant Director. Contains all tracking data (unclassified at source).
65. Reuters; June 19, 1961. Edinburgh Evening Dispatch; June 19, 1961.
66. Air Force Cambridge Research Laboratories, Radars and Flying Saucers. 2 July 1962.
67. Borden, R. C. & Vickers, T. K., Technical Development Report No. 180; A Preliminary Study of Unidentified Targets Observed On Air Traffic Control Radars. (Civil Aeronautics Administration Technical Development and Evaluation Center, Indianapolis, Indiana, September 1952).
68. U. S. Air Force, Radar Storm Detection. (Washington, D.C., 6 August 1945).
69. Air Force Cambridge Research Laboratories, Report 63-434, 1963.
70. Skolnik, Merrill J., Introduction to Radar Systems. (McGraw-Hill, 1962), ppg. 551-552.

Physical & Physiological Effects

71. Keyhoe, op. cit., p. 174.
72. Michel, op. cit., p. 44
73. Ibid., p. 58
74. Ibid., p. 76
75. Ibid., ppg. 82-83
76. Ibid., ppg. 90-92
77. Ibid., p. 97
78. Ibid., p. 131
79. Ibid., p. 130
80. Ibid., p. 133
81. Ibid., p. 143
82. Ibid., p. 145
83. Ibid., p. 154
84. Ibid., p. 158
85. Ibid., p. 177
86. Ibid., p. 181
87. Ibid., p. 184
88. Ibid., p. 198
89. Report obtained by Leonard H. Stringfield, Cincinnati, Ohio. (See Section VII).
90. Ibid.
91. Indianapolis Star; August 27, 1955.
92. Reports on file at NICAP.
93. Lincoln Evening Journal & Nebraska State Journal; November 8, 1957.
94. APRO Bulletin; September 1959.
95. Associated Press; February 20, 1958
96. Report obtained by William D. Leet, Pres., Bluegrass NICAP Affiliate.
97. Reported by Dr. Askold Ladonko, Caracas, Venezuela, NICAP Adviser.

SECTION IX

THE AIR FORCE INVESTIGATION

Abstract

NICAP contends that the Air Force has practiced an intolerable degree of secrecy and withholding of information in its public policies on the UFO subject, and refuses to allow an independent evaluation of its data. There are two general schools of thought on the reasons for this secrecy:

(1) That the Air Force has obtained significant proof of UFO reality, and is withholding its evidence until the public can be psychologically prepared under a program guided by some higher agency;

(2) That the withholding of information is not because of any special knowledge on the subject, but results more or less unconsciously from red tape, lack of continuity to the UFO project, differences of opinion within the Air Force, etc.

In either case, the secretive public information policies are symptomatic of the general governmental secrecy which has mushroomed since World War II, and must be viewed in that context. Since official secrecy has become so commonplace, almost an accepted way of life, the topic is extremely complex. For the sake of simplicity, this section is presented mostly in outline form:
  A. Background of Government Secrecy
  B. Air Force Regulations & Policies
     1. History of the UFO Project
  C. Air Force Statements About Its UFO Investigation/NICAP Rebuttals
  D. Sample UFO Cases Involving Aspects of Secrecy.

A. GOVERNMENT SECRECY

It is a generally conceded fact in Washington that government secrecy, since World War II, has grown by leaps and bounds. Even high-ranking officers in the Pentagon, in testimony to Congress, state that there is considerable over-classification of information. Sometimes it appears to be a case of the tail wagging the dog.

There is no simple solution to this problem, though it should be a matter of concern to anyone who believes in democracy. It is worth examining the structure of this secrecy, to pinpoint some aspects of it which have been uncovered by Congressional investigators, scholars and newsmen.

The Cold War burden plainly has put a severe strain on the traditional American belief in freedom of information. Censors can (and sometimes do) make a case that almost any information released in this technological age is of value to a potential enemy. Often information is withheld in the name of the "public interest." But who defines the "public interest?"

Rep. John E. Moss (D.-Calif.), Chairman of the Government Operations Subcommittee on Government Information, has long been a champion of the public's "right to know." Hearings by his subcommittee over the past several years have brought out many specific instances of unwarranted secrecy, especially by the Executive Branch. The subcommittee was chartered on June 9, 1955. A year later, the parent committee unanimously adopted House Report No. 2947, which included a study of Defense Department secrecy. The report stated:

"The study of the Defense Department so far shows that the informational policies and practices of the Department are the most restrictive--and at the same time the most confused--of any major branch of the Federal Government." [2]

Two recent books indicate that there has been no appreciable change in Defense Department information practices. Clark R.

Mollenhoff, Pulitzer Prize-winning reporter for Cowles Publications, in his 1963 book Washington Cover-Up, states what he believes is the crux of the problem: ". . . the arbitrary secrecy of 'executive privilege' . . . There would be 'managed news' as long as executive departments and independent regulatory agencies were able to invoke an arbitrary secrecy to prevent the press and Congress from reviewing the record--and as long as newspapers indolently accepted the management." [2]

Power In Washington, by Douglass Cater, also probes Washington "sub-governments" and their influence on government policies. According to reviewer James MacGregor Burns, Cater considers the "military-industrial complex" (so phrased by President Eisenhower) a sub-government. Part of it is "news managers in the Pentagon who try to influence public opinion." [3]

In summary, these aspects of the secrecy brought out by the Moss subcommittee particularly concern us:

* The Defense Department, in practice, claims executive privilege to withhold information from Congress and the public; existing directives leave the decision in specific cases to an arbitrary judgment by the Defense Department.

* Because of over-classification, the public often is not kept properly informed.

* By existing regulations, Defense Department personnel are forced to justify release of information and are not required to justify withholding of it. (A natural desire on the part of individuals to avoid trouble on controversial issues by not releasing information about them results in excessive secrecy).

A more pervasive tendency has developed among the military services to issue reassuring statements, rather than facts; generalized statements putting the best face on the matter (as far as the agency is concerned), rather than useful detail. In short, the concept of "public information" has been perverted to public relations, which tries to put across a favorable idea or image rather than to inform.

B. AIR FORCE REGULATIONS & POLICIES

1. Regulations Governing the UFO Investigation

Air Force Regulation 200-2, "Intelligence; Unidentified Flying Objects (UFOs), . . . establishes the responsibility and procedure for reporting information and evidence on [UFOs] and for releasing pertinent information to the general public."

Paragraph 3c, rather than furnishing objective guidelines, biases the investigation by clearly implying that all UFOs are explainable as misidentified conventional objects. (Thus the investigation assumes its own conclusion). Contrary to the oft-repeated public relations announcements about the investigation being "completely objective and scientific," the regulation states what the conclusion of the investigation must be:

"c. Reduction of Percentage of UFO 'Unknowns.' Air Force activities must reduce the percentage of unknowns to the minimum. Analysis thus far has provided explanation for all but a few of the sightings reported. These unexplained sightings are carried statistically as unknowns. If more immediate, detailed objective data on the unknowns had been available, probably these too could have been explained. . . [Due to subjective factors] it is improbable that all of the unknowns can be eliminated."

Paragraph 9 explicitly states that, in the area of occurrence, only explained cases may be released to the public:

"In response to local inquiries resulting from any UFO reported in the vicinity of an Air Force base, information regarding a sighting may be released to the press or the general public by the commander of the Air Force base concerned only if it has been positively identified as a familiar or known object." Follow-up queries about unexplained cases are to be referred to the Office of Information Services in the Pentagon (which seldom releases detailed information on a specific case unless it has been widely publicized).

Paragraph 11 restricts Air Force personnel from publicly discussing UFOs: "Air Force personnel, other than those of the Office of Information Services, will not contact private individuals on UFO cases nor will they discuss their operations and functions with unauthorized persons unless so directed, and then only on a 'need-to-know' basis."

JANAP 146 is a Joint Chiefs of Staff directive: "Communications Instructions for Reporting Vital Intelligence Sightings [CIRVIS] From Airborne and Waterborne Sources." In addition to military aircraft and surface vessels, the directive also applies to civil aircraft under certain conditions.

Chapter II, Section I, paragraph 201 includes, under information to be reported, (1) (c) "Unidentified flying objects."

Section III, "Security: 210. Military and Civilian. a. All persons aware of the contents or existence of a CIRVIS report are governed by the Communications Act of 1934 and amendments thereto, and Espionage Laws. . . The unauthorized transmission or revelation of the contents of CIRVIS reports in any manner is prohibited."

The effect of this directive, relative to UFOs, is to silence even commercial airline pilots cooperating with the intelligence network, once they have made a UFO report through official channels. It is, of course, also binding on all military personnel.

2. Regulations Concerning Release

of Information

There are only three classifications of military or national defense information authorized directly by law: Top Secret, Secret and Confidential. The types of information, and procedures of classification, are carefully spelled out. Legitimate security needs clearly necessitate withholding certain types of information from the general public. Theoretically, the public interest is protected by the limitations on the types of information which can be classified.

In practice, military (and other) agencies have adopted other quasi-legal means of withholding additional information from the public for reasons of their own. "Executive privilege" and the so-called "administrative classification" is the gray area of secrecy, where no clear standards delimit the withholding of information. The particular agency itself becomes both judge and jury in deciding what the public ought to know.

Any business (the U.S. Government is the world's largest business organization) may have justifiable reasons for withholding certain types of information beyond those which are clearly concerned with national defense. Personal information which if released might unfairly damage an individual's reputation, for example, might be considered private information. Files of correspondence or personnel records, in most cases, could be considered private information (unless needed for the defense of an individual on trial or for other overriding considerations).

However, there is a great potential for abuse of a system which, in effect, allows arbitrary withholding of government information from the public. To the maximum possible extent, government business should be public business. Clearly, the system is continually abused and "administrative classifications" are used to conceal facts which might embarrass an agency, or which might throw a spotlight on government activities that a significant segment of the public would oppose. The system continues to encroach on the public's right to know what its government is up to.

Worst of all, such pseudo-classifications as "For Official Use Only" are rapidly being given status by default, largely unchallenged by Members of Congress or the press. Many Air Force regulations, for example, (using a free interpretation of Federal Law) authorize Air Force personnel to judge what information they may withhold "in the public interest." About this practice Clark Mollenhoff said: "The broad right of arbitrary

withholding information is not something that any officials should be permitted to arrogate to themselves." [4]

Air Force Regulation 11-30, "Administrative Practices; Custody, Use and Preservation of DOD [Department of Defense] Official Information Which Requires Protection in the Public Interest."

The euphemistic phrase "in the public interest" is repeated in paragraph 1, which explains the "Reason for Issuing Regulation." Among other things, the regulation is intended to "assure the proper. . . use of official information which in the public interest should not be given general circulation." In spite of outlining some apparently worthy uses of this administrative classification, the regulation nevertheless does give blanket authority to withhold information whenever someone in the Air Force considers it to be "in the public interest." It is difficult to imagine how the public benefits by this arrangement.

Air Force Regulation 11-7, "Administrative Practices; Air Force Relations With Congress."

This regulation goes one step further than AFR 11-30, and claims the authority to withhold "For Official Use Only" information from Congress in some cases.

After stating that most "For Official Use Only" information not given to the public is given to Congress, the regulation continues:

"However, the considerations set forth [in AFR 11-30] which preclude making information available to the public may raise a question, in rare instances, as to whether the particular information requested may be furnished to Congress, even in confidence . . ." This, it must be emphasized, refers to information whose release in no way endangers national security--or else it would be legally classified "Top Secret," "Secret," or "Confidential." This indicates the extent to which the Air Force has taken upon itself the right to decide what the public--and even Congress-- should know.

Chronological History of the Air Force UFO Project

[One of the most informative sources regarding the conduct of the UFO investigation is the book Report on Unidentified Flying Objects, (Doubleday, 1956), by Capt. Edward J. Ruppelt, who headed the investigation from September 1951 to September 1953. Page references to this book are indicated after some of the following entries].

Early Investigation

July 1947: The Air Force began investigating UFO reports seriously after sightings by airline pilots, other qualified observers.

September 23, 1947: The Chief of Air Technical Intelligence Center (ATIC) sent a letter to the Air Force Commanding General stating the conclusion of ATIC that UFOs were real, and urging the establishment of a permanent project to analyze future reports. (p. 31)

January 22, 1948: Project "Sign" (popular name "Saucer") established at Wright-Patterson AFB, Ohio, to investigate UFO reports.

September 1948: Top Secret "Estimate of the Situation", concluding UFOs were interplanetary, sent from ATIC to Air Force Chief of Staff, General Hoyt S. Vandenberg. (Report was kicked back for additional proof; later declassified and burned). (ppg. 62-63, 67)

February 11, 1949: Project name changed to "Grudge." Because of internal disagreement about the significance of UFOs, reports were then "evaluated on the premise that UFOs couldn't exist." (ppg. 85-88)

April 27, 1949: Project Saucer report released: About 30% of the sightings investigated to date were said to be explained as conventional objects. An equal number, the report said, probably would be explainable after further probing.

December 27, 1949: Project Grudge report released: Explained away all reports to date as delusions, hysteria, hoaxes and crackpot reports. Announcement that project had disbanded.

Phase Two

1950-51: This period has been called the "Dark Ages" of UFO investigation. Following the Project Grudge report, the project was not disbanded. However, those who believed in a more positive investigation could not win support for their views--until late in 1951 when the situation was reviewed partly due to public protests.

September 15, 1951: Lt. Jerry Cummings, and a Lt. Col. from ATIC, were called to Washington to brief a General (and a disgruntled group of industrialists and scientists) about the conduct of the investigation. Received orders to set up a new project. (ppg. 128-130)

September 1951: Capt. Edward J. Ruppelt became chief of the newly revitalized project.

October 27, 1951: New project officially established. (p. 154).

March 1952: Project Grudge had become a full-fledged organization, the "Aerial Phenomena Group." Soon thereafter, the code name was changed to "Blue Book." (p. 176)

April 1952: Al Chop appointed public information officer for UFOs.

Air Force Letter 200-5 gave Project Blue Book authority to cut red tape, contact any Air Force unit in the U.S. without going through channels; provided for wire transmission of reports to ATIC, followed with details via Air Mail.

Life article "Have We Visitors From Space?", inspired by several top officers in the Pentagon. (ppg. 177-178)

May 8, 1952: Capt. Ruppelt and a Lt. Col. from ATIC briefed Air Force Secretary Thomas K. Finletter for one hour. (p. 185)

Mid-June 1952: Capt. Ruppelt briefed General Samford, Director of Intelligence, others; given directive to take further steps to obtain positive identification of UFOs. (ppg. 196-199)

Mid-July 1952: Every Air Force installation in U.S. swamped with UFO reports. (p. 205)

August 1952: Study of UFO maneuvers initiated, to determine whether objects displayed intelligent control. (ppg. 250-251)

November 1952: Panel of four scientists convened at ATIC to make preliminary review of accumulated reports. Recommended convening panel of top scientists. (p. 264)

January 12, 1953: The Air Force (reportedly with the assistance of the Central Intelligence Agency) convened a panel of top scientists to weigh the accumulated evidence. The panel was to decide whether the evidence indicated UFOs were interplanetary, whether it was all explainable, or whether the project should continue and seek better data. (p. 275). A study of UFO maneuvers concluding the objects were interplanetary was presented to the panel by Maj. Dewey Fournet. (p. 285)

January 17, 1953: The conclusions of the scientific panel were not made public at the time. Since then, two conflicting versions have been released:

Conclusions Reported by Ruppelt, 1956

The panel recommended that the UFO project be expanded, the investigative force quadrupled in size and staffed by trained scientists; that tracking instruments be established all over the

country, and that the public be told "every detail of every phase" of the investigation. The scientists believed this program would "dispel any of the mystery" created by military security procedures, and also keep the investigation on a scientific basis. The recommendations were not adopted. (ppg. 293-298)

Summary Released by Air Force, 1958

The panel concluded that UFOs constituted no "direct physical threat to national security," there was no evidence of "foreign artifacts capable of hostile acts," and no "need for the revision of current scientific concepts." The panel recommended "immediate steps to strip the Unidentified Flying Objects of the special status they have been given and the aura of mystery they have unfortunately acquired." The panel suggested "an integrated program designed to reassure the public of the total lack of evidence of inimical forces behind the phenomena."

Phase Three

The 1958 summary issued by the Air Force Office of Public Information--five years after the fact--first released the names of the scientists on the panel: H. P. Robertson, Luis W. Alvarez, Lloyd V. Berkner, S. A. Goudsmit, and Thornton Page.

Exactly what transpired at the conclusion of this meeting is not clear, though it is strongly suggested that the whole story has not been told. If the decision of the panel had been clearly negative, as the 1958 summary implies, there would have been no reason to be so secretive about it. On the contrary, there would have been every reason to make an immediate public announcement.

What is known about the affair is the public manifestation of the UFO project following the meeting. After a period of apparent serious interest in gathering better data (which supports Ruppelt's version of the panel conclusions), the Air Force began debunking UFOs. Since then the Air Force does not admit to having the slightest shred of evidence that anything at all out of the ordinary is taking place. Concurrently, a noticeable public relations policy has been adhered to by the Air Force through the Public Information Office: A policy of public reassurance. Members of Congress or citizens who request current information on the subject are told repeatedly that UFOs do not present any danger, or threat to the national security.

About the same time as the panel meeting, or shortly thereafter, the Air Force (reportedly through its own RAND Corporation) had an independent study conducted. This resulted in the Project Blue Book "Special Report No. 14." What relationship this had to the scientific panel meeting is not known. However, the introduction to the Blue Book report states (p. vii): "The special study which resulted in this report started in 1953. . .the information cut-off date was established as of the end of 1952."

August 26, 1953: AF Regulation 200-2 issued by Secretary of Air Force; procedures for reporting UFOs, restrictions on public discussion.

December 1, 1953: The Air Force announced in Washington it had set up cameras around the country equipped with diffraction gratings to analyze the nature of light from UFOs.

January 6, 1954: Reporters seeking information on UFOs were banned from Wright-Patterson AFB. [Cleveland Press]

February 23, 1954: Scripps-Howard papers said the Air Force had worked out a plan with commercial airline companies to report sightings quickly.

May 15, 1954: General Nathan F. Twining, Air Force Chief of Staff, stated the best brains in the country were working on the UFO problem; Air Force could not explain 10 per cent of the sightings. [Quoted by United Press; Amarillo, Texas].

May 5, 1955: Project Blue Book "Special Report No. 14" declassified.

October 25, 1955: Summary of Blue Book report released to press; linked with statement that Air Force would soon have its own saucer-shaped aircraft, the AVRO disc. (The AVRO disc project subsequently was scrapped without producing a flying model). Reported no evidence that UFOs "constituted a threat to the security of the United States. . ."

1956-1957: UFOs all but faded out of the news. Queries to the Air Force were answered by a "fact sheet" referring back to the 1955 report. A 1957 "fact sheet" stated the unexplained cases had been reduced "from approximately 10% in 1954 to 3%, as of now."

November 1957: When the "flap" of UFO reports began about November 1 [See Section XII; November 1957 Chronology], "fact sheets" were issued on the letterhead of the Department of Defense, Office of Public Affairs. These emphasized the percentages of explained cases, and again the lack of evidence of "a threat to the security of the country."

1958-1959: "Fact sheets" were issued approximately semi-annually reiterating the above position.

December 24, 1959: Air Force Inspector General brief to Operations and Training Commands: "UFOs Serious Business." Stated that UFO investigators on base level "should be equipped with binoculars, camera, geiger counter, magnifying glass and have a source for containers in which to store samples."

August 15, 1960: "Air Force Information Policy Letter; For Commanders," Vol. XIV, No. 12, issued by Office of Secretary of Air Force. Under title "AF Keeping Watchful Eye on Aerospace," stated, "There is a relationship between the Air Force's interest in space surveillance and its continuous surveillance of the atmosphere near Earth for unidentified flying objects--'UFOs.'"

1960-1961: Through its spokesman in the Pentagon, Lt. Col. Lawrence J. Tacker, the Air Force began answering critics of its UFO program publicly. Late in 1960, Col. Tacker's book Flying Saucers and the U.S. Air Force (Van Nostrand) was published, with a foreword by General Thomas D. White, Air Force Chief of Staff. Col. Tacker went on a public tour to publicize the book, appearing on radio and television, and giving lectures. Examples--

December 5, debate with NICAP Director on Dave Garroway's network television program.

December 18, interview on Westinghouse network radio program, "Washington Viewpoint."

March 17, 1961, lecture ot Aero Club of Buffalo, N.Y.

March 1961, article in Argosy magazine.

Col. Tacker used the strongest language to date in denouncing critics of the UFO investigation. Their claims were "absolutely erroneous;" "a hoax;" "sensational theories;" the work of "amateur hobby groups." NICAP's evidence was "drivel," its claims "ridiculous" and it was making "senseless accusations."

In April 1961, after being associated with the UFO project for over three years, Col. Tacker was shipped to Europe on "routine reassignment."

June 1961: The outspoken new policy, if that is what it was, apparently backfired. Angered by Col. Tacker's attitude, NICAP members and other citizens deluged Congress with requests for an investigation of the Air Force project. Congressional hearings were contemplated [See Section XIII] but never came about. Instead, Air Force Congressional Liaison personnel briefed key Congressional committees in private.

February 6, 1962: The Air Force issued the last "fact sheet" (No. 179-62) of the old style, then dropped that format.

1963-1964: In the past two years, packets of information-- including some details of specific cases--have been substituted for the generalized "fact sheets." The unexplained cases for each year are briefly described. (In the new "fact sheets", the "unknown" category has been rendered meaningless by the inclusion of vague and imcomplete cases. Formerly the term "unknown" was applied to the most detailed and inexplicable cases from the best observers. Now the distinction between "unknowns", and cases which lack detail or apparently have natural explanations, has been blurred.)

SUMMARY

1947-1949: Serious investigation, conclusions UFOs real and interplanetary..

1950-1951: These conclusions challenged on basis of lack of proof; "explain-away" approach adopted by investigators.

1952-1953: After review of situation, new serious investigation started; evidence uncovered led many high-ranking officers to conclude UFOs were interplanetary.

1954 to date: Evidence again challenged as "proof," this time by panel of scientists. Conflicting versions of whether expanded investigation was recommended (and adopted) to obtain more data. Public relations program adopted to assure public UFOs posed no danger, or threat to national security.

C. Air Force Statements/NICAP Rebuttals

Over the past ten years, the Air Force has had considerable correspondence with citizens unsatisfied by the official conclusions and attitudes about UFOs. The letters have reflected Air Force thinking and the philosophy of their investigation at various stages. The letters often have been more specific than the "fact sheets," but fewer people are aware of their contents.

The left-hand column below contains Air Force statements about its UFO investigation, general and specific. The right-hand column contains NICAP rebuttals, comments, or other data refuting the Air Force statements.

(Note the recurrence in these letters, and the detailed cases following, of certain types of answers given by the Air Force. These include counter-to-fact, "shotgun," and "zig-zag" answers. "Shotgun" refers to a fusillade of explanations given for one UFO sighting, e.g., that it was either a balloon, an aircraft, or the planet Venus. "Zig-zag" answers are those in which the press is given a quick explanation for public consumption; this explanation is later quietly changed one or more times. These techniques result in a sort of patchwork explanation for a given case. If Venus cannot explain one aspect of a sighting, then perhaps a balloon or aircraft can.)

"NOTHING WITHHELD"

"The allegation that the Air Force is withholding vital UFO information has no merit whatsoever. The press release approach is considered censorship by some UFO organizations, because they do not receive individual attention from the Air Force, they contend that we are withholding vital information. The Air Force was compelled to adopt the press release approach because in the past when factual information was furnished to certain writers of UFO books, upon their individual request, our action was interpreted as granting approval and clearance for the books in which the information was used." (Maj. Gen. W. P. Fisher, USAF, Director of Legislative Liaison, to Senator Harry Flood Byrd, 1-20-59).

"As stated in the material recently forwarded to you, limited resources preclude the distribution of case summaries to individuals and private organizations. Summaries of findings are published only when deemed necessary. (Maj. Maston M. Jacks, USAF, Public Information Division, Office of Information, to Charles R. Culbertson, 8-1-63).
NICAP: These letters admit that specific information is not given out; only generalized summaries. Conflicting reasons given for this: "limited resources" or alleged "misuse" of the material. The use of public information is no concern of the Air Force. It is standard procedure in the Defense Department to stamp disclaimers on factual material stating DOD is not responsible for "factual accuracy or opinion" in the use of the material.

"No reports of unidentified flying objects have been withheld. . . As Director of this Committee [NICAP], Major Donald E. Keyhoe, Marine Corps, Retired, has already received all the information in the hands of the United States Air Force. . ." (Maj. Gen. Joe W. Kelly, USAF, Director of Legislative Liaison, to Rep. Peter Frelinghuysen, 9-12-57).

Asked to provide data on specific cases which had not been furnished to NICAP, General Kelly replied: "I assure you the Air Force never intended to turn over 'official use only' files to your organization." (11-15-57) NICAP: This has been standard practice; public announcements that UFO information is not classified, but refusal to provide specific information when requested.

"The Department of the Air Force does not 'edit' or 'splice' film submitted by private citizens. When the Department receives such a film, it does make the necessary studies, analyses, and duplication of the film. When this work has been completed, it has been the consistent practice of the Department to return the film to the person who submitted it." (Major Lawrence J. Tacker, USAF, Executive Officer, Public Information Division, Office of Information Services, to Eli Bernzweig, 10-10-58).

Photographs which the owners allege were either edited, spliced, or not returned to them by the Air Force [See Section VIII; Photographs]: Aug. 15, 1950, Great Falls, Montana. Nick Mariana: Reported best frames of color movie film missing when returned by Air Force. July 2, 1952, nr Tremonton, Utah. D. C. Newhouse: Reported frames of movie film showing a single UFO moving away over the horizon, missing when film returned by Air Force. July 29, 1952, Miami, Fla. Ralph Mayher:

USAF STATEMENTS

On December 1, 1957 at about 3 p.m. Ralph Benn of Los Angeles, using a 3x telephoto lens, took about six and a half feet of Kodachrome film showing four of six objects—resembling those in the Tremonton, Utah film—which made repeated passes over the area.

Benn described the objects as dull white and oval shaped and said they moved slowly west at constant speed. Other passes —one described as "very fast" — were observed by Benn's children.

EXTRACT FROM NICAP MEMBERSHIP BULLETIN

"There is no truth to allegations that the Air Force withholds or otherwise censors information vital to public understanding or evaluation of the nature of unidentified flying objects (UFO). (Lt. Col. William J. Lookadoo, USAF, Public Information Division, Office of Information, to Miss Miriam Brookman, 7-19-62).

ASKANIA CINETHEODOLITE

"We are interested in the truth concerning reported sightings and are fully aware of our obligation to keep the public informed on such matters." (Hon. Richard E. Horner, Assistant Secretary of the Air Force for Research and Development, to Richard Tuttle, 7-3-58).

THE 1947 & 1948 DOCUMENTS

"There has never been an Air Force conclusion that flying saucers were real and were interplanetary space ships. The Alleged 1948 document in your letter is non-existent." (Maj. Gen. W. P. Fisher, USAF, Director of Legislative Liaison, to Larry W. Bryant, 10-27-58).

"With regard to Mr. Maccubbin's reference to the 1948 top secret report which he states officially concluded that UFOs were 'real,' no such report exists. . .There never has been an official Air Force report with the conclusion Mr. Maccubin indicates." (Colonel Carl M. Nelson, USAF, Congressional Inquiry Division, Office of Legislative Liaison, to Rep. Porter Hardy, Jr., 3-31-60).

REBUTTALS

Reported submitting 16 mm movie film to Air Force for analysis; film never returned. Dec. 1, 1957, Los Angeles, Calif. Ralph Benn: Reported several splices in his 8 mm film and two or three frames missing when returned by Air Force.

Film Data reportedly analyzed by USAF, but never released to public [See Section VIII]: Apr. 27, 1950; White Sands, N.M., Cine-theodolite film of UFO, also observed visually. May 29, 1950; White Sands, Cine-theodolite films (2) of one or more UFOs, also observed visually. July 14, 1951; White Sands, Movie film (35mm) of UFO, also seen visually, tracked on radar. Sept. 20, 1952; North Sea, three color photographs taken on board an aircraft carrier. Aug. 12, 1953, Rapid City, S.D., gun camera film of UFO also seen visually, tracked on radar. Aug. 31, 1953; Port Moresby, New Guinea, movie film of UFO taken by aviation official. May 24, 1954; nr Dayton, Ohio, photograph of circular UFO taken by Air Force photoreconnaisance plane.

"It is my belief that one of the objectives of your organization [Air Research Group] is the public dissemination of data on unidentified flying objects. . . this is contrary to Air Force policy and regulations." (Capt. Gregory H. Oldenburgh, USAF, Information Services Officer, Langley AFB, Va., to Larry W. Bryant, 1-23-58).

Existence of 1948 Top Secret document reported by Capt. Ruppelt; described as a thick document on legal-size paper with a black cover. [Report on Unidentified Flying Objects, p. 62]
Existence of 1948 document confirmed by Dewey J. Fournet, former Major, USAF, Pentagon Monitor of the UFO investigation [See photostat]. Existence of 1947 letter by ATIC stating UFOs were real, reported by Ruppelt [p. 85].

Dewey J. Fournet (see photostat for complete statement): ". . .I would like to confirm the existence of two USAF documents which were recently denied by an official USAF representative. These are: 1.

"It is believed that the documents you refer to are the first estimates of the UFO situation prior to the establishment of the project. These early documents did indicate that UFOs were probably real, in the sense that they were objects and/or phenomena, but did not in any way indicate that they were interplanetary space vehicles." (Major William T. Coleman, Jr., USAF, to George W. Earley, 9-7-61)

"There is no record of an alleged Top Secret document by (sic) the late Mr. Ruppelt, as suggested. It is true that an early estimate, probably 1948, of the UFO situation was prepared by the Intelligence Division of the then Air Materiel Command. It is not known exactly what this estimate consisted of in the way of conclusions or leads thereto. It cannot be positively stated that such a document existed." (Col. Carl M. Nelson, USAF, Chief, Congressional Inquiry Division, to Senator B. Everett Jordan, 9-20-61).

An intelligence summary on UFOs prepared in 1948 by the organization which later became the Air Technical Intelligence Center at Wright-Patterson AFB. 2. An intelligence analysis on specific aspects of UFO data which I prepared in 1952 while acting as UFO program monitor for Headquarters USAF, Washington, D. C."

DEWEY J. FOURNET, JR. BATON ROUGE, LA.

MR. FOURNET IS A FORMER AIR FORCE MAJOR WHO WAS AIR FORCE HEADQUARTERS MONITOR OF THE PROJECT BLUE BOOK UFO INVESTIGATION DURING 1952. IN THIS CAPACITY HE ACTED AS LIAISON OFFICER BETWEEN THE DAYTON, OHIO, PROJECT AND THE PENTAGON.

IN ONE WAY OR ANOTHER, MR. FOURNET WAS INVOLVED IN ALL OF THE MAJOR UFO INVESTIGATIONS DURING THIS PERIOD. HE SUPERVISED THE ANALYSIS OF THE UTAH FILMS, AND WAS INTIMATELY FAMILIAR WITH THE HISTORY OF UFO INVESTIGATION PRIOR TO THAT TIME.

MR. FOURNET HAS SERVED AS A MEMBER OF THE NICAP BOARD OF GOVERNORS SINCE 1957. HE HAS STATED THAT THE WHOLE UFO SUBJECT "SHOULD BE INVESTIGATED AND ANALYZED INTENSIVELY" AND THAT IT "IS INDEED WORTHY OF /SCIENTISTS'7 SERIOUS ATTENTION."

ON THE FOLLOWING PAGE 112 HIS COMMENTS CONCERNING A RECENT AIR FORCE STATEMENT ALLEGING THAT THE UTAH MOVIE FILM IMAGES WERE IDENTIFIABLE AS SEAGULLS.

Statement by Former Air Force UFO Project Monitor

At the request of Major Keyhoe, I would like to confirm the existence of two USAF documents which were recently denied by an official USAF representative. These are:

1. An intelligence summary on UFOs prepared in 1948 by the organization which later became the Air Technical Intelligence Center at Wright-Patterson AFB.

2. An intelligence analysis on specific aspects of UFO data which I prepared in 1952 while acting as UFO program monitor for Headquarters USAF, Washington, D.C.

Since both documents were classified when I last saw them, I am not at liberty to reveal their contents. I would also like to add a qualification about #2: I completed it in rough form just a few hours before my departure from Washington (following my release from active duty) and turned it over to one of my associates in the Directorate of Intelligence. Therefore, I never saw it in its published form. However, since I had prepared it - as well as other reports which I recorded on tape - at the specific request of my Branch and Division Chiefs, I am certain that it was published.

Another word of caution is necessary on the latter document: I prepared it primarily as a weapon for use against the apathy and/or bias on the subject which prevailed in certain official quarters. Although the processes of logic employed would stand up under ordinary circumstances, they become somewhat tenuous and difficult to defend completely when applied to the task in question. The important point should be, therefore, that such a document did exist - not that it did or did not establish anything about UFOs.

There is also a question about the report prepared by the panel of civilian scientists convened in January 1953 to examine the UFO data. I met with this panel during part of its deliberations; this was during the week when I was being processed off active duty. Since I had departed by the time the panel adjourned, I did not see any report which it may have prepared. However, since it was convened for the specific purpose of reviewing all available data and making recommendations on the UFO program, it must necessarily have left some sort of report, undoubtedly written. (I have since been informed that it did, although let me repeat that I never saw it.)

Dewey J. Fournet, Jr.
Baton Rouge, La.
May 4, 1958

USAF STATEMENTS

REBUTTALS

BLUE BOOK:
"SCIENTIFIC & OBJECTIVE"
"Some cases arise which, on the basis of information received, are of a weird and peculiar nature. The objects display erratic movements and phenomenal speeds. Since maneuvers and speeds of this kind cannot be traced directly to aircraft, balloons, or known astronomical sources, it is believed that they are reflections from objects rather than being objects themselves... Reflections may be projected to clouds and haze both from the ground and air. Many things which are common to the sky have highly reflective qualities, such as balloons, aircraft, and clouds." ("Fact sheet," November 1957).

NICAP: Air Force logic appears to be that, if something is observed which out-performs conventional aircraft and balloons, it must not be a real solid object. The "objective" Air Force investigation denies the possibility that UFOs could maneuver as reported, in effect concluding that all witnesses have been deluded. The hypothesis that UFOs represent a superior technology--and may be space ships--is not even considered. The "investigation" therefore consists of searching for the conventional phenomenon--or phenomena--most nearly resembling the reported UFO. If none is found, complex speculative "light reflection" theories are invoked.

"...the Air Force does not proceed with an investigation unless the sighting is reported directly to the Air Force." (Col. George M. Lockhart, USAF, Congressional Inquiry Division, Office of Legislative Liaison, to Senator Harrison A. Williams, Jr., 2-21-63)

NICAP: A scientific investigation of any phenomenon would set out to gather objective and quantitative data about that phenomenon. It would not ignore potentially valuable data merely because it was not reported through official channels.

"Four frames from the films taken by Mr. Diaz in Venezuela [Dec. 1962--See Section VIII] were forwarded to the Air Force for evaluation. However, the negatives of these frames were not submitted and therefore, without them, it has been impossible to make any investigation." (Maj. Maston M. Jacks, USAF, Public Information Division, Office of Information, to Richard Hack, 12-31-63).

NICAP: There is no such thing as negatives of movie film. Upon learning of this statement, NICAP had its adviser in Caracas, Dr. Askold Ladonko, contact Mr. Diaz again. The film was loaned to the Air Force attache with permission to make copies or stills if desired, and was returned intact with no frames missing. Apparently the attache did not have a copy of the film made; just four stills.

"The images on the photographs which were made by the U.S. Coast Guard on 16 July 1952 at Salem, Mass., were evaluated as being due to a double exposure." (Maj. Carl R. Hart, USAF, Public Information Division, Office of Information, to George D. Fawcett, 2-12-63).

"The unidentified flying objects in the photographs taken at Salem, Mass., on July 16, 1952 have been evaluated as light reflections on the window through which the photos were taken." (Maj. Maston M. Jacks, USAF, Public Information Division, Office of Information, to John P. Speights, 8-5-63).

"The Long Beach sighting of November 5, 1957 [See Section XII; Nov. 1957 Chronology] has been evaluated as possible reflections on sheet-ice, from either the sun or from lightning. Also there was a balloon in the area, and there were 10 aircraft in the vicinity. . ." (Maj. Maston M. Jacks, USAF, Public Information Division, Office of Information, to Herbert S. Taylor, 11-18-63)

NICAP: A good example of "shotgun" explanation for a sighting which is difficult to explain in conventional terms; in this case, six shiny circular objects making sharp turns and maneuvers. It is obvious guesswork, hardly a "scientific" evaluation. This is one of many similar cases during the November 1957 "flap" which the Air Force lists as "explained."

Re: April 8, 1956 sighting by Capt. Raymond Ryan, American Airlines pilot; "The Air Force concluded that the object viewed during this sighting was the planet Venus." (Air Force "fact sheet", 1963).

NICAP: In a taped description of his sighting, Capt. Ryan states that the UFO zoomed through a 90 degree arc from off his wingtip to dead ahead. Control tower operators reported seeing a silhouette of a UFO. [See transcript, Section V]

"The objects which appeared in the film taken at Great Falls, Montana on 15 August 1950 were identified as F-94 aircraft." (Maj. Carl R. Hart, USAF, Public Information Division, Office of Information, to George D. Fawcett, 2-12-63).

The F-94 aircraft were observed by the photographer behind him coming in for a landing. Photogrammetric analysis [See Section VIII] states there are "several factors which make such a hypothesis quite strained." Persistence of reflection from alleged aircraft "would require a very rare coincidence of airplane maneuver."

"The Air Technical Intelligence Center reports concerning the Washington Airport Control Center sighting of July 1952 state there were radar blips observed and that they were caused by a temperature inversion." (Maj. Gen. W. P. Fisher, USAF, Director of Legislative Liaison, to Senator Kenneth B. Keating, 6-19-59).

NICAP: Gen. Fisher failed to mention that visual observations often coincided with the unexplained radar blips; that the degree of inversion was insufficient to account for the sightings; and that Project Blue Book classified the sightings as "unknown," contrary to public announcements at the time. [Report on Unidentified Flying Objects, Ruppelt, p. 226; also see Section XII]

"...the Air Force feels that public hearings would merely give dignity to the subject out of all proportion to which it is entitled. The sensation seekers and the publishers of science fiction would profit most from such hearings, and in the long run we would not accomplish our objective of taking the aura of mystery out of UFOs." (Maj. Gen. W. P. Fisher, USAF, Director of Legislative Liaison, to Senator A.S. "Mike" Monroney, 6-4-59).

NICAP: Nothing would remove the "aura of mystery" about UFOs more rapidly than Congressional hearings. Presumably, the Air Force believes hearings would prove its case. If so, the alleged "myth" of UFOs would be punctured. Sensationalists and opportunists thrive only because of public confusion about UFOs. Hearings could help to establish the facts and clarify the entire picture. Continued refusal to give out detailed information encourages an "aura of mystery."

"The Air Force has a tremendous task in defending this country against weapon systems which we know exist. To divert more men and money from this mission into a greatly enlarged program for investigation of and defense against UFOs would jeopardize the security of this country against a known threat and would, in our opinion, be grossly imprudent." (Col. Carl M. Nelson, USAF, Congressional Inquiry Division, Office of Legislative Liaison, to Senator Philip A. Hart, 4-8-60).

NICAP: These letters pinpoint the real issue between the Air Force and its scientific critics. No one denies that the Air Force mission is to defend the country against attack, and that this is an important mission. The thinking is clear: UFOs are evaluated in the light of being a potential threat to the country. If preliminary investigation satisfies the Air Force the country is not under attack, "an understandably lower priority is placed on the further evaluation of the sighting." But what about scientific investigation of the reported objects thereafter? The Air Force should not be expected to carry through a job for which it is

111

"The UFO investigative role is intimately associated with the air defense role of the United States. As such, the first thing to be determined is the threat potential of an unidentified flying object. When this determination has been made (none of the over 7,000 sightings have proven inimical or hostile) an understandably lower priority is placed on the further evaluation of the sighting. I'm sure you will agree that the security of the nation is and must be our primary concern." (G. Wise, for Maj. William T. Coleman, Jr., USAF, UFO Project Officer, Public Information Division, to Fred Kempf, 8-17-61).

not fitted: scientific investigation of a phenomenon. Yet, as the agency officially charged with investigation of UFOs, the Air Force is under pressure to do just that. Intelligence techniques are not sufficient for scientific investigation. The full resources of the scientific community, including tracking instrumentation specifically for that purpose, would be required. Once satisfied that a given UFO poses no threat, the Air Force investigators apparently search for the most plausible conventional explanation. When none can be found, the "shotgun" approach is used. Clearly, this is not a scientific investigation.

D. Sample UFO Cases Involving Aspects of Secrecy

Red Bluff, California

The sighting of a UFO Aug. 13, 1960, by California Highway Patrolmen [Section VII] described a highly maneuverable, elliptical object. Toward the end of the observation, a second similar object was observed.

In a letter to a NICAP member, the Air Force stated: "The findings [are] that the individuals concerned witnessed a refraction of the planet Mars and the two bright stars Aldebaran and Betelgeux. . . [temperature inversions] contributed to the phenomena as the planet Mars was quite low in the skies and the inversion caused it to be projected upwards." (9-16-60).

In a letter to NICAP, the Air Force stated: "It is an impossible task to determine what the exact light source was for each specific incident, but the planet Mars and the star Capella were the most probable answers for these sightings." (10-6-60). The change of identification occurred about the time NICAP reported, in a special bulletin for October, 1960, that the first three named astronomical objects all were below the horizon at the time of the sighting. As it happens, the star Capella is the only one named which was above the horizon at the time of the sighting.

NICAP recently telephoned the office of a California Senator and confirmed that the state is on Daylight Saving Time (P.D.T.) from April 26 to October 25. The sighting began at 11:50 p.m. (P.D.T.), Aug. 13. At that time, the planet Mars was about one hour (i.e., about 15 degrees) below the eastern horizon. It is completely absurd to suppose that it could in any way account for the sighting. Aldebaran did not rise until about 1 a.m., Betelgeux about 3 a.m.

As for Capella, which was barely above the horizon when the sighting began, no star, by the wildest stretch of imagination, could give the appearance of a large ellipse a few hundred feet off the ground, nor could it maneuver as described by the police officers. [See Section VII] Also, the objects disappeared below the eastern horizon at the end of the sighting, whereas Capella would have risen about 35 degrees in that period. The Air Force explanation of this case is one of the most strained and counter-to-fact on record.

UTAH FILM

In 1963, the Air Force circulated an information sheet labelled "Ode D 'Classic' -- Seagulls" (See photostat) suggesting that there was a "strong possibility" that the UFOs filmed by Delbert C. Newhouse on July 2, 1952, were seagulls. By the end of the statement, after baldly assuming that actual seagulls "undoubtedly" showed up in some of the frames, the conclusion was stated more positively: There is "little reasonable doubt" that the UFOs actually were seagulls. The author refers to the "unani-

mity of opinion" of those who analyzed the film.

As a matter of fact, there is virtually no support for this identification. Mr. Newhouse, a Navy chief photographer (aviation), viewed the UFOs at relatively close range at first. They were shiny, perfectly disc-shaped objects. By the time he was able to unpack his camera, the objects had receded into the distance, but he was still able to capture them on film.

When the new Air Force information sheet was issued, NICAP forwarded a copy to Board Member Dewey J. Fournet, Jr. Mr. Fournet is a former Air Force Major who monitored the UFO program for the Pentagon. While on active duty with the Air Force, he handled the Utah movie film, helped arrange for its analysis, was conversant with the analyses conducted and their results. The following are excerpts from his reply to NICAP:

"This [document] was apparently written by someone only very superficially acquainted with the Tremonton movie case -- someone who obviously didn't bother to study the case history in any detail, or by someone who is purposely distorting the facts of the case. . . .

"There were two different analyses made of the movies shortly after I received them in 1952, both by the most qualified military photoanalytical labs then in existence. One was by the Wright-Patterson AFB photo lab and the other by the Navy photo lab at Anacostia. . . . The W-P lab concluded that the objects were not airplanes or balloons and probably not birds. The Navy lab concluded that they were not any of these. In neither case was there anything even remotely hinting that birds of any type had been identified in any frames of the movie. . . .

"The 'unanimity of opinion' to which the author of "Ode D" refers must certainly be a recent development. There most certainly was no such unanimity among the original parties in this case that the objects were probably seagulls. Quite to the contrary, the majority concluded that they were probably not birds, although some of us conceded this possibility if certain corollary assumptions were made: [That the witness was lying or unreliable; that despite his photographic experience, the witness panned his camera opposite to the direction the lone object was flying.]

"The 'Ode D' author apparently is unaware of or intentionally omitted reference to Newhouse's statement. . . he described [the UFOs] as 'two pie pans, one inverted on top of the other.' . . .

"Overall, whether the USAF author realized it or not, it would be necessary to conclude that Newhouse was lying in many of his statements in order to conclude that the Tremonton objects were birds. If I recall correctly, the unanimous opinion of the intelligence officers was that he was completely sincere and somewhat reserved. I have never heard anyone claim anything to the contrary. . . ."

ODE D "CLASSIC" - SEAGULLS
(FROM COLORED MOTION PICTURE FILM)

TREMONTON, UTAH INCIDENT
2 July 1952

At approximately 1110 on 2 July 1952 while driving in the vicinity of Tremonton, Utah, Chief Petty Officer Delbert C. Newhouse's wife noticed a group of objects in the sky that she could not identify. She asked him to stop the car and look. There was a group of about ten or twelve objects that bore no relation to anything he had seen before milling about in a rough formation and proceeding in a westerly direction. He opened the luggage compartment of his car and got his camera out of a suitcase. Loading it hurriedly, he exposed approximately thirty feet of film. There was no reference point in the sky, and it was impossible for him to make any estimate of speed, size, altitude or distance. Toward the end one of the objects reversed course and proceeded away from the main group. He held the camera still and allowed this single one to cross the field of view, picking it up again and repeating for three or four such passes. By this time all of the objects had disappeared. He stated that he expended the balance of the film late that afternoon on a mountain somewhere in Idaho.

The original film was analyzed by a photo reconnaissance laboratory shortly after the sighting. The conclusion reached was that a strong possibility existed that the bright spots of light appearing on the film were caused by seagulls soaring in thermal air currents. The credibility of the conclusion was undoubtedly supported by the presence of identifiable seagulls in some of the frames.

This conclusion was further strengthened by movies of seagulls, taken at various distances, which showed them as bright spots of light similar to those in the Newhouse film.

A recent analysis (1956) of the Newhouse film, made by USAF photo specialists totally unaware of the nature or previous history of this case, yielded the opinion that the bright spots of light on the film were bird reflections on the strong sunlight.

The unanimity of opinion present in all evaluations made in this case leaves little reasonable doubt that the UFO's in the Newhouse films were, indeed, seagulls.

The Sheffield Lake Case

Early on the morning of Sept. 21, 1958, a domed, disc-shaped UFO was observed a few feet above the ground outside a house in Sheffield Lake, Ohio. The main witness was Mrs. William Fitzgerald. Other residents in the area reported UFO sightings that morning. After a superficial investigation, the Air Force reported a completely counter-to-fact explanation (also incorporating the "shotgun" approach): Mrs. Fitzgerald had been fooled by a train headlight, plus a spotlight on a Coast Guard ship on Lake Erie. After a careful investigation, the Akron UFO Research Committee published a documented report, "The Fitzgerald Report" (P.O. Box 5242, Akron 13, Ohio), refuting the Air Force statements.

Air Force:

"The investigation revealed that a railroad track ran near the home of Mrs. Fitzgerald. The night of Mrs. Fitzgerald's sighting, a train passed the house at approximately the same hour of the reported sighting. The train had a rotating headlight which, under some conditions, would produce unusual effects. Contact was also made with Chief Bosun's Mate William Schott of the Coast Guard Station, Lorain, Ohio. Chief Schott reported that he was using his spotlight in an attempt to attract the attention of another ship, and that the light was directed toward the shore in the general direction of Mrs. Fitzgerald's house. . .The weather at the time of the incident was a misty rain with haze and smoke.

"The conclusion of the Air Force investigators was that the combination of moving lights, noise of the train and prevailing weather account for the illusion experienced by Mrs. Fitzgerald. The Air Technical Intelligence Center, after evaluating the evidence in this case, concurred with the conclusion of the investigators." (Maj. Gen. W. P. Fisher, USAF, Director, Legislative Liaison, to Rep. A. D. Baumhart, Jr., 10-31-58).

The Air Force logic is apparent: UFOs are not real objects and can all be explained in terms of honest but deluded witnesses. Mrs. Fitzgerald only thought she saw a distinct disc-shaped domed object. She must have been fooled by some local light. A bright train headlight, or Coast Guard spotlight shining through mist and haze could be the cause.

Akron UFO Research Committee:

Checking each point of the Air Force statements, the Akron group found many errors and omissions. Gen. Fisher had also told Congressman Baumhart that one of the confirmatory witnesses listed by Mrs. Fitzgerald had stated she had not seen anything unusual that night. Later, the witness signed a statement, reproduced in the Akron report, that she had confirmed the sighting to Air Force investigators: A round object with a "hump" or dome. The investigators, she stated, then decided not to have her fill out a report form.

* The railroad track is situated so that no train headlights ever shine into the window of Mrs. Fitzgerald's house. Although urged to do so by the Akron group, the Air Force investigators made no attempt to check this.

* At the time of the UFO sighting, Chief Schott's ship was about 5-1/2 miles from Mrs. Fitzgerald's house. Lake Erie is not even visible from her house, being obscured by trees and other houses.

Through Ohio Congressmen, the Air Force was asked to explain these discrepancies. Various spokesmen for the Air Force reiterated their confidence in the "competence" of their investigators and that their findings were "accurate and adequate." Maj. Lawrence J. Tacker, Pentagon UFO spokesman, in a letter to the Akron group, labelled their report ". . . the erroneous charges [of] amateur organizations." He added, "Further, we are not interested in your theories or science fiction approach to this subject." (1-14-59).

When pressed by Congressman Baumhart for "a more complete report" on the incident, the Air Force was totally unresponsive. The Congressman was sent a form reply defending the Air Force position against the "mistaken beliefs" of UFO groups which make "sensational claims and contentions." The same form letter has been sent to Members of Congress repeatedly.

Redmond, Oregon

When a UFO sighting by Federal Aviation Agency (FAA) personnel on Sept. 24, 1959, at Redmond, Ore., airport [See Section V] was reported in the press, NICAP made a thorough investigation. Information was obtained from the FAA, the Weather Bureau and the IGY World Data Center at Cornell University. A taped interview of the witnesses was obtained by members in the area. The essence of the report was that a round object had descended and hovered, moved quickly to a new position, then shot up into clouds emitting a flame trail as jet interceptors approached. The jets were scrambled because, according to FAA logs, an Air Force radar station was also tracking a UFO at the time.

When queried about the official explanation for this sighting, the Air Force replied: "The Portland Oregon UFO sighting of 24 September 1959 is carried on the records of ATIC as 'insufficient information.' The ATIC account of the sighting fails to reveal any evidence of radar tracking or any success of the attempted intercept. It is the ATIC opinion that this object was probably a balloon as evidenced by its relatively long period in the area (more than an hour), and the fact that, unless equipped with reflectors, balloons are not good radar reflectors. The average direction and strength of the wind at the time of the sighting was south at 15 knots [NICAP: The UFO reportedly moved south, where it showed on radar after the visual sighting had ended]." (Maj. Lawrence J. Tacker, USAF, Public Information Division Office of Information, 1-19-60).

NICAP obtained wind data from the U.S. Weather Bureau showing steady winds from the southeast throughout the morning, from 3-7 knots, until nearly five hours after the sighting. No balloon had been launched locally at the time of the sighting, and even if one had been, it almost certainly would have travelled on a northerly course. Later, the Air Force dropped the balloon explanation.

After NICAP publicity on the case drew Congressional attention, the Air Force issued a much more detailed account (admitting that six jet interceptors had been scrambled, but denying that radar had tracked a UFO). Air Force letters to Members of Congress attributed the radar sighting to an error on the part of their Ground Control Intercept radar station. "It was determined by the four senior controllers on duty during the period of the search that this radar return on the ground station scope was a radar echo from a gap filler antenna located on a mountain at the 8010-foot level. This radar return did not move during the entire period of the search. [NICAP: The FAA logs state, "Altitude has been measured on height finder at altitudes that vary from 6000 to 54,000 feet."] . . . The fact that this radar return did not move is in complete disagreement with ground observers who sighted the UFO visually. They all testified it maneuvered rapidly and at times hovered." (Col. Gordon B. Knight, Chief, Congressional Inquiry Division, Office of Legislative Liaison, to Senator Warren G. Magnuson, 4-27-60.)

On March 25, 1960, the Pentagon UFO spokesman had written to NICAP that ". . . because of the information contained in the FAA logs, your correspondence and the copies of the logs have been forwarded to ATIC for possible additional consideration. . . Based upon all the present data on this sighting, the finding of 'insufficient data' is definitely valid." As of Col. Knight's April 27, 1960, letter to Senator Magnuson, the case still was classified as "insufficient data."

An Air Force information sheet circulated in 1963 attributes the UFO to "the refraction of light from the planet Venus." (The sheet also accuses NICAP of "exploitation" of the FAA logs which contradicted the Air Force story). NICAP astronomy advisors had already checked this possibility, and knew Venus was prominent in the eastern sky that morning. The witnesses were queried on this specific point and stated they did not see Venus during the UFO sighting, but did see it and identify it afterwards.

NICAP concedes that, if the radar target was perfectly stationary throughout, it was not the UFO observed visually. When trying to establish the balloon explanation, the Air Force emphasized the long period of observation (The FAA log indicates the visual sighting lasted about 10 minutes.) When dissociating the radar sighting from the visual sighting, the Air Force emphasized the high maneuverability of the UFO. Finally, the UFO which "maneuvered rapidly and at times hovered" has been explained as the planet Venus.

FEDERAL AVIATION AGENCY

Redmond Oregon.
Jan. 15, 1960

TO WHOM IT MAY CONCERN.

The following in the original records on file at this facility
and is all the information contained in this record concerning
UFO sighted September 24, 1959. Taken from log of this date.
1259Z
Robert Dickerson Redmond city police reported strange bright
light descending rapidly north of the station. At several
hundred feet it stopped and hovered for several minutes. He
drove toward it on the Prineville highway and turned in toward
the airport. At this time the light turned orange and it moved
to the northeast of the station very rapidly. Relocated
approximately 10 miles northeast of the station estimated 3000
feet.
1310Z
Reported object to Seattle Air Route Control Center. We continued
to observe UFO. Stayed very steady and projected long tongues
of red, yellow and green light. These tongues of light varied
in length and extended and retracted at irregular times.
Observed high speed aircraft approaching from southeast. As
aircraft approached UFO took shape of mushroom, observed long
yellow and red flame from lower side as UFO rose rapidly and
disappeared above clouds estimated 14,000 feet, scattered layer.
UFO reappeared south of Redmond approximately 20 miles estimated
25,000 feet. Seattle Air Route Control Center advised radar
contacted UFO at 1420Z located 25 miles south of Redmond at
52,000 feet. No further sightings made at this station.
1511Z
Seattle Air Route Control Center advised UFO still 25 miles south
of Redmond, various altitudes from 6,000 to 52,000 feet.

L.E. Davis
Chief, Redmond Air Traffic
Communication Station.

OLDEN MOORE

At the height of the November, 1957, "flap," [See Section XII],
a resident of rural Montville, Ohio, had a close-range sighting of
a UFO. The report quickly spread to newspaper reporters, area
Civil Defense officials and others. The witness, Olden Moore,
stated that not only was he interrogated by representatives of the
Federal Government, but also he was taken to Washington, D.C.,
and questioned repeatedly over a three-day period. At the conclusion, he was sworn to secrecy.

After more than three years' observance of this, he decided
the need for revealing his story superceded the need for secrecy,
so he told his story to newspaper reporter Don Berliner, then
of the Painesville (Ohio) Telegraph, on Jan. 21, 1961.

Moore stated that, within two weeks of the sighting, he was taken
to Youngstown (Ohio) AFB by car, then to Wright-Patterson
AFB by helicopter, and from there to an air base within 20-30
minutes drive of Washington, D.C. (probably Andrews AFB) in
a small Air Force transport plane. At all times he was accompanied by two government representatives.

During his stay in Washington, he was quartered in a hotel-
like room with one of the government men, who impressed Moore
as being there for the purpose of keeping an eye on him. Questioning and interviewing took place in the basement of the building
in which he stayed. (The U.S. Court House fits the description.
Upstairs are hotel-like jury rooms; in the basement are many
offices, including those of U.S. Marshals.) The only time he was
permitted to leave the building prior to departure was for a
brief guided tour of some historic and scenic areas (which proved
highly impressive to one who had never before seen the Nation's
Capital.)

The interrogation, according to Moore, was not so much a
question-and-answer session, as a corroboration by him of details
of his experience, i.e. "was the thing you saw a such-and-such?"
His answer, in almost every instance, was affirmative. This led
him to conclude that his questioners were less interested in
learning what he had seen than in finding out how much he had
detected. He said he got the definite impression that those
asking the questions were quite familiar with what he had seen.

At the end of the third day of questions, Moore was required
to sign a statement promising never to tell of his trip to Washington. Upon returning home, all he would tell the newspapers was

that he had talked with some officials at home and others elsewhere. His wife said he was taken to Washington, but Moore did
not confirm this at the time.

Don Berliner, who interviewed Moore in 1961, was highly
impressed by his sincerity, lack of sensationalism, and his awareness of the seriousness of revealing information he had promised
to keep secret. This material was not published by Mr. Berliner
at the time because of its sensitive nature. However, Mr. Moore
did offer to tell his story to any Committee or Subcommittee
of Congress which might be interested.

Allegedly, the Air Force (government spokesmen on this subject)
has withheld nothing from the public. The implication of Moore's
story is that considerable information has been withheld. A
Congressional inquiry into this matter would appear to be fully
justified.

The 1956 sighting of a huge disc by the crew of a Navy transport
over the Atlantic [See Section IV] was followed by the personal
visit to the aircraft commander by a government scientist. The
man took a set of photographs out of a briefcase and showed
them to the pilot, asking him to point out the object he saw. The
Commander quickly identified one of the pictures as the machine
he had seen, whereupon the unnamed scientist put the picture back,
refused to comment further, and departed. [Report obtained
by R. Adm. D. S. Fahrney, USN, Ret.].

The obvious implication of this incident is that someone in
the government has considerably more information about UFOs
than has been released by the Air Force. It tends to substantiate
Olden Moore's report.

The Sheneman Case

On Aug. 1, 1955, W. M. Sheneman, proprietor of a radio and TV
store, arrived at his home near Willoughby, Ohio, (20 miles east of
Cleveland). As he got out of his car, he saw a large circular
object, with a red light on the front rim, descend rapidly over a
nearby field. It stopped at an estimated 800 feet altitude and shot
two beams of light toward the ground. As the glow illuminated
the ground, Mr. Sheneman saw several "windows" around the edge
of the hovering disc. He fled into the house, but returned after
a minute with his wife for another look. The craft had become dark
and was hovering about 200 feet above the house; from this vantage
point, he estimated its diameter at 80-100 feet. It then began
to move away, revealing a dome on top lit by a white glow from
within. Mrs. Sheneman reported hearing a soft humming sound.

Following report of the incident to the Air Force in 1956, the
Sheneman's were visited by a major from ATIC, who told them
they had seen a test of a Canadian Avro vertical-lift device developed for the U.S. Air Force. To back up his claim, the
officer displayed a glossy print purportedly showing the craft in flight.
This was, in fact, an artist's conception of what the Avro disc
might look like, as the first example was not completed until
1959. The major tried for three hours to convince Mr. and Mrs.
Sheneman that they had seen the Avro and to sign a statement to
that effect, but they refused.

While definitely resembling the public idea of a "flying
saucer," the 18-foot Avro VZ-9V failed to achieve its design
performance of vertical take off and high-speed flight. Wind-
tunnel and free-flight tests demonstrated that it would not fly
out of ground effect, and was therefore limited to an altitude of
several inches and top speed of about 35 mph. [5]

The Kinross Case

On the night of November 23, 1953, an unidentified flying object
was detected over Lake Superior by Air Defense Command radar.
An F-89C all-weather interceptor was scrambled from Kinross
AFB, near the Soo Locks in northern Michigan. Guided by radar,
the jet sped northwest across the lake on an intercept course.
On the radar screen, ground controllers saw the F-89 close in
on the UFO blip, and then the two blips merged and faded from
the screen. From all appearances, the aircraft and the UFO had
collided. No trace of the jet has ever been found.

The last radar contact with the F-89 showed it to be at 8000
feet, 70 miles off Keeweenaw Point, and about 160 miles northwest of Soo Locks. Later, the Air Force reported that the
"UFO" was identified by the F-89 as a Royal Canadian Air
Force C-47. After identifying the friendly plane, the Air Force
states, the F-89 turned back to base. From that time, "nothing of
what happened is definitely known." [Air Force information

sheet; copy on file at NICAP]. The C-47 was "on a flight plan from Winnipeg, Manitoba, to Sudbury, Ontario, Canada." [Air Force letter to NICAP member, 4-2-63].

The original report released by the Air Force PIO at Truax AFB, Wisc., stated that contact was lost with the F-89 when it appeared to merge with the UFO. There is no mention of tracking the jet after that.

In 1961, a NICAP member wrote to the RCAF concerning the Kinross incident to verify the C-47 identification. The reply stated:

"Thank you for your letter of April 4 requesting information regarding an 'Unidentified Flying Object' on November 23, 1953.

"A check of Royal Canadian Air Force records has revealed no report of an incident involving an RCAF aircraft in the Lake Superior area on the above date." (Flight Lt. C. F. Page, for Chief of the Air Staff, RCAF, to Jon Mikulich, 4-14-61).

Later, another NICAP member wrote to the RCAF and received an even more specific denial that any Canadian aircraft was intercepted by a U.S. jet. The spokesman added: ". . . as you stated the C-47 was travelling on a flight plan taking it over Canadian territory; this alone would seem to make such an intercept unlikely." (See photostat).

There are two interpretations of what happened over Lake Superior that night: (1) Air Force radar tracked a UFO, the F-89 closed in to investigate, collided with or was in some manner destroyed by the UFO (as indicated by the blips merging on radar, the fact that radar contact was lost after the blips merged, and the fact that no trace of the fully-equipped all-weather aircraft has been found.); or (2) Air Force radar tracked a temporarily unidentified RCAF plane, the F-89 intercepted it, made the identification and then crashed for unknown reasons.

The latter explanation does not account for what was observed on radar; it assumes that expert radar men cannot read radar scopes. The RCAF has no record of such an incident, although a flight plan allegedly was filed. If there was such a flight, it would have been entirely over Canadian territory. Because of international identification networks between Canada and the U.S., its flight plan would have been known to the radar stations and there would have been no need for the intercept mission to begin with. The F-89 was originally reported to be chasing an "unidentified object."

The Air Force information sheet on this case states: "It is presumed by the officials at Norton AFB [Flying Safety Division] that the pilot probably suffered from vertigo and crashed into the lake." Judging by weather reports at the time, the pilot would have been on instruments, so that vertigo (dizziness resulting from visual observation) would be an extremely unlikely explanation. Even if the F-89 was not on instruments at the time, there is no explanation why radar tracked it 160 miles out over the lake and then lost contact just after the blips appeared to merge.

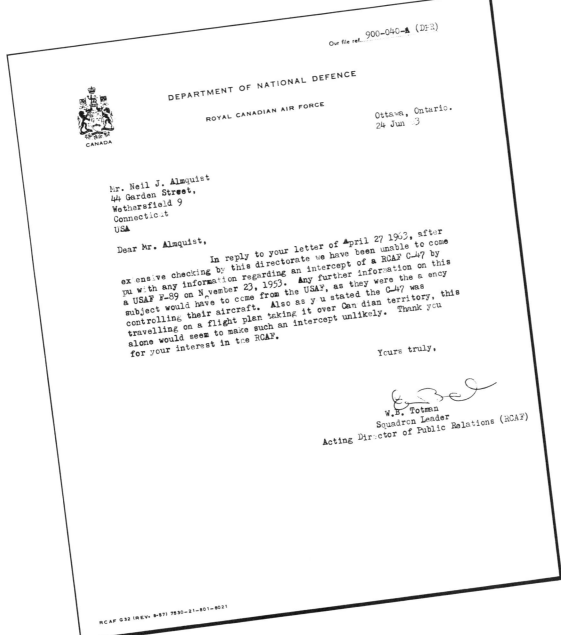

Our file ref. 900-040-A (DPR)

DEPARTMENT OF NATIONAL DEFENCE

ROYAL CANADIAN AIR FORCE

Ottawa, Ontario.
24 Jun 3

Mr. Neil J. Almquist
44 Garden Street,
Wethersfield 9
Connecticut
USA

Dear Mr. Almquist,

In reply to your letter of April 27 1963, after extensive checking by this directorate we have been unable to come up with any information regarding an intercept of a RCAF C-47 by a USAF F-89 on November 23, 1953. Any further information on this subject would have to come from the USAF, as they were the agency controlling their aircraft. Also as you stated the C-47 was travelling on a flight plan taking it over Canadian territory, this alone would seem to make such an intercept unlikely. Thank you for your interest in the RCAF.

Yours truly,

W. B. Totman
Squadron Leader
Acting Director of Public Relations (RCAF)

RCAF G32 (REV. 8-57) 7530-21-801-6021

The Killian Case

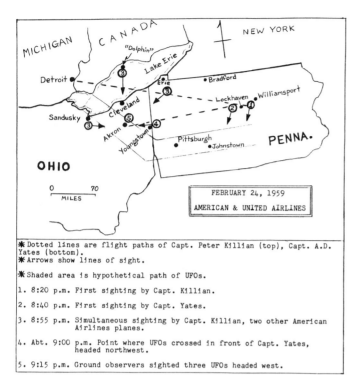

❋ Dotted lines are flight paths of Capt. Peter Killian (top), Capt. A.D. Yates (bottom).
❋ Arrows show lines of sight.

❋ Shaded area is hypothetical path of UFOs.

1. 8:20 p.m. First sighting by Capt. Killian.
2. 8:40 p.m. First sighting by Capt. Yates.
3. 8:55 p.m. Simultaneous sighting by Capt. Killian, two other American Airlines planes.
4. Abt. 9:00 p.m. Point where UFOs crossed in front of Capt. Yates, headed northwest.
5. 9:15 p.m. Ground observers sighted three UFOs headed west.

Capt. Peter Killian, American Airlines pilot, was one of several pilots who reported observing three UFOs above Pennsylvania, Feb. 24, 1959. [See Section V]. While travelling westward across the state, Capt. Killian and the other pilots saw the UFOs flying a parallel course to the south. The Air Force later stated that the pilots had seen Air Force bombers refueling from a tanker aircraft.

Reconstructing the sighting (see map), it is possible to trace a hypothetical, but very consistent, picture of the UFOs' flight path. Around 8:20 to 8:40 p.m., from Central Pennsylvania, the UFOs were observed to the SSW paralleling the westerly course of the airliners. Their distance, of course, is unknown. But based on subsequent observations, it is a reasonable supposition that the UFOs were over southern Pennsylvania, in the vicinity of Pittsburgh and Johnstown.

Around the same time that Capt. A. D. Yates, United Airlines, saw the UFOs turn and head northwest in the vicinity of Akron, three American Airlines pilots simultaneously saw the objects (8:55 p.m.). Their lines of sight converge on the Cleveland-Akron area. By 9:20 p.m., the Akron UFO Research Committee had received reports from ground observers, describing three UFOs headed west. Capt. Killian continued to observe the UFOs until he began his landing approach at Detroit, about 120 miles northwest of Akron.

In a letter to Senator Harry Flood Byrd, dated 6 May 1959, Maj. Gen. W. P. Fisher (Air Force Director of Legislative Liaison) stated:

"The investigation of this incident revealed that an Air Force refueling mission, involving a KC-97 and three B-47 aircraft, was flown in the vicinity of Bradford, Pennsylvania, at the time of the sighting by Capt. Killian. The refueling operation was conducted at 17,000 feet altitude at approximately 230 knots true air speed (about 265 mph) for a period of approximately one hour."

Assuming that this is a completely accurate statement, the Air Force could lay to rest this "flying saucer" report once and for all by publishing the exact flight plan of the refueling mission. Surely, at this late date there would be no compromising of security. On the surface, the explanation is plausible (except for the back-and-forth motion of the third UFO in line). The distance from the area of Johnstown, Pa., to Detroit is approximately 250 miles, which is consistent with the distance that would be covered by the refueling tanker. On closer analysis, however, there are several discrepancies in this explanation:

(1) Bradford, Pa., given as a geographical reference point for the refueling mission, is north of the flight paths of the American and United airliners. All the pilots saw the UFOs to the south. If the refueling mission actually took place over southern Pennsylvania (which would have to be the case to account for the reported facts), why wasn't Pittsburgh or Johnstown given as a reference point? Bradford is virtually the full width of the state away from the apparent location of the UFOs.

(2) Triangulation shows that (from the line of Capt. Killian's flight path in Central Pennsylvania) the tanker and other aircraft would have to be within 12 miles of Capt. Killian's position for a sighting angle of 15 degrees to place them at approximately 17,000 feet altitude. Even allowing for a 1/3 error in estimation of angle, the aircraft would have to be within 20 miles to the south of Capt. Killian. This is inconsistent with the observation by Capt. Yates, farther to the south, who also saw the UFOs to his south as he travelled all the way to the Pennsylvania-Ohio border.

(3) Triangulation of the simultaneous sighting by the three American Airlines pilots is even more damaging to the tanker explanation. The three lines of sight converge on the general Akron area, where ground sightings also tend to confirm the distance from Capt. Killian's aircraft. From the position of Capt. Killian's plane at the time of the simultaneous observation, the distance to Akron is approximately 70 miles.

$$\tan 15 \text{ degrees} = \frac{x}{70}$$

$$x = 70 \tan 15 \text{ degrees}$$
$$x = 18.1 \text{ miles}$$
$$x = 95,568 \text{ feet (altitude of UFOs)}$$

Even allowing for a 2/3 error in angle estimation:

$$x = 70 \tan 5 \text{ degrees}$$
$$x = 6.1 \text{ miles}$$
$$x = 32,208 \text{ feet (altitude of UFOs)}$$

(4) The American Airlines pilots checked after landing and learned that no jet tankers were in the area. (Taped statement by copilot on file at CSI, New York). Capt. Killian is also quoted by the Air Force as stating that a check with Air Traffic Control showed no three aircraft in the area (see below).

(5) Several aspects of the Air Force handling of this case suggest a desire to explain it away, including issuance of typical counter-to-fact explanations.

Before any representatives of the Air Force contacted Capt. Killian to obtain his report, the Air Force first suggested he had been fooled by the belt of the constellation Orion seen through breaks in the overcast. (There was no overcast). This statement was issued from ATIC three days after the sighting. An anonymous spokesman implied that UFO witnesses often proved to be drunks (N.Y. Herald-Tribune; March 1, 1959).

On March 20 (more than three weeks after the sighting) the Air Force issued a statement from Washington alleging that the airline pilots had seen a refueling mission. (One critic of the USAF UFO investigation wryly suggested to NICAP that it took the Air Force three weeks to locate some of its own planes). The refueling mission explanation has since been given all inquiring Members of Congress.

When contacted by the press about the tanker explanation, Capt. Killian gave a strong rebuttal: "If the Air Force wants to believe that, it can," Capt. Killian said. "But I know what a B-47 looks like and I know what a KC-97 tanker looks like, and I know what they look like in operation at night. And that's not what I saw." [See Notes, Section V]

Later, the Air Force began circulating a copy of a statement (unsigned) which it alleges was obtained from Capt. Killian by American Airlines:

Departing Newark 1910 arriving Detroit 2252.

It was approximately 2045 I noticed these three lights off my left wing in the vicinity of Bradford, Pennsylvania. I was flying 8,500 VFR on top of broken clouds. Visibility was unlimited with no upper clouds observed. It was extremely difficult to ascertain the distance of the lights. The color of the lights were from a yellow to a light orange. The intensity of the lights also changed from dim to a bright brilliant. Sometimes the interval of the three lights were identical to the Belt of the constellation Orion. Occasionally the rear lights lagged somewhat behind. Also changed altitudes. During the 40 minutes of observation, the three lights occasionally came forward from a 9 o'clock position to 11 o'clock position and then fell back to the original 9 o'clock position. Also occasionally the lights extinguished completely alternating from one to another, sometimes the whole three were extinguished and during this whole operation, as I mentioned before, the lights changed in intensity. This motion was not only seen by myself but four crew members and passengers on board and also by two other airplanes in the area.

The only possible explanation other than flying saucers could be a jet tanker refueling operation. Never having witnessed refueling operation at night, I am not aware of the lighting of the jet tanker.

My air speed during this complete flight was 250 knots indicated. I also do not know the air speed of tankers during operation if this could be so. I contacted ATC to find out if they had any airplanes on a clearance and no three airplanes were given.

In attempting to resolve the contradictions, NICAP once again telephoned Capt. Killian. Mrs. Killian stated to the NICAP Director that Capt. Killian had been instructed not to say any more about the sighting. She indicated he was angry about being silenced, and felt his rights were being denied.

Officially, the case has been "explained" as a refueling mission. The facts obtained before Capt. Killian was silenced (including his own public denial of that explanation), the above triangulations, and the type and timing of the Air Force statements all cast doubt on the validity of the explanation.

Though it may seem far-fetched to those unfamiliar with UFO history to suppose that the Air Force would have any motive for a deliberate cover-up, the former chief of the Air Force UFO project, himself, reported many similar incidents. A good parallel to the Capt. Killian sighting is described by Capt. Edward J. Ruppelt (Report on Unidentified Flying Objects, ppg. 119-120). When a report came in from airline pilots that their plane had been buzzed by a cigar-shaped object as they were taking off from Sioux City, Iowa [See Section V; 1-20-51], Capt. Ruppelt witnessed the reaction by Air Force investigators. The sighting was treated as a joke; the "investigator" merely located an Air Force bomber near Sioux City and blamed it for the sighting. Capt. Ruppelt acknowledged the absurdity of this answer: a bomber buzzing an airliner in an airport traffic pattern. There was no investigation; only an arbitrary and counter-to-fact "explanation."

The Ryan Case

On April 8, 1956, an American Airlines flight, headed west across New York state, saw and followed a UFO. After notifying an Air Force Base in the vicinity, the pilot, Capt. Raymond Ryan, was requested to follow the UFO until jet interceptors could reach the scene. In a taped interview [see transcript of sighting detail, Section V], Capt. Ryan admitted going off course and following the UFO as far as Oswego, N.Y., on the shore of Lake Ontario, before giving up the chase.

Although Capt. Ryan stated the UFO zoomed through a 90 degree arc from off his wingtip to dead ahead, the Air Force later blamed the sighting on the planet Venus. NICAP asked the then Civil Aeronautics Administration and the Civil Aeronautics Board for an investigation. CAA, CAB and American Airlines all denied that Capt. Ryan departed from his course. The Air Force does not admit asking Capt. Ryan to follow the UFO. [Taped interview

of Capt. Ryan and all other documentation, on file at NICAP].

November 1957 Press Release

On November 15, 1957, after two weeks of highly publicized UFO sightings, the Air Force issued news release No. 1108-57. Out of hundreds of current sightings, five cases were listed and debunked: 1. Levelland, Tex.; 2. Alamogordo, N. Mex. (James Stokes); 3. Coast Guard Cutter, Gulf of Mexico; 4. White Sands, N. Mex. (Army jeep patrols); 5. Kearney, Nebr. (Reinhold Schmidt).

Two, the Kearney incident and the sighting by James Stokes at White Sands, were labelled hoaxes. The first case no doubt was a hoax, but there is not the slightest evidence of a hoax in the White Sands case. At last report, Mr. Stokes was still employed as a research engineer at White Sands in good standing.

The Levelland sightings were attributed to "weather phenomena of electrical nature, generally classified as 'Ball lightning' or 'St. Elmo's fire,' caused by stormy conditions in the area. . . ." The two are totally different phenomena. The Air Force stated it was able to locate only three persons who saw the "big light." Actually, there were at least 10 witnesses who similarly described elliptical objects. [See Section XII, Nov., 1957 Chronology]

The Coast Guard sighting was attributed to "aircraft, and possible spurious radar returns." [See Section XII]

The Army jeep patrols sightings were evaluated as "astronomical." The release said: "Astro plots indicate Venus is at magnitude at the time, place and direction of the first patrol's observation, and the Moon, with scattered clouds, was in general direction of the second patrol's observation." [See Section XII]

With the exception of the Levelland sightings and the one fairly obvious hoax, the remaining cases all involve personnel under military control. This selection of cases could be significant. A few days after the November sightings began, the Air Force had rushed out a general news release stating that in 10 years of UFO investigation "the number of unknowns has been reduced to less than 2%." Both news releases bear all the earmarks of public relations utterances designed to reassure the public that (1) the Air Force is conducting a thorough scientific investigation, and (2) nothing truly unexplainable is being seen. Inside of two weeks, the Air Force found answers to hundreds of reports. The time factor, alone, casts doubt on the thoroughness of investigation and validity of the explanations.

NOTES

1. Committee on Government Operations, U.S. House of Representatives, Availability of Information From Federal Departments and Agencies. (House Report No. 1884, 1958), p. 2
2. Mollenhoff, Clark R., Washington Cover-Up. (Popular Library, 1963), p. 73
3. Burns, James MacGregor, "The Eagle's Wings Need Realigning," Book Week, March 8, 1964. [Review of Power in Washington, by Douglass Cater (Random House, 1964)]
4. Mollenhoff, op. cit., p. 12
5. NASA Technical Note D-1432

SECTION X

FOREIGN REPORTS

"Although we tend to think of flying saucers as peculiarly American, they are international in scope. England has had more reported sightings, per square mile of territory, than has the United States. France has had its share, not only sporadically, but also in one apparently major wave in the fall of 1954. Brazil, Spain, Italy, Australia, Canada and even several Iron Curtain countries have also been the sources of reports."-- Dr. J. Allen Hynek, Chief scientific consultant to Air Force on UFOs [Yale Scientific magazine, April 1963]

A Survey of Foreign UFO Activity, Public Interest, and Official Attitudes

United States press coverage has sometimes given the impression that UFOs are wholly, or mostly, a native phenomenon. This is completely disproved by the evidence below. Nearly every nation on earth has had reports of sightings from reputable witnesses. Most have had official investigations, usually by military departments rather than scientific agencies. Organizations exist on every continent, privately pursuing the study of UFOs.

Wherever man travels on the globe, UFOs have been sighted. Ships at sea have reported strange objects [For example see Section II; U.S.S. Supply case]. Although not many reports have been made in the polar regions, this is no doubt due to the small populations and lack of opportunity for observations in these areas. It is worth noting that increased population in Antarctica, at scientific bases, has resulted in some reports. Even the natives of remote islands in the South Pacific have reported UFOs.

The following survey is a small sample of thousands of world-wide UFO reports, official statements and significant opinions. The section is divided by geographical regions: A. Western Hemisphere; B. Eastern Hemisphere; C. Oceana and Antarctica.

A. WESTERN HEMISPHERE
NORTH AMERICA

Canada has had a history of UFO sightings closely paralleling that of the U.S. Early reports led to acceptance of UFOs as a reality and establishment of a government laboratory to investigate them, in the period 1952-53.

On April 16, 1952, RCAF Intelligence "went on record as believing that 'flying saucers' could not be laughed off as optical illusions." The spokesman termed UFOs a "bona fide phenomenon." Dr. Peter Millman, noted Dominion astrophysicist, stated: "We can't laugh off these observations." [1]

In the fall of 1953 the government Department of Transport announced establishment of a flying saucer laboratory designed to prove or disprove UFO reports. The laboratory, with scientific equipment to detect gamma rays, magnetic fluctuations, radio noises, etc., was headed by engineer W.B. Smith, later a member of the NICAP Panel of Advisers.

After the official project was closed in 1954 because of "embarrassing" publicity, Mr. Smith issued a statement: "The conclusions reached by Project Magnet and contained in the official report were based on a rigid statistical analysis of sighting reports and were as follows: There is a 91% probability that at least some of the sightings were of real objects of unknown origin. There is about a 60% probability that these objects were alien vehicles." [2]

Typical Canadian Sightings

July 9, 1957: An attorney in Hamilton, Ontario, with another witness watched a glowing white elliptical object speed overhead from SW to NE, about 9:05 p.m. [3]

December 12, 1957: Capt. J.A. Miller, Trans-Canada Airline pilot, flying between Toronto and Windsor about 7 p.m., saw a whirling orange oval object at about 2000 feet altitude, moving at "a terrific rate of speed." The UFO flashed across Lake Erie and was seen over a wide area before swinging back over the lake and disappearing. Other witnesses included employees of Windsor airport and police from every detachment in Southern Essex County. [4]

April 12, 1959: Control tower operators at St. Hubert Air Base, Montreal, and many others about 8 p.m. watched a reddish UFO which hovered over the base for several minutes, then darted away to the north. An RCAF spokesman stated: "It was a genuine UFO as far as we are concerned." [5] About the same time residents of north Montreal saw a red UFO, alternately described as round and cigar-shaped, which hovered low over a field, then climbed rapidly emitting "fiery sparks" from the underside.

Later official statements also paralleled U.S. policy. In a 1960 letter to a NICAP member, Group Captain L.C. Dilworth, for the Chief of the Air Staff, RCAF, stated: "The RCAF has recently implemented the JANAP 146 (D) procedure for the reporting of vital intelligence sightings [including UFOs; see Section IX] ... Needless to say, the RCAF in concert with American forces is interested in all such reports and evaluation is done on a systematic basis. While the outcome of individual evaluations is not made public, you may rest assured that any threat to the security of Canada or the United States will be reflected in appropriate military plans." [6]

In 1961, RCAF Station Comox, British Columbia, stated in a letter to a NICAP member: "Most UFOB reports terminating at Headquarters are unclassified and there should be no reason to suspect that information on this subject is being withheld from the public. Such phenomena pose no threat to the safety of North America in so far as is known by this Headquarters ... Station Comox does not receive directives which apply to the USAF AFR 200-2. This unit, however, does have a reporting guide to be used when phenomena is [sic] reported." [7]

(As in U.S. statements, note the emphasis on assurances that UFOs pose no threat, implying that the inquirer's letter is motivated by fear rather than curiosity.)

In 1961 the Canadian Defence Minister, Douglas S. Harkness wrote a NICAP member that official investigations "have not revealed positive evidence of anything which might affect national welfare and which could not be attributed to possible natural phenomena or mistaken identity." As of 1963, "The Air Officer Commanding Air Defence Command, is charged with the military investigation of Unidentified Flying Object reports. ... Information compiled by the RCAF, pertaining to this matter [UFOs], is not available to the public." [8]

Alaska has had many UFO sightings [See Section XI; Chronology]. In a typical case February 14, 1960, airline employees and others in Nome about 4:40 p.m. saw a silvery tube-shaped object spouting orange flame from the tail. The UFO moved ENE, then curved up and away "as if it were manned and controlled." Another similar UFO was sighted at Unalakleet the same day, moving rapidly NW and leaving contrails. [9] (Five days later the U.S. Air Force stated the objects were meteors.)

Three USAF F-94 jet interceptors pursued a UFO January 22, 1952 which had been tracked on ground and airborne radar at a northern Alaska radar outpost. [See Section VIII; Radar].

(Alaska, of course, is now one of the United States, and is covered in this Section because of its geographical location).

Mexico: In 1949-1950, during the sighting wave which occurred in that period, there were many press reports of UFOs sighted over Mexico. Example: Los Angeles News, March 14 & 15, 1950, Mexico City (UP) -- Hundreds of persons said they saw four flying saucers over Mexico City, and one at Monterrey. Witnesses included trained aircraft observers and meteorologists. [See Section V]

Many additional sightings in past 12 years.

In 1958, Mr. Rafael Aveleyra, Minister of the Embassy of Mexico, Washington, in a letter to NICAP stated: "Please be advised that in accordance with the information just received from my Government, no reports have been received of unidentified flying objects within the area of Mexico, therefore no official investigation has been made." [10]

CENTRAL AMERICA

UFOs have been sighted regularly over the Gulf of Mexico, Caribbean Sea, and Central America [See December 6, 1952 Gulf of Mexico case; Coast Guard Cutter Sebago case, November 5, 1957, Section VIII; etc.] On January 23, 1959, the New York Times reported that a bright silver unidentified object, which had arced across the sky above the Panama Canal, had been tracked by U.S. radar.

A NICAP member in El Salvador, who visited the NICAP office in 1961, informed us that UFO sightings were very common in her country, and that they were a regular topic of conversation, in schools and elsewhere.

SOUTH AMERICA

The same is true of most South American countries, at least five of which have active UFO organizations. Two, Argentina and Brazil, have treated the subject more frankly and openly than any other nations.

Argentina: A letter to NICAP from the Argentine Embassy dated October 10, 1958, requested information about the structure, scope and aims of NICAP, because "the creation of an agency similar to NICAP, with the same objectives, is under consideration by Argentine Air Force officials." [11]

Strong Argentine interest in UFOs is not surprising considering the well-documented cases which have occurred there. At Cordoba Airport, November 25, 1954, two luminous objects which hovered for nearly an hour were reported by Dr. Marcos Guerci, chief of the meteorological service; Carlos Bassoli, control tower operator; and many others. One UFO was roughly semi-circular, appearing like a disc on edge, the other circular. Dr. Guerci stated he believed he had observed "something foreign to our knowledge," according to the official report released by the Argentine Embassy. [12]

The most recent series of sightings in Argentina (as this is being written) began in May 1962, continuing throughout the year. The incidents included reported landings with resultant markings and stains on the ground, highly maneuverable luminous phenomena, electro-magnetic effects, and other typical UFO features. [See Section XII; Argentine Chronology]

On May 22, 1962, UFOs were sighted four times in a period of about 35 minutes by a flight of Navy pilots in the vicinity of Espora Naval Air Base. In one instance, about 7:20 p.m., student pilot Roberto Wilkinson reported that a luminous object trailing his plane lit up his cockpit, and his radio-electric transmission failed as the UFO passed below his aircraft. [13]

Sightings continued throughout the summer, many concentrated around aircraft and airports. Over Floresta District, September 8, 1962, Lt. (j.g.) Juan Jose Vico sighted a "burnished metal" lenticular UFO making smooth and apparently controlled maneuvers, according to the report.

Investigations of the 1962 sightings by military authorities brought forth two statements. Capt. Luis Sanchez Moreno, investigating for the Navy, told the press the Navy had been constantly concerned about UFOs since the great wave of global sightings in 1952. Following the sightings by Navy personnel in May 1962, the investigation report released by the Argentine Embassy concluded: "The testimonies of Naval Air Officer pilots and personnel of the Flying Course indicate the existence of abnormal luminous phenomenon."

In addition to receiving good cooperation from the Embassy, NICAP is indebted to Mr. Thomas Williams, Fundacion Williams, Buenos Aires; Mr. Christian Vogt, Secretary of the "Comision Observadora de Objetos Voladores No Identificados (CODOVNI)" and Ing. William Kalocai, Director of the "Centro Investigador de Fenomenos Espaciales (C.I.F.E.)," Bahia Blanca, [14] for details of many Argentine UFO cases. At Ezeiza International Airport, Buenos Aires, December 22, 1962, a UFO was sighted about 3:00 a.m. Tower operators Horacio Alora and Mario Pezzutto were watching an Aerolineas Argentinas plane which was about to take off, and an approaching DC-8 jet operated by Panagra (a division of Pan American Airways).

One of the operators was radioing landing instructions when the jet Captain suddenly broke in:

"What's that thing at the end of the runway?"

An instant later, the same question came from one of the Argentine airliner pilots. Operator Alora turned and saw a large round object, glowing with an intense fiery light, at the head of runway 1-0-2-8. It had evidently descended while he and Pezzutto were watching the two airliners.

Because of the UFOs' brilliant glow, Alora could not tell whether it had actually touched down or was hovering just above the runway. At the moment he turned, the UFO rose about ten meters, hovering briefly. Then, rapidly accelerating, it took off on a northeast course. Before it disappeared, it was also seen by Operator Pezzutto.

During the 1962 sightings around Buenos Aires, as well as in remote areas of the country, key cases were reported freely on television. Argentina's treatment of the UFO question provides an interesting contrast with the secretive policy of the U.S. Government.

Brazil: UFO activity has been virtually constant in Brazil during the past 10-15 years. The number and quality of sightings has been at least equal to that of the U.S., and since 1952 sightings have been reported much more openly than in this country.

In 1958, the majority of experienced UFO investigators, many of whom had published bulletins or headed small UFO groups, formed the "Comissao Brasileira de Pesquisa Confidencial Sobre Objetos Aereos Nao Identificados (CBPCOANI)," a top level commission to promote scientific investigation of UFOs on an international basis. Members of the Commission include Dr. J. Escobar Faria (Attorney and author), a NICAP Adviser; Dr. Olavo Fontes, (M.D.), adviser to the Aerial Phenomena Research Organization (APRO), Tucson, Arizona; Prof. Flavio Pereira, President (also President of the Scientific Council, Brazilian Interplanetary Society); Cmdr. A.B. Simoes (airline official and writer). Significantly, the Commission includes representatives of the Brazilian armed services. As in Argentina, UFOs are considered an important problem justifying the formation of civilian-military agencies for continuous investigation.

Virtually every large coastal city, military base, and airport of Brazil has been visited by UFOs, and witnesses have included high-ranking officers, public officials and scientists.

A formation of "circular silver-colored" objects, apparently "mechanical" devices, were observed by FAB (Brazilian Air Force) officers and men, as well as airline personnel and civilians, as they sped over Porto Alegre AFB, October 24, 1954. [15]

```
(SAUCER)
    PORTO ALEGRE, BRAZIL.--THE AIR FORCE BASE HERE REPORTED THAT
"CIRCULAR, SILVER-COLORED" OBJECTS MOVING AT TREMENDOUS SPEEDS HAD
BEEN SIGHTED OVER THE BASE LAST SUNDAY.
    A STATEMENT DISTRIBUTED BY THE BASE COMMAND SAID THE PHENOMENON
WAS REPORTED IMMEDIATELY TO THE AIR MINISTRY IN RIO DE JANEIRO WITH A
REQUEST FOR INVESTIGATION.
    THE STATEMENT SAID THE BODIES WERE NOT CELESTIAL "BECAUSE THEIR
MOVEMENTS APPEARED MECHANICAL AND INTERMITTENT." NO BALLOONS WERE
ALOFT AT THE TIME, THE BASE ADDED.
    "IT WAS IMPOSSIBLE TO CALCULATE THE ALTITUDE OR VELOCITY AT WHICH
THE OBJECTS MOVED, BUT THE SPEED WAS GREATER THAN ANY OF WHICH THE BASE
HAS KNOWLEDGE. THEIR GENERAL SHAPE WAS CIRCULAR, SILVER-COLORED AND
SHIMMERING."
    THE STATEMENT SAID THE OBJECTS WERE OBSERVED BY OFFICERS AND ENLISTED
MEN OF THE AIR BASE, BY PERSONNEL OF THE VARIG AIRLINE AND BY A NUMBER
OF CIVILIANS IN THE CITY, BETWEEN 1 P.M. AND 6 P.M. SUNDAY.
                                                    10/27--PA306P
```

A startling incident on November 21, 1954, was reported on the front pages of newspapers in South and Central America, and in England, but apparently not in the U.S. A Brazilian airliner in flight near Rio de Janeiro, at night, encountered 19 glowing saucer-shaped objects. The UFOs flew at high speed within about 300 feet of the plane causing a panic among the passengers.

The crew had to act forcibly to calm the passengers and continue the flight safely. [16]

Another extremely important incident, January 16, 1958, was only sketchily reported in a few U.S. papers. Near Trindade Isle off the Brazilian east coast, the Almirante Saldanha, an IGY oceanographic vessel, saw and photographed a maneuvering disc-shaped UFO which made several passes over the area [See Section VIII; Photographs]. Marine photographer Almiro Barauna, officers and men on deck, sighted the UFO and Barauna obtained four good exposures of the object. The film was developed on board ship, the witnesses confirming that the Saturn-shaped images (disc with central flange) corresponded to what they had observed.

The impressive evidence created a stir in the Brazilian Congress. At first the Navy was cautious and secretive about the incident, but the President of Brazil, Mr. Juscelino Kubitschek, intervened at the request of a reporter and the photographs were published in the press. [17]

Both airline and military pilots in Brazil have often reported UFOs:

June 30, 1957. An airliner enroute from Belo Horizonte to Rio de Janeiro, at 6:30 p.m., encountered a glowing red-orange disc-like object. Capt. Saul Martins later told the press the UFO maneuvered all around the DC-3, pacing it, flying above and below it. One of the many passengers who also witnessed the object was a renowned Brazilian writer, Prof. Aires de Mata Machado Filho. [18]

July 4, 1957. A REAL Airlines plane enroute from Campos to Victoria, capital of Espirito Santo State, was paced by a circular UFO. The pilot, Cmdr. Delgado, said that when his plane and the UFO were passing through clouds, brightly lighted apertures like windows became visible on the object. When they left the clouds, these markings disappeared. The UFO had raised portions on top and bottom. [See Section IX; Patterns].

August 14, 1957. Near Joinville, at 8:55 p.m., a Varig Airlines C-47 enroute from Porto Alegre to Rio de Janeiro was approached by a luminous object. The pilot, Cmdr. Jorge Campos Araujo, said his co-pilot first noticed the UFO pacing the plane to the left. As they watched, the UFO suddenly sped ahead and crossed just in front of the plane. Then it hovered briefly, and dove into the undercast at about 5,700 feet. (The plane was flying at 6,300 feet). At the moment when the strange object hovered briefly, the engines of the airliner began coughing and missing, and the cabin lights dimmed. When the UFO moved away, the aircraft electrical system returned to normal. [See Section VIII; Electro-Magnetic Effects].

Cmdr. Araujo described the UFO as "shaped like a saucer with a kind of cupola or dome on top of it. The whole cupola glowed with an intense green light. The flattened base glowed with a less intense yellowish luminosity." [19]

November 4, 1957. Capt. Jean Vincent de Beyssac, flying a Varig Airlines C-46 near Ararangua at 1:20 a.m., noticed a red light to the left. The plane was at 7,000 feet above a layer of stratus clouds. Both Capt. de Beyssac and his co-pilot watched curiously as the light increased in size. When the pilot decided to investigate and started to press his rudder, the UFO suddenly leaped through an arc of about 45 degrees and appeared much larger in size. Capt. de Beyssac went into an 80 degree left turn for a closer look. About midway of the turn, the object began glowing more brilliantly and the pilot smelled smoke in the cabin. While the crew hastily looked for fire, the UFO vanished. It was then discovered that the ADF (direction finder), right generator and transmitter-receiver had burned out simultaneously. [20]

May 27, 1958. Near the Bahia State coast, a Varig airliner piloted by Cmdr. Bittar, was approached by a brightly luminous UFO with ball-like projections on the underside. The object maneuvered under the plane, hovered, then dove toward the sea. [21]

July 14, 1959. A Brazilian Air Force pilot checked on a hovering light observed from the control tower at Pampulha, Belo Horizonte, Minas Gerais State at the request of the tower operator. After landing, the pilot reported that the unidentified light had followed him for about an hour while he was enroute from Pico do Couto. The control tower operator then fired some flares in the direction of the UFO, and it changed color from white to amber to intense green. Then it turned white again, and darted upwards, disappearing in the darkness. [22]

July 24, 1961. At night in the vicinity of Ilha Grande, Cmdr. Jose Guilherme Saez, pilot of a VASP Airlines "Scandia" flying at 7,000 feet, saw a luminous object which he first believed was a meteor. "I radioed the Santa Cruz Air Force Base and Sao Paulo airport," Cmdr. Saez stated. "Suddenly the object changed direction, from the left to our right. Then I saw it quite near our Scandia." The object remained visible several minutes. During this time, Cmdr. Saez said, "The UFO did not describe curves, but made angular turns. It moved up and down, back and forth, in all directions." [23] (cf., sighting by Capt. Hull, Capital Airlines, November 14, 1956; Section I).

At times, Brazil has been one of the least secretive governments in regard to release of UFO information. High officials have often openly admitted their serious concern with UFOs.

As in the case of several countries, there is evidence that the Embassies in Washington, either yielding to the wishes of the U.S. Government or for political reasons of their own, sometimes debunk the subject in spite of serious official concern of their governments at home. In 1959, Maj. Gen. Antonio Barcellos, Air Attache of the Brazilian Embassy, wrote a NICAP member: "The Brazilian Government does not accredit or acknowledge any reports of unidentified flying objects ... it considers the question of UFO to be in the same category as that of Santa Claus. Therefore, if anyone in Brazil has ever cited what they consider to be a UFO, they would probably not report to any official agency, but if they did try to make such a report, they would find that it would not be accepted." [24]

Other South American Countries

The history of UFO reports in the other South American countries is very similar to that of Argentina and Brazil.

In Valparaiso, Chile, October 28, 1959, Juan Fruto (Director of a local Astronomical Association), C. Ventura (civil aviator), and others about 9:15 p.m. sighted a luminous orange concave disc performing evolutions in the sky. [25]

Cases of electro-magnetic effects [See Section VIII] have been noted in Argentina, Brazil, Chile, Peru and Venezuela. On January 30, 1958, a lawyer and his wife, near Lima, Peru, saw a circular UFO hovering an estimated 500 meters above the highway. As their automobile passed beneath the object, the car lights went out. Truck drivers and others on the same highway also witnessed the UFO. Passengers on a bus felt an electric shock, and the bus motor failed as the UFO was seen. [26]

A NICAP Subcommittee (investigative unit) is operative in Santiago, Chile, headed by Prof. Juan E. Gatica Salinas, astrophysicist. Other members of the unit are professors of mathematics and physics, and students. The Subcommittee is divided into three groups which make scheduled observations of the sky from different observatories, increasing the chances of obtaining triangulations of a UFO.

In Montevideo, Uruguay, Milton W. Hourcade is one of the directors of the "Centro de Investigacion de Objetos Voladores Inidentificados (C.I.O.V.I.)." The group has investigated and compiled reports in Uruguay for many years, periodically exchanging data with NICAP.

One of the cases investigated by C.I.O.V.I. occurred May 5, 1958, near San Carlos. About 3:40 p.m., Carlos A. Rodriguez, an experienced and reputable pilot, was flying his piper aircraft in the vicinity of Capitan Curbelo Naval Air Base when he noticed a brilliant glowing object approaching his plane. The UFO stopped an estimated 2000 meters away and, according to the report, "it rocked twice in a balancing motion." [cf., Oct. 2, 1961, Salt Lake City, Utah, pilot sighting; Section I]. The object was shaped like a child's top, symmetrical above and below. As he closed to about 700 meters, Rodriguez felt intense heat in the cockpit and was forced to open the windows and door of the plane and remove his jacket. The UFO then took off, accelerating rapidly eastward toward the sea, leaving a thin vapor trail. [27]

Venezuela has been the scene of so much UFO activity that as of 1963, according to a NICAP member who visited Caracas, the sight of huge glowing objects lighting up mountain tops around the city was no longer considered noteworthy. Active in UFO investigation around Caracas are Dr. Askold Ladonko (NICAP Adviser) and Horacio Gonzalez Ganteaume (NICAP member). In December 1962 over an unexplored jungle area near famous Angel Falls, a UFO was photographed on 8 mm movie film by

Mr. Ali Diaz. Diaz was aboard a DC-3 plane carrying vacationists on a tour to view the beautiful scenery. Dr. Ladonko and Gonzalez Ganteaume notified NICAP, interviewed Diaz, and encouraged analysis of the film.

During June 1963 a Spanish speaking NICAP member from New York City, Mr. Jose A. Cecin, flew to Caracas and borrowed the original film. Analysis of it currently is being arranged by NICAP. [See Section VIII]. Viewed at the NICAP office by the staff and several members, the movie shows an eerie, brilliant yellow, tear-drop shaped light rising from the base of Auyantepuy Mountain, oscillating back and forth as it accelerates across the mountain, blue sky and clouds.

(During his visit to Caracas, Mr. Cecin was told of an incident in which a prominent citizen was driving through a rural area when he saw a large disc hovering over a field where several peasants were working. He excitedly called their attention to it. "We know about it," they replied casually. "It comes here every day. It doesn't bother anyone.")

Venezuela also has a history of sightings by airline pilots and other experienced observers. An orange light closed in on a Venezuelan airliner at 6:45 p.m., January 2, 1955, in the vicinity of Punta San Juan. When the UFO was at close range, a bright light from it shone into the cockpit of the plane intermittently. [28]

A month later, February 2, an Aeropost Airlines plane was bound for Merida from Maiquetia. At the controls was Capt. Dario Celis; co-pilot was B.J. Cortes. About 11:15 a.m., a round, glowing green "apparatus" approached the plane, rotating counter-clockwise. Around its center was a reddish ring which emitted flashes of brilliant light. Above and below the ring, markings like portholes were visible. Capt. Celis banked his plane toward the UFO. Instantly, the object whirled downward, levelled off, and sped away. During the sighting, Capt. Celis attempted to report the object by radio, but his communication was cut off. [29]

July 2, 1960, near Maiquetia, a Venezuelan Airlines Super-Constellation was arriving from Spain about 3:00 a.m. Flying at 10,000 feet about 20 degrees N, 68 degrees W (near Puerto Rico), the pilot and crew noticed a bright luminous object angling toward the plane at about their altitude. After paralleling the plane for several minutes, the object suddenly shot away at terrific speed. The pilot reported the sighting to the press upon landing. [30]

A Professor of Engineering, Central University, reported a UFO September 15, 1960. Prof. German Alvarez, in Carrizales, Miranda State, watched a luminous object sweep across the sky for about three minutes, after 7:30 p.m. The UFO accelerated in a curved course. Before disappearing behind mountains, it appeared as two objects. [31]

Formations of UFOs, about 16 objects in all, passing from east to west between 4:00 and 6:00 p.m. were witnessed by many people in the Parque del Este, Caracas, February 11, 1962. One witness, Sr. Emiro Ayesta, ran to the Humboldt Planetarium in the park where Sr. Carlos Pineda of the Planetarium staff witnessed one of the UFOs. Sr. Pineda described it as "a body giving off a brilliant light, moving at great altitude as if towards the moon." [32]

B. EASTERN HEMISPHERE

Scandinavia

The earliest well-publicized UFO reports from Scandinavia were the so-called "ghost rockets" observed in Sweden during the summer and fall of 1946. Military authorities adopted secrecy reminiscent of wartime in dealing with reports of the objects, banning publication of the location of sightings, and requiring newspapers to use the dateline "somewhere in Sweden." [33]

Mysterious fireballs and cigar-shaped UFOs were observed all summer. [34] Finally, in October the defense ministry announced that it had been unable to discover the origin or nature of the "ghost rockets." Of 1000 reports studied, about 80% were attributed to "celestial phenomena." But, the report continued, radar detected some "which cannot be the phenomena of nature or products of imagination, nor be referred to as Swedish planes..." [35]

In May 1954, Mutual news commentator Frank Edwards (now a NICAP Board Member) reported an item from Stockholm: "Swedish military authorities sent special crews into north Sweden where scores of residents have reported strange glowing objects maneuvering over forests at low altitude during the week of May 10...Military men who have seen the things say they were not planes of any type."

After the crew of a Swedish airliner reported a wingless circular UFO over southern Sweden December 17, 1953, the defense department ordered a full scale investigation. Capt. Ulf Christiernsson, former RAF pilot, said: "It was an entirely unorthodox, metallic, symmetrical and circular object." The UFO was seen speeding over the town of Haessleholm in the main commercial airlane between Stockholm and Copenhagen. [36]

In 1961 Mr. Sven Schalin, aeronautical engineer in Linkoping, became NICAP Adviser for Sweden. In his acceptance letter, Mr. Schalin stated: "UFOs very definitely have been sighted also in this country. A 'flap' seemed to occur around January 1959, the whole period starting perhaps in July 1958 and ending about June 1959. Obviously the Swedish Intelligence Center in Stockholm knows what is going on but the usual debunking policy is strictly followed."

During Operation Mainbrace, extensive naval maneuvers in the North Sea on and about September 20, 1952, UFOs were sighted in the vicinity on several occasions. [See Section XII; Operation Mainbrace Chronology] On the 20th, a silvery disc of metallic appearance was observed passing swiftly over the Allied fleet. Wallace Litwin, an American newsman on board the aircraft carrier "Franklin Roosevelt," took three color photographs of the UFO. As far as is known, the pictures have never been published and no explanation of the incident was offered.

Norway, Finland and Denmark also have had their share of UFO sightings. During an aerial expedition to take photographs of a solar eclipse, June 30, 1954, Norwegian scientists and others on board three planes observed and photographed two "enormous" silvery discs which gave a metallic glint. [Section I]

In 1958, replying to a NICAP query, the Norwegian Embassy stated: "Our Air Force's UFO material is mainly of security graded nature and cannot be put to the disposal of NICAP." [37]

During the winter of 1958, observers on the Finnish-Soviet border reported circular and cigar-shaped luminous objects maneuvering over Soviet territory near the Arctic Circle. Brilliantly glowing spherical "missiles," some of which moved vertically up and down, also were reported. [38]

While "Operation Mainbrace" was in full swing nearby in the North Sea during September 1952, a shining apparently metallic disc was seen on the 20th by three Danish Air Force officers. About 7:30 p.m., the UFO sped over Karup Airfield, Denmark, disappearing in clouds to the east.

On November 20, 1957, during the rash of UFO sightings in the Western hemisphere [see Section XI] Air Force officers and many civilians near Bernholm, Denmark, saw a UFO flashing red and green lights as it swooped low above the water and over the island. At times the object hovered motionless. No sound could be heard. The Danish newspaper "Familie-blad" reported the sightings.

September 11, 1956: Allied intelligence experts were reported to be investigating radar sightings of "mysterious objects" which had been tracked for three weeks over the Baltic Sea by a NATO radar station on Bernholm Island, Denmark. The UFOs followed a curved course traveling about 2000-2500 m.p.h. [See Section VIII; Radar]

England

The policy of the British Air Ministry has been identical to that of the U.S. Although claiming their investigations have proved that almost all UFO sightings have mundane explanations, the Air Ministry firmly refuses to release the case histories. When NICAP requested information about specific cases in 1957, the Air Ministry replied: "We regret that we are unable to release any information on the radar sighting at West Freugh in Scotland on 4th April...We cannot release any information on the B.O.A.C. or the Flt. Lt. Salandin sightings. Air Ministry policy has not changed since those sightings were made." [39]

In a 1963 letter to a NICAP member, the Air Ministry stated: "Because of our defense responsibilities we investigate reports of UFOs as they come in whenever there is sufficient information for this to be done. I am afraid, however, that we cannot undertake to provide details of any particular reports which have been received." [40]

Unofficially, a totally different picture of British opinion is available. Dozens of very active UFO organizations exist in England, many publishing bulletins. The largest and most professional magazine is the "Flying Saucer Review," published in London. The groups exist because of a long history of good UFO sightings in the British Isles, many involving trained observers.

The Royal Air Force, one of the most highly respected air forces in the world, has contributed a number of sightings. One of the most prominent proponents of UFOs in England is Air Chief Marshal Lord Dowding, head of the RAF fighter command during the Battle of Britain. In a by-line article for the London Sunday Dispatch (July 11, 1954), Lord Dowding stated: "I am convinced that these objects do exist and that they are not manufactured by any nation on earth. I can therefore see no alternative to accepting the theory that they come from some extra-terrestrial source."

"RAF Flying Review," unofficial but authoritative and highly regarded aviation publication in London, has treated the UFO subject seriously and urged a more thorough investigation.

The fact that UFOs were being taken seriously in England was first widely known in 1957. The London Reynolds News reported June 16:

"In room 801 of what was once the Hotel Metropole, Britain's Air Ministry is investigating Flying Saucers -- and that's official . . . At airfields all over Britain, fighter planes are kept ready to intercept, and if necessary engage, any unidentified flying object within combat range . . . [the room's] existence was admitted last night by an Air Ministry spokesman. He disclosed that it has been investigating Flying Saucer reports since 1947. 'We have something like 10,000 on our files,' he said."

A few of the reports which have concerned British authorities: Topcliffe, September 20, 1952 (Reuters) -- "A flying saucer entered the eight-nation Baltic area maneuvers ["Operation Mainbrace"] here today. The RAF base here reported to maneuver headquarters that an unidentifiable silver circular object had been sighted 15,000 feet above the airfield. The object, which appeared five miles behind a Meteor jet fighter [piloted by Lt. John W. Kilburn], maintained a slow forward speed before descending in a swinging pendulum motion. Then it began a rotary motion about its own axis and accelerated at an incredible speed in a westerly direction but later turned southeast. It was seen by RAF officers and men on the airfield."

Another RAF pilot encountered a UFO October 4, 1954. Flight Lt. J.R. Salandin of the 604th Fighter Squadron, flying a Meteor jet out of North Weald, Essex, nearly collided head-on with a huge, metallic appearing object. The UFO was shaped like two saucers pressed together, one inverted on top of the other. At the last second, it flipped to one side and streaked past at tremendous speed. Two round UFOs had been sighted speeding between two other Meteor jets in the vicinity just before Lt. Salandin's sighting. [41]

An object described as a "bright yellow light varying in intensity some 200 feet from the ground" was reported hovering over London Airport February 26, 1959. (Some accounts called it a "yellow disc.") Control tower operators and other airport personnel saw the object, studying it through binoculars. The official report to the Air Ministry concluded, the object "then climbed away at high speed."

(On March 6, conflicting theories were advanced by Air Ministry and Airport officials. Some believed the UFO was the planet Venus distorted by clouds; others that it was the "nose cone light" of a civilian aircraft).

An Aer Lingus (Irish International Airlines) pilot reported a globe-shaped unidentified object which flew beneath his Viscount May 21, 1962, above southern England. While flying from Cork to Brussels at about 17,000 feet, Capt. Gordon Pendleton and First Officer J.P. Murphy saw the UFO approaching head-on. They estimated the rate of closure at about 1200 m.p.h. The UFO sped past about 3,000 feet below the airliner at close to 700 m.p.h. "I could see it quite clearly," Capt. Pendleton said. "It definitely had no wings. It was brown, appeared to be round

and had a number of projections, looking rather like some kind of radio antennae, on its surface. I have never seen anything like it before." [42]

The European Continent

On the Continent, UFOs have been sighted in virtually every country. In Switzerland, businessman J.H. Ragaz, publisher of "Weltraumbote," has supported NICAP's investigation as well as publicizing European UFO activity. Many sightings of typical UFOs have taken place in Switzerland.

Other small countries, such as Austria, also have experienced UFO activity:

May 15, 1954, Vienna (Reuters) -- Three discs in wedge formation reported by five persons.

December 19, 1954, Vienna (INS) -- Several witnesses reported UFOs moving at great speed above the capital. "Austrian authorities are reportedly taking these observations seriously. Police received orders to report any strange flying objects."

The "Nederlandse Studiekring Voor Ufologie" has been active for several years in Amsterdam, Holland. Mr. A.F. van Wieringen, a member of its board, is also a NICAP member and correspondent. A recent report investigated by his group involved a Royal Dutch Air Force pilot who chased a UFO January 29, 1962, over eastern Holland. After sighting the object and seeing it on the radar set of the F-86, the pilot radioed his base. He was informed that the UFO was also being tracked by ground radar. Following instructions, he tried to make radio contact with the unidentified object, but there was no response. Arming his "Sidewinder" rocket, the pilot tried to close in, but the UFO swiftly pulled away before he could fire, and disappeared within seconds.

On the night of August 6-7, 1952, Will Jansen, a marine engineer and designer, was visiting in Kerkrade, Holland. Just after midnight a disc-shaped craft with visible superstructure swooped down to low altitude, hovered, zig-zagged and sped away. A second disc-shaped UFO, similar in outline, was then seen hovering farther away. Finally it tilted up vertically and shot up out of sight. [43]

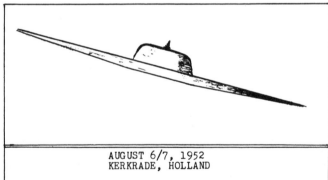

AUGUST 6/7, 1952
KERKRADE, HOLLAND

FIRST OF TWO DISCS OBSERVED BY WILL JANSEN, MARINE ENGINEER. "CABIN" PROTRUDED FROM UNDERSIDE TOO ON SECOND UFO.

Numerous UFO sightings in France have been thoroughly investigated and documented by Aime Michel, mathematician and engineer. (Author of "The Truth About Flying Saucers," Criterion Books, N.Y., 1956; and "Flying Saucers and the Straight Line Mystery," Criterion, 1958). Since 1958, M. Michel has joined forces with Rene Hardy, engineer at Drivomatic Laboratories in Paris, and other scientists to form a scientific commission to study UFO reports. Both Michel and Hardy also serve as NICAP Advisers.

On June 13, 1952, a very prominent bright orange-red light hovered in the sky, visible from Le Bourget airport. About 1:00 a.m., after hovering for an hour, the UFO began moving and crossed the sky southwest of the field, accelerating rapidly. Witnesses included M. Navarri, pilot of an approaching plane; M. Veillot and M. Damiens, control tower operators. [44]

At a military meteorological station in Villacoublay, August 29, 1952, a UFO was tracked by theodolite and the observation carefully logged. The object alternately hovered, and moved erratically. [45]

New Yorker magazine, in a "Letter From Paris" column, October 23, 1954 recounts many UFO sightings during the summer and fall of that year. Witnesses included the Mayor of Briancon, gendarmes, sailors, taxi-drivers and other citizens. The European "flap" of fall 1954 is one of the most intense concentrations of UFO activity on record. [See Aime Michel's books, cited above, for details]

At Orly Field, Paris, February 17, 1956, a UFO was tracked on radar and seen by an Air France pilot. "They [radarmen at Orly] said the object showed up on radar screens at an estimated speed of about 1700 mph., then hovered at various points over the capital." [46]

Also in Paris, September 26, 1957, an American Embassy officer and his wife watched a reddish-orange elliptical UFO for twenty minutes around 7:00 p.m. The sighting was later reported to NICAP in confidence. [47]

Germany: In 1963, Major Artur W. Heyer, air attache at the German Embassy, answered a NICAP member's query: "I have been informed that no information with regard to your questions is available and that there is no official West German Government policy or agency concerning unidentified flying objects (UFOs)." "However," he concluded: "I am sorry to give you this reply and I think your request deals with a matter which has not yet been exploited sufficiently." [48]

Over Fursten-Feldbruck November 23, 1948, a bright red UFO was seen by a USAF pilot and tracked by ground and air radar. The UFO was clocked at 900 mph., and climbed 23,000 feet in a matter of minutes, far exceeding the performance of any known aircraft. [See Section VIII; Radar]

London Daily Mail, July 5, 1954: "Berlin is seeing saucers regularly. Allied officials there are investigating the appearance of mysterious objects over the city. German eyewitnesses claim that a formation of three fast-moving objects can regularly be seen whenever the sky over Berlin is clear. The objects, described as "small and dislike," are said to appear between 10 and 11 p.m., at extremely high altitudes."

In recent years, German NICAP members have contributed UFO information to NICAP regularly. Martin Bruckmann, engineering student, at about midnight November 19, 1956 observed seven bright, blue-white elliptical objects in V-formation moving rapidly east to west over Frankfurt. [49]

In Kirchberg, Hunsruck, at 3:30 p.m., May 25, 1958, Gunter Henn (Master of Business Administration) with another person watched a glistening silver object, circular with spoke-like markings. The UFO descended on a slant, them moved horizontally into clouds. [50]

The NICAP Adviser for West Germany, at Wolfsburg, is Dr. Helmut H. Damm, a German-born American citizen currently employed in Germany as a management consultant in engineering. He holds the degree of Doctor of Mechanical Engineering. During World War II he served as a systems and field instructor, and design engineer, in the Rocket Division of the German Army.

Dr. Damm took a survey of UFO interest in West Germany during 1962. Results:

* Air Force headquarters at Bonn stated they had no personnel or funds to devote to UFO investigation.

* The German Research Institute for Aeronautics also stated they were doing no work on UFOs, but appeared interested and openminded in discussing the subject.

* The daily newspaper "Bild" stated it was greatly interested in obtaining more facts and new evidential reports for publication.

* On the whole, Dr. Damm found individuals and agencies poorly informed on the subject.

At least two eminent German scientists who have been employed in the U.S. since World War II are outspoken believers that UFOs are space ships from another planet. Prof. Hermann Oberth in 1954 began an American Weekly article (October 24) in these words: "It is my thesis that flying saucers are real and that they are space ships from another planet." Upon his return to Germany in November 1958, after being employed by the U.S. at Huntsville, Alabama, Prof. Oberth repeated his belief that "very intelligent beings" have been observing the earth for a long time. [51]

Dr. Walther Riedel, former chief designer and research director of Peenemunde rocket center in Germany, directed the Civilian Saucer Investigation of Los Angeles. CSI was the first prominent UFO investigation group in the U.S., publicized by Life and Time early in 1952. Dr. Riedel stated: "I'm convinced saucers have an out-of-world basis." (Another prominent member of CSI was philosopher Gerald Heard, author of Is Another World Watching? Harpers, 1950).

Reports in southern Europe and over the Mediterranean Sea have been as frequent as in any other area of the world. (For example, see New York Times; March 30, 1950, "More Flying Saucers in Mediterranean, Orient.") The sightings which received the most attention in the press and were best documented, however, were those during the fall 1954 European "flap".

Around 7:00 p.m., September 17, 1954, a large circular object, (shaped like a truncated cone) trailing smoke and making a series of explosive sounds, was observed along a 15-mile stretch above the Mediterranean coast west of Rome. International News Service (INS) reported that an Italian Air Force radar station at Practica Dimare, 40 miles southwest of Rome, tracked the UFO for 39 minutes at an altitude of 3600 feet. The UFO flew slowly at first, then accelerated rapidly and disappeared straight up at great speed.

Mrs. Clare Booth Luce, then U.S. Ambassador to Italy, was among dozens of witnesses to a UFO phenomenon over Rome, October 28, 1954. A luminous round object sped across the sky, followed by a fall of fine cotton-like particles from the sky. Mrs. Luce said: "I saw something, but I don't know what it was." An Associated Press reporter, Maurizio Andreolo, described the UFO as being "like a moon dashing across the sky at fantastic speed...silently." [52]

Several UFOs, some described as spear-shaped and some egg-shaped, sped over Belgrade, Yugoslavia shortly after 6:15 a.m., October 25, 1954. (The same or similar objects were also seen in Austria and Italy that day.) Witnesses included Vladimir Ajvas, aeronautical engineer; Stjepan Djitkol, Air Force Captain; and members of the staff at Zemun Airport.

United Press reported from Belgrade, October 27: "Authorities announced today they were making a 'serious investigation' of the flight over Yugoslavia Monday of objects which looked and acted like nothing described in the standard aviation reference books. . . . The reports under investigation were that shiny 'ellipsoidal' objects zipped through the Yugoslav skies trailing bluish tails for about an hour after sunrise Monday. Scientists in astronomical observatories who witnessed the flights concluded that the objects could not have been meteors, and probably were not any form of 'heavenly body' . . .'"

Barcelona, Spain, November 12, 1958 (AP): "A group of scientists here has founded the interplanetary studies center to investigate 'unexplained phenomena in space and unidentified objects in the skies' . . ." The President of the "Centro do Estudios Interplanetarios," Mr. Eduardo Buelta, established contact with NICAP late in 1958 offering collaboration and setting up an exchange of information.

Palma Observatory on the Spanish Island of Majorca (or Mallorca), in the Balearic Islands (off the east coast of Spain in the Mediterranean Sea) sighted a UFO at 9:33 a.m., May 22, 1960. The report, cabled to NASA in Washington, described a white triangular object about 1/4 the size of the moon spinning on its own axis as it flew on a steady course. NICAP efforts to obtain more information from the Observatory went unanswered.

Africa

The vast African continent has been visited repeatedly by unidentified flying objects showing characteristics similar to those seen all over the world. One of the earliest and most spectacular reports on record concerns the sighting of a huge cigar-shaped UFO which hovered over famous Mt. Kilimanjaro February 19, 1951. The UFO was photographed from an East African Airways plane flying in the vicinity. After remaining motionless for a considerable period of time, the object suddenly climbed steeply and disappeared. The movie film was developed and reportedly showed a clear and sizeable image of the object, according to the Natal Mercury.

The sighting was detailed in the Nairobi Sunday Post, February 25, 1951, by Capt. Jack Bicknell, pilot of the East African Airways plane. Extracts from Capt. Bicknell's report: "The Lodestar plane left Nairobi West at 7:00 a.m. At 7:20 a.m., the radio officer (D. W. Merrifield) drew my attention to a bright object like a white star hanging motionless about 10,000 feet above Kilimanjaro. My first reaction was to say nothing. We watched it for three minutes. Then we told the passengers about it. One of them had a very powerful pair of binoculars with him and he began to study it. In the meantime, we put a radio message through to Eastleigh describing it. Eastleigh asked us to check whether it was a meteorological balloon. I then examined it for several minutes through the binoculars. . [At this point the plane had approached to within about 50 miles of the mountain]. . .

"Through the glasses I saw a metallic, bullet shaped object which must have been over 200 feet long. At one end was a square-cut vertical fin. Its colour was a dull silver, and at regular intervals along the fuselage were vertical dark bands. Its whole outline was clear and sharp and there was no haziness about it at all. . It was absolutely stationary, and remained that way for 17 minutes. . [Capt. Bicknell states that two passengers were taking photographs at this time] . . .

"Then it began to move eastwards, rising as it did so. It disappeared at about 40,000 feet. . . The machine left no vapour trail, and it had no visible means of propulsion. . . My impression was that it was definitely a flying machine of some kind."

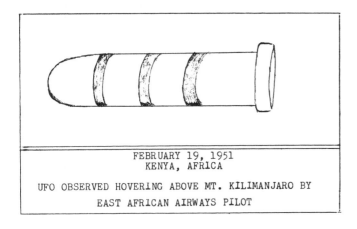

FEBRUARY 19, 1951
KENYA, AFRICA

UFO OBSERVED HOVERING ABOVE MT. KILIMANJARO BY

EAST AFRICAN AIRWAYS PILOT

New Yorker magazine, October 23, 1954 reported a UFO sighting by the Administrator of Danane, French West Africa on September 19th of that year. He, his wife, a doctor, and others saw an object described as an "oval flying machine" with a dome, and lights like searchlights.

In populous South Africa, scientists, aviation personnel, police and many others have reported UFO sightings. At the Upington Meteorological Station, Cape Province, December 7, 1954 the Officer-in-Charge, Mr. R. H. Kleyweg, tracked a white semi-circular UFO through a theodolite for about a minute. Then the object began moving too fast to track. "I have followed thousands of Meteorological balloons," Mr. Kleyweg said. "This object was no balloon." [53.]

During the North and South American "flap" in November 1957 [See Section XII], hundreds of people in the Southern Transvaal area witnessed an "enormous" cylindrical UFO. On the night of November 5, the object was observed hovering in the sky. South African Air Force searchlights in Dunnotar pinpointed the UFO, which then "withdrew" behind clouds, according to witnesses. [54.]

At Johannesburg, April 11, 1958, H. F. Daniels (airport instrument inspector) and others watched a reddish-white UFO above the north horizon at night, moving back and forth east and west. "I have worked with aircraft for 18 years," Mr. Daniels said, "and the thing I saw was certainly no conventional plane. The speed was phenomenal and it sometimes became completely stationary, changing color from white to blood red." [55.]

Many other African UFO sightings, some from French air bases and scientific stations, are recorded by Aime Michel.

Far East

Because of language difficulties, NICAP has not been able to compile as many reports from the Far East (except in the Australia-New Zealand area), but it is known that UFOs are often seen and that UFO groups exist in most countries. A query to the Nationalist Chinese Government, referred to the Taiwan Weather Bureau, brought the following reply in 1963:

"The Mission for the observation on unidentified flying objects should be assigned to a Military Agency such as National Civil Defense Organization in order to meet the emergencies. The Government will inform the public on the sightings of UFOs when the situation is necessary. . . At present no conclusion on the observation of UFOs has been reached or an official report. . . announced to the public." [56.]

An unclassified Air Force intelligence report in NICAP possession describes a U.S. Air Force sighting of a "large round object" somewhere in the Far East in December 1956. A jet pilot experienced radar jamming as he closed on the UFO, and saw it flash away easily outdistancing his jet. [Section I.]

On September 15, 1954, in Manbhum, Bihar, India, Mr. Ijapada Chatterjee (manager of a mica mine) and hundreds of others watched a saucer-shaped object descend to an altitude of about 500 feet. The UFO hovered, then soared upwards at terrific speed causing a tremendous gust of wind. The object was seen over a mine which has supplied beryllium for the U.S. Atomic Energy Commission. [57.]

A book entitled "The Mystery of the Flying Saucers Revealed," published in Indonesia in 1961, contains a foreword by the Air Force Chief of Staff, Air Chief Marshal S. Suryadarma, which discloses that UFOs have often been reported by Indonesian Air Force personnel. The author is Col. J. Salatun, Secretary of the Indonesian Joint Chiefs of Staff and member of the Supreme People's Congress. NICAP checked with the Indonesian Embassy and verified the positions of both men.

In Japan and Korea, notably during the Korean War, UFOs have often been sighted by U.S. Air Force and other military personnel.

October 15, 1948: The crew of an F-61 night fighter over Japan tracked on radar and saw the silhouette of a UFO shaped "like a rifle bullet" (cf., Mt. Kilimanjaro sighting, above) which repeatedly accelerated out of reach of the fighter. [Section VIII; Radar.]

January 29, 1952: Bright, rotating, disc-shaped UFOs seen by B-29 crews near Wonsan and Sunchon, Korea. [58.]

March 29, 1952: Small shiny disc maneuvered around USAF F-86 in flight north of Misawa, Japan. [Section I.]

August 5, 1952: Dark circular UFO with bright body light hovered near control tower at Oneida AFB, Japan, sped away, dividing into three sections. [Section VIII; Radar.]

October 13, 1952: Elliptical UFO hovering in clouds near Oshima, Japan, sighted by Major William D. Leet, USAF, and his engineer; object sped away after 7 minutes. [Section III.]

December 12, 1962: Five school girls in Amagaski City, at 4:30 p.m., saw a brightly glowing UFO. Asked to draw independently what they had seen, all five sketched a Saturn-shaped disc. [59.]

AUSTRALIA--NEW ZEALAND

Another hotspot of UFO activity has been the Australia--New Zealand area. The great number of UFO sightings in this region (about the same southern latitudes as Brazil - Uruguay - Argentina) and the amount of public interest in them can only be suggested in this limited survey of foreign reports. [60.]

As in many other countries, UFOs are "officially" nonexistent. A 1963 letter to a NICAP member from A. B. McFarlane, Secretary, Department of Air, Commonwealth of Australia states: "From time to time reports of unidentified flying objects are received and investigated by the Royal Australian Air Force, but details of individual investigations have not been made public.". . . The letter goes on to quote a 1960 speech in Parliament by Minister for Air, Hon. F. M. Osborne: "Nearly all [UFO reports] are explainable on a perfectly normal basis. . . only three or four per cent cannot be explained on the basis of some natural phenomenon, and nothing that has arisen from that three or four percent. . . gives any firm support for the belief that interlopers from other places in this world or outside it have been visiting us." [61.]

The New Zealand Embassy in 1963 said their government had never stated any policy on UFOs and that "a policy on this subject has never been warranted."

In mid-December 1954 a Royal Australian Navy pilot was flying back to Nowra air base after dark when "two strange aircraft resembling flying saucers" took up formation with him. The pilot called Nowra air control, whose radar showed three objects flying together. The pilot identified himself by moving according to pattern. Upon landing, the pilot said the two UFOs were much faster than his Seafury fighter. [62.]

As a result of hundreds of similar UFO reports, there are a number of UFO groups in Australia. NICAP member Peter E. Norris, an attorney in Melbourne, heads the Victorian Flying Saucer Research Society, which publishes "Flying Saucer Review" (not to be confused with a publication of the same name in London).

On October 16, 1957 Air Marshal Sir George Jones sighted a UFO resembling a balloon with a white light on the bottom, except that it sped past silently at an altitude of about 500 feet. "Nothing can shake me from my belief in what I saw," he said. Interviewed by Mr. Norris, he admitted he had no explanation for the sighting. Sir George Jones is the former Commander-in-Chief of the RAAF.

During the November 1957 "flap" in the western hemisphere, Australia also was flooded with sightings. Mr. Norris reported that "during early November UFO reports came from all Australian states except Tasmania."

The most prominent UFO organization in New Zealand is Civilian Saucer Investigation headed by Harold H. Fulton, a Sergeant in the Royal New Zealand Air Force. Mr. Fulton is now a NICAP Adviser. C.S.I. publishes a bulletin named "Space Probe," however, it has recently been suspended while Mr. Fulton has been on a tour of active duty with the RNZAF. Over the years, Mr. Fulton has contributed dozens of good cases to NICAP and actively publicized serious UFO evidence in his country.

A National New Zealand Airlines plane was enroute to Auckland, N.Z., from Wellington on the night of October 31, 1955. At the controls was Capt. W. T. Rainbow. The co-pilot was S. G. Trounce. A bright object, changing color repeatedly, came from behind the plane on a parallel course, flew alongside, passed the plane and disappeared in the distance. Capt. Rainbow estimated the UFOs' speed at about 850 mph. The strange object, unlike any aircraft, pulsated in colors of red, yellow, orange, and blue.

One of the potentially most important pieces of evidence for UFOs is a secret motion picture film purporting to show a saucerlike UFO climbing steeply over Port Moresby, New Guinea. The film was taken August 31, 1953 by Mr. T. C. Drury, Deputy Regional Director of Civil Aviation. According to Reuters news agency, the film was sent to Air Technical Intelligence Center in Dayton, Ohio, for analysis. The USAF analysis report has never been released.

C. OCEAN & ANTARCTIA

UFOs have been sighted at sea, in the islands of the major oceans, and in Antarctica. Reports from ships' officers are of unusual interest because they are experienced sky observers, familiar with the stars and planets and other astronomical and atmospheric phenomena.

A well-qualified scientific observer aboard an ice-breaker in Admiralty Bay, Antartica, sighted a luminous object which divided into two parts while flying on a level course below an overcast. This phenomenon was observed by Rubens J. Villela, Brazilian meteorologist, March 16, 1961. [Section VI.]

Pacific Ocean

Two objects "like small moons" were observed June 18, 1957 about 150 miles off San Francisco. Capt. C. O. Wertz, Roy Melton, electrician, and other crew members of the freighter "Hawaiian Fisherman" at 8:00 p.m., watched the objects pacing the freighter. Then 15 minutes later a third UFO joined the first two, making a V, and followed the ship. [63.]

A missionary, and four natives in a separate location, in the Fiji Islands witnessed a circular white UFO which descended and hovered about 20 feet above the sea during the night of October 8, 1957. The UFO was revolving and gave off a blinding beam of light as the natives approached it in their boat. The natives reported seeing a man-like figure on top of the object. [64.]

Trans-Oceanic pilots have often sighted strange aerial phenomena, but are reluctant to talk about their experiences. Capt. Willis T. Sperry, American Airlines pilot whose plane was circled by an elliptical UFO May 29, 1950 [Section V.] stated in 1951:

"I have talked to just as many pilots who have seen strange occurrences while flying and have not reported it, as have reported the incident. The ones who did not report it feared adverse publicity. . . Several P.A.A. [Pan American Airways] pilots have seen unexplained objects far from land - one near Australia, several between the mainland of California and Hawaii, and two that I talked to out there [in the Far East] said they saw an object close enough so they could describe it in some detail. . ." [65.]

The sighting of a formation of UFOs east of Hawaii by the crews of several aircraft July 11, 1959 was reported widely by Associated Press, United Press International and Hawaiian newspapers. NICAP interviewed several of the civilian witnesses; the crews of Air Force planes were not available.

Capt. George Wilson, Pan American Airways, gave the following account: "While flying a Boeing Stratocruiser at 20,000 feet on a 224 degree heading [about 900 nautical miles northeast of Honolulu] a large and bright light appeared on the horizon at 11 o'clock position [SSW]. The large bright light was flanked by 3 or 4 smaller lower magnitude lights in a line below, behind and to the left of the main vehicle. The lights passed from 11 o'clock to 10 o'clock position, the formation made an abrupt right turn and disappeared to the south."

The co-pilot, Richard Lorenzen, and Flight Engineer Bob Scott, also saw the UFOs. Lorenzen commented that "the rate of closure with us was much greater than any I had ever experienced before. It was not until the object turned that I was able to distinguish the smaller lights associated with it."

First Officer D. W. Frost, on another Pan American flight in the vicinity, reported essentially the same phenomenon. The UFOs were also observed by Air Force bomber crews, a Slick Airways plane, and a Canadian Pacific airliner. Capt. Lloyd Moffatt, pilot of the Canadian airliner, told the press: "You can take it from me they were there. I never saw anything like it in my life and there are four of us who saw the same thing at the same time."

For about 10 minutes at 7:00 a.m. (Honolulu time), September 21, 1961, two airliners and a U.S. ship at sea observed a UFO simultaneously. The object passed overhead, apparently at extremely high altitude, angling southeasterly above the North Pacific. (See map.)

Reports from the Federal Aviation Agency, and the U.S. Navy Oceanographic Office publication "Notice to Mariners," establish the following facts.

At 1700 Greenwich Mean Time, the S. S. Iberville, north and east of Midway Island, noticed a white object about 20 degrees above the NW horizon. Its apparent angular size was about 1 degree (twice the apparent size of the full moon). For about 10 minutes, the UFO was observed passing over the ship headed southeast. As it neared the ship's meridian, it resembled a huge halo with a bright object in the center. The apparent size increased to over four times the size of the full moon. [See Notice to Mariners report, reproduced below.]

At the same time, a British Overseas Airways Corporation (BOAC) airliner about 800 miles northeast of the ship saw the object overtake the plane. From a steep angle above the plane, the UFO continued southeasterly and disappeared over the horizon. Capt. R. F. Griffin described the UFO as "like a large smoke ring about 2 degrees in diameter [about 4 times the size of the full moon]." He said the center of the ring was clear sky, and once a star was visible through it. A ray of light seemed to project downward from the object.

A Pan American Airways plane, about 400 miles southeast of Capt. Griffin's position, confirmed the report. The pilot reported a doughnut-shaped object moving easterly about 10 degrees above the horizon. [66.]

The Soviet Union announced a few days later that they had successfully test fired a multi-stage carrier rocket over the pacific (exact date not on record). However, the reported size of the UFO was far too large to be explained as a rocket payload.

NORTH PACIFIC

Second Officer William C. Ash of the American S.S. *Iberville*, Capt. M. O. Vinson, Master, reported the following:

"At 1700 G.M.T. on September 21, 1961, while in lat. 31°30′ N., long. 175°30′ E., a few minutes before morning twilight, a white opaque mass about twice the size of a full moon appeared in the northwest at an elevation of about 20°. It continued to climb toward the zenith and at about an elevation of 40° the mass opened gradually to appear as a huge halo with a satellite in the center having very nearly the brightness of a first magnitude star. By the time it reached the zenith it had more than doubled in size reaching its maximum at the zenith and then diminishing as it proceeded to the southeast. As it diminished it continued to decrease in size but did not appear to shrink into a corona as it had appeared but rather faded out completely at an elevation of approximately 20°. The entire mass was in view for approximately 8 to 10 minutes."

Weather partly cloudy, wind NW force 2, slight sea and small NW swell, temperatures: dry 74° F., wet 67° F., sea 79° F.

(N.M. 43/61.)

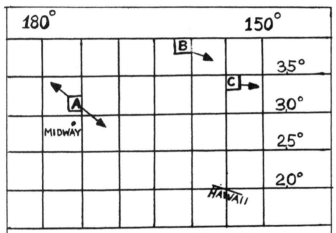

Distance Midway to Hawaii:
1312 Statute Miles

A. Position of S.S. Iberville

B. Position of BOAC Airliner

C. Position of PAA Airliner

(Lines of sight indicated by Arrows)

Atlantic Ocean

About 150 miles south of Goose Bay, Labrador, above the North Atlantic, another BOAC pilot observed UFO activity June 30, 1954. Capt. James Howard described the sighting to the London Sunday Chronicle:

"I had taken off from Idlewild airfield New York at 5 o'clock... headed northeast across the St. Lawrence River... It was 9:05 p.m. Labrador time and we were about twenty minutes' flying time northeast of Seven Islands when I first sighted the thing."

The UFO first appeared as a "dark blob" in the distance, similar to a flak burst, with smaller objects around it. "As near as I can describe it," Capt. Howard said, "it was something like an inverted pear suspended in the sky." The object was to the port side of the Stratocruiser, in a westerly direction.

Capt. Howard pointed out the UFO to his co-pilot, Lee Boyd, and they noticed that it was moving on a course parallel to the plane. The smaller objects were stretched out in a line, in front of and behind the larger object.

Anticipating the questions that would come when he reported this, Capt. Howard counted the smaller objects several times. "Six. Always six. Sometimes there were three stretched out in front and three behind. Sometimes five stretched out in line ahead and only one behind."

To rule out a flight of normal aircraft, Capt. Howard radioed Goose Bay. A minute later they replied: "No other traffic in your area." When he described the UFOs, Goose Bay said they would send a fighter to investigate.

As the pilots continued to watch, the large UFO appeared to change shape. "It turned into what looked like a flying arrow - an enormous delta-winged plane turning in to close with us." The object appeared to grow larger, as if coming closer, but then changed shape again and seemed to hold its distance. Now it appeared more flattened and elongated, as the smaller objects continued to maneuver around.

The other members of the crew crowded forward to watch: George Allen, navigator; Doug Cox, radio officer; Dan Godfrey, engineer; and Bill Stewart, engineer. They all saw it, as did the stewardess Daphne Webster and many of the passengers.

The navigator lined the UFOs up with the window frame, and reported that they pulled ahead of the plane once, then dropped back. This reduced the possibility that the "objects" actually were some kind of illusion.

In a short time, the fighter pilot called in and said he was about 20 miles off at higher altitude. Capt. Howard confirmed that the UFOs were still pacing his plane. When the fighter pilot asked how they looked, Capt. Howard turned to look again. The small satellite objects had suddenly vanished. He asked the navigator what had happened. Allen replied: "It looked to me as though they went inside the big one."

At that moment, the remaining UFO began to diminish rapidly in size, apparently moving away at terrific speed. In a matter of seconds, the UFO diminished to a pinpoint, then disappeared. Eighteen minutes had elapsed since the first sighting.

Capt. Howard called it "the strangest eighty-mile journey of my life."

When they landed at Goose Bay, the crew was interrogated by a U.S. Air Force intelligence officer.

"It was a solid thing," Capt. Howard concluded. "I'm sure of that. Maneuverable and controlled intelligently - a sort of base ship linked somehow with those smaller attendant satellites. . . It must have been some weird form of space ship from another world."

NOTES

1. Ottawa Journal
2. Copy of statement on file at NICAP
3. Report on file at NICAP
4. Windsor Daily Star; December 13, 1957
5. United Press International; April 13, 1959
6. Letter on file at NICAP
7. Letter on file at NICAP
8. Statements by Wing Commander William M. Lee, Director of Public Relations, RCAF, on file at NICAP
9. Fairbanks Daily News-Miner; February 16, 1960. Anchorage Daily News; February 16, 1960. Anchorage Daily Times; February 15, 1960
10. Letter on file at NICAP
11. Letter, signed by Lt. Col. Arnoldo C. Tesselhoff, Assistant Air Attache, on file at NICAP
12. Stringfield, Leonard H., Inside Saucer Post. . .3-0 Blue. (Privately published: 4412 Grove Avenue, Cincinnati, Ohio, 1957), p. 83
    CRIFO Newsletter, June 1955, L. H. Stringfield, Ed.
13. Official report from Argentine Embassy, on file at NICAP
14. C.I.F.E. has twenty counselor members, among them Army, Navy and Naval Air Force officers on active duty. Collaborating members include directors of astronomical and astronautical centers.
15. Keyhoe, Donald E., Flying Saucer Conspiracy. (Henry Holt, 1955), p. 212
16. Ibid., p. 26.   London Daily Sketch, November 22, 1954

17. Diairo de Sao Paulo; February 22, 1958
18. Diairo Popular; July 7, 1957
19. APRO Bulletin; September 1959. Brazilian newspapers; August 20, 1957
20. Pilot interviewed by Cmdr. A. B. Simoes, Sao Paulo, Brazil
21. O Estado de Sao Paulo; May 28, 1958
22. Report officially logged at airport and relayed to Brazilian Air Force. Obtained for NICAP by J. Escobar Faria, Adviser in Sao Paulo
23. Report obtained by J. Escobar Faria, Sao Paulo
24. Letter on file at NICAP
25. El Mercurio; October 28, 1959
26. El Universal; January 31, 1958
27. Report on file at NICAP
28. APRO Bulletin; April 1955
29. Keyhoe, Donald E., op. cit., p. 249
30. Ultimas Noticias; July 3, 1960
31. Report on file at NICAP
32. El Universal; February 13, 1962
33. New York Times; July 28, 1946
34. See New York Times; August 11, 1946; Associated Press; August 11, 1946; Stockholm Aftenbladet; August 13, 1946
35. New York Times; October 11, 1946
36. United Press; December 18, 1953
37. Letter, signed by Col. O. B. Engvik, Air Attache, on file at NICAP
38. Christian Science Monitor; January 29, 1959
39. Letter on file at NICAP
40. Letter on file at NICAP
41. RAF Flying Review; July 1957. London Illustrated News; December 2, 1954
42. Irish Times; May 22, 1962. Reuters News Agency; May 22, 1962
43. Letter to CSI of Los Angeles, on file at NICAP
44. Michel, Aime, The Truth About Flying Saucers. (Criterion, 1956), ppg. 165-166
45. Ibid., p. 169ff
46. Los Angeles Times; February 19, 1956
47. Report on file at NICAP, available to Congressional investigators
48. Letter on file at NICAP
49. Report on file at NICAP
50. Report on file at NICAP
51. United Press International; November 7, 1958
52. Associated Press; October 28, 1954
53. Natal Mercury (Durban); January 28, 1955
54. New Zealand Herald; November 7, 1957 (Datelined Johannesburg)
55. Johannesburg Sunday Times; April 13, 1958
56. Letter, signed by Kenneth T. C. Cheng, Director of Taiwan Weather Bureau, on file at NICAP
57. Information obtained by Rev. Albert H. Baller, NICAP Board Member, from Indian newspaper
58. Life; April 7, 1952. Newsweek; March 3, 1952
59. Report and sketches published in Japan International UFO Investigation, J. I. Takanashi, Editor; Toyonaka, Osaka, Japan. (8-9-2, Sakurazuka-Higashi)
60. For additional data on UFO sightings in Australia, New Guinea and New Zealand, see: Maney, Charles A. & Hall, Richard, Challenge of Unidentified Flying Objects (Willard Courts #504, Washington, D.C. 20009); Chapter 3, "Recent Sightings in the Pacific."
61. Letter on file at NICAP
62. Auckland Star; December 16, 1954 (N.Z.P.A., Reuters)
63. San Francisco newspapers; June 19, 1957
64. Manila Bulletin; November 6, 1957
65. Popular Science; August 1951
66. Reports on file at NICAP

SECTION XI

THE UFO CHRONOLOGY

19th Century

Roman numerals in brackets indicate numbers of other Sections which contain information about a given case in this Chronology.

August 6, 1860--Norfolk, Va. Two objects, one red and one green, flew overhead together, moving with an undulating motion.

1877--England. Three meteor-like objects moving together with "remarkable slowness" flew across the sky, visible about three minutes, "moving with the same velocity and grade of regularity. . [as] a flock of wild geese." [Credit: Charles Fort, from Report of the British Association, 1877-152]

July 3, 1884--Norwood, N.Y. Saturn-shaped UFO (globe with central ring) flew slowly overhead. [Credit: Charles Fort, from Science Monthly, 2-136]

1896-1897--Mysterious "Airship" reported all across United States.

Early 20th Century

February 28, 1904--Formation of three maneuvering objects sighted by U.S.S. Supply in North Pacific off San Francisco. [II]

December 22, 1909--Worcester, Mass. "Mysterious Airship" emitting a bright beam of light appeared moving SE to NW, hovered over city, moved away. Seen again two hours later; hovered, moved away to south and turned east. Observed over Boston and Lynn, Mass. next night. [N.Y. Tribune, 12-23-09; N.Y. Sun, 12-24-09]

July 19, 1916--Unidentified luminous object shaped like a dirigible observed over Huntington, W. Va. [Credit: Charles Fort, from Scientific American, 115-241]

Early 1918--Near Waco, Texas. Reddish cigar-shaped object, with no motor or rigging, passed silently from SW to NE.

1923--Greencastle, Indiana. Revolving red object passed overhead from NE to SW. Two witnesses currently are college professors.

January 1924--Oklahoma. White oval-shaped object lit up ground, moved out of sight over horizon.

August 5, 1926--Himalayan Mountains. Explorer Nicholas Roerich and others in his caravan observed a shiny oval-shaped object move overhead, changing course. [I]

November 1928--Milton, N.D. A UFO, round "like an inverted soup plate," sped overhead emitting rays of light which illuminated the ground and startled cattle.

January 1, 1931--Cobden, Ont., Canada. UFO sighted in early morning, had bright light on front which lit up tree-tops, flashing lights on rear. Object made sweeping curve, sped up and climbed out of sight.

April or May 1932--Durham, N.Y. Aluminum-like disc with periphery of yellowish lights or "portholes" on underside.

1932 or 1933--Oakland, California. About seven brilliant objects in a group flew from 30 degrees elevation in the east to 45 degrees elevation in the west, in an arc. Witness now college graduate, former USAF pilot.

World War II "Foo-Fighter" Era

August 29, 1942--Columbus, Miss. Control tower operator at Army Air Base saw two round reddish objects hover over field. [III]

Approx. 1943--Washington, D.C. Sighting of UFO formation by Metropolitan policeman. [VII]

March 1944--Carlsbad, N.M. Air Force pilot saw fast-moving UFO speed out of sight over horizon. [III]

Summer 1944--Normandy, France. Los Angeles columnist George Todt, in a party of four Army officers including a Lt. Col., watched a pulsating red fireball sail up to the front lines, hover for 15 minutes, then move away. [IV]

July 1944--Brest, France. Two men of the 175th Infantry Regiment, 29th Infantry Division, saw a large rectangular object with no apparent source of propulsion move steadily over the front lines and out to sea. The UFO at one point passed in front of the moon, briefly obscuring it from view. [IV]

August 10, 1944--Sumatra. Sighting of maneuvering UFO which paced B-29 during mission. [III]

October 1944--Southeast Holland. Field Artillery officer and men saw a brilliant object moving from NW to SW, crossing an arc of about 90 degrees in about 45 minutes. [IV]

November 1944--France. 415th Night Fighter Squadron pilot saw formation of round objects. [III]

December 1944--Austria. B-17 pilot and crew, on a lone wolf mission, were followed by an amber-colored disc. [III]

January 1945--Germany. Another 415th Night Fighter Squadron pilot was followed by three red and white lighted objects over Germany. [III]

January 2, 1945--The New York Times carried an AP dispatch from France about several recent "foo-fighter" sightings. Lt. Donald Meiers said he had twice been followed by UFOs. [III]

March 1945--Aleutian Islands. Fourteen men on the U.S.A.T. Delarof (an attack transport) saw a dark spherical object which rose out of the water, circled the ship and flew away. An official report on the incident was sent to Washington. [IV]

May 1946--LaGrange, Florida. A Navy gunnery and radar officer observed a dark elliptical object which moved slowly overhead, disappearing in a cloud bank. [I]

July-August 1946--Swedish "Ghost rocket" sightings. [X]

August 1, 1946--Florida. Observation of cigar-shaped UFO by Air Corps transport pilot. [III]

1947

[See Section XII, June-July 1947 "Flap," for additional details]

June 23, 1947--Cedar Rapids, Iowa. Railroad engineer saw 10 shiny disc-shaped objects, very high, fluttering along in a string toward NW. [XII]

June 24, 1947--Mt. Ranier, Wash. Kenneth Arnold sighting. [V] Term "Flying saucer" coined.

June 28, 1947--Nr Lake Mead, Nevada. USAF F-51 pilot reported a formation of 5-6 circular objects. [III]

June 28, 1947--Maxwell AFB, Ala. Zig-zagging light seen by pilots, intelligence officers. [III]

June 29, 1947--White Sands, N.M. Naval rocket expert, at test grounds observed a silvery disc. [IV]

July 4, 1947--Portland, Oregon. Police and many others saw many UFOs in formations and singly beginning about 1:05 p.m. [II, XII]

July 4, 1947--Nr. Boise, Idaho. United Airlines pilot and crew, enroute to Portland, Ore., saw 9 disc-like UFOs. [V]

July 4, 1947--Seattle, Wash. Coast Guard yeoman took first known photograph of UFO, a circular object which moved across the wind. Photo shows round dot of light. [VIII, XII]

July 4, 1947--Redmond, Oregon. Car full of people saw four disc-shaped UFOs streak past Mt. Jefferson. [XII]

July 6, 1947--Fairfield-Suisun AFB, Calif. Pilot reported "oscillating" UFO which shot across sky. [III]

July 6, 1947--S. Central Wyoming. Aviation engineer saw oval UFO. [VI]

July 8, 1947--Series of sightings over Muroc AFB and Rogers Dry Lake, secret test base, California:

Morning: Two spherical or disc-like UFOs joined by a third object. [XII]

            Crew of technicians saw white-aluminum UFO with distinct oval outline descending, moving against wind. [II]

Afternoon: Thin "metallic" UFO climbed, dove, oscillated over field, also seen by test pilot in vicinity. [XII]

            F-51 pilot watched a flat object "of light-reflecting nature" pass above his plane. No known aircraft were in area. [XII]

July 9, 1947--Nr. Boise, Idaho. Newspaper aviation editor saw flat circular UFO maneuver in front of clouds. [VII]

July 10, 1947--S. New Mexico. A "top astronomer" of the U.S. observed a bright white elliptical UFO. [II, VI]

Capt. Edward J. Ruppelt, head of Air Force UFO investigation from 1951-53; "By the end of July (1947) The UFO security lid was down tight. The few members of the press who did inquire about what the Air Force was doing got the same treatment that you would get today if you inquired about the number of thermonuclear weapons stock-piled in the U.S. atomic arsenal. . . (At ATIC there was) confusion almost to the point of panic." (Report on Unidentified Flying Objects, p. 39)

Summer 1947--Pittsburg, Kansas. Navy Commander observed a disc-shaped UFO. [IV]

August, 1947--Media, Pa. Air Force pilot watched a disc hover, speed away. [V]

September 23, 1947--Air Technical Intelligence Center letter stating UFOs are real sent to Commanding General of Air Force. (IX)

October 14, 1947--Muroc AFB. California. First piloted supersonic flight in plane, Capt. Yeager flying X-1 rocket-powered aircraft.

December 8, 1947--Las Vegas, Nevada. Moving reddish UFO emitted flash of light, shot upwards out of sight. [XII]

1948

January 7, 1948--Fort Knox, Ky., Mantell case. Air National Guard pilot killed in crash of F-51 during UFO pursuit. Also sighting at Lockburne AFB, Ohio, later same afternoon, UFO maneuvering erratically up and down. [V]

January 22, 1948—Project Sign (or "Saucer") established by Air Force. UFO reports sent to Air Materiel Command, Ohio, for investigation.

April 5, 1948--White Sands, N.M. Scientists watched disc-shaped UFO, one-fifth the size of the full moon, streak across sky in series of violent maneuvers. (No details reported).

May 28, 1948--Air Force transport reported being buzzed by 3 UFOs. [III]

July 1948--Pasco, Wash. Private pilot saw disc diving and climbing away at high speed. [V]

July 4, 1948--Nr. Longmont, Colorado. Revolving silver circular object soared upward at "terrific speed." [XII]

Summer 1948--Erie, Pa. Engineer saw elliptical UFO which flew horizontally, then ascended rapidly. [VI]

Summer 1948--Easton, Pa. Physicist watched 3 luminescent greenish discs cross sky. [VI]

Summer 1948--Labrador. UFO tracked on radar at 9000 m.p.h. [VIII]

July 23, 1948--Nr. Montgomery, Ala. Chiles-Whitted, Eastern Airlines sighting of rocket-like UFO with exhaust, square ports along side. [V]

August 1948--Air Technical Intelligence Center Top Secret "Estimate of the Situation," concluding UFOs were interplanetary space ships, sent to Air Force Chief of Staff. (IX)

October 1, 1948--Fargo, N.D. Air National Guard F-51 pilot had "dogfight" with a small flat, circular UFO. [V]

October 15, 1948--Japan. Crew of F-61 night-fighter tracked on radar and saw silhouette of UFO shaped "like a rifle bullet" which repeatedly accelerated out of reach of the fighter. [VIII]

November 1, 1948--Goose Bay, Labrador. UFO tracked by radar at 600 mph [VIII]

November 6, 1948--Japan. Two UFOs, like planes in "dogfight" tracked on radar. [VIII]

November 18, 1948--Nr. Washington, D.C. Air Force pilot flying out of Andrews AFB, chased oval-shaped UFO for 10 minutes. [III]

November 23, 1948--Fursten-Feldbruck, Germany. Bright red UFO tracked by ground and air radar, seen visually by U.S. AF pilot. [VIII]

December 3, 1948--Fairfield-Suisun AFB, Calif. Ball of light ascending, seen by pilot. [III]

1949

January 1, 1949--Jackson, Miss., Cigar-shaped UFO crossed path of private plane, accelerated rapidly and sped away. [V]

April 24, 1949--White Sands, N.M. General Mills balloon personnel tracked elliptical UFO with theodolite. [I]

April 27, 1949--Project "Saucer" Report released by Air Force: Space visitors considered "improbable," but many unexplained cases. 30% probably conventional objects.

April 30, 1949--First installment of Saturday Evening Post article by Sidney Shallett. "What You Can Believe About Flying Saucers."

May 9, 1949--Time article called UFO witnesses "spinners of yarns."

June 5, 1949--Walter Winchell column: "The New York World-Telegram has confirmed this reporter's exclusive report of several weeks before -- which newspapermen have denied -- about the flying saucers. Said the front page in the World-Telegram: 'Air Force people are convinced the flying disk is real. The clincher came when the Air Force got a picture recently of three disks flying in formation over Stephensville, Newfoundland. They outdistanced our fastest ships. . . . "

June 10, 1949--White Sands, N.M. Two round white UFOs maneuvered around a missile in flight. (Confirmed by Capt. R. B. McLaughlin, USN) [II]

July 3, 1949--Longview, Wash. Navy Commander, others, watched disc pass above air show. [IV]

August 1949--N.M. Astronomer Clyde Tombaugh, discoverer of the planet Pluto, observed elliptical pattern of 6-8 rectangles cross the sky. [VI]

Fall 1949--At a key atomic base, a high AF officer was involved in the radar tracking of 5 apparently metallic UFOs which flew S over the base at tremendous speed and great height. [II]

October 23, 1949--Nr. Baja, Calif. Air Force pilot saw four discs in formation. [III]

December 27, 1949--Air Force issued Project "Grudge" Report (Technical Report No. 102-AC-49/15-100) explaining away all UFO reports to date as delusions, hysteria, hoaxes, and crackpot reports. Announcement that project had disbanded. (IX)

1950

January 1950--True magazine article "Flying Saucers Are Real," by Maj. Donald E. Keyhoe, suggested UFOs are of extraterrestrial origin.

February 2, 1950--Davis-Monthan AFB, Arizona. Bomber pilot chased UFO which left smoke trail. [III]

February 22, 1950--Key West, Fla. Navy pilots, others, saw glowing UFO, confirmed by radar. [IV]

March 1950--True article "How Scientists Tracked a Flying Saucer," by Cmdr. R. B. McLaughlin, USN, reported April 24, 1949 White Sands sighting. (I)

March 8, 1950--Dayton, Ohio. A round UFO seen by the crew of a TWA airliner, was tracked on radar, and chased by two F-51s. [VIII]

March 10, 1950--Orangeburg, S.C. Disc hovered over city, sped away. [XII]

March 13, 1950--Clarksburg, Calif. Saucer-shaped object descended, hovered with swaying motion, moved away. [IV]

March 13, 1950--Mexico City, Mexico. Airport observers saw 4 UFOs, one through theodolite. [V, X]

March 16, 1950--Dallas, Texas. Navy Chief Petty Officer at Naval Air Station saw a flat oval UFO pass under a B-36 bomber. [IV]

March 17, 1950--Farmington, N. Mex. Retired Army Captain, others, saw dozens of discs gyrating in sky. [IV]

March 18, 1950--Nr. Bradford, Ill. Private pilot watched illuminated oval pass his plane. [V]

March 20, 1950--Nr. Little Rock, Ark. Chicago & Southern Airlines pilots watched a circular UFO with "portholes" arc above their plane. [II]

March 26, 1950--Reno, Nevada. CAA control tower operator saw maneuvering light source. [V]

March 26, 1950--Nr. Washington, D.C. Former Air Force aircraft inspector dove his plane at disc which zoomed up into overcast. [V]

April 9, 1950--Shelby, N.C. Round UFO in level flight, suddenly climbed away. [XII]

April 24, 1950--Balearic Islands. Photograph of alleged UFO. [VIII]

April 27, 1950--White Sands, N. Mex. UFO spotted by ground observers just after a test missile had fallen back to earth, photographed by Askania Cinetheodolite. [VIII]

April 27, 1950--Goshen, Ind. TWA airliner paced by disc-like reddish UFO. [V]

May 11, 1950--McMinnville, Oregon. Shiny silver disc hovered, two photographs taken. [VIII]

May 20, 1950--Flagstaff, Ariz. Astronomer/meteorologist observed a "powered" disc-like object from the grounds of Lowell Observatory. [I]

May 29, 1950--Nr. Washington, D.C. American Airlines pilots saw dark elliptical UFO circle airliner. [V]

May 29, 1950--White Sands, N. Mex. UFO spotted by two theodolite stations just before firing of a missile. Object tracked and photographed by both stations. [VIII]

June 12, 1950--California. Geologist saw disc-shaped object loop around plane. [VI]

June 21, 1950--Hamilton AFB, Calif. UFO buzzed control tower several times. [III]

June 24, 1950--California desert. Cigar-shaped UFO paced United Airlines plane for 20 minutes. [V] Navy pilot reported cigar-shaped UFO. [IV]

June 30, 1950--Nr. Kingman, Kansas. Rotating disc hovered, sped away when car approached [XII]

July 1950--Flying magazine article, "Flying Saucers -- Fact or Fiction?" summarized recent UFO sightings by pilots.

July 1950--Cincinnati, Ohio. CAA flight engineer observed a "wingless, fuselage-shaped" UFO. [V]

July 11, 1950--Osceola, Ark. Two Navy aircraft watched domed disc pass in front, confirmed by radar. [IV]

August 15, 1950--Great Falls, Mont. Nick Mariana took motion pictures of 2 UFOs (The "Montana film," later shown in the documentary movie "UFO"). [VIII]

October 3, 1950--Pomona, Calif. Disc-shaped UFO reported by scientist. [VI]

October 5, 1950--San Fernando, Calif. California Central Airlines plane buzzed by wing-like UFO. [V]

November 27, 1950--Huron, S.D. CAA personnel saw hovering maneuvering UFO. [V]

November 27, 1950--Evansville, Wisc. Flying instructor reported six elliptical objects in loose echelon formation. [V]

December 1950--Nr. Cheyenne, Wyo. USAF officer saw aluminum-like oval UFO. [III]

December 27, 1950--Bradford, Ill. Trans-World Airways pilot watched light source perform violent and erratic maneuvers. [V]

1951

January 16, 1951--Nr. Artesia, N. Mex. General Mills personnel tracking a Skyhook balloon saw two disc-shaped objects approach rapidly, tip on edge, circle the balloon, and speed off over the NW horizon. [I]

January 20, 1951--Nr. Sioux City, Iowa. A dark cigar-shaped UFO with white and red body lights buzzed a Mid-Continent Airlines plane. [V]

February 14, 1951--Alamogordo, N. Mex. Two Air Force pilots, while watching a large balloon, saw a flat, round white object hovering at high altitude. [III]

February 19, 1951--Kenya, Africa. A large cigar-shaped UFO hovering over Mt. Kilimanjaro was observed and photographed from an aircraft. [X]

February--Look magazine article: Dr. Urner Liddel, Office of Naval Research, stated "There is not a single reliable report of

an observation which is not attributable to the cosmic balloons (plastic "Skyhook" research balloons)."

May 22, 1951--Nr. Dodge City, Kansas. American Airlines pilot observed maneuvering star-like object. [V]

June 1, 1951--Dayton, Ohio. Wright-Patterson AFB official watched disc make sharp turn. [III]

July 14, 1951--Nr. White Sands, N. Mex. A UFO which sped near a B-29 was tracked on radar, observed visually and photographed. [VIII]

July 23, 1951--March Field, Calif. Radar-visual sighting of silvery object circling high above aircraft. [VIII]

Summer 1951--Augusta, Ga. Air Force pilot flying F-51 "attacked repeatedly" by flying disc. [III]

August 1951--Central, N. Mex. Mining engineer sighted two discs with "portholes." [VI]

August 3, 1951--Nr. Pinckney, Mich. NICAP Adviser saw a glowing, yellowish UFO which moved on an undulating course. [VI]

August 11, 1951--Portland, Ore. Former Air Force fighter pilot observed formation of three discs. [V]

August 25, 1951--Lubbock, Texas. Formations of luminous objects passed overhead several consecutive nights; V-formation photographed. [VIII]

August 26, 1951--Washington State. Air Force radar station tracked UFO at 900 m.p.h. on two different radar sets. [VIII]

August 1951--Popular Science. Editors surveyed witnesses to choose most plausible explanations for UFOs; 70% believed they were intelligently controlled devices, either man-made or extraterrestrial.
September 1951--Capt. Edward J. Ruppelt, new chief of Project Blue Book, the Air Force UFO investigation.

September 10, 1951--Nr. Sandy Hook, N.J. Two AF pilots in a T-33 jet trainer chased a "perfectly round and flat" silvery UFO traveling at an estimated 900 mph [III]

September 23, 1951--Nr. March AFB, Calif. F-86 jets circled below an unidentified object, unable to reach its altitude. [III]

Fall 1951--Korea. UFO circled fleet, tracked on 14 ships' radars, departing at over 1000 mph. [VIII]

October 9, 1951--Terre Haute, Indiana; Nr. Paris, Illinois. A fast-moving UFO shaped like a flattened sphere was sighted two minutes apart by a C.A.A. employee and a private pilot. Project Blue Book plotted the sighting and concluded both had been the same object which was an "unknown." [V]

October 10-11, 1951--Nr. Minneapolis, Minn. Two sightings of UFOs by General Mills, Inc., supervisor of balloon manufacture, and other balloon personnel, from an aircraft. [VI]

November 7, 1951--Lake Superior. Steamship Captain and crew watched elongated orange object with six glowing "portholes" speed towards Ontario. [XII]

November 9, 1951--After 7 sightings of green fireballs in 11 days Dr. Lincoln LaPaz, Institute of Meteoritics, said: "There has never been a rate of meteorite fall in history that has been one-fifth as high as the present fall. If that rate should continue, I would suspect the phenomenon is not natural. . . (they) don't behave like ordinary meteorites at all." (Associated Press)
November 10, 1951--Albuquerque, N.M. The eighth fireball in 13 days was seen here and as far away as Wyoming. (United Press)

1952

1952--London, Ont., Canada. Astronomer observed elliptical UFO with 2 bright body lights. [VI]

January 20, 1952--Fairchild AFB, Wash. Two master sergeants (intelligence specialists), reported a large, bluish-white spherical object with a long blue tail which flew below a solid overcast. [III]

January 21, 1952--Mitchel AFB, N. Y. Navy TBM pilot chased a dome-shaped, white circular object which accelerated and pulled away [IV].

January 22, 1952--North Alaska Radar outpost. Ground radar and three F-94 interceptors' radar tracked a distinct target. [VIII]

January 29, 1952--Wonsan, Korea. B-29 paced by a bright disc-shaped orange object. (Similar sighting by another B-29 crew same night 80 miles away over Sunchon.) [III, X]

February 20, 1952--Greenfield, Mass. Congregational Minister saw three very bright silver objects, apparently spherical, traveling in a perfect V. [VII]

March 3, 1952--Dr. Walter Riedel, former German Rocket Scientist at Peenemunde: "I'm convinced saucers have an out-of-world basis." (Life; April 7, 1952.)

March 10, 1952--Oakland, Calif. Inspector of Engineering Metals watched two dark, wing (or hemisphere) shaped objects pass overhead, one swaying back and forth like pendulum. [VI]

March 29, 1952--Nr. Misawa, Japan. Small shiny disc made pass at an F-84, observed by second Air Force pilot. [I]

March 29, 1952--Butler, Missouri. Chairman of Industrial Commission of Missouri saw cylinder-shaped, silver UFO. [VII]

April 7, 1952--Life article. "Have We Visitors From Space?" (cleared by Air Force Commanding General.) strongly suggested UFOs are interplanetary.

April 8, 1952--Nr. Big Pines, Calif. Disc-like UFO observed by TV network engineer. [VI]

April 17, 1952--Nellis AFB, Nevada. Large group of circular UFOs. [III]

April 23, 1952--Watertown, Mass. Engineer saw high-speed maneuvering UFO. [VI]

May 7, 1952--Barra da Tijuca, Brazil. Photographs of alleged UFO. [VIII]

May 8, 1952--Atlantic Ocean off Jacksonville, Fla. Pan-American Airways pilot and copilot saw light, 10 times the size of a landing light, come head-on, streak past left wing. [V]

May 8, 1952--Project Blue Book Chief and two Colonels briefed Air Force Secretary Finletter on UFOs for one hour. (Report on Unidentified Flying Objects, Ruppelt, p. 185.)

May 13, 1952--National City, Calif. Convair design engineers, ex-Navy pilot, and amateur astronomer observed luminescent white circular object descend rapidly, circle area. [I]

June, 1952--Tombstone, Ariz. Navy pilot watched a disc hover, speed away. [IV]

June 1952--Air Force reported to be taking the UFO problem seriously partly because a lot of good UFO reports were coming in from Korea. Pilots were seeing silver spheres or disks, and radar in Japan, Okinawa, and Korea had tracked unidentified targets. (Report on Undentified Flying Objects, Ruppelt, p. 192.)

June 1, 1952--Los Angeles, Calif. Crew of Hughes Aircraft Co., radar test section tracked unidentified target at 11,000 ft.; UFO suddenly tripled its speed. [VIII]

June 9, 1952--Time article by Dr. Donald H. Menzel, "Those Flying Saucers," "Light reflections" given as explanation.

June 13, 1952--Le Bourget, France (airport). Control tower operators and pilot watched brilliant light source cross sky SW of field after hovering for about an hour. [X]

June 18, 1952--California. UFO paced B-25 for 30 minutes. [II, III]

June 19, 1952--Goose Bay, Labrador. Radar-visual sighting of reddish object. [VIII]

July 1952 "Flap"

[See Section XII for more detailed chronology]

Summer 1952--MacDill AFB, Florida. USAF Colonel, B-29 pilot investigated radar target, saw glowing ellipse which reversed direction and sped away. [III]

July 1, 1952--Boston, Mass. Two silvery cigar-shaped objects reported moving SW. [XII]

July 1, 1952--Fort Monmouth, N.J. Radar-visual sighting of two UFOs; objects hovered, sped away SW. [VIII]

July 2, 1952--Tremonton, Utah. Navy Warrant Officer D.C. Newhouse photographed group of 12 to 14 objects maneuvering in formation at high speed. [VIII]

July 10, 1952--Nr. Korea. Crew of Canadian destroyer "Crusader", saw and tracked on radar two shiny discs. [VIII, X]

July 12, 1952--Chicago, Ill. Air Force weather officer, many others at Montrose Beach saw large red object with small white lights on side reverse course directly overhead. [III]

July 13, 1952--Nr. Washington, D.C. National Airlines pilot radioed CAA that he was being approached by a blue-white light. Object came to within 2 miles, hovered at same altitude. Pilot switched on all lights; UFO took off, upwards. [V]

July 14, 1952--Newport News, Virginia. Pan-American Airways pilots watched formation of 6 discs make sharp turn below airliner joined by 2 more discs. [V]

July 16, 1952--Hampton, Va. Aeronautical research engineer watched rendezvous of four amber colored objects. [VI]

July 16, 1952--Salem, Mass. Seaman at Coast Guard Air Station photographed four brilliant white lights. [VIII]

July 18, 1952--Nr. Denver, Colo. American Airlines pilot watched unidentified lights speed back and forth. [V]

July 18, 1952--Patrick AFB, Florida. Two officers, weathermen, several others saw four amber-colored lights circling near the field. [III]

July 19, 1952--Porto Maldo, Peru. Photograph of oval UFO taken by customs official. [VIII]

July 19/20, 1952--Washington, D.C., CAA radar sightings; visual confirmation by airline pilots. [XII]

July 23, 1952--Braintree, Mass. Bluish-green UFO circling at high speed observed by radar, ground observers, F-94 pilot. [VIII]

July 23, 1952--Culver City, Calif. Aircraft-plant employees reported a silvery elliptical UFO accompanied by two small discs. [II]

July 24, 1952--Nr. Carson Sink, Nevada. Two Air Force colonels in B-25 saw formation of three delta wing silver objects traveling at estimated speed of over 1000 mph. [III]

July 26, 1952--California. Radar-visual sighting. Jet chased large, yellow-orange light. [VIII]

July 26/27, 1952--Washington, D.C. Radar and visual sightings. [XII]

July 27, 1952--Ann Arbor, Mich. Biologist reported "flotilla" of rocket-like UFOs. [VI]

July 27, 1952--Manhattan Beach, Calif. Aeronautical engineer, others, observed group of UFOs changing position in formation. [VI]

July 28, 1952--Wisconsin-Minnesota. Ground Control Intercept radar, Air Force pilot, plane spotter of G.O.C., tracked several UFOs. [VIII]

July 29, 1952--Air Force press conference in Washington, D.C., headed by Major General John A. Samford, UFOs explained away as weather phenomena. (Transcript on file at NICAP.)

July 29, 1952--Miami, Florida. Movies taken of high-speed UFO; film submitted to Air Force, never released. [VIII]

August 1, 1952--Nr. Yaak, Montana. Air Defense Command radar tracked UFO; sighted visually a dark, cigar-shaped object. [VIII]

August 1, 1952--Sharonville, Ohio. Brilliant white disc observed at low altitude. Others reported oval object. [XII]

August 1, 1952--Albuquerque, N.M. Scripps-Howard Staff Writer watched UFOs change position in formation. [VII]

August 3, 1952--Hamilton AFB, California. Pilots on ground, radar, plane spotters tracked two silvery discs "dogfighting". [III, VIII]

August 5, 1952--Haneda AFB, Japan. Circular UFO tracked on radar, chased by jets. [III, VIII]

August 5, 1952--Baltimore, Md. Experienced amateur astronomer observed two copper-like discs. [VI]

August 6/7, 1952--Kerkrade, Holland. Marine engineer and designer saw two disc-shaped objects with superstructures. [X]

August 13, 1952--Tucson, Ariz. Air Force officer reported formation of bright UFOs. [III]

August 13, 1952--Dallas, Texas. Airlines Chief Pilot chased maneuvering light. [V]

August 20, 1952--Congaree AFB, S.C. Air Defense Command radar tracked UFO at 4,000 mph. [VIII]

August 22, 1952--Elgin, Illinois. USAF jets, guided by Ground Observer Corps, chased a pulsating yellowish light. [VII]

August 24, 1952--Nr. Hermanas, New Mexico. Air Force Colonel piloting F-84 saw two round silvery objects; one climbed straight up 2,000-3,000 feet. [III]

August 28, 1952--Le Roy, N.Y. Disc circled airliner vertically. [II]

August 28, 1952--Atlanta, Ga. Police watched maneuvering UFO. [VII]

August 29, 1952--Villacoublay, France. Unidentified bright blue light observed through theodolite; once appeared as luminous white bar edged with black. [X]

September 9, 1952--Portland, Oregon. Two oval objects observed in searchlight beam. [XII]

September 16, 1952--Belle Glade, Florida. Circular object with row of lights on underside passed low overhead; cattle bolted. [XII]

September 19, 1952--North Sea. Spherical UFO photographed from U. S. Navy aircraft carrier participating in "Operation Mainbrace," NATO maneuvers. [XII]

September 20, 1952--Topcliffe, Yorkshire, England. Silvery disc followed Meteor jet, descended with pendulum motion. [See "Operation Mainbrace" chronology, Section XII.]

September 22, 1952--Fairfax County, Va. Police observed 3-4 UFOs maneuvering erratically. [VII]

September 30, 1952--Edwards AFB, California. Aviation photographer, others, observed two discs alternately hovering and darting around. [VI]

October 11, 1952--Newport News, Va. Ground Observer Corps spotter saw disc-shaped UFO with "dome". [XII]

October 12, 1952--Palo Alto, Calif. V-formation of six apparent discs. [V]

October 13, 1952--Oshima, Japan. Air Force pilot and engineer saw round object in cloud formation; object became elliptical in appearance, sped away disappearing in seconds. [III]

October 27, 1952--Gaillac, France. Hundreds of citizens saw 16 UFOs in formation surrounding a cigar-shaped object. "Angel's hair" fell. [VIII]

October 29, 1952--Richmond, Va. Venezuelan Airlines pilot watched luminous UFO speed past plane. [V]

October 29, 1952--Hempstead, L. I., N. Y. Two F-94 pilots saw object which maneuvered at high speed. [III]

Fall 1952--N. Y. to Puerto Rico. Three Pan American Airways pilots watched UFO hover, speed away. [V]

November 16, 1952--Nr. Landrum, S. C. Hundreds of people saw a huge disc, watched through binoculars by air-traffic controller.

November 25/26, 1952--Panama Canal Zone. Two UFOs tracked by defense radar. [VIII]

December 4, 1952--Laredo, Texas. USAF F-51 pilot chased glowing white object which made tight turns, head-on passes at plane. [III]

December 6, 1952--Nr. Galveston, Texas. Air Force B-29 tracked UFOs at speeds up to 9000 mph, saw speeding blue-white lights. [VIII]

December 8, 1952--Chicago, Ill. Aircraft paced by row of unidentified lights. [V]

December 10, 1952--Nr. Hanford, Washington, Radar-visual sighting of round, white UFO with "windows." [VIII]

December 15, 1952--Goose Bay AFB, Labrador. Radar-visual sighting of reddish UFO which changed to white as it maneuvered. [VIII]

December 29, 1952--Northern Japan. Colonel, other USAF pilots, radar detected rotating UFO. [III]

1953

1953--Anaco, Venezuela. Avensa Airlines pilot reported round gray object paced plane. [X]

1953--Navy Carrier-based Squadron of attack planes approached by rocket-shaped UFO. [IV]

January 9, 1953--Northern Japan. Pilot and radar observer of an F-94 jet interceptor saw and tracked a rotating UFO. Air base Commander, Col. George W. Perdy, stated there was "remarkable corroboration as to description of the cluster of lights by people widely separated who hadn't so much as talked to one another." [III]

January 9, 1953--Santa Ana, Calif. V-formation of blue-white lights banked near USAF bomber. (III)

January 22, 1953--Santa Fe New Mexican: "A fireball expert said today Russia may be scouting the United States and other parts of the world with strange new guided missiles. Dr. Lincoln LaPaz said a good many shreds of evidence point to green fireballs sighted throughout the world being a type of missile - possibly of Soviet make." (Associated Press)

January 26, 1953--New Mexico radar site. Very bright reddish-white UFO observed and tracked on radar. [VIII]

January 27, 1953--Livermore, Calif. Pilot watched shiny circular object in high speed climb. [V]

January 28, 1953--Albany, Ga. Air Force F-86 pilot saw a definite circular UFO pass below his plane, confirmed by radar. [VIII]

January 29, 1953--Presque Isle, Me. Gray oval UFO seen by USAF pilots. [III]

January 30, 1953--Yuma, Ariz. Gyrating light ascending steeply, observed by scientist. [VI]

February 1, 1953--Terre Haute, Indiana. Sighting by USAF pilot (no details released). [III]

February 6, 1953--Rosalia, Wash. USAF bomber reported a circling UFO. [III]

February 7, 1953--Korean area. Radar-visual sighting by USAF pilot, maneuverable bright orange light. [III, VIII]

February 9, 1953--Virginia-N. C. border. Marine Corps pilot chased rocket-like object. [IV]

February 11, 1953--Tunis-Tripoli. USAF transport paced by UFO. [III]

February 13, 1953--Fort Worth, Texas. Radar-visual sighting by B-36 crew. [VIII]

February 16, 1953--Nr. Anchorage, Alaska. Reddish UFO approached, paced USAF transport. [III]

February 17, 1953--Elmendorf AFB, Alaska. UFO chased by jet, accelerated away. [III]

March 7, 1953--Yuma, Arizona. Discs observed by Air Force officers at gunnery meet. [III]

Spring 1953--Laredo, Texas. Air Force instructor flying T-33 watched circling cigar-shaped object make right-angle turn. [III]

May 5, 1953--Yuma, Ariz. Scientist observed silvery disc; concentric rings visible through Polaroid glasses. [VI]

May 21, 1953--Prescott, Ariz. Veteran private pilot saw 8 discs. [V]

May 23, 1953--Union of S. Africa. South African headquarters announced in November that on May 23, radar had tracked an unidentified object near the Cape at over 1000 mph. [VIII]

July 9, 1953--Columbus, Ohio. Circular, silver UFO seen at North American Aviation plant. [VII]

July 24, 1953--Mt. Vernon, Ohio. Large silver object circled over town. [VII]

July 31, 1953--Port Clinton, Ohio. Unidentified white light viewed through field glasses. [VII]

Summer 1953--Yaak, Montana. Radar-visual sighting of six UFOs in formation. [VIII]

August 1, 1953--Toledo, Ohio. UFO, changing color, flickered and jumped in sky. [VII]

August 9, 1953--Moscow, Idaho. Three F-86 fighters pursued a large glowing disc reported by Ground Observer Corps. [VII]

August 12, 1953--Rapid City, S. D. Simultaneous sighting of UFO by ground and airborne radar, visual. [I]

August 14, 1953--Columbus, Ohio. Lighted object came straight down out of sky, stopped, then sped out of view. [VII]

August 15, 1953--Crestline, Ohio. Circling light changed color, white, red, green. [VII]

August 21, 1953--Maumee, Ohio. Black oval with green and red lights around perimeter. [VII]

August 23, 1953--Columbus, Ohio. Red and white object moving very slowly upward, observed by Ground Observer Corps.

August 26, 1953--Air Force Regulation 200-2 issued by Secretary of AF Harold E. Talbott: procedures for reporting UFOs, restrictions on public discussion by Air Force personnel. (IX)

August 31, 1953--Port Moresby, New Guinea. Motion picture film purporting to show saucer-like object climbing steeply, taken by aviation official. [VIII]

September 7, 1953--Cleveland, Ohio. Technical writer watched rotating triangle pass overhead (cf., May 22, 1960, Majorca sighting). [VII]

September 7, 1953--Vandalia, Ohio. Two Navy fighter pilots saw a brilliant white object speed below their planes, then climb rapidly out of sight. [IV]

September 11-13, 1953--Chiloquin, Ore. Police Chief, others, watched top-like UFOs three consecutive nights. [VII]

September 24, 1953--Bexley (Columbus), Ohio. Ground Observer Corps report: silvery disk followed plane. [VII]

October 18, 1953--English Channel. Airline pilots saw a UFO "like two shallow saucers with their rims together." [V]

October 29, 1953--Lt. Col. F. K. Everest in F-100 Super-Sabre set speed record, 755.149 mph.

October 30, 1953--Mt. Vernon, Ohio. Round, silver object circled at low altitude. [VII]

November 3, 1953--London, England. A huge apparently metallic UFO, "completely circular" and white, was tracked on radar and observed visually through a telescope by the 256th Heavy Anti-Aircraft Regiment. [VIII]

November 12, 1953--Canadian Government announcement of flying saucer observatory (Project Magnet) near Ottawa.

November 14, 1953--Nr. Toledo, Ohio. UFO flashing various colors observed climbing. [VII]

November 23, 1953--Kinross AFB, Michigan. Air Force F-89 vanished while pursuing UFO over Lake Superior. [VIII, IX]

December 1, 1953--Air Force announced in Washington it had set up "flying saucer" cameras around the country equipped with diffraction gratings to analyze nature of UFO light sources.

December 13, 1953--Central Ohio. Rocket-like UFO with white lights at both ends observed by Ground Observer Corps. [VII]

December 16, 1953--Toledo, Ohio. Group of lights changing from red to white, each appearing to revolve. [VII]

December 17, 1953--Sweden. Defense high command ordered a full scale investigation of sightings of a wingless circular object which sped over southern Sweden. [X]

1954

1954--Dayton, Ohio. Air Force Lt. Colonel saw two maneuvering UFOs. [III]

January 1, 1954--Australian Airline pilot saw huge, apparently metallic, elliptical UFO. [V]

January 4, 1954--Quantico, Va. Red revolving or blinking lights, hovering and moving soundlessly at tree-top height reportedly seen for six nights above Marine Corps base. [IV]

January 6, 1954--Cleveland Press headline: "Brass Curtain Hides Flying Saucers." Reporters seeking information were banned from Wright-Patterson AFB, Ohio.

February 13, 1954--Jim G. Lucas of Scripps-Howard, reported that representatives of major airlines would meet in Los Angeles with Military Air Transport Service Intelligence officers to discuss speeding up UFO reporting procedures. "Airline pilots are asked not to discuss their sightings publicly or give them to newspapers," Lucas said.

(In a follow-up report, Feb. 23, Scripps-Howard papers said that "the nation's 8500 commercial airline pilots have been seeing a lot of unusual objects while flying at night, here and overseas." Plans for a detailed reporting system were agreed upon so Air Force jets could quickly investigate. Each airline was to have an "internal security specialist" for liaison between civilian and military organizations.)

February 15, 1954--Dorothy Kilgallen column: "Flying saucers are regarded as of such vital importance that they will be the subject of a special hush-hush meeting of world military heads next summer."

March 1954--Rouen, France. Disc-shaped UFO photographed.

March 24, 1954--Baltimore, Md. Maneuvering formation of UFOs observed by Civil Defense official. [VII]

March 24, 1954--Florida. Marine Corps jet pilot saw round object streak downward, stop, speed away when pursued. [IV]

April 16, 1954--Grand Canyon, Ariz. School superintendent, explorer, watched elongated UFO with "portholes" pass overhead. [VII]

April 26, 1954--Newburyport, Mass. Round UFO making sharp turn observed by architect. [VII]

May 1954--True article, "What Our Air Force Found Out About Flying Saucers"; by Edward J. Ruppelt, former UFO Project Chief.

May 10, 1954--Northern Sweden. Week of UFO sightings investigated by military authorities. Scores of residents reported strange glowing objects maneuvering low over forests.

May 13, 1954--Washington, D. C. Several large glowing objects maneuvered over National Airport for three hours; observed visually and on radar. [VIII]

May 14, 1954--Nr. Dallas, Texas. Marine Corps pilots chased formations of 16 UFOs. [IV]

May 15, 1954--Vienna, Austria. Three discs in formation. [X]

May 24, 1954--Dayton, Ohio. Photo officer and scanner on RB-29 saw and photographed circular UFO below plane. [III]

May 30, 1954--Bainbridge, N. Y. Silvery elliptical UFO with four "portholes" accelerated and shot away. [XII]

June 1, 1954--Nr. Boston, Mass. TWA pilot en route from Paris, control tower operators, saw large white disc. [V]

June 11, 1954--Nr. Baltimore, Md. Huge glowing object seen by GOC observers; alternately hovered, moved rapidly. [VII]

June 23, 1954--Columbus-Vandalia, Ohio. Round white light followed Air National Guard F-51. [V]

June 26, 1954--Idaho Falls, Idaho. Brilliant light source flared up over AEC station, climbed out of sight. [XII]

June 30, 1954--Mobile, Alabama. UFO observed from tower of Brookley AFB, tracked on radar. [VIII]

June 30, 1954--Nr. Oslo, Norway. Two silvery disks observed and photographed from eclipse expedition planes. [VIII]

June 30, 1954--Nr. Goose Bay, Labrador. Airliner crew saw large UFO with smaller satellite objects. [X]

July 3, 1954--Albuquerque, N. M. Nine green spheres sighted visually, tracked on radar. [VIII]

July 8, 1954--Lancashire, England. British astronomer saw a silvery object with 15-20 smaller satellite objects. [II]

July 11, 1954--Hunterdon, Pa. USAF bombers reported a disc. [III]

July 28, 1954--North Atlantic. Dutch ship observed disc with apparent portholes. [XII]

August 28, 1954--Oklahoma City, Okla. Fifteen UFOs in precise triangular formation observed by hundreds of citizens, Tinker AFB radar. [VIII]

August or September, 1954--New York State. Round UFO tracked on radar, plotted across state by Ground Observer Corps. [VII]

September 7, 1954--Origny, France. Hovering luminous disc fled when lights were shone at it. [II]

September 9, 1954--Nelson, N.Z. Hovering disc photographed. [VIII]

September 15, 1954--Bihar, India. Gray disc hovered, emitted smoke and climbed away at high speed. [X]

September 16, 1954--Nr. Roanoke, Va. Shiny, round object buzzed radio tower; transmitter failed to operate properly. [VIII]

September 17, 1954--Rome, Italy. Thousands of citizens, Italian Air Force radar watched disc-like object which departed upwards. [VIII]

September 19, 1954--Danane, French West Africa. Officials watched oval UFO with dome and "searchlights". [X]

September 20, 1954--Cuyahoga Falls, Ohio. Dark saucer-shaped UFO arced overhead, levelled off and moved into distance. [XII]

October 1954--Cherry Valley, N. Y. Engineer sighted maneuvering disc. [I]

October 3, 1954--Nr. Waben, France. UFO paced car. [II]

October 4, 1954--North Weald, Essex, England. Saturn-shaped disc buzzed RAF Meteor jet. [X]

October 7, 1954--Isles-sur-Suippes, France. UFO shaped like "giant artillery shell" with "portholes"; landing or near-landing case. [XII]

October 22, 1954--Marysville, Ohio. School principal, teacher, 60 students saw silver cigar-shaped UFO with "portholes" hover over school, then speed away; "angel's hair" fell. [VIII]

October 23, 1954--New Yorker magazine. "Letter From Paris" column detailed recent French sightings.

October 24, 1954--Prof. Herman Oberth's American Weekly article, "Flying Saucers Come From A Distant World."

October 24, 1954--Porto Alegre, Brazil. Formation of silver, circular objects sped over Air Force base. [X]

October 25, 1954--Belgrade, Yugoslavia. High speed objects some egg-shaped seen by hundreds. [X]

October 28, 1954--Rome, Italy. Mrs. Clare Booth Luce, American Ambassador, others sighted luminous, round UFO. [X]

Fall 1954--Korea. Marine Corps weather observer saw 7 discs oscillating in formation. [XII]

November 5, 1954--Lookout Point, N.Z. Orange elliptical object with blue "portholes" observed. [XII]

November 12, 1954--Louisville, Ky. Spherical object moved quickly south, hovered for long period. [VIII]

November 21, 1954--Rio de Janeiro, Brazil. Crew, passengers of Brazilian airliner saw 19 glowing UFOs. [X]

November 25, 1954--Cordoba, Argentina. Meteorologist, control tower operator at airport watched two hovering luminous objects (official report from Argentine Embassy). [X]

November 26, 1954--Matasquan, N. J. Formation of round objects. (Confidential report from college professor.) [VII]

Millville, N. J. Disc with four body lights. [II]

December 3, 1954--Wilmington, N. C. Civil Aeronautics Administration personnel watched round, yellowish UFO through binoculars. [V]

December 5, 1954--North East, Pa. Domed object with double row of square "ports" hovered low over Lake Erie. [XII]

December 7, 1954--Upington, Cape Province, So. Africa. Meteorologist tracked white hemispherical object with theodolite. [X]

December 15, 1954--Nr. Nowra, Australia. Royal Australian Navy pilot paced by two UFOs, confirmed on radar. [VIII]

December 19, 1954--Vienna, Austria. High-speed UFOs reported. [X]

December 20, 1954--Pontiac, Mich. Red-orange circular UFO, with white glow from "portholes" at front, sped overhead. [XII]

1954 or 1955--Coos Bay, Oregon. District Judge observed maneuvering disc. [VII]

1955

1955--Virginia, nr. Washington, D. C. Navy pilot observed domed disc. [IV]

January 2, 1955--Nr. Punta San Juan, Venezuela. Airliner en route to Maracaibo approached by luminous UFO. [X]

February 2, 1955--Nr. Merida, Venezuela. Aeropost Airlines pilot reported a top-shaped object with "portholes" and central ring paced airliner. [X]

February 11, 1955--Miami to New York. Pan American Airways flight saw two reddish-green objects speed past under wing. [V]

April 22, 1955--Tintinara, Australia. Saturn-shaped UFO made sharp turn, ascended. [XII]

April 24, 1955--Albuquerque, N. Mex. April 23 (AP) Dr. Lincoln LaPaz: "I'm sure the yellow-green fireballs aren't ordinary meteorite falls. I've been observing the skies since 1914, and I've never seen any meteoric fireballs like them."
During the week of April 3-9, five green fireballs were reported in New Mexico and two in northern California. After a number of sightings reported about mid-morning April 5, LaPaz said: "This is a record. We believe we have it narrowed from the many reports to three. But they were seen within a very few minutes of each other. . ."

May 25, 1955--Alexandra Park, London, England. Circular, luminous object approached B-47, quickly reversed direction and shot away. [II]

June 16, 1955--Eastern U. S. UFOs observed over wide area, jets scrambled. [III]

June 17, 1955--Nr. Adelaide, Australia. Silver oblong UFO viewed through binoculars; hovered; moved away behind clouds as an aircraft neared. [XII]

July 9, 1955--Santa Catalina Channel, Calif. Family aboard boat saw a round cylinder, greyish and white, surrounded by a "haze of fumes." UFO zig-zagged upward, then sped away. [XII]

July 17, 1955--Canton, Ohio. Disc hovered, climbed away as airliner approached. [XII]

July 26, 1955--Lasham, Hants, England. Members of British Gliding Association watched boomerang-shaped object (or flattened triangle) hover above glider then speed away. [XII]

July 26, 1955--Washington, D. C. A brilliant round object with trail 4 or 5 times its own length approached National Airport, stopped, oscillated, and moved off at high speed. Ceiling lights at airport went out when object approached; returned to operation when UFO left. [VIII, XII]

July 29, 1955--Cincinnati, Ohio. Zigzagging UFO made shrill sound. [VII]

August 6, 1955--Cincinnati, Ohio. Oval-shaped UFO observed ascending at high speed. [XII]

August 21, 1955--Chalmette, La. Glowing-white Saturn-shaped object hovered, rotating; turned sideways and shot away. [XII]

August 23, 1955--Cincinnati, Ohio. SAC jets "dogfight" with UFOs first detected by radar. White spheres and discs observed by Ground Observer Corps. [VIII]

August 28, 1955--Yonkers, N. Y. Board of Education official and others saw a white Saturn-shaped object through a telescope. [XII]

October 2, 1955--Akron and Alliance, Ohio. Hovering disc-like UFO observed over wide area. [VII]

October 28, 1955--Galloway, England. Disc with row of blue lights on rim, maneuvered slowly over car on lonely road. [XII]

October 31, 1955--Nr. Auckland, N. Z. Bright object passed National Airlines DC-3. [X]

November 1, 1955--Mojave Desert, Calif. Astronomer observed cigar-shaped UFO and smaller disc. [VI]

November 2, 1955--Williston, Fla. Police, others saw as many as six oval-shaped objects in formation. [VII]

November 5, 1955--Cleveland, Ohio. Minister observed elliptical UFO with square "windows". [VII]

November 9, 1955--Philadelphia, Pa. Newspaper photographers and others saw 12 silvery-white round objects in formation. [VII]

November 14, 1955--San Bernardino Mts., Calif. Pilot saw a globe of white light approach plane, blinked landing lights; object blinked in seeming response, reversed course. [V]

November 20, 1955--Oak Ridge, Tenn. Two shiny, elliptical UFOs "like two dirigibles" traveled over restricted area. [IX]

November 23, 1955--Spirit Lake, Iowa. Ground Observer Corps spotters reported a brilliant object which changed color, moved erratically. [VII]

December 6, 1955--Ashfield & Greenfield, Mass. Several people watched a cigar-shaped object with long rows of brilliant, reddish body lights, moving slowly south. [XII]

December 11, 1955--Nr. Jacksonville, Fla. Navy jets in dogfight with round, reddish UFO. [IV]

December 29, 1955--New Britain, Conn. Shiny object hovered, sped away. [XII]

1956

1956--North Atlantic. Large disc paced Navy transport. [IV]

January 17, 1956--Orangeville, Canada. Disc-shaped UFO seen at close range; rings of light visible on bottom. [XII]

January 22, 1956--Gulf of Mexico, nr. New Orleans. Pan American Airways flight engineer saw a large elongated object, emitting yellow flame or light, pass aircraft from horizon to behind a weather front. [V]

February 17, 1956--Paris, France. Large UFO tracked on radar at Orly Airport, observed by airline pilot as red light source. [VIII]

March 5, 1956--Honolulu, Hawaii. UFO formation photographed. [VIII]

April 8, 1956--Nr. Schenectady, N. Y. American Airlines pilot followed UFO across state. [V, IX]

June 27, 1956--Trieste, Italy. Luminous object hovered, sped away. [XII]

July 19, 1956--Hutchinson, Kansas. Naval Air Station reported tracking "a moving unidentified object" on radar, observed visually by state police as "teardrop shaped" light source. [VIII]

Noticeable maneuvers of UFO "vertically and horizontally over a wide area of the sky" mapped by Wichita Eagle.

July 19, 1956--Phoenix, Ariz. Luminous round object hovered, sped away. [XII]

July 29, 1956--Pasadena, Calif. Hovering/speeding light seen by Ground Observer Corps, tracked on radar. [VII]

August 1956--Boulder City, Nevada. Research technician observed formation of five flat, circular UFOs. [VI]

August 8-19, 1956--Connecticut. Concentration of sightings over 12-day period. Retired fire department engineer in Hartford saw an oblong UFO with halo (August 8); an egg-shaped UFO was seen over West Redding (August 11); unidentified white lights reported over West Hartford by Ground Observer Corps (August 14);

August 19, 1956--Newington, Conn. Fiery object made turn, dimmed, window-like markings became visible. [XII]

August 20, 1956--Citrus Heights, Calif. Man & wife saw 25 or more bright, Saturn-like UFOs in a rough semi-circle formation. [XII]

August 21, 1956--Wyoming-Montana. Dumbbell-shaped UFOs approached plane. [VII]

September 4, 1956--Copenhagen, Denmark. Radar tracking of several UFOs at about 1800 mph. [VIII]

September 6, 1956--Pasadena, California. Western Airlines pilot reported erratically moving white lights to Air Defense Command; visual confirmation from ground. [V]

September 11, 1956--Baltic Sea. Radar sightings of "mysterious objects": flying at speeds of 2,000 to 2,500 mph., in a curved course, during previous three weeks. (Altus (Okla.) Times-Democrat; 7-11-56.)

Early November 1956--Malibu, Calif. Flat oval object with three window-like markings on underside flew low, through searchlight beam. [XII]

November 8, 1956--Miami, Florida. Pan American Airways radar tracked a UFO at 4000 mph. [VIII]

November 14, 1956--Nr. Mobile, Alabama. Capital Airlines pilot sighting of maneuvering light. [I]

November 19, 1956--Frankfurt, Germany. V-formation of blue-white, elliptical UFOs. [X]

November 24/25, 1956--Nr. Pierre, South Dakota. (Widespread UFO sightings for several days.) State police chased UFO, Air Force jets scrambled. [VII]

December 1956--Far East. Air Force jet pilot tracked UFO on radar; observed visually as "large round object." [I]

December 27, 1956--Los Angeles, Calif. Real estate investor saw three spherical UFOs reflecting sunlight. [VII]

1957

January 21, 1957--Army Intelligence report on "large shiny metal ball," disc, other UFOs over APO Army base. [IV]

January 24, 1957--Indiana. Commercial pilot and many others saw four brilliant white lights, in-line formation; trailing object larger, egg-shaped and pulsating. [V]

February 13, 1957--Burbank, California. Police received many calls about oval-shaped objects over city. Officer Robert Wells, who went to investigate, confirmed sighting. [XII]

March 8, 1957--Nr. Houston, Texas. UFO paced plane, moved up and down at high speed. [V]

March 9, 1957--Nr. San Juan, Puerto Rico. Pan American Airways pilot took evasive action as fiery round, greenish-white object passed plane. [V]

March 23, 1957--Long Beach, California. Four UFOs tracked on CAA radar, widespread visual sightings. [VIII]

March 29, 1957--Off East Coast, Florida. Pan American Airways pilot observed brilliant pulsating light, confirmed by radar. [V]

April 4, 1957--Wigtownshire, Scotland. Three radar posts tracked a UFO which flashed across the sky at 60,000 feet, dove to 14,000 feet, circled and sped away. [VIII]

May 12, 1957--Moab, Utah. Round, blue-green UFO sped past below observer's altitude. [IV]

June 15, 1957--Lancashire, England. Saturn-like UFO with "portholes" observed through telescope in bright daylight. [XII]

June 18, 1957--Jackson, Mississippi. Physics professor sighted UFO with "a halo of light around it and what appeared to be three portholes." [VI]

June 18, 1957--Pacific Ocean, 150 miles off San Francisco. Captain and crew of freighter Hawaiian Fisherman saw three brightly lighted objects "like small moons." [II]

June 30, 1957--Belo Horizonte, Brazil. Disc-like object paced, maneuvered around airliner. [X]

July 1957--Azusa, California. "Disc with amber lights around edge made wobbling vertical descent. [XII]

July 1, 1957--Avon, Mass. Cigar-shaped UFO with green lights like windows. [XII]

July 4, 1957--Nr. Campos, Brazil. Disc with dome and portholes paced airliner. [X]

July 9, 1957--Hamilton, Ont., Canada. Attorney saw speeding, white elliptical UFO. [X]

July 31, 1957--Calistoga, California. Businessman watched two erratically maneuvering brilliant white objects. [VII]

August 1, 1957--Toronto, Ontario, Canada. Large glowing object hovered 20 minutes, sped away. [VII]

August 14, 1957--Nr. Joinville, Brazil. Varig Airlines pilot observed domed disc, which affected aircraft engines. [X]

August 15, 1957--Woodland Hills, California. Retired Navy pilot watched disc wobble, climb away. [IV]

August 20, 1957--Fujisawa City, Japan. Cylindrical UFO observed above beach, photographed. [VIII]

September 17, 1957--Ft. Devens, Mass. Army report on eight round, orange UFOs which flew over base, one oscillating up and down. [IV]

September 26, 1957--Paris, France. Confidential report, from U.S. Embassy officer and wife, of bright elliptical UFO. [X]

October 7, 1957--Cape Canaveral, Fla. White oval object seen near Cape for second consecutive night. [XII]

October 8, 1957--Bua Province, Fiji Islands. Natives in small boat saw UFO descend vertically, hover about 20 feet above sea.

October 8, 1957--Nr. Boston, Mass. Pan American Airways pilot saw a brilliant object flying at high speed in daylight. [V]

October 15, 1957--Fountain County, Indiana. Farmer reported silver disc which hovered over his combine as he worked in field; combine engine failed when UFO rose. [VIII]

October 16, 1957--Australia. Round UFO sighted by former Commander-in-Chief of Royal Australian Air Force. [X]

October 21 (or 29), 1957--Nr. London, England. RAF pilot sighted UFO near atomic base, confirmed by radar. [VIII]

October 22, 1957--Pittsburgh, Pa. Family saw six UFOs in two separate groups, changing position in formation. [II]

October 23, 1957--Kent, England. Disc travelling on edge. [XII]

November 1957 "Flap"

[See Section XII for detailed November 1957 Chronology]

November 2, 1957--Levelland, Texas. Elliptical UFOs sighted repeatedly on or near roads, many cars stalled.

November 3, 1957--White Sands, N.M. Army Jeep patrol sightings; UFO observed twice near old atomic bunker.

November 4, 1957--Alamogordo, N.M. James Stokes, White Sands engineer, watched elliptical UFO swoop over mountains, car stalled.

November 4, 1957--Elmwood Park, Illinois. Reddish elongated object at low level pursued by police in squad car.

November 5, 1957--Gulf of Mexico, off New Orleans. Coast Guard cutter Sebago repeatedly tracked UFO on radar, once saw planet-like speeding light. About same time, airman at Keesler AFB, Miss., saw elliptical UFO accelerate rapidly and disappear in clouds. [VIII]

November 5, 1957--East St. Louis, Illinois. Three Alton & Southern Railroad employees saw two silvery, egg-shaped UFOs.

November 5, 1957--Haverhill, Mass. Ground Observer Corps reported a circular or spherical glowing object which appeared to vibrate up and down and from side to side while hovering. [VII]

November 5, 1957--Long Beach, California. Air Force Major, others at Municipal Airport saw 6 shiny circular UFOs "changing course instantaneously without loss of speed like planes in a dogfight."

November 6, 1957--Nr. Danville, Illinois. State Police chased UFO for 15 miles, experienced radio failure.

November 6, 1957--Nr. Atlanta, Ga. Three truckers independently reported seeing reddish elliptical objects on the road.

November 6, 1957--Montville, Ohio. Olden Moore case; low, hovering Saturn-like disc, abnormal radioactivity later detected in area. [IX, XII]

November 7, 1957--Lake Charles, Louisiana. Silvery disc hovered, car motor failed.

November 7, 1957--El Paso, Texas, Times: "Some of the nation's top scientists are 'pretty shook up' about the mysterious flying objects sighted in New Mexico and West Texas skies this week, said Charles Capen (a scientist at White Sands). 'This is something that hasn't happened before,' (he said)."

November 10, 1957--Hammond, Indiana. Police chased an elongated UFO; electromagnetic interference reported.

November 11, 1957--Nr. Los Angeles, California. Airline passenger saw elliptical UFO flying low over ground below plane. [VII]

November 11, 1957--San Fernando Valley, Calif. Rocketdyne engineers observed three UFOs climbing at high speed. [VI]

November 15, 1957--Carthage, Tenn. Highway patrolman, sheriff, others saw many flashing revolving red lights which moved around slowly, hovered. [VII]

November 22, 1957--Canutillo, Texas. Silvery UFO sped back and forth, ascended. [VII]

December 12, 1957--Chatham, Windsor area, Canada. Trans-Canada Airlines pilot, many police, saw orange oval UFO curving rapidly at low altitude. [X]

December 1957--Pacific Ocean. Photograph of alleged disc-shaped UFO. [VIII]

December 1, 1957--Los Angeles, California. Formation of oval UFOs photographed. [VIII]

December 12, 1957--Tokyo, Japan. Radar-visual sighting of vari-colored UFO, jets scrambled. [VIII]

December 16, 1957--Old Saybrook, Conn. Elliptical UFO with "portholes." [XII]

1958

January 3, 1958--Hawaii. Group of round UFOs reportedly photographed. [VIII]

January 9, 1958--Marion, Illinois. Three reports of seven red lighted objects in straight line formation. [II]

January 16, 1958--Trindade Isle, Brazil. Saturn-shaped UFO observed and photographed from on board IGY ship Almirante Saldanha. [VIII]

January 30, 1958--Lima, Peru. Lawyer and family saw a circular UFO hover; car headlights went out. [VIII, X]

February 2, 1958--N.S.W., Australia. Elliptical UFO with two "porthole" like markings. [XII]

February 9, 1958--Troy, Michigan. Oval UFO photographed. [VIII]

March 3, 1958--Nr. Marshall, Texas. Family saw two bright, planet-like objects with 6 or 7 smaller lights moving around them. [II]

March 8, 1958--Korea. Air Force radar tracked slowly descending UFO. [VIII]

March 20, 1958--Henrietta, Missouri. Saturn-like disc descended, hovered, moved away. [XII]

April 2, 1958--Columbus, Ohio. Cigar-shaped UFO with long row of "portholes or windows." [XII]

April 4, 1958--Santa Monica, Calif. Cigar-shaped UFO with "windows" observed in rapid vertical climb. [XII]

April 7, 1958--Newport Beach, California. Police watched two UFOs with flashing body lights, maneuver near coastline. [VII] Similar sightings for two nights in El Toro and Santa Ana.

April 9, 1958--Cleveland, Ohio. Nine yellow UFOs in V-formation; split into two groups (5 and 4). [II]

April 11, 1958--Johannesburg, S. Africa. Airport instrument inspector, others watched reddish-white UFO arc back and forth. [X]

April 14, 1958--Albuquerque, N. Mex. Air Force Staff Sergeant saw large formation of unidentified lights. [III]

May 5, 1958--San Carlos, Uruguay. Well-known pilot watched a brilliant object come near his plane, felt intense heat. [X]

May 17, 1958--Ft. Lauderdale, Florida. UFO sped away when light was shone at it. [II]

May 25, 1958--Kirchberg, Hunsruck, Germany. Circular silvery UFO observed moving through clouds. [X]

May 27, 1958--Bahia State Coast, Brazil. Varig Airlines pilot watched a brightly luminous circular object maneuver under his plane. [X]

June 4, 1958--Sarasota, Florida. White oval-shaped object zig-zagged overhead. [XII]

June 23, 1958--Nr. England AFB, Louisiana. State policeman photographed two round UFOs. [VIII]

July 17, 1958--Chitose AFB, Japan. Radar-visual sighting of circling reddish light. [III]

July 26, 1958--Durango, Colorado. Ground Observer Corps Supervisor spotted a round silvery object moving "at tremendous speed." [VII]

Summer 1958--Air Force Base. Southwest United States. Two maneuvering UFOs evaded jet interceptors. [VIII]

August 11, 1958--Chautauqua Lake, N. Y. Engineering pr[of]sor observed unidentified lights arranged as if on oval ob[ject] [VI]

August 17, 1958--Kansas City, Kansas. Dome-shaped disc [with] "portholes" followed jets, hovered. [XII]

August 24, 1958--Westwood, N. J. Police reported a circu[lar] orange UFO which hovered, sped away. [VII]

September 7, 1958--Mission, Kansas. Publisher saw w[hite] disc speed overhead. [VII]

September 8, 1958--Offutt AFB, Omaha, Nebraska. Air For[ce] Major, other officers, observed rocket-like UFO with satell[ite] objects. [III]

September 21, 1958--Sheffield Lake, Ohio. Disc hovered ne[ar] ground. [IX]

October 2, 1958--Nr. Blairstown, New Jersey. Zoologist watche[d] disc circling and maneuvering. [VI]

October 3, 1958--Nr. Rossville, Ind. Crew of freight trai[n] reported four disc-like objects followed train for over an hour[,] reacted to light. [II]

October 7, 1958--Nantucket, Mass. Ship's Master, others watched a grayish oval object hover for several minutes, then climb away at high speed. [VII]

October 12, 1958--Aurora, Illinois. Police reported several yellowish UFOs moving in all directions. [VII]

October 26, 1958--Baltimore, Maryland. Hovering elliptical UFO flashed, shot up out of sight. [XII]

October 26, 1958--Lafayette, Indiana. Research chemist saw 2-3 bright objects pass through field of telescope. [VI]

November 1958--Dewline radar tracked UFO which descended, moved horizontally, climbed out of radar beam. [VIII]

November 5, 1958--Conway, N. H. Hovering light suddenly sped away. [XII]

December 20, 1958--Dunellen, New Jersey. Police patrol observed a bright red, pulsating elliptical object which approached, hovered, then "went straight up like a shot." [I]

1959

January 1, 1959--Newport Beach, California. County Harbor Department guards watched UFO split in four parts; two rose vertically at high speed, one headed SE, one remained stationary. [XII]

January 8, 1959--Nr. Walworth, Wisconsin. Former control tower operator and flight controller saw UFO descend slowly, then speed away like meteor. [V]

January 13, 1959--Pymatuning Lake, Penna. UFO hovered over truck causing electrical failure. [II, VIII]

January 23, 1959--Panama. Bright silver object arced across sky, tracked by U.S. radar. [VIII]

February 4, 1959--Gulf of Mexico. Reddish light sped back and forth across course of Pan American Airways plane, then disappeared at high speed in vertical climb. [V]

February 9, 1959--Imperial Beach, California. Bright UFO with halo filmed. [VIII]

February 24, 1959--Pennsylvania. American and United Airlines planes paced by three glowing objects. [V, IX]

February 26, 1959--London, England. Air Traffic Controllers, others saw a bright yellow disc which hovered for 20 minutes above airport, then climbed away at high speed. [X]

April 3, 1959--Ocoee, Florida. Treasury enforcement officer saw UFO ascending and descending. [VII]

April 12, 1959--Montreal, Canada. St. Hubert Air Base Control Tower Operators, others saw red light which hovered over base, then darted away. [X]

May 14, 1959--Des Moines, Iowa. UFO hovered, sped away. [XII]

June 3, 1959--Nr. Bloomington, Indiana. Torpedo-shaped UFO hovered, dove out of sight. [XII]

June 11, 1959--Henderson, Nevada. Security officers observed a formation of four disc-like objects. [VII]

June 27, 1959--New Guinea. Anglican priest and natives reported seeing figures on top of hovering disc. (XIV)

July 8, 1959--Columbus, Indiana. Family in car chased three pulsating object seen moving slowly at low altitude in V-formation. (Two WTTV employees saw similar formation few minutes earlier, 25-30 miles away.) [II]

Pacific Ocean, 900 miles NE of Hawaii. Pan
crews, other pilots, watched UFO with satellite
p turn. [X]

Nr. Ridgecrest, California. Electronics mechanic
U. S. Naval Ordnance Test Station saw three
which alternately hovered and moved at high
ert to the Southwest. [IV]

ite *—Blenheim, N. Z. Domed disc descended, hovered.*

59--Pampulha, Belo Horizonte, Minas Gerais State.
ject followed FAB (Brazilian Air Force) B-26,
airport. [X]

, 1959--Nr. Emmitsburg, Maryland. Planet-like UFO
k off straight up. [XII]

r 7, 1959--Wallingford, Kentucky. Bluish disc-like
ver ground, observed by mail carrier, rose suddenly
way; left stained ring on ground. [XII]

ber 24, 1959--Redmond, Oregon. Federal Aviation
ersonnel watched disc hover near airport, ascend into
s interceptors approached. [V]

r 7, 1959--Nr. Forrest City, Arkansas. Kentucky Air
l Guard pilot chased glowing object. [V]

ber 20, 1959--Key West, Florida. Navy enlisted men
d two UFOs rendezvous, speed away. [IV]

ober 28, 1959--Valparaiso, Chile. Astronomer, others,
ved maneuvering orange disc. [X]

ecember 24, 1959--Air Force Inspector General's Brief issued
Operations and Training Commands: "UFOs SERIOUS BUSI-
SS"; UFO investigating officers to be equipped with geiger
nters, camera, binoculars, other equipment.

1960

1960--Cincinnati, Ohio. Kentucky Air National Guard pilot
chased round UFO. [V]

February 1960--Dr. S. Fred Singer (Special space adviser to
President Eisenhower) supported the view that the Martian moon
Phobos might be artificial; added: "I would be very disappointed
if it turns out to be solid." (ASTRONAUTICS Magazine)

February 3, 1960--Intervale, New Haven. Former Air Force
PT Boat Commander watched UFOs rendezvous, travel in formation. [VII]

February 5/6, 1960--Hollywood, California. Several witnesses
(about 11:15 p.m. each night) saw a distinct round UFO hover and
maneuver slowly. [Los Angeles NICAP Subcommittee investigation report on file.]

February 14, 1960--Nome, Alaska. Airline employee, others,
saw a silvery rocket-like object with orange flame trail curving
up and away "as if it were manned and controlled." A similar
second UFO was sighted at Unalakleet moving rapidly NW leaving
contrails. [X]

February 16, 1960--Laguna Beach, California. Retired chemical
manufacturing company executive observed rendezvous of two
oval UFOs. [VII]

March 4, 1960--Dubuque, Iowa. Flying instructor saw three
glowing blue-white elliptical objects, in-line formation. [V]

April 25, 1960--Plymouth, N.H. Former Town Selectman saw
bright red cigar-shaped UFO hover, speed away. [VII]

May 4, 1960--Sarasota, Florida. Cigar-shaped UFO with four
window-like markings sighted by architect. [XII]

May 18, 1960--Wellington, N.Z. Cigar-shaped UFO with
"portholes." [XII]

May 22, 1960--Majorca Isle, Mediterranean Sea. Palma
Observatory reported morning observation of a white triangular
UFO, about one-fourth the size of the moon, spinning on its axis.
[VI]

May 24, 1960--Ocumare del Tuy, Venezuela. Several doctors,
a topographer and policemen saw three UFOs, in-line formation,
which landed in a heavily wooded area on a hilltop; diamond-
shaped scorched marking found at landing site. [VIII]

June 8, 1960--New York City. Elliptical UFO sighted by
biochemist. [VI]

July 1, 1960--Nr. Leefe, Wyoming. Hovering disc like "two
dinner plates face to face," ascended and sped away. [XII]

July 2, 1960--Nr. Maiquetia, Venezuela. Pilot and crew of
Venezuelan Airlines Super-Constellation arriving from Spain,
reported plane was followed by a luminous UFO. [X]

July 24, 1960--Portville, N. Y. State policeman reported two
dumbbell-like UFOs. [X]

August 13, 1960--Red Bluff, California. State Police reported
highly maneuverable elliptical UFO. [VII]

August 13-18, 1960--California. Concentration of UFO sightings,
mostly in north, including many police witnesses. (See Section XII)

August 15, 1960--Policy letter to Commanders, from office of
Secretary of Air Force: The USAF maintains a "continuous sur-
veillance of the atmosphere near Earth for unidentified flying ob-
jects -- UFOs."

August 16, 1960--Oak Forest, Illinois. Former Air Force
pilot saw disc-like UFO which hovered, bobbed around. [V]

August 25, 1960--Mystery satellite seen for several days, photo-
graphed by Grumman Aircraft Corporation.

August 26, 1960--Mesa, Arizona. UFO observed by chemistry
teacher, pilot. [VII]

September 4, 1960--Lexington, Kentucky. Former Strategic
Air Command radar technician saw a glowing sphere traveling
from horizon to horizon. [V]

September 5, 1960--Sonoma County, California. Sheriffs observed six vari-colored UFOs flying in V-formation. [VII]

September 15, 1960--Carrizales, Venezuela. Professor of
engineering observed accelerating luminous object. [X]

September 28, 1960--Arlington, Texas. Aeronautical engineer
observed erratically maneuvering UFO. [V]

About October 3, 1960--Canadian Broadcasting Corporation
newscast (October 10): "The sighting of six flying saucers and a
'mother ship' has been reported from the Australian island state
of Tasmania. A Church of England minister says he saw the
mysterious craft nearly one week ago, but was reluctant to report
them. The clergyman finally did report the matter when other
people in the area said today, they too had seen strange objects in
the sky."

October 9, 1960--Longpoint, Illinois. Minister and others saw
a golden, elliptical UFO hover, move away. [VII]

October 27, 1960--Lexington, Kentucky. Attorney saw disc
hover, move away. [VII]

November 24, 1960--Ohio. White elliptical UFO observed by
scientist. [VI]

December 5, 1960--Major Donald E. Keyhoe, USMC, ret., (NICAP
Director) debated Lt. Colonel Lawrence J. Tacker (Air Force UFO
spokesman) on Dave Garroway's "Today" program.

December 14, 1960--Brookings Institution report discussed ef-
fects of meeting extraterrestrial life: "It is possible that if the
intelligence of these creatures were sufficiently superior to ours,
they would choose to have little if any contact with us. . . " (New
York Times, Dec. 15, 1960)

1961

January 1961--Missile Base. Hovering, maneuvering UFO
tracked on radar during missile test. [VIII]

January 10, 1961--Benjamin, Texas. Glowing red, zig-zagging
UFO observed from air by pilot (also from ground by others);
maneuvered and landed on large overgrown field. [V]

January 22, 1961--Eglin AFB, Florida. An elliptical UFO,
metallic looking, approached from over the Gulf, made a U-turn
and sped back over the Gulf. Photographed on 8 mm movie film
by a businessman. [VIII]

February 5-7, 1961--Maine. Many reports of strange lights
flashing around in sky. Some blinked and moved up and down.
Portland Press Herald editorial, Feb. 9: "Mysterious objects 'lit
up like a ball of fire and going fast' zoom over Portland. Uniden-
tified shapes with green, yellow and red lights hover over Bruns-
wick then dart away with 'unbelievable quickness.' Strange things
are happening. . . The military had us just about convinced that no
such objects existed. The only trouble was that many people -
good, reliable observers - continued to see these things."

February 7, 1961--Kennebunkport, Maine. The president of
an advertising agency saw a bright red hemispherical UFO
which hovered, then suddenly sped away. [VII]

February 28, 1961--Nr. Lakeville, Mass. A bright yellow elongated UFO with dark red edge, surrounded by black "smoke", was seen after witnesses heard a roaring noise. House lights failed as UFO made two passes over area. [VIII]

March 16, 1961--Antarctica. Meteorologist observed a fireball-like object, multi-colored, below overcast. [VI]

April 9, 1961--Kingsville, Texas. Round red UFO descended, hovered, sped away. [XII]

May 1961--Joint statement by 21 American Scientists released by NICAP. Calls for open investigation of UFOs without secrecy, the need for a more thorough investigation shown by circumstantial evidence. States the Air Force should have more straightforward information policy, specifically to give out all facts on major UFO sightings.

May (first week) 1961--Union Mills, Indiana. Hemispherical UFO with "portholes", on road; took off as car approached. [XII]

May 19, 1961--Long Beach, Calif. Twelve shiny UFOs maneuvered erratically over the area at 3:50 p.m., with an odd fluttering motion; then two loud "skyquakes" were heard. [XII]

May 20, 1961--Tyndall AFB, Florida. Air Police observed unidentified light diving and climbing. [III]

May 25, 1961--Shepperton, Middlesex, England. Domed UFO with "portholes." [XII]

May 29, 1961--Newark, Ohio. Boy filmed unidentified light. [VIII]

June 4, 1961--Blue Ridge Summit, Pa. A cigar-shaped or long elliptical UFO with a cluster of smaller UFOs was observed by a librarian. First motionless, the smaller objects then streaked across the sky to the large UFO and all vanished behind trees. [VIII]

June 19, 1961--Exeter, England. A "flying object" was reported to have hovered for more than an hour above an airport. Officials said: "We do not know what it is. It was seen on the radar screen and we have had it under observation for some time. We think it is pretty big. It appears to be shining brightly and is about 50,000 feet up." [VIII]

July 4, 1961--Akron, Ohio. A glowing green and white object dove at a plane, stopped suddenly and climbed away at tremendous speed. (July 5, same pilot sighted similar object; also seen visually and tracked on radar at Cleveland airport). [V]

July 24, 1961--Ilha Grande, Brazil. An intensely luminous UFO maneuvered sharply around a VASP Airlines plane. [X]

August 4, 1961--Letter to NICAP member from Rep. Thomas W. Downing: "The Bureau manager (of Newsweek) informs me that his information indicates that an investigation of the UFO phenomenon is being contemplated by the Science and Astronautics Committee. The information that I was provided indicates that Congressman Joseph E. Karth of Minnesota may serve as Chairman of the three-man Subcommittee." (See Section XIII)

August 17, 1961--Stillwater, Minn. A V-formation of yellowish lights (or V-shaped UFO with body lights) passed behind trees at low altitude. [II]

September 13, 1961--Crawfordsville, Indiana. 4:00 a.m. Three people reported a round, orange UFO which moved rapidly east to west, stopped and hovered for 5 minutes, then accelerated rapidly disappearing in the distance. [XII]

September 19/20, 1961--Nr. N. Woodstock, N.H. Disc-shaped UFO seen at close range; "beings" reportedly visible through windows. (XIV)

September 21, 1961--Pacific Ocean, nr. Wake Island. Airline pilots, ship, reported a bright white circular UFO. [X]

October 2, 1961--Salt Lake City, Utah. Disc-shaped UFO maneuvered away from investigating aircraft. [I]

October 12, 1961--Indianapolis, Indiana. Spherical UFO with a row of pulsating lights viewed from many angles by different observers. [XII]

October 21, 1961--Nr. Datil, N. Mex. Four lights paced car, maneuvered, shot away upward. [II]

October 30, 1961--Ligonier, Penna. Engineer observed four luminous blue discs with bands of lights or "portholes" on outer periphery. [I]

November 1961--Green Bank, W. Va. Government (National Academy of Sciences) sponsored secret discussions on space life, possibility of communicating with other worlds. (New York Times; February 4, 1962)

November 22, 1961--Nr. Grafton, N.D. Metallurgist obse___ a hovering, grayish cigar-shaped UFO with "portholes".

1962

January 29, 1962--Eastern Holland. Radar-visual sightin___ Dutch AF F-86 pilot. [X]

February 9, 1962--Ashton Clinton, Beds., England. Disc-l___ UFO with apparent dome, "portholes", hovered low over ro___ [VIII, XII]

February 11, 1962--Parque del Este, Caracas, Venezuela. Fo___ mations of UFOs, about 16 objects in all, were observed ___ many people. Sr. Carlos Pineda, at nearby Humboldt Planetariu___ witnessed one of the UFOs, described as "a body giving off___ brilliant light. . . moving at great altitude as if towards th___ moon." [X]

February 20, 1962--Col. John Glenn orbital flight, Project Mer___ cury.

April 24 & 25, 1962--Philadelphia, Penna. Series of UFO___ sightings over area. April 24: Circular UFO with body lights,___ apparent dome on top, shafts of white light directed downward___ from base. Center section had rotating row of square "windows."___ [XII]

April 30, 1962--X-15 flight, piloted by Joe Walker; Photograph___ (no visual sighting) of 5 or 6 "disc-shaped or . . . cylindrical" objects. Slides later shown in Seattle conference. NICAP unable to obtain prints.

May 1962--At least twelve UFOs sighted in Argentina in May. Official reports and newspaper chronology given NICAP by Argentine Embassy include four sightings by Argentine Navy pilots, two reported landing cases. (See Section XII; Argentine Chronology.)

May 18, 1962--Pompano Beach, Florida. Cigar-shaped UFO, brilliantly lighted below, dark on top. Hovered, sped away. [VII]

May 20, 1962--Defiance, Ohio. Scientist, others, watched maneuvering light source, brilliant blue changing to yellow. [VI]

May 21, 1962--England. Irish International Airlines pilot watched spherical UFO pass below aircraft. [X]

May 24, 1962--Astronaut Scott Carpenter, Project Mercury orbital flight.

May 26, 1962--Westfield, Mass. "Round, slightly oval, bright red object, giving off sparks from top and bottom. Center. . . yellowish or white. . .case is listed as unidentified." (Air Force Project Blue Book 1962 Summary.)

May 27, 1962--Palmer, Alaska. Two triangular UFOs, diving and climbing. Unidentified. (Air Force Project Blue Book 1962 Summary.)

June 30, 1962--Richmond, Va. Circular red object with some white observed 10 minutes. Went from 20 degree elevation, 169 degrees azimuth to 13-1/2 degree elevation, 132 degrees azimuth. Unidentified. (Air Force Project Blue Book 1962 Summary)

July 10, 1962--New Iberia, Louisiana. Disc-shaped UFO with rotating dome on top swept low over Naval Auxiliary Air Station, slowed over area of runway and hangar, then climbed out of sight at 20 to 30 degrees angle accelerating rapidly. [IV]

July 17, 1962--X-15 flight, Maj. Bob White pilot. Photographs and visual sighting of unidentified object "like a piece of paper," gray-white. Observed to left of aircraft "going along with the ship" for about 5 seconds, then "darted above and behind the plane."

July 30, 1962--Ocean Springs, Miss. "Diamond-shaped object, mostly round, sometimes rectangular. Color bright cherry red varying in intensity as it maneuvered. Performed intricate maneuvers. Moved slowly, sometimes stationary -- then darted up and over, etc." Case listed as unidentified. (Air Force Project Blue Book 1962 Summary.)

August 2, 1962--Liberal, Kansas. Series of brightly lighted colored objects seen by airline pilot, airport personnel, and passengers at airport. [V]

September 8, 1962--Floresta, Argentina. "Burnished metal" lens-shaped UFO sighted by Argentine Navy pilot. [X, XII]

Northeast New Jersey Concentration

September 15-28, 1962--Northeast New Jersey, across the Hudson River from New York City, was the scene of a definite flurry of sightings of UFOs, with the heaviest concentration in the Oradell-Hawthorne area.

At 6 p.m., ex-Navy electronics officer, J. J. McVicker reported two "silver dollars" apparently revolving as they passed over W. Nyack, N.Y. At about 7:55 p.m., five boys reported a disc which hovered over the Oradell reservoir, touched down on it, then took off silently at high speed. Later, two other boys said they had seen a very bright light moving back and forth over the edge of the reservoir, following which a loud explosion was heard.

-- 4 a.m.; Two Westwood, N.J., policemen reported a 7-8 second observation of a huge object, round at the top and tapering to a cone.

4:45 a.m.; Two Oradell policemen reported a brilliant light in the sky.

7:55 p.m.; A family in Hawthorne watched a greenish disc descend low over their house.

20 -- Early in the morning, a watchman, William Stock, of Hawthorne, reported a saucer-shaped object which hovered and moved from side to side as it shone bright enough to illuminate a huge area.

ber 21 -- At 3:40 a.m., William Stock and four invited policemen spent a half hour watching a round object with two apparently revolving body lights. At 4 a.m., two policemen, between Hawthorne and North Haledon, watched a bright light revolving and moving up and down and from side to side for about 35 minutes.
That night, 4 young persons in Hawthorne reported seeing a bright star-like object with light beams coming from it.

eptember 23 -- In the middle of the day a Hawthorne woman and her son saw an oblong, silvery object, for about 10 seconds.

September 24 -- Early in the morning, a group consisting of the head of an independent news agency, a photographer and numerous policemen watched, for 10 minutes, an object which changed from red to silver to green and back to red. In the evening, a Hawthorne patrolman watched a light approach, hover for 15 minutes and then move away.

September 28 -- Police from seven counties reported seeing UFOs between 2:30 and 3:30 a.m. Most reported three objects which changed color.

September 18, 1962--Northeast Ohio. Six policemen sighted UFOs about the same time. One hovering object, two maneuvering. [VII]

October 3, 1962--Chicago, Ill. City of Chicago official watched circular UFO with dome move across lower half of moon. [VII]

October 25, 1962--Delta, Colorado. Police dispatcher saw round glowing object from radio room window. State patrolman and Cedaredge Marshal observed two UFOs "like an inverted umbrella with a number of bright, tail-like appendages." [VII]

November 19, 1962--Tampa, Florida. Three star-like objects approached horizontally, hovered. "Impression was that objects were under intelligent control at all times." Unidentified. (Air Force Project Blue Book 1962 Summary.)

December 12, 1962--Amagasaki City, Japan. Five students saw, and independently sketched, Saturn-shaped UFO. [X]

December 21, 1962--Angel Falls, Venezuela. Bright teardrop-shaped light apparently rising from jungle floor filmed from aircraft. [VIII]

December 22, 1962--Buenos Aires, Argentina. At Ezeiza Airport, pilots and control tower operators saw circular UFO rise from end of runway. [X]

1963

January 5, 1963--The National Academy of Sciences, Space Science Board, released a report (Pub. No. 1079) urging that a search for extraterrestrial life "be proclaimed the top-priority scientific goal of our space program."

January 24, 1963--Lexington, Ky. Post Office safety engineer saw a round UFO traveling east to west, and a delta-wing aircraft north to south. UFO's line of flight intersected aircraft path at right angles. [Report via Bluegrass NICAP Affiliate, Lexington, Ky.]

February 5, 1963--Nr. Washington, D. C. Private pilot, newsman passenger, watched a pulsating yellow-white light maneuver around their plane. [V]

February 15, 1963--SE of Melbourne, Australia. Farmer watched disc-shaped object with dome descend through rain clouds, hover, then climb away; cattle bolted. [Witness interviewed by Attorney Peter Norris, NICAP member.]

March 11, 1963--Oahu, Hawaii. Brilliant light headed west and leaving a trail observed by many people just after 8:00 p.m. Two National Guard pilots flying jets about 40 miles west of Honolulu reported UFO was "much higher" than their altitude of 40,000 feet and moving "very fast." Possibly an observation of the recently announced A-11. (At 7:28 p.m., Pacific Time, a newsboy in El Sobrante, California, saw two oval-shaped yellow lights pass over the San Francisco Bay area from north to south, traveling at high speed.)

March 12, 1963--Paine, Chile. Members of the Santiago NICAP Subcommittee observed a pulsating luminous white sphere about 7:50 p.m. The UFO moved from north to south, disappearing in the distance after about a minute.

May 21, 1963--Nr. Mt. Gambier, Australia. Unconfirmed report that a brilliant light followed a car. A youth stated the object was at side of road, rose suddenly as he approached, hovered overhead, then followed car. The Dominion, Adelaide, reported May 22 this was "the second report of such an occurrence in a week."

May 23, 1963--Sunnyvale, Calif. Bluish disc observed hovering and circling slowly, apparently at tree-top height; rose vertically and disappeared. [Report via Bay Area NICAP Subcommittee.]

June 16, 1963--Palmerston, North City, N.Z. A college student observed two brilliant lights descending in zig-zag fashion. The UFOs hovered stationary for about 5 seconds, then "suddenly shot off at very great speed, at first in level flight across my front, then climbed up into the sky at approximately 45 degrees to disappear." [Witness interviewed by NICAP Adviser Harold H. Fulton.]

June 18, 1963--Niagara Falls, N. Y. An unidentified object flashing various colors moved around erratically for over two hours. Witnesses in separate locations described the maneuvers similarly. About 10:00 p.m., the UFO moved from west to east, reversed direction and headed back west. Later, it headed southeast rising higher in the sky. Local astronomers and airport officials could not account for the object. [Report from NICAP member.]

June 19, 1963--Burlington, Mass. An unidentified white light was observed descending, changing color; finally appeared silvery. The UFO then circled the area, disappearing behind objects on the visible horizon. [Report via Walter N. Webb, Boston NICAP Adviser.]

June 21, 1963--Chicago, Ill. A student saw a gray, apparently spherical UFO with a central row of yellow lights. Apparently at low altitude, the object made a "sizzling sound" as it moved east, turned sharply and disappeared to the north. [Witness filed NICAP report form.]

June 26, 1963--Pine Crest, Calif. Four glowing greenish objects with halos were observed by a technician, many others. Three objects moving westerly were approached by a similar object from the west. The fourth object stopped and hovered as the three approached, split formation, and continued west. Then the fourth object continued east. [Report via Bay Area NICAP Subcommittee.]

June 26, 1963--Rockland, Mass. About 1:00 a.m., witnesses attracted by a loud roar observed a Saturn-shaped UFO. The object hovered, then moved away horizontally. The shape was observed in silhouette, partly illuminated by a white light on top and orange light on bottom. [Witnesses interviewed by NICAP member Raymond Fowler.]

July 1963--Boston, Mass. An advertising plane caused several erroneous UFO reports. (Aircraft identified by NICAP Adviser, Walter N. Webb.)

July 18, 1963--Sunnyvale, Calif. A technical writer for United Technology Center saw a disc-shaped UFO hovering in the sky.

He exposed 8 mm color film of the object using a 36 mm tele-photo lens. (A few frames of the film were submitted to NICAP, but the image is too small to show detail.) When four jet inter-ceptors converged on the UFO (three from the west and one from the east), it drifted westward tilting back and forth, "then pulled up in a short arc and shot up out of sight in an estimated three seconds." [Report via Bay Area NICAP Subcommittee.]

July 20, 1963--Springfield, Ill. About 7:50 p.m., a shiny silver object was observed hovering at high altitude. The UFO moved up and down, back and forth, but remained in the same area of the sky. About dusk, the object (now resembling a bright star) began moving across the sky, picking up speed, and disappeared in the distance. [Witness filed NICAP report form.]

August 1, 1963--Garston, Herts., England. A former RAF pilot, and flying instructor, observed a triangular UFO which hovered for a long period of time, then climbed out of sight. An air traffic controller four miles away also observed the UFO. [FLIGHT International, 15 August 1963.]

Illinois Sightings

From August 4 into mid-month, there was a flurry of UFO sight-ings, mostly in southern Illinois. An advertising plane in the Chicago area caused some erroneous reports about the same time. Once the reports had been publicized, the planet Jupiter also was reported as a UFO on a few occasions. The Vincennes, Indiana, NICAP Subcommittee investigated several of the key cases, sub-mitting taped interviews and investigation reports.

August 4, 1963--Wayne County, Illinois. Ronald Austin (18) and his girl friend, returning home from a drive-in theater, noticed a large white object at tree-top level pacing the car. At one point, the UFO crossed the road ahead of the car. During the closest pass, a whining noise drowned out the car radio. Ronald was ter-rified by the experience, and needed medical attention. (Police and others later saw a light in the sky, probably the planet Jupiter.)

August 7, 1963--Nr. Fairfield, Ill. Chauncey Uphoff and Mike Hill had their attention attracted to a UFO when Uphoff's dogs began barking. Looking up, they saw a yellow-orange diamond-shaped object traveling west to east. The UFO made a sharp turn, headed toward the observers, changing color from orange to gray, and finally to blue-white. The object continued its U-turn, tilting on edge, and turned southeast. After hovering briefly, the UFO took off at a 45 degree angle toward Grayville.

August 9, 1963--Mount Vernon, Ill. Former Mayor Harry Bishop watched a large, bright red light follow a car along Centralia road. When the car stopped, the UFO stopped and hovered, then moved away at right angles to its original course.

August 6, 1963--Sanford, Florida. Orvil Hartle, Chairman of the LaPorte, Indiana NICAP Subcommittee, on a brief visit to Florida, observed a UFO. He obtained a full report with signa-tures of 13 additional witnesses. The object appeared in the northwest sky first as a red, then a white moving light. To the west, the star-like light hovered, then moved south. To the south, the object began a series of gyrations and pulsated on and off, visible intermittently. It moved up and down, back and forth, once emitting a flare of greenish-white light.

August 13, 1963--Honolulu, Hawaii. While vacationing in Hawaii, a chemist observed a UFO and reported it to NICAP. Dr. Richard Turse, Princeton, N.J., about 11:30 p.m., saw a round reddish object pass overhead from southwest to northeast. The UFO "traveled across the sky at great speed making two sharp turns at the same time."

August 13, 1963--Nr. Ellsworth, Maine. A family and their housekeeper observed an elliptical object, apparently on the ground adjoining Molasses Pond, for more than an hour. Body lights were visible along its length, and rays of light shone upward from each end of the object occasionally. [Witnesses interviewed by Walter N. Webb, NICAP Adviser.]

August 18, 1963--Ft. Kent, Maine. A silvery disc-shaped UFO was seen by two young boys, whose parents agreed they must have seen something unusual. The disc passed from north to south, emitting a hum intermittently.

September 14, 1963--Susanville, Calif. (Satellite object [ ] see Section II.) Round UFO accelerated, joined a "long" ob[ ] "An unusual report from a competent witness. Unidentifi[ ] (Air Force Project Blue Book 1963 Summary.)

September 20, 1963--Huntsville, Arkansas. A rancher repo[ ] watching an egg-shaped UFO moving eastward about 10 degr[ ] above the southern horizon. Through binoculars, a dark s[ ] was visible near the top of the object. As it proceeded west, [ ] UFO dimmed, turning orange, and faded from view after 10-[ ] minutes. [Witness reported sighting to NICAP.]

September 26, 1963--Sunnyvale, Calif. Police officer, ma[ ] others, observed a gray disc with central bright spot, moving [ ] a westerly course at high speed. [VII]

October 4, 1963--East Hartland, Conn. State Representativ[ ] L. B. Martin, about 1:00 p.m., saw a silvery triangular objec[ ] with a row of black dots across the leading edge. The UF[ ] passed overhead, emitting a flame-like tail, at an estimate[ ] speed of 2000 mph. [Report obtained by NICAP-CONN Affiliate.[ ]

October 23, 1963--Meridian, Idaho. Shiny disc hovered, emit-ting "loud pulsating sound," maneuvered across sky and disap-peared. Unidentified. (Air Force Project Blue Book 1963 Sum-mary.)

October 31, 1963--Daylston, Victoria, Australia. A deliveryman on his rounds at 4:15 a.m., was frightened by a UFO which approached his van, turned and followed his course just ahead. The object seemed to be 8-12 feet long, glowing orange and red. It then darted to the side of the road, continuing to pace the van for a while, finally zooming ahead over a hill and apparently de-scending. It was not seen again. Other witnesses reported seeing a maneuvering light at the time of the sighting.

November 3, 1963--Corona, N. Y. A Pan American Airways mechanic, about 1:30 a.m., noticed a star-like object maneuvering across the northern sky. The light moved rapidly, slowed and seemed to "shudder," then changed course by about 45 degrees. Finally it made a 90-degree turn, accelerated, turned again and disappeared from view. [Report obtained by New York NICAP Subcommittee.]

November 12, 1963--Port Huron, Michigan. Deputy Sheriffs chased a low-flying UFO which first appeared as a white flashing light. At times the object seemed to have a "big divided window" on it. When the UFO hovered, the deputies approached and flashed their squad car light. Then a flashing red light became visible on the UFO. The object finally moved away to the northwest making a motor-like sound. Other residents reported a flashing light and "high-pitched" or "whining" noises at the same time.

November 14, 1963--Carson City Nevada. A huge bluish-green disc was seen hovering in the northwest sky about 4:45 a.m. Mrs. Blanche Pritchett said she was listening to her radio when a bright light shining through her drapes caused her to look outdoors. As she watched the hovering object, her radio went off. A brilliant shaft of light from the UFO illuminated a hill-top. Suddenly the UFO blacked out and disappeared, after which the radio resumed playing. Other residents reported odd glows in the sky that morning. [VIII]

November 20, 1963--Neche, N.D. Two high school girls re-ported that a bright orange, oval-shaped object circled their car at night while they were en route home. They were on highway 55 east of town when they first saw the UFO. It appeared to be surrounded by a light haze. The glowing object sped across in front of the car and circled around the side before disappearing to the southeast.

December 2, 1963--Grand Rapids, Michigan. A motorist stopped at a traffic light about 9:30 a.m., noticed a strange object "glittering in the sun." Then the object tipped on edge (revealing a disc shape) and quickly sped away to the southeast. The shape was "like a pancake."

December 5, 1963--Nr. Carrasco, Uruguay. An oval UFO, metallic-looking like aluminum, was observed hovering in the clear morning sky by hundreds at a resort. One description said the object "balanced gently in the air."

SECTION XII

PATTERNS

An attempt was made to find groups of Unknowns for which the observed characteristics were the same. No such groups were found...An intensive study, aimed at finding a verified model or models of "flying saucers"...led to the conclusion that neither goal could be attained using the present data...the data conclusively failed to reveal even a rough model...the data as a whole failed to reveal any marked patterns or trends. — Statement by U.S. Air Force (From Project Blue Book Special Report No. 14, 1955, ppg. 91-94)

The many obvious patterns which appear in UFO sighting data are summarized under the following general types:

A. Physical Appearance
B. Maneuvers
C. Flight Characteristics
D. Concentrations With Time

(See also patterns of formations, Section II).

A. PHYSICAL APPEARANCE

Shape

The Air Force Project Grudge Report of December 1949 (Technical Report No. 102-AC-49/15-100) concluded, on the basis of intelligence reports of UFOs, that the objects were of three basic types:

(1) "The most numerous reports indicate daytime observation of metallic disc-like objects roughly in diameter ten times their thickness."

(2) Rocket-like objects.

(3) "Sharply defined luminous objects" appearing as lights at night.

Thirteen years of UFO sightings have been added to the record since this evaluation was made. A statistical study of the cases listed in the chronology of this report [Section XI], covering a period of 22 years beginning with 1942, indicates that the above pattern is well-established.

Statistics Based on Cases in Section XI (1942-1963)

Description	Number of cases	Percentage of Total
Geometrical (disc, ellipse, triangle...)	333	58.0%
Rocket-like or Cigar-shaped	48	8.3%
Light Source	140	24.3%
Other/None	35	6.1%
Radar (No visual)	19	3.3%
Total Number of Cases:	575	

[Between 1947 and 1952, the Air Force investigated 2199 cases; 46.9% were elliptical UFOs, 5.2% rocket-like. The study did not have a separate category for discs. See Project Blue Book Special Report No. 14, page 197, tables A140-A146].

The cases of geometrical objects break down as follows:

Shape	Number of Cases	Percentage of Total (575)
1. Disc	149	26%
2. Round (spheres or discs)	96	17%
3. Oval/elliptical	77	13%
4. Triangular	11	2%
Total Geometrical	333	

If we make the reasonable assumption that some of the UFOs in categories 2 and 3 were discs seen in perspective, the possible range of generally flat circular objects observed becomes:

	Minimum	Maximum
Number of Cases	149	322
Percentage of Total	26%	56%

One particular type of disc, whose shape occasionally has been compared to the planet Saturn, has been sighted periodically since 1947. It resembles a flattened sphere (sometimes with a centrally located surrounding ring). The following list, including one 1884 sighting, shows that many independent witnesses have used very similar terminology in describing the symmetry of the discus-shaped UFO.

Date	Location	Witness	Description
July 3, 1884	Norwood, N. Y.	---	"Globe surrounded by a ring"
July 12, 1947	Over Utah Lake	Pilot	"Much like two saucers face to face"
July 2, 1952	Nr Tremonton, Utah	Navy photographer	"Like two pie-pans, one inverted on top of the other" Section VIII
October 18, 1953	Over English Channel	Airline Pilots	"Like two saucers, with rims together"
January 8, 1954	Hamilton, Victoria, Australia	---	"Like two saucers, the upper inverted"
October 4, 1954	Northweald, Essex, England	RAF Flight Lieutenant	"Like two saucers pressed together" [Section X]
August 21, 1955	Chalmette, Louisiana	Housewife	"Like two soup plates put together"
August 28, 1955	Yonkers, N. Y.	Board of Education official	"Circular-dome-shaped like Saturn"

Note: These drawings are hypothetical constructions, generalized from hundreds of UFO reports. They are intended to indicate basic shapes which have been reported, and are not necessarily completely accurate in every detail. Additional details sometimes reported, such as "portholes," projections, body lights, etc., are not portrayed. The general types shown do represent with reasonable accuracy virtually all UFOs which have been reliably described in any detail. Examples of each type appear in the left-hand column.

UFO SHAPE	BOTTOM VIEW	BOTTOM ANGLE		SIDE VIEW	
		A	B	A	B
1. FLAT DISC A. 10-54 Cox 7-2-52 Newhouse B. 7-9-47 Johnson 7-14-52 Nash	○	oval		"lens-shaped"	"coin-like"
2. DOMED DISC A. 9-21-58 Fitzgerald 4-24-62 Gasslein B. 5-11-50 Trent 8-7-52 Jansen	○	"hat-shaped"		"World War I helmet"	
3. SATURN DISC (Double dome) A. 10-4-54 Salandin 1-16-58 Trindade 10-2-61 Harris B. 8-20-56 Moore	A ◎ B ⬯	"Saturn-shaped" "diamond-shaped"			
	elliptical or "winged oval"				
4. HEMISPHERICAL DISC 9-24-59 Redmond 1-21-61 Pulliam 2-7-61 Walley	○	"parachute"		"mushroom" "half moon"	
5. FLATTENED SPHERE 10-1-48 Gorman 4-27-50 Adickes 10-9-51 C.A.A.	○				sometimes with peak
6. SPHERICAL (Circular from all angles) 3-45 Delarof 1-20-52 Baller 10-12-61 Edwards	A ○ metallic-appearing ball	B ball of glowing light			
7. ELLIPTICAL 12-20-58 Arboreen 11-2-57 Levelland 8-13-60 Carson	"football" "egg-shaped"				
8. TRIANGULAR 5-7-56 G.O.C. 5-22-60 Majorca	◁			"tear-drop"	
9. CYLINDRICAL (Rocket-like) 8-1-46 Puckett 7-23-48 Chiles	"cigar-shaped"	**10. LIGHT SOURCE ONLY** "star-like" or "planet-like"			

Date	Location	Witness	Description
November 5, 1955	Cleveland, Ohio	Minister	"Like two saucers, the uppermost inverted and resting on the edges of the lower one" [Section VII.]
August 20, 1956	Citrus Heights, California	Family	"Like two soup bowls, one inverted on top of the other"
August 20, 1957	Nr Trujillo, Venezuela	Lawyers	"Like two soup plates clamped together by their rims"
November 6, 1957	Nr Montville, Ohio	Plasterer	"Like a saucer with another inverted one resting on top..." [Section XII]
January 16, 1958	Trindade Isle, Brazil	Ship's crew	"A flattened sphere encircled at the equator by a large ring..." [Section VIII]
March 20, 1958	Henrietta, Mo.	---	"One saucer inverted over another"
July 1, 1960	Nr Leefe, Wyoming	---	"Shape of two dinner plates face to face"
October 2, 1961	Salt Lake City, Utah	Businessman/pilot	"Shaped like a pair of saucers, one turned upside down on top of the other" [Section I]

Color

UFOs observed in daylight rarely have shown any particular color. Common descriptions have been "silver" or "white". Occasionally some "glow" or "shine" has been observed in daylight or twilight, appearing to be self-illumination rather than reflection. At night, UFOs have most often appeared as bright light sources, occasionally as silhouetted objects (sometimes with body lights). The color of the light sources or body lights have ranged across the spectrum, and sometimes UFOs have shown more than one color or changed color during the observation. (See part C of this section for color change study.)

Frequency of Reported Colors

Daylight or Twilight	NICAP (575 Cases)		Air Force* (2199 Cases)	
Silver or Metallic	88	15.3%	389	17.7%
White	81	14.1%	517	23.5%
Reflective (shiny or bright)	34	5.9%	---	-----

Continued				
Gray	19	3.3%	5	.2%
Silhouette (dark or black)	31	5.4%	57	2.6%
Night or Twilight				
Red	62	10.8%	179	8.1%
Orange	25	4.3%	221	10.1%
Yellow	28	4.9%	159	7.2%
Green	21	3.7%	144	6.5%
Blue	26	4.5%	93	4.2%
Purple	0	0.0%	5	.2%

[*Project Blue Book Special Report No. 14, page 143, table A65]

"Portholes"

An often observed feature of UFOs seen at relatively close range is markings, apertures, or lights on the body of the object. The appearance is that of "portholes" or "windows", as many of the witnesses have stated. In the sample of 50 "porthole" cases charted here, the markings are of three general types:

(a) Circular; (b) Rectangular (or square); (c) Row of lights; [(d) Not specified.]

Date & Location	Time	UFO & Maneuvers	Number & Pattern
April or May 1932 Durham, N.H.	---	Silvery, saucer-shaped; passed slowly overhead.	(c) on underside of edge
July 23, 1948 Montgomery, Ala.	2:45 a.m.	Cigar-shaped, fiery exhaust; sped past airliner, rose.	(b) two rows [Section V.]
August 20, 1949 Las Cruces, N.M.	10:45 p.m.	6-8 rectangles arranged in elliptical pattern, apparent connecting glow.	(b) Section VI
March 31, 1950 Little Rock, Ark.	9:29 p.m.	Circular with flashing light on top; arced above airliner.	(a) 8-10 in circular pattern on underside [Section V]
August 31, 1951 Matador, Texas	12:30 p.m.	Pear-shaped; spiraling climb.	(d) "porthole" on side.

Date & Location	Time	UFO & Maneuvers	Number & Pattern
November 7, 1951 Lake Superior	Evening	Bright orange, oval; high speed, horizontal flight.	(a) 6 spaced in two rows of three each on underside.
September 16, 1952 Belle Glade, Fla.	About 4:30 a.m.	Circular disc	(c) Red and amber lights alternately spaced around outside rim, on underside.
October 27, 1952	2:05 a.m.	Elliptical, trailing sparks; landed at deserted airport.	(b) 4 on top following curve of surface.
April 16, 1954 Grand Canyon, Ariz.	10:20 p.m.	Cigar-shaped UFO with bright light on front.	(c) 5 along side [Section VII]
May 30, 1954 Bainbridge, N.Y.	4:50 p.m.	Elliptical, silvery.	(a) 4 in line along major axis
July 28, 1954 Atlantic Ocean	8:15 p.m.	Luminous disc, top gray, underside bright.	(c) around edge.
September 20, 1954 Cuyahoga Falls, Ohio	---	Circular, dark object; moderate speed, curved, then followed straight path.	(c) 6-8 lights
October 7, 1954 Isles-sur-Suippes, France	Early a.m.	Elongated object	(d) dim light emanating from "portholes" illuminated object.
October 14, 1954 Hobbs, N.M.	8 p.m. to 9:20 p.m.	5 semicircles of "pearly" lights.	(c) Semicircles bisected by row of lights.
November 5, 1954 Lookout Point, N.Z.	---	Orange, elliptical.	(d) blue portholes.
December 5, 1954 Northeast, Penna.	1:40 to 1:50 a.m.	Domed object giving off brilliant orange glow.	(b) double row below dome.
December 20, 1954 Pontiac, Mich.	Night	Circular object, bright orange/dull red; fast.	(b) semicircle of ports or slits.
February 2, 1955 Maiquetia-Merida, Venezuela	11:15 a.m.	"Saturn" disc, rotating; near airliner.	(d) above, below ring. [Section X.]
June 17, 1955 Adelaide, Australia	2:15 to 2:45 p.m.	Silver, oblong; slight movement.	(c) 2 bright spots along length.
Octbber 28, 1955 Galloway, England	---	Disc with revolving rim; very slow.	(c) Bluish lights on rim.
November 5, 1955 Cleveland, Ohio	6 to 6:30 p.m.	Elliptical; hovered, cruised slowly.	(b) 8 "windows" clearly visible. [Section VII.]
December 6, 1955 Ashfield, Mass.	4:15 p.m.	Cigar, smoke trails; slow.	(c) Long rows of brilliant red lights.
August 19, 1956 Newington, Conn.	11:20 p.m.	Fiery object; slow, reversed direction.	(b) 4 "windows" in line.
Early November, 1956 Malibu, Calif.	8:30 p.m.	Oval, brilliant white object. Approximately 5,000 ft. alt. Underside clearly visible.	(b) 3 evenly spaced on outer rim. Three oblong outlined "windows" on underside
June 15, 1957 Lancashire, England	5:06 p.m. GMT	Saturn-like, silvery blue	(b) 4 visible below ring; rectangular with rounded ends.
June 18, 1957 Jackson, Miss.	---	Object with halo of light.	(d) 3 "portholes".
July 1957 Azusa, Calif.	2:30 a.m.	Disc; wobbling descent	(c) amber lights at edges.
July 1, 1957 Avon, Mass.	10:00 p.m.	Cigar-shaped UFO.	(c) green "windows".
November 5, 1957 New York, N.Y.	4:30 a.m.	Domed disc; hovered, sped away	(d) "Portholes" on dome; number & type not specified.
November 6, 1957 Marion, Indiana	7:30 p.m.	Cigar; hovered, then outran jet.	(c) String of very bright lights.
December 16, 1957 Old Saybrook, Conn.	2:00-3:00 a.m.	Elliptical object; (Ports visible only while UFO not glowing, during hovering).	(b) 4 spaced along horizontal axis.
January 14, 1958 Sarasota, Fla.	7:30 p.m.	White glowing object	(c) about 10 "ports" or "windows".
February 2, 1958 NSW, Australia	7:45 p.m.	Elliptical; flame trail.	(a) 2 portlike markings.

Date & Location	Time	UFO & Maneuvers	Number & Pattern
April 2, 1958 Columbus, Ohio	9:00 to 11:00 p.m.	Cigar-shaped.	(c) long row of "portholes or windows".
April 4, 1958 Santa Monica, Cal.	7:15 p.m.	Cigar-shaped; shot straight up.	(d) "windows"
April 7, 1958 Santa Ana, Calif.	---	Large glowing object; slow.	(c) string of lights.
April 9, 1958 Newport Beach, Cal.	9:30 p.m.	2 deltas; hovered, flew away.	(c) row of 6 flashing red lights on edges. [Section VII.]
August 17, 1958 Kansas City, Kans.	2:00 p.m.	Dome-shaped disc; followed jets, hovered.	(a) row of about 5 "portholes".
May 4, 1960 Sarasota, Fla.	9:15 a.m.	Yellow elliptical object.	(b) 4 evenly spaced "windows", square, slightly rounded corners.
May 18, 1960 Wellington, N.Z.	---	Cigar-shaped object.	(d) "portholes".
August 18, 1960 Redlands, Calif.	1:45 a.m.	Disc with small dome.	(c) red lights around edge.
August 24, 1960 Rumney, N.H.	9:15 p.m.	Cigar-shaped, self-luminous.	(c) 4 blinking lights which changed from orange to yellow.
November 3, 1960 Price County, Wis.	4:30 p.m.	Aluminum like disc with dome on top. On ground; rose above trees, took off at high speed, (humming noise).	(b) several around circumference.
December 25, 1960 Cottonwood, Minn.	11:45 p.m.	Hemispherical disc (convex surface downward) with dome on top.	(b) row at base of dome.
Between May 2 and May 5, 1961 Union Mills, Ind.	10:00 p.m.	Object about 8' high, 10' to 15' diameter, inverted bowl shape; took off from road.	(a) oblong "windows" around top with flashing red lights coming from them. Lights changed to steady flourescent when object rose.
May 25, 1961 Shepperton, Middlesex, England	Between 10:00 and 10:30 p.m.	Domed object first appearing as brilliant point of yellow light in West.	(a) row of 3 "portholes".
November 22, 1961 Near Grafton, N.D.	7:00 p.m.	Cigar-shaped object, steady red light at upper end and flashing white light at other end.	(b) even row with yellow light. [Section VI.]
February 9, 1962 Ashton Clinton, Beds., England	About 3:30 a.m.	Disc-like reflective object with hazy dome; hovered low above road. White halo appeared as object took off at high speed.	(b) black markings "like portholes or air vents."
April 24, 1962 Philadelphia, Pa.	7:45 p.m.	Circular object, dome on top; moving slowly E to W, estimated altitude 50'. (shafts of white light directed downward from base).	(b) Center section was rotating row of "square windows".
April 25, 1962 Philadelphia, Pa.	8:00 p.m.	Brilliantly lighted circular object low in southern sky moving slowly West. Green light on top.	(c) Row of yellow "window-like lights" disappeared and reappeared periodically.

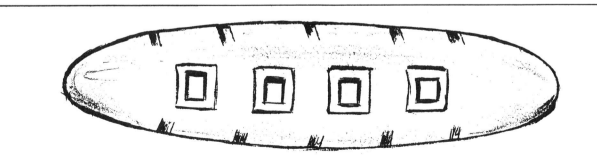

UFO WITH "PORTHOLES," SARASOTA, FLORIDA
OBSERVED BY ARCHITECT; MAY 4, 1960

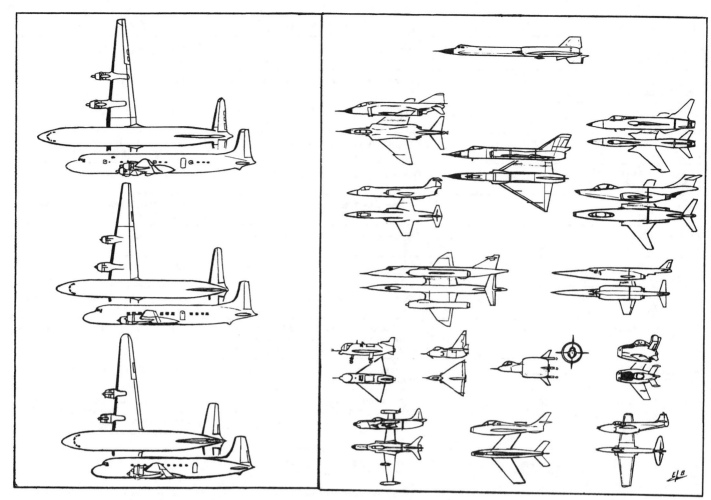

Aircraft designs show similarities and differences comparable to the variety of UFO types. Left (from bottom to top): DC-4, DC-6, and DC-7. Right: Top, A-11. Second row, F4F "Phantom"; F-106 "Delta Dart"; F-105 "Thunderchief." Third row, F-104 "Starfighter"; F-101 "Voodoo." Fourth row, British T-188 (high speed research); X-3 "Stiletto." Fifth row, British VTOL; X-13; French "Coleopter" VTOL; XF-85 "Goblin." Sixth row, F-94 "Starfire"; F-84F "Thunderstreak"; P-59.

Comparing the UFO shape to type of "porthole", to determine whether a particular type of UFO tended to have a particular type of "porthole", the findings were largely negative. The UFOs reported as cigar-shaped (11 cases) did not have rectangular "portholes" — with one exception (November 22, 1961).

Circular or disc-shaped objects (19 cases) were reported as having circular "ports" in 4 cases, rectangular in 6 cases, rows of lights in 7 cases.

Elliptical or oval UFOs (10 cases) were reported as having rectangular "ports" in 5 cases, circular in 3 cases, rows of lights in 1 case.

The most striking consistency or pattern to "porthole" reports is the description of their arrangement on the body of the UFO. In no case were the lights or markings arranged haphazardly. On the contrary, in every case the "portholes" were arranged either in straight lines, or circular patterns (most often around the curved surface).

In many cases the "portholes" were arranged exactly along the major axis of UFOs which presented elliptical outlines to the observer.

The "row of lights" cases, alone, consist of two basic types: (1) Lights on or adjacent to the edge of a disc. (In two cases, witnesses reported the lights were just below the disc edge, on the underside of the UFO.) (2) Lights along the length of cigar-shaped UFOs.

The position and geometrical arrangement of the "portholes," and the light usually associated with these markings, strongly suggest that they are indeed ports or vents. They could well be actual windows, particularly those of distinctly square or round construction. The "row of lights" cases are subject to several different interpretations: (1) Lighted windows seen at greater distance; (2) Running lights, such as those on normal aircraft; Exhaust or propulsion vents.

B. MANEUVERS

A study of hundreds of UFO reports has revealed several recurring maneuver patterns. These include:

* Hovering (or very slow motion) and sudden rapid acceleration.
* Circling and pacing of human vehicles. [Section II.]
* UFOs rendezvousing, then operating together [e.g., Aeronautical Engineer report, July 16, 1952, Section VI; Airline Pilot report, July 14, 1952, Section V]
* Satellite objects, associated with and maneuvering around larger central parent objects. [Section II.]

Numerous examples of these features appear in previous sections, especially Section II which discusses the evidence that UFOs are intelligently guided. A number of rendezvous cases is included in the formation chart, Section II, and other examples may be found throughout the report.

The remaining feature, hovering followed by rapid acceleration, occurs so regularly that it can practically be considered a defining characteristic of a "UFO." No man-made objects or known natural objects can perform in the manner described. The objects which were observed performing this maneuver were predominantly the typical discs and ellipses so often reported.

The following table lists one hundred sample cases between 1947 and 1962, illustrating this feature.

Hovering and Acceleration Cases		
Date	Location	Description
7-9-47	Nr Boise, Idaho	Disc maneuvering slowly, turned on edge, "shot straight up." [Section VII.]

Date	Location	Description
7-10-47	Southern New Mexico	Astronomer saw elliptical UFO hovering and wobbling, reported a "remarkably sudden ascent"; estimated 600 to 900 mph. [Section II.]
8-47	Media, Pa.	Hovered, flipped over showing it was disc; second later shot from mid-sky over the horizon in 3 to 4 seconds. [Section V.]
12-8-47	Las Vegas, Nevada	Pilots at night saw reddish light moving at moderate speed; flashed bright green and "shot up at tremendous speed."
7-4-48	Nr Longmont, Colo.	Round, silvery object, revolving; hovered for several seconds, soared upward at terrific speed.
3-10-50	Orangeburg, S.C.	Publisher and others saw bright disc hover over city for 15 minutes, speed away leaving trail.
3-8-50	Dayton, Ohio	Round UFO hovered at high altitude; pursued by interceptors, streaked vertically upward. [Section VIII.]
3-26-50	Nr Washington, D.C.	Private pilot saw metallic disc below his plane, dove at it; UFO zoomed up into broken clouds. [Section V.]
3-26-50	Reno, Nevada	CAA tower operator saw brilliant UFO hover, move slowly, shoot upward into clouds. [Section V.]
4-9-50	Shelby, N.C.	Round aluminum-like UFO moving horizontally for two minutes, shot straight up.
5-29-50	Nr Washington, D.C.	After circling airliner and hovering, elliptical UFO sped east at "fantastic speed." [Section V.]
6-30-50	Nr Kingman, Kans.	Rotating saucer-shaped UFO hovered; took off with terrific acceleration as minister (former USAF pilot) started to drive his car under it.
1-20-51	Nr Sioux City, Iowa	Rocket-like object flew alongside DC-3, suddenly shot up out of sight [Section V.]
2-19-51	Mt. Kilimanjaro, Africa	Cigar-shaped UFO with vertical bands, hovering, sighted by airline pilot and crew; after 15 to 20 minutes suddenly shot straight up. [Section X.]
8-51	Nr Murray, Ky.	Silver, roughly triangle-shaped object hovered, then shot straight up.
10-9-51	Nr Paris, Ill.	Disc-like UFO hovering, as pilot turned toward it, UFO began to pick up speed, shot off toward NE. [Section V.]
Early 1952	Cleveland, Ohio	Red light hovered; took off at high speed when chased by plane. [Section V.]
1-21-52	Mitchel AFB, N.Y.	Disc circling and climbing slowly; pilot gave chase, UFO accelerated rapidly and pulled away out to sea. [Section IV.]
1-29-52	Wonsan, Korea	Revolving disc paralleled B-29 for five minutes, pulled ahead, shot away at sharp angle. [Section X.]
2-20-52	Greenfield, Mass.	Minister watched three round silvery UFOs hover, suddenly speed away disappearing in seconds. [Section VII.]
3-29-52	Nr Misawa, Japan	USAF pilot saw small disc maneuver close to plane, pass in front, shoot out of sight in near vertical climb. [Section I.]
6-1-52	Los Angeles, Calif.	Radar tracking of target at 11,000 feet, which suddenly tripled speed and climbed rapidly about 35,000 feet per minute. Other maneuvers followed. [Section VIII.]
6-13-52	Le Bourget, France	Pilot, control tower operator, saw bright orange-red object speed away after hovering for about an hour. [Section X.]
7-1-52	Fort Monmouth, N.J.	Radar-visual sighting of two shiny objects which approached slowly from NE, hovered for about 5 minutes, then sped off with a terrific burst of speed to the SW. [Section VIII.]
7-5-52	Nr Richlands, Washington	Airline pilots saw "perfectly round disc" hover, accelerate and speed away. [Section V.]
7-13-52	Washington, D.C.	Airline pilot report from CAA study: "The object came to within two miles of the aircraft and hovered at the same altitude. Pilot switched on all lights, ball of light took off, going up and away." [Section XII; July 1952 Chronology.]
7-18-52	Patrick AFB, Fla.	After 4 UFOs circled area and flew away, two approached base, hovered; circled, accelerated at terrific speed and flashed away to West. [Section XII; July 1952 Chronology.]
7-22-52	New Smyrna Beach, Fla.	Metallic disc hovered about 10 seconds, shot away in abrupt fast climb. [Section XII; July 1952 Chronology.]
7-23-52	Culver City, Calif.	Elliptical UFO hovered (2 smaller objects emerged, rejoined) and climbed straight up at tremendous speed. [Section II.]
7-26-52	California	USAF F-94C chased UFO, got radar lock-on, saw large orange light; each time jet tried to close, UFO would suddenly pull away at terrific speed, then slow down again until jet began to gain. [Section VIII; Radar.]
8-1-52	Bellefon-taine, Ohio	USAF jet pilots climbed toward hovering UFO which accelerated and disappeared at high speed. [Section VIII; Radar.]
8-5-52	Haneda AFB, Japan	Dark circular object with bright lights hovered near control tower; suddenly accelerated and sped away dividing into three units. [Section VIII; Radar.]
8-6/7-52	Kerkrade, Holland	Disc hovered, accelerated rapidly and climbed away at high speed. Another disc hovered, zigzagged, sped away. [Section X.]
8-29-52	Villacoublay, France	In two separate instances, observers at a meteorological station, using a theodolite, observed circular UFOs which first hovered, then streaked away. [Section X.]
9-20-52	Topcliffe, England	Disc which had followed Meteor jet to field hovered rotating; then accelerated and vanished to SE. [Section XII; "Operation Mainbrace" Chronology]

Date	Location	Description
10-11-52	Newport News, Va.	Disc-shaped object with "dome" hovering for 20 minutes, reported to Langley Field. As two jets neared on intercept, UFO tilted up, accelerated, shot away.
10-13-52	Oshima, Japan	USAF pilot observed disc hovering in clouds for seven minutes; then saw it speed away to West, disappearing in seconds. [Section III.]
2-16-53	Nr Anchorage, Alaska	USAF C-47 pilot observed bright red light (first below horizon, ruling out stars and planets); object approached, hovered for 5 minutes. Plane gave chase, UFO accelerated and shortly vanished. [Section III.]
11-10-53	Knutsford, England	UFO with ports or "windows" first hovered, then moved North at very high speed.
3-9-54	Cincinnati, Ohio	Elliptical UFO hovered about 8 minutes; accelerated rapidly, disappearing in seconds in near vertical climb.
3-24-54	Florida	Marine Corps pilot banked toward hovering round UFO to try for gun camera pictures; object took off at terrific speed. [Section IV.]
5-27-54	Somerset, England	Glowing UFO hovered for about 2 minutes, took off at high speed.
5-30-54	Bainbridge, N.Y.	Silver elliptical UFO with four "ports" moved slowly on horizontal course; accelerated rapidly and climbed out of sight in seconds.
6-26-54	Idaho Falls, Idaho	Brilliant light flared up above AEC station, hovered several seconds, then zoomed up out of sight.
7-3-54	Albuquerque, N.M.	Nine spherical UFOs, glowing green observed north of station; hovered, "then proceeded 340° at approximately 2,600 mph." [Section VIII; Radar.]
7-28-54	Atlantic Ocean off New York City	Officers of Dutch liner observed disc with spots of light around edge hovering just over sea about 40° off port bow; UFO then shot up into clouds.
9-9-54	Nelson, New Zealand	Three discs hovered over mud flats; two tipped on edge, streaked up vertically; third followed shortly afterward. [Section VIII; photographs.]
9-15-54	Bihar, India	Saucer-shaped UFO descended and hovered at about 500 feet altitude; emitted "smoke" and "soared upwards at an incredible speed." [Section X.]
9-17-54	Nr Rome, Italy	Disc-like UFO flew along Italian coast, tracked by radar, hovered. "Suddenly it shot upward...straight up into the sky...What was strange was the object's ability to 'park' in midair for several minutes." (Eyewitness account quoted by INS.)
10-3-54	Rue de Fleury, France	Dome-shaped UFO hovered motionless for minutes; suddenly accelerated at tremendous speed and disappeared to SSW.
10-22-54	Marysville, Ohio	School principal and teacher watched cigar-shaped UFO hover over school, saw "angel's hair" fall. UFO took off rapidly disappearing horizontally. [Section VIII.]
11-12-54	Oolitic, Ind.	White ball-like object made explosive sound, moved South at rapid rate; stopped and hovered for about 1-1/2 hours.
4-22-55	Tintinara, Australia	Silver spherical object surrounded by flange (Saturn-shaped) moving very slowly over road; turned about 90°, accelerated, and climbed rapidly.
5-25-55	London, England	Circular object rapidly approached B-47, stopped above it for about 5 seconds; pulled to one side, reversed direction, hovered for about 8 second, shot away at high speed.
7-9-55	Santa Catalina Channel, Calif.	Cylindrical UFO, turning rapidly on own axis, hovered for 16 minutes; then zigzagged upward at high speed into clouds.
7-17-55	Canton, Ohio	Disc (domed on top and bottom) hovered; airliner neared, UFO went straight up and disappeared into an overcast. [1]
7-26-55	Washington, D.C.	Brilliant round UFO approached airport, stopped; oscillated, and moved off at high speed. [Section VIII; E-M Effects.]
7-26-55	Hants, England	Boomerang-shaped UFO "rather like a flattened triangle" hovered above a glider for about 30 seconds, then sped away to NW "swooped down very fast, and disappeared behind trees on the horizon." [2.]
8-6-55	Cincinnati, Ohio	Blinding white ovoidal object sitting on ground suddenly ascended and streaked away at incredible speed to NW.
8-21-55	Chalmette, La.	Disc with ring (Saturn-type) hovered, rotating slowly; began moving, tilted on edge, shot away.
12-29-55	New Britain, Conn.	Shiny object hovered at high altitude for about 5 minutes, then sped away.
1-17-56	Orangeville, Canada	Disc-shaped UFO (giving appearance of three concentric rings) hovered; glowed more intensely, began moving horizontally, shot up in spiral motion, disappearing in 5 to 6 seconds.
2-17-56	Orly Airport, France	UFO tracked on radar, and seen visually as a bright light, approached at high speed; bobbed around area hovering at various points for several hours, then departed at high speed. [Section X.]
6-27-56	Trieste, Italy	Numerous persons near the sea coast reported a luminous UFO which hovered about 10 seconds, then shot away at high speed to the NE.
7-19-56	Phoenix, Arizona	Round object, apparently spherical, hovered; lower hemisphere dimmed, object sped away.
1-21-57	Army base	Captain and Master Sergeant watched two UFOs maneuvering close together at high altitude; one shot away at very high rate of speed in level flight. Disc-shaped. [Section IV.]

Date	Location	Description	Date	Location	Description
2-13-57	Burbank, Calif.	Several oval UFOs observed maneuvering over city at various times night of February 13/14. Police officer said UFOs would dart across sky, hover briefly, then speed away. Woman reported oval object emitting light beams; "then it went straight up and disappeared."	4-12-59	Montreal, Canada	Reddish UFO hovered over air base for several minutes, darted away to North. [Section X.]
			5-14-59	Des Moines, Iowa	UFO hovered, later streaked away. [3.]
10-8-57	Fiji Islands	Circular UFO which descended and hovered low over water seen from separate locations by minister, natives; natives reported seeing figure of man on object, blinding light; then UFO shot straight up and disappeared.	6-3-59	Nr Bloomington, Indiana	Bright torpedo-shaped UFO hovered at angle for 6 to 8 minutes; dove toward earth disappearing below horizon.
			8-24-59	Nr Emmitsburg, Maryland	Brilliant white planet-like UFO, hovered over 2 minutes; took off straight up at terrific speed.
10-23-57	Kent, England	White disc dropped through cloud cover on edge, hovered just under clouds; shot North still on edge, then tilted (showing as a relatively thin line) and climbed rapidly into clouds.	9-7-59	Wallingford, Ky.	Disc-like UFO hovered low over ground; rose abruptly, sped away horizontally.
11-2-57	Nr Seminole, N.M.	Lights seen on road ahead of car; motor stalled and headlights failed as driver neared object; then lights suddenly rose into sky and sped away. [Other similar cases in November 1957; See Chronology this Section.]	9-24-59	Redmond, Oregon	Disc observed by police officer descended, hovered several minutes, shifted abruptly to new position; spouted "flames" from underside and rose quickly into scattered clouds. [Section V.]
11-6-57	Marion, Indiana	Cigar-shaped UFO with string of bright lights; hovered, then moved away at high speed.	4-25-60	Plymouth, N.H.	Bright red cigar-shaped UFO with vertical bands of light hovered in eastern sky; suddenly moved South at high speed, lighting tree branches as it passed. [Section VII.]
12-16-57	Old Saybrook, Conn.	Elliptical UFO with four square "ports" hovered just above ground; then began moving, accelerating rapidly to East. Witness reported seeing forms of two robot-like figures through "ports").	7-1-60	Nr Leefe, Wyoming	Disc approached from South, hovered over slag dump; ascended and took off to South at "tremendous speed."
5-5-58	San Carlos, Uruguay	Disc-like UFO approached plane, hovered; as pilot tried to close on object, it darted away East toward the sea. [Section X.]	7-2-60	Nr Maiquetia, Venezuela	Luminous UFO paralleled Venezuelan Airlines Super-Constellation for 20 minutes, suddenly shot away at terrific speed. [Section X.]
8-24-58	Westwood, N.J.	Police saw glowing orange circular UFO; first motionless, then moved East rapidly, disappearing in seconds. [Section VII.]	9-28-60	Arlington, Texas	Star-like UFO, moved slowly relative to stars; suddenly sped away horizontally. [Section V.]
10-7-58	Nantucket, Mass.	From ship's log: Unknown object "remained stationary for a minute or more, then shot up and away to the NE and disappeared out of sight at a rapid rate of speed." [Section VII.]	10-3-60	Cressy, Australia	Gray cigar-shaped UFO with vertical bands (5 to 6 satellite objects associated) hovered just below cloud cover, rose rapidly into clouds. [Section II.]
10-26-58	Baltimore, Md.	Egg-shaped UFO hovered above bridge; suddenly shot straight up into sky making explosive sound.	2-7-61	Kennebunkport, Maine	Bright red dome-shaped UFO hovered for two minutes; suddenly accelerated, disappearing swiftly in East. [Section VII.]
11-5-58	Conway, N.H.	Bright light like "red beacon" hovered in sky for about 15 minutes; then accelerated and sped away.	4-9-61	Kingsville, Texas	Round bright red UFO descended rapidly through overcast, hovered for a few minutes; emitted black "smoke" and sped off to SE disappearing in overcast.
12-20-58	Dunellen, N.J.	Police saw bright red elliptical UFO approach from West, hover; zoom "straight up like a shot." [Section I.]	9-13-61	Crawfordsville, Ind.	Round orange UFO approached rapidly, stopped and hovered for 5 minutes; light intensity increased, UFO accelerated rapidly sped away.
1-1-59	Newport Beach, California	Round rotating UFO (or four close together) hovered, then split into four UFOs, two of which rose vertically at extreme speed. Another headed SE and fourth remained stationary.	10-2-61	Salt Lake City, Utah	Disc hovered; as plane approached, object rose quickly like elevator, moved away, hovered again; finally moved up and shot away to West at "extremely accelerated speed." [Section I.]
			10-12-61	Indianapolis, Ind.	Spherical UFO with row of lights like ports, hovered; spiralled upward, hovered, sped away to South.
1-8-59	Nr Walworth, Wisc.	Round UFO descended slowly; suddenly sped off on horizontal path at high speed, trailing sparks. [Section V.]	2-9-62	Bedfordshire, England	Disc with black markings like "portholes or air vents" hovered above road, moved slowly ahead of car; glow appeared around object, it "veered" to right and took off at high speed. [Section VIII.]

Date	Location	Description
5-18-62	Ft. Lauderdale, Fla.	Cigar-shaped UFO hovered; began moving slowly SW, changed direction and flashed away to West. [Section VII.]
9-15-62	Oradell, N.J.	Disc-shaped UFO darted back and forth, touched down on reservoir; moments later took off at high speed.
9-21-62	Hawthorne, N. J.	Circular UFO (apparently a disc) hovered; began moving when spotlight shone at it, sped away rapidly.

Over 60% of the UFOs which maneuvered in this manner, therefore, were the typical circular and oval objects so often described in UFO reports.

A disc can present either a perfectly circular outline or, if viewed from an angle, an oval or roughly elliptical outline. Assuming that a certain percentage of the UFOs reported as round or elliptical/oval actually were discs viewed from an angle, we have from 35% minimum to 66% maximum disc-shaped objects.

At any rate, objects described as disc-shaped or round constitute 55% of the cases.

C. FLIGHT CHARACTERISTICS

(1) Study of Color Changes Related to Motion

A special study was made of cases in which UFOs reportedly changed color during flight. A sample of 82 color change cases was accumulated. In addition, 25 cases of change in luminosity or brightness (some overlapping the color changes) were singled out for examination. Could any pattern be discovered relating these changes to the motion or maneuvers of UFOs?

No attempt was made to discover what relation might exist between type or shape of UFO and color patterns. The large majority of color change cases occurred at night, when the UFOs mostly appeared as light sources only.

(*) The colors observed during acceleration were isolated. (*) Shifts of color toward the red and violet ends of the spectrum were studied in relation to hovering, acceleration, etc. (*) Cases in which white, or dark (absence of color) constituted one predominating color were examined as a class. (*) Luminosity changes were similarly analyzed.

Red	Orange	Yellow	Green	Blue	Indigo	Violet

Color Spectrum

Results:

Though it is admittedly a small sample and may not be significant, the 25 cases of luminosity change yielded the most promising pattern. In all except two cases, the luminosity change occurred during acceleration or direction change. (The sequence of events was not clear in one exception. The UFO flared up brilliantly sometime during the observation, as it moved back and forth at low altitude.)

In 18 cases the luminosity increased with acceleration. (In two of these cases, the opposite was also observed: dimming during deceleration.)

In 2 additional cases (for a total of 4) decrease of luminosity was observed. (One occurred as the UFO made a turn; dimming caused window-like lights to become visible on object. One occurred just before hovering luminous sphere accelerated and sped away; lower hemisphere dimmed.)

In 3 cases, pulsating or blinking lights were observed. (One, pursued by an aircraft, sped up and the light became steady. One pulsated from bright to dim twice while hovering. One pulsated more brightly as it began a series of erratic maneuvers.)

A secondary pattern, more difficult to assess because of inexact descriptions in many sightings, is suggested by the data. Careful interrogation of witnesses on this point in future sightings (or appropriate tracking instrumentation) would provide a test of it.

Hypothesis: That the colors of UFOs which undergo change during acceleration shift toward the red end of the spectrum.

From the original sample of 82 cases, it could be determined that in a minimum of 23 cases (28%), the color change occurred during - and seemed to be associated with - acceleration. These cases were broken down into three categories:

(a) Change from one specific color to another (10 cases). In 9 out of 10 cases the color shift was toward red, (7 shifting to red, 2 to amber). The remaining case was a red UFO which gave off a green flash of light while changing direction, but not changing to that color.

(b) Change, specific color to or from white (10 cases). In all 10 cases the color shifted white to or from red/orange (5 each way).

(c) Change, specific color to or from dark (3 cases). In all 3 cases the color shifted dark to or from red/orange (2 from dark to red/orange, 1 from orange to dark).

In 21 of the 23 color change cases related to acceleration, red/orange was either the first or last color observed in the sequence. In two cases, the color shifted to red, then back toward the violet end of the spectrum, to blue or green.

The only other conclusion of possible significance is that the data (primarily U. S. cases) failed to verify the prediction of Lt. Plantier's theory reported by Aime Michel, that UFOs should give off green luminescence during sharp turns. [4]

Only one confirming instance of this was found.

(2) Oscillation

a. Wobble on Axis

A regular feature of UFOs, observed periodically since the first U.S. reports, is the tendency of the objects to wobble much as a spinning top does when it begins to slow down. The sample of 35 cases in this chart is not the result of an exhaustive search; no doubt, there are many more. However, it was impractical to search the thousands of UFO reports on record for this one feature without use of an expensive punchcard system. In the listed cases, the following points stand out:

* The UFOs which show this feature, with few exceptions, are disc-shaped.
* The wobble does not necessarily occur only during hovering or slow flight.
* With few exceptions, the observations of this feature occurred during relatively close-range sightings in daylight.

Date	Location	Description
6-23-47	Cedar Rapids, Iowa	10 shiny discs "fluttering along in a string."
7-6-47	Fairfield-Suisan AFB, California	USAF pilot saw UFO "oscillating on lateral axis."
7-8-47	Rogers Dry Lake, California	Round metallic UFO; "rotation or slow oscillation" while moving slowly. [Section II.]
7-10-47	Southern New Mexico	Elliptical UFO sighted by astronomer, "wobbled" while hovering. [Section II.]
7-12-47	Utah Lake, Utah	Group of discs fluttered and stabilized alternately.
Summer 1948	Erie, Penna.	Disc wobbled while flying straight course; (accelerated and climbed away). [Section VI.]
7-26-49	Mitchell, Nebraska	Saucer-shaped UFO whirling, "occasionally tipping."
4-9-50	Shelby, N.C.	Round aluminum-like UFO wobbled along on course for 2 minutes, then shot straight up.

Date	Location	Description
10-51	Anderson, Indiana	Large group of discs individually tilted back and forth in unison.
3-29-52	Misawa, Japan	USAF pilot observed small disc near plane which fluttered, "rocked back and forth in 40-degree banks" while moving slowly. [Section I.]
4-5-52	Hensley AFB, Texas	Circular metallic object moving at high speed, "wobbled" in flight.
4-17-52	Cassopolis, Mich.	Oval-shaped UFO moving at high speed with "wobbling motion."
5-13-52	Greenville, S. C.	Several oval-shaped UFOs in diamond formation "wobbled in flight." [5]
8-1-52	Sharonville, Ohio	Brilliant milk-white disc flying slowly, with "tendency to wobble."
8-14-52	Coral Gables, Fla.	Bright white luminous object with orange ring, hovered; wobbled back and forth every few seconds.
9-9-52	Portland, Ore.	Two oval or disc-shaped UFOs hovering; one wobbled.
9-20-52	Topcliffe, England	Silver disc rotated and wobbled. [Operation Mainbrace Chronology, this section]
9-9-54	Nelson, New Zealand	Three discs hovered, wobbled, rose at high speed. [Section VIII; Photographs.]
3-2-55	Tucson, Arizona	Elongated UFO passed overhead with "loping or rocking motion."
3-28-55	Joseph City, Ariz.	Large group of UFOs maneuvering like jets in a dogfight, split up, began moving with "strange fluttering motion."
7-26-55	Washington, D. C.	Round UFO approached airport, hovered and oscillated before speeding away.
3-20-56	Washington, D. C.	Three discs, silvery-white; tilted in "wobbling" motion, moved up and down.
7-56	Washington, D. C.	Three discs, one with "a pronounced wobble," leaving visible trails and flying "in definite formation."
7-14-56	Arlington, Va.	Amateur astronomers watched object larger than stars or planets for four minutes; object had "wobbling motion."
8-20-56	Citrus Heights, Calif.	Large group of Saturn-shaped UFOs in rough semi-circle formation, individually wobbling.
12-18-56	Barberton, Ohio	UFO arced across sky from E to W; when it slowed and hovered, "it wobbled and had erratic movement."
7-57	Azusa, Calif.	Disc-shaped UFO with row of amber lights on rim descended with wobbling motion.
8-15-57	Woodland Hills, Calif.	Disc hovered 6 minutes, rocked from side to side and rose straight up out of sight. [Section IV.]
11-29-57	Sarasota, Florida	Round orange object "wobbled" and hovered for about 2 minutes, moved away.
5-5-58	San Carlos, Uruguay	Brilliant top-shaped UFO approached, stopped; "rocked twice" before speeding away. [Section X.]

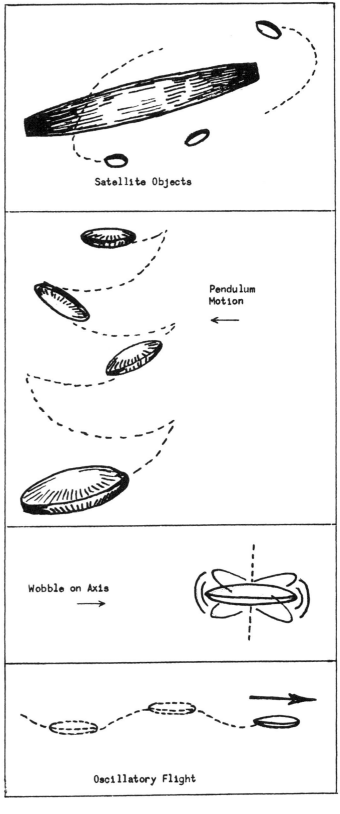

Satellite Objects

Pendulum Motion

Wobble on Axis

Oscillatory Flight

11-8-59	Biloxi, Miss.	Disc-like UFO; edges "flipped or fluttered" as it flew steady course (later spiraled, turned sharply.)
2-16-60	Laguna Beach, Calif.	Oval UFO "wobbled...on an axis through its center and at right angles to its course" as it slowed down approaching a second UFO. [Section VII.]
5-19-61	Long Beach, Calif.	Shiny UFOs maneuvered erratically, with "odd fluttering motion."

Date	Location	Description
10-2-61	Salt Lake City, Utah	Disc-shaped UFO seen by pilot, hovered "with slight rocking motion." [Section I.]
7-9-62	West New York, N. J.	Disc with rotating central ring "hovered with swaying motion."

b. Pendulum/Falling Leaf Motion

A curious, but fairly common, flight characteristic of UFOs is a pendulum-like motion (swaying back and forth) during hovering, slow climb, or descent. Witnesses frequently have compared this to the gyrations of a falling leaf.

<u>Sample Cases:</u>

October 11, 1951. J.J. Kaliszewski (then Supervisor of balloon manufacture for General Mills, Inc.) and Dick Reilly were flying near Minneapolis, Minnesota, observing a balloon at 6:30 a.m. They noticed a bright glowing object overhead moving at high speed from east to west. The UFO had a dark undersurface, and a halo of light. Finally it slowed, and started climbing "in lazy circles." Kaliszewski: "The pattern it made was like a falling oak leaf inverted." [Section VI.]

February 9, 1957. At 1:00 a.m. in Philadelphia, Pennsylvania, Roger Standeven observed a white oval-shaped UFO with a red light visible on top. The object would stop, "fall like a leaf," speed up again, and repeat the sequence, gaining altitude each time it sped up.
[For other examples; See Section XI, Chronology: 9-20-52, 9-26-54, 11-25-56, 2-28-61.]

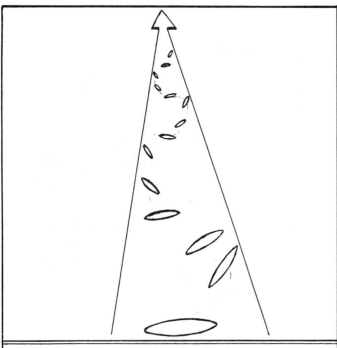

POHANG, KOREA; Fall 1954

U.S. Marine Corps Weather Observer John A. Potter observed a formation of seven bright orange UFOs moving north to south about 11:00 p.m. The objects, travelling at "a very rapid pace," individually fluttered from side to side as pictured.

(c) Side-to-Side Oscillation

A very similar pendulum-like motion, occurring as a UFO travels in a horizontal plane (rather than ascending or descending) has been noticed occasionally. It consists of a side-to-side oscillation as the UFO proceeds in a constant direction.

<u>Sample Cases:</u>

(c) Side-to-Side Oscillation

Date	Location	Description
3-29-50	Ironwood, Mich.	Round UFO moving with "slipping and sliding sideways" motion. [Section V.]
10-9-50	Nr Williamstown, Vermont	Two cylindrical UFOs swinging back and forth like "flying pendulums."
3-10-52	Oakland, Calif.	Two dark hemispherical UFOs, one following straight-line course, second swaying back and forth "like a pendulum" across the path of the first. [Section VI.]
10-54	Pohang, Korea	Formation of 7 discs; individually "fluttered," swaying from side to side.
9-22-56	Williston Plains, No. Dak.	UFO (appearing alternately circular and delta-shaped) moved slowly past, oscillating from side to side.
10-30-61	Derry, Penna.	Four luminous blue discs "oscillated" from side to side, on constant course. [Section I.]
6-19-62	London, England	Disc "oscillated" from side to side, "hesitating sometimes and practically stopping in midair," on constant course.

<u>Sample Cases:</u>

b. Pendulum/Falling Leaf Motion

Date	Location	Description
6-24-47	Mt. Ranier, Wash.	Nine flat shiny UFOs moved with skipping motion.
7-7-47	Nr Medford, Ore.	Disc on edge moved S to N along eastern horizon, bouncing up and down "as if following contour of hills." [Section XII; July 1947 Chronology.]
1-7-48	Columbus, Ohio	Round or oval UFO in level flight estimated at over 500 mph., making "elevator-like" motions.
5-29-51	Downey, Calif.	Large formation of glowing UFOs, maneuvered, moved with undulatory "skipping" motion.
8-3-51	Nr Pinckney, Mich.	Yellow light "moving in an undulating path." [Section VI.]

(3) Violent & Erratic Maneuvers

In a sample of 40 cases in which erratic maneuvers were reported, there is a noticeable repetition of certain motions which appear to be characteristic of many UFOs. All of the cases involve UFOs which abruptly altered direction and/or speed, usually more than once during the observation. Of the total, 63 percent occurred during night hours.

<u>Reported Shapes:</u>

43 percent round or elliptical UFOs, 50 percent light souces only (no shape discernible).

<u>Witnesses:</u>

28 percent scientific or experienced; 33 percent good; 39 per cent average.

Hovering and Bobbing UFOs

In 14 cases (35 per cent) the UFOs jumped or "bobbed" around while hovering in one general area of the sky, moving abruptly up and down, side to side. The words "bobbing," "erratic," and "jerky" regularly appear in the reports. Sometimes the maneuvers are compared to the bouncing of a ping-pong ball. At least one witness said the motion was like the bobbing of a float on a fishline.

VIOLENT AND ERRATIC MANEUVERS

Observer Ratings: A = Scientific or experienced;   B = Good;   C = Average

Date & Location		Time	Number and Description	Maneuvers	Observer Rating
9-1897	Canada	---	(1) light source	"tacking and veering"	?
4-5-48	White Sands, New Mexico	---	(1) disc, 1/5 size of moon	"streaked...series of violent maneuvers."	A
4-8-49	Los Angeles, Calif.	day	(1) silvery disc	high speed, "zig-zagged"	C
4-9-49	Tucson, Arizona	4-5 p.m.	(1) bright orange light source	hovered, bobbed around arcing back and forth, up and down	B
7-50	Cincinnati, Ohio	1:45 p.m.	(1) cigar-shaped	climbed rapidly, stopped 10 seconds, dived, levelled off, moved away horizontally [Section V.]	A
10-10-51	Croix Falls, Wisc.	10:00 a.m.	(1) glowing cigar-like object	dove, levelled off, sharp left turn, climbed steeply and shot away [Section VI.]	A
5-13-52	San Diego, Calif	8:55 p.m.	(1) luminous, circular	erratic darting side to side, undulatory course, circled. [Section I.]	A
6-12-52	Le Bourget, France	3:30 p.m.	(1) silver, egg-shaped	hovered, violent jerks up & down, rocked back & forth, darted away	B
7-1-52	Washington, D. C.	noon	(1) gray, shape not specified	hovered 8 minutes, arced back & forth about 15°, returning to original position, slowly dropped out of sight	A
7-16-52	Hampton Roads, Virginia	9:00 p.m.	(4) amber light sources	Two spun around each other rapidly, joined by two others, moved jerkily when moving slowly [Section VI.]	A
7-19-52	Quebec, Canada	2:30 to 3:00 p.m.	(2) blue-white light sources	Bobbed up & down, back & forth, maintained 3° separation	C
8-7-52	Kerkrade, Holland	Early a.m.	(2) disc-shaped with flat dome	One swooped down, hovered, zig-zagged & shot away; second hovered, tilted up & shot away. [Section X.]	A
9-28-52	Scandinavia	---	(1) luminous, emitted sparks	Moved with irregular jerks, visible one hour, satellite objects visible at one point.	C
10-17-52	S. France	12:50 p.m.	(About 30), 1 large cylinder and many Saturn-like discs	Discs moved in pairs, zig-zagged ("angel's hair" fell) [Section VIII.]	B
10-27-52	S. France	5:00 p.m.	(17) 1 cigar surrounded by 16 discs with domes	Discs moved in pairs, zig-zagged ("angel's hair" fell) [Section VIII.]	B
8-22-54	Chicago, Ill.	---	(1) half-moon shaped	Hovered, darted erratically in various directions, up & down...	C
9-23-55	Mt. Washington, Ohio	---	(2) red light sources	Stopped near hilltop, began independent motions, jumping up & down; one moved back & forth	C
10-3-55	Denver, Colorado	8:00 p.m.	(1) yellow-orange light source	Rapid pulsation, square turns, sudden stops & spurts of speed	C
11-7-55	Montrose, Calif.	6:30 p.m.	(1) elliptical, lights on each end	circled, hovered, ascended & descended...	B
11-23-55	Spirit Lake, Iowa	5:45 p.m.	(1) vari-colored light source	Moved erratically up & down, hovered 10 minutes...[Section VII.]	A
12-12-55	Branford, Conn.	10:30 p.m.	(1) large light source, flare-like flashes	Bobbed around in various directions	C
2-17-56	Paris, France	night	(1) large red light source	Sped into area, hovered, bobbed around sky for several hours; tracked by radar, seen visually. [Section X.]	A

Date & Location		Time	Number and Description	Maneuvers	Observer Rating
8-23-56	New Orleans, La.	8:35 p.m.	(1) orange light source, green flashes	Steady course, sudden reversal, violent zig-zagging...	B
11-5-57	Haverhill, Mass.	4:30 p.m.	(1) disc	Hovered, vibrated up & down, side to side [Section VII.]	A
1-10-58	New Orleans, La.	8:20 p.m.	(1) orange light source	Zig-zagged across lake at high speed.	C
4-11-58	S. Africa	night	(1) white light source, bright red when hovering	Moved back & forth in steady 30° arc, occasionally hovered. (cf., 7-1-52; Wash., D.C.)	B
4-14-58	Hot Springs, Ark	1:00 p.m.	(1) silver cigar, divided into parts	Hovered 2 minutes, split into 2 parts which moved jerkily in opposite directions at high speed came back together several times, then 3 parts...	B
4-16-58	Lincoln, Nebraska	4:00 to 6:30 a.m.	(9) round light sources, 1 large	Moved back & forth, up & down, as group moved E to W	C
6-4-58	Sarasota, Florida	8:50 p.m.	(1) white oval	High speed zig-zag path, S to N	B
8-3-58	Ontario, Canada	1:15 a.m.	(1) star-like light source	High speed W to E, zig-zagged several directions, then continued E.	C
8-9-58	Detroit, Mich	8:15 to 12:00 p.m.	(1) light source	bobbed and circled erratically, sometimes at high speed	B
5-17-59	New Orleans, La.	9:35 p.m.	(1) oblate, blue-white	Zig-zagged across sky, N to S	B
8-10-59	Wayne, Penna.	7:30 p.m.	(1) disc with dome	High speed with "quick & jerky" motions, generally moved in one direction	C
11-8-59	Ellensburg, Wash.	12:30 to 1:45 a.m.	(1) oval, pulsating,	Hovered, floated few lengths (repeatedly)...sharp turns	C
8-13-60	Red Bluff, Calif.	11:45 p.m.	(2) red elliptical, emitting red beam	Hovered, sharp reversal of direction, erratic maneuvers [Section VII.]	B
1-10-61	Benjamin, Texas	night	(1) light source	Zig-zag flight, appeared to land (observed from airplane) [Section V.]	B
2-28-61	Nr Lakeville, Mass.	3:20 a.m.	(1) yellow, elongated, dark red edge, black smoke	"Rolled back & forth" bobbed around, while moving in one general direction	C
7-1-61	Sacramento, Calif.	night	(1) star-like light source, pulsating	Spun, zig-zagged & stopped, moved back and forth	C
7-24-61	Ilha Grande, Brazil	night	(1) brightly luminous object	"...made angular turns...moved up & down, back & forth, in all directions.." [Section X.]	A
7-7-62	Dorchester, Mass.	10:30-11:00 p.m.	(1) yellow ellipse	Dropped, hovered, moved, hovered, rose...	C

Zigzagging UFOs

Another pattern is of UFOs zigzagging across the sky, usually in constant motion rather than hovering in one general area. Twelve cases (30 per cent).

Maneuvering UFOs

Most of the remaining cases involve motions which can only be described as "maneuvering." These include UFOs which circled, darted here and there, climbed, dove, and reversed course.

D. Concentrations with Time

The word "flap" has been applied to one feature of UFO activity: periodical surges of sightings with attendant publicity. "Flap" originally was a military slang word indicating a high degree of excitement and confusion, such as might result from the unannounced visit of a V.I.P. to a military base. Its adaptation to similar reactions related to UFO sightings is very appropriate.

The UFO "flaps" have involved elements of sudden news media attention to UFO sightings concentrated in a short period of time, or relatively small geographical area; resurgence of public interest in UFOs (frequently introducing larger numbers of erroneous reports from inexperienced observers); confusion about the interpretation of these events. Analytically, it is not clear whether so-called "flaps" result from and feed on publicity, or vice versa. Does the occurrence of a "flap" really indicate a sudden increase in UFO sightings? Or does it merely represent occasional attention to something which is going on virtually all the time?

Sometimes there have been concentrations of sightings which were widely publicized. At other times there have been concentrations which received little or no publicity (these shall be termed "concentrations" rather than "flaps" here). It appears that "flaps" are the combined products of concentrated UFO activity plus a sudden outbreak of publicity and more thorough news coverage. If so, this would tend to give a false picture of total UFO activity.

News coverage and publicity have been spotty and erratic over the years, largely reflecting the degree of official attention to UFOs. In this connection, it is interesting to note that during the past six years the Air Force has constantly debunked UFOs; during that period no real "flap" has occurred in the United States. In the same period, concentrations have occurred.

The following chart probably gives a more accurate picture of real increases and decreases of UFO activity.

FLAPS (Based on U.S. publicity)	CONCENTRATIONS	YEAR	PERIOD	MAIN LOCATIONS
X		1947	June-July	Western United States
	X	1950	First Half	Midwest, West, & SW U.S.
X		1952	July-August	Eastern United States
	X	1952	Sept.-October	Europe
	X	1954	April-December	World-Wide
	X	1954	October	France
	X	1955	August	Midwest United States
X		1957	November	Midwest, Southwest U.S., South America
	X	1959	June-August	Pacific Ocean, Australia, New Guinea, New Zealand
	X	1960	August	Northern California
	X	1962	May, July-August	Argentina
	X	1962	September	New Jersey

June-July 1947

The first major wave of UFO sightings in the United States began in June 1947. Kenneth Arnold, a private pilot flying near Mt. Ranier, Washington, first reported a sighting to the press. On June 24 he observed 9 flat, shiny objects which fluttered and skipped along as if in a chain. In describing the sighting to newsmen, he said the strange objects flew "like a saucer skipped across water." Newsmen promptly dubbed the objects "flying saucers," and the name stuck.

In the next three weeks, similar objects were spotted all over the country, but reports were concentrated in the northwest. Later research in library files, by a NICAP member traveling around the country, uncovered 125 separate UFO reports for June and July. These covered 25 states, with 30% coming from Washington.

Washington	38
Colorado	16
Idaho	11
Utah	8
Oregon	6
California	5
New Mexico	3
Wyoming	2
Arizona	2
	91

Ninety-one (72% of total) came from states west of the 100 degrees W longitude line. East of that line, Oklahoma had 9 reports, other states had only one or two.

The Air Force Project Blue Book Report, released in 1955, lists for the same period:

June — 13 sightings, 4 unknown

July — 40 sightings, 8 unknown

53 Total

The following chart lists the main sightings of this period.

DATE	LOCATION	TIME	NUMBER	SHAPE	COLOR	OBSERVERS	ACTIONS	SECTION
1947								
June 23	Iowa-Cedar Rapids	---	10	Discs	Shiny	Railroad Engineer	Fast, fluttered	
" 24	Wash.-Mt. Ranier	1400	9	Flat	Bright	Pilot (private)	Fluttered, skipped	
" 24	Ore.-Cascade Mtns.	---	5-6	Discs	Shiny	Prospector, Contractor	Banked	
" 25	N.Y.-Glens Falls	---	1	Disc	Red, blue	County Deputy Treasurer	Unspecified	
" 26	Ariz.-Grand Canyon	---	1	Ball	Silver	M. D.	High speed	
" 28	Nev.-Lake Meade	1515	5-6	Circular	Unspec.	Pilot (USAF)	Formation off wing	III.
" 28	Ala.-Montgomery	2120	1	Light	Bright	4 USAF Officers	Zig-zag, 90° turn	III.
" 29	N.Mex.-Rocket test site	---	1	Disc	Silver	Rocket expert	Flew straight	IV.
July 1	N.Mex.-Albuquerque	---	1	Disc	Bluish	Chamber of Commerce Executive	Zig-zag	
" 4	Ore.-Redmond	1100	4	Discs	Unspec.	Car full	High speed	
" 4	Ore.-Portland	1305	3-30	Discs	Shiny	Police, Pilots (private)	Oscillated	II.
" 4	Wash.-Seattle	1745	1	Circular	White	USCG Yeoman	Across wind	VIII.
" 4	Idaho-Hauser Lake	'1900	1	Disc	Unspec.	Over 200 persons	Circled, shot up	

DATE	LOCATION	TIME	NUMBER	SHAPE	COLOR	OBSERVERS	ACTIONS	SECTION
" 4	Idaho-Boise	2100	9	Discs	Silhouetted	Airliner crew	2 groups, apart	V.
" 6	Calif.-Long Beach	1315-1330	1	Disc	Brilliant	WW I Pilot, teacher	Side-slipped	
" 6	S. Central Wyoming	1445	1	Oval	Unspec.	Aviation engineer	Steady flight	VI.
" 7	Wash.-Tacoma	1430-1500	3	Unspec.	Red-purple blue-white	2 policemen	Spinning, threw sparks	VII.
" 7	Ore.-Medford	1720	1	Disc	Blue-white	Radar technician	S to N on edge	
July 8	Calif.-Muroc (Edwards) AFB	0930	3	Spheres or discs	Silvery	Pilots	Est. 300 mph.	III.
" 8	Calif.-Rogers Dry Lake	1150	1	Hemisphere	White	AF technicians	Descending, oscillating	II.
" 8	Calif.-Edwards AFB	1200	1	Thin	Metallic	USAF Test Pilot, others	Dove, climbed, oscillated	III.
" 9	Nr Boise, Idaho	Day	1	Disc	Dark	Pilot/aviation editor	Climbed, turned on edge	VII.
" 10	N. Mex.-(South)	1647	1	Ellipse	White	Astronomer	Wobbled	VI.
" 13	Ohio-Dayton	---	1	Cone	Bright	Mfg. Pres./Am. Astronomer	High speed	
" 13	Mass.-Gardner	1748	1	Disc	Silver	Interior decorator	Tilted, accelerated rapidly	VII.

The 1952 "Flap"

The year of 1952 saw the greatest wave of UFO reports in the United States; a wave which carried with it a major group of simultaneous radar-visual sightings of objects displaying outstanding speed, maneuverability and persistence.

By official Air Force figures (Project Blue Book, Special Report No. 14), there were 1501 sightings during the year which were reported through official channels. As an indication of a much larger total number of sightings, one Ground Observer Corps Filter Center (Columbus, Ohio), covering about 1% of the continental U.S., reported 70 UFOs during six weeks at the height of the activity in mid-summer (on-the-spot count by NICAP member).

Project Blue Book Chief, Capt. E.J. Ruppelt stated that as of July 21, when the tide approached flood stage, "We were getting an average of 40 reports a day, 1/3 of which were unidentified." [6]

The early part of the year was marked by a number of interesting events:

January 29 — An Air Force pilot flying north of Misawa, Japan, in a practice intercept mission, watched a small disc pace one of the jet interceptors, then climb steeply away. [Section I.]

May 13 — In National City, California, two aeronautical engineers, an ex-Navy pilot and an amateur astronomer watched a round, white UFO descend at meteor-like speed; the UFO then levelled off and circled the area, darting erratically from side to side. [Section I.]

The first of more than a dozen simultaneous radar-visual observations occurred just after midnight, June 19, at Goose Bay AFB, Labrador. A light—first, red, then changing to white—hovered briefly. When it appeared to oscillate, its image on the radar scope flared up. Then it returned to its original size and disappeared. [Section VIII; Radar.]

On the first of July, the pace began to quicken. Capt. Ruppelt later stated, "By July 1 were were completely snowed under with reports." [7.]

At Fort Monmouth, N.J., three radar instructors and 12 trainees tracked two objects on an SCR 584 radar set as they hovered at 50,000 feet for about five minutes. Viewers outside saw two shiny objects at the same time. [Section VIII; Radar.] Later that day, in Washington, D.C., hundreds of persons, including a physics professor from George Washington University,

watched a dull grey object for about eight minutes, as it hovered, with an occasional movement to the side and return.

The next day, July 2, Navy photographer W/O Delbert Newhouse took color movies of 12 disc-shaped UFOs maneuvering in a group at high speed near Tremonton, Utah. [Section VIII; Photographs.]

After a week of nationwide activity, there began a period marked by almost daily accounts of almost unprecedented reliability and detail.

At 3:00 a.m., on the morning of July 13, Captain W. Bruen, National Airlines, reported to Washington, D.C., ARTC Center that a blue-white light was approaching his aircraft. He was 60 miles SW of National Airport. The UFO "came up to altitude of aircraft, hovered two miles to left of northbound aircraft. Pilot turned on all lights. Ball of light took off, going up and away." [From Civil Aeronautics Administration Report. See Section VIII; Radar.]

Group sightings played a significant part in the 1952 "flap", with some patterns appearing. Near Newport News, Va., July 4, the pilots of a Pan American Airways DC-4 watched a formation of six red discs speed below their plane, turn sharply and speed away, joined by two more discs. [Section V.]

Over a three-day period, July 16-18, there were three observations of groups of four UFOs. (See below).

An American Airlines pilot, Capt. Paul L. Carpenter, was approaching Denver, Colorado enroute to Chicago on the night of July 17/18. Capt. James Smay, on a flight ahead, radioed back and reported some odd lights maneuvering in the area. About 2:45 a.m., while at 17,000 feet over Denver, Capt. Carpenter noticed a speeding yellowish light to the south. It darted from a compass bearing of about 165 degrees (SSE) to about 180 degrees (S). About a minute later, a light sped back toward the east from about 195 degrees (SSW) to about 180 degrees. Simultaneously, two more lights sped from south to the south-southwest. Moments later, two lights were observed headed from south-southwest to south.

To Capt. Carpenter, it seemed that some unidentified objects were speeding back and forth, reversing direction sharply. The objects maneuvered over an arc of 30 degrees. Assuming they were over Colorado Springs, Capt. Carpenter estimated the speed at 3000 mph. If they were farther away, he pointed out, the speed would be even more fantastic.

Washington, D.C.

The first of several well-publicized nights of radar-visual sightings in the Washington, D.C., area began about 11:40 p.m., July 19, at National Airport. Ground observers and military and civilian pilots observed unidentified lights while as many as ten strange blips were on radar scopes. Radar indicated hovering, sudden accelerations and great speeds until near dawn. Objects followed and passed incoming airliners, often seen by pilots and crews. USAF F-94 interceptors arrived at 3 a.m., after reportedly being delayed to check on UFOs over New Jersey, but the objects had left the scene (confirmed by radar), returning when the jets departed.

About 1:00 a.m., July 20, Capt. S.C. (Casey) Pierman, piloting Capital Airlines Flight #807 had just taken off from Washington National Airport and was swinging around to head south. At the airport, radar controllers had been noticing unidentified targets on the sets for some time. They had recalibrated the sets and were now convinced the targets were legitimate. Chief Controller Harry Barnes called Capt. Pierman and asked him to check for objects. Pierman, in the vicinity of Martinsburg, W. Va., agreed and quickly called back: "There's one, and there it goes!"

In a detailed interview published later, Barnes stated: "His [Pierman's] subsequent descriptions of the movements of the objects coincided with the position of our pips [radar targets] at all times while in our range."

In the next fourteen minutes, Capt. Pierman reported six such lights, "like falling stars without tails" which "moved rapidly up, down, and horizontally. Also hovered." [C.A.A. Report. See Section VIII; Radar.]

Two hours later, Capt. Howard Dermott on incoming Capital Flight #610 reported that a light followed his aircraft from the vicinity of Herndon, Va., to 4 miles west of the airport. Radar sets both in the control center and the tower at National Airport showed the object.

Again the following weekend, radar targets and maneuvering lights appeared. On the night of July 26/27, from 4 to 12 objects were tracked at various times between 8:00 p.m. and 1:20 a.m. on radar sets at the CAA control center, Washington National Airport tower, and Andrews AFB, Md. Lights were seen individually and in groups, both from the air and the ground.

Air Force interceptors were called in, and criss-crossed the area from 10:25 p.m. to 1:20 a.m. The pilots observed fast-moving lights where radar told them to look. One, Lt. William Patterson, was badly frightened when a group of glowing objects surrounded his interceptor. As the CAA radar operators watched the blips on the scope cluster around his plane, the pilot asked them in a scared voice what he should do. There was a stunned silence; no one answered. After a tense moment, the UFOs pulled away and left the scene. (Incident confirmed by Al Chop, then Air Force spokesman on UFOs. Taped statement on file at NICAP).

The dramatic visual sightings of unexplained lights in the same places that radar showed unexplained objects were later attributed to unusual weather conditions. Ground lights refracted by inverted layers of cool and heated air (temperature inversions) were said to account for the visual sightings. The same conditions were said to cause refraction of the radar beams causing simultaneous false radar targets. Unfortunately for this theory, the stable air conditions required to produce persistent light (refracted from a ground source) are inconsistent with the reported rapid motions of the observed lights across the sky and large angular displacements. [See Radar analyses, Section VIII.]

At the time of the Washington radar-visual sightings, the NICAP Director consulted both a civilian scientist and an Air Force radar expert about the degree of temperature inversion necessary to produce false radar targets. The scientist stated the inversion would have to be 10 degrees Fahrenheit (about 6 degrees Centigrade), and much larger to produce strong radar effects. The Air Force expert, who had made a special study of temperature inversions, stated it would take an inversion of 5-10 degrees Centigrade.

The following weather information was obtained from the National Weather Records Center by the New York City NICAP Affiliate (photo-copy on file at NICAP).

"For the dates of interest to you, upper air observations were made at Silver Hill Observatory, Maryland rather than at Washington National Airport, but these locations are sufficiently near each other for Silver Hill to be representative of the general area of interest.

"In the data which follow, local time is given, temperature difference is given in degrees Centigrade and altitude is given as altitude above mean sea level. To convert to altitude above station level, 88 meters would be subtracted from the metric altitudes given below.

"July 18, 1952, 10 P.M. observation: An inversion from the surface to 210 meters. Temperature at top of inversion was 1.7 degrees warmer than at base of inversion. No other significant inversion below 20,000 feet.

"July 19, 1952, 10 A.M. observation: No significant inversion below 20,000 feet.

"July 19, 1952, 10 P.M. observation: An inversion from the surface to 340 meters. Temperature at top of inversion was 1.7 degrees warmer than at base of inversion. There was an isothermal condition (no temperature change) between 2,780 and 3,100 meters.

"July 25, 1952, 10 P.M. observation: An inversion from the surface to 320 meters. Temperature at top of inversion was 4 degrees warmer than at base of inversion. There was another inversion between 1,700 and 1,940 meters and in this case the temperature at top of inversion was 8 degrees warmer than at base of inversion.

"July 26, 1952, 10 A.M. observation: Two minor inversions. One between 1,060 and 1,230 meters, temperature at top 0.8 degree warmer than at base. One between 2,370 and 2,530 meters, temperature at top 0.9 degree warmer than at base.

"July 26, 1952, 10 P.M. observation: An inversion from the surface to 360 meters. Temperature at top of inversion was 1.1 degrees warmer than at base of inversion. There was another inversion between 1,310 and 1,370 meters where the temperature at top was 0.7 degree warmer than at base of inversion . . . "

/s/ Roy L. Fox
Director "

The unusual concentration of UFO activity in the Washington, D.C. area continued on July 29, as radar tracked unidentified targets for almost six hours. Unlike the first two nights, there were few visual sightings of these objects.

During the afternoon of July 29, the Air Force attempted to quiet the national concern which by now had grown to unprecedented proportions. In the heaviest attended Washington press conference since World War II, USAF Intelligence Chief Maj. Gen. John A. Samford explained that the UFOs tracked and seen in the Washington area were the result of the refraction of light and radar waves by atmospheric temperature inversions. (Transcript on file at NICAP.) Weeks later, after scientists had made it clear that the inversions on the nights of the Washington sightings had been grossly insufficient to cause highly qualified radar observers to err so drastically, the Air Force re-classified these objects as "unknown."

Although they received less publicity after the Air Force press conference, UFO sightings continued at a high rate throughout August.

As the flood of reports was beginning to wane, late in the month, an Air Force Colonel, flying an F-84 between Hermanas, N. Mex., and El Paso, Tex., on the morning of August 24, saw two round, silvery objects flying abreast. One made a right turn in front of the jet, then both disappeared over Hermanas. They reappeared over El Paso. One was seen to climb straight up for several thousand feet.

The Colonel stated, "From their maneuvers and their terrific speed, I am certain their flight performance was greater than any aircraft known today." (Statement from Air Force Intelligence Report.)

Date	Time	Location	Description
1	7:30 a.m.	Boston, Mass.	USAF Capt., others saw two silvery cigar-shaped UFOs headed SW across city.
1	9:30 a.m.	Ft. Monmouth, N.J.	Visual & radar sighting of two shiny UFOs which hovered at 50,000 ft. for 5 minutes, shot away SW.
2	11:10 a.m.	Nr Tremonton, Utah	Warrant Officer Newhouse filmed 12-14 disc-shaped UFOs. [Section VIII; Photographs]
5	6:00 a.m.	Nr Richlands, Wash.	Airline pilots saw "perfectly round disc" hover, accelerate and speed away. [Section V.]
8	10:00 p.m.	Nr Wilkes-Barre, Pa.	CAA equipment man reported domed UFO. [Section V]
10	---	Nr Korea	Canadian destroyer watched two shiny revolving discs speed across sky, tracked by radar at distance of 7 miles.
10	---	Nr Quantico, Va.	National Airlines plane at 2000 feet reported slow moving brilliantly lighted object.
12	9:42 p.m.	Chicago, Ill.	USAF Captain (weather officer) and hundreds of others saw large red light with smaller white body lights make 180 degree turn directly overhead, and move away over horizon. [8]
12/13	3:00 a.m.	Nr Washington, D. C.	Airline pilot watched UFO hover, take off upward.
14	8:12 p.m.	Newport News, Va.	Airline pilots watched six discs maneuver below airliner, turn sharply, speed away joined by 2 more discs. [Section V.]
16	9:35 a.m.	Salem, Mass.	Coast Guard photographer filmed four brilliant round lights arranged in rough V.
16	9:00 p.m.	Hampton Roads, Va.	High-ranking government scientist observed four maneuvering yellowish lights. [Section VI.]
17/18	2:00 a.m.	Washington, D. C.	Chief Engineer, WRC Radio, saw 6-7 bright orange discs which sped along in single file, then each in turn veered sharply upward and disappeared.
17/18	2:45 a.m.	Nr Denver, Colo.	Airline pilot watched 3-6 lights speed back and forth, making apparent sharp reversals of flight.
18	10:45 p.m.	Patrick AFB, Fla.	USAF officers, weathermen, others, watched four amber-colored lights maneuvering near the base.
18/19	midnight	River Edge, N. J.	Associated Press staff writer, saw reddish-orange ball of light move steadily overhead NW to SE in direction of Washington.
19/20	11:40 p.m.	Washington, D. C.	National Airport CAA radar began picking up unidentified targets.
	1:00 a.m.	Nr Washington, D. C.	Outbound airline pilot checked radar targets for CAA, saw maneuvering objects coinciding with radar.
	early morning	Andrews AFB, Md.	USAF personnel saw unidentified orange light.
	3:00 a.m.	Nr Washington, D. C.	Inbound airline pilot watched light follow plane to within 7 miles of airport; UFO confirmed by radar.
	5:40	Radar sightings ended.	
20	mid-evening	Andrews AFB, Md.	USAF radar operators at weather tower tracked ten UFOs for 15-20 minutes; objects approached runway, scattered, made sharp turns and reversals. [Section VIII; Radar.]
21	10:30 a.m.	Atlanta, Ga.	Colonel commanding Dobbins AFB announced detection of a UFO by radar. The object passed over the area at about 50,000 feet traveling about 1200 mph. [9.]
22	5:47 p.m.	New Smyrna Beach, Fla.	Private pilot and his wife saw a metallic-appearing disc which hovered about 10 seconds, then shot away in abrupt fast climb.
22/23	night and early morning	New England and New Jersey	Many reports of discs and maneuvering lights. Westfield, Maine: Ground observer Corps reported three discs (different sizes) headed SW; Nahant, Mass: Coast Guardsman saw two discs circle station, head out to sea.

Date	Time	Location	Description
23	---	Culver City, Calif.	Unofficial report of elliptical silvery UFO seen by aircraft workers; launched two small discs which maneuvered, returned on board; parent object climbed straight up out of sight.
	---	Braintree, Mass	UFO tracked on radar, seen by ground observers as blue-green light. F-94 saw and chased UFO, locked on with radar, UFO pulled away and disappeared. [10]
	11:35 p.m.	South Bend, Indiana	Capt. Harold Kloth, USAF, saw two blue-white objects arc over the city.
24	3:40 p.m.	Nr Carson Sink, Nev.	Two USAF Colonels (both Command Pilots) saw three triangular objects in tight V formation; approached their B-25 at one o'clock position, banked past less than 1000 yards away at estimated speed of over 1000 mph. Investigation showed no aircraft, balloons or other devices in area. "Unknown." [11]
26/27	8:00 p.m. after midnight	Washington, D. C.	UFOs tracked by CAA radar, chased by jet interceptors; some visual sightings.
	8:15 p.m.-9:46 p.m.		Civilian pilots saw glowing white lights moving at high speed on four occasions:
		Nr Andrews AFB, Md. Nr Herndon, Va. Beltsville, Md. Nr Andrews AFB, Md.	National Airlines pilot, United Airlines pilot, CAA inspection aircraft pilot, CAA inspection aircraft pilot. [12]
	10:25 p.m.	Newcastle, Delaware	Fighters appeared on CAA radarscopes, were vectored on unknowns; one saw four lights ahead of him but could not catch them.
	10:49 p.m.	About 10 miles E of Mt. Vernon, Va.	Same pilot saw "steady white light"; light disappeared in about a minute.

In a special article for International News Service, July 29, CAA Radar Specialist James Ritchey (who tracked the unidentified targets both weekends) said that one of the airline pilots mentioned above got close to a UFO. "He reported to us that he sighted a yellow light that appeared to turn red and then back to yellow again," Ritchey said. "The object appeared to be about two miles away and to be flying parallel with him. Radar confirmed that he was between two and three miles from the object."

The Washington Post (July 28, 1952) reported that long-range radar at Andrews AFB registered the UFOs from about 7:30 p.m. (EST) to about 11:00 p.m. (The CAA report on Washington radar sightings, although it has a column for that purpose, does not mention any Air Force radar sightings on either July 19/20 or July 26/27).

Date	Time	Location	Description
26	night	California	Air Defense Command radar tracked a UFO, F-94C scrambled, locked on with radar, crew saw large yellow-orange light. Ground and airborne radar both showed that when jet would get close, UFO would suddenly accelerate and pull away, then slow down and let jet catch up again. Object "Unknown" [13].
27	10:40 a.m.	Ann Arbor, Mich.	Scientist observed 15 glowing UFOs in formation. [Section VI.]
27	6:35 p.m.	Manhattan Beach, Calif.	Eight people, including aviation engineer, watched maneuvers of seven discs in formations of two and three. [Section VI.]
27	7:30 p.m.	Riverdale, Md.	Air Force Lt. Wales, Andrews AFB, saw dark disc moving slowly NE with "oscillating rolling motion." Clouds were moving SE. UFO entered base of clouds. [CAA Report. See Section VIII; Radar.]
	10:00	Andrews AFB, Maryland	Air Force Major Turlin reported unidentified yellow light which "moved slowly, stopped, flickered, moved in arc." [CAA Report]
27/28	1:00-5:00 a.m.	South Central Indiana	Round UFOs with visible "exhausts" were seen by police, Civil Defense, military personnel and hundreds of citizens in 20 or more counties.
	1:00 a.m.	Shelby County, Indiana	State policemen at opposite ends of county watched a maneuvering starlike object which alternately hovered, moved up and down, back & forth.
	3:00 a.m.	Franklin, Indiana	Civil Defense and police saw one orange and one white light chasing each other as if in a dogfight.
	2:30 a.m.	Nr St. Paul, Minn.	Air Force radar tracked UFOs, which appeared visually to pilots as rapidly moving lights. [14]
28	7:55 a.m.	Geneva, N. Y.	Hovering elliptical UFO sighted. Vapor trails, apparently from interceptors, converged on object, it rose straight up and disappeared into cloud bank.

Daily papers headlined story that Air Defense Command had ordered its jet pilots to pursue, and if necessary "shoot down," UFOs sighted anywhere in country (15).

28/29	1:30-5:00 a.m.	Washington, D. C.	Many unidentified targets tracked by CAA radar in belt 15 miles wide, objects moving SE. Eight to twelve UFOs on radar scopes at one time.
	3:00 a.m.	Washington, D. C.	Eastern Airlines pilot was asked to check on radar targets, reported seeing nothing. CAA official said the targets disappeared from the radar screen when the plane was in their area, "then came back in behind him." [16]
29	day	Chicago, Ill.	U. S. Rocket Society president wired Defense Department and President Truman urging them to restrain pilots from shooting at UFOs. "Should they be extraterrestrial, such action might result in the gravest consequences..." Rumors that many prominent scientists wired President Truman expressing similar views.
29	day	Washington, D. C.	*Air Force called press conference on UFO sightings,*

attended by more than 40 reporters. Suggested UFOs were probably temperature inversions or unexplained natural phenomena causing radar mirages, but announced USAF was calling in top scientists to evaluate sightings; setting up special grid cameras to determine nature of light from UFOs. Stressed lack of any menace to country.

29	noon	Los Alamos, N.M.	Shiny, apparently metallic UFO watched by ground observers through binoculars. Jet interceptors scrambled, observers saw UFO turn and move behind the jets. [17]
	afternoon	Albuquerque, N.M.	Air Force Reserve Colonel, at Los Alamos Atomic Energy Commission station, saw a yellowish elliptical object speed overhead. [18]
	3:00 p.m.	Nr Washington, D. C.	Air Force pilot sighted three round white UFOs 10 miles SE of Andrews AFB, Maryland. CAA Report. Other UFOs tracked by CAA radar during afternoon.
	9:35 p.m.	Miami, Florida	Marine Corps photographer obtained 40 feet of movie film showing a UFO; image described as "bowl-shaped with a projection on top." [Section VIII; Photographs.]
	About 10:45 p.m. (EST)	Michigan	Air Defense Command radar tracked a UFO, moving at 550 knots. Chased by F-94's; one got a radar lock-on; bright flashing light seen at the same time, same position. [19]
30	day	Washington, D. C.	International News Service reported:

"Radar experts and weather scientists today declined to endorse the Air Force theory that 'flying saucers' are ground objects reflected in the sky under freak atmospheric conditions. (CAA radar men) maintained that what they have seen were 'unknown objects,' twisting and swerving in an unexplainable pattern. . . A Weather Bureau official said that reflections due to such inversion ordinarily would appear on a radar screen as a steady line, rather than as single objects such as were sighted on the airport radarscope."

The Operation Mainbrace Sightings

After UFO reports in the United States had begun to taper off in August 1952, a wave of sightings began in Europe. All over the continent, strangely maneuvering objects were seen in the skies. A particularly interesting series of reports came from the vicinity of the "Operation Mainbrace" NATO maneuvers then in progress.

The maneuvers commenced September 13, and lasted 12 days. "Units of 8 NATO governments and New Zealand participated, including 80,000 men, 1,000 planes and 200 ships . . . in the vicinity of Denmark and Norway ..." They were directed by British Admiral Sir Patrick Brind. "It was the largest NATO maneuver held up until that time." (Information from U.S. Navy).
September 13 - The Danish Destroyer "Willemoes," participating in the maneuvers, was north of Bornholm Island. During the night, Lt. Cmdr. Schmidt Jensen and several members of the crew saw an unidentified object, triangular in shape, which moved at high speed toward the southeast. The object emitted a bluish glow. Cmdr. Jensen estimated the speed at over 900 mph [20]

Within the next week, there were four important sightings by well-qualified observers. (Various sources differ by a day or two on the exact dates, but agree on details. There is no question about the authenticity of the sightings; the British cases were officially reported by the Air Ministry, the others are confirmed by reliable sources. All occurred on or about September 20).

About September 20 - A British Meteor jet was returning to the airfield at Topcliffe, Yorks., England just before 11:00 a.m. As he approached for landing, a silvery object was observed following him, swaying back and forth like a pendulum. Lt. John W. Kilburn and other observers on the ground said that when the Meteor began circling, the UFO stopped. It was disc-shaped, and rotated on its axis while hovering. Suddenly, the disc took off westward at high speed, changed course, and disappeared to the southeast. The Air Ministry announced it was investigating. [21]
About September 20 - Personnel of the U.S. Aircraft Carrier Franklin D. Roosevelt, participating in the Mainbrace maneuvers, observed a silvery, spherical object which was also photographed. (The pictures have never been made public). The UFO was seen moving across the sky behind the fleet. Reporter Wallace Litwin took a series of color photographs, which were examined by Navy Intelligence officers. The Air Force UFO project chief, Capt. Ruppelt stated: "[The pictures] turned out to be excellent ... judging by the size of the object in each successive photo, one could see that it was moving rapidly." The possibility that a balloon had been launched from one of the ships was immediately checked out. No one had launched a balloon. [22]
September 20 - At Karup Field, Denmark, three Danish Air Force officers sighted a UFO about 7:30 p.m. The object, a shiny disc with metallic appearance, passed overhead from the direction of the fleet and disappeared in clouds to the east. [23]
September 21 - Six Royal Air Force Pilots flying a formation of jets above the North Sea observed a shiny sphere approaching

162

from the direction of the fleet. The UFO eluded their pursuit and disappeared. When returning to base, one of the pilots looked back and saw the UFO following him. He turned to chase it, but the UFO also turned and sped away. [24]

September 27/28 - Throughout western Germany, Denmark, and southern Sweden, there were widespread UFO reports. A brightly luminous object with a comet-like tail was visible for a long period of time moving irregularly near Hamburg and Kiel. Once, three satellite objects were reported moving around a larger object [cf., Section II; Satellite Object cases]. A cigar-shaped object moving silently eastward also was reported. [25]

The November 1957 "Flap"

When the Soviet Union launched the first earth satellite, October 4, 1957, Americans suddenly became "space (and sky) conscious." Amateur astronomers and average citizens strained for a glimpse of the barely visible sphere. However, there was no particular increase of UFO reports. The whole month of October produced no more than 4-5 substantial UFO cases in the United States. One of the most intriguing accounts, never fully investigated, described a whitish oval-shaped object observed in the vicinity of Cape Canaveral on the nights of October 6 and 7. [26]

Immediately following the launching of the dog-carrying Sputnik II, late on the evening of November 2 (Eastern Standard Time), the country was suddenly inundated with UFO reports. The sightings actually began before word of the satellite launching was flashed to the western world. Most of the significant reports concerned very large, usually elliptical objects, observed on or near the ground (not merely fleeting lights in the sky). The possibility that hysteria played a part in the reports which followed cannot be ruled out entirely. But clearly it is not the whole answer. Reliable witnesses soberly described plainly observed UFOs, and the press gave their stories very full coverage.

Before the sightings began to taper off two weeks later, eager citizens began to introduce many erroneous reports. After elliptical UFOs were reported daily in the press for a week, people began to scan the sky hoping to see one for themselves. The planet Venus, glowing prominently in the early evening sky to the WSW, was often reported as a UFO by inexperienced sky observers. To complicate matters, there was a spectacular auroral display the evening of November 6, which was also visible unusually far south. The flashing red auroral lights, in some cases, were transformed into "UFOs." An occasional fireball (exceptionally bright and long-lasting meteor) flashed through the skies, adding to the confusion.

The features of the UFO reports which defied explanation were the consistent descriptions of red to reddish-orange, egg-shaped (roughly elliptical) objects on or near the ground, and electrical failures experienced in their vicinity. For the month of November, NICAP has records of 118 apparently reliable

sightings. In approximately one of every three cases, electro-magnetic (E-M) interference was reported. Subsequent research showed that E-M effects associated with UFOs were not uncommon, [Section VIII].

By November 3, newspapers were full of UFO reports; by November 5 the reports were given banner headlines. Also on the 5th, the Air Force issued a special press release to the effect that no evidence of UFOs had been found and all except 2% of the reports had been explained. The release did not even mention the sightings then in progress. A second press release November 15, after which the reports virtually died out, listed and debunked five specific cases which had been widely publicized. [Section IX].

An Air Force press release nearly a year later (No. 986-58) listed 414 sightings for November 1957. About 64% (266) were explained as stars and planets, aircraft and balloons. Only four were listed as "unknown;" 70 as "insufficient data." The Air Force gave no weight to reports of electro-magnetic interference, later stating "the number of cases involving car stallings is negligible." (Air Force letter on file at NICAP)

Anything reported to the Air Force as a UFO is included in their statistics. This procedure makes it a foregone conclusion that only a comparatively small percentage of total reports might remain which would be difficult to fit into a known category. NICAP considers it a more meaningful approach to first weed out fairly obvious reports of meteors, etc., then to study the remainder of more substantial reports as a group. The percentage of mistaken observations is considered irrelevant.

November 1957			
	Sightings	Explained	Insufficient data	Unknown
Air Force:	414	340	70	4

NICAP: After weeding out process, 118 cases not readily attributable to conventional objects or phenomena.

The following chronology lists the 118 cases which appear to be authentic and presently unexplainable, plus a few unverified or probably explainable incidents (in italics) to give a more complete picture of what was being reported at the time. The information is drawn from many sources, including signed or taped reports, investigation reports compiled by NICAP personnel, and newspaper and radio reports when cross-checks have given reasonable assurance the data is reliable.

Because of the flood of published information on UFOs at the time, it is likely that minor inaccuracies or inconsistencies will subsequently be discovered. On the whole, the picture given is believed to be essentially accurate. Collectively, the reports are too widespread and consistent to be ignored. They have not been adequately explained in conventional terms, and apparently cannot be so explained.

THE NOVEMBER 1957 "FLAP"
Chronology

Date	Location	Time	Description
1	Nr Coleman, Texas (200 miles SE of Levelland)	2:00 a.m.	Oblong, reddish object hovered, maneuvered over area, seen by 4 members of oil drilling crew.
1	Sandia Mountains, New Mexico	6:20 a.m.	Secretary saw glowing oblong object which hovered, then rose out of sight.
1	Nr Campbellsville, Kentucky	4:30 p.m.	Boy Scout executive: elongated luminous white UFO, accelerated and sped away.
1	Johannesburg, South Africa	Day	Two UFOs, one a reflective disc; one flew S at high speed, 2nd hovered, then followed first.
2	Amarillo, Texas	8:30 p.m.	UFO reported on road south of city; car engines stalled. (Later, pilot reported UFO to control tower.)
2	Nr Seminole, New Mexico	About 8:30 p.m.	Motorist reported to sheriff he saw lights on road, car lights and engine failed; object on road suddenly rose and sped away.
2	Clemens, North Carolina	9:12 p.m.	Woman saw elliptical UFO, bright yellow, speed behind cloudbank.
2/3	Levelland, Texas	About 10:50 p.m.	Torpedo-shaped object, making loud explosive noise, rose from field and passed low over truck. Truck lights and engine failed. (Pedro Saucedo)

163

Date	Location	Time	Description
2/3	Pettit, Texas (Near Levelland)	----	Two grain combines failed as UFO passed.
2/3	Nr Levelland, Texas	About midnight	Large elliptical object on road; car lights and engine failed; UFO rose; when it blinked out, headlights came back on. (Jim Wheeler)
2/3	Nr Levelland, Texas	About Midnight	Man saw UFO on road, car lights and engine failed. (Jose Alvarez)
2/3	Nr Levelland, Texas	12:05 p.m.	Glowing blue-green object on road, car lights and engine failed. (Newell Wright)
2/3	Nr Levelland, Texas	12:15 a.m.	Elliptical UFO on road; car lights and engine failed each time object pulsated to bright phase; UFO rose straight up with explosive sound. (Frank Williams)
2/3	Nr Levelland, Texas	12:45 a.m.	Round, glowing orange UFO landed, changed to blue-green; truck lights and engine failed; UFO took off straight up. (Ronald Martin)
2/3	17 miles N of Levelland, Texas	About 1:00 a.m.	Fire Marshal Ray Jones reported seeing a "streak of light," car lights dimmed and engine "almost died."
2/3	Nr Levelland, Texas	1:15 a.m.	Elliptical UFO on road, truck lights and engine failed; UFO rose with a "thunderclap." (James Long)
2/3	Levelland, Texas	1:30 a.m.	Sheriff Weir Clem and deputy saw oval red light while investigating reports of same.
3	White Sands, New Mexico	3:00 a.m.	Army jeep patrol reported elliptical UFO which descended, hovered.
3	Cincinnati, Ohio	About 6:00 p.m.	Round white UFO leaving reddish trail, just above treetops; rose rapidly out of sight.
3	Scotia, Nebraska	About 6:00 p.m.	Boy saw oblong object with apparent antenna, at low altitude as if about to land; object circled (emitting hum) and moved away. (Boy felt numbness.) [Section VIII].
3	Nr Calgary, Alberta, Canada	7:00 p.m.	Very large blinking light passed over car; motor coughed and headlights flickered.
3	White Sands, New Mexico	8:00 p.m.	Second Army jeep patrol reported UFO maneuvering above test base.
3	Nr Monroe, Louisiana	Night	Bright object hovering near ground reported to police; UFO "suddenly rose rapidly straight up and vanished into the sky."
3	Barahona, Dominican Republic	----	Numerous people observed disc-shaped UFOs from an estimated distance of 100 yards; objects hovered about 2 minutes, moved away rapidly.
3	Johannesburg, South Africa	----	Cylindrical UFO observed hovering for 2 hours; ascended out of sight.
3/4	Ararangua, Brazil	1:20 a.m.	Airline pilot saw red light describe arc near plane; aircraft electrical equipment affected. [Section X]
3/4	Sao Vicente, Brazil	2:00 a.m.	Disc approached, hovered near Itaipu Fort; sentries severely burned. [Section VIII]
3/4	Elmwood, Illinois	About 2:30 a.m.	Police chased elongated reddish UFO; cruiser lights affected.
3/4	N.M. desert	4:30 a.m.	Salesman saw round ball of red light size of moon, hovering, moving slowly above desert.
4	Nr Orogrande, New Mexico	1:10 p.m.	James W. Stokes, high altitude research engineer at White Sands, saw elliptical UFO sweep across highway twice; car radio and engine failed.
4	Stinnet, Wisconsin	4:45 p.m.	Minister, others, saw silvery disc move slowly overhead.
4	Kodiak, Alaska	10:00 p.m.	Policeman saw fiery red object trailing greenish-yellow vapor pass low over school; interference on cruiser radio.
4	Toronto, Ontario, Canada	----	Television interference (audio); viewers were called outdoors to see UFO.
4	Johannesburg, South Africa	Night	Cylindrical UFO caught in searchlight beams.
November 5 (By time zones) Eastern Standard Time			
5	Philadelphia, Pennsylvania	Early morning	Fiery disc in sky; electric power failed.
5	New York, New York	4:30 a.m.	Disc with dome and visible "portholes" hovered, sped away.
5	S. Springfield, Ohio	About 4:50 a.m.	Police saw brilliant blue light in sky; two cars had engine trouble.
5	Fort Oglethorpe, Georgia	3:10 p.m.	Round, brilliant orange UFO hovered, revolving; television blacked out.
5	Norfolk, Virginia	4:00 p.m.	White glaring object (no shape discernible) sped overhead at "a pretty good clip;" observed by electric power company employees.
5	Haverhill, Mass.	4:30 p.m.	GOC spotters watched disc-like UFO bob around in sky. [Section VII]
5	Aiken, Georgia	Night	Bright yellowish cigar-shaped object observed twice, finally disappeared over horizon.

Date	Location	Time	Description
5	Port Arthur, Ontario, Canada	7:30 p.m.	Brilliant elliptical object observed travelling at high speed, low on horizon.

Central Standard Time:

Date	Location	Time	Description
5	Galesburg, Illinois	About 4:30 a.m.	Orange elliptical object hovered, then moved away slowly to the north.
5	Gulf of Mexico	5:10 a.m.	Coast Guard cutter Sebago began tracking UFO on radar; brilliant planet-like UFO seen visually at 5:21 a.m. [Section VIII; Radar]
5	Keesler AFB, Mississippi	About 5:20 a.m.	Airman saw elliptical UFO travel S to N, accelerate rapidly and enter clouds.
5	Wichita Falls, Texas	10:00 a.m.	Oblong UFO observed moving back and forth, in and out of rain clouds.
5	E. St. Louis, Illinois	11:45 a.m.	Two silvery elliptical objects passing overhead at high speed, observed by Southern Railroad employees.
5	Nr Kearney, Nebraska	----	TWA airline pilot reported seeing high-speed, brightly lighted object.
5	Hedley, Texas	Dusk	Pulsating bluish-green object seen low above ground, television affected.
5	Nr Wabash, Indiana	6:12 p.m.	UFO with lights in circular pattern made three passes low over barn, emitting humming sound.
5	Dauphin, Manitoba, Canada	6:20 p.m.	UFO variously described as round and silvery, orange and egg-shaped, reported by about 20 people over wide area.
5	Winnipeg, Manitoba, Canada	6:40 p.m.	Shiny silver UFO hovered, moved from side to side; left toward SW emitting slight trail, as RCAF aircraft were seen approaching.
5	Nr Ringwood, Ill.	Evening	Luminous round object bobbing up and down, followed car for some time; one witness reported "swishing" noise from object.
5	Red Bank, Tenn.	6:30 p.m.	Glowing, pulsating object at edge of overcast; finally ascended out of sight.
5	Houston, Texas	6:25 p.m.	Bright planet-like object moved overhead in zig-zag, irregular course.
5	Houston, Texas	7:00 p.m.	Round white object about 1/4 size of moon, passed overhead and over SE horizon in 15 seconds, making roaring noise.
5	Nr San Antonio, Texas	Abt 9:30 p.m.	Car lights, engine and radio failed; driver then saw elliptical UFO hovering above field; object ascended rapidly, levelled off and sped away.
5	Kansas City, Mo.	11:15 p.m.	Round, reddish-orange UFO passed from SE to SW.

Mountain Standard Time:

Date	Location	Time	Description
5	Alamogordo, N.M.	4:34 p.m.	Civilian radar technician saw orange cigar-shaped object hovering in west.
5	Hobbs, N.M.	7:30 p.m.	Two separate reports of light which paralleled car, passed directly over car; car lights and engines failed.

Pacific Standard Time:

Date	Location	Time	Description
5	Nr Dixon, Calif.	2:30 a.m.	Trucker reported meteor-like object which descended rapidly, slowed and hovered, pulsating.
5	Nr Sacramento, Calif.	3:00 a.m.	Bluish-green elliptical object moving vertically.
5	Long Beach, Calif.	Abt 3:50 a.m.	Six shiny circular objects maneuvering "like planes in a dogfight," reported by AF Major.
5	Corona del Mar, California	6:04 p.m.	Bright circular orange object, like a "jack-o-lantern," hovered above ocean.

Southern Transvaal, Africa:

Date	Location	Time	Description
5	Dunnotar, Transvaal, and vicinity	Night	Hundreds watched an "enormous" hovering cylindrical object; observers said UFO "withdrew" behind clouds when searchlights pinpointed it.

November 6 (by time zones)

Eastern Standard Time:

Date	Location	Time	Description
6	*United States*	*Evening & night*	*Spectacular auroral display observed over wide area. Caused many erroneous UFO reports by citizens who had been reading about sightings for days.*
6	Atlanta, Ga.	5:27 a.m.	Orange, oval-shaped object, darted behind cloud, reappeared, moved out of sight behind buildings.
6	*Florida West Coast*	*5:20-5:30 a.m.*	*Widespread sightings of "ball of fire;" possible meteor.*
6	Toronto, Ont., Canada	7:00 a.m.	Cigar-shaped object with fins near front moved from E to W leaving trail; turned N, then S. [Cf., January 20, 1951 pilot sighting, Section V.]
6	Toronto, Ont., Canada	7:15 a.m.	Shiny cigar-shaped object; alternately hovered, moved slowly.
6	100 mi. north of Ottawa, Canada	9:00-9:30 p.m.	A group of electronic technicians and ham radio operators saw a huge brightly-lighted sphere projecting beams of light, hovering above hill; two radios failed, except for rapidly modulated strong single tone picked up on one frequency. UFO finally disappeared into clouds.

Date	Location	Time	Description
6	Nr Montville, Ohio	11:20 p.m.	Olden J. Moore saw flattened spherical object with conical projection on top descend toward field; above-normal radiation later detected by Civil Defense.

Central Standard Time:

Date	Location	Time	Description
6	Nr Pell City, Alabama	Abt 4:30 a.m.	Milkman saw glow in sky, car engine failed; left to obtain aid and saw oblong object hovering low above ground.
6	Houston, Texas	4:30 a.m.	Reddish elliptical UFO moving at high speed observed as car engine failed.
6	*Dante, Tenn.*	*6:30 a.m.*	*Reported landing of elliptical object, four human-like figures seen. (not verified by NICAP.)*
6	Richmond, Ind.	----	Reddish elliptical UFO, changing to green and blue, reported by employees at police truck weighing station; UFO zig-zagged S in eastern sky.
6	Dugger, Ind.	Night	Iron worker reported brilliant round object hovered low overhead, moved up and away to west; witness treated for eye inflammation. [Section VIII.]
6	Marion, Ind.	About 7:30 p.m.	Many residents saw cigar-shaped object with string of very bright lights hovering; then moved away at high speed.
6	Nr Danville, Ill.	Night	State Troopers chased brilliant white UFO for 15 miles, experienced failure of their short wave radio; during chase, object changed color to amber, then bright orange. [Section VII.]
6	Western Springs, Illinois	8:04 p.m.	Brilliant orange light with corona effect moved S, accelerated (emitting short trail), turned east and moved out of sight.
6	Chattanooga, Tenn.	8:05 p.m.	Large reddish-orange light leaving short trail observed moving S to N.

Mountain Standard Time:

Date	Location	Time	Description
6	Santa Fe, N.M.	12:01 a.m.	Elliptical UFO passed low over car emitting a hum; car engine, clock, and wristwatch stopped. (Joe Martinez)
6	*Western U.S. & Alberta, Canada*	*6:00-9:00 p.m.*	*Several observations of irregular lights; probably explainable as aurora.*

Pacific Standard Time:

Date	Location	Time	Description
6	*Anaheim, Calif.*	*12:10 a.m.*	*Moving reddish light appearing and disappearing, photographed by Edwin G. Leadford (See Section VIII) Description resembles aurora.*
6	Palm Springs, California	5:06 p.m.	Shiny circular object leaving trail approached, doubled back over mountains.

November 7 (by time zones)

Eastern Standard Time:

Date	Location	Time	Description
7	Thompson, Ohio	6:15 a.m.	Orange UFO shaped like flattened sphere, glowing brilliantly; hovered, moved away.
7	Atlanta, Ga.	9:35 a.m.	Reddish elliptical object hovered.
7	Washington, D. C.	Abt 6:30 p.m.	Magazine staff member watched hovering red light suddenly move east at high speed, turn north, stop, then move on out of sight.
7	Nr Erie, Pa.	9:45 p.m.	Seven people watched row of brilliant lights with bright green light at rear sweep over the area twice in few minutes.

Central Standard Time:

Date	Location	Time	Description
7	*Nr Meridian, Miss.*	*7:25 a.m.*	*Large elliptical object reported on highway by trucker, who said three small beings approached him. (Story not verified by NICAP.)*
7	Lake Charles, La.	7:45 a.m.	Car engine failed; silvery disc seen hovering low overhead then sped away.

Mountain Standard Time:

Date	Location	Time	Description
7	Nr Orogrande, N.M.	9:30 p.m.	Family reported observing cylindrical UFO; car's speedometer apparently affected as object passed overhead.

Pacific Standard Time:

Date	Location	Time	Description
7	Palm Springs, California	5:40-6:25 a.m.	Two people watched first a cigar-shaped object, then a sphere, maneuver over area.

- -

Date	Location	Time	Description
8	Au Sable Forks, N. Y.	2:55 p.m.	Silvery reflective object, alternating from round to oval (like a disc oscillating from side to side) pacing a bomber; observed from ground.
8	Orgueil, France	Abt 6:30 p.m.	Disc-shaped UFO with dome, hovered, rotated, moved away and disappeared with sudden burst of speed.
9	Lafayette, La.	9:15 a.m.	Eastern Airlines pilot, crew, watched round silvery object hovering just below cloud layer; object vanished suddenly after 3 minutes.

Date	Location	Time	Description
9	Sacramento, California	3:45 p.m.	Three disc-shaped objects observed bobbing up and down, circling, in eastern sky.
9	Nr White Oaks, N.M.	7:30 p.m.	Car lights failed as bright light approached; object then changed course and sped away.
9	Entre Rios Province, Argentina	10:55 a.m.	Four luminous objects emitting brilliant trails moved rapidly overhead N to S, crossing 40 degrees and disappearing in 10-12 minutes.
10	Madison, Ohio	Abt 1:25 a.m.	Mrs. Leita Kuhn watched brilliant UFO hovering low overhead; rash, eye damage, other physiological effects reported to NICAP. [Section VIII.]
10	Hammond, Ind.	7:00 p.m.	Police chased elongated object; loud beeping sound interfered with cruiser radios, television blackout reported. [Section VII.]
11	Strum, Wisconsin	8:20 a.m.	Silver, tube-shaped object, no trail, moved slowly overhead toward NW.
11	Nr Los Angeles, California	Day	Elliptical, silvery UFO observed moving low above desert, from airliner approaching Los Angeles. [Section VII.]
11	San Fernando Valley, California	4:20 p.m.	Three elliptical silvery objects climbing at high speed observed by aeronautical engineers. [Section VI.]
11	Pittsburgh, Pennsylvania	5:00 p.m.	Moonwatch observers saw two round shiny objects leaving long fire-like trails, moving easterly.
12	Fitchburg, Mass.	12:35 a.m.	Many people watched two bright lights approach from opposite directions, hover together, bobbing up and down.
12	Rumney, N.H.	10:20 p.m.	Car engine failed, lights went out; man saw red light moving away.
12 or 13	Hazelton, Pa.	----	Television disrupted as UFO seen.
14	Sacramento, California	Abt 5:00 p.m.	Brilliant oval UFO moving across eastern sky and into heavy cloudbank, seen by employees of Signal Depot.
14	Tamuroa, Ill.	----	Very bright circular object hovering, making sputtering or explosive sounds; gave off three flashes, electric power failed in area.
14	Austin, Texas	8:00 p.m.	Bright round object, moved up and down, from side to side.
14	San Bernardino Mts., Calif.	Night	"Globe of white light" observed by pilot; blinked in seeming response to his signals. [Section V.]
15	Smith County, Tennessee	6:45-9:30 p.m.	State Police, sheriff, others repeatedly saw flashing, revolving red lights which hovered, moved around slowly. [Section VII.]
15	Wheaton, Md.	8:00 p.m.	Two prominent, self-luminous objects in echelon passed from NE to SW at high speed.
15	Cachoeira, Brazil	2:00 p.m.	Car engines failed, UFO hovering low above ground.
16	Lemmon, S.D.	Night	UFO followed train into railroad yard, hovered, then sped away; railroad phones and automatic block system failed.
20	Nr McMinnville, Tennessee	Abt 10:00 p.m.	Flashing red light passed low over sheriff's car; calling in other police, sheriff gave chase; unable to catch UFO.
21	Compton, N.H.	6:05 p.m.	Brilliant oblong object moved rapidly overhead to E, stopped and hovered, pulsating; later sped west.
22	Canutillo, Texas	Abt 4:00 p.m.	Hovering silvery UFO sped up, moved back and forth, climbed out of sight. [Section VII.]
23	Tiro, Ohio	6:30 p.m.	Disc-like object paced car, swung back and forth, up and down.
25	Mogi Mirim, Brazil	Abt 10:00 p.m.	City lights failed as 3 circular UFOs passed overhead.
26	Baton Rouge, Louisiana	11:15 a.m.	Three flat silvery objects in V-formation, moving slowly W in the northern sky.
30	Murphysboro, Illinois	Afternoon	Three white oval objects in V-formation moving rapidly west.

Date	Number	E-M	Main Locations
1	4	0	----------------
2*	7	6	Texas--New Mexico
3*	14	6	Levelland, Texas
4	9	6	New Mexico, Brazil
5	31	7	California, Texas
6	16	6	Illinois--Indiana
7	7	2	Scattered
8	2	0	----------------
9	4	1	----------------
10	2	1	----------------
11	4	0	----------------
12**	3	2	----------------
13	0	0	----------------
14	4	1	----------------
15	3	1	----------------
Sub-Totals	110	39	

(From the 16th through the 30th, not more than one substantial case per day is on record, and one E-M case.)

| 16-30 | 8 | 1 | ---------------- |
| Totals, 1-30: | 118 | 40 | |

* Cases on night of November 2/3 whose times are given as "about midnight" are included in November 2.
**Case with uncertain date included under November 12.

Levelland, Texas

The first series of sightings to be widely publicized, and the most intensive single concentration, occurred on the night of November 2/3 in and around Levelland, Texas. The first recorded sighting was at about 10:50 p.m.; the last at 1:30 a.m. In less than three hours, there were 10 very similar sightings within a radius of 20 miles around Levelland. (see map).

Why should reddish elliptical UFOs which caused cars to stall suddenly be reported from one small Texas town? No answer is apparent. Within a few hours after the last Levelland sighting, an Army jeep patrol at White Sands proving grounds, about 300 miles to the west, reported an elliptical UFO which descended and hovered. (See below). The following account of the Levelland reports was compiled by Walter N. Webb, NICAP Adviser.

Levelland is an oil and cotton town, population about 10,000, located in northwest Texas 32 miles west of Lubbock, in plains country. Early on November 3 its sheriff, Weir Clem, suddenly found himself cast into national prominence following a rapid series of nightmarish reports.

At 10:50 p.m. Officer A. J. Fowler received a phone call from a "terrified" farmhand, Pedro Saucedo. He and a friend, Joe Salaz, were driving on Route 116 about 4 miles west of Levelland when they saw a flash of light in a field. "We didn't think much about it," Saucedo said, "but then it rose up out of the field and started toward us, picking up speed. When it got nearer, the lights of my truck went out and the motor died. I jumped out and hit the deck as the thing passed directly over the truck with a great sound and a rush of wind. It sounded like thunder, and my truck rocked from the blast. I felt a lot of heat."

When the object had passed, Saucedo got up and watched it go out of sight toward Levelland. It was "torpedo-shaped, like a rocket," and about 200 feet long. As the UFO moved into the distance, the truck lights came back on. Saucedo was able to start the truck and drive to a telephone. Ptn. Fowler thought his caller was drunk and shrugged off the report.

About an hour later, the phone rang again. Jim Wheeler, driving on Route 116 about 4 miles east of town had come upon a 200-foot egg-shaped thing sitting on the road. The brightly lit object cast a glare over the area. As he approached the object, his lights and motor died. When Wheeler started to get out of his car, the UFO rose into the sky. As its light blinked out, the car lights came back on.

Another call came from Jose Alvarez at Whitharral, 11 miles north of town. Driving on Route 51, he had approached a similar glowing object on the road and his motor and lights had failed.

At 12:05 a.m., Newell Wright (who did not report the experience until the next day, and then only at his parents' urging) had "motor trouble" while driving toward Levelland on Route 116 from the east. His ammeter began jumping, the motor gradually died, then the lights went out. Puzzled, Wright got out and lifted the hood to check his battery and wires. Finding nothing wrong, he closed the hood and turned around. For the first time, he noticed an oval object sitting on the road ahead of the car. The object appeared to be over 100 feet long, and was glowing a bluish-green. Frightened, Wright jumped in the car and frantically tried to get it started, without success. Then he sat helplessly watching the object, hoping someone would drive up. After several minutes, the UFO rose "almost straight up," veered to the north, and disappeared almost instantly. The car then started without difficulty.

Meanwhile, another telephone report was made at 12:15 a.m. Frank Williams had encountered a similar object on the road close to the position where Alvarez had seen it. He also experienced motor and headlight failure. The light from the UFO was pulsating steadily on and off; each time it came on, Williams' lights went out. Finally it rose swiftly with a noise like thunder, and disappeared. Then the car functioned normally.

By this time, Sheriff Clem and other police officers had begun searching the roads around Levelland, as reports continued to come in. At 12:45 a.m., Ronald Martin saw a glowing reddish UFO descend and land on Route 116 ahead of his truck, then turn to bluish-green. The electrical system of the truck failed. When the object took off, it turned reddish again.

About 1:15 a.m., James Long encountered a glowing egg-shaped object on a farm-to-market highway just north of town. His engines and lights failed. Then the object rose quickly and sped away.

About 1:30 a.m., Sheriff Clem and his deputy were searching on the same road. Near where Long had seen the UFO, Clem saw an oval light "like a brilliant red sunset" streak across the road about 300 yards ahead of his car, lighting up the pavement. Fire Marshal Ray Jones, farther to the north, had a similar experience sometime after 1:00 a.m.; his lights dimmed and motor "almost died, then started up again."

The Pettit incident, same night, was uncovered during an investigation by NICAP member James Lee. Two grain combines, each with two engines, failed as a UFO was observed passing.

An impressive feature of these reports is that the witnesses (in most cases) were going about their business when the UFOs intruded upon the scene. There is no evidence that the witnesses were searching the sky or otherwise expecting to see anything unusual. Their independent reports told a consistent story.

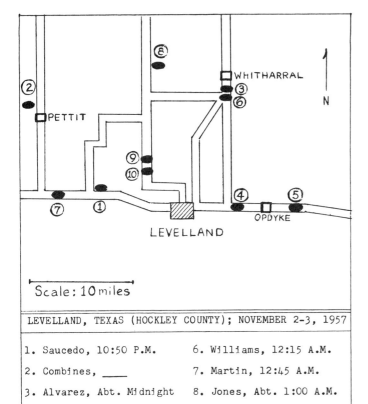

Scale: 10 miles

LEVELLAND, TEXAS (HOCKLEY COUNTY); NOVEMBER 2-3, 1957

1. Saucedo, 10:50 P.M.	6. Williams, 12:15 A.M.
2. Combines, _____	7. Martin, 12:45 A.M.
3. Alvarez, Abt. Midnight	8. Jones, Abt. 1:00 A.M.
4. Wheeler, Abt. Midnight	9. Long, 1:15 A.M.
5. Wright, 12:05 A.M.	10. Clem, 1:30 A.M.

White Sands Military Police Patrols

At 3:00 a.m. (MST) - 4:00 a.m. Levelland time - November 3, two military policemen on routine patrol at the White Sands missile range, reported an egg-shaped UFO which descended over the base. A report on this case, and a similar sighting next evening, was issued to the press November 4 by 1st Lt. Miles F. Penney, Commanding Officer of the Stallion Site Camp north of the base headquarters.

Cpl. Glenn H. Toy and Pfc. James Wilbanks, patrolling in a jeep, noticed a "very bright object" high in the sky. The object descended to a point about 50 yards above a bunker which was used during the first atomic bomb explosion. Then its light blinked out. A few minutes later the light flared up again, becoming bright "like the sun," dropped toward the ground on a slant about 3 miles away and disappeared. According to Lt. Penney, the M.P.'s described the UFO as egg-shaped, and about 75-100 yards in diameter. A search party later was unable to find any trace of the object.

[On November 5, in an open session with Public Information Officer William Haggard and newsmen (reported by International News Service), Cpl. Toy stated: "It looked like a completely controlled landing."]

That evening, about 8:00 p.m., Sp. 3/C Forest R. Oakes and Sp. 3/C Barlow, on another two-man jeep patrol, reported seeing an unidentified light hanging above the old A-bomb bunker. Oakes described it as "200 or 300 feet long. . . very bright." The patrol was about 2-3 miles west of the bunker. As the M.P.'s watched, the UFO took off climbing at a 45 degree angle, its light pulsating on and off. Moving slowly, sometimes stopping, the UFO gradually diminished to a point of light "like a big star," and finally disappeared.

White Sands Engineer

About 17 hours after the second jeep patrol sighting at White Sands, James Stokes, a high altitude research engineer at the base, watched an elliptical UFO maneuver over the area. While driving toward El Paso, Texas, on Highway 54, near Orogrande, N.M. (at the southeast corner of the Proving Grounds, about 15 miles from the Missile Test Center), Stokes began experiencing motor trouble. As the motor failed and he coasted to a stop, he noticed other cars ahead of him stopped on the roadside with people looking up and pointing to the sky.

Climbing out of his car, Stokes also looked up and saw a large, whitish egg-shaped object moving in and out of clouds to the northeast, in the direction of the Sacramento Mountains. The UFO made a shallow dive, turned and crossed the highway a few miles ahead. As the UFO flashed by, Stokes felt a wave of heat. (His face later appeared "sunburned.")

Moving at fantastic speed, the featureless object turned sharply and disappeared over the Organ Pass west of the base. In a taped interview broadcast on station KALG, Stokes estimated the speed at 2500 mph. It was "definitely a solid object," he said.

Declining to speculate on what the object was, Stokes said, "I just hope we're ready for whatever it is." [27]

Next day sightings reached a peak with numerous reports from all over the country. Included was the radar-visual sighting by the Coast Guard Cutter Sebago, south of New Orleans. [Section VIII; Radar.] Stories of alleged encounters with "spacemen" began to be reported, including a claim by a grain salesman in Nebraska who said he had met German-speaking beings in a landed spaceship. The story was subsequently discredited when it was learned that the "witness" had a prison record. (Later, he was convicted of two counts of swindling elderly women out of large sums of money in California).

On the 6th, a similar report came from Dante, Tennessee, where a young boy reported a landed "spaceship" at 6:30 a.m. Human-like figures were walking near the ship, he said, and their voices sounded like German which he had heard on television. (About the same time, a few reports of "little men" associated with landed craft also began to circulate). NICAP was unable to investigate the Tennessee report sufficiently to pass judgment on it. Some of the story is plausible, but lacking concrete proof and substantiation by other witnesses, we cannot accept it as authentic. [See Section XIV.]

A more thoroughly investigated case (without the "spacemen" aspect) occurred on the night of the 6th. The case also includes the implication of high-level knowledge of UFOs, which is kept secret from the public.

The Olden Moore Case

About 11:20 p.m., Olden Moore, a plasterer, was returning to his home in Huntsburg, Ohio, from Painesville, driving on Route 86. He noticed a bright star-like light approaching, apparently following the course of the road. As the light got brighter and brighter, Moore pulled to the side of the road to watch, and switched off his ignition. (When his story was first publicized, some erroneous news reports were circulated that his motor had failed.) Moore was later interviewed by NICAP member C. W. Fitch in Cleveland, and gave a detailed statement:

"In a matter of seconds from the time I first saw the object it was over a large field at the intersection of Hart Road and Route 86. While it was still high in the air, it [the light] seemed to split apart and one section moved upward out of my range of vision. The other descended slowly and silently into the field adjoining the road, where it loomed big like a house in front of me. In the darkness I could not discern whether it was actually resting on the ground or hovering just above it.

"It appeared to be perhaps 50 feet across and 20 feet from the top to the bottom. It was round and shaped like a saucer with another inverted one resting on top of the lower saucer. It had an inverted cone-shaped dome in the center of the top part. It was mirror-like. . . surrounded by a bluish-green mist or haze, through which it glowed like the dial of a luminous watch. It began to pulsate, first glowing brightly and then dimming with rythmic repetition.

"I sat in my car and watched the strange object for about 15 minutes, then got out and walked toward it to get a closer look. My feelings at the time were more of curiosity than of anything else, in fact, I do not recall having any feeling of fear. I was so amazed at what I was seeing that I was filled with a sensation of wonderment and curiosity which occupied my mind completely.

"The sky was clear and the moon shining brightly and the surface of the object reflected the moonlight. It appeared to be of a very shiny substance, though I cannot say whether it was metallic or not. . . As I got closer I heard a humming or ticking sound like that of an electric meter. About halfway up to it the thought crossed my mind that no one would believe me if I told them what I saw so I decided I would try to get someone else there as a witness. I stopped, returned to my car and drove home to get my wife. Though I made a hurried trip, when we got back to the field about twenty minutes later the object was gone."

Next morning Mrs. Moore phoned the sheriff and reported the incident, since Moore had been reluctant to report it. Moore was subsequently interviewed by Sheriff Louis A. Robusky, Geauga County; Civil Defense Officials; newsmen and others.

Kenneth Locke, Lake County Civil Defense Director, led an investigating party to the site of the report next day. At the point where the UFO was observed, Locke found small markings about 1-1/2 inches deep. Each marking consisted of three holes arranged in a triangular pattern with a fourth hole outside of the lines of the triangle. NICAP Adviser Ralph C. Mayher (then associated with the news department of station KYW) made a plaster cast of one set of the holes. The cast was turned over to Richard Gray, research physicist at Case Institute of Technology for examination. It was reported that the markings could have been made by some very heavy type of tripod.

Locke took a geiger counter reading at 2:00 p.m. (about 15 hours after the sighting). An area about 50 feet in diameter showed a reading of 150 microroentgens per hour above normal background radiation at the center of the area. At the perimeters, the reading tapered off to about 20-30 microroentgens per hour above normal. A second reading at 5:00 p.m. showed that the radiation at the center of the area had dropped off to 20-25 microroentgens per hour above normal, and the count at the perimeter was now normal. The 2:00 p.m. reading was approximately 10 times greater than the normal background radiation for the area, which is 15-20 microroentgens per hour.

A few weeks later the news leaked out that Moore had been taken to Washington, D.C., where "high officials in the Defense Department" interrogated him. Later probing uncovered that Moore alleged he had been sworn to secrecy after being shown films and slides of UFOs, but felt that he had kept silent long enough. He described the experience in detail to a NICAP member. [See Section IX.]

Other witnesses reported UFOs in the area the night of Moore's sighting. Because of this, the physical evidence, and Moore's sound reputation, his story would appear to warrant the attention of Congressional investigators. If his story is accurate merely in broad outline, the implication is obvious: Highly important information about UFOs is being withheld from the public.

August 1960; Northern California

An intensive concentration of UFO sightings occurred over a six day period in northern California. Dozens of witnesses, including at least 14 police officers, reported typical disc, elliptical and cigar-shaped UFOs. The state police sighting of a highly maneuverable ellipse, which shone red beams of light toward the ground the night of August 13, was reported on the front page of state newspapers and on the newswires.

Chronology of Main Cases:

Aug. 13-14   Hollywood. 10:30 p.m. Red elliptical UFO passed overhead, hovering once.
Willow Creek. After 11:00 p.m. Circular red UFO approached, circled, dove, climbed away.
Red Bluff. 11:50 p.m.-2:05 a.m. State policemen reported reddish elliptical UFO which made "unbelievable" maneuvers. [See Section I.] Second UFO reported during latter part of sighting.

Aug. 16-17   Corning. 8:30 p.m. Two cigar-shaped objects flashing red and white lights passed from E to NE.
Eureka. 9:30 p.m. Group of 6-8 white and red lights maneuvering in formation. Air Force explanation: aircraft refueling mission.

Corning. About 9:50 p.m. Bomerang-shaped UFO passed from SW to NW, twice emitting bursts of white light.
Mineral. About 11:00 p.m. Dozens of witnesses, including Tehama County police officers, watched six brightly lighted objects "dipping and diving and moving at simply unbelievable speed" in the southern sky. Objects alternately hovered, speedily changed position.
Concord and Pleasant Hill. 11:40 p.m. to 12:15 a.m. Circular UFO flashing red and blue lights maneuvered over area, hovering, moving up and down, side to side.
Near Healdsburg and Santa Rosa. Early A.M. Deputy Sheriff observed "flattened ball, dull red and crimson on the edges," hovering and moving slowly about 5 degrees above horizon.

Aug. 17-18   Roseville. Night. Two oblong lighted objects bobbed around in sky for an hour; witnesses included police captain and sergeant.
Folsom. UFO with two bright white lights on front, red lights at rear, maneuvered over area off and on for two hours at night; whining noise "like spinning top" heard.
Dunsmuir. 12:10 a.m. Oblong reddish UFO with associated smaller yellow light descended, then rose and sped away. High-pitched sound "like rushing wind" heard.
Redlands. 1:45 a.m. Oval-shaped UFO with dome and row of red lights on edge, maneuvering slowly in sky.

August 18   Honeydew (Humboldt Co.) 9:54 p.m. The postmaster watched a delta-shaped object, clearly visible for more than 2 minutes. UFO approached, made sharp turn and moved away. Red glow visible on front, lights on inside of V.

LIST OF CALIFORNIA POLICE WITNESSES, Aug. 13-18, 1960

State Highway Patrolmen:	Stanley Scott
	Charles A. Carson
Tehama County Sheriff's Office:	Deputy Clarence Fry
	Deputy Montgomery
	Chief Criminal Investigator A. D. Perry
	Deputy Bill Gonzalez
Sonoma County Sheriff's Office:	Deputy William Baker
	Deputy Lou Doolittle
Plumas County Sheriff's Office:	Deputy Robert Smith
Roseville, Placer County:	Captain Hugh McGuigan
	Sergeant James Hall
Mt. Shasta Police:	Officers Pete Chinca,
	Jack Brown,
	George Kerr

Argentine Concentration, 1962

(Sources: Argentine Embassy, Washington, D. C. Also Argentine newspapers: Buenos Aires Herald, La Razon, La Nacion and La Prensa).

May 11 - Photograph of a UFO taken by a reporter of the "La Nueva Provincia." (Another photograph was taken by one Miguel Thome at some unspecified time during this concentration).

May 11 - Rear Admiral Eladio M. Vazquezant and Captain A. Molinari, Navy officers at the U. S. Military Mission in Espora, confirmed that they had seen a UFO about 7:40 p.m., possibly the same one that was photographed.

May 12 - Truck drivers traveling toward La Pampa about 4:10 a.m. reported seeing a UFO on the ground which looked like "a brightly lighted railroad car." As the trucks neared, the UFO took off showing flickering body lights. It emitted a red flash, rose quickly, and separated into two bodies which flew off in different directions. Navy Capt. Luis Sanchez Moreno investigated and interrogated witnesses. They said light seemed to come through small windows in the UFO. Samples of a grayish substance found at the site were taken to Puerto Belgrano Naval Base for analysis. (Capt. Sanchez Moreno told the press the Navy had been investigating UFOs since 1952, and he had personally observed UFOs with other witnesses in Mar del Plata, "mobile bodies with incredible speed and irregularity of movement.")

May 12 - The Navy Department received reports from four people who sighted a UFO about 4:30 a.m., while traveling by automobile. The UFO illuminated the car like daylight; one of the passengers had to undergo treatment for eye damage.

May 13 - Many residents of Cordoba witnessed a bright elongated UFO passing overhead at high speed about 4:30 a.m. Two women in a car then saw a glowing object in woods near the road.

May 14-16 - Several UFO reports from Bahia Blanca, La Rioja, and La Barrera. In the latter location, 4-5 elliptical UFOs in a line were sighted by Dr. Jorge M. Vallina and others.

May 18 - A highly luminous reddish UFO flew over an airport early in the morning at such a low altitude that tongues of "flame" were easily visible on the object.

May 22 - A formation of Navy planes near Espora Naval Air Base had several UFO sightings over a 35 minute period. The formation was headed by an instructor, Lt. Galdos.

7:10 p.m. Student pilot Eduardo Figueroa saw an orange object moving on an oscillatory path below the visible horizon.

7:20 p.m. Student pilot Roberto Wilkinson, flying at 4000 feet, reported that his cockpit was suddenly illuminated by an object astern. A luminous UFO then passed below his plane and was lost from sight in city lights. During the observation, his radio transmitter failed to operate.

7:30 p.m. The flight instructor, Lt. Rodolfo Cesar Galdos, was asked by the control tower whether he saw an object in the sky. "At about 30 degrees above the horizon over Bahia Blanca he saw a disc or luminous circular spot, orange colored and of an apparent diameter of a small moon. . . The object was moving to the south, obscured at times by the lights of Punta Alta."

7:45 p.m. Lt. Jose A. Ventureira and Ensign Eduardo Vigier, in the control tower, watched a luminous object about 10 degrees above the horizon. The UFO "moved vertically and horizontally and 15 seconds later disappeared in the horizon."

About May 24 - La Pampa woman rancher reported landed UFO and two robot-like beings.

May 24 - The astronomical observatory at Cordoba announced that it was collecting reports on the UFOs to try to determine what they are.

May 24 - Medical Capt. Constantino Nunez of the National Atomic Energy Agency was reported to be in Bahia Blanca to take part in the official investigation. La Nacion stated he flew to the landing site by helicopter. (The Agency next day said they had sent no one to investigate the UFO reports, and denied that Capt. Constantino Nunez was one of their employees.)

May 25 - La Prensa reported that results of the Navy analysis of samples taken from the May 12 landing site were released. No radioactive elements were present. (No other details given). The analysis report was said to confirm results already obtained from scientists of the National University of the South.

(NICAP has no record of reports in June)

Second Series:

July 17 - La Razon reported that five UFOs were sighted by airport employees and farmers in the lake region of San Carlos de Barilocha, maneuvering in the sky in broad daylight. Radio messages were sent to all aircraft in the vicinity requesting eye-witness reports. (Embassy report dates incident: July 7).

July 24 - La Razon reported that three mathematics and astronomy students in Cordoba obtained 9 clear photographs of a UFO. Photographic experts reportedly declared the pictures authentic.

August 2 - Numerous witnesses at Camba Punta airport near Corrientes, including the airport director Luis Harvey, sighted an obviously controlled UFO. Advised by telephone that the strange object was approaching, Harvey cleared the landing strip. A "perfectly round" UFO approached the field at high speed, stopped and hovered for about 3 minutes. Rays of blue, green, and orange light were visible projecting from the UFO. When the observers attempted to move closer, the UFO took off at high speed.

August 2 - An engineer and his wife traveling from La Plata to Chascomus about 1:40 a.m., noticed a reflection of light on the hood of their truck. Then they saw a cylindrical UFO, emitting red sparks, which flew parallel to them at low altitude for about 15 kilometers. The engineer told reporters he believed the UFO was "some space vehicle from another planet."

August 23 - A newsman of the "Saporiti" information agency and his wife saw two luminous spheres approaching his house on a zig-zag course. The movement of the UFOs, which were close together, were "rhythmic and violent." They left an intensely luminous trail and made no noise. After about 4 minutes, the UFOs disappeared upwards at high speed.

September 8 - Navy Lt. (j.g.) Juan Jose Vico, in the Floresta district, saw a "burnished metal" disc-shaped UFO maneuvering so smoothly that he stated it must have been manned or "tele-controlled."

(Embassy report lists additional sightings, with no detail, on May 23, Bahia Blanca; May 25, General Pico, La Pampa; July 19, Parana, Entre Rios; July 31, Misiones (4 towns); July 9, Mar del Plata; Sept. 9, Santa Lucia, San Juan).

NOTES

1. From Air Force Intelligence Report
2. London Daily Sketch; July 27, 1955
3. Associated Press; May 15, 1959
4. Michel, Aime, The Truth About Flying Saucers. (Criterion, 1956), ppg. 206-207
5. From Air Force Intelligence Report
6. Ruppelt, Edward J., Report on Unidentified Flying Objects. (Doubleday, 1956), p. 217
7. Ibid., p. 201
8. Ibid., p. 204
9. International News Service; Atlanta, July 25, 1952
10. From Air Force Intelligence Report
11. From Air Force Intelligence Report
12. United Press; July 27 & 28, 1952
13. From Air Force Intelligence Report
14. From Air Force Intelligence Report
15. United Press; Washington, July 28, 1952
16. United Press; July 29, 1952
17. From Air Force Intelligence Report
18. From Air Force Intelligence Report
19. From Air Force Intelligence Report
20. United Press, Associated Press; September 15, 1952
21. Reuters; September 20, 1952
22. Ruppelt, op. cit., p. 257
23. Michel, op. cit., p. 133
24. Ruppelt, op. cit., p. 258
25. United Press; Stockholm, September 29, 1952
26. United Press; October 8, 1952
27. Writer's Digest; December 1957

SECTION XIII

CONGRESS & THE UFOs

Copies of this report have been sent to all Members of Congress. If you agree that the UFO subject ought to be probed by Congress, letters to your own Congressman or Senators would help to bring about action. We also invite the support and encouragement of individual Members of Congress, and will cooperate fully in any reasonable investigation which they deem appropriate.

It is our firm conviction that the Congress is the logical place for the UFO problem to be ironed out. Our efforts to deal directly with the Air Force, to resolve the issue without sensational publicity, have been rebuffed. Still, we believe the matter can be settled in an unsensational manner without making the Air Force a scapegoat. Air Force errors and misinformation on the UFO subject should be corrected (as should any NICAP errors), so that the public can be reliably informed. Beyond that, the Air Force has a serious mission to perform and NICAP has no desire to criticize.

UFOs, we believe, are a matter for scientific inquiry. The Air Force, through intelligence procedures, has concluded UFOs represent no danger or threat to the national security. Therefore, there is no reason why the scientific community should not have complete access to UFO data and be encouraged to study the problem from the scientific standpoint. The fact that NICAP (including a large number of scientists and engineers) disagrees with the Air Force about the nature of UFOs should not be construed as an "attack" on the Air Force. Only dispassionate scientific investigation can settle the dispute about the significance of UFOs.

NICAP's criticisms of the Air Force are directed only at its specific policies on the UFO subject; particularly its dogmatic and "authoritative" approach to the subject, and seeming resentment of legitimate requests for more detailed data which would allow independent study of the phenomenon.

Soon after NICAP was formed in late 1956, one of the main goals established was to press for Congressional hearings as a step toward bringing scientific attention to UFOs. Hearings, it was felt, would clarify the problem and bring out information about the scope and seriousness of the phenomenon. Hoaxters would be exposed, and serious fact separated from misinformation. Then it would be possible for scientists and others to lend their skills to a thorough investigation, without fear of ridicule. An equally important result would be a more regular flow of reliable information to the public.

At first, there was only scattered interest in UFOs among Members of Congress. As NICAP began to publish solid information, sending occasional reports to Congress, interest picked up. NICAP members also began to write their Senators and Congressmen urging them to look into the subject. In June 1960, NICAP sent a confidential report to Members of Congress outlining the accumulated evidence. Congressional interest reached a peak in 1961, when the House Committee on Science & Astronautics began to look into the matter.

Serious discussion of UFO hearings continued until, late in the year, Chairman Overton Brooks died. About the same time, NICAP had nearly exhausted its financial resources (always slim), and was forced to send an emergency appeal to its members. The response was excellent, but it was too late to allow effective use to continue the drive for hearings.

A misunderstanding with the Chairman of the UFO Subcommittee about Congressional protocol, at the peak of interest, also was a setback. However, the misunderstanding was cleared up and the Subcommittee Chairman was willing to proceed with hearings, if approved by the new parent committee Chairman. The new Space Committee Chairman opposed UFO hearings.

Then, in answer to letters about UFOs, the House Science & Astronautics Committee began stating that the subject was not in their jurisdiction, referring inquiries to the House Armed Services Committee. The Chairman of that Committee also opposed UFO hearings.

Since early 1962, neither Committee has taken any action on UFOs. However, interest has been shown by individual Members of Congress, including an increasing number of Senators. The problem has been to find an appropriate Committee Chairman who is willing to undertake an investigation. At the present time, it appears that the Senate Committees on Space and Armed Services offer the best chance, although interest could also be revived in the House Committee.

Chronological List of Statements by Members of Congress

(From letters to NICAP members; copies on file at NICAP)

1957

Senator Barry Goldwater (R. Ariz.) - August 31, 1957

"I am an Air Force Reserve Officer and have been one for the past 27 years and, consequently, I am, indeed, interested in unidentified flying objects. I, frankly, feel that there is a great deal to this and I have discussed it often with many Air Force Officers. . ."

1958

Congressman William H. Ayres (R. Ohio) - January 28, 1958

"Congressional investigations have been held and are still being held on the problem of unidentified flying objects and the problem is one in which there is quite a bit of interest. . .Since most of the material presented to the Committees is classified, the hearings are never printed. When conclusions are reached they will be released if possible. . ."

Congressman Ralph J. Scott (D. N.C.) - March 13, 1958

"I quite agree with you that the general public should be allowed information thus far known about Flying Objects except, of course, in the case where they might become unduly alarmed or panicked by such a revelation. . .you can readily understand and appreciate the seriousness of such a reaction. If this information could be presented to the American public in such a way as to appeal to reason and not to emotion, I think it would be a good thing. . ."

Senator George Smathers (D. Fla.) - June 26, 1958

"The subject of flying saucers is one in which we all share a great interest. No legislation is pending in the Congress at the present time to require that information on the subject be made public, but you may be sure that your interest in the matter will have my attention should it come before the Senate. . ."

Congressman Thomas Ludlow Ashley (D. Ohio) - July 14, 1958

"I have made a number of inquiries of the Air Force relative to its activities in connection with these unidentified flying objects, but have invariably received comment that evidence to date is too inconclusive to sustain any theory but that these objects are 'hoaxes, hallucinations, or normal meteorological manifestations.' I share your concern over the secrecy that continues to shroud our intelligence activities on this subject, and I am in complete agreement with you that our greatest national need at this time is the dissemination of accurate information upon which responsible public opinion can be formulated. . ."

1959

From "Senate Cloakroom" Newsletter of Senator J. Glenn Beall (R. Md.) - March 23, 1959

"Hello, Outer Space! Who's There? -- Definite, serious steps are being made by the Space agency leading to the sending of a rocket to Venus, one of our close little family of planets, 'clustered' about our sun (which is but one of millions of such suns, which we call 'stars'). We'll get to Venus. Nevertheless, there are those who dismiss the idea of 'flying saucers' from other planets as preposterous. Isn't it stupid -- and conceited -- for us human beings to think no one else in the universe is as intelligent as we are?

"A famous physicist, when asked if it were possible for the planet Earth to be destroyed by nuclear power, answered: 'Yes, it theoretically could happen, but it isn't as if the Earth were one of the major planets.'"

Senator Stuart Symington (D. Mo.) - April 17, 1959

"There is little doubt that the American public has sound reason for being confused about the existence and nature of these phenomena. While I am not in a position to comment on any particular report, I am certain it would be in the interest of public understanding if a current and objective evaluation of this situation were issued.

"There are undoubtedly some objects observed directly or on radarscopes which are not subject to positive analysis. However, the public should be given all information which would not adversely affect our national security."

Congressman Dante B. Fascell (D. Fla.) - May 12, 1959

"There are many areas where unrealistic policy keeps vital information from the American people. . .Certainly, accurate information concerning so-called unidentified flying objects, within the proper bounds of National Security, should be made available immediately to the American people. . ."

Congressman George P. Miller (D. Calif.) - May 15, 1959

"I am concerned, as are most Americans, with unidentified flying objects. Surely the public should be kept informed about them. On the other hand, nothing should be done to create fear in the minds of the public if a reasonable explanation can be made. There may be cases where so-called unidentified flying objects are part of our scientific research in the problem of outer space and missile development. This could not rightfully be disclosed to the public because it would immediately tip our hand to our enemy. . ."

Congressman Walter H. Moeller (D. Ohio) - May 15, 1959

"I cannot help but feel that there may be some justification behind some of the UFO reports. I also feel that if there is any information available within the Government which has not been released to the American public it should be made known. I have every confidence that the American people would be able to take such information without hysteria. The fear of the unknown is always greater than fear of the known. . ."

Senator George Smathers (D. Fla.) - May 19, 1959

"I have noted your comments and the articles you marked with specific reference to government 'secrecy' concerning UFOs. . . I would not oppose open hearings on this subject for I believe the public is entitled to know the facts that can be divulged without violating our national security. . ."

Congressman William J. Randall (D. Mo.) - September 1, 1959

"Personally, I have always felt that maybe there was some substance in what is described as 'UFO' or 'Unidentified Flying Objects.' I am not certain what Committee would have proper jurisdiction, but I must stress what difficulty we have in getting information even on foreign military aid, on the theory it is strategic or constitutes classified or top secret information. . ."

1960

Senator Thomas J. Dodd (D. Conn.) - February 27, 1960

"Thank you for your recent letter concerning unidentified flying objects. This is a matter which has always aroused my interest and curiosity."

In a telecast March 14, Senator Dodd enlarged on his statement in answer to a newsman's question: "UFOs have never been accurately explained. I think there is as much reason to believe that there is something to them as there is for believing that there is not. There is certainly reason for thinking we don't have all the facts and certainly the Senate committee dealing with space should have all the facts."

Congresswoman Gracie Pfost (D. Idaho) - March 25, 1960

". . .regarding flying objects. I am interested in this subject also, and you will want to know that after conversing with the Air Force Department I am not completely satisfied with the information they gave me. . ."

Congressman J. Carlton Loser (D. Tenn.) - April 8, 1960

". . .relative to the present policy of the Air Force in handling the problem of unidentified flying objects. . .I am in full accord with what you say about the necessity for full disclosure of pertinent information to be made our people on any subject of such national importance. . ."

Congresswoman Florence P. Dwyer (R. N.J.) - April 26, 1960

"I am not one of those who arbitrarily dismiss 'flying saucers' as figments of the imagination. I take them seriously, and I certainly would have no objections to a careful and reasonable investigation of this phenomenon. Too many intelligent and thoroughly responsible people, who have been in positions to observe such unidentified foreign objects, have testified to their conviction that such objects exist for me or anyone else to deny the validity of their observations. Under careful supervision, and with the proper safeguards, I would think that a Congressional investigation would be a worthwhile undertaking. . ."

June 1960: NICAP began sending a summary of its evidence to Members of Congress.

Congressman Joseph E. Karth (D. Minn.) - August 24, 1960

"As a member of the House Committee on Science and Astronautics, I, of course, have had contact with high Air Force officers and have had opportunity to hear their comments on and off the record on the subject of unidentified flying objects. Despite being confronted with seemingly unimpeachable evidence that such phenomena exist, these officers give little credence to the many reports on the matter. When pressed on specific details the experts refuse to answer on grounds that they are involved in the nation's security and cannot be discussed publicly. . .I will continue to seek a definite answer to this most important question."

Congressman Edgar W. Hiestand (R. Calif.) - September 19, 1960 (to Secretary of Air Force)

"I am wondering if we ought now reexamine our policy with regard to Unidentified Flying Objects. Won't you kindly suggest to your associates that the matter be considered? I am apprehensive that right now, in the middle of a campaign, some concrete and well-documented incident may occur, and a sensational revelation could really hurt. After all, although the UFOs are unknown devices, there seems to be enough evidence available to convince that they are real rather than imaginary. Therefore what harm could complete frankness do?. . ."

Congressman John V. Lindsay (R. N.Y.) - October 25, 1960

". . .with regard to suppressing information covering sightings of unidentified flying objects. . .such matters are of vital importance. . .the security of the United States does not always demand total secrecy in the gathering of information vital to our needs. The American people are fully capable of understanding the nature of these problems. . ."

Congressman John W. McCormack (D. Mass.) - November 4, 1960 [See photostat]

JOHN W. McCORMACK
12TH DIST., MASSACHUSETTS

EUGENE T. KINNALY
Administrative Assistant

BOSTON OFFICE:
JAMES V. HARTNEY
SECRETARY

WASHINGTON OFFICE:
MARTIN SWEIG
SECRETARY

Congress of the United States
House of Representatives
Office of the Majority Leader
Washington, D. C.

November 4, 1960

Major Donald E. Kehoe
National Investigations Committee on Aerial Phenomena
1536 Connecticut Avenue, N.W.
Washington, D. C.

Dear Major:

      I am in receipt of your letter of October 28, with enclosure. I am glad you wrote me on the subject matter mentioned in your letter and the enclosure. Some three years ago as Chairman of the House Select Committee on Outer Space out of which came the recently established NASA, my Select Committee held executive sessions on the matter of "Unidentified Flying Objects." We could not get much information at that time, although it was pretty well established by some in our minds that there were some objects flying around in space that were unexplainable.

      I assume you have written a letter to the Members of the House and Senate Committee on Science and Astronautics, if not I suggest you do so.

Sincerely yours,
John W. McCormack

Senator Alan Bible (D. Nev.) - December 6, 1960

"Dear Major Keyhoe: Thank you for sending on to me the Confidential Report on Unidentified Flying Objects.

"I found this Report to be very interesting and I certainly do appreciate your thoughtfulness in making it available to me."

1961

Senator Wallace F. Bennett (R. Utah) - February 16, 1961

"Dear Major Keyhoe: Thank you for your letter of February 12, concerning unidentified flying objects.

"Certainly, this is an area which deserves our careful study and I hope that the Air Force will not keep any essential facts from the public."

The Late Senator Estes Kefauver (D. Tenn.) - March 30, 1961

"Uncertainty over UFOs certainly exists and I think it is wise to keep an open mind about them. I occasionally hear from Major Keyhoe who is with the National Investigations Committee on Aerial Phenomena here in Washington, and while I am not able to evaluate the Committee's work, I think it should be continued. . ."

Congressman Daniel B. Brewster (D. Md.) - April 21, 1961

"The Air Force has consistently said, after extensive investigations, that it can find no information to support the contention of some that Unidentified Flying Objects are under intelligent control. . .In this connection, the Air Force has also said that it has no classified information which would show, or tend to show, such intelligent control. In my judgment, this is the salient point to be remembered in connection with any allegations that classified information, which is pertinent to the point under consideration, is being suppressed. Repeated inquiries and other efforts by the Committee failed to disclose any derogatory information on this point. Under all prevailing circumstances, it is my current judgment that the Committee should not undertake a Congressional investigation of Unidentified Flying Objects. . ."

Congressman Horace R. Kornegay (D. N.C.) - May 3, 1961

"I had a very interesting conference with Major Keyhoe [NICAP Director], and I am continuing to urge the Majority Leader, Mr. McCormack, and the Committee Chairman, Mr. Overton Brooks, to hold hearings to bring all data and new information up to date relative to Unidentified Flying Objects."

Senator Harry F. Byrd (D. Va.) - May 9, 1961

"As you know, I am a member of the Senate Armed Services Committee, and this Committee is frequently briefed on the subject matter of your communication. Access to U.F.O. files is necessarily restricted. . ."

Congressman Perkins Bass (R. N.H.) - May 17, 1961

"I have just been put on a small 3-man subcommittee of the House Space Committee to investigate this UFO situation. We will hear various witnesses from the Air Force, NASA, and other Defense Department officials, but these will probably not be public hearings. . .and would appreciate your sending me along any particular points or questions I might ask of these Defense Department officials which might throw more light on the matter and answer some of the questions in your own mind. . ."

June: News stories began to appear stating that the House Committee on Science & Astronautics was considering holding hearings on UFOs.

Waterbury (Conn.) Republican, June 20: Bulkley Griffin, reporting from Washington, said the House Space Committee would conduct hearings, "according to present plans of Chairman Overton Brooks. He is designating a subcommittee to hear witnesses. Rep. Joseph E. Karth, (D.Minn.), will head the subcommittee it is stated. . .The question whether all the subcommittee sessions will be secret or whether some will be public, has not been finally decided."

In their column June 26, Robert S. Allen and Paul Scott reported: "The Unidentified Flying Objects, that have been mysteriously appearing over the U. S. for years, are going to be investigated by the House Space Committee."

July 3, Newsweek, in its "Periscope" column, reported that a three-man House subcommittee would soon start a UFO probe, beginning with Air Force reports.

(By August 6, Bulkley Griffin reported a hitch in the investigation. In a story headlined "Flying Object Probe Out This Session," the Waterbury Republican said no investigation would be held. "The Air Force is understood to have succeeded in blocking it. . .(Rep.) Karth has declared he won't serve unless some public hearings are permitted and (Chairman) Brooks has always been against public hearings. It is believed, however, that the Air Force, as usual, has been urging against any UFO hearings at all.")

Congressman Thomas N. Downing (D. Va.) - August 4, 1961

"The Bureau manager of Newsweek informs me that his information indicates that an investigation of the UFO phenomenon is being contemplated by the Science and Astronautics Committee. The information that I was provided indicates that Congressman Joseph E. Karth of Minnesota may serve as Chairman of the three-man Subcommittee. . ."

Senator Leverett Saltonstall (R. Mass.) - August 18, 1961

"I can assure you that Congressional hearings have been held on UFOs, and the responsible committees continue to receive up-to-date reports."

Congressman Dominick V. Daniels (D. N.J.) - September 12, 1961

"I have discussed your letter with Congressman Karth and I understand that attention will be focused on the UFO problem during the next Congressional session. Presumably many of the issues which you raise will be investigated at that time. . ."

Congressman Joseph E. Karth (D. Minn.) - September 19, 1961 (To Major Keyhoe, after misunderstanding about Congressional protocol was cleared up.)

"Now that we better understand each other, I would hope we could properly proceed with a hearing early next year - providing the new chairman authorizes hearings."

Congressman Joseph E. Karth (D. Minn.) - October 3, 1961

"Chairman Brooks with whom I had the agreement to conduct hearings, as you know, has passed away. What the new Chairman will decide, I do not yet know. Sorry I cannot answer your question, as to whether or not hearings relative to unidentified flying objects will definitely be held, in a positive manner at this time..."

Congressman Bruce Alger (R. Tex.) - November 28, 1961

"I have studied some of Major Keyhoe's works and have discussed this matter with a number of people in my office in Washington. Certainly, I will not dismiss the questions which have been unanswered, but I am afraid we will have little success in getting more information from the military services. This does not mean that I will stop trying. . .''

Congressman Charles A. Mosher (R. Ohio) - December 18, 1961
"We are advised by Mr. Karth's secretary that no action is scheduled as yet concerning hearings by a UFO subcommittee. Mr. Karth was named chairman to such a subcommittee by the late Congressman Overton Brooks. . .The decision to create such a committee. . .now rests with the new chairman. . .Congressman George Miller."

1962

AUGUST 6, 1961 Waterbury (Conn.) Republican

Flying-Object Probe Out This Session

By BULKLEY GRIFFIN

WASHINGTON, D. C. — No House investigation of the Unidentified Flying Objects (UFOs) will be held this session. The Air Force is understood to have succeeded in blocking it.

U. S. Rep. Joseph E. Karth, D-Minn., chairman of the subcommittee that was picked to probe the UFO situation, predicted that hearings will be held in the next session of Congress, which starts next January. Karth may get the backing of House Leader John W. McCormack, D-Mass., in this plan.

Meantime, Sen. Henry M. Jackson, D-Wash., the former chairman of the Democratic National Committee, may call some witnesses before the Senate Preparedness Subcommittee before the present session ends. These would be Government officials and such brief UFO hearings, if held, would be closed, said the senator.

Chairman Overton Brooks D-La. of the House Space Committee, who selected the Karth subcommittee, gives various reasons for not wanting that body to start action. Karth has declared he won't serve unless some public hearings are permitted and Brooks has always been against public hearings.

It is believed however that the Air Force, as usual, has been urging against any UFO hearings at all. The Air Force is the sole official investigator and reporter on UFO sightings. Its repeated story is that all the sightings can be explained away as familiar objects misidentified.

Despite the Air Force pressure and prestige, men like House Leader McCormack, Adm. R. H. Hollenkoetter, former head of the Central Intelligence Agency, a considerable number of veteran pilots, a few former Pentagon officials who were close to the UFO situation while in the Pentagon and other experts in the field of the atmosphere and its sights, all disagree with the Air Force.

These persons hold that certain of the sightings constitute something real and unknown, and demand investigation. Leader McCormack, Adm. Hillenkoetter and others believe the Air Force has been withholding some information. The move for congressional hearings will continue, it is indicated at the Capitol.

Congressman Horace R. Kornegay (D. N.C.) - January 3, 1962
"I am returning to you Flying Saucers: Top Secret [by Maj. Donald E. Keyhoe] along with my expression of gratitude for your lending it to me. I found it very interesting.
"I shall return to Washington on January 8 and look forward to conferring with Mr. Miller, Chairman of the Space Committee, and others on that Committee in connection with the matter of holding hearings on unidentified flying objects in accordance with our earlier conversation here in Greensboro. . ."

Congressman W. M. Abbitt (D. Va.) - January 31, 1962
"I am very much in accord with your sentiments and am hopeful that we can get the [UFO] hearings started in the not too distant future. . ."

Congressman W. Pat Jennings (D. Va.) - February 1, 1962
"The Air Force, it seems, is taking the whole subject seriously, which is important at the moment because of the need to maintain our Nation's defense in an ever-ready state. It would be helpful to hear more of the background on these objects, and I shall await the action of the Space Subcommittee with interest. . ."

Congressman Hugh J. Addonizio (D. N.J.) - February 1, 1962
". . .concerning the subject of UFOs. . .It is a pleasure to cooperate in the matter. I have expressed my deep personal interest in early and open hearings to the Committee and I shall keep in touch with developments. . ."

Congressman George P. Miller (D. Calif.), Chairman, Committee on Science and Astronautics - February 2, 1962
"I don't intend at this time to conduct any hearings on UFOs since that subject really is not a scientific, research and development, nor space related activity. I should think that the subject matter of UFOs is really in the jurisdiction of the Armed Services Committee since the Air Force has been given the responsibility to investigate all such unusual aerial phenomena. . ."

Congressman Carl Vinson (D. Ga.), Chairman, Committee on Armed Services - February 7, 1962
"While it remains true that some aerial phenomena remain unexplained, the great majority of the reports which have been investigated have been subject to a valid scientific explanation. As I have previously said, we have found no evidence to substantiate the allegation that such vehicles are under intelligent control. . ."

Charles F. Ducander, Executive Director & Chief Counsel, Committee on Science and Astronautics, House of Representatives - March 27, 1962
"At the present time, the Committee agenda does not include any investigations of UFOs. In addition, I must be candid and tell you that the Chairman has no plans for scheduling this type of investigation in the foreseeable future."

Congressman Odin Langen (R. Minn.) - July 5, 1962
"It would be my hope and desire that facts in this instance [UFOs] may be brought out at an early date so the controversy may be cleared up. . . "

Congressman John B. Anderson (R. Ill.) - July 12, 1962
"I would certainly have no objection to an investigation of AF-UFO policies. . ."

Senator Jacob K. Javits (R. N.Y.) - July 19, 1962
". . .regarding unidentified flying objects. Reports of investigations made by the Department of the Air Force and National Aeronautics and Space Administration indicate there is no foundation to these allegations. . ."

Congressman Harlan Hagen (D. Calif.) - July 20, 1962
"I have read with interest your comments regarding unidentified flying objects. This is a subject which has been of interest to me for some time and I am asking the Air Force to furnish me with its reaction to your remarks, and for a statement of its position with respect to the subject. . ."

Senator Kenneth B. Keating (R. N.Y.) - July 23, 1962
"I do feel that more information should be available to the general public on this matter, and would favor, of course, some Senatorial hearings on UFO problems."

Congressman Emilio Q. Daddario (D. Conn.) - September 13, 1962
"I would certainly be interested in any information [on UFOs] that can be developed by the Committee or by the scientific investigators."

Senator Thomas J. Dodd (D. Conn.) - September 26, 1962
"I believe that hearings would be a good way to help clear up the differences of opinion that exist with respect to UFOs. Perhaps the Senate Aeronautical and Space Sciences Committee will be able to conduct hearings, or another possibility is the Senate Preparedness Subcommittee. . ."

In September, NICAP published an issue of the UFO Investigator (membership publication) containing an outline and preview of this report. Copies were sent to all Members of Congress. Sample reactions:

Congressman W. R. Poage (D. Tex.) - September 22, 1962
"I have long been disturbed by these UFOs. I would be very much interested in seeing the accumulation of facts which you have assembled. . ."

Congressman E. C. Gathings (D. Ark.) - September 24, 1962
"I shall be interested in seeing a copy of the report your Committee is preparing for Congressional distribution. . ."

Congressman F. Edward Hebert (D. La.) - September 24, 1962
"I shall certainly appreciate receiving a copy of your report when it becomes available. . ."

Congressman Thomas N. Downing (D. Va.) - September 24, 1962
"Thank you for writing to enclose a copy of the "UFO Investigator", and to also bring to my attention your plans to submit a report on your Committee's five-year investigation of Unidentified Flying Objects. I very much appreciate your thoughtfulness. . ."

Congressman Charles Raper Jonas (R. N.C.) - September 25, 1962
"If you care to send me the 128-page report on your five-year investigation, I will be glad to have it. . ."

––––––––––––

Senator Jacob K. Javits (R. N.Y.) - October 25, 1962
"I appreciate your views regarding the aerial phenomena. As you know, the Department of Defense and NASA have repeatedly denied the existence of such objects."

Congressman John E. Moss (D. Calif.) - Chairman, Government Information Subcommittee - December 19, 1962
"The Subcommittee has no authority to go into the over-all question of unidentified flying objects, but other Congressional committees may well look into it."

Congressman Richard H. Poff (R. Va.) - December 31, 1962
"I am not satisfied that the Air Force has disclosed all the information which it has assembled, and I am hopeful that the Armed Forces Committee (of which I am not a member) will see fit to conduct an appropriate investigation. . ."

1963

Senator Milward L. Simpson (R. Wyo.) - January 8, 1962
"I have not yet been able to determine that any Congressional Committee plans to hold hearings on the UFO problem, but something may develop after the 88th Congress convenes. I do know that the Senate Armed Services Committee plans early hearings on the entire defense posture and it is possible that the question of unidentified flying objects will be brought up during this investigation. . ."

Senator Gaylord Nelson (D. Wis.) - January 14, 1963
"I share your belief that there should be no unnecessary secrecy surrounding the matter [of UFOs] and will do what I can to see to it that relevant facts are brought out and made available to the public."

Congressman John F. Shelley (D. Calif.) - January 28, 1963
"I share the concern of my colleagues in Congress about the gravity of the UFO problem. . .my genuine desire to see positive action taken to lessen the danger caused by UFOs to air travel and our national security."

Senator William Proxmire (D. Wis.) - January 31, 1963
"The NICAP report [outline] is a fine document which does much to substantiate the allegation made. You probably noted my remarks that 'The very fact that so many inexplicable incidents have occurred is reason enough for a thorough investigation.' I am going to contact the Department of Defense on this matter..."

Congressman Clark MacGregor (R. Minn.) - May 28, 1963
"I would certainly agree with Senator Keating that more information should be available to the public. I would favor Congressional hearings [on UFOs] which, of course, would require action by the Congressional majority leadership. . ."

Senator Birch Bayh (D. Ind.) - May 29, 1963
"I too am interested in these aerial phenomena. Some people tend to discount UFOs, but I feel that any such unknown objects bear investigation. . ."

Senator Vance Hartke (D. Ind.) - June 5, 1963
"I agree. . .that a full explanation of the 'Flying Saucers' seems due. . ."

Senator Kenneth B. Keating (R. N.Y.) - June 28, 1963
"I want to assure you that as a high officer in the military myself, I am not overawed or overimpressed by some of the conclusions reached by Air Force officers. As you know, I have no hesitancy in taking issue with other government agencies as to the dangers facing our country. . .I am sorry that there seems to be nothing which I can add to the UFO situation at the present time."

Congressman Glenn Cunningham (R. Nebr.) - August 8, 1963
"I think it quite possible that the Air Force is withholding information about at least a certain number of these [sightings] because I have found that the military services in the past have sometimes acted in a secretive way in other matters when there was really no justification for it. . ."

Senator Len B. Jordan (R. Idaho) - August 16, 1963
"Since you are a member of NICAP, I would welcome any information you might provide me which would improve my knowledge of this very mysterious phenomenon. . ."

SECTION XIV

THE PROBLEMS & THE DANGERS

The human reactions to UFO reports very nearly have prevented a rational investigation of these phenomena. Neither the rabid "believers" nor the dogmatic skeptics favor a scientific review of the UFO problem. Both think they have the answer. To the neo-religious cultists, largely centered in southern California, UFOs are the vessels of saintly beings from space (or another dimension) come to aid us through troubled times. To the skeptics, UFOs are a figment of the imagination dreamed up by unstable individuals unable to face up to the realities of the day. Neither of these positions is tenable on the basis of the evidence acquired to date.

On the basis of the evidence in this report, NICAP has concluded that UFOs are real, and that they appear to be intelligently controlled [Section II]. We believe it is a reasonable hypothesis that UFOs (beyond those explainable as conventional objects or phenomena) are manifestations of extraterrestrial life. The evidence to date is too sketchy to allow any conclusions about what the pilots of UFOs (if any) look like or what their purposes may be in visiting the earth, if UFOs are in fact spaceships. Once UFOs are accepted as a reality, perhaps it will be possible to obtain some of the answers to these fascinating questions.

The problems of UFO investigation, and the inherent dangers, are discussed below, followed by recommendations for solutions to the problems. The basic problem of UFOs is the lack of attention to something which, if true, could be of very great significance indeed to the whole human race. Most skeptics, in the final analysis, base their conclusions on a seemingly inadequate and highly prejudiced investigation [Section IX]. Quite often, skeptics point to the cultists as (allegedly) the source of the whole UFO problem. Only a superficial analysis of the cultist claims is necessary to make one a skeptic, because it is easy to see that they present beliefs and faith rather than evidence. Ergo, there are no UFOs. Thus the cultists (and opportunists, and con-men) obscure the real issues, and mislead critical-minded people into believing that there is no evidence for UFOs.

The basic danger associated with UFOs is a danger to the very fabric of society if UFOs are in fact real unexplained objects maneuvering in our atmosphere. There is a danger of a reverse delusion - fooling ourselves into believing nothing of any significance is being seen. There is a danger of an unprepared public, and the possibility of widespread panic if an external danger or threat to our way of life is suddenly imposed upon us without some prior knowledge of what has been learned about UFOs. Without psychological preparedness, a sudden confrontation with extraterrestrial beings (for example) could have disastrous results.

If there is deliberate secrecy being practiced by authorities (rather than a semi-conscious failure to face up to facts), this would appear to be inexcusable. Secrecy breeds fear and paves the way for panic, by introducing false fears and causing people to substitute imagination for reality. The danger of continuing such a policy was pointed out by NICAP Adviser Morton Gerla, a professional engineer: "This shortsighted policy results in delaying the solution of the UFO mystery, leaving both military and civilian populations unprepared for whatever steps may eventually have to be taken, whether peaceful or hostile. In the event of action being forced upon our government or people by UFO initiative, public confidence in a government following a policy of secrecy prior to being forced into action would be shattered, perhaps with catastrophic results to morale."

THE IMPLICATIONS OF UFOs

Why are UFOs important? Because if they are real (not explainable as a variety of conventional objects), it is generally conceded that they are most likely space ships. Their presence in our skies would naturally be a matter of utmost concern to all nations on earth.

In spite of the fact that UFOs are not "officially" recognized, it is plain that they - and the general idea of some day encountering extraterrestrial beings - have inspired considerable scientific thought and speculation. As a result of our entrance into the Space Age, the idea of UFOs has rapidly become plausible.

The hypothesis that UFOs are space ships has important implications for humanity. Many questions are raised - philosophical, religious and technological. What effect would contact with extraterrestrials have on our society? What relationship would - or should - we have with such beings? What should our behavior toward them be? What effects would their detection have on our technology and industries?

Of all groups which would have an immediate concern about UFOs, pilots obviously are one of the first whose careers and interests would be affected. To obtain the reaction of this group, we asked two NICAP Advisers their opinions on what pilots would most want to know about UFOs if it was suspected that they were space ships.

Mr. L. Dan Sheridan, Jr., former Marine Corps fighter pilot, replied with these questions:

"What is their performance?"

"Are they controlled and who and what controls them?"

"Are they hostile?"

"Are they responsible for the many unexplained crashes and/or loss of aircraft?"

"What is their mission?"

"Are they subject to destruction and/or death?"

"Is there any basis of contact?"

"Why has the fact of their existence been covered up for so long?"

John F. McLeod (Major, USAFR, active in Civil Air Patrol Search & Rescue Squadron, graduate of Harvard University in the field of psychology) replied:

"Because of their special training and experience, pilots in general are better able to report and evaluate aerial phenomena, including possible UFO sightings, than most other groups. A pilot would normally be more exposed to conditions in which such phenomena might occur, he would be more likely to be able to report the details of such phenomena accurately, and he would be more likely to be able to judge the true nature of conditions pertinent to such phenomena.

I believe that, in general, pilots would want to know the following basic data about any report to the effect that UFOs were actually spacecraft:

1. Their type and source of motive power
2. Their origin
3. Their speed and other performance characteristics
4. The nature of their occupants

In short, the average experienced pilot would, I believe, be more interested in the technical facts of such a situation than in any sensational effect it might have. . ." Commenting on pilots as observers of UFOs, Mr. McLeod added, "An experienced pilot's ability to adapt to an unusual situation in the air should enable him to retain an objective attitude after his initial surprise, and his interest should stimulate physical thresholds of awareness regarding the data to be learned from the situation . . ."

RELIGION

From the viewpoint of religion, Rev. Albert Baller (German Congregational Church, Clinton, Mass.), a NICAP Board Member, had this to say:

"What our fate will be [if we come into contact with extra-terrestrial beings] will depend upon whether there will ever be close enough contact with intelligences from extraterrestrial realms to matter. The very possibility, however, is certainly being envisaged by some scientific experiments now being made. For example, various experiments being carried out at public expense to invent a means of communication between humans and porpoises! The main purpose of these experiments is said to be to prepare ourselves for the time when our interplanetary vehicles shall take us to other worlds and other intelligent beings. Not, of course, that we anticipate that such other beings will confront us speaking the language of porpoises. But to have broken the "porpoise speech code" will give us some insights into breaking other completely foreign speech codes.

"What will such contact mean, if it comes, to our thinking? The question asserts itself especially if you are, as I am, a minister of religion. What will such contact do to our theological conceptions? What will it mean in terms of our beliefs about God, Christ, Salvation, the unique nature of Man? Here, again, one can only guess. But based on the record of man's reaction to other such challenges over the centuries, we may expect this one to be taken in stride too. For this will not have been the first time, by any means, that humankind has had to stretch its thinking and feeling to encompass the wider revelation. . ."

TECHNOLOGY

Mr. Robert Purdy, Metallurgical Engineer, through a NICAP member suggested what a few of the effects on technology, industry and science would be if we establish contact with an advanced race of beings:

"In my certain field, metallurgy, of course the first problem most likely to be solved would be a metal so strong, so light, so heat resistant, it could only be dreamed of before this event. The present space programs could be speeded up such that we might be taking our first trip to Mars within several months. Our present corrosion problem which costs this country over 8 billion dollars a year could be reduced to practically nothing. Perhaps another method of obtaining pure metal other than from its ore would be discovered. These suggestions are only a few of the vast number of possibilities such an event would bring into focus."

Dr. Fred C. Fair (professor emeritus of engineering, New York University) a NICAP Adviser, commented on the technology displayed by UFOs, deduced from reported observations:

"Astronomers and chemists agree that the only metallic elements found on stars and planets are the same as the ones that occur on earth. No planet has a supply of a super metal foreign to the earth. Consequently, if the metallic materials used in the construction of the body of the UFO and of the machinery and mechanisms within it are more durable than alloys produced on earth, it would indicate that the art and science of Metallurgy at the source of these UFOs is in advance of the corresponding art and science on earth.

"Without the opportunity of inspecting a UFO, we can infer that the metal parts are superior to any alloy now produced on earth, as shown by the durability and superior performance of the vehicle and the machinery within it. The mechanism of these objects is so nearly perfect that all of them, or at least almost all of them have functioned perfectly while in the area of visibility from the surface of the earth, or while within the earth's gravitational field. Malfunctions of a very few of these objects may account for some of the green fireballs and space explosions that have been reported from time to time. . .

"UFOs have been clocked by competent observers using adequate equipment at speeds in excess of 17,000 miles per hour. This is beyond the speed that an earth-made controllable and steerable vehicle can attain. Nor is it expected that such speeds may be developed in the foreseeable future. Much has been written concerning the type of organisms that must be within a UFO that can withstand the huge G forces that occur when such objects abruptly change their course through ninety or more degrees while maintaining high velocity. The extreme maneuverability of these huge craft operated at high velocity has been a source of wonder from the time of the earliest observations. Why does a UFO seem to be not subject to the law of inertia? How, without

collision, can the forward motion of any object be stopped immediately; and instantaneously assume a new and at times a directly opposite direction? The momentum of any solid body, having mass, would seem to make such a tactic impossible. . .

"What little we know at present of the Unknown Flying Objects indicates a technology in several fields which has reached a state of development far beyond that attained on earth."

SOCIAL AND MORAL CONSIDERATIONS

In 1963 a NICAP member posed a hypothetical question to the U. S. Department of Justice: "If a human being killed a space man, in a moment of panic and fear, would this be murder? Or could the person defend his action on the legal ground that he had not committed homicide since the being was not 'human'?"

On July 11, Assistant Attorney General Norbert A. Schlei replied: ". . .as a matter of information, it does not seem likely that present criminal laws against homicide would play a primary role in restraining attacks by excited citizens if the situation you describe were to arise. Since criminal laws are usually construed strictly, it is doubtful that laws against homicide would apply to the killing of intelligent, man-like creatures alien to this planet, unless such creatures were members of the human species. Whether killing these creatures would violate other criminal laws - for instance, the laws against cruelty to animals or disorderly conduct - would ordinarily depend on the law of the particular state in which the killing occurred. . .until it is clearer what problems of safety, health or commerce such creatures might bring, there is little basis for describing the kinds of laws which might prove appropriate."

Replying to the same question, Professor James P. Whyte, School of Law, College of William and Mary, agreed with Mr. Schlei. Assuming for discussion that UFOs are occupied, he said, the question is whether they are occupied by human beings sufficiently similar to homo sapiens.

"The intelligence of these occupants might or might not be a factor," said Prof. Whyte. "It is just as much homicide to kill an idiot as it is to kill a genius."

Another problem of making contact with, and attempting to communicate with, extraterrestrial beings has been suggested by NICAP Adviser, Dr. Robert L. Hall (social psychologist), and others. That is the possibility of such beings not having a form similar to ours. Our earth-bound analogies (and our egos) tend to make us think in terms of the human form. Some anthropologists and biologists, in fact, have argued that extraterrestrials would very likely have to resemble us in some ways, because of certain physical structures of the human body which led to the development of human intelligence. But, again, this development could have been only one of many possible ways in which intelligent life can develop.

It has been suggested that intelligent life forms might, for example, be of microscopic size - or amorphous blobs. If extraterrestrials who traveled to earth were not humanoid in form, it is conceivable that man could come "face to face" with a space being and not recognize him as an intelligent creature. The question is often asked, "If UFOs are real (i.e., space ships carrying intelligent beings), why haven't they landed?" The answer is that no one knows for sure whether any beings from other planets have landed on earth and, if they did, whether they would be recognizable as such.

Commenting about space travel and extraterrestrial life, Dr. Edward Teller in a lecture at the University of California said, "Where is everybody? It is possible that it's a form of life that we may not recognize as such, and isn't it even more possible that we in our galaxy may just be suburbans living on a God-forsaken outpost?" [1]

In a discussion of the necessary training, and expected behavior, of men who will travel through space, Dr. Harold D. Lasswell (Yale social scientist) states in his concluding remarks: "All the foregoing rests, of course, on the assumption that earth's inhabitants will be able to execute programs of the kind under discussion, which is no foregone conclusion. The implications of the unidentified· flying objects (UFO) may be that we are already viewed with suspicion by more advanced civilizations and that our attempts to gain a foothold elsewhere may be rebuffed as a threat to other systems of public order." [2]

Problems of Scientific Investigation

The atmosphere of ridicule surrounding the subject of UFOs, largely due to the activities of the cultists, has prevented many of the best qualified analysts from lending their talents to a meaningful scientific investigation. Also, a myth has developed in some scientific quarters that there is nothing in UFO evidence that scientists can come to grips with; no quantitative data or concrete evidence. This position is based on quicksand, since no real scientific effort has been made to acquire such data. It is, in fact, not a reasoned position at all, but a presumption. How can these skeptics be so sure until someone <u>tries</u> to obtain better data with instruments? The evidence presented in this report strongly suggests that an organized and instrumented study of UFOs would be very fruitful. If not, then these skeptics would have a solid basis for their currently illogical position.

Some skeptics base their position on the alleged fact that modern tracking instruments have not detected UFOs. On the contrary, UFOs have been tracked with theodolites and filmed at White Sands, N.M. [Section VIII; Photographs], tracked on radar at Cape Kennedy, and by Air Force and civilian radar all over the world. [Section VIII; Radar]. There has been a tendency to rationalize, or suppress, any puzzling data. Interpretation of unexplained objects detected by instruments has been left to guesswork.

In the summer of 1963, Richard Hall (NICAP Assistant Director) and Walter N. Webb (NICAP astronomy Adviser) visited a mutual friend in Columbus, Ohio. A. B. Ledwith, engineer and former member of the Smithsonian Institution satellite tracking program, provided some information which illustrates one of the problems of UFO investigation.

While on the satellite project, Ledwith had made a particular point of studying reports of unidentified flying objects which came from the Nunn-Baker camera sites around the world. In particular, he carefully checked each photograph showing an unidentified light source to see if the "UFOs" could be explained in conventional terms. Many, he found, could not. Several of the photographs showing unexplained objects tracked by the Smithsonian cameras were turned over to NICAP.

Ledwith emphasized that the photographs did not prove anything; often it was impossible to completely rule out a stray aircraft, which conceivably could have been captured on film. But the images, nevertheless, were unexplained and no one had reported aircraft in the area. Ledwith also ran into the common skeptical tendency to assume the images <u>must be</u> aircraft, or something conventional.

The Smithsonian teams were tracking satellites. If something else which did not fit the satellite track showed up on the film, it was ordinarily assumed to be a film defect, a meteor, or aircraft. Very little careful checking was done to determine the likelihood of these explanations.

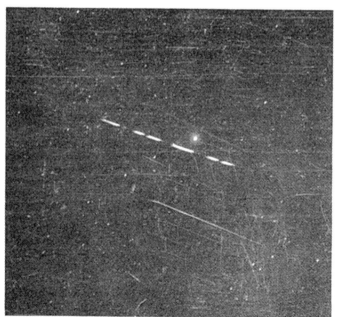

Japanese Site Photograph: UFO?

On April 14, 1959, the Nunn-Baker camera site at Tokyo Mitaka, Japan, was attempting to track Vanguard 2 (launched February 17, 1959). The developed film showed a bright unexplained object, in the wrong position for the satellite. This was Smithsonian observation number SC5-498 (data on file at NICAP). Photograph reproduced here shows prominent trail left by object.

Landings and Near-Landings

The most controversial aspect of the UFO subject is the question of the validity of claims that UFOs have actually landed, in some instances, and that occupants have been seen. On one extreme are fantastic science-fiction sounding claims of sojourns through space with noble beings who have come to aid earthmen through fearsome times. (Such claimants have been labelled "contactees.") Dr. Carl Jung [3] and other psychologists have pointed out the cultist aspect of these claims, the apparent wishful thinking, and formation of a neo-religion which espouses the "New Age" philosophy. On the other extreme are reports from seemingly reliable people, with no obvious axe to grind, who claim to have witnessed the landing or near-landing of strange craft (usually of general elliptical or circular shape).

Although there is a vast difference between the types of people who have made the claims on either extreme, and in the types of experience they depict, the confusion around the UFO subject in general makes it nearly impossible to distinguish between the types. If you seem to treat seriously <u>any</u> of these cases, you seem to be accepting <u>all</u> of them. The most ardent believers and the most severe skeptics both tend to assume that either all such stories are true, or all who claim they are true are crackpots. Unfortunately, life is not that simple and it is not possible at this stage of investigation to make any sweeping judgments.

As long as UFO reports are not investigated scientifically, not quickly and thoroughly checked out, doubt will remain. The confusion also leaves an open field for opportunists and charlatans who, it should be noted, are very active in "contactee" circles.

Since NICAP has concentrated on investigating factual reports of straightforward UFO observations by reputable people, our investigation of landing, near-landing, and "contactee" reports has not been exhaustive. However, it has been more extensive than many people realize. Our policy has been to quietly investigate the controversial cases to the best of our ability without engaging in polemics about them. When facts about these cases have, in our estimation, been fairly conclusively established, we have reported them. In so doing, we have not passed judgment on the whole spectrum of landing claims. Some cases have proved to be fairly obvious hoaxes, others have involved key "witnesses" of dubious background and engaged in dubious activities.

One of the most famous "contactees" made a claim in 1958 which NICAP thoroughly investigated, and disproved. One of this person's alleged "witnesses" masquerades as a Ph.D. and a knowledgeable anthropologist. He is neither. One self-styled evangelist "contactee" engaged in blatant misrepresentation of himself while relating a wild tale of contact with spacemen. Later he was convicted in Los Angeles of selling Doctor of Divinity degrees, mainly to other "contactees." Another was convicted in California of stock fraud. All four, perhaps significantly, claimed meetings with the idealized human-type "spacemen."

Some landings and near-landing cases are more plausible than others. Some may eventually prove to be honest mistakes of some kind. But as long as it is considered a reasonable hypothesis that some UFOs are space ships, it is logical to suppose that some form of contact with extraterrestrial beings is possible. For the moment, we are ignoring other problems which might prevent or delay contact, such as total dissimilarity between us and extraterrestrials, different psychological make-up, etc.

If our hypothesis to explain UFOs is correct, then landing and near-landing reports from seemingly reputable people become the most important cases of all; and this extraterrestrial hypothesis is based on a considerable accumulation of solid evidence presented in this report. But lack of recognition even to solidly established, straightforward UFO sighting reports of a less sensational nature makes objective investigation of these potentially sensational ones nearly impossible.

Some UFO investigators, impatient with NICAP's "conservative" policy of starting from the beginning and building up a solid case, have argued that investigation of the landing reports may be the only way to conclusively prove the extraterrestrial hypothesis. Perhaps they are right, but we believe that such an investigation will not be possible until the UFO problem generally attains scientific recognition.

Some borderline cases which have neither been proved nor disproved, are worth mentioning as possibly authentic close-up observations of seeming vehicles or craft. They are selected solely as examples of cases in which preliminary investigation turned up no derogatory information about the witnesses, and no glaring errors in their stories. We readily concede that cases of claimed contact with, or close-up observation of, beings in landed vehicles demand the closest scrutiny and the most painstaking investigation, which has seldom been possible to date.

These cases should not be taken out of context and used to imply either that NICAP accepts them at face value, or that we are gullible. On the contrary, we have been criticized by other UFO groups for our often voiced skepticism and demand for strong objective evidence in landing cases. It is a fact of human nature, we believe, that the more sensational or unorthodox a claim is, the stronger the evidence will have to be to convince people generally of its truth. We do not uncritically accept all reports without careful investigation and meaningful evidence. Rather, when the reports come from seemingly reputable people and are made with reasonable objectivity, we believe only that they deserve serious attention and far more thorough investigation.

Close-up Observations:

June 27, 1959 New Guinea
Witnesses: Rev. William B. Gill and local natives
Color: Brightly lit, shaft of blue light shining upward from center.
Dimensions: About 35 feet diameter.
Distance: About 450 feet.

July 13, 1959 New Zealand
Witness: Mrs. Frederick Moreland
Color: Silhouetted, orange and green body lights.
Dimensions: About 20 feet diameter, 4-5 feet high.
Distance: About 40-50 yards.

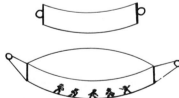

September 20, 1961 New Hampshire
Witnesses: Mr. & Mrs. Barney Hill
Color: Silhouetted, bluish-white fluorescent glow from windows, red light on each side.
Dimensions: About as large as a 4-engine airliner.
Distance: About 100 feet.

RECOMMENDATIONS

Summarizing the main problems and dangers associated with the UFO phenomenon, these points stand out:

* Doubt about the scientific adequacy of the Air Force investigation; lack of access to the specific detailed cases in Air Force files.

* The dangers of having a basically <u>military</u> organization responsible for overall evaluation of a <u>scientific</u> problem; the intrusion of military secrecy preventing the scientific community from reviewing the methods of investigation and reasoning employed by Air Force investigators.

* The possibility of ignoring, or rationalizing away, facts which may have important effects on the human race, for good or ill.

* As previously pointed out by NICAP, the danger of accidental war resulting from misinterpretation of objects on radar scopes, a possibility made more likely by the general confusion and doubt surrounding the subject of UFOs.

* Continued exploitation of the public by con-men and opportunists who thrive because of the confusion and doubt.

* The threats to society posed by an unprepared and ill-informed public; the psychological preparation, and general planning for any eventuality needed if UFOs are in fact manifestations of extraterrestrial life.

One solution to all these problems would be a scientific and political review of the entire UFO situation. The main purposes would be clarification of the facts, and evaluation of those facts. This would require a program designed to (1) study the accumulated facts to date (including the detailed reports in Air Force files); (2) taking steps to insure that future reports are quickly and scientifically evaluated (encouraging citizens, and particularly scientists, engineers and pilots, to make immediate and full reports without fear of ridicule or reprisal; frank and full reporting of all data and evaluations to the public; open and serious treatment of UFO reports generally, as phenomena worthy of careful scientific attention).

The framework for a scientific review of UFOs could take many forms, and would not necessarily require huge appropriations of funds. (Some government grants to encourage specific evaluations might prove to be desirable.) Judging by public interest in UFOs displayed in letters to NICAP, there are hundreds of competent personnel who would almost certainly contribute their talents to a program of this nature.

√ A simple directive to scientists and engineers at White Sands, Cape Kennedy and other government establishments could require personnel manning tracking equipment to attempt to track and record on instruments any UFOs observed in the vicinity. If something unexplained is tracked accidentally, this too should be reported. (Reports could be sent to some central office, such as the NASA Office of Life Sciences, or a university science department, and made available to any interested scientists).

√ Cooperation of existing astronomical societies, and such instrument programs as Smithsonian Institution's meteorite camera network in the western U. S., could be requested.

√ All reports from military sources, particularly pilots, could be sent to the central agency after deletion of legitimately classified portions of the intelligence reports.

√ Commercial airlines; General Mills, Inc., balloon trackers; etc., all could be encouraged to report sightings.

The Air Force, of course, has a legitimate interest in anything that flies or anything with a threat potential to the country. Air Force liaison with this program would be desirable, and in fact civilian scientists (perhaps a special panel for the particular purpose) could assist the Air Force in an immediate evaluation of threat potential - in secret if necessary.

However, once it is determined that a given UFO report is not evidence of an attack on the country, all except legitimate security data on the case should be made public immediately. If the object or phenomenon is definitely explainable, the explanation and all evidence and reasoning leading thereto, should be reported. If the phenomenon is not immediately explainable, the report should be released as <u>unevaluated data</u> which any and all investigators could then evaluate independently.

Interpretation of the accumulating unexplained reports could then be accomplished (without any "aura of mystery") through the normal channels of scientific endeavor: scientific journals and papers. (A "special status" <u>is</u> given to UFO reports when they are not evaluated through normal scientific channels). Perhaps this program would cause a 24-hour sensation in the popular press, but it would soon become a matter of routine. Any conclusions reported by an individual scientist, or scientific agency, would then be the responsibility of that individual or agency and subject to the review (for accuracy and sound logic) of the entire scientific community.

If the evidence mounted, and a scientific consensus gained sway indicating UFOs might be space ships, initiation of a full government program - indeed an international program - would be fully justified.

In addition to putting existing tracking equipment to work to help provide a final solution to the UFO problem, precedents exist which would make civilian participation feasible (and desirable in restoring confidence that the problem is receiving serious attention and is being adequately investigated). A program, which NICAP could organize to supplement the investigation, could be patterned after the Ground Observer Corps aircraft spotting and Moonwatch satellite tracking networks - manned by civilian volunteers. Minimum standards of experience and/or training could be established. A Moonwatch telescope grid, sound detection equipment, field investigation units, etc., could be manned 24 hours a day.

If existing government and military facilities, combined with a civilian volunteer network, were coordinated in a positive effort to gather and evaluate reliable data, this would be a crucial scientific experiment. The data gathered very likely would prove or disprove the reality of UFOs as a unique phenomenon. Regardless of what the answer proved to be, the data no doubt would be extremely useful to science (atmospheric physics, meteorology, etc.) and national defense (a constant watch on the sky, and no doubt - with experience - ability to more rapidly identify and weed out reported phenomena which are not enemy weapons).

Politically, it would be necessary to examine and review the current UFO program and to take any action or pass any legislation necessary to give a legal foundation to this, or a similar program designed to end the UFO controversy and establish the facts.

Contact and Communication

As we come nearer to making manned space voyages, the question of communicating with extraterrestrials takes on increasing importance. NICAP therefore endorses such programs as an enlarged Project Ozma (attempt to intercept intelligent communications from space), and studies of the language system of porpoises as a model for efforts to translate the language of alien beings.

In general, a great deal more thought should be given to such questions as Space Law; moral questions such as raised in the Justice Department letter involving behavior toward extraterrestrial beings; and problems raised by the increasing likelihood of eventual contact with extraterrestrial societies.

By our standards, these societies might be "advanced" or "backwards" technologically, politically, morally, or any combination of these parameters. In some cases, physical and intellectual contact might be disastrous, either to our society or theirs. In other cases, contact might be unilaterally or mutually beneficial. Some might lead to interplanetary war, others to association with extremely intelligent and wise beings who could help us solve our problems of war, hunger and ignorance. In short, the possibilities are endless. But they are well worth exploring for many reasons -- including the possibility that the first such contact may be imminent.

Detection of UFOs

Dr. James C. Bartlett, Jr., (experienced amateur astronomer, member of Association of Lunar and Planetary Observers) a NICAP Adviser, was asked to suggest ways in which scientists might be able to determine the extent and nature of UFO activity:
"It seems to me that an important first step would be a willingness to recognize the UFO problem for what it really is, namely a universally reported phenomenon for which an impartial scientific investigation is required. . .
"Now the primary objection to UFO reports, as most scientists think of such things, is that the raw data almost never permit of measurement. It should be carefully noted, however, that this is not the same as saying that the data are therefore worthless as evidence; though such is the position commonly taken by those scientists who reject them. Rather it is to be expected as the necessary consequence of chance sightings which are completely unpredictable as to time and place.
"Scientists could make a real contribution therefore by working in collaboration with a program designed to eliminate the element

of surprise, and at the same time provide means of measuring apparent position, size, and velocity, and especially parallax. Such a program is entirely feasible, though admittedly difficult.

"The suggested technique is the division of the celestial sphere into sectors, each sector to be assigned to a team of qualified observers who would keep watch over their sector for a specified period of time each day or night. Instrumentation adequate to the task might consist of high power prism binoculars, a theodolite, a 3-inch refractor using a straight view with erecting eyepiece, a camera, and a magnetic compass.

"The source of observing personnel, it is suggested, is to be found in the more or less worldwide distribution of astronomical societies and groups which are quite capable of furnishing both the instrumentation and observers qualified to make the necessary measurements. Moreover, memberships are sufficiently large to make the personnel problem manageable.

"Ideally, a 24-hour patrol of all sectors covering 360 degrees of the celestial sphere is indicated; but in practice this would be impossible. Consequently, many UFOs could still go undetected; but in any sustained program of regular observation, as outlined above, it is certain that some would be "caught" and the required measurements obtained.

"The work of professional observatories then would be to scientifically evaluate the measured data, which could hardly be rejected on the commonly assigned ground of vagueness. Perhaps a given professional group could act as evaluation center for the entire project in any given country.

"Such a program is feasible, though it will require immense labor to set up; but certainly the game is worth the candle. It might or might not discover what UFOs really are; but at minimum it could certainly determine what they are not. We could at least hope to be relieved of the profoundly learned nonsense which hitherto has characterized alleged "scientific" evluations, and which thinks it quite natural that experienced airline pilots should mistake a mirage for a cigar-shaped craft with lighted cabins and jet exhaust."

Discussing ways in which we might attempt to detect extraterrestrial life, Prof. Ronald Bracewell, Stanford University radio-astronomer, "suggests that the nearest [intelligent] community may well be over 100 light-years away. In this event, he feels that advanced societies might send probes, instead of just signals, to likely stars. These probes would presumably contain transmitting and receiving apparatus, designed either to listen for us or to make contact with us, and would go into orbit about target stars. Upon some positive detection, a signal with information would be transmitted back to the home star. We might, then, look and listen for probes within our own solar system." [4.]

In any normal situation, no one would question the sanity and reliability of the group of witnesses named in this report. But the UFO problem because it is controversial, and because mystical or crackpot UFO groups are publicized all out of proportion, appears to be a special case. Unthinking skeptics often take the easy way out by assuming that there must be "something wrong" with people who report UFOs. (Another type of skeptic refuses to come to grips with the UFO problem because he unconsciously fears his system of beliefs might be upset if UFOs are real). The notion that UFO reports originate with a small group of cultists, or crackpots, or any other small and uniform segment of our society, is refuted by the reports in this document.

One skeptical school of thought holds that UFO witnesses do not really see what they think they see. Through careless or inexpert observation, they are fooled by conventional objects, or phenomena. The observed performance of UFOs, obviously beyond earthly capabilities if true, is illusory. But radar in many cases has recorded unidentified objects exceeding the performance of earthly devices. Photographs in some cases have shown unidentifiable objects also observed visually. And, perhaps more significant than may be realized at first, reputable persons from all walks of life and all types of backgrounds (technical and non-technical, religious and non-religious, pilots, businessmen, police officers, celebrities, and the man on the street) all have seen and reported very much the same thing consistently for at least the past 17 years. If delusion is the answer to UFOs, then our whole society is deluded.

NOTES

1. New York World Telegram & Sun; June 23, 1960.
2. Lasswell, Harold D., "Men In Space." Annals of the New York Academy of Sciences, Vol. 72, Article 4; April 10, 1958.
3. Jung, Carl G., Flying Saucers: A Modern Myth of Things Seen In the Skies. (Routledge & Kegan Paul, London, 1959).
4. Seybold, Paul G., A Survey of Exobiology; Memorandum RM-3178-PR.   (The Rand Corporation, March 1963), ppg 31-32.